Disney
Voice Actors

ALSO BY THOMAS S. HISCHAK

*Broadway Plays and Musicals: Descriptions and
Essential Facts of More Than 14,000 Shows through 2007*
(McFarland, 2009)

*American Plays and Musicals on Screen: 650 Stage
Productions and Their Film and Television Adaptations*
(McFarland, 2005)

Disney Voice Actors
A Biographical Dictionary

Thomas S. Hischak

McFarland & Company, Inc., Publishers
Jefferson, North Carolina, and London

LIBRARY OF CONGRESS CATALOGUING-IN-PUBLICATION DATA

Hischak, Thomas S.
Disney voice actors : a biographical dictionary / Thomas S. Hischak.
     p.   cm.
Includes bibliographical references and index.

ISBN 978-0-7864-6271-1
softcover : 50# alkaline paper

1. Voice actors and actresses — Biography — Dictionaries.
2. Walt Disney Company.   I. Title.
PN1998.2.H594 2011   791.4092'2 — dc23   [B]   2011035289

BRITISH LIBRARY CATALOGUING DATA ARE AVAILABLE

© 2011 Thomas S. Hischak. All rights reserved

*No part of this book may be reproduced or transmitted in any form
or by any means, electronic or mechanical, including photocopying
or recording, or by any information storage and retrieval system,
without permission in writing from the publisher.*

Front cover: *foreground* Dory; *left* Ellen DeGeneres (recording voice of Dory)
and co-director Andrew Stanton in *Finding Nemo*, 2003 (both from Photofest);
background © 2011 Shutterstock

Manufactured in the United States of America

*McFarland & Company, Inc., Publishers
Box 611, Jefferson, North Carolina 28640
www.mcfarlandpub.com*

For Cathy,
still my favorite voice

Acknowledgments

I would like to thank Mark Robinson, Robert Bro, Tony Butala, Walden Hughes, Stuffy Singer, and Cathy Hischak for their help, as well as Ron Mandelbaum at Photofest.

TABLE OF CONTENTS

Acknowledgments
vi

Preface
1

Voice Actors
3

Voice Guide to Disney Animated Films and Characters
235

Voice Guide to Favorite Disney Characters
266

Bibliography
274

Index
275

Preface

Walt Disney had been making animated short films for six years before *Steamboat Willie* opened at the Colony Theatre in New York City on November 18, 1928. Those previous shorts had been silent, of course, and were based on familiar fairy tales such as *Little Red Riding Hood, Puss in Boots, Cinderella*, and *Jack and the Beanstalk*. After making a short version of *Alice in Wonderland,* Disney created his own Alice character and made a series of shorts with a live-action Alice, played by Virginia Davis, who inhabited an animated world. No one expected Alice to talk, just as it was natural that the animated characters she met were silent. When talking pictures burst onto the scene in 1927, Disney was not interested in having his characters speak. After all, most of them were animals and inanimate objects and they did not talk in real life. What interested Disney about the new sound technology was the ability to use music and sound effects. This wish to synchronize animated action and sound is what inspired *Steamboat Willie.* There is no dialogue in the eight-minute film but there is a series of sound effects and a musical soundtrack with a fifteen-piece orchestra playing throughout. Mickey's squeaks, Minnie's squeals, Captain Pete's growls, and the parrot's squawks are the only sounds made by the characters and for those characters you needed performers. The film animation actor was born.

Disney himself provided the voice of Mickey in the early years as the character progressed from squeaking sounds to dialogue. Using his thin falsetto voice, Disney was simply providing one minor production element needed to turn out cartoons. After all, action supported by music and sound effects was everything; talking was unimportant. This attitude continued through the Silly Symphony shorts and other innovative Disney movies that experimented with music and motion, many of them not requiring any speech at all. But audiences fell in love with Mickey Mouse and wanted him and his friends to talk. Like it or not, actors were going to be more and more necessary. For two decades Disney insisted that the actors who voiced his characters be unknowns. He did not want audiences to identify a particular voice outside of the animated character. But that changed with *Alice in Wonderland* (1951) when the familiar voices of stars Ed Wynn and Jerry Colonna were easily recognized by moviegoers. Furthermore, the animation artists were inspired by the facial aspects and the physical gestures of the actor when animating the cartoon character. Today the actors who voice animated movies are often filmed in the sound studio and the artists use the footage to help connect such movements with the actors' voices. How far animation acting has come since Mickey's squeaks over eighty years ago!

This book is about the 943 actors over the period of those eighty years who have voiced characters for Disney animated films. Some of these performers were rarely if ever seen in live-action movies while others moved easily back and forth from cartoons to live action. Some of these actors are famous and familiar names, others are obscure and long forgotten. Several were Disney regulars who provided voices for film after film, sometimes playing three or four characters in each movie. Some performers voiced the same character, such as Donald Duck or Jiminy Cricket, in several short and feature length films. I call them all "unseen stars" because the sound of their voices is forever linked with beloved Disney characters. Few know the name of the actress who voiced the evil Queen in *Snow White and the Seven Dwarfs* and even fewer know what she looked like; but we can never forget her cold, haughty voice as she questioned her Magic Mirror. (The actress, by the way, was Lucille LaVerne. She was sixty-five years old when she did the voice of the Queen and also that of the old Witch that she turns into. It was LaVerne's last film. See her entry for other details.) Today the leading roles in Disney feature films are often played by well-known actors but we still hear the characters even as we recognize the voices. Nathan Lane's Timon or Tom Hanks' Woody, for example, have a life beyond the familiar actors that we know from live-action movies, television, or the stage. They are part of a long tradition of unforgettable Disney characters who resound in our ears as well as in our visual memory.

As a way of keeping the book from getting too long or too thinned out, I have selected only actors who voiced Disney feature films or movie shorts. Today Disney projects include network television programs, cable TV specials, and made-for-DVD releases, and these involve hundreds of additional voice actors. By limiting the book to movie voices it is possible to go into more depth with each performer. If an actor who provided the voice for a feature film also was heard in the video sequel or in a television series, that information is included in the entry, as well as other voice-over credits outside of Disney and their work in different media. Each entry gives some biographical information (if available) and describes the various animated characters portrayed for Disney. The key word here is animated. The character must be animated, whether it be hand-drawn, stop-motion, or computer generated. So in films that mix live action and animation, such as *Song of the South* or *Who Killed Roger Rabbit*, only the actors for the animated characters are discussed. Similarly, several of the Muppet films were produced by the Disney studio but those cloth creatures are not, by definition, animated and so are not included. The scope of the book covers every feature-length Disney film since 1937 with animation in it, as well as every Disney cartoon or animated short that was first released in a movie theatre. The first part of the book consists of the voice actors' entries in alphabetical order. The second part is composed of two Voice Guides — to Disney animated films and characters listed by film (features and shorts), and to favorite Disney characters, listed by genre, then character. Using the two sections the reader may look up either an actor or a character and also learn about other films in which a performer can be heard.

It is hoped that the reader will discover what I have learned in preparing this book: The actors who provided the voices for the Disney films make up a remarkable collection of talent, versatility, and productivity. I was continually amazed at how certain actors played so many different characters, how others found endless variety portraying the same character types, and how so many of them have left something indelible for future generations of moviegoers. There is something eternal about a Disney animated film, and these men, women, and children who provided the voices for so many unforgettable characters are indeed stars, unseen as they may be.

VOICE ACTORS

Abbott, John (1905–1996) A British actor who spent much of his fifty-year career in American movies and television, he provided the voice of Akela, the leader of the pack of wolves, in *The Jungle Book* (1967). He was born John Kefford in London and made his first film in 1936 and years later appeared in some of the earliest television programs in England. By the 1940s he was in Hollywood and played supporting roles in over sixty films, including *Mrs. Miniver* (1942), *Mission to Moscow* (1943), *Jane Eyre* (1943), *Cry of the Werewolf* (1943), *Saratoga Trunk* (1945), *Anna and the King of Siam* (1946), *Humoresque* (1946), *The Woman in White* (1948), *Madame Bovary* (1949), *The Merry Widow* (1952), *Rogue's March* (1953), *Omar Khayyam* (1957), and *Gigi* (1958). Abbott turned to American television in the 1950s and appeared on hundreds of episodes of TV series over the next three decades, including *Crusader, Studio 57, Matinee Theatre, Peter Gunn, Have Gun—Will Travel, Gunsmoke, The Rifleman, Bonanza, Alfred Hitchcock Presents, The Farmer's Daughter, The Beverly Hillbillies, Perry Mason, The Man from U.N.C.L.E., The Munsters, Lost in Space, Star Trek, The Wild Wild West, Medical Center,* and *Holmes and Yo-Yo*.

Adams, Amy (b. 1974) A versatile, strawberry blonde actress-singer of films and television, she voiced the naive heroine Princess Giselle in the animated portion of *Enchanted* (2007) and appeared on screen as the princess in the live-action sections as well. Amy Lou Adams was born in Aviano, Italy, to American parents stationed overseas in the military, and grew up in Castle Rock, Colorado. She had ambitions to become a ballet dancer but found work in musicals in dinner theatres before making her screen debut in *Drop Dead Gorgeous* (1999). Subsequent roles in *Psycho Beach Party* (2000), *Catch Me If You Can* (2002), and *The Wedding Date* (2005), as well as appearances on the TV series *Buffy the Vampire Slayer, Smallville, Dr. Vegas,* and *The West Wing,* did not bring her much recognition, but her performance in the low-budget independent movie *Junebug* (2005) earned her many plaudits. Adams' breakout film was *Enchanted*, which also revealed her singing talents, and led to major roles in such movies as *Charlie Wilson's War* (2007), *Miss Pettigrew Lives for a Day* (2008), *Doubt* (2008), *Night at the Museum: Battle of the Smithsonian* (2009), *Julie & Julia* (2009), *Leap Year* (2010), and *The Fighter* (2010). Her other television credits include the series *The Office* and providing voices for the cartoon series *King of the Hill.* Over 300 actresses auditioned for the role of Giselle in *Enchanted.* The character is something of a spoof of the sweet heroine Snow White and the famous song "Whistle While You Work" is satirized in *Enchanted*'s "Happy Working Song." Similarly, Adams impersonates the soprano trilling of Adriana Caselotti, the voice of the original Snow White, though Adams' singing register is not nearly as high as the would-be opera singer Caselotti. Perhaps the most charming part of Adams' performance in *Enchanted* is the way she maintains a cartoon attitude and persona in a very realistic New York City setting, slowly becoming less cartoonish as she matures.

Adler, Bruce (1944–2008) A Jewish character actor and singer who was busy on the stage, he provided some of the singing for the Genie in *Aladdin* (1992). He was born in New York City, the son of two actors in the Yiddish theatre, and was on stage as a child in both Yiddish and English-language productions. After serving in the army, Adler made his Broadway debut as the peddler Ali Hakim in the 1979 revival of *Oklahoma!*, then went on to featured roles in *Oh, Brother!* (1981), *Those Were the Days* (1990), *Crazy for You* (1992), and several musicals Off Broadway and across the country. Adler's one-man show *Song and Dance Man* was popular in New York and on the road. He provided the singing for minor characters in the movie *Beauty and the Beast* (1991) then was hired by Disney to sing some of the high notes that Robin Williams could not reach in the opening "Arabian Nights" number and other songs in *Aladdin.* Adler did the same thing for the video *Aladdin and the King of Thieves* (1995). In both cases he was able to imitate Williams' voice so well that it is difficult to tell where the comic stops and Adler starts.

Adler, Charles (b. 1956)   A prolific voice artist who has been heard on hundreds of episodes of TV cartoons since the 1980s, he supplied the voices for two of the Weasels, the Pig Driver, the Peasant, and other characters in the Mickey Mouse featurette *The Prince and the Pauper* (1990). Growing up in New Jersey, Massachusetts, and New York, Adler picked up the different dialects around him and has used them throughout his career. He began working in animation when he did voices for the videos *My Little Pony* (1984) and *My Little Pony: Escape from Catrina* (1985). Adler's first TV series was *The Smurfs*, followed by dozens of other shows, including *G.I. Joe, The Transformers, My Little Pony 'n Friends, Jem, BraveStar, The Flintstone Kids, The Real Ghost Busters, Midnight Patrol: Adventures in the Dream Zone, TaleSpin, Yo Yogi!, Darkwing Duck, Tiny Toon Adventures, Family Dog, The Little Mermaid, Bonkers, Aladdin, Sonic the Hedgehog, Swat Kats: The Radical Squadron, Capitol Critters, The Mask, Mighty Ducks, Timon and Pumbaa, Rocko's Modern Life, Earthworm Jim, Jungle Cubs, Eek! The Cat, Space Goofs, Aaahh!!! Real Monsters, Cow and Chicken, Spawn, I Am Weasel, Rugrats, Danger Rangers, Jakers! The Adventures of Manny Rivera, Loonatics Unleashed, G.I. Joe: Resolute*, and *The Super Hero Squad Show*. Among the many animated films and videos he has voiced are *The Pound Puppies* (1985), *Rainbow Brite and the Star Stealer* (1985), *My Little Pony: The Movie* (1986), *G.I. Joe: The Movie* (1987), *The Chipmunk Adventure* (1987), *The Little Troll Prince* (1987), *The Good, the Bad, and Huckleberry Hound* (1988), *Christmas in Tattertown* (1988), *The Little Mermaid* (1989), *Defenders of Dynatron City* (1992), *Aladdin* (1992), *Once Upon a Forest* (1993), *Hollyrock-a-Bye Baby* (1993), *Yogi the Easter Bear* (1994), *The Bears Who Saved Christmas* (1994), *The Flintstones Christmas in Bedrock* (1996), *Aladdin's Arabian Adventure: Creatures of Invention* (1998), *Rusty: A Dog's Tale* (1998), *The Rugrats Movie* (1998), *The Wacky Adventures of Ronald McDonald: Visitors from Outer Space* (1999), *The Rugrats: All Growed Up* (2001), *Charlotte's Web 2: Wilbur's Great Adventure* (2003), *The Happy Elf* (2005), *Transformers: Revenge of the Fallen* (2009), and *The Haunted World of El Superbeasto* (2009). Adler is also an accomplished dialogue director, voice director, and casting director.

Adlon, Pamela (b. 1966)   A television and film actress who has become a busy voice artist since the 1990s, she did the voices for the "cool" high schoolers Trevor, Taylor, and Tyler in *Teacher's Pet* (2004). She was born Pamela F. Segall in New York City and made her screen debut as one of the Pink Ladies in the movie *Grease 2* (1982). The next year she was featured in nine episodes of the TV series *The Facts of Life*, followed by appearances in such television shows as *Night Court, The Jeffersons, ER, The Redd Foxx Show, ALF, Wiseguy, 21 Jump Street, Life Goes On, Murder One, Down the Shore, Unscripted, Lucky Louie, Boston Legal, Monk*, and *Californication*. Aldon has also been in several films, including *Growing Pains* (1984), *Say Anything* (1989), *After Midnight* (1989), *Gate II: Trespassers* (1990), *The Adventures of Ford Fairlane* (1990), *Bed of Roses* (1996), *Sgt. Bilko* (1996), *Plump Fiction* (1997), *Eat Your Heart Out* (1999), *Vampire Hunter D* (2000), *Lucky 13* (2005), *Dino Man* (2010), and a handful of TV-movies. Yet she has been busier in animated television and movies, voicing characters in such cartoon series as *Phantom 2040, Quack Pack, 101 Dalmatians, Jungle Cubs, Adventures from the Book of Virtues, Spawn, Recess, Pepper Ann, Time Squad, The Oblongs, Jakers!, The Adventures of Piggley Winks, Squirrel Boy, Teacher's Pet, The Drinky Crow Show*, and *WordGirl*, but she is most known as the voice of Bobby Hill on *King of the Hill*. Adlon can also be heard in the animated videos and movies *Kiki's Delivery Service* (1989), *FernGully: The Last Rainforest* (1992), *Edith Ann: A Few Pieces of the Puzzle* (1994) and its sequels, *Princess Mononoke* (1997), *The Wacky Adventures of Ronald McDonald: Scared Silly* (1998) and some of its sequels, *O Christmas Tree* (1999), *Recess: School's Out* (2001) and its sequels, *The Trumpet of the Swan* (2001), *Final Flight of the Osiris* (2003), *Brother Bear* (2003), *Chicken Little* (2005), and *Tinker Bell* (2008) and its sequels.

Alan, Lori (b. 1966)   A very active actress and voice artist since the 1990s whose comic delivery is unique, she supplied the voice of Bonnie's Mom who works at the Sunnyside Daycare Center in *Toy Story 3* (2010). She was born Lori Alan Denniberg in Potomac, Maryland, and began her career doing stand-up comedy and appearing in regional theatre productions. Alan made her television debut on an episode of *Law & Order* in 1990 and within a few years was in demand for her lively and comic voices. Among her TV cartoon series are *Swat Kats: The Radical Squadron, Fantastic Four, The Angry Beavers, Animaniacs, Silver Surfer, Johnny Bravo, The Grim Adventures of Billy & Mandy, Stroker and Hoop, Rick and Steve the Happiest Gay Couple in All the World, Chowder*, and *Hey, Arnold!*, but she is probably best known as the voice of the whale Pearl Krabs on *SpongeBob SquarePants* and the news anchor Diane Simmons on *Family Guy*. Alan can be seen in a handful of films and on such television series as *Boston Common*, *Touched by an Angel*, *Will & Grace*, *Friends*, *Six Feet Under*, *Cory in the House*, *Days of Our Lives*, *Southland*, and *The Closer*. Among the animated films and videos she has voiced are *Virtual Oz* (1996), *Toto Lost in New York* (1996), *The SpongeBob SquarePants Movie* (2004), *Family Guy Presents Stewie Griffin: The Untold Story* (2005), *WALL-E* (2008), and *Cloudy with a Chance of Meatballs* (2009).

Alaskey, Joe (b. 1949)   A versatile voice artist since the 1980s who is able to recreate the voices of cartoon characters of the past, he provided the voices of two Warner Brothers favorites, fiery cowboy Yosemite Sam and the Southern-accented rooster Foghorn Leghorn, in cameo performances in *Who Framed Roger Rabbit* (1988). Alaskey excels at impersonating many of Mel Blanc's voices, such as Bugs Bunny, Daffy Duck, Sylvester, Tweety Bird, and Marvin the Martian, and has voiced dozens of new characters as well. Among his many TV cartoon series are *Where's Waldo?*, *The Little Mermaid*, *Tiny Toon Adventures*, *Duckman: Private Dick/Family Man*, *Extreme Ghostbusters*, *Casper*, *Buzz Lightyear of Star Command*, *Time Squad*, *Samurai Jack*, *Teamo Supremo*, *Rugrats: All Growed Up*, *Duck Dodgers*, *Loonatics Unleashed*, *Avatar: The Last Airbender*, and *Mighty Mouse, the New Adventures*. Alaskey can also be heard in many animated films and videos, including *Bugs Bunny's Lunar Toons* (1991), *A Wish for Wings That Work* (1991), *Tiny Toon Adventures: How I Spent My Vacation* (1992), *Tiny Toons Spring Break* (1994), *Casper* (1995), *Carrotblanca* (1995), *Marvin the Martian in the Third Dimension* (1996), *A Rugrats Vacation* (1997), *The Rugrats Movie* (1998), *Tweety's High-Flying Adventure* (2000), *Scooby-Doo and the Cyber Chase* (2001), *Balto: Wolf Quest* (2002), *Rugrats Go Wild* (2003), *Looney Tunes: Stranger Than Fiction* (2003), *Hare and Loathing in Las Vegas* (2004), *Daffy Duck for President* (2004), *Bah Humduck! A Looney Tunes Christmas* (2006), *Justice League: The New Frontier* (2008), and *The Haunted World of El Superbeasto* (2009). He has appeared in a few films and television shows but most of his live-action movie credits are vocal, such as the voices of Richard M. Nixon in *Forrest Gump* (1994) and Jackie Gleason in *King of the World* (2000).

Albertson, Jack (1907–1981)   A tall, thin character actor usually assigned to supporting roles on stage, television, and in the movies, he was the voice of the stubborn hunter Amos Slade in *The Fox and the Hound* (1981). Albertson was born in Malden, Massachusetts, went into vaudeville as a song-and-dance man, and also worked in burlesque. He made his Broadway debut in 1940 in the musical revue *Meet the People*, followed by appearances in *Strip for Action* (1942), *Allah Be Praised!* (1944), *The Lady Says Yes* (1945), *The Cradle Will Rock* (1947), *Tickets, Please!* (1950), and *Top Banana* (1951), but he didn't find fame until the end of his stage career with memorable roles in *The Subject Was Roses* (1964) and *The Sunshine Boys* (1972). Albertson made his film debut in 1938 and appeared in a handful of movies, such as *The Harder They Fall* (1956), *Period of Adjustment* (1962), *Days of Wine and Roses* (1962), *The Subject Was Roses* (1968), and *The Poseidon Adventure* (1972), though he is probably best remembered as Grandpa Joe in *Willy Wonka and the Chocolate Factory* (1971). He was busier on television where he performed in dozens of specials and series between 1950 and 1980, including *Toast of the Town*, *Damon Runyon Theatre*, *December Bride*, *Yancy Derringer*, *The Thin Man*, *Have Gun—Will Travel*, *The Many Loves of Dobie Gillis*, *Pete and Gladys*, *Room for One More*, *Ensign O'Toole*, *Mister Ed*, *Gunsmoke*, and *Grandpa Goes to Washington*, but he was most known as the "man" Ed Brown on *Chico and the Man*. Albertson was able to bring a crusty villainy to the role of Amos in *The Fox and the Hound*, a character modeled after co-director Art Stevens. Yet the actor was also able to convey the human side of this slow-to-like character. *The Fox and the Hound* was Albertson's last film.

Albright, Hardie (1903–1975)   A versatile actor who was busy on the stage, then in the movies, and finally on television, he provided the voice of Adolescent Bambi in *Bambi* (1942) even though he was forty years old at the time. Hardie Hunter Albright was born in Charleroi, Pennsylvania, the son of vaudevillians, and was on the stage as a child. He was educated at Carnegie Tech then became a member of Eva Le Gallienne's distinguished stage repertory company. Albright appeared on Broadway in such productions as *Saturday Night* (1926), *The Three Sisters* (1926), *The Merchant of Venice* (1928), and *The Greeks Had a Word for It* (1930) before making his screen debut in *Young Sinners* (1931). Over the next fifteen years he acted in over fifty films, including *So Big!* (1932), *A Successful Calamity* (1932), *White Heat* (1934), *The Scarlet Letter* (1934), *Carolina Moon* (1940), *The Pride of the Yankees* (1942), and *Angel on My Shoulder* (1946). Albright left show business after World War II and taught at UCLA for several years, writing books about acting and directing. In the 1960s he turned to television, appearing in dozens of TV series such as *Gunsmoke*, *Perry Mason*, *Rawhide*, *Twilight Zone*, *Leave It to Beaver*, *Dennis the Menace*, *Bewitched*, and *Hazel*.

Alden, Norman (b. 1924)   A prolific and flexible television actor who has appeared in hundreds of episodes in over one hundred different TV series, he supplied the voice of the brawny bully Sir Kay in *The Sword in the Stone* (1963). He was born in Fort Worth, Texas, and was educated at Texas Christian University after serving during World War II. Alden made his television debut in 1957 and over the next fifty years acted in such diverse series as *Leave It to Beaver, Manhunt, The Adventures of Rin Tin Tin, Tightrope, Not for Hire, The Lawless Years, Hennesey, Bonanza, Dr. Kildare, Combat!, Batman, Family Affair, Rango, The Andy Griffith Show, My Three Sons, The Mod Squad, Kung Fu, The Streets of San Francisco, Switch, Operation Petticoat, Eight Is Enough, Charlie's Angels, Falcon Crest, Hunter, Cagney & Lacey, JAG,* and *Murder, She Wrote,* although he is probably best remembered as Coach Leroy Fedders in *Mary Hartman, Mary Hartman*. He also appeared in many movies, including *Hear Me Good* (1957), *The Walking Target* (1960), *Operation Bottleneck* (1961), *The Nutty Professor* (1963), *The Patsy* (1964), *Andy* (1965), *Chubasco* (1967), *All the Loving Couples* (1969), *Ben* (1972), *Kansas City Bomber* (1972), *The Hindenburg* (1975), *I Never Promised You a Rose Garden* (1977), *Semi-Tough* (1977), *Borderline* (1980), *Back to the Future* (1985), *They Live* (1988), *Ed Wood* (1994), *Patch Adams* (1998), and many made-for-TV movies. Alden can be heard doing voices in the animated film *The Transformers: The Movie* (1986) and in the TV series *Super Friends, Rugrats,* and *The All-New Super Friends Hour*.

Alexander, Ernie Even though he appeared in nearly 200 films from the end of the silent period to the mid–1940s, next to nothing is known about the actor who provided the voice of John Weems, the anxious father of a infant prodigy, in the "Baby Weems" section of *The Reluctant Dragon* (1941). Alexander made his screen debut in 1926 and played bit parts in a variety of movies for two decades. He can be spotted in such films as *Marianne* (1929), *Our Blushing Brides* (1930), *I Surrender Dear* (1931), *Winner Take All* (1932), *Young Ironsides* (1932), *Beauty for Sale* (1933), *George White's Scandals* (1934), *Operator 13* (1934), *Death on the Diamond* (1934), *Forsaking All Others* (1934), *Shipmates Forever* (1935), *Here Comes Trouble* (1936), *Find the Witness* (1937), *Topper* (1937), *Love Is a Headache* (1938), *Test Pilot* (1938), *Tell No Tales* (1939), *Judge Hardy and Son* (1939), *Little Nellie Kelly* (1940), *Blossoms in the Dust* (1941), *The Pride of the Yankees* (1942), *For Me and My Gal* (1942), *Unexpected Riches* (1942), *Benjamin Franklin, Jr.* (1943), *Du Barry Was a Lady* (1943), *I Dood It* (1943), and *Casanova Brown* (1944).

Alexander, Jason (b. 1959) The short, stocky comic actor with a wise-cracking persona, he has found success in character roles in all major media including many voices for animated television series and films, most memorably as the wisecracking gargoyle Hugo in *The Hunchback of Notre Dame* (1996). Born Jason Scott Greenspan in Newark, New Jersey, he briefly attended Boston University before making his Broadway debut in the musical *Merrily We Roll Along* (1981). He began his film career the same year in *The Burning* and his television career three years later as the recurring character of Harold Stickley in the drama series *ER*. Although Alexander often returned to the New York stage and has made a number of movies, he has been most successful on television where he was featured as the obnoxious George Costanza on the long-running series *Seinfeld* in the 1990s, and was a regular on such shows as *Bob Patterson, Listen Up,* and *Curb Your Enthusiasm*. He has also acted in many TV specials, such as the musicals *Bye Bye Birdie* (1995), *Cinderella* (1997), and *A Christmas Carol* (2004). Alexander returned to the New York stage in such productions as *Forbidden Broadway* (1983), *The Rink* (1984), *Personals* (1985), *Broadway Bound* (1986), *Jerome Robbins' Broadway* (1989), and *Accomplice* (1990). On screen he has played mostly sidekicks or comic supporting characters in such movies as *The Coneheads* (1993), *The Adventures of Rocky and Bullwinkle* (2000), and *How to Go Out on a Date in Queens* (2006). Among Alexander's many voice credits for TV animated series are *Dinosaurs, Aladdin, Hercules, Dilbert, Duckman: Private Dick/Family Man,* and *The Legend of Tarzan*. He has also done voices for the animated films and videos *Jingle Bells* (1999), *Madeline: Lost in Paris* (1999), *101 Dalmatians II: Patch's London Adventure* (2003), and *Farce of the Penguins* (2006). The gargoyle Hugo in *The Hunchback of Notre Dame*, named after author Victor Hugo who wrote the original book, is perhaps the least French character in the film, his delivery more in the style of an American stand-up comic. Purists found the talking gargoyles the most offensive aspect of Disney's version, the wise-cracking Hugo most of all. That aside, Alexander gives a very funny performance as his crass behavior is contrasted by the more debonair Victor and the more maternal Laverne, his fellow gargoyles. Hugo has been compared to Philoctetes in *Hercules* (1997), another helpful, rough, American-like character in a foreign setting.

Alexander, Stan A child actor who provided the voice for Young Flower the Skunk in *Bambi* (1942), he made no further movies or television programs.

Allen, Barbara Jo (1906–1974) A radio, film, and television comedienne and actress with a long career, she provided the voices for the good fairy

Fauna in *Sleeping Beauty* (1959) and the complaining Scullery Maid in *The Sword in the Stone* (1963), as well as the elephant Goliath II's Mother in the animated short *Goliath II* (1960). She was born in New York City and studied at the Sorbonne in Paris before moving to Los Angeles to live with her uncle when her parents died. Although Allen was a dark-haired beauty, her versatile voice talents found her work playing old maids, crotchety club women, and other unattractive types on the radio. She performed with Jerry Colonna, Jack Benny, and Al Jolson, and was a favorite with Bob Hope who put her on his show many times and took her with him on his USO tours. Allen became famous for the prim, scatterbrained caricature Vera Vague who she played in movie shorts in the late 1930s and often producers just wanted her to continue to voice the caricature and play variations of her on screen. She made over fifty films, including *The Women* (1939), *Melody Ranch* (1940), *Kiss the Boys Goodbye* (1941), *Lake Placid Serenade* (1941), *Mrs. Wiggs of the Cabbage Patch* (1942), *Priorities on Parade* (1942), *Girl Rush* (1944), *The Opposite Sex* (1956), and *Born to Be Loved* (1959), as well as many comedy shorts as Vera Vague. She also appeared on such early television shows as *The James Melton Show, Follow the Leader, The Greatest Man on Earth, Maverick,* and *Hey, Jeannie!* In the planning of *Sleeping Beauty*, the three good fairies were to be identical looking but have different voices. The animators found that they lacked character so three individual looks were created for Flora, Fauna, and Merryweather. Fauna is the most amiable of the three fairies and Allen's vocals are warm and friendly. After voicing *The Sword in the Stone*, Allen retired, saying she could not escape the popularity and limitations of being Vera Vague.

Allen, Rex (1920–1999)   A popular cowboy crooner and actor in radio, on screen, and on television, he did the voices of the singing narrator and the cocky inventor Windwagon Smith in the cartoon short *The Saga of Windwagon Smith* (1961). He was born Elvie Rex Allen in Tucson, Arizona, and began as a singer in vaudeville. After singing on the radio and working in rodeo shows, he was signed by Republic Pictures for a series of Western musicals, often playing himself and paired with character actor Slim Pickens. Among his two dozen movies are *The Arizona Cowboy* (1950), *Hills of Oklahoma* (1950), *Silver City Bonanza* (1951), *Utah Wagon Trail* (1951), *I Dream of Jeanie* (1952), *South Pacific Trail* (1952), *Old Overland Trail* (1953), *Shadows of Tombstone* (1953), *Rails into Laramie* (1954), *Tomboy and the Champ* (1961), and *Swamp Country* (1966). Allen had his own television show, *Frontier Doctor*, and appeared on such series as *The Red Skelton Hour, The Virginian,* and *Hold the Back Page*. He narrated over fifty Disney wildlife adventure films, shorts, and episodes on the TV series *Walt Disney's Wonderful World of Color*, including *The Legend of Lobo* (1962), *The Incredible Journey* (1963), *An Otter in the Family* (1965), *Charlie, the Lonesome Cougar* (1967), *My Family Is a Menagerie* (1968), and *Ringo, the Refugee Raccoon* (1974). Allen can also be heard narrating the animated movie *Charlotte's Web* (1973). Biography: *Rex Allen: The Arizona Cowboy*, Paula Simpson-Witt, Snuff Garrett (1989).

Allen, Tim (b. 1953)   A smiling actor and comedian who has found major success on both the big and little screen, perhaps his most popular role is the toy spaceman Buzz Lightyear in *Toy Story* (1995) and its sequels. He was born Timothy Alan Dick in Denver, Colorado, the son of a real estate salesman, and was educated in Western Michigan University for a career in television production. After a jail term for drug possession, he started to do stand-up comedy in clubs and eventually appeared on cable television. This exposure led to the role of handyman Tim Taylor in the sit-com *Home Improvement* which ran eight years and made him famous. Allen's film credits include *The Santa Clause* (1994), *Jungle 2 Jungle* (1997), *Galaxy Quest* (1999), *The Santa Clause 2* (2002), *Christmas with the Cranks* (2004), *The Shaggy Dog* (2006), *The Santa Clause 3: The Escape Clause* (2006), and *Crazy on the Outside* (2010). He reprised his Buzz Lightyear in *Toy Story 2* (1999), *Toy Story 3* (2010), briefly as the Buzz Lightyear Car in *Cars* (2006), and in the video *Buzz Lightyear of Star Command: The Adventure Begins* (2000). The character of Buzz Lightyear was based on the central character of *Tin Toy* (1989), an Academy Award–winning short made by Pixar while it was still developing its computer animation technology. The short was about some toys in a child's bedroom and served as the inspiration for *Toy Story*. Buzz was originally a wind-up tin toy but it was felt a more high-tech toy was needed to threaten Woody's leadership in the story. The spaceman was first named Larry Lunar then Buzz Lightyear after Apollo astronaut Buzz Aldrin and the toy's facial features are very close to those of John Lasseter, the movie's director. Casting Allen as the voice of Buzz was playing against type since the actor usually played everyday people, mostly hassled fathers. The role had originally been offered to actor-comic Billy Crystal who turned it down and has since stated it is the biggest regret of his career. A few years after *Toy Story* was released, Crystal eagerly signed up to voice Pixar's *Monsters, Inc.* (2001). Other actors considered to voice Buzz were Jim Carrey, Bill Murray, Chevy

Chase, and Paul Newman, but this first Pixar feature had a modest budget and could not afford them. Newman later voiced *Cars* (2006). Allen has written three books of comedy nonfiction. Biography: *Tim Allen Laid Bare*, Michael Arkush (1995).

Allister, Claud (1888–1970) An English actor of stage and screen who excelled at playing very British stereotypes in the grand manner, he provided the voice for the absent-minded, poetry-loving old knight Sir Giles in *The Reluctant Dragon* (1941) and the Sherlock Holmes–like Water Rat in "The Wind in the Willows" section of *The Adventures of Ichabod and Mr. Toad* (1949). He was born William Claud Michel Palmer in London and was on the London stage before he made his screen debut in 1929. Soon Allister was in Hollywood where he played monocled, stuffy Brits and other character types in over sixty films, including *Bulldog Drummond* (1929), *Monte Carlo* (1930), *The Private Life of Henry VIII* (1932), *The Awful Truth* (1937), *Captain Fury* (1939), *Lillian Russell* (1940), *Charley's Aunt* (1941), *Quartet* (1948), and *Kiss Me, Kate* (1953). Allister's vocals for Sir Giles in *The Reluctant Dragon* are mockingly British, very upper-crust, and rather silly. For the Holmesian rat-sleuth in "The Wind in the Willows," Allister sported a droll impersonation of Basil Rathbone who played Holmes in several films; Rathbone also narrated *The Adventures of Ichabod and Mr. Toad*. Sir Giles makes a cameo appearance in the film *Who Framed Roger Rabbit* (1988) with many other past Disney characters.

Allman, Elvia (1904–1992) A film and television character actress with many credits over a period of nearly sixty years, she began her screen career voicing the cheerful bovine Clarabelle Cow in the Disney shorts *Mickey's Mellerdrammer* (1933) and *Mickey's Fire Brigade* (1935). She was born in Enochville, North Carolina, and worked in radio for several years, playing comic characters on serials and doing commercials. It is unknown how many times Allman voiced Clarabelle since actors were rarely credited in the early cartoons. She is credited as the voice of the Lady Chef on the radio in both *Donald's Ostrich* (1937) and *Pluto's Dream House* (1940). Allman also voiced some cartoons for Warner Brothers, such as the first Porky Pig short *Porky's Moving Day* (1936), and *I Only Have Eyes for You* (1937), *I Wanna Be a Sailor* (1937), and *Little Red Walking Hood* (1937). She first appeared on screen in *Road to Singapore* (1949) and played supporting roles in such movies as *A Night at Earl Carroll's* (1940), *Sis Hopkins* (1941), *Carolina Blues* (1944), *Week-End with Father* (1951), *You Can't Run Away from It* (1956), *The Pleasure of His Company* (1961), *Breakfast at Tiffany's* (1961), *The Nutty Professor* (1963), *Honeymoon Hotel* (1964), and the TV movies *Halloween with the Addams Family* (1977) and *The Adventures of Huckleberry Finn* (1981). Among the many television series she appeared in are *The George Burns and Gracie Allen Show*, *I Married Joan*, *Blondie*, *December Bride*, *The Bob Cummings Show*, *Bachelor Father*, *Mister Ed*, *Dennis the Menace*, *The Jack Benny Program*, *The Dick Van Dyke Show*, *The Beverly Hillbillies*, *Petticoat Junction*, *The Doris Day Show*, *Private Benjamin*, *Alice*, and *Murder, She Wrote*, but she is perhaps most recognized as the candy factory boss in the famous *I Love Lucy* episode with the chocolates on the conveyor belt. Right before she retired, Allman returned to the Disney studios and voiced Clarabelle the Cow one last time for the Mickey Mouse featurette *The Prince and the Pauper* (1990).

Allwine, Wayne (1947–2009) A sound editor at the Disney studios, he voiced mostly one character but an important one — Mickey Mouse — from 1983 to Allwine's death twenty-six years later. Wayne Anthony Allwine was born in Glendale, California, and began his career as a musician in his own band that toured the country. He began working for Disney in 1979 when he worked in the music department and on the sound editing for the feature film *The Black Hole*(1979), followed by the cartoon short *Mickey's Christmas Carol* (1983). Allwine also sound edited such films as *Something Wicked This Way Comes* (1983), *Country* (1984), *Innerspace* (1987), and *Star Trek V: The Final Frontier* (1989). Only two actors, Walt Disney and James MacDonald, had voiced Mickey up until 1983 so when MacDonald was preparing to retire he coached Allwine who first provided the voice for the mouse in *Mickey's Christmas Carol*. Allwine subsequently played Mickey in dozens of videos and shorts, in over one hundred episodes of the animated TV series *Mickey Mouse Works*, *House of Mouse*, and *Mickey Mouse Clubhouse*, and in the feature films *Who Framed Roger Rabbit* (1988), *A Goofy Movie* (1995), and *Fantasia/2000* (1999). His two non–Mickey voice credits are one of the Henchmen in *The Black Caldron* (1985) and the Thug Guard in *The Great Mouse Detective* (1986). Allwine was married to Russi Taylor, a voice artist who did the vocals for Minnie Mouse.

Almanzar, James (1934–2002) A television character actor who was mostly seen in Westerns, he provided the voice of one of the thick-headed Henchmen in *The Black Caldron* (1985). James Roland Almanzar was born in Las Vegas, New Mexico, and made his TV debut in an episode of *Hawaiian Eye* in 1960. Over the years he appeared in such series as *Daniel Boone*, *The Iron Horse*, *The*

Man from U.N.C.L.E., *The Wild Wild West*, *The High Chaparral*, *Here Come the Brides*, *Mission: Impossible*, *Ironside*, *Gunsmoke*, and *How the West Was Won*. His movie credits include *The Hostage* (1967), *Charro!* (1969), *Herbie Rides Again* (1974), *Gus* (1976), *Pony Express Rider* (1976), *The Apple Dumpling Gang Rides Again* (1979), and *The Devil and Max Devlin* (1981).

Anderson, Stephen J. An animator, scriptwriter, and director of animated videos and films, he supplied the voices for the mysterious Bowler-Hat Guy, the grandfather Bud who likes to wear his clothes backwards, and dippy Cousin Tallulah in *Meet the Robinsons* (2007) which he directed. The Texas native was educated at the California Institute of the Arts and began working for Disney as a writer on the films *Tarzan* (1999), *The Emperor's New Groove* (2000), and *Brother Bear* (2003). Anderson worked on the animation for *The Brave Little Toaster to the Rescue* (1997) and *Bolt* (2008), as well as the videos *Easter Egg Morning* (1991), *The Nome Prince and the Magic Belt* (1996), and *Loose Tooth* (1997). The TV cartoon series *The Itsy Bitsy Spider* was his first directorial credit, followed by the videos *Toto Lost in New York* (1996), *Underground Adventure* (1997), and *Journey Beneath the Sea* (1997). Anderson can be heard voicing minor characters in *The Emperor's New Groove* and *Bolt*. For some years he was a story instructor at the Cal Arts. Movie star Jim Carrey was set to voice the villain Bowler Hat Guy in *Meet the Robinsons* but at the last minute decided to make the movie *The Number 23* (2007), so director Anderson voiced the role himself and it is a very Carrey-like performance filled with hyperactivity and vocal pyrotechnics.

Andretti, Mario (b. 1940) One of the most famous names in auto racing, a winner of every major race in the States, he provided the voice for the Ford Fairlane named Mario Andretti in *Cars* (2006). Mario Gabriele Andretti was born in Istria in present-day Croatia and emigrated with his family to America in 1955. He was soon racing professionally and went on to win the Indy 500, Daytona 500, the International Race of Champion series, the CART, and the Formula One World titles. Andretti has made many television appearances over the years and played himself in such series as *It Takes a Thief*, *The Pretender*, and *Home Improvement*. He was one of several real-life race car figures to do voice work for *Cars*. Autobiography: *Andretti* (1994); biography: *Mario Andretti: A Driving Passion*, Gordon Kirby (2001).

Andrews, Julie (b. 1935) One of America's favorite leading ladies who appeared in landmark musicals on Broadway and on television, as well as many musicals and non-musical movies, her only voice credit for Disney is narrating the opening animated sequence of *Enchanted* (2007). She was born Julia Elizabeth Wells in Walton-on-Thames, England, the daughter of entertainers, and sang on the stage as a young girl. Her surprisingly adult soprano voice made her an unusual attraction and by the age of twelve Andrews was performing professionally in London concerts and pantomimes. She first came to America in 1954 to recreate her role as Polly in the London musical spoof *The Boy Friend* and was immediately singled out. She scored a major triumph as Eliza Doolittle in *My Fair Lady (1956)*, first on Broadway and then in London. While appearing in the show in New York, Andrews played the title role in Rodgers and Hammerstein's original television musical *Cinderella* (1957). In 1960 she shone again on Broadway as Queen Guenevere in *Camelot* (1960). Andrews made an auspicious screen debut as *Mary Poppins* (1964), beginning her remarkable Hollywood career. She had her greatest screen success as Maria in *The Sound of Music* (1964), the role she has been most identified with ever since. Among her numerous other films are *The Americanization of Emily* (1964), *Hawaii* (1966), *Thoroughly Modern Millie* (1967), *Star!* (1968), *Darling Lili* (1969), *10* (1979), *Victor/Victoria* (1982), *The Princess Diaries* (2001), and *The Princess Diaries 2: Royal Engagement* (2004). She returned to the New York theatre in the Off Broadway revue *Putting It Together* (1993) and in the Broadway version of *Victor/Victoria* (1995). Andrews can be heard in the animated movies *Shrek 2* (2004), *Shrek the Third* (2007), *Shrek Forever After* (2010), and *Despicable Me* (2010), as well as in the video *The Cat That Looked at a King* (2004). She has also appeared in many television specials, a handful of TV dramas, and her own series *Julie*. Under the pen name Julie Edwards, she has written several children's books, and has penned an autobiography: *Home: A Memoir of My Early Years* (2009). Biographies: *Julie Andrews*, Robert Windeler (1997); *Julie Andrews: An Intimate Biography*, Richard Stirling (2009).

Andrews, Maeve A child performer who was one of the two children who voiced the baby superhero Jack-Jack Parr in *The Incredibles* (2004), she has no other film or television credits. The character's name comes from the nickname "Jack Jack" that director Brad Bird gave one of his sons.

The Andrews Sisters A trio of sibling harmony singers and arguably the most famous sister act of all time, the trio sang the narrative ballad "Johnny Fedora and Alice Blue Bonnet" in one animated section of *Make Mine Music* (1946) and the musical tale of "Little Toot" in *Melody Time* (1948). Patti (b. 1918), LaVerne (1911–1967), and Maxene (1916–1995) Andrews were born in Minneapolis to Norwegian-Greek parents and were put on the stage as youngsters, winning talent contests with their precision singing. The threesome grew up touring in vaudeville and then as adults were featured with bands, finding great success recording hit records such as "Bei Mir Bist Du Schoen" and "The Beer Barrel Polka" in the late 1930s; all in all, they sold over 75 million records. The Andrews Sisters made their screen debut in the Ritz Brothers vehicle *Argentine Nights* (1940) and became stars in *Buck Privates* (1941) when they sang "Boogie Woogie Bugle Boy." Playing themselves, the sisters were never the top-billed stars in their films but they never failed to stop the show with their singing. Their other movies include *Hold That Ghost* (1941), *In the Navy* (1941), *What's Cookin'?* (1942), *Private Buckaroos* (1942), *Give Out, Sisters* (1942), *Always a Bridesmaid* (1943), *Follow the Boys* (1944), *Moonlight and Cactus* (1944), *Hollywood Canteen* (1944), and *Road to Rio* (1947). The trio was very popular on radio, where they had their own show, and later on television. After LaVerne's death in 1967, the surviving sisters performed together on occasion, most memorably in the Broadway musical *Over Here!* (1973). On her own, Maxene appeared on tour as old Berthe in *Pippin* and in the Off Broadway revue *Swingtime Canteen* (1995). The sisters' vocals in the two anthology films *Make Mine Music* and *Melody Time* represent the trio at the peak of their powers and the two sequences they narrated in song are musical highlights in those two movies. Memoir: *Over Here, Over There: The Andrews Sisters*, Maxene Andrews (2005); biography: *The Andrews Sisters: A Biography and Career Record*, Harry Nimmo (2007).

Angel, Heather (1909–1986) A British actress who was in Hollywood from the advent of the talkies to the 1960s, she voiced Alice's very proper elder Sister in *Alice in Wonderland* (1951) and the London mother Mrs. Darling in *Peter Pan* (1953). She was born Heather Grace Angel in Oxford, England, and had experience on the London stage before coming to the States and getting a role in the film *Bulldog Drummond* (1929). She was cast as British or Irish characters in such films as *The Hound of the Baskervilles* (1932), *Berkeley Square* (1933), *Charlie Chan's Greatest Case* (1933), *Orient Express* (1934), and *The Informer* (1935), followed by *The Three Musketeers* (1935), *The Last of the Mohicans* (1936), *Daniel Boone* (1936), *Pride and Prejudice* (1940), *Suspicion* (1941), and many other movies. Angel found fame as Phyllis Cavering in *Bulldog Drummond Escapes* (1937) and reprised the role in four more Bulldog Drummond movies. She turned to television in the late 1950s and for the next twenty years appeared on a variety of TV series, including *Studio 57, Perry Mason, Peyton Place*, and *Family Affair*.

Angel, Jack (b. 1930) A prolific voice artist since the 1970s who can be heard on hundreds of episodes of TV cartoons, he supplied the voices of Squeeks the Caterpillar in *The Fox and the Hound* (1981), the toy Shark in *Toy Story* (1995), and the rock creature Chunk who is one of Lotso's henchmen in *Toy Story 3* (2010). He was born in Modesto, California, and began his career on radio, eventually getting his own show in Los Angeles. Angel began his voice artist career with the animated short *The Legend of Paul Bunyan* (1973) and within a few years he was voicing the TV cartoon series *The All-New Super Friends Hour*. Among the many other series he worked on are *Challenge of the Super-Friends* and its various sequels and spinoffs, *The Dukes, Voltron: Defender of the Universe, Pole Position, G.I. Joe, The Transformers, Crime Story, Peter Pan and the Pirates, TaleSpin, Where's Waldo?, Goof Troop, Darkwing Duck, Bonkers, Sonic the Hedgehog, The Legend of Prince Valiant, Spider-Man, Pokémon*, and *Avatar: The Last Airbender*. He can be heard in many animated videos and films, including *Metric Meets the Inchworm* (1974), *J-Men Forever* (1979), *Nutcracker Fantasy* (1979), *The Furious Funcycle* (1980), *Voltron: Fleet of Doom* (1986), *The Transformers: The Movie* (1986), *G.I. Joe: The Movie* (1987), *Sport Goofy in Soccermania* (1987), *Who Framed Roger Rabbit* (1988), *Dino-Riders in the Ice Age* (1989), *The Little Mermaid* (1989), *Land of Enchantment* (1990), *DuckTales: The Movie—Treasure of the Lost Lamp* (1990), *Beauty and the Beast* (1991), *An American Tail: Fievel Goes West* (1991), *Porco Rosso* (1992), *Aladdin* (1992), *Balto* (1995), *The Hunchback of Notre Dame* (1996), *Hercules* (1997), *A Bug's Life* (1998), *Tarzan* (1999), *The Iron Giant* (1999), *Toy Story 2* (1999), *The Trumpet of the Swan* (2001), *Spirited Away* (2001), *Monsters, Inc.* (2001), *Rapsittie Street Kids: Believe in Santa* (2002), *Lilo & Stitch* (2002), *Treasure Planet* (2002), *Ice Age: The Meltdown* (2006), *Cars* (2006), and *Horton Hears a Who!* (2008). He has also voiced many video games.

Anselmo, Tony (b. 1967) An animator-turned-actor, he has been the voice of Donald Duck since 1986. He was born in Salt Lake City, Utah, and studied animation at the California Institute of the Arts before joining the Disney studio as an animator. While working on the animation for such movies as *The Black Cauldron* (1985), *The Great Mouse Detective* (1986), *Oliver & Company* (1988), and *The Little Mermaid* (1989), he befriended voice artist Clarence Nash who taught him how to create the Donald Duck sounds. After Nash's death, Anselmo was asked to voice Donald in the TV special *DTV Valentine* (1986) and from that point on he has been the sole voice for the character. His Donald has been heard in such animated shorts as *The Prince and the Pauper* (1990), *Mouseworks Opera Box* (1999), and *How to Haunt a House* (1999), in a series of *Disney Sing-Along* videos , and in such video movies as *Down and Out with Donald Duck* (1987), *Mickey's House of Villains* (2001), *Kingdom Hearts* (2002), *Mickey's Twice Upon a Christmas* (2004), *The Lion King 1½* (2004), *Kingdom Hearts II* (2005), and *Mickey's Adventures in Wonderland* (2009). Anselmo can be heard on the TV cartoon series *DuckTales, Quack Pack, Mickey Mouse Works, House of Mouse*, and *Mickey Mouse Clubhouse*, and in the feature films *Who Framed Roger Rabbit* (1988), *A Goofy Movie* (1995), and *Fantasia 2000* (1999). Anselmo has joined with voice artist Russi Taylor and provided voices for Donald's nephews Huey, Dewey, and Louis on television and on videos, and he voiced the Thug Guard in *The Great Mouse Detective*. Even as he did voice work, Anselmo continued working as an animator and contributed to *Beauty and the Beast* (1991), *Aladdin* (1992), *The Lion King* (1994), *Pocahontas* (1995), *The Hunchback of Notre Dame* (1996), *Hercules* (1997), *Mulan* (1998), *Tarzan* (1999), *Fantasia 2000, The Emperor's New Groove* (2000), *Treasure Planet* (2002) *Home on the Range* (2004), and some videos.

Arnett, Will (b. 1970)   A Canadian actor with stage and film experience but is mostly known for his television roles, he provided the voice for Horst, the fierce-looking German *sous chef* with the deadly thumb, in *Ratatouille* (2007). William Emerson Arnett was born in Toronto, Canada, and trained at the Tarragon Theatre there and at the Lee Strasberg Theatre and Film Institute in New York City. He was featured in many television pilots that were not picked up by the networks but was seen on such series as *Sex and the City, The Mike O'Malley Show, Third Watch, Boston Public, The Sopranos*, and *Law & Order: Special Victims Unit* before finding acclaim as George "Gob" Bluth II in *Arrested Development*. Arnett was later featured in episodes of *Will & Grace, Odd Job Jack, Sesame Street, 30 Rock*, and *Running Wilde*, and has done voices for such cartoon series as *Danny Phantom, All-Star American Destiny Trek, Freak Show, King of the Hill*, and *Sit Down Shut Up*. Among Arnett's film credits are *Southy* (1998), *The Acting Class* (2000), *Despacito* (2004), *Monster-in-Law* (2005), *Runaway Vacation* (2006), *Let's Go to Prison* (2006), *Blades of Glory* (2007), *The Brothers Solomon* (2007), *G-Force* (2009), *When in Rome* (2010), and *Jonah Hex* (2010), as well as voices in the animated movies *Ice Age: The Meltdown* (2006), *Horton Hears a Who!* (2008), *Monsters vs. Aliens* (2009), and *Despicable Me* (2010).

Asner, Ed (b. 1929)   A favorite actor from television and film who is expert at playing grumpy, no-nonsense characters, he provided the voice of the disgruntled senior citizen Carl Fredrickson who sets off for South America in *Up* (2009). He was born Yitzhak Edward Asner in Kansas City, Missouri, and grew up across the river in the state of Kansas, later getting his education at the University of Chicago and beginning his career on the stage in that city. While serving with the U.S. Army Signal Corps, he toured to army bases in plays then later moved to New York City and appeared on stage in a few productions, including *The Threepenny Opera* (1956) Off Broadway and *Face of a Hero* (1960) on Broadway. Asner made his television debut in 1957 and over the next four decades acted in dozens of series, mini-series, and TV-movies. Among his television series are *Naked City, Route 66, Dr. Kildare, Ben Casey, The Defenders, Mr. Novak, Burke's Law, Gunsmoke, The Fugitive, Judd for the Defense, The F.B.I., Ironside, The Name of the Game, The Mod Squad, Insight, Off the Rack, The Bronx Zoo, The Trials of Rosie O'Neill, Hearts Afire, Thunder Alley, Roseanne, Mad About You, The Closer, The X-Files, Curb Your Enthusiasm, ER, The Practice, Center of the Universe, Studio 60 on the Sunset Strip*, and *The Cleveland Show*, but he will always be remembered as TV producer Lou Grant on *Mary Tyler Moore* for seven years and in the spinoff series *Lou Grant* for five years. Asner was also featured is such mini-series and made-for-TV films as *Rich Man, Poor Man* (1976), *Roots* (1977), *The Life and Assassination of the Kingfish* (1977), *The Gathering* (1977), *Yes, Virginia, There Is a Santa Claus* (1991), *Gone in the Night* (1996), *Pope John Paul XXIII* (2002), and *The Man Who Saved Christmas* (2002). His many films include *Kid Galahad* (1962), *The Slender Thread* (1965), *Gunn* (1967), *Change of Habit* (1969), *They Call me MISTER Tibbs* (1970), *Skin Game* (1971), *Gus* (1976), *Fort Apache the Bronx* (1981), *Daniel* (1983), *JFK* (1991), *The Fanatics* (1997), *Basil* (1997), *Academy Boyz* (1997), *Hard Rain* (1998), *The Bachelor* (1999), *Mars and Beyond* (2000), *Bring Him Home* (2000), *Above Suspicion* (2000), *The Animal* (2001), *Elf* (2003), *The Commission* (2003), *Sleeping Dogs Lie* (2005), *Gigantic* (2008), and *Sheeba* (2010). In the late 1980s Asner took up voice work and voiced hundreds of episodes of TV cartoons and animated films. Among the series he has voiced are *Fish Police, Sonic the Hedgehog, Animaniacs, Bonkers, Batman,*

Dinosaurs, Captain Planet and the Planeteers, Gargoyles, The Magic School Bus, Freakazoid, Recess, Life with Louie, The Angry Beavers, Spider-Man, Hercules, The Simpsons, Superman, Buzz Lightyear of Star Command, The Wild Thornberrys, Family Guy, King of the Hill, Johnny Bravo, The Grim Adventures of Billy & Mandy, Duck Dodgers, Justice League, W.I.T.C.H., WordGirl, and *The Boondocks.* Asner reprised his Carl Fredrickson in the video short *Dug's Special Mission* (2009) and can also be heard in such animated movies and videos as *Pinocchio and the Emperor of the Night* (1987), *3×3 Eyes* (1991), *Happily Ever After* (1993), *Gargoyles: The Heroes Awaken* (1995) and several of its sequels, *Spider-Man: Sins of the Fathers* (1996), *A Christmas Carol* (1997), *Our Friend Martin* (1999), *The Sissy Duckling* (1999), *Olive, the Other Reindeer* (1999), *Lolo's Cafe* (2006), *Christmas Is Here Again* (2007), and *Superman/Batman: Apocalypse* (2010). He returned to the stage on occasion, starring in *Born Yesterday* on Broadway in 1989. Although Asner was a familiar face to Americans, he was not the model for Carl Fredricksen in *Up*. The animators wanted a combination of film actors Spencer Tracy and Walter Matthau for the look of Carl. It was a first of sorts for the central character in an animated film to be a grumpy old man but Asner managed to be sympathetic and endearing even as he grumbled. The scriptwriters likened Carl to Scrooge in that he is not very likable but manages to redeem himself. When *Up* was dubbed for France, the octogenarian singer Charles Aznavour voiced the character of Carl.

Atkinson, Rowan (b. 1955) One of the most distinctive and physical of British comics and one who does not always depend on dialogue for his comedy, he provided the voice for the fussy hornbill Zazu, chief-of-protocol for the Pride Lands, in *The Lion King* (1994). Rowan Sebastian Atkinson was born in Consett, England, the son of a farmer, and studied electrical engineering at Newcastle University and Oxford University even as he wrote and performed in comedy revues. One of these revues received some attention at the Edinburgh Festival in 1976, leading to Atkinson's own BBC radio show *Atkinson People*. Moving on to television he found international success with the series *Not the Nine O'Clock News, The Black Adder, Mr. Bean,* and *The Thin Blue Line*. Atkinson reprised his Black Adder and Mr. Bean characters in a series of TV specials which have become cult favorites. Among his film credits are *Dead on Time* (1983), *Never Say Never Again* (1983), *The Witches* (1990), *Four Weddings and a Funeral* (1994), *Bean* (1997), *Scooby-Doo* (2002), *Love Actually* (2003), *Keeping Mum* (2005), and *Mr. Bean's Vacation* (2007). Atkinson's unusual voice can be heard in the TV cartoon series *Mr. Bean* which he also wrote. The directors of *The Lion King* considered (and in some cases actually auditioned) just about every major British actor for the role of Zazu, including Patrick Stewart, Simon Callow, and all five surviving Monty Python performers: John Cleese, Eric Idle, Terry Gilliam, Terry Jones, and Michael Palin. They selected Atkinson after watching some of his Mr. Bean comedy sketches, even though the character of Mr. Bean rarely speaks. Atkinson's vocals for the hornbill Zazu are stuffy British which contrast nicely with the more American voices of Mufasa and Simba. Biography: *Rowan Atkinson*, Bruce Dessau (2000).

Attenborough, Tom The English boy actor who voiced the British lad Christopher Robin in *The Tigger Movie* (2000), his only other credit is doing the voice of Harry Potter in two of the *Harry Potter* video games.

Atwell, Roy (1878–1962) A stage actor-singer with many silent and talking film credits, he provided the voice of Doc, the leader of the dwarfs, in *Snow White and the Seven Dwarfs* (1937). He was born in Syracuse, New York, and was educated at the Sargent School of Acting before working in vaudeville then making his New York legit stage debut in 1901. Atwell appeared in twenty Broadway productions, mostly musicals, such as *Moonshine* (1905), *Marrying Mary* (1906), *The Mimic World* (1908), *The Firefly* (1912), *The Laughing Husband* (1914), *Here Comes the Bride* (1917), *Apple Blossoms* (1919), *Helen of Troy, New York* (1923), *Americana* (1926), *John Murray Anderson's Almanac* (1929), *Strike Me Pink* (1933), and *On to Fortune* (1935). He started making silent film shorts in 1922 then played character parts in features and musical shorts when sound came in, including *The Harvester* (1936), *Varsity Show* (1937), *Honolulu* (1939), *The Fleet's In* (1942), *Abie's Irish Rose* (1946), and *Where There's Life* (1947). Atwell also acted in radio, sang with light opera companies, and wrote popular songs. The character of Doc uses some of Atwell's characteristics. In vaudeville, the performer often substituted the first syllables of consecutive words (called spoonerisms) and mispronounced words so they had a different meaning (called malaprops) for comic effect, and a few of these show up in Doc's dialogue in *Snow White and the Seven Dwarfs*.

Auberjonois, René (b. 1940) A small, lithe character actor who has appeared on stage, screen, and television in everything from Shakespeare to campy musicals, he has often stolen the show in supporting roles, as he did as the manic chef Louie in *The Little Mermaid* (1989). Auberjonois was born in New York City to French-Canadian parents and studied at Carnegie Mellon University in Pittsburgh before getting professional experience in regional theatre. He made an impressive New York debut in *King Lear* (1968) followed by other classical roles for the New York Shakespeare Festival. Auberjonois shone in the Broadway musicals *Coco* (1969), *Big River* (1985), *City of Angels* (1989), and *Dance of the Vampires* (2002), as well as in many plays. He made his film debut in *Lilith* (1964) followed by dozens of features, including *Brewster McCloud* (1970), *McCabe & Mrs. Miller* (1971), *Pete 'n' Tillie* (1972), *The Hindenberg* (1975), *King Kong* (1976), *Eyes of Laura Mars* (1978), *Where the Buffalo Roam* (1980), *Walker* (1987), *Star Trek VI: The Undiscovered Country* (1991), *The Ballad of Little Jo* (1993), *Batman Forever* (1995), *Inspector Gadget* (1999), *The Patriot* (2000), *The Princess Diaries* (2001), and *Eulogy* (2004). Auberjonois has provided voices for hundreds of cartoon episodes on television, such as *The Smurfs*, *Snorks*, *The Super Powers Team: Galactic Guardians*, *DuckTales*, *Miracles of Jesus*, *Darkwing Duck*, *The Pirates of Dark Water*, *Aladdin*, *Mighty Max*, *The Wild Thornberrys*, *The Legend of Tarzan*, *The Mummy: The Animated Series*, *Justice League*, *Xiaolin Showdown*, and *Avatar: The Last Airbender*, as well as reprising his Chef Louie in the series *Marsupilami* (1993), *The Little Mermaid* (1994), and *House of Mouse* (2002). He can also be heard in the animated films and videos *The Last Unicorn* (1982), *Billy the Kid* (1989), *Little Nemo: Adventures in Slumberland* (1989), *The Miracles of Jesus* (1991), *Cats Don't Dance* (1997), *An American Tale: The Treasure of Manhattan Island* (1998), *The Little Mermaid II: Return to the Sea* (2000), *Joseph: King of Dreams* (2000), *Commander and Conquers: Renegade* (2002), *Tarzan and Jane* (2002), *Geppetto's Secret* (2005), and *Uncharted 2: Among Thieves* (2009). Auberjonois has been a regular on several live-action TV series, including *Benson*, *Star Trek: Deep Space Nine*, *Judging Amy*, and *Boston Legal*, and appeared in many TV movies, such as Disney's *Geppetto* (2000) in which he played the diabolical Professor Buonragazzo.

Audley, Eleanor (1905–1991)   A durable television actress active from the 1950s through 1970, she voiced two classic Disney villains: Cinderella's cold-blooded stepmother Lady Tremaine in *Cinderella* (1950) and the wicked fairy Maleficent who turns herself into a dragon in *Sleeping Beauty* (1959). She was born Eleanor Zellman in New York City and trained for a stage career but ended up on the radio where she was very busy throughout the 1940s. She made her movie debut in 1949 and the next year voiced *Cinderella*, followed by appearances in such films as *Starlift* (1951), *Prince of Players* (1955), *All That Heaven Allows* (1955), *Home Before Dark* (1958), *A Summer Place* (1959), *The Pleasure of His Company* (1961), *The Unsinkable Molly Brown* (1964), and *Hook, Line and Sinker* (1969). Audley was much more successful on television where she played mothers, society matrons, and other character parts in dozens of series, including *Father Knows Best*, *The George Burns and Gracie Allen Show*, *The Millionaire*, *The Loretta Young Show*, *Richard Diamond: Private Detective*, *Perry Mason*, *The Many Loves of Dobie Gillis*, *Have Gun—Will Travel*, *The Dick Van Dyke Show*, *Wagon Train*, *The Beverly Hillbillies*, *Hazel*, and *My Three Sons*, though she is most remembered as Eddie Albert's obnoxious mother on *Green Acres*. She played Cinderella's stepmother a second time in a radio play called *The Six Shooter* (1953) which reset the tale in the wild West. Audley can be heard as the voice of Madame Leota in the Haunted Mansion in the Disney theme parks. The two Disney villains that Audley voiced are surprisingly different. Lady Tremaine in *Cinderella* possesses no supernatural powers, has no henchmen, and uses no violence. Yet her villainy is chilling in a quiet but deadly manner. Audley rarely raises her voice or moves beyond a slow, steady pace in her line readings. Maleficent in *Sleeping Beauty* is more actively sinister, letting her haughty voice revel in sarcasm and threats. Audley's performance here is more complex; the evil fairy has moments of high triumph and low cunning and one can almost hear the dragon she will become in Audley's vocal work. Actress Jane Fowler was the live-action model for Maleficent but it was Audley's commanding voice that helps make the character so unforgettable.

Backus, Jim (1913–1989)   A distinctive and popular character actor and voice artist who shone in movies, on television, and was heard in cartoons for over a period of fifty years (most memorably as Mr. Magoo), he provided the voice of wily Milton the Cat in the Pluto cartoon short *Plutopia* (1951). James Gilmore Backus was born in Cleveland, Ohio, and trained at the American Academy of Dramatic Arts in New York where he started working in radio. He was cast in two Broadway plays, *Hitch Your Wagon* (1937) and *Too Many Heroes* (1937), while he had his own radio show where he developed the character of the upper-class snob Hubert Updyke III, a type he would often play in films and on television. Backus was heard on screen before he was seen, voicing characters for the cartoons *Where Will You Hide?* (1948) and *A-Lad-in His Lamp* (1948). The next year he voiced the nearsighted Mr. Magoo for the first time in the short *Ragtime Bear* (1949), a beloved character he would reprise in over fifty cartoon shorts, on television, and on animated videos. He made his live-action movie debut in *One Last Fling* (1949), followed by more than eighty films, including *Father Was a Fullback* (1949), *Easy Living* (1949), *A Dangerous Profession* (1949), *Ma and Pa Kettle Go to Town* (1950), *M* (1951), *His Kind of Woman* (1951), *I'll See You in My Dreams* (1951), *Pat and Mike* (1952), *Don't Bother to Knock* (1952), *I Love Melvin* (1953), *Deep in My Heart* (1954), *Rebel Without a Cause* (1955), *Francis in the Navy* (1955), *Meet Me in Las Vegas* (1956), *The Opposite Sex* (1956), *The Girl He Left Behind* (1956), *The High Cost of Loving* (1958), *Ice Palace* (1960), *The Errand Boy* (1961), *Zotz!* (1962), *The Wonderful World of the Brothers Grimm* (1962), *Critic's Choice* (1963), *Sunday in New York* (1963), *Billie* (1965), *Hurry Sundown* (1967), *Hello Down There* (1969), *Crazy Mama* (1975), *Pete's Dragon* (1977), *C.H.O.M.P.S.* (1979), and *Prince Jack* (1985), as well as many TV-movies. Backus appeared on television as early as 1949 and over the decades acted in dozens of series, among them *I Married Joan*, *The Web*, *Conflict*, *Climax!*, *Playhouse 90*, *The Untouchables*, *77 Sunset Strip*, *Hot Off the Wire*, *Maverick*, *McKeever and the Colonel*, *The Beverly Hillbillies*, *Burke's Law*, *I Spy*, *Blondie*, *Nanny and the Professor*, *The Brady Bunch*, *Joe Forrester*, *Police Story*, *CHiPs*, *Fantasy Island*, and *Trapper John, M.D.*, but he will always be remembered as the aristocratic Thurston Howell III in *Gilligan's Island* for three years and in its several film and TV sequels. In addition to voicing Mr. Magoo on the cartoon series *Mister Magoo*, *The Famous Adventures of Mr. Magoo*, and *What's New, Mr. Magoo?*, he provided voices for such TV series as *The Bugs Bunny Show*, *The Bugs Bunny/Road Runner Hour*, *The New Adventures of Gilligan*, *Gilligan's Planet*, *The Bugs Bunny and Tweety Show*, and *Merrie Melodies: Starring Bugs Bunny and Friends*. Backus can also be heard in the animated movies and videos *1001 Arabian Nights* (1959), *Yes, Virginia, There Is a Santa Claus* (1974), *The Enchanted Journey* (1984), and many Mr. Magoo videos, in particular the holiday favorite *Mr. Magoo's Christmas Carol* (1962). Memoirs: *Rocks on the Roof* (1958), *What Are You Doing After the Orgy?* (1962), *Only When I Laugh* (1965), *Backus Strikes Back* (1984), and *Forgive Us Our Digressions* (1998), all with Henny Backus (his wife).

Baddeley, Hermione (1906–1986)   A British comedienne with a long career on the stage who livened up many a movie and television show with her frumpy, crusty Cockney characters, she voiced the eccentric Parisian millionaire Madame Adelaide Bonfamille in *The Aristocats* (1970). She was born Hermione Youlanda Ruby Clinton-Baddeley in Broseley in the Shropshire region of England and was on the stage by the time she was six, making her London stage debut at the age of twelve. While her first love was the theatre and she performed in hundreds of plays in England, she also started making films in 1927 and was on British television beginning in 1949. By the 1960s Baddeley was working in both British and American movies but by the 1970s she was most known for her many TV series in the States, in particular her outspoken Mrs. Naugatuck in *Maude*. Among her many movies are *Passport to Pimlico* (1949), *A Christmas Carol* (1951), *Tom Brown's Schooldays* (1951), *The Pickwick Papers* (1952), *Room at the Top* (1959), *Midnight Lace* (1960), *The Unsinkable Molly Brown* (1964), *Mary Poppins* (1964), *The Adventures of Bullwhip Griffin* (1967), *The Happiest Millionaire* (1967), *C.H.O.M.P.S.* (1979), and *There Goes the Bride* (1980). Her distinctive Cockney voice can be heard in the animated film *The Secret of Nimh* (1982). Baddeley's only Disney animated role was quite against type. Not only was Madame Bonfamille in *The Aristocats* not British but she was upper-class French gentility, though eccentric enough to want to leave her entire fortune to her cats. Autobiography: *The Unsinkable Hermione Baddeley* (1984).

Bader, Diedrich (b. 1966)   A character actor who has voiced many television cartoon series, he provided the voice of the snide Veteran Cat in *Bolt* (2008). He was born Karl Diedrich Bader in Alexandria, Virginia, the son of a diplomat and a sculptor, grew up in Paris, France, and returned to the States to attend the North Carolina School of the Arts. Before finishing college he was acting on such TV series as *Star Trek: The Next Generation*, *21 Jump Street*, *Cheers*, *The Fresh Prince of Bel-Air*, *Quantum Leap*, *Center of the Universe*, *Bones*, and *Outsourced*, but he is most remembered as Oswald Lee Harvey on *The Drew Carey Show* for nine years. Bader's film credits include *The Beverly Hillbillies* (1993), *Teresa's Tattoo* (1994), *Office Space* (1999), *Evil Alien Conquers* (2002), *Napoleon Dynamite* (2004), *Miss Congeniality 2: Armed & Fabulous* (2005), *Cattle Call* (2006), and *Meet the Spartans* (2008). His deep, husky voice has been heard in hundreds of episodes of such animated series as *Gargoyles*, *Hercules*, *The Simpsons*, *Pepper Ann*, *Buzz Lightyear of Star Command*, *The Zeta Project*, *Kim Possible*, *The Replacements*, *The Grim Adventures of Billy & Mandy*, *Higglytown Heroes*, *Batman*, *King of the Hill*, *The Penguins of Madagascar*, *The Secret Saturdays*, *Batman: The Brave and Bold*, and *Kung Fu Pandas: Legends of Awesomeness*, as well as the films and videos *Hercules: Zero to Hero* (1999), *Barok the Magnificent* (1999), *Olive, the Other Reindeer* (1999), *Buzz Lightyear of Star Command: The Adventure Begins* (2000), *Recess: School's Out* (2001), *Ice Age* (2002), *The Country Bears* (2002), *Dinotopia:*

The Quest for Ruby Sunstone (2005), *Surf's Up* (2007), and *Open Season 2* (2008).

Bailey, G. W. (b. 1944) A character actor who has often played roles much older than himself on television and film, he provided the voice of Rusty, the Sheriff's dog, in *Home on the Range* (2004). He was born George William Bailey in Port Arthur, Texas, and attended Lamar University and Texas Tech in Lubbock before leaving school to become a professional actor. (In the 1990s he finally finished a theatre degree at Southwest Texas State University.) Bailey worked in regional theatre, where his prematurely-graying hair made him ideal for older characters, before making his television debut in 1975, appearing in a variety of TV series before finding wide recognition as Sergeant Luther Rizzo on *M*A*S*H*. He was also featured in the series *St. Elsewhere*, *The Jeff Foxworthy Show*, *The Closer*, and *Goodnight, Beantown*, as well as many mini-series and made-for-TV movies. Among Bailey's movie credits are *A Force of One* (1979), *Runaway* (1984), *Short Circuit* (1986), *Mannequin* (1987), *Write to Kill* (1991), *Brothers, Dogs and God* (2000), and *Cake: A Wedding Story* (2007), but he is most remembered as Lt. Thaddeus Harris in *Police Academy* (1984) and four of its sequels.

Bailey, Pearl (1918–1990) The smooth-voiced African American nightclub singer and recording star made only a handful of stage, television, and film appearances but each one was memorable, as was her acting and singing vocals for the wise and motherly owl Big Mama in *The Fox and the Hound* (1981). Bailey was born in Newport News, Virginia, the daughter of a preacher, and she started singing in vaudeville and cabarets as a teenager. By the 1940s she was singing in Manhattan's finest supper clubs and in 1946 she made her Broadway debut in *St. Louis Woman*. Bailey also appeared in the musicals *Arms and the Girl* (1950), *Bless You All* (1950), and *House of Flowers* (1954), but her greatest Broadway triumph was as a wisecracking Dolly Levi in *Hello, Dolly!* (1967 and 1975). Although she had appeared on screen in specialty bits in *Variety Girl* (1947) and *Isn't It Romantic?* (1948), she got to play more memorable supporting roles in *Carmen Jones* (1954), *St. Louis Blues* (1958), and *Porgy and Bess* (1959). Bailey appeared on many television specials during her long career, including appearances on *Disneyland* (1981). During the preparation of *The Fox and the Hound*, the animators were concerned about developing a wise owl character that was not just a repeat of similar owls in *Bambi* (1942), *The Sword in the Stone* (1963), and the *Winnie the Pooh* shorts. Once Pearl Bailey was cast to do the vocals, they patterned the owl after the singer's easy-going persona and made the character not so much a sage as a friendly neighbor with good common sense. Bailey's singing also set the laid-back tone for the story. Autobiographies: *The Raw Pearl* (1968), *Between You and Me* (1989)

Bakalyan, Richard (b. 1931) A tough-looking character actor who moved from playing juvenile delinquents to adult thugs during his long career, he provided the voices of two Disney birds: the put-upon M. C. Bird who is tormented by civilization in the short *It's Tough to Be a Bird* (1969) and the pint-sized sparrow Dinky in *The Fox and the Hound* (1981). He was born in Watertown, Massachusetts, and had a run-in with the law as a teenager. Bakalyan made his screen debut in 1954 and soon was playing youthful trouble makers in *The Delinquents* (1957), *The Delicate Delinquent* (1957), *Dino* (1957), *The Brothers Rico* (1957), *The Cool and the Crazy* (1958), *Juvenile Jungle* (1958), and other films. He was also cast as juveniles in many television series, including *Official Detective*, *The Lineup*, *The Walter Winchell File*, *Mike Hammer*, and *The Lawless Years*. As Bakalyan matured, he was given a variety of roles but often he was still cast as the heavy. Among his many other movies are *Up Periscope* (1959), *The Errand Boy* (1961), *Robin and the 7 Hoods* (1964), *None but the Brave* (1965), *Von Ryan's Express* (1965), *The St. Valentine's Day Massacre* (1967), *The Computer Wore Tennis Shoes* (1969), *Charley and the Angel* (1973), *Chinatown* (1974), *The Shaggy D.A.* (1976), *Return from Witch Mountain* (1978), *The Mask Maker* (2000), and *Art School Confidential* (2006). He was kept even busier on television where he appeared in dozens of series between 1957 and 2008, such as *The Many Loves of Dobie Gillis*, *The Rebel*, *The Untouchables*, *Combat!*, *Batman*, *Gunsmoke*, *Mannix*, *Cannon*, *Switch*, *Emergency!*, *Barnaby Jones*, *The Rockford Files*, *CHiPs*, *Charlie's Angels*, *Vega$*, *Cagney & Lacey*, *Matlock*, *Hunter*, *Baywatch Nights*, *Cold Case*, and *My Name Is Earl*.

Baker, Joe (1928–2001) A popular British television star, he voiced the red-headed, red-bearded English settler Lon in *Pocahontas* (1995). He was born in London, the son of British vaudevillians, and worked as a stand-up comic, pantomime actor, impressionist, and musical theatre actor on the London stage before finding notoriety on BBC television. After starring in the TV shows *The Joe Baker Show*, *Baker's Half Dozen*, *My Man Joe*, and *Crackerjack*, he emigrated to the States in 1975 and appeared on such American television series as *Mrs. Columbo*, *Fantasy Island*, *Matt Houston*, *Trapper John M.D.*, *Highway to Heaven*, *Coach*, *Doogie Howser M.D.*, and *Acapulco H.E.A.T.* Baker also acted in the movies *The Apple Dumpling Gang Rides Again* (1979), *C.H.O.M.P.S.* (1979), *Waxwork* (1988),

Bugsy (1991), *Waxwork II: Lost in Time* (1992), *Robin Hood: Men in Tights* (1993), *Freaked* (1993), *Dumb & Dumber* (1994), and *Art House* (1998). He can be heard in the TV cartoon series *The Skatebirds, The Robonic Stooges, The Big Show*, and *The Kwicky Koala Show*, as well as the videos *Fred and Barney Meet the Thing* (1979), *Fred and Barney Meet the Shmoo* (1979), *The Flintstones: Wind-Up Wilma* (1981), and *Adventures in Odyssey: Shadow of a Doubt* (1993).

Bale, Christian (b. 1974) A British actor who found success in the movies as a teenager and has become a major star as an adult, he voiced the young English settler Thomas who discovers the humanity of the Native Americans in *Pocahontas* (1995). Christian Charles Philip Bale was born in Haverfordwest in Wales, the son of an English commercial pilot, and grew up in several different countries, allowing him to pick up different accents. At the age of ten he was performing on the London stage, then was featured in the television movie *Anastasia: The Mystery of Anna* (1986) and the Swedish film *Mio in the Land of Faraway* (1987). Bale became internationally known as the English teenager Jamie Graham who is caught up in World War II in Asia in the movie *Empire of the Sun* (1987), followed by notable performances as teens in *Henry V* (1989), *Newsies* (1992), *Swing Kids* (1993), and *Royal Deceit* (1994), as well as in the TV movies *Treasure Island* (1990) and *A Murder of Quality* (1991). He moved into young adulthood in *Little Women* (1994) then moved back and forth from big-budget Hollywood projects and small (and often controversial) independent films. Among his many other screen credits are *The Portrait of a Lady* (1996), *The Secret Agent* (1996), *A Midsummer Night's Dream* (1999), *American Psycho* (2000), *Shaft* (2000), *Equilibrium* (2002), *The Machinist* (2004), *Batman Begins* (2005), *The New World* (2005), *Rescue Dawn* (2006), *The Prestige* (2006), *3:10 to Yuma* (2007), *The Dark Knight* (2008), *Terminator Salvation* (2009), *Public Enemies* (2009), and *The Fighter* (2010). Bale can be heard in the English version of the animated film *Howl's Moving Castle* (2004). Biography: *Christian Bale: From Bad Man to Batman*, Cheung Harrison (2011).

Ball, Sherwood A pop, soul, and rock singer-musician associated with various bands throughout his career, he has sung and done voices for films, including *The Nightmare Before Christmas* (1993) in which he voiced the skinny Mummy and one of the quartet of Vampires. Born in California into a musical family (his father is strings musician Ernie Ball and his great-grandfather Ernest Ball composed "When Irish Eyes Are Smiling"), he began acting at a young age, appearing as a kid in the film *Follow Me, Boys!* (1966) and the TV series *Make Room for Grandaddy* in 1970. As an adult Ball mostly pursued music, composing and singing in bands and writing and/or singing songs for such movies as *Three for the Road* (1987), *Let It Ride* (1989), *Always* (1989), *Down the Drain* (1990), *Solar Crisis* (1990), *Out for Justice* (1991), *Killer Tomatoes Strike Back!* (1991), and *Skins* (1994). as well as for the television series *The Chipmunks, Hangin' with Mr. Cooper*, and *Jake and the Fatman*. He can be heard in the animated videos *Little Nemo: Adventures in Slumberland* (1989) and *The Chipmunks' Rockin' Through the Decades* (1990), and seen in the films *Solar Crisis* (1990) and *102 Dalmatians* (2000). Ball has done many speaking and singing TV commercials throughout his career and was the announcer for Toyota ads for over ten years.

Bana, Eric (b. 1968) A handsome Australian actor who has found popularity in the States, he voiced the hammerhead shark Anchor in *Finding Nemo* (2003). He was born Eric Banadinovich in Melbourne, Australia, and began his career as a stand-up comic doing impersonations of celebrities in Sydney clubs and later on Australian television. His various characterizations on the series *Full Frontal* and *Eric* made him very popular in his native country, but it was his performances in such movies as *Chopper* (2000), *Black Hawk Down* (2001), *Troy* (2004), *Munich* (2005), *The Other Boleyn Girl* (2008), *Star Trek* (2009), and *The Time Traveler's Wife* (2009) that made him an international star.

Barclay, Don (1892–1975) A beefy character actor who appeared in over eighty movies between 1915 and 1964, he voiced the palace Doorman in *Cinderella* (1950) and the saucy Card in the Queen of Hearts' garden in *Alice in Wonderland* (1951). He was born Donn Van Tassel Barclay in Ashland, Oregon, and made his screen debut in the silent short *That Little Band of Gold* (1915). His chubby figure and expressive face made him ideal for comedy and he made the transition to sound movies with no difficulty. Among his many talkies are *Frisco Kid* (1935), *Man Hunt* (1936), *Kid Galahad* (1937), *Outlaw Express* (1938), *The Oklahoma Kid* (1939), *Frankenstein Meets the Wolf Man* (1943), *Thank Your Lucky Stars* (1943), *Shine on Harvest Moon* (1944), *My Darling Clementine* (1946), *The Long Grey Line* (1955), and *Mary Poppins* (1964). Barclay also provided various voices for *One Hundred and One Dalmatians* (1961).

Bardsley, Grant (b. 1967) A British child actor mostly on television in the United Kingdom, he voiced the young hero Taran, the pig keeper who dreams of becoming a warrior, in *The Black Cauldron* (1985), his only voice credit. Bardsley appeared as one of the children in the film *The Blue Bird* (1976) and that same year made his British television debut. He played young boys in such mini-series as *Wuthering Heights* (1978), *The Famous Five* (1978), *Tales of the Unexpected* (1980), and *To Serve Them All My Days* (1980), retiring from acting in 1989. Bardsley was fourteen years old when he voiced *The Black Cauldron*, the same age as the hero Taran, and it is a solid performance, retaining youthful excitement but also a maturing sense of responsibility.

Barnes, Christopher Daniel (b. 1972) An actor and voice artist since he was a teenager, he provided the voice for the hero Prince Eric in *The Little Mermaid* (1989). He was born in Portland. Maine, and began his television career at the age of twelve under the name C. B. Barnes, appearing in such series as *As the World Turns, Starman, The Golden Girls,* and *Day by Day.* Although he was only seventeen when *The Little Mermaid* was made, the directors thought he sounded much older and cast him in the major role. Prince Eric is not in the film as much as Ariel and her friends so he is given little chance to develop his character. But the dialogue and Barnes' casual, very accessible vocals keep Eric from being the stiff, vague prince with which former Disney heroines fell in love. Barnes voiced characters in the television cartoon series *Captain Planet and the Planeteers, Spider-Man, Jackie Chan Adventures,* and *Sonic Underground,* and voiced another royal hero, Prince Charming, in the videos *Cinderella II: Dreams Come True* (2002) and *Cinderella III: A Twist in Time* (2007). As an adult, Barnes appeared in such TV series as *Empty Nest, Blossom, Clueless, Malcolm & Eddie, 7th Heaven, Touched by an Angel,* and *Beverly Hill, 90210,* and played Greg Brady in the film *The Brady Bunch Movie* (1995) and its sequel *A Very Brady Sequel* (1996).

Barr, Roseanne *see* **Rosanne**

Barrie, Barbara (b. 1931) A diminutive and perky singer-actress who specialized in comedies and musicals on Broadway as well as many series on television, she voiced Hercules' foster mother Alcemene in *Hercules* (1997). She was born Barbara Ann Berman in Chicago and was educated at Southwestern University in Georgetown, Texas, and the University of Texas at Austin before going to New York and studying acting at the Herbert Berghof Studio. Barrie made her Broadway debut and her television bow in 1955. She shone in such New York stage productions as *The Crucible* (1958), *Twelfth Night* (1969), *Company* (1970), *The Prisoner of Second Avenue* (1972), *California Suite* (1976), *Isn't It Romantic* (1984), and *After-Play* (1995), and has been seen in dozens of TV series, including *The Phil Silvers Show, Love of Life, Naked City, The Defenders, Ben Casey, Ironside, McMillan & Wife, Barney Miller, Breaking Away, Reggie, Double Trouble, thirtysomething,* and *Suddenly Susan,* as well as many mini-series and made-for-TV movies. Barrie reprised her Alcmene in the TV series *Hercules* as well as in the video *Hercules: Zero to Hero* (1999). In addition to a handful of movies, such as *Giant* (1956), *The Caretakers* (1963), *Breaking Away* (1979), *Private Benjamin* (1980), and *Judy Berlin* (1999), Barrie is a successful author of fiction and non-fiction books.

Bart, Roger (b. 1962) A small, lively character actor with a continual smirk who has shone in several Broadway musicals, he provided the singing voice for Young Hercules in *Hercules* (1997), introducing the song "Go the Distance." He was born in Norwalk, Connecticut, and educated at the Mason Gross School of Arts at Rutgers University. Bart made his Broadway debut in 1987 as a replacement for the role of Tom Sawyer in *Big River,* then appeared on television shows such as *Law & Order* before returning to play major roles on Broadway in *Triumph of Love* (1997), *You're a Good Man, Charlie Brown* (1999), *The Producers* (2001), *The Frogs* (2004), and *Young Frankenstein* (2007). Bart was a regular on the TV series *Bram and Alice* and *Desperate Housewives,* and his film credits include *The Stepford Wives* (2004), *The Producers* (2005), *American Gangster* (2007), *Harold & Kumar Escape from Guantanamo Bay* (2008), and *Law Abiding Citizen* (2009). He can be heard as the singing voice of the mischievous pup Scamp in the video sequel *Lady and the Tramp II: Scamp's Adventure* (2001).

Bartlett, Peter (b. 1942) A stage character actor known for doing unusual and demanding plays who later found success on television, he provided the voice for Prince Naveen's overly-ambitious valet Lawrence in *The Princess and the Frog* (2009). The Chicago native made his Broadway debut in *A Patriot for Me* (1969), followed by *Gloria and Esperanza* (1970), *Boom Boom Room* (1973), *Beauty and the Beast* (1994), *Voices in the Dark* (1999), *Never Gonna Dance* 2003), *The Frogs* (2004), and *The Drowsy Chaperone* (2006), as well as such Off Broadway productions as *The Crazy Locomotive* (1977), *The Learned Ladies* (1991), *Jeffrey* (1993), *The Naked Truth* (1994), *Don Juan in Chicago* (1995), *The Most Fabulous Story Ever Told* (1998), *Rude Entertainment* (2001), and *What's That Smell? The Music of Jacob Sterling* (2008). Bartlett did not make his television bow until he was fifty-two years old, appearing in the series *The Cosby Mysteries,*

Law & Order, Ed, and *Law & Order: Criminal Intent*, and he is best known as Nigel Bartholomew-Smythe on the soap opera *One Life to Live*. He can also be seen in the films *Jeffrey* (1995), *Meet the Parents* (2000), *Get Well Soon* (2001), and *The Producers* (2005).

Barty, Billy (1924–2000) Hollywood's favorite "midget" actor and the founder of the organization Little People of America, he voiced the cowardly Australian rodent Baitmouse in *The Rescuers Down Under* (1990). He was born William John Bertanzetti in Millsboro, Pennsylvania, and made his screen debut at the age of three in the Mickey Rooney comedy short *Mickey's Eleven* (1927). The teaming of the two tiny performers was so successful that Barty co-starred as Mickey's Brother in over fifty more shorts, then went on to act in such features as *Daddy Long Legs* (1931), *Gold Diggers of 1933* (1933), *Footlight Parade* (1933), *Bride of Frankenstein* (1935), *A Midsummer Night's Dream* (1935), *Three Wise Fools* (1946), *Jungle Jim in Pygmy Island* (1950), *The Clown* (1953), *The Wonderful World of the Brothers Grimm* (1962), *Roustabout* (1964), *Harum Scarum* (1965), *The Perils of Pauline* (1967), *Pufnstuf* (1970), *The Day of the Locust* (1975), *W. C. Fields and Me* (1976), *The Amazing Dobermans* (1976), *The Happy Hooker Goes to Washington* (1977), *Rabbit Test* (1978), *Foul Play* (1978), *Legend* (1985), *Tough Guys* (1986), *Body Slam* (1986), *Rumpelstiltskin* (1987), *Snow White* (1987), *Masters of the Universe* (1987), *Willow* (1988), *Life Stinks* (1991), and *Outlaws: The Legend of O. B. Taggart* (1994). Curiously, Hollywood's most famous Little Person was not in the movie that employed more midgets than any other: *The Wizard of Oz* (1939); though Barty was later featured in the movie *Under the Rainbow* (1981) about the making of that classic film. He made his television debut in 1951 and appeared on many shows, including the series *The Dennis Day Show, The Spike Jones Show, The Colgate Comedy Hour, Circus Boy, Shirley Temple Theatre, Peter Gunn, Rawhide, Roman & Martin's Laugh-In, Get Smart, The Red Skelton Hour, The Bugaloos, Sigmund and the Sea Monsters, Phyllis, Chico and the Man, The Love Boat, Fantasy Island, CHiPs, Little House on the Prairie, Hart to Hart, The Munsters Today, Jack's Place, Frasier*, and *L.A. Heat*. Barty also voiced the TV cartoon series *Wildfire, DuckTales*, and *The New Batman Adventures*. In addition to founding the Little People of America in 1957, he also established the charitable Billy Barty Foundation in 1975 and campaigned for the passing of the Americans with Disabilities Act. Biography: *Within Reach: An Inspirational Journey into the Life, Legacy and Influence of Billy Barty*, Michael Copeland (2002).

Baskett, James (1904–1948) Forever remembered as the warm-hearted African American character actor-singer who played Uncle Remus in *Song of the South* (1946) and introduced the Oscar-winning song "Zip-a-Dee-Doo-Dah," he also voiced the animated character of Brer Fox in that film (as well as one sequence as Brer Rabbit) and provided the singing and speaking voice for one of the crow quartet in *Dumbo* (1941). Baskett was born in Indianapolis, Indiana, the son of a barber, and started to study to become a pharmacist until he ran out of money so he went to New York City where he found jobs on the stage, later appearing in the Broadway musicals *Hot Chocolates* (1929) and *Deep Harlem* (1929). Baskett made his movie debut in *Harlem Is Heaven* (1932) and went on to play roles in such films as *Gone Harlem* (1938), *Straight to Heaven* (1939), *Comes Midnight* (1940), *Revenge of the Zombies* (1943), and *The Heavenly Body* (1944). He was also heard on a handful of radio shows in the 1940s, including the *Amos 'n' Andy Show* where he voiced the character of lawyer Gabby Gibson for four years. *Song of the South* afforded Baskett his most beloved role. He originally auditioned for the voice of an animated butterfly but he so impressed Disney and his crew that eventually he played leading roles in both the live-action and animated sections of the movie. As the live-action Uncle Remus, Baskett is easygoing, comfortable, warm, and boasts a deep soothing voice. As the animated Brer Fox, his vocals are hyperactive, high-pitched, and shrill. The fox is a comic villain who always fails yet is endearing in an odd way, just like the forever-unsuccessful Wile E. Coyote in the Warner Brothers cartoons. During the recording of *Song of the South*, actor Johnny Lee, who voiced Brer Rabbit, was called away to promote the film and the sequence about a "Laughing Place" needed to be done. Baskett imitated Lee's characterization and did the speaking and singing voice of the rabbit for that scene. *Song of the South* was Baskett's last film. He reprised his performance on a 1947 radio broadcast of *The Hedda Hopper Show* then died the next year.

Bassett, Angela (b. 1958) The acclaimed African American actress who has played many real-life characters on television and in the movies, she provided the voice for the kindly Mildred who runs the orphanage in *Meet the Robinsons* (2007). Angela Evelyn Bassett was born in New York City, raised in St. Petersburg, Florida, and educated at the Yale School of Drama before beginning her career on the New York stage. She appeared in the Off Broadway productions of *Black Girl* (1986) and *Henry IV Part I* (1987) and was on Broadway in *Joe Turner's Come and Gone* (1988); she later returned to the New York stage as Lady Macbeth in *Macbeth* (1998). Bassett made her television debut in 1985 and was first noticed the next year in the cult sci-fi series *F/X*, followed by such series as *The Cosby Show*, *Ryan's Hope*, *A Man Called Hawk*, *thirtysomething*, *Alias*, and *ER*. She won more praise for her films and TV movies, playing Katherine Jackson in *The Jacksons: An American Dream* (1992), Dr. Betty Shabazz in *Malcolm X* (1992), Tina Turner in *What's Love Got to Do with It* (1993), and the title role in *The Rosa Parks Story* (2002). Among her other film credits are *Boyz n the Hood* (1991), *Passion Fish* (1992), *Vampire in Brooklyn* (1995), *Waiting to Exhale* (1995), *How Stella Got Her Groove Back* (1998), *Music of the Heart* (1999), *Boesman and Lena* (2000), *Mr. and Mrs. Smith* (2005), *Nothing but the Truth* (2008), and *Notorious* (2009). Memoir: *Friends: A Love Story*, with Courtney Vance (her husband), (2006); biography: *Angela Bassett*, Dawn FitzGerald (2001).

Baucom, Bill (1910–1981) A television actor who appeared mostly in Westerns in the 1950s, he provided the voice for the aging bloodhound Trusty in *Lady and the Tramp* (1955). His television credits include the series *Judge Roy Bean*, *Annie Oakley*, *Alfred Hitchcock Presents*, *The Life and Legend of Wyatt Earp*, *M Squad*, *26 Men*, and *Gunsmoke*. The old hound dog Trusty, who bores the other dogs with stories of his days tracking down escaped criminals, is one of the most lovable of Disney sidekicks. Audiences were so taken with him that when he is crushed by the dog pound wagon trying to save Tramp, the effect was shocking. So Walt Disney insisted Trusty be added to the epilogue scene at Christmas, showing that he was not killed by the wagon. Baucom's slow Southern drawl in the vocals was among Trusty's many endearing qualities.

Bauer, Cate (b. 1922) A British stage actress, she provided the voice for the London canine Perdita who gives birth to the fifteen dalmatian puppies in *One Hundred and One Dalmatians* (1961). The London-born Bauer's only other film or television credit is appearing in one episode of the BBC TV series *The Third Man* in 1959.

Beaird, Barbara (b. 1948) A child performer in films and television who retired from acting at the age of fourteen, she supplied the voice for the pudgy, forever-hungry dalmatian pup Rolly in *One Hundred and One Dalmatians* (1961). She was born in Waco, Texas, and was spotted by a talent agent when her family was vacationing in California. Beaird played little girls in the movies *The Man in the Net* (1959), *Toby Tyler, or Ten Weeks with a Circus* (1960), and *Flaming Star* (1960), as well as episodes of the television series *Steve Canyon*, *Death Valley Days*, *Fibber McGee and Molly*, *Startime*, *The Danny Thomas Show*, *Wagon Train*, *Rawhide*, and *Dr. Kildare*.

Beal, John (1909–1997) A handsome leading man of stage and screen whose six-decade-long career also included many television appearances, he was the voice of Adult Jeremiah who is the Narrator of *So Dear to My Heart* (1948). He was born James Alexander Bliedung in Joplin, Missouri, and was studying art in New York City when he turned to acting, making his Broadway debut in 1931. Among his early Broadway credits are *Wild Waves* (1932), *Another Language* (1932), *She Loves Me Not* (1933), *Russet Mantle* (1936), *Miss Swan Expects* (1939), and *Liberty Jones* (1941). Beal made his screen bow in the 1933 film version of *Another Language* then played romantic leads in such movies as *The Little Minister* (1934), *Laddie* (1935), *Les Misérables* (1935), *M'Liss* (1936), *We Who Are About to Die* (1937), *The Man Who Found Himself* (1937), *Madame X* (1937), *The Arkansas Traveler* (1938), and *The Cat and the Canary* (1939). He continued to find good roles as he matured, including the films *Doctors Don't Tell* (1941), *One Thrilling Night* (1942), *Edge of Darkness* (1943), *Key Witness* (1947), *Chicago Deadline* (1949), *My Six Convicts* (1952), *Remains to Be Seen* (1953), *The Vampire* (1957), *The Sound and the Fury* (1959), *Ten Who Dared* (1960), *The House That Cried Murder* (1973), *Amityville 3-D* (1983), and *The Firm* (1993). Beal began doing television series as early as 1949 and over the decades acted in dozens of shows, including *Lights Out*, *Schlitz Playhouse*, *Kraft Theatre*, *Inner Sanctum*, *Goodyear Playhouse*, *Studio One in Hollywood*, *The Ann Sothern Show*, *The Millionaire*, *The Loretta Young Show*, *Bonanza*, *The United States Steel Hour*, *The Defenders*, *The Doctors and the Nurses*, *Dark Shadows*, *Kojak*, *The Waltons*, *The Blue Knight*, *The Streets of San Francisco*, and *Family*, as well as such mini-series as *Lincoln* (1974), *The Adams Chronicles* (1976), and *Eleanor and Franklin* (1977). He returned to Broadway in *Calculated Risk* (1962), *Billy* (1969), *In the Matter of J. Robert Oppenheimer* (1969), *Our Town* (1969), *The Changing Room* (1973), *The Crucible* (1991), *A Little Hotel on the Side* (1992), *The Master Builder* (1992), *The Seagull* (19920, and *Three Men on a Horse* (1993).

Beatty, Ned (b. 1937) A pudgy, prolific character actor of over one hundred films who usually plays genial characters, he provided the voice for the seemingly-friendly but sinister toy Lots-O-Huggin' Bear in *Toy Story 3* (2010). He was born in Louisville, Kentucky, and raised in nearby St. Matthews where he sang in barbershop quartets and churches before going on the stage. After appearing in an outdoor drama and regional theatre in Kentucky, Beatty appeared on Broadway in *The Great White Hope* (1968). He made a memorable film debut in *Deliverance* (1972) and was immediately in demand for a variety of supporting roles, often rural and amiable types, and became one of the busiest actors in Hollywood. Among his many notable films are *The Life and Times of Judge Roy Bean* (1972), *White Lightning* (1973), *W. W. and the Dixie Dancekings* (1975), *Nashville* (1975), *Gator* (1976), *Network* (1976), *Silver Streak* (1976), *Exorcist II: The Heretic* (1977), *Wise Blood* (1979), *Superman II* (1980), *The Incredible Shrinking Woman* (1981), *Stroker Ace* (1983), *Back to School* (1986), *The Big Easy* (1986), *Hear My Song* (1991), *Prelude to a Kiss* (1992), *Rudy* (1993), *Radioland Murders* (1995), *Cookie's Fortune* (1999), *Life* (1999), *Where the Red Fern Grows* (2003), *Shooter* (2007), *Charlie Wilson's War* (2007), and *The Killer Inside Me* (2010). Beatty has also been featured in dozens of TV-movies, most memorably *The Execution of Private Slovik* (1974), *Tail Gunner Joe* (1977), *Friendly Fire* (1979), *Guyana Tragedy: The Story of Jim Jones* (1980), *All the Way Home* (1981), *A Woman Called Golda* (1982), *Back to Hannibal: The Return of Tom Sawyer and Huckleberry Finn* (1990), *T Bone N Weasel* (1992), *Lincoln* (1992), and *Homicide: The Movie* (2000). He has acted in such television series as *The Waltons*, *Kojak*, *Gunsmoke*, *Lucas Tanner*, *M*A*S*H*, *Hunter*, *The Rockford Files*, *The Streets of San Francisco*, *Syysznyk*, *Highway to Heaven*, *Avonlea*, *The Boys*, *Roseanne*, *Homicide: Life on the Street*, and *Law & Order*. Beatty has returned to the stage on occasion, acting in regional theatres and starring on Broadway in *Cat on a Hot Tin Roof* (2003) which he also played to acclaim in London. The character of Lots-O-Huggin' Bear in *Toy Story 3* was originally planned to be a Care Bear doll from the 1980s but "Lotso" turned out to be so devious that the idea was dropped. (Lotso actually made a cameo appearance in the first *Toy Story* film but never spoke.) Like the old prospector Stinky Pete in *Toy Story 2* (1999), Lotso is one of those particularly disturbing Disney villains who appear so warm and friendly at first but are later revealed to be sinister and deadly. Beatty was ideally cast because he usually played likable characters on screen. Yet when the true Lotso is revealed, Beatty's vocals are disturbingly menacing. Biography: *Ned Beatty*, Lambert M. Surhone, Miriam T. Timpledon, Susan F. Marseken (2010).

Beaumont, Kathryn (b. 1938) A British child actress who retired from acting before adulthood, she voiced two major Disney heroines: the inquisitive Alice in *Alice in Wonderland* (1951) and the adventurous Londoner Wendy Darling in *Peter Pan* (1953). She was born in London but spent World War II in North Wales where her father was a broadcaster. Soon after returning to London, Beaumont was signed by MGM and went to Hollywood where she appeared in child roles in such movies as *On an Island with You* (1948), *The Secret Garden* (1949), and *Challenge to Lassie* (1949). Walt Disney thought the ten-year-old girl looked and sounded just like Alice so she not only voiced and sang for the character but was filmed in scenes from the script so that the animators could copy her movements and facial expressions. Two years after *Alice in Wonderland* was released, she did the singing and speaking voice for Wendy in *Peter Pan*. Beaumont reprised both roles on *Lux Radio Theatre* broadcasts in 1951 and 1953. Although Alice and Wendy are both Victorian Londoners of about the same age, they are very different characters and Beaumont's performances differ as well. Her Alice is smart and observant but also prim, complaining, and condescending at times. Beaumont's Wendy is romantic, adventurous, and very accepting of others. It is definitely the same voice in each film but very different in tone. Beaumont stopped acting after *Peter Pan* in order to finish her schooling and later attended the University of Southern California to become a teacher. Upon graduation she began her thirty-year teaching career, returning after retirement to reprise her Alice in the videos *Villain's Revenge* (1999) and *Kingdom Hearts* (2002), and two episodes of *House of Mouse* (2002). She recorded all the dialogue for grown-up Wendy in the sequel *Return to Never Land* (2002) but the producers thought she sounded too old for the young wife and mother so Kath Soucie was hired to re-record the role for the final print. Beaumont also played some minor characters in the video *101 Dalmatians II: Patch's London Adventure* (2003).

Beck, Erica (b. 1992) A child performer in television and film, she provided the voice of the flapjack octopus Pearl in *Finding Nemo* (2003). Erica Lulu Beck was born in Lakewood, California, and was only two years old when she voiced a child in the English version of the Japanese animated film *The Raccoon War* (1994). She can he heard as one of the children in *Lilo & Stitch* (2002) and has appeared on the TV series *Unfabulous*, *ER*, and *iCarly*.

Bedard, Irene (b. 1967) A statuesque leading lady who has played strong-willed Native American characters in film and on television, she provided the speaking voice for the title heroine in *Pocahontas* (1995). She was born in Anchorage, Alaska, of Inupiat Inuit and Métis ancestry, and studied musical theatre at The University of the Arts in Philadelphia. Bedard made her television debut in the made-for-TV film *Lakota Woman: Siege at Wounded*

Knee (1994), followed by such theatrical features as *Squanto: A Warrior's Tale* (1994), *Navajo Blues* (1996), *Song of Hiawatha* (1997), *6/29* (1998), *Naturally Native* (1998), *Smoke Signals* (1998), *Wildflowers* (1999), *Your Guardian* (2001), *Paris* (2003), *Greasewood Flat* (2003), *Miracle at Sage Creek* (2005), *Cosmic Radio* (2007), *Tortilla Heaven* (2007), and *The Red Chalk* (2007). Among her television credits are the series *The Marshall, Profiler, The Outer Limits, The Agency,* and *Into the West.* The character of Pocahontas is the first Disney animated heroine to be based on a real person, though it is far from a historically accurate portrayal. The real Pocahontas was only about ten years old when John Smith came to the New World and, although legend states she saved Smith's life, there is no evidence that the two ever fell in love. The romance in *Pocahontas* may have been fabricated but the film sought to portray the Native Americans with some accuracy, casting actors of tribal ancestry to do the voices and giving the characters Native American features rather than European ones. Historically accurate or not, Pocahontas is one of the most fully realized Disney heroines. Bebard was the physical model for Pocahontas as well as the voice of the character, and her performance is a lovely blend of passion and dignity. Bedard reprised her Pocahontas in the video sequel *Pocahontas II: Journey to a New World* (1998) and she played Pocahontas' mother in the live-action movie *The New World* (2005). She can also be heard on the television cartoon series *Adventures from the Book of Virtues, The Real Adventures of Jonny Quest, Roughnecks: The Starship Troopers Chronicles, Higglytown Heroes, The Spectacular Spider-Man,* and *What's New, Scooby-Doo?*

Bedford, Brian (b. 1935) The distinguished British actor with a subtle and crystal-clear voice who has spent much of his career doing the classics at the Stratford Shakespeare Festival in Canada, he occasionally appears on Broadway and in films, such as the animated feature *Robin Hood* (1973) in which he voiced the title character. Bedford was born in Morley, England, and educated at the Royal Academy of Dramatic Art before making his London debut in 1956. He made an auspicious Broadway bow in *Five Finger Exercise* (1959) and returned to the New York theatre for such productions as *The Private Ear* (1963), *The Unknown Soldier and His Wife* (1967), *The Misanthrope* (1968 and 1983), *Private Lives* (1969), *The School for Wives* (1971), *Two Shakespearean Actors* (1992), *Timon of Athens* (1993), *The Moliere Comedies* (1995), *London Assurance* (1996), *Tartuffe* (2002), and *The Importance of Being Earnest* (2011). Bedford became an American citizen but spends most of his time in Canada playing the most demanding comic and tragic roles at the Stratford Festival where he also directs on occasion. His film and television appearances are limited but usually memorable, such as *The Pad and How to Use It* (1966), *Grand Prix* (1966), and *Nixon* (1995) on the large screen, such diverse television series as *Ben Casey, Coronet Blue, Judd for the Defense, Cheers, The Equalizer, Alfred Hitchcock Presents, Nanny and the Professor,* and *Frasier,* and the TV-movies and mini-series *Androcles and the Lion* (1967), *The Last Best Year* (1990), *Scarlett* (1994), *More Tales of the City* (1998), *Mr. St. Nick* (2002), *and A Christmas Carol* (2004). Bedford's Robin Hood for Disney is not a dashing ruffian like Errol Flynn but more reserved, more British, and subtly sly, appropriate for a fox. His vocals are energetic but always gentlemanly. Critics have complained that the outlaw is the least interesting character in the film but, in fact, Robin acts as straight man for his rambunctious cohorts and the silly villains. Originally the British performer Tommy Steele was hired to voice Robin Hood but after a few recording sessions it was clearly not working and he was replaced by Bedford.

Behn, Peter (b. 1934) A child actor who provided the voice of Young Thumper the Rabbit in *Bambi* (1942), he did not continue in show business. He is the son of screenwriter and children's book author Harry Behn and as a toddler he appeared in the movie short *Jungle Juveniles* (1937). After working on *Bambi,* Behn's family moved to Arizona and then Connecticut where he was educated at Phillips Academy and Yale. He later became a successful real estate broker in Vermont. Behn was located by the Disney studio for the fiftieth anniversary of *Bambi* and appeared in the TV special *The Making of "Bambi"* (1994). One of the most beloved scenes in *Bambi* is Thumper's ice skating on the frozen pond. Ice skating champions Donna Atwood and Jane Randolph were filmed skating and falling and the animators used this footage in their work. The character was originally called Bobo until an animator came up with the idea of the rabbit's foot thumping when he got excited. Thumper is one of the very few characters in the film who is not in the original Felix Salten novel.

Belack, Doris (b. 1926) A veteran television character actress who has also been on the stage and in several movies, she provided the voice of the mayor, Mrs. Tippi Dink, in *Doug's 1st Movie* (1999). She was born in New York City and started her television career in 1956 on the soap opera *The Edge of Night.* Belack's other daytime drama credits include *Another World, One Life to Live,* and *The Doctors,* as well as other series such as *The Patty*

Duke Show, Barney Miller, Baker's Dozen, Family Ties, Remington Steele, The Golden Girls, Laurie Hill, Family Album, Sisters, Cosby, Law & Order, and *Sex and the City*. She was frequently on the New York stage, acting in many productions Off Broadway and on Broadway in such plays as *Semi-Detatched* (1960), *Last of the Red Hot Lovers* (1969), *Bad Habits* (1974), *The Trip Back Down* (1974), *Cheaters* (1978), and *The Cemetery Club* (1990). Belack has appeared in such movies as *Looking Up* (1977), *Tootsie* (1982), *Fast Forward* (1985), *Batteries Not Included* (1987), *Opportunity Knocks* (1990), *What About Bob?* (1991), *Naked Gun 33⅓: The Final Insult* (1994), *The Odd Couple II* (1998), and *Delirious* (2006). She first voiced Mrs. Dink in the TV cartoon series *Doug* and *Disney's Doug*.

Bennett, Jeff (b. 1962) A prolific voice actor who can be heard in over 500 television episodes and many animated videos, he provided the singing voice for the Centipede in *James and the Giant Peach* (1996), the voice for Captain Hook's pirate accomplice Mr. Smee in *Return to Never Land* (2002), the chipmunk Pip in the animated Andalasia portion of *Enchanted* (2007), and the animal shelter guard Lloyd in *Bolt* (2008). Jeff Glenn Bennett was born in Burbank, California, and worked as a singer before he started doing voices for Japanese cartoons in 1984. He appeared in a few television series before he concentrated on voice work, providing voices for a variety of characters in dozens of animated series, including *Where's Waldo?, Raw Toonage, Bonkers, Batman, The Legend of Prince Valiant, The Little Mermaid, The Mask, Gargoyles, Animaniacs, Timon and Pumbaa, Mighty Ducks, 101 Dalmatians, Hercules, Pinky and the Brain, House of Mouse, The Legend of Tarzan, Dexter's Laboratory, The Powerpuff Girls, Samurai Jack, Dave the Barbarian, Lilo & Stitch, Duck Dodgers, The Adventures of Jimmy Neutron: Boy Genius,* and *Codename: Kids Next Door, Kim Possible, American Dragon: Jake Long, The Replacements, Curious George, The Marvelous Misadventures of Flapjack,* and *The Penguins of Madagascar,* but he is mostly known as the title character in *Johnny Bravo*. Among Bennett's many animated movie and video credits are *Kiki's Delivery Service* (1989), *Batman: Mask of the Phantasm* (1993), *A Hollywood Hounds Christmas* (1994), *The Return of Jafar* (1994), *The Land Before Time III: The Great Valley Adventure* (1994) and six of its sequels, *Aladdin and the King of Thieves* (1995), *Mighty Ducks the Movie: The First Face-Off* (1997), *Pfish and Chip* (1997), *Beauty and the Beast: The Enchanted Christmas* (1997), *Pocahontas II: Journey to a New World* (1998), *Mickey's Once Upon a Christmas* (1999), *An American Tail: The Mystery of the Night Monster* (1999), *An Extremely Goofy Movie* (2000), *Lady and the Tramp II: Scamp's Adventure* (2001), *Balto: Wolf Quest* (2002), *Winnie the Pooh: A Very Merry Pooh Year* (2002), *Tarzan and Jane* (2002), *The Jungle Book 2* (2003), *Atlantis: Milo's Return* (2003), *Stitch! The Movie* (2003), *The Lion King 1½* (2004), *Mulan II* (2004), *Chicken Little* (2005), *Kingdom Hearts II* (2005), *Curious George* (2006), *Brother Bear 2* (2006), *The Fox and the Hound 2* (2006), *The Little Mermaid: Ariel's Beginning* (2008), *Tinker Bell* (2008), *Curious George 2: Follow That Monkey!* (2009), *Tinker Bell and the Lost Treasure* (2009), and *Tinker Bell and the Great Fairy Rescue* (2010).

Bennett, Marjorie (1896–1982) An Australian actress whose career in the States stretched from silent films to 1980s television, she voiced the generous cow Princess who helps feed the puppies in *One Hundred and One Dalmatians* (1961). She was born in York, Australia, and was in Hollywood by 1917 acting in such silents as *The Midnight Patrol* (1918), *Naughty, Naughty* (1918), and *Hugon, the Mighty* (1918). Bennett did not return to movies until after World War II, appearing as housekeepers, landladies, charwomen, and society ladies in a variety of films, including *Dressed to Kill* (1946), *Monsieur Verdoux* (1947), *June Bride* (1948), *Perfect Strangers* (1950), *The Man Who Cheated Himself* (1950), *Limelight* (1952), *So Big* (1953), *Sabrina* (1954), *Athena* (1954), *Young at Heart* (1954), *The Cobweb* (1955), *Strange Intruder* (1956), *Man of a Thousand Faces* (1957), *Holiday for Lovers* (1959), *Ocean's Eleven* (1960), *A Thunder of Drums* (1961), *Saintly Sinners* (1962), *What Ever Happened to Baby Jane?* (1962), *Girls! Girls! Girls!* (1962), *Mary Poppins* (1964), *36 Hours* (1965), *Billy the Kid versus Dracula* (1966), *Coogan's Bluff* (1968), *Stacey* (1973), *Charley Varrick* (1973), and *The North Avenue Irregulars* (1979). She acted in hundreds of television episodes, including the series *The Gale Storm Show, Adventures in Paradise, The Real McCoys, Zane Grey Theatre, The Many Loves of Dobie Gillis, Alfred Hitchcock Presents, Pete and Gladys, The Jack Benny Program, Twilight Zone, The Joey Bishop Show, My Living Doll, Dr. Kildare, F Troop, Ironside, Room 222, Mission: Impossible, Adam-12, Night Gallery, McMillan & Wife, Happy Days, Kojak, Phyllis, CHiPs,* and *Barney Miller*.

Benson, Jodi (b. 1961) A vivacious actress-singer from the stage with a crystal-clear, engaging singing voice, she provided the voices for the aquatic heroine Ariel in *The Little Mermaid* (1989), the Tour Guide Barbie in *Toy Story 2* (1999), and Molly's doll Barbie who falls for Ken in *Toy Story 3* (2010). She was born Jodi Marzorati in Rockford, Illinois, and educated at Millikin University before going to New York where she was featured in the short-lived Broadway musicals *Smile* (1986) and *Welcome to the Club* (1989). After winning the role of Ariel from a field of 500 candidates, Benson continued to voice characters in the television cartoon series *Pirates of the Dark Water*, *Pepper Ann*, *Hercules*, *The Wild Thornberrys*, *Batman Beyond*, *Duck Dodgers*, *The Grim Adventures of Billy & Mandy*, and *Camp Lazlo*, as well as in the animated films and videos *P. J. Sparkles* (1992), *Thumbelina* (1994), *A Christmas Carol* (1997), *The Mighty Kong* (1998), *Hercules: Zero to Hero* (1999), *Joseph: King of Dreams* (2000), *Lady and the Tramp II: Scamp's Adventure* (2001), *Rapsittie Street Kids: Believe in Santa* (2002), *Balto: Wolf Quest* (2002), *101 Dalmatians II: Patch's London Adventure* (2003), and *Balto III: Wings of Change* (2004). The character of Ariel is the first in a new line of Disney princesses who are determined to be more than a victim of fate and villains and are not dependent on princes to save them. She is young yet gains maturity (and even a subtle sexual awakening) during the course of the film. The directors wanted a singer-actress since so much of her character was musical. Benson's extensive stage experience got her the job and the resulting performance is one of the very best in the Disney canon. She reprised her Ariel in the videos *Giggles* (1999), *Wish Upon a Starfish* (1999), *The Little Mermaid II: Return to the Sea* (2000), *Mickey's Magical Christmas: Snowed in at the House of Mouse* (2001), *Disney Princess Party: Volume III* (2005), and *The Little Mermaid: Ariel's Beginning* (2008), as well as the animated series *The Little Mermaid* and *House of Mouse*. Benson returned to Broadway in *Crazy for You* in 1992 and has performed in many musicals in national and international tours.

Benson, Robby (b. 1956) The boyish movie and television actor who later turned to directing, he provided the voice of the tormented Beast in *Beauty and the Beast* (1991). He was born Robin David Segal in Dallas, Texas, the son of a writer and actor-singer, and raised in New York City where he began acting professionally at the age of ten. While appearing in such Broadway productions as *Zelda* (1969), *The Rothschilds* (1970), and *The Pirates of Penzance* (1981), Benson acted in television soap operas and played teens in such movies as *Jeremy* (1973) *Ode to Billy Joe* (1976), *One on One* (1977), and *Ice Castles* (1978). As an adult he usually played sensitive but determined heroes in the movies and then on television. His other film credits include *Walk Proud* (1979), *The Chosen* (1981), *Running Brave* (1983), *Rent-a-Cop* (1987), and *Deadly Exposure* (1993), and among the TV series he appeared on are *Tough Cookies*, *Seinfeld*, *American Dreams*, and *Sabrina, the Teenage Witch*. The animators of *Beauty and the Beast* took aspects of various animals to come up with the look of the Beast: the head and beard of a buffalo, the body of a bear, the mane of a lion, the brow of a gorilla, and the legs and tail of a wolf. Instead of casting an actor with a deep, growly voice to do the vocals for the Beast, the directors chose Benson who has a light voice. They then altered his recording, added the growls from recordings of real lions and panthers, and mixed them together. Benson's true voice is only heard at the end of the movie when the Beast turns back into a prince. Benson reprised his Beast in the videos *Beauty and the Beast: The Enchanted Christmas* (1997), *Belle's Magical World* (1998), *Mickey's Magical Christmas: Snowed in at the House of Mouse* (2001), *Kingdom Hearts* (2002), and *Kingdom Hearts II* (2005), as well as in the TV cartoon series *House of Mouse*. He has also provided voices for such series as *The Legend of Prince Valiant*, *Batman*, *Exosquad*, and *The Magic School Bus*, as well as the videos *King's Quest: Heir Today, Gone Tomorrow* (1992), *Dragonheart: A New Beginning* (2000), *The Life and Adventures of Santa Claus* (2000), and *The Christmas Lamb* (2000). In the 1990s, Benson took up directing for television and has helmed such series as *Evening Shade*, *Thunder Alley*, *Ellen*, *Friends*, *The Naked Truth*, *Jesse*, *The Huntress*, and *8 Simple Rules*. He has semi-retired from show business and has taught at New York University, Appalachian State University, and the University of North Carolina.

Bergen, Bob (b. 1964) An in-demand voice artist who has provided the voice for Porky Pig since 1990, he voiced Bucky the Squirrel in *The Emperor's New Groove* (2000). The St. Louis native began his career as a teenager dubbing the English dialogue for the Japanese cartoon *Lupin the Third: The Castle of Cagliostro* (1979). Soon he was heard in films providing voices for animated features and shorts as well as for live-action movies such as *Gremlins* (1984), *Problem Child* (1990), *Total Recall* (1990), *Look Who's Talking Now* (1993), and *The Santa Clause* (2002). Bergen has regularly supplied additional voices for Disney animated features, playing minor roles in such films and videos as *The Hunchback of Notre Dame* (1996), *Pocahontas II: Journey to a New World* (1998), *A Bug's Life* (1998), *Tarzan* (1999), *Toy Story 2* (1999), *Monsters, Inc.* (2001), *Lilo & Stitch* (2002), *Treasure Planet* (2002), *Brother Bear* (2003), *Cars* (2006), *WALL-E* (2008), *Tinker Bell* (2008), *Up* (2009), and *Tinker Bell and the Lost Treasure* (2009), as well as such non–Disney movies and videos as *Bugs Bunny's Funky Monkeys* (1997), *The Iron Giant* (1999), *Spirited Away* (2001), *Scooby-Doo and the Cyber Chase* (2001), *Ice Age: The Meltdown* (2006), *Happily N'Ever After* (2006), *Horton Hears a Who!* (2008), and *Cloudy with a*

Chance of Meatballs (2009). He first voiced Porky Pig in the TV cartoon series *Tiny Toon Adventures* and reprised his characterization in the series *Duck Dodgers,* in several videos such as *Looney Toons Racing* (2000), *Looney Toons: Reality Check* (2003), *Looney Toons: Stranger Than Fiction* (2003), and *Bah Humduck! A Looney Toons Christmas* (2006), and in the film *Space Jam* (1996). Bergen reprised his Bucky in the sequel *The Emperor's New Groove 2: Kronk's New Groove* (2005), as well as in the TV series *The Emperor's New School,* and he can be heard in other cartoon series, including *The Legend of Prince Valiant, Spider-Man, The Powerpuff Girls, Sabrina the Animated Series, Johnny Bravo,* and *Robot Chicken.* He is also the voice of Luke Skywalker on many *Star Wars* video games.

Bergman, Mary Kay (1961–1999) A versatile voice actress who excelled at comic cartoon characters in her short career, her first movie job was voicing one of the gushing village maidens dubbed Bimbette in *Beauty and the Beast* (1991). She was born in Los Angeles, the daughter of an artist who painted animation cels for Max Fleischer cartoons, and began her career doing radio commercials in 1986. Bergman studied theatre at UCLA for a time and then worked as a receptionist and secretary while auditioning for acting jobs. Her ability to impersonate famous actors and characters got her noticed by the Disney studio who was looking for someone to replace Adriana Caselotti. The aging singer-actress had been voicing Snow White ever since making *Snow White and the Seven Dwarfs* in 1937 and someone new was needed to voice promotional work and cartoon appearances by Disney's first princess. Bergman was hired and voiced Snow White for everything from television spots to ice shows. After working on *Beauty and the Beast,* Bergman quickly found work on television, voicing such series as *Family Dog 2, The Little Mermaid, Fantastic Four, Extreme Ghostbusters, Captain Planet and the Planeteers,* and *Family Guy,* but she was most known for providing voices for most of the female characters in the adult cartoon series *South Park.* She returned to Disney to voice Quasimodo's gypsy mother in *The Hunchback of Notre Dame* (1996), the Earthquake Lady and other characters in *Hercules* (1997), various minor roles in *Mulan* (1998), and did the yodeling for the cowgirl doll Jessie in *Toy Story 2* (1999). Bergman's many animated videos and movies include *The Bear Who Saved Christmas* (1994), *Wanna Be a Dingo Finder* (1995), *Someone in the Kitchen* (1996), *Pony Express Rider* (1996), *Scooby-Doo on Zombie Island* (1998), *Rusty: A Dog's Tale* (1998), *South Park: Bigger, Longer & Uncut* (1999), *Deep Blue Sea* (1999), *Alvin and the Chipmunks Meet Frankenstein* (1999), *The Scooby-Doo Project* (1999), *Buzz Lightyear of Star Command* (2000), *The Life & Adventures of Santa Claus* (2000), *Lady and the Tramp II: Scamp's London Adventure* (2001), and *Balto: Wolf Quest* (2002), the last five being released after Bergman's death by suicide.

Beswick, Quinn (b. 1987) A pre-teen actor with a handful of credits before he gave up acting, he supplied the voice for the "Lost Boy" Slightly in *Return to Never Land* (2002). The Los Angeles native appeared in the TV-movie *Heartless* (1997), the films *Family Tree* (1999) and *The Secret Sea* (2002), and provided the voice of Charlie Brown in the TV special *It's the Pied Piper, Charlie Brown* (2000).

Bettin, Val (b. 1923) An American actor often cast in British roles on the stage, on radio, in films, and on television, he provided the voice of Basil's fellow mouse sleuth and friend, Dr. David Q. Dawson, in *The Great Mouse Detective* (1986). He was born Valentin Bettin in La Crosse, Wisconsin, and studied acting at the Royal Academy of Dramatic Art in London before returning to the States to be a drama teacher. In 1953 he took up acting professionally and was heard on the radio and performed in regional theatre for many years. Bettin did not make his film debut until he was fifty-seven years old, appearing in *Somewhere in Time* (1983), followed by *The Man Who Wasn't There* (1983) and *Entertaining Angels: The Dorothy Day Story* (1996). Most of his television work has been voicing animated series such as *Gargoyles, Mighty Ducks, W.I.T.C.H.,* and *Aladdin.* Bettin voiced the Sultan in the last one, a role he also played in the videos *The Return of Jafar* (1994) and *Aladdin and the King of Thieves* (1995). He can also be heard in the animated movie *Shrek* (2001). The character of Dawson in *The Great Mouse Detective* is drawn from Sherlock Holmes' Dr. Watson and patterned after the actor Nigel Bruce who often portrayed Watson on screen. Bettin's vocals do not use Bruce's sputtering, blundering phrases that became the character actor's trademark but he does allow for a bit of British bluster in his line readings which contrast nicely with Basil's more intellectual way of speaking.

Billingsley, Dick (b. 1975) A child actor who made his television debut at the age of three and retired from acting at the age of twelve, he voiced the young mouse Tiny Tim in *Mickey's Christmas Carol* (1983) and the young kangaroo Roo in *Winnie the Pooh and a Day for Eeyore* (1983). Richard W. Billingsley played toddlers and kids in the television series *The Young and the Restless, Archie Bunker's Place, Days of Our Lives, Simon & Simon,*

The Love Boat, and *Valerie's Family*, as well as in the TV-movies *Like Normal People* (1979), *Obsessed with a Married Woman* (1985), *Destination America* (1987), and *After the Promise* (1987).

Bing, Herman (1889–1947)   A thickly accented, easily excitable German character actor whose comic hysterics were useful in over one hundred films, he provided the voice of the bombastic circus Ringmaster in *Dumbo* (1941). He was born in Frankfurt, Germany, and was a circus clown and performer in vaudeville before beginning his film career in his native land. Bing arrived in Hollywood just as sound was coming in and was quickly picked up for dialect roles, overemphasizing his German accent for comic effect. Among his screen credits are *Anna Christie* (1931), *Footlight Parade* (1933), *The Cat and the Fiddle* (1934), *The Merry Widow* (1934), *Twentieth Century* (1934), *In Caliente* (1935), *The Night Is Young* (1935), *Every Night at Eight* (1935), *Rose Marie* (1936), *The Great Ziegfeld* (1936), *Maytime* (1937), *The Great Waltz* (1938), *Sweethearts* (1938), *Bluebeard's Eighth Wife* (1938), *Bitter Sweet* (1940), *Broadway Melody of 1940* (1940), *The Devil with Hitler* (1942), *Where Do We Go from Here?* (1945), *I Was a Criminal* (1945), and *Night and Day* (1946). When Bing's career started to collapse in the mid-1940s, he committed suicide. His brother Rudolf Bing (1902–1997) was the General Manager of the New York Metropolitan Opera for twenty-two years.

Bird, Brad (b. 1957)   A successful director and writer of animated films, he has occasionally provided voices for his projects, most memorably the haughty fashion designer Edna E. Mode in *The Incredibles* (2004) and the food critic's dry butler Ambrister Minion in *Ratatouille* (2007), writing and directing both movies. Born Phillip Bradley Bird in Kalispell, Montana, he grew up in Portland, Oregon, and begin his training as an animator when he was fourteen years old. Bird studied at Cal Arts then began as a Disney animator, working on *The Fox and the Hound* (1981) and other projects. He also worked on such television shows as *The Simpsons* and wrote scripts for and directed the *Amazing Stories* series. Throughout his career Bird provided a miscellaneous voice when needed and when he was directing *The Incredibles* he filled in the voice for Edna who was going to be played by actress-comic Lily Tomlin; the result was so hilarious that Tomlin didn't think she could be as funny and his performance was retained in the film. The character of Edna is somewhat based, both physically and vocally, on the prodigious Hollywood costume designer Edith Head. Bird's other voice credits include Don Carlo in the Tim Burton short *Doctor of Doom* (1979). He is the father of child actors **Nicholas Bird**, who voiced the role of the young sea turtle Squirt in *Finding Nemo* (2003) and the Boy on the tricycle in *The Incredibles*, and **Michael Bird**, who voiced Violet's heartthrob Tony Rydinger, the cutest guy in the class, in *The Incredibles*.

Black, Sam (b. 1962)   A computer software engineer who works on the visual effects in animated movies, his only acting credit is voicing the shaved, accident-prone monster George Sanderson in *Monsters, Inc.* (2001). Under the name Samuel Lord Black he has worked on the movies *A Bug's Life* (1998), *Toy Story 2* (1999), *Monsters, Inc.*, *Finding Nemo* (2003), and *The Incredibles* (2004).

Blacque, Taurean (b. 1941)   An African-American stage actor with some film and television credits, he voiced Sykes' deadly Doberman pinscher thug Roscoe in *Oliver & Company* (1988). He was born Herbert Middleton, Jr., in Newark, New Jersey, and trained at the New Federal Theatre in Manhattan, going on to act on Broadway in *The River Niger* (1973) and *We Interrupt This Program* (1975), and in the Off Broadway productions of *Orrin* (1975), *Welcome to Black River* (1975) and *So Nice They Named It Twice* (1976). Blacque made his television debut in 1976 and appeared on such series as *What's Happening!*, *Sanford and Son*, *The Tony Randall Show*, *Good Times*, *The Bob Newhart Show*, *Taxi*, *The White Shadow*, *The Love Boat*, *Gabriel's Fire*, *In the Heat of the Night*, *Dream On*, and *The Client*, but he is best remembered as Detective Neal Washington on *Hill Street Blues* for six years. Among his film credits are *House Calls* (1978), *Rocky II* (1979), *Beyond Death's Door* (1979), *The Hunter* (1980), *DeepStar Six* (1989), and *Nowhere Road* (2002), as well as a number of TV-movies. Blacque has often returned to the regional stage, most frequently to the Alliance Theatre in Atlanta.

Blanc, Mel (1908–1989)   Perhaps America's most famous and versatile voice artist who created and voiced many memorable cartoon characters, his only Disney credits are the hiccups for the cat sidekick Gideon in *Pinocchio* (1940), Raja the Tiger in the short *Goliath II* (1960), and the cameos of several Warner Brothers characters in *Who Framed Roger Rabbit* (1988). Melvin Jerome Blanc was born in San Francisco and grew up in Portland, Oregon, starting his career on radio in 1927. He was soon in demand for his character voices and ability to create any kind of sound. On *The Jack Benny Program*, for example, he voiced human characters as well as a parrot, a polar bear, and even Benny's rickety Maxwell automobile. Blanc had his own CBS radio program, *The Mel Blanc Show*, in the 1940s even as he continued to do voices for other shows.

He began working with Warner Brothers in the late 1930s and created some of its most popular cartoon characters, including Bugs Bunny, Porky Pig, Daffy Duck, Tweety Bird, the cat Sylvester, Yosemite Sam, the rooster Foghorn Leghorn, Marvin the Martian, and the skunk Pepé le Pew. He also worked for Hanna-Barbera, contributing characters to *The Flintstones*, *The Jetsons*, *Tom and Jerry*, and other series, and for Universal he played Woody Woodpecker. His other television series include *Mr. Magoo*, *The Dick Tracy Show*, *Lippy the Lion and Hardy Ha Har*, *The Peter Potamus Show*, *The Magilla the Gorilla Show*, *The Secret Squirrel Show*, *The Pink Panther Show*, *Where's Huddles?*, *Captain Caveman and the Teen Angels*, *Heathcliff*, *Buck Rogers in the 25th Century*, and *The Flintstone Kids*. All in all, he voiced over one hundred characters in approximately one thousand cartoons over a period of fifty years. Blanc was also an accomplished comic actor and audiences got to see as well as hear him in such movies as *Broadway Melody of 1940* (1940), *A Wave, a WAC and a Marine* (1944), *Neptune's Daughter* (1949), *Kiss Me, Stupid* (1964), and *How's Your Love Life?* (1971), and in the television series *The Jack Benny Program*, *Angel*, *Dennis the Menace*, *The Many Loves of Dobie Gillis*, *The Beverly Hillbillies*, and *Curiosity Shop*. It is interesting to consider why this master of voices did not work for Disney more often. Some of the reason may go back to *Pinocchio*. Blanc was hired to voice the comic cat Gideon who was a speaking character, but by the final cut Gideon was mute and only his hiccups remained. When Blanc returned to the Disney studio years later, he voiced Daffy Duck, Tweety Bird, Bugs Bunny, Porky Pig, and Sylvester for *Who Framed Roger Rabbit*, his last film credit. Autobiography: *That's Not All, Folks!* with Philip Basbe (1989).

Blessed, Brian (b. 1937) An oversized British character actor from the classical stage who has played many boisterous, bigger-than-life characters, he supplied the voice for the deceiving jungle guide Clayton who is really a poacher in *Tarzan* (1999). He was born in Mexborough, England, the son of a miner, and worked at various blue-collar jobs before training at the Bristol Old Vic Theatre School. Blessed went on to play many roles in the classical repertoire as well as modern works, such as the original London productions of *Cats* (1981) and *Chitty Chitty Bang Bang* (2002). He made his television debut in 1963 and was featured on many series and TV dramas before finding international recognition as Augustus Caesar in the BBC miniseries *I, Claudius* in 1976. His other series and miniseries include *The Three Musketeers*, *Cold Comfort Farm*, *Arthur of the Britons*, *Boy Dominic*, *Z Cars*, *The Little World of Don Camillo*, *The Black Adder*, *Return to Treasure Island*, *My Family and Other Animals*, *Doctor Who*, and *The History of Tom Jones, a Foundling*. Among his many notable films are *Till Death Do Us Part* (1969), *The Trojan Women* (1971), *Man of La Mancha* (1972), *King Arthur, the Young Warlord* (1975), *Flash Gordon* (1980), *High Road to China* (1983), *Henry V* (1989), *Robin Hood: Prince of Thieves* (1991), *Much Ado About Nothing* (1993), *The Bruce* (1996), *Hamlet* (1996), *Devil's Harvest* (2003), *As You Like It* (2006), and *Back in Business* (2007). Blessed's deep, booming voice can be heard as narrator in many films and he provided voices for both live-action and animated films and videos such as *Asterix and the Big Fight* (1989), *Freddie as F.R.0.7.* (1992), *Star Wars: Episode I—The Phantom Menace* (1999), *The Legend of Tamworth Two* (2004), and *Agent Crush* (2008), as well as the TV cartoon series *Dennis the Menace*, *The Big Knights*, *Kika & Bob*, and *Family Guy*. Blessed is also an adventurer who has written about climbing Mount Everest and his other pursuits in non-fiction books. Patrick Stewart and Ian McKellen were both considered for the voice of the villain Clayton in *Tarzan*, a character who appears in Edgar Rice Burroughs' original book. The directors decided on Blessed because they wanted a voice that was lower and more sinister than Tarzan's. Ironically, the one time in the movie that Tarzan does his famous Tarzan yell, it was recorded by Blessed. Autobiography: *Dynamite Kid* (1992).

Bletcher, Billy (1894–1979) A small actor with a big voice, the comic performer appeared in several films starting in the silent era but he was most adept at voicing villains in hundreds of animated shorts, most memorably the snarling Big Bad Wolf in Disney's *The Three Little Pigs* (1933) and in its sequels. Born William Bletcher in Lancaster, Pennsylvania, the five-foot, two-inch actor made his screen debut in the short *A Sticky Affair* (1916), followed by several other silents. He appeared in a number of Mack Sennett comedies and then teamed up with Billy Gilbert for some shorts for Hal Roach. His diminutive size and full baritone voice made him ideal for character parts in the talkies and he appeared in small roles in dozens of feature films, most memorably as the Chief of Police in *Babes in Toyland* (1934), Shorty in *High, Wide and Handsome* (1937), the dwarf Gorza in *The Lost City* (1935), and Spanky's father in some of the *Our Gang* comedies. Bletcher provided voices for over 300 animated shorts between 1931 and 1956. Among his different voices for Disney shorts were the gruff Pete in many Mickey Mouse and Donald Duck cartoons, the foolish King Midas in the *The Golden Touch* (1935), the sinister Dirty Bill in *The*

Robber Kitten (1935), and the authoritative Judge Owl in *Who Killed Cock Robin?* (1935), as well as one of the crass Clowns in the feature film *Dumbo* (1941). The evolution of the character of Pete over the years is interesting. The large, cat-like creature was first seen in the silent *Alice* shorts, then he appeared as Captain Pete in the first Disney sound film *Steamboat Willie* (1928). Over the years his name often changed, from Black Pete to Pegleg Pete to Pierre to just Pete, as he took on different shapes and jobs, always the aggressive adversary to the hero. Bletcher voiced Pete in thirty cartoons between 1928 and 1953. He also voiced many cartoons for Warner Brothers and other studios, providing voices for heavies in a series of Porky Pig cartoons, Spike the Bull Dog in several Tom and Jerry cartoons, and the Spider in *Bingo Crosbyana* (1936). Sometimes Bletcher also did the voice for actors in live action films, such as providing the deep voice for Zorro in a series of Republic Pictures in the late 1930s (and later on radio) and speaking for the Munchkin Mayor in *The Wizard of Oz* (1939). His last years were spent in television and his final appearance was as Pappy Yokum in a TV version of *Li'l Abner* (1971). Bletcher can be considered the first Disney villain voice and he laid the groundwork for dozens of actors to imitate over the decades.

Blethyn, Brenda (b. 1946)   A British character actress who has played just about every kind of mother imaginable, she voiced the worried mother elephant Mama Heffalump in *Pooh's Heffalump Movie* (2005). She was born Brenda Anne Bottle in Ramsgate, England, and worked for British Rail before taking acting lessons at the Guildford School of Acting. She began her new career on the stage and by 1975 was performing with the Royal National Theatre, going on to become a much-acclaimed figure in the London theatre. Blethyn's television work in the 1980s made her a familiar face in the British Isles, in particular her performances in *BBC2 Playhouse*, *Death of an Expert Witness*, *Play for Today*, *Who Dares Wins*, *Chance in a Million*, and *That Certain Feeling*. It was her films in the 1990s that made Blethyn internationally known. Among her movie credits are *The Witches* (1990), *A River Runs Through It* (1992), *Secrets & Lies* (1996), *Little Voice* (1998), *Saving Grace* (2000), *Lovely & Amazing* (2001), *Undertaking Betty* (2002), *Beyond the Sea* (2004), *Pride and Prejudice* (2005), *Atonement* (2007), *The Calling* (2009), and *Dead Man Running* (2009). Her later TV series and mini-series in Britain and the States include *Alias Smith & Jones*, *Outside Edge*, *The Budda of Suburbia*, *War and Peace*, *Between the Sheets*, *Law & Order: Special Victims Unit*, and *The New Adventures of Old Christine*. Blethyn reprised Mama Heffalump in the video *Tigger & Pooh and a Musical Too* (2009) and she can also be heard in *The Wild Thornberrys Movie* (2002) and *Bob the Builder: The Knights of Fix-a-Lot* (2003). Autobiography: *Mixed Fancies* (2007).

Bliss, Lucille (b. 1916)   A veteran voice artist from the early days of television, she provided the voice for the spoiled stepsister Anastasia in *Cinderella* (1950) and the Commercial Singer on the television screen in *One Hundred and One Dalmatians* (1961). The native New Yorker made her movie debut in 1950 voicing *Cinderella* and that same year was cast as the voice for the title character in *Crusader Rabbit*, the first animated cartoon series on television. She was also heard in the series *The Flintstones*, *The Space Kidettes*, *Duck Dodgers*, *Vavatar: The Last Airbender*, *Invader ZIM*, and as Smurfette in *The Smurfs* and its many video spin-offs. Bliss provided voices for such animated films and videos as *A Kiddies Kitty* (1955), *A Waggily Tale* (1958), *The Tiny Tree* (1975), *A Flintstones Christmas* (1977), *The Flintstones Little Big League* (1978), *Casper the Friendly Ghost: He Ain't Scary, He's Our Brother* (1979), *The Secret of Nimh* (1982), *The Great Bear Scare* (1983), *Betty Boop's Hollywood Mystery* (1989), *Who Saves the Village?* (2005), and *Robots* (2005).

Block, Bobby   A child voice actor on television since 2002, he provided the voice of the young Piggy in *Home on the Range* (2004). Block has appeared on the TV series *In-Laws*, *Malcolm in the Middle*, *All That*, *According to Jim*, and *Monk*, and has been heard in the cartoon series *Whatever Happened to Robot Jones?* and in the animated films and videos *Shrek* (2001), *Charlotte's Web 2: Wilbur's Great Adventure* (2003), and *Finding Nemo* (2003).

Blondell, Gloria (1915–1986)   A wide-eyed blonde actress of films and television, she provided the voice of Daisy Duck in five Disney shorts in the 1940s. She was born in New York City, the younger sister of movie actress Joan Blondell, and made her screen debut in 1938. Although she played a major role in *Accidents Will Happen* (1938), her film career suffered because of her similarity to her more popular sister. Blondell appeared in minor roles in such movies as *The Spider's Web* (1938), *The Lady Objects* (1938), *The Sap Takes a Wrap* (1939), *Model Wife* (1941), *Don't Bother to Knock* (1952), *White Lightning* (1953), and *God Is My Partner* (1957). She had more success in television where she was a regular on *The Life of Riley* and appeared on other series, including *I Love Lucy*, *Crossroads*, *Wanted: Dead or Alive*, and *Thriller*. Blondell first voiced Daisy Duck in the cartoon

Donald's Crime (1945), followed by *Cured Duck* (1945), *Donald's Double Trouble* (1946), *Donald's Dilemma* (1947), and *Crazy Over Daisy* (1950). She also voiced the role of Gloria in the early 1960s TV cartoon series *Calvin and the Colonel*. Blondell occasionally acted on the stage, as in the Broadway plays *Three Men on a Horse* (1935) and *Iron Men* (1936).

Blore, Eric (1887–1959) A round, owlish character actor from England, he was a master at playing stuffy and fussy British butlers, hotel managers, clerks, waiters, and valets, and lent his distinctly nasal voice for the character of adventurer J. Thaddeus Toad in the "Wind in the Willows" portion of the animated double feature *The Adventures of Ichabod and Mr. Toad* (1949). Blore was born in London and began his career as an insurance agent before going on the stage in comic roles in plays and musicals. He made his Broadway debut in 1923 and was seen in such musicals as *Andre Charlot's Revue* (1924), *Charlot Revue* (1925), *Gay Divorce* (1932), and *Ziegfeld Follies* (1943). Blore had made some films in England before making his Hollywood debut in 1926 and with the coming of sound he was ideal as a comic foil in talkies, making over eighty features during the next twenty-five years. Among his screen credits are *Flying Down to Rio* (1933), *Top Hat* (1935), *The Good Fairy* (1935), *Swing Time* (1936), *Shall We Dance* (1937), *Road to Zanzibar* (1941), *The Shanghai Gesture* (1941), *The Lady Eve* (1941), *Happy Go Lucky* (1943), *Romance on the High Seas* (1948), and *Fancy Pants* (1950). Blore's vocals for Mr. Toad in the animated "The Wind in the Willows" are deliciously chaotic. He uses his haughty English dialect yet there is nothing "stiff upper lip" in this wild and carefree character who enjoys life even when he leaves destruction in his path. The animators utilized Blore's round face and large mouth when designing the character, adding the gloves, hat, and spats that Blore usually wore in his films.

Boardman, Thelma (1909–1978) An actress whose only films were for Disney during a brief time in the late 1930s and early 1940s, she voiced Minnie Mouse in four cartoon shorts and Mrs. Quail in *Bambi* (1942). Boardman made her movie debut as the voice of Donald's Angel in the short *Donald's Better Self* (1938). She can also be heard as Minnie opposite Walt Disney's Mickey Mouse in *The Little Whirlwind* (1941), *The Nifty Nineties* (1941), *Mickey's Birthday Party* (1942), and *Out of the Frying Pan into the Firing Line* (1942).

Bottone, Bob A voice actor in television, he provided the voice for the corrupt Assistant to the polluter Bluff in *Doug's 1st Movie* (1999). Bottone can be heard in the TV cartoon series *The Adventures of the Galaxy Rangers* and *Courage the Cowardly Dog*.

Braff, Zach (b. 1975) A film and television actor, producer, and director mostly known for doing all three jobs on the TV series *Scrubs*, he provided the voice for the young rooster hero Ace "Chicken Little" Cluck in *Chicken Little* (2005). Zachary Israel Braff was born in South Orange, New Jersey, the son of a lawyer and a clinical psychologist, and educated at Northwestern University. He acted in plays Off Broadway, did commercials, and made a few movies before finding fame as Dr. John "J. D." Dorian on *Scrubs*. Braff wrote, directed, and appeared in the popular small-budget movie *Garden State* (2004). His other film acting credits include *Manhattan Murder Mystery* (1993), *Endsville* (2000), *Blue Moon* (2000), *The Last Kiss* (2006), *The Ex* (2006), and *The High Cost of Living* (2010). In the original storyboard for *Chicken Little*, the title character was to be a girl. Once the plot changes were made to accommodate a male Chicken Little, Michael J. Fox, David Spade, and Matthew Broderick were considered for the role. In the end, the directors went with Braff who gave a vivid performance voicing the very nontraditional hero.

Bragger, Klee (b. 1984) A child performer who became a television voice artist, he provided the voice for the mean Tourist Kid in *A Goofy Movie* (1995). The Los Angeles native made his television debut at the age of eleven in the sit-com *Love & War* and the same year appeared on *Frasier*. For two years Bragger supplied the voice of Digger Sam in the cartoon series *Recess* as well as in the videos *Recess: School's Out* (2001), *Recess: All Growed Down* (2003), and *Recess: Taking the Fifth Grade* (2003).

Breaux, Marc (b. 1925?) A recognized film, television, and stage dancer-turned-choreographer who often worked with his wife Deedee Wood, he provided the voice of the Cow in the animated section of *Mary Poppins* (1964). Marc Charles Breaux was born in Carenco, Louisiana, and danced on Broadway in *Kiss Me, Kate* (1948), *Catch a Star* (1955), *Li'l Abner* (1956), and *Destry Rides Again* (1959); he and Wood served as assistants to choreographer Michael Kidd for the last two. Both of them co-choreographed *Do Re Me* (1960) then he did the dances for *Minnie's Boys* (1970) and *Lovely Ladies, Kind Gentlemen* (1970), as well as directing the television musical *Goldilocks* (1970). Wood and Breaux staged the imaginative dances for *Mary Poppins* and co-choreographed *The Sound of Music* (1965), *The Happiest Millionaire* (1967), *Chitty Chitty Bang Bang* (1968), and *Huckleberry Finn*

(1974). The two also choreographed many television specials, including the TV version of *Of Thee I Sing* (1972). Breaux alone choreographed the films *The Slipper and the Rose* (1976) and *Sextette* (1978). He rarely performed in the movies but while working on the dances for *Mary Poppins* he made a vocal cameo by voicing the Cow in the animated sequence that he choreographed.

Brenner, Eve A television character actress often playing grandmothers, she supplied the voice of Queen Moustoria, the Queen Victoria–like mouse monarch in *The Great Mouse Detective* (1986). Among her television credits are the series *The Twilight Zone, The Adventures of McGee and Me, Adam 12, Star Trek: The Next Generation, Star Trek: Voyager, Ally McBeal, The X-Files, ER, Cold Case, I'm in the Band,* and *Dr. Quinn, Medicine Woman.* Brenner has appeared in a handful of movies, including *Murder in the First* (1995), *Finding Kelly* (2000), *Monkey Love* (2002), and *Play the Game* (2008).

Breslin, Spencer (b. 1992) A child performer who has continued to work as an adult actor, he voiced Cubby, one of the "Lost Boys," in *Return to Never Land* (2002). He was born in New York City, the son of a telecommunications executive, and made his television debut at the age of five, appearing in such series as *Soul Man, Law & Order, Trinity, Kate Brasher, Center of the Universe,* and the mini-series *Storm of the Century.* Breslin found more notoriety on the big screen, getting noticed in such films as *The Kid* (2000), *Meet the Parents* (2000), *Ozzie* (2001), *The Santa Clause 2* (2002), *The Cat in the Hat* (2003), *Raising Helen* (2004), *The Princess Diaries 2: Royal Engagement* (2004), *The Shaggy Dog* (2006), and *The Santa Clause 3: The Escape Clause* (2006), as well as several TV-movies. He continues to act and also performs in an alternative rock trio called The Dregs.

Briggs, Paul A visual effects animator who has worked for Disney since 1995, he provided the voice for the fumbling frog hunter Two Fingers in *The Princess and the Frog* (2009). Briggs has helped create the special visual effects for the animated films *The Hunchback of Notre Dame* (1996), *Hercules* (1997), *Mulan* (1998), *Lilo & Stitch* (2002), *Brother Bear* (2003), *Bolt* (2008), and *The Princess and the Frog.*

Bright, Charles The young actor who voiced Andy as a little boy on the family videos and the character of Peatey, one of the three plush peas-in-a-pod, in *Toy Story 3* (2010), he has no other film or television credits yet, but he did supply the voice of Peatey on the video game of *Toy Story 3.*

Brill, Fran (b. 1946) A voice artist and puppeteer who was on *Sesame Street* for thirty-eight years, she voiced the art teacher Mrs. Petigrew in *Doug's 1st Movie* (1999). Frances Joan Brill was born in Chester, Pennsylvania, the daughter of a physician, and was educated at Boston University before acting in regional theatres and in New York City. She appeared in several Off Broadway plays, including *What Every Woman Knows* (1975), *Look Back in Anger* (1980), *Skirmishes* (1982), *Hyde in Hollywood* (1989), and *Desdemona* (1993), and on Broadway in *Red, White and Maddox* (1969). In 1970 Brill created and voiced the character of Zoe and other puppets for *Sesame Street* and stayed with the children's show until 2008. During this time she acted in such television series as *How to Survive a Marriage, The Guiding Light, Family, Barnaby Jones, Kate & Allie, Law & Order,* and *The West Wing.* Brill's film credits include *Being There* (1979), *Old Enough* (1984), *Midnight Run* (1988), *What About Bob?* (1991), and *City Hall* (1996). In addition to *Sesame Street*, she has voiced characters for the TV series *The Muppet Show, Dog City,* and *Doug,* and can be heard on such movies and videos as *The Great Santa Claus Switch* (1970), *Muppet Picker Upper* (1975), *The Muppet Show: Sex and Violence* (1975), *My Little Pony* (1984), *The Muppets Take Manhattan* (1984), *A Muppet Family Christmas* (1987), *The Adventures of Super Grover* (1987), *Big Bird Brings Spring to Sesame Street* (1987), *Jim Henson's Dog City: The Movie* (1989), *Sesame Street: Rock & Roll* (1990), *The Tale of Peter Rabbit* (1991), *Elmo Saves Christmas* (1996), *Cinderelmo* (1999), *The Adventures of Elmo in Grouchland* (1999), *Sesame Beginnings: Beginning Together* (2006), *Elmo's World: All About Faces* (2009), as well as many *Sesame Street* sing-along and instructional videos.

Broderick, Matthew (b. 1962) The forever-boyish-looking leading man who first became a star playing teenagers in film and on Broadway, he provided the voice for the lion hero Adult Simba in *The Lion King* (1994) and its video sequels. The native New Yorker is the son of stage and television actor James Broderick (1928–1982) and he studied acting with Uta Hagen. Broderick made his first film *Max Dugan Returns* (1983) when he was twenty-one and soon won attention as the teenage whiz in *War Games* (1983). He made his Broadway debut the same year as the wisecracking youth Eugene in *Brighton Beach Memoirs*, a role he continued in *Biloxi Blues* (1985). Moving back and forth from the stage to the screen, Broderick shone on Broadway in the musicals *How to Succeed in Business Without Really Trying* (1995) and *The Producers* (2001), which he filmed in 2005, as well as in many plays on and Off Broadway. One of the few "teen" movie stars to remain popular into adulthood, he has appeared in many films, including *Ferris Bueller's Day Off* (1986), *Torch Song Trilogy* (1988), *Glory* (1989), *Election* (1999), *Inspector Gadget* (1999), *You Can Count on Me* (2000), *The Stepford Wives* (2004), and *Deck the Halls* (2006). Broderick reprised his Simba performance in the video movies *The Lion King 2: Simba's Pride* (1998) and *The Lion King 1½* (2004), and provided voices for two non–Disney animated films: Tack the Cobbler in *The Princess and the Cobbler* (1993) and the adventurous mouse Despereaux in *The Tale of Despereaux* (2008). The character of Simba has been compared to that of Hamlet, another hero who must decide between revenge or denial. Adult Simba is more reticent than other Disney heroes and his flash of bravery at the end of the movie does not come easily. This lion has to earn his stature and rank in *The Lion King*, as opposed to simply being a prince who simply inherits valor and the throne.

Brodie, Don (1904–2001) A tall, mustachioed character actor whose career stretched from early talkies to 1980s television, he provided the voices of Donald's Devil in the shorts *Donald's Better Self* (1938) and *Donald's Decision* (1942), and the Carnival Barker in *Pinocchio* (1940). He was born in Cincinnati, Ohio, and made his first movie in 1931, followed by supporting roles in over 200 films, including *You Said a Mouthful* (1932), *The Kennel Murder Case* (1933), *Fugitive Lovers* (1934), *Gold Diggers of 1935* (1935), *The Call of the Savage* (1935), *The Little Red Schoolhouse* (1936), *Turn Off the Moon* (1937), *The Last Express* (1938), *The Rookie Cop* (1939), *Broadway Melody of 1940* (1940), *Road to Singapore* (1940), *The Great Dictator* (1940), *Yumpin' Yimminy!* (1941), *They Got Me Covered* (1943), *Mr. Lucky* (1943), *Mr. Blandings Builds His Dream House* (1948), *Street Corner* (1948), *On the Loose* (1951), *Fear Strikes Out* (1957), *Diary of a Madman* (1963), *How to Commit Marriage* (1969), *Little Big Man* (1970), *Blackenstein* (1973), *Escape to Witch Mountain* (1975), *Eat My Dust* (1976), and *Goodnight, Sweet Marilyn* (1989). Among the many television series he appeared in are *Dick Tracy*, *Climax!*, *It's a Great Life*, *I Love Lucy*, *Sky King*, *Cheyenne*, *Circus Boy*, *Peter Gunn*, *Mister Ed*, *Run for Your Life*, *Get Smart*, *Lassie*, *My Three Sons*, *Bracken's World*, *The Name of the Game*, *Adam-12*, *McCloud*, and *Murder, She Wrote*. Brodie also worked as a dialogue coach and legend has it that he was the model for the Old Hag Witch in *Snow White and the Seven Dwarfs* (1937).

Brooks, Albert (b. 1947) The satirical comedian who developed into a character actor specializing in nebbish roles, he provided the voice for the uptight, overprotective clownfish father Marlin in *Finding Nemo* (2003). He was born Albert Lawrence Einstein in Beverly Hills, California, the son of show business parents, and briefly attended Carnegie Mellon University in Pittsburgh before starting his career as a stand-up comic. After making many nightclub, concert, and television appearances and writing-performing two successful comedy records, Brooks turned to directing short films and television spots but he found more fame as an actor in such movies as *Taxi Driver* (1976), *Private Benjamin* (1980), *Unfaithfully Yours* (1984), *Broadcast News* (1987), *Mother* (1996), and *The In-Laws* (2003). He directed, wrote, and appeared in the movies *Real Life* (1979), *Modern Romance* (1981), *Lost in America* (1985), *Defending Your Life* (1991), and *The Muse* (1999). He found a new popularity on television voicing characters for the animated series *The Simpsons* for fifteen years then appeared on *Weeds*. Brooks' voice can be heard in the movies *Terms of Endearment* (1983) and *Doctor Dolittle* (1998), and the animated *The Simpsons Movie* (2007). In the original version of *Finding Nemo*, the death of Marlin's wife was not revealed until a flashback later in the movie. This resulted in Marlin coming across as an annoying worrywart; once the loss of his spouse was shown at the beginning of the film, Marlin's character made more sense. Marlin is named not so much after the fish but after Marlin Drive not far from the Pixar Studio's home in San Francisco. Co-director Andrew Stanton had Brooks in mind for Marlin from the start, though William H. Macy was considered for the part for a while. Although Brooks had voiced cartoons, he was hesitant about doing a feature length animated movie because he liked working off of other actors and knew in animation that one usually did voices alone in a studio. Making *Finding Nemo* was not a pleasant experience for him and he has not returned to movie animation since.

Brooks, Breanna The young actress who voiced the rich and spoiled Charlotte La Bouff as a child in *The Princess and the Frog* (2009) has also acted in the films *False Hope* (2007), *The Last Lullaby* (2008), *The Longshots* (2008), and *Stanley DeBrock* (2010), as well as the television movie *Front of the Class* (2008) on the *Hallmark Hall of Fame*.

Brophy, Edward (1895–1960) A bald, raspy-voiced character actor who specialized in playing gangsters on screen, he supplied the voice of Dumbo's friend, the streetwise Timothy Q. Mouse, in *Dumbo* (1941). He was born in New York City and educated at the University of Virginia before making his screen debut in 1919 with bit parts in silent films while he worked as a security guard at a studio. Brophy first got screen recognition in the Buster Keaton film *The Cameraman* (1928) and when sound came in he was in demand for character parts with a thick New Yorkese accent. Among his over one hundred movies are *Doughboys* (1930), *Parlor, Bedroom and Bath* (1931), *Freaks* (1932), *The Whole Town's Talking* (1935), *Naughty Marietta* (1935), *China Seas* (1935), *Varsity Show* (1937), *A Slight Case of Murder* (1938), *Golden Boy* (1939), *The Bride Came C.O.D.* (1941), *All Through the Night* (1941), *Air Force* (1943), *The Falcon's Adventure* (1946), *Bundle of Joy* (1956), and *The Last Hurrah* (1958). Brophy appeared in a handful of television series in the 1950s, most memorably *Damon Runyon Theatre*. Like Jiminy Cricket in *Pinocchio*, Timothy Q. Mouse is the wisecracking pal of the hero. Yet in *Dumbo*, Timothy is a very distinct character, unlike Jiminy or Disney's most famous mouse Mickey. The animators were inspired by Brophy's Brooklynese pronunciation of words and cocky manner of speech. Also, since the title character never speaks, Timothy's conversations with Dumbo are all one-sided, yet Brophy makes the scenes feel like a two-character dialogue.

Brown, Julie (b. 1954) A television writer and comic actress who has also produced some of her own series, she provided the voice of high school student Lisa who is glimpsed kissing her boy friend Chad in *A Goofy Movie* (1995). The native of Van Nuys, California, made her television debut on an episode of *Happy Days* in 1980 and that same year made her first film, *Any Which Way You Can*. Brown's other screen credits include *The Incredible Shrinking Woman* (1981), *Police Academy 2: Their First Assignment* (1985), *Nervous Ticks* (1992), *Clueless* (1995), *Like Mike* (2002), and *Fat Rose and Squeaky* (2006). After appearing in such TV series as *Laverne & Shirley*, *Newhart*, and *Get a Life*, she was featured in her own series *Just Say Julie*. Subsequent television credits include *The Edge, Clueless, Strip Mall*, and *Paradise Falls*. Brown can be heard in such cartoon series as *Tiny Toon Adventures, Batman, Animaniacs*, and *Happily Ever After: Fairy Tales for Every Child*, as well as in the animated videos *Wakko's Wish* (1999) and *Elise: Mere Mortal* (2002).

Browne, Roscoe Lee (1925–2007) A deep-voiced, charismatic African American actor who worked in all media in both the classics and new works, he lent his full, resounding voice to two Disney animated features: as the British-accented bulldog Francis in *Oliver & Company* (1988) and the severe First Mate Mr. Arrow in *Treasure Planet* (2002). He was born in Woodbury, New Jersey, and educated at Lincoln University, Middlebury College, and Columbia where he was a star athlete in track. Browne taught French and literature at Lincoln before making his professional acting debut at the New York Shakespeare Festival in 1956. He was one of the first African Americans to frequently play traditionally-white roles in Shakespeare in New York. Among his many notable stage credits are *Aria de Capo* (1958), *The Blacks* (1961), *Brecht on Brecht* (1962), *The Ballad of the Sad Cafe* (1963), *Benito Cereno* (1964), *Danton's Death* (1965), *The Dream on Monkey Mountain* (1971), *My One and Only* (1983), and *Two Trains Running* (1992). Browne made his film debut in 1962 and his television bow the next year and he appeared in many TV programs over the years, including *Mannix, The Name of the Game, All in the Family, Maude, Miss Winslow and Son, Soap, Falcon Crest, A Different World*, and *Static Shock*. Among his film credits are *The Connection* (1962), *Black Like Me* (1964), *Topaz* (1969), *The World's Greatest Athlete* (1973), *Uptown Saturday Night* (1974), *Legal Eagles* (1986), *The Mambo Kings* (1992), *Dear God* (1996), and *Behind the Broken Words* (2003). Because of his deep voice, Browne served as narrator on several films and television specials but he got to voice characters in the animated series *Visionaries: Knights of the Magical Light, The Real Ghostbusters, The Pirates of Dark Water*, and *The Wild Thornberrys*. The canine Francis in *Oliver & Company* is a delicious paradox: a street mutt with very sophisticated speech and tastes. Patrick Stewart was considered for the role but instead it went to Browne whose deep musical voice allows the paradox to work so well.

Buchanan, Stuart (1894–1974) A deep-voiced announcer who worked mainly in radio, he supplied the voice for Humbert the gruff Huntsman who cannot bring himself to kill Snow White in *Snow White and the Seven Dwarfs* (1937). Buchanan can be heard as an announcer in the films *Super-Speed* (1935) and *Saludos Amigos* (1943).

Bumpass, Rodger (b. 1951) A voice artist who has worked on many television cartoons and movies, he provided the voice of the weary waiter Mosquito in *A Bug's Life* (1998) and various minor characters in *The Hunchback of Notre Dame* (1996), *Hercules* (1997), *Tarzan* (1999), *Toy Story 2* (1999), *The Emperor's New Groove* (2000), *Monsters, Inc.* (2001), *Treasure Planet* (2002), *Brother Bear* (2003), and *Cars* (2006). A native of Jonesboro, Arkansas, Bumpass can be heard in the cartoon series *The Chipmunks, The Real Ghostbusters, TaleSpin, Raw Toonage, Bonkers, Timon and Pumbaa, 101 Dalmatians, The Angry Beavers, The Fairly Odd Parents, ChalkZone, Teen Titans, Invader ZIM, SpongeBob SquarePants*, and *Mighty Mouse, the New Adventures*, as well as the animated videos and movies *Heavy Metal* (1981), *Pedal to the Metal* (1992), *Theodore Rex* (1995), *Pocahontas II: Journey to a New*

World (1998), *The Iron Giant* (1999), *Forgotten Realms: Icewind Dale* (2000), *Spirited Away* (2001), and *The SpongeBob SquarePants Movie* (2004).

Bupp, Tommy (1924–1983)   A child actor who made over one hundred movies between 1934 and 1942, he voiced the Sailor Doll in the Silly Symphony cartoon *Broken Toys* (1935). He was born Edmond Thomas Bupp in Norfolk, Virginia, to a family of child performers, and made his screen debut at the age of ten as one of the *Our Gang* kids. Bupp played newsboys, street kids, schoolboys, and sometimes leading child roles in a wide variety of films, including *It's a Gift* (1934), *Little Men* (1934), *Babes in Toyland* (1934), *Arizona Bad Man* (1935), *Ginger* (1935), *Roarin' Guns* (1936), *San Francisco* (1936), *Piccadilly Jim* (1936), *The Longest Night* (1936), *Make Way for Tomorrow* (1937), *Hittin' the Trail* (1937), *The Cherokee Strip* (1937), *Love Is on the Air* (1937), *Tex Rides with the Boy Scouts* (1937), *Swing Your Lady* (1938), *Reformatory* (1938), *Nancy Drew — Detective* (1938), *Little Orphan Annie* (1938), *Outside These Walls* (1939), *No Place to Go* (1939), *The Way of All Flesh* (1940), and *Naval Academy* (1941). He can also be heard in the animated short *Happy Days* (1936). Bupp retired from acting at the age of eighteen and spent his adult life in the wholesale electric business.

Burghardt, Arthur (b. 1947)   A busy actor and voice artist since the 1980s, he supplied the voice of Pete, the gruff Captain of the Guard, in the Mickey Mouse featurette *The Prince and the Pauper* (1990). He made his film debut in *Network* (1976) but did not have much of a movie career, finding work instead on the television soap opera *One Life to Live* and such series as *Diff'rent Strokes*, *Hardcastle and McCormick*, *Santa Barbara*, *Knots Landing*, *Hill Street Blues*, *The Jeffersons*, *The Fall Guy*, *Good Sports*, and *Los Luchadores*. Burghardt was kept even busier doing voices for dozens of TV cartoon series, including *Scooby-Doo and Scrappy-Doo*, *G.I. Joe: A Real American Hero*, *Super Friends*, *Saturday Supercade*, *The Chipmunks*, *G.I. Joe: The Revenge of Cobra*, *Challenge of the GoBots*, *Robotix*, *The Transformers*, *The Real Ghostbusters*, *A Pup Named Scooby-Doo*, *Tom & Jerry Kids Show*, *Fievel's American Tails*, and *Conan*. He can also be heard in such animated movies and videos as *Cabbage Patch Kids: First Christmas* (1984), *Robotix* (1985), *Bigfoot and the Muscle Machines* (1985), *GoBots: War of the Rock Lords* (1986), *The Transformers: The Movie* (1986), *G.I. Joe: Arise, Serpentor, Arise!* (1986), *Transformers: Five Faces of Darkness* (1986), *G.I. Joe: The Movie* (1987), *Christmas in Tattertown* (1988), *Star Kid* (1997), and *The Wild Thornberrys: The Origin of Donnie* (2001), as well as several video games.

Burnham, David   A tenor with many musical theatre and concert credits, he was the singing voice of one of the idiot Willie Brothers in *Home on the Range* (2004). Burnham has recorded Broadway songs, sung with various orchestras, and appeared on Broadway in *Wicked* (2003) and *The Light in the Piazza* (2005).

Burton, Corey (b. 1955)   A busy voice actor for Disney and other companies, he can be heard in hundreds of TV cartoon episodes and in several feature films, including such roles as the diminutive husband Wendell in *A Goofy Movie* (1995), the brutish Guard in *The Hunchback of Notre Dame* (1996), one of the Titans and other voices in *Hercules* (1997), the Announcer for "Woody's Round-Up" show in *Toy Story 2* (1999), the French geologist Gaetan "the Mole" Moliere in *Atlantis: The Lost Empire* (2001), Captain Hook in *Return to Never Land* (2002), the multi-eyed Onus in *Treasure Planet* (2002), and the corrupt realtor Harvey Fenner in *The Princess and the Frog* (2009). He was born Corey Gregg Weinberg in Los Angeles and studied radio acting before winning a Disney contest looking for someone who could imitate the late Hans Conried's voice. He started doing voices for animated characters in 1980 and first worked for Disney imitating Bill Thompson's voice as Professor Owl for the "Disney Sing-Along" videos. Burton was so adept at imitating other voice actors that he inherited such Disney roles as Ludwig Van Drake, Captain Hook, The White Rabbit, the chipmunk Dale, the Mad Hatter, Ranger Audubon J. Woodlore, and others for videos and television cartoon series. He can also be heard in such feature-length videos as *Aladdin and the King of Thieves* (1995), *Hercules: Zero to Hero* (1999), *Cinderella II: Dreams Come True* (2002), *Kingdom Hearts* (2002), *101 Dalmatians II: Patch's London Adventure* (2003), *Atlantis: Milo's Return* (2003), *Stitch! The Movie* (2003), *The Lion King 1½* (2004), *The Nightmare Before Christmas: Oogie's Revenge* (2004), *Kingdom Hearts II* (2005), *Disney Princess Enchanted Tales: Follow Your Dream* (2007), and *Kingdom Hearts: Birth by Sleep* (2010). Among his many Disney TV series credits are *DuckTales*, *Chip N' Dale's Rescue Rangers*, *TaleSpin*, *Adventures of the Gummi Bears*, *Animaniacs*, *Bonkers*, *Goof Troop*, *Mighty Ducks*, *Timon and Pumbaa*, *Hercules*, *Buzz Lightyear of Star Command*, *Mickey Mouse Works*, *Kim Possible*, *The Adventures of Jimmy Neutron: Boy Genius*, and *The Emperor's New School*. Of his many non-Disney series, he is most known as the voice of Count Dooku and other characters on the animated *Star Wars: The Clone Wars*, as well as such programs as *G.I. Joe*, *The Transformers*, *Superman*, *The New Woody Woodpecker Show*, *Batman Beyond*,

Jackie Chan Adventures, Justice League, and *James Bond, Jr.* Burton's voice has been heard at several Disney theme park attractions, including Universe of Energy, Pirates of the Caribbean, It's Tough to Be a Bug, Mr. Toad's Wild Ride, Goofy About Heath, and Cranium Command.

Burtt, Ben (b. 1948) The pioneering sound designer, mixer, and editor who has created the special sound effects for many sci-fi and adventure films, he provided the voices for the dirty hardworking little trash-collecting robot WALL-E (Waste Allocation Load Lifter: Earth Class) and his nemesis, the clean-freak robot M-O (Microbe-Obliterator), in *WALL-E* (2008). He was born in Jamesville, New York, and educated at Allegheny College and the University of California School of Cinematic Arts. Burtt worked for LucasFilms for twenty-eight years, creating such memorable sound effects as the droids and other non-human creatures in the *Star Wars* movies, the weird special sounds in such films as *Invasion of the Body Snatchers* (1978) and *Raiders of the Lost Ark* (1981), and the vocals for the title alien in *E.T.: The Extraterrestrial* (1982). He has designed or edited the sound in such notable movies as *Death Race 2000* (1975), *More American Graffiti* (1979), *The Dark Crystal* (1982), *Howard the Duck* (1986), *Willow* (1988), *Always* (1989), *Blue Planet* (1990), *Munich* (2005), and *Star Trek* (2009). Burtt has also worked as editor on some of the *Star Wars* films and the TV series *The Young Indiana Jones Chronicles*. He reprised his WALL-E and M-O in the animated short *BURN-E* (2008) and provided the voices for minor characters in the first and sixth episodes of *Star Wars*, but his most famous "voice" was programming the electronic sounds for the droid R2-D2 in the *Star Wars* series. Although the character of WALL-E is the main character in the film, his dialogue is sparse and his ability to gesture and make facial expressions is very limited. Yet the animators and voice actor Burtt managed to make the little mechanical hero very expressive and endearing. They were inspired by the bespectacled, hopelessly romantic little guys that Woody Allen played in his films. The binocular eyes do suggest Allen's glasses at times. Although the name WALL-E is an acronym for his job, the name also is a nod to Walter Elias Disney.

Buscemi, Steve (b. 1957) The prolific film and television director and actor who often plays fast-talking, street-wise characters, he provided the voices for the evil chameleon-like monster Randall Boggs in *Monsters, Inc.* (2001) and the corrupt businessman Wesley who buys the stolen cattle from Alameda Slim in *Home on the Range* (2004). He was born in Brooklyn, New York, and worked as a fire fighter for four years before performing professionally Off Off Broadway and with the experimental Wooster Group. Buscemi made his screen debut in 1985 and soon was featured in colorful roles in such films as *Parting Glances* (1986), *Kiss Daddy Goodnight* (1987), *New York Stories* (1989), *Slaves of New York* (1989), *King of New York* (1990), *Miller's Crossing* (1990), *Barton Fink* (1991), *Billy Bathgate* (1991), *Reservoir Dogs* (1992), *Rising Sun* (1993), *The Hudsucker Proxy* (1994), *Desperado* (1995), *Fargo* (1996), *Escape from L.A.* (1996), *Con Air* (1997), *The Wedding Singer* (1998), *The Big Lebowski* (1998), *Armageddon* (1998), *Deadrockstar* (2002), *I Now Pronounce You Chuck & Larry* (2007), and *Grown Ups* (2010). Among the television series he has appeared in are *Not Necessarily the News, Miami Vice, The Equalizer, The Sopranos, 30 Rock,* and *Boardwalk Empire*, as well as the mini-series *Lonesome Dove* (1989). Buscemi can be heard on the TV cartoon series *The Simpsons* and supplied voices for the films *Monster House* (2006), *Charlotte's Web* (2006), *Igor* (2008), and *G-Force* (2009). He has directed a few movies as well as TV episodes, including *Oz, The Sopranos, 30 Rock,* and *Nurse Jackie*. He got the role of the creepy monster Randall in *Monsters, Inc.*, because John Goodman, who voiced Sulley in the film, recommended him. Buscemi and Goodman had been teamed effectively in three previous films.

Butala, Tony (b. 1938) A child actor and singer who later found wide success as a group vocalist, he voiced Tootles, the Lost Boy wearing the skunk skin, in *Peter Pan* (1953). Anthony Francis Butala was born in Sharon, Pennsylvania, and sang on the radio as a child before going to California to sing with the Robert Mitchell Boys' Choir. As a member of that group he sang on screen in *On Moonlight Bay* (1951) and *White Christmas* (1954), and he appeared in *The 5,000 Fingers of Dr. T* (1953) and did the singing voice for Tommy Rettig in the leading role of that movie. His other film credits are *The War of the Worlds* (1953) and *Dragstrip Riot* (1958). When he was a teenager, Butala left acting and sang with different all-guy quartets, most famously The Letterman, making many recordings and television appearances, and performing in concert into the next century. He founded and currently oversees the Vocal Group Hall of Fame and Museum in his Pennsylvania hometown. Like most of the original cast of *Peter Pan*, Butala reprised his performance on a *Lux Radio Theatre* broadcast soon after the movie version was released.

Butcher, Paul (b. 1994) A child actor with a long list of credits, he supplied the voice of the fat student Stanley who has the volcano exhibit at the science fair in *Meet the Robinsons* (2007). Paul

Matthew Hawke Butcher was born in Los Angeles, the son of retired NFL line backer Paul Butcher, and started acting at the age of seven. He made his television debut on an episode of *The Bernie Mac Show*, followed by appearances on such series as *Power Rangers Wild Force*, *Providence*, *Six Feet Under*, *ER*, *That 70's Show*, *NYPD Blue*, *Bones*, *The King of Queens*, *Without a Trace*, *American Dad*, *Criminal Minds*, and most memorably in *Zoey 101*. Among Butcher's movie credits are *Landspeed* (2002), *Hollywood Homicide* (2003), *Imaginary Friend* (2006), *The Number 23* (2007), and *The Legacy* (2010). He can be heard on the TV cartoon series *Avatar: The Last Airbender*, *The Mighty B!*, and *King of the Hill*, as well as the animated films and videos *Ice Age: The Meltdown* (2006), *Over the Hedge* (2006), *Barnyard* (2006), *Holly Hobbie and Friends: Christmas Wishes* (2006), *He's a Bully, Charlie Brown* (2006), *Holly Hobbie and Friends: Secret Adventures* (2007), and *Holly Hobbie and Friends: Best Friends Forever* (2007).

Butler, Daws (1916–1988)   A prolific voice artist who played characters in over 200 animated shorts and another 200 episodes of TV cartoons, he voiced the Turtle and one of the Penguins in the animated section of *Mary Poppins* (1964). He was born Charles Dawson Butler in Toledo, Ohio, and grew up in Oak Park, Illinois, where as a teenager he did impersonations of famous people in talent shows, nightclubs, and in theatre revues. After serving in the Navy during World War II, he went to California where he worked in radio then with Stan Freberg on television in the puppet show *Time for Beanie* which later became the popular cartoon series *Cecil and Beanie*. Butler played characters in some of Freberg's best-selling comedy records while he began voicing cartoon characters such as Huckleberry Hound, Yogi Bear, Quick-Draw McGraw, Snagglepuss, and many others. He also did dozens of TV commercials and voiced such popular characters as Captain Crunch and Snap (of Snap, Crackle and Pop). Among the many cartoon series he can be heard on are *Rocky and His Friends*, *The Bugs Bunny Show*, *The Bullwinkle Show*, *The Huckleberry Hound Show*, *The Yogi Bear Show*, *Wally Gator*, *Lippy the Lion and Hardy Har Har*, *The Woody Woodpecker Show*, *The Flintstones*, *The Banana Splits Adventure Hour*, *Wacky Races*, *Bailey's Comets*, *The Jetsons*, and *Yogi's Treasure Hunt*, as well as many television specials that featured these characters. In his later years Butler ran acting workshops teaching young actors how to do voice work for animation. It is curious that Butler, who worked with several different studios over a long period of time, voiced only one Disney film in his career.

Buttram, Pat (1915–1994)   A popular comic actor with a thick Southern drawl who found success in radio, films, and television, he was a favorite voice in Disney animated features with such roles as the military-minded farm dog Napoleon in *The Aristocats* (1970), the doltish wolf, the Sheriff of Nottingham, in *Robin Hood* (1973), the lazy muskrat Luke in *The Rescuers* (1977), the fox-hating dog Chief in *The Fox and the Hound* (1981), the tough cowpoke Bullet #1 in *Who Framed Roger Rabbit* (1988), and the obnoxious Possum Park Emcee in *A Goofy Movie* (1995). He was born Maxwell Emmett Buttram in Addison, Alabama, and, as a teenager, visited the Chicago World's Fair in 1933 and was interviewed on the local radio, sending its listeners into hysterics with his hayseed humor. Buttram was hired on the spot by the station and found national fame on the popular *National Barn Dance* radio program. He made his movie debut in 1948 and went on to make many Westerns as the comic sidekick for Gene Autry, also appearing in Autry's television show in the 1950s. Buttram concentrated on television thereafter, acting in dozens of TV series, none of his portrayals becoming as beloved as his sly salesman Mr. Haney in *Green Acres*. His distinctive voice can be heard in the animated series *Tiny Toon Adventures* and *Garfield and Friends*, and the videos *The New Misadventures of Ichabod Crane* (1979) and *The Good, the Bad, and Huckleberry Hound* (1988). Buttram died soon after finishing the vocals for the film *A Goofy Movie*. Biography: *Pat Buttram: The Rocking Chair Humorist*, Sandra Graham (2006).

Buzzi, Ruth (b. 1936)   A popular television comedienne whose homely face and farcical expressions made her ideal for broad comedy, she provided the singing voice for the horse Frou-Frou in *The Aristocats* (1970) and voiced the German Mouse in *The Rescuers* (1977). Ruth Ann Buzzi was born in Westerly, Rhode Island, the daughter of a mortuary owner, and studied acting at the Pasadena Playhouse before beginning her career in comedy revues and Off Broadway musicals. Her portrayal of several small comic roles in the Broadway musical *Sweet Charity* (1966) led to appearances on such television programs as *The Garry Moore Show*, *The Entertainers*, *The Steve Allen Comedy Hour*, and *That Girl*, as well as many commercials. It was as one of the regulars on *Rowan and Martin's Laugh-In* that Buzzi became a national favorite, her character of the repressed spinster Gladys Ormphby becoming so popular that she reprised her in the animated TV series *Baggy Pants and the Nitwits*. She has acted in several movies but was busier in television, providing voices for such cartoon series as *Linus! The Lion Hearted*, *The Smurfs*, *The*

Chipmunks, The Berenstain Bears, Pound Puppies, The Savage Dragon, The Angry Beavers, and *Sheep in the Big City,* as well as the videos and movies *I Go Pogo: The Movie* (1980), *Milroy: Santa's Misfit Mutt* (1987), *Rockin' with Judy Jetson* (1988), *Pound Puppies and the Legend of Big Paw* (1988), *Marvin: Baby of the Year* (1989), *I Yabba-Dabba-Do!* (1993), and *Hollyrock-a-Bye Baby* (1993). Buzzi can also be heard singing the operatic spoof "When the Buzzards Return to Hinckley Ridge" in the Disney short *It's Tough to Be a Bird* (1969).

Byner, John (b. 1938) A comic actor and impressionist with as many facial expressions as he has different voices, he played both the cowardly furry creature Gurgi and the hot-tempered, sometimes-invisible Fair Folk critter Doli in *The Black Caldron* (1985). He was born John Thomas Biener in New York City, the son of an auto mechanic, and began his career as a stand-up comic in Greenwich Village nightclubs. Soon he was doing his comedy and impressions of famous people in the top nightspots in New York and Las Vegas, also appearing on television variety shows hosted by Merv Griffin, Steve Allen, and Ed Sullivan. Byner played characters in such TV sit-coms as *Get Smart, The Mothers-in-Law, The Odd Couple, Maude, Soap, Married with Children, Dharma & Greg,* and *Love, American Style,* as well as his own show in 1972. Because of his vocal agility, he was in great demand for voicing cartoons and contributed to many animated series, including *Garfield and Friends, Duckman: Private Dick/Family Man, The Angry Beavers, Aaahh!! Real Monsters, Wat Kats: The Radical Squadron,* and *The Pink Panther.* His animated movies and video credits include *The Ant and the Aardvark* (1969) and its fourteen sequels, *Aesops' Fables* (1971), and *A Wish for Wings That Work* (1991), Byner's work in *The Black Cauldron* is impressive. His Gurgi has a funny, barely-discernible voice reminiscent of Donald Duck while his excitable Doli has squeaky and punctuated vocals.

Cabot, Sebastian (1918–1977) The round, bearded British character actor with a gentlemanly demeanor, he supplied the voices of the Medieval vassal Sir Ector in *The Sword in the Stone* (1963) and the wise panther Bagheera in *The Jungle Book* (1967). Charles Sebastian Thomas Cabot was born in London and left school to work as a garage mechanic, professional wrestler, chef, and chauffeur before turning to acting. He made his screen debut in 1935 and appeared in several British films, most memorably *Othello* (1946), *The Captain's Paradise* (1953), and *Romeo and Juliet* (1954), before going to Hollywood and finding recognition in supporting roles in such movies as *Kismet* (1955), *Westward Ho the Wagons!* (1956), *Johnny Tremain* (1957), *The Time Machine* (1960), and *The Family Jewels* (1965). Cabot found greater success in television, appearing in many series, including *Gunsmoke, Zorro, Bonanza, Twilight Zone, Checkmate, The Beachcomber, My Three Sons, Circle of Fear,* and *McCloud,* but he is most remembered as the valet Mr. French on *Family Affair* for five years. Much in demand as a narrator because of his smooth, deep voice, he narrated the first *Winnie the Pooh* short in 1966 and continued with all the subsequent cartoons until his death. Cabot can also be heard doing character voices in the video *The City That Forgot About Christmas* (1974).

Calame, Niketa (b. 1980) The African American teenager who voiced the lioness Young Nala in *The Lion King* (1994), the Los Angeles native was in the film *CB4* (1993) and later in *Viewfinder* (2006) and *Moments* (2009). She studied at the Actors Studio and the University of California at Santa Cruz.

Caldwell, Zoe (b. 1933) An intense, vibrant actress who has excelled in classic and modern plays on three continents, she brought her commanding persona to the voice of the Grand Councilwoman in *Lilo & Stitch* (2002). She was born Ada Caldwell in Hawthorn, Australia, where she began acting professionally before going to England in 1958. Caldwell played classic characters in such celebrated companies as the Shakespeare Memorial Theatre, Royal Court, Royal Shakespeare Company, Stratford Shakespeare Festival in Canada, and Guthrie Theatre in Minneapolis. She made her Broadway debut in 1965 and returned for such memorable productions as *Slapstick Tragedy* (1966), *The Prime of Miss Jean Brodie* (1968), *Colette* (1970), *The Dance of Death* (1974), *Medea* (1982), *Lillian* (1986), and *Master Class* (1995). Caldwell's film and television credits are few but impressive and she is also a respected stage director. She reprised her Grand Councilwoman in the TV series *Lilo & Stitch* and in the videos *Stitch Experiment 626* (2002), *Stitch! The Movie* (2003), *Stitch's Great Escape* (2004), and *Leroy & Stitch* (2006). Autobiography: *I Will Be Cleopatra: An Actress's Journey* (2001).

Callahan, Julius A bearded, offbeat character actor and something of a jack of all trades, he did the voices of the saucier Lalo who is afraid of rats and the crass advertising agency guru Francois Dupuis in *Ratatouille* (2007). He was born in Denver, Colorado, and grew up in Nigeria, France, the Netherlands, and other places around the world, After studying at Lewis and Clark College in Oregon, he worked on the radio, designed shoes for Nike, produced record albums, painted murals for civic places, and promoted the sound of hip hop across the States. The singer-actor turned to acting in 2003 and has appeared on such television series as *The Practice, Deadwood, Strong Medicine, Joan of Arcadia, CSI: Miami, Judging Amy, Alias, Arrested Development, CSI: Crime Scene Investigation,* and *Cold Case*. Callahan's movie credits include *The Princess Diaries 2: Royal Engagement* (2004), *Lemony Snicket's A Series of Unfortunate Events* (2004), *Mr. & Mrs. Smith* (2005), *Rebound* (2005), *Art School Confidential* (2006), *Shanghai Kiss* (2007), and *Unemployed* (2008). He often returns to Nigeria to present arts programs and performs in concert and on television.

Callas, Charlie (b. 1924) The rubber-faced comedian and actor of movies and television, he provided the indecipherable sounds of the friendly dragon Elliott, the only animated character in the live-action movie musical *Pete's Dragon* (1977). He was born in Brooklyn, New York, and after serving in World War II he began his career as a drummer with Tommy Dorsey, Claude Thornhill, Buddy Rich, and other band leaders. In the 1960s Callas turned to stand-up comedy, finding success in nightclubs and on television where he appeared on everything from talk shows to variety specials to quiz programs. He played characters on such TV series as *The Munsters, The Monkees, The Snoop Sisters, Switch, The Love Boat, Hart to Hart, It Takes Two, Cagney & Lacey, L.A. Law, Silk Stalkings, Cybill,* and *Beggars and Choosers*. Callas was also featured in a number of movies, including *The Big Mouth* (1967), *Silent Movie* (1976), *High Anxiety* (1977), *History of the World: Part I* (1981), *Hysterical* (1983), *Dracula: Dead and Loving It* (1995), and *Crooks* (2002). Originally the title creature in *Pete's Dragon* was to be invisible, not seen by anyone except the boy Pete, and even the moviegoers would not get a glimpse of him until the last scene. As much as the filmmakers tried to make this work, the idea was thought to be too frustrating for viewers and the dragon Elliott was animated and placed in the live-action film. Callas' vocals, consisting of a variety of squeaking and gurgling sounds, kept the dragon from being too human yet Callas still managed to communicate Elliott's thoughts and feelings.

Callow, Simon (b. 1949) A distinguished English character actor, writer, and theatre director, he provided the voice of the snobby British Grasshopper in *James and the Giant Peach* (1996). Simon Phillip Hugh Callow was born in London and attended Queen's University of Belfast before leaving school to act at the Drama Centre London. He performed with various theatre companies throughout Great Britain and found wide acclaim when he played Mozart in the original production of *Amadeus* (1979) at the Royal National Theatre. He continued to act on stage even as he appeared on many British television programs and made his screen debut as Schikaneder in the 1984 film version of *Amadeus*. Among Callow's many notable films are *A Room with a View* (1985), *Maurice* (1987), *Mr. and Mrs. Bridge* (1990), *Four Weddings and a Funeral* (1994), *Jefferson in Paris* (1995), *Ace Ventura: When Nature Calls* (1995), *Shakespeare in Love* (1998), *Bright Young Things* (2003), *The Phantom of the Opera* (2004), and *Natural Selection* (2010), as well as many English and American TV-movies and mini-series such as *David Copperfield* (1986), *The Crucifer of Blood* (1991), *The Woman in White* (1997), *Around the World in 80 Days* (1999), *The Mystery of Charles Dickens* (2000), *Hans Christian Anderson: My Life as a Fairy Tale* (2001), and *Angels in America* (2003). He can be heard in the animated films and videos *The Reluctant Dragon* (1987), *Animated Epics: Don Quixote* (2000), and *Christmas Carol: The Movie* (2001). Callow has written books on such topics as acting, directing, Charles Laughton, Charles Dickens, and Orson Welles, and he is also a recognized director of plays and musicals on the British stage. Memoir: *Being an Actor* (2003).

Campbell, Colin (1883–1966) A short, lively character actor who usually played Scottish types, he provided the voice of the jovial, polite Mole in "The Wind in the Willows" portion of the animated double bill *The Adventures of Ichabod and Mr. Toad* (1949). Campbell was born in Falkirk, Scotland, and was appearing in British films by 1915. By the time sound came in he was in Hollywood and acted in small roles in some fifty movies, including *Big Boy* (1930), *The Dark Angel* (1935), *Mrs. Miniver* (1942), *The Lodger* (1944), *The Two Mrs. Carrolls* (1947), *The Lost World* (1960), and *My Fair Lady* (1964). In the 1950s Campbell turned to television and appeared in many drama anthology programs such as *Schlitz Playhouse of Stars, Alfred Hitchcock Presents,* and *The Twilight Zone*. The Mole in "The Wind in the Willows" is the assistant to the Sherlock Holmes–like Rat and Campbell's vocals suggest actor Nigel Bruce who was Dr. Watson to Basil Rathbone's Holmes in several films.

Campbell, Tevin (b. 1976) A popular rhythm and blues singer and songwriter who first found fame as a teenager in the 1990s, he supplied the speaking and singing voice of the dog-like rock star Powerline in *A Goofy Movie* (1995). Tevin Jermod Campbell was born in Waxahachie, Texas, and at the age of fourteen had his first number one single on the charts with "Tomorrow (A Better You Better Me)." Award-winning, best-selling albums and singles have followed. Campbell has acted on occasion, appearing in the television series *The Fresh Prince of Bel-Air* and *Moesha*, in the TV-movie *Wally and the Valentines* (1989), and in the film *Grafitti Bridge* (1990). He also appeared on Broadway in the musical *Hairspray* in 2009. In *A Goofy Movie*, he sings the songs "Stand Out" and "I2I" as Powerline, a character patterned after the teen idol that he once was. Biography: *Tevin Campbell*, Lambert M. Surhone, Miriam T. Timpledon, Susan F. Marseken (2010).

Campos, Bruno (b. 1973) The appealing Brazilian-born actor who is a romantic idol in American television and movies, he provided the voice of the handsome but irresponsible Prince Naveen of Maldonia in *The Princess and the Frog* (2009). He was born in Rio de Janeiro, Brazil, the son of an international banker, and grew up in Canada, the United States, and his native country. Campos was educated at the Interlochen Arts Academy in Michigan and at Northwestern University and began his career back in Brazil, getting noticed in the movie *O Quatrilho* (1995) which was an international hit. Two years later he was in the States and acting in such television series as *Chicago Sons, Suddenly Susan, Cybill, Jesse, Leap Years, Will & Grace, ER, The D.A., Boston Legal, Nip/Tuck, Castle, Royal Pains, Private Practice*, and *The Closer*. Campos also appeared in the films *Dopamine* (2003), *Blue Moon* (2005), *Cold Feet* (2005), *Crazylove* (2005), and *Wake* (2009), as well as the TV-movies *Mimic 2* (2001), *Miss Miami* (2002), *The Wedding Album* (2006), and *Night Life* (2008). Naveen in *The Princess and the Frog* is not a typical Disney prince. He is handsome and dashing but he is also immature, self-centered, and not at all interested in marriage. Yet he makes no pretense of being noble and does not try to fool Tiana and other characters into thinking he is any better than he seems. The transformation his character goes through is as great as his change from prince to frog and back to prince. Campos' funny and endearing performance must be credited with making Prince Naveen so appealing during all the steps of this transition.

Candido, Candy (1913–1999) The growly-voiced character actor who specialized in villains or their sidekicks, he supplied the voices for the stern Indian Chief in *Peter Pan* (1953), Maleficent's Goon in *Sleeping Beauty* (1959), the crocodile Captain of the Guards in *Robin Hood* (1973), Madame Medusa's crocodile bullies Brutus and Nero in *The Rescuers* (1977), and Ratigan's peg-legged henchman Fidget the Bat in *The Great Mouse Detective* (1986). He was born Jonathan Joseph Candido in New Orleans, Louisiana, and began his career as a bass player and singer with Ted Fio Rito's Orchestra and soon was a favorite on Jimmy Durante's radio show, his deep voice often proclaiming "I'm feeling mighty low." Candido appeared as a band member in several movie musicals, such as *Sadie McKee* (1934), *Roberta* (1935), *Broadway Gondolier* (1935), *Something to Sing About* (1937), *Cowboy from Brooklyn* (1938), *Rhythm Parade* (1942), *Campus Rhythm* (1943), *Sarge Goes to College* (1947), and *Riding High* (1950), as well as bit parts in other films. He can also be heard in the animated movies *The Phantom Tollbooth* (1970), *Heavy Traffic* (1973), and *Hey Good Lookin'* (1982), and in the TV cartoon series *Mighty Mouse, the New Adventures*. The character of the bat henchman Fidget in *The Great Mouse Detective* was developed using Candido's facial features. The actor's deep, throaty vocals were perfectly devious but on listening to the recording the directors felt his voice was so low that it might not carry well. So the filmmakers speeded up the tapes and Candido's voice was raised to a slightly higher pitch.

Candy, John (1950–1994) The oversized comic actor who usually played lovable buffoons on television and on the screen, he voiced the cockeyed seagull Wilbur in *The Rescuers Down Under* (1990). John Franklin Candy was born in Toronto, Canada, and acted on stage and in some Canadian television before becoming one of the cast members of the Toronto comedy troupe Second City. When the group appeared on television in the series *SCTV*, Candy found national recognition for his wide repertory of comic characters and impersonations of celebrities. He was featured in many movies before his premature death from a heart attack at the age of forty-four. Among his many notable films are *The Silent Partner* (1978), *1941* (1979), *The Blues Brothers* (1980), *Stripes* (1981), *Splash* (1984), *Brewster's Millions* (1985), *Spaceballs* (1987), *Planes, Trains & Automobiles* (1987), *The Great Outdoors* (1988), *Uncle Buck* (1989), *Home Alone* (1990), *Only the Lonely* (1991), *JFK* (1991), *Boris and Natasha* (1992), *Cool Runnings* (1993), and *Canadian Bacon* (1995). In addition to his six years on *SCTV*, Candy also appeared on the television series *The David Steinberg Show, Coming Up Rosie, King of Kensington, Tales of the Klondike, The New Show, The Dave Thomas Comedy Show*, and *Shelley Duvall's Bedtime Stories*. He can be heard in the animated film *Heavy Metal* (1981). Because Jim Jordan, who had voiced the seagull Orville in *The Rescuers* (1977) had died in 1988, it was decided not to reprise Orville but replace him with his brother Wilbur, allowing Candy to develop his own character for the bird. While Orville was a bit grouchy and disapproving, Candy's Wilbur is more fun-loving and amiable in the comic's distinctive style. The actor's last job was in Disney's *Pocahontas* (1995). He voiced a comic turkey named Redfeather, but after Candy's death the character was eliminated from the film. Also, all the other animals in the movie had their dialogue removed in order to make *Pocahontas* more realistic. Biography: *Laughing on the Outside: The Life of John Candy*, Martin Knelman (1998).

Canney, Wayne A professional musician who supplied the voice of John Walker, the stern Principal of Dash's school, in *The Incredibles* (2004), he has no other film or television credits.

Carlin, George (1937–2008) The popular bearded stand-up comic and writer whose pointed sense of humor remained on the cutting edge for over forty years, he provided the voice for Fillmore, the hippie Volkswagon bus, in *Cars* (2006). George Denis Patrick Carlin was born in New York City and grew up in various places across the country. He started doing stand-up comedy and soon distinguished himself for his political astuteness and anti-establishment point of view. Always controversial, Carlin still managed to find popularity in concerts and on television from the 1960s until his death. In addition to his hundreds of TV appearances on talk shows and variety programs (including his own show in 1994), he appeared in such movies as *With Six You Get Eggroll* (1968), *Car Wash* (1976), *Outrageous Fortune* (1986), *Bill & Ted's Excellent Adventure* (1989), *Bill & Ted's Bogus Journey* (1991), *The Prince of Tides* (1991), *Dogma* (1999), and *Scary Movie 3* (2003). Carlin also acted in the television series *Shining Time Station* and its spinoffs, voiced the animated series *Bill & Ted's Excellent Adventures* and *The Simpsons*, and can be heard on the videos *Tarzan II* (2005), and *Happily N'Ever After* (2006). The character of the hippie bus Fillmore in *Cars* was inspired by Carlin's stage and real-life persona. Fillmore was originally named Waldmire after the hippie artist Bob Waldmire who illustrated many postcards and maps of Route 66 (the original title of the film). Waldmire is a strict vegetarian and did not give permission to use his name, afraid that the character might become a toy given with a McDonald's Happy Meal. The new name Fillmore was taken from the Fillmore Auditorium, a popular music venue for counterculture groups in the 1960s and 1970s. Carlin wrote several books including his memoir *Last Words* with Tony Hendra (2009). Biography: *George Carlin's Alter Ego by His Alter-Ego*, Bill Brennan (2009).

Carmichael, Jim A story director and layout artist in Hollywood and later in television, he provided the speaking and singing voice for one of the quartet of Crows in *Dumbo* (1941). Carmichael worked on the animation for the Disney cartoons *Sea Scouts* (1939) and *Pantry Pirate* (1940), as well as the non–Disney *Grape Nutty* (1949). Among the TV cartoon series he story directed were *Cattanooga Cats*, *The Amazing Chan and the Chan Clan*, *The Flintstones*, and *The Addams Family*. He has no other voice credits outside of *Dumbo*.

Carr, Darleen (b. 1950) A singer-actress mostly on television from the 1960s to the late 1990s, she voiced the singing Girl from the Indian village who attracts Mowgli at the end of *The Jungle Book* (1967). She was born Darleen Farnon in Chicago, the daughter of a musician and an actress, and first started acting on television in 1963, going on to appear on such series as *The John Forsythe Show*, *Mayberry R.F.D.*, *The Smith Family*, *The F.B.I.*, *The Rookies*, *Medical Center*, *The Streets of San Francisco*, *Barnaby Jones*, *Miss Winslow and Son*, *Simon & Simon*, and *Star Trek: Deep Space Nine*, but she is mostly remembered as Mary Lou Springer on *Bret Maverick*. Carr made a handful of movies, including *Monkeys Go Home!* (1967), *The Impossible Years* (1968), and *Death of a Gunfighter* (1969), and she dubbed some of the singing for the children in *The Sound of Music* (1965). She can also be heard in the TV cartoon series *G.I. Joe*, *Darkwing Duck*, *The Pirates of Dark Water*, and *The Real Adventures of Jonny Quest*, as well as in the animated videos *Joshua and the Battle of Jericho* (1986) and several others in the Bible series, *The Halloween Tree* (1993), *The Secret of Nimh 2: Timmy to the Rescue* (1998), and *Lands of Lore III* (1999). Her sister is actress Charmian Carr who was featured in *The Sound of Music*.

Carrere, Tia (b. 1967) A stunningly attractive actress-singer-songwriter on both television and in film, she voiced Lilo's older sister and guardian Nani in *Lilo & Stitch* (2002). She was born Althea Rae Duhinio Janairo in Honolulu, Hawaii, and did some modeling before making her television debut as Miss Philippines in an episode of *Cover Up* in 1985. She went on to appear in such series as *General Hospital*, *The A-Team*, *MacGyver*, *Anything but Love*, and *Married with Children*, but got more attention when she started to make films, including *Aloha Summer* (1988), *Wayne's World* (1992), *Rising Sun* (1993), *Wayne's World 2* (1993), *True Lies* (1994), *Top of the World* (1998), *Merlin: The Return* (2000), *The Last Guy on Earth* (2006), and *Wild Cherry* (2009). Carrere was featured in later television series such as *Murder One*, *Relic Hunter*, *Curb Your Enthusiasm*, and *CSI: Miami*. Being a native Hawaiian, Carrere knew the islands well and was able to make suggestions to the writers of *Lilo*

& Stitch on dialogue and dialect matters. She reprised her Nani in the videos *Stitch! The Movie!* (2003), *Lilo & Stitch 2: Stitch Has a Glitch* (2005), *Leroy & Stitch* (2006), and the TV series *Lilo & Stitch*. She can be heard doing voices in the cartoon series *Happily Ever After: Fairy Tales for Every Child, Hercules, Megas XLR, Johnny Bravo, Duck Dodgers,* and *American Dragon: Jake Long*, as well as the videos *The Night of the Headless Horseman* (1999) and *Aloha, Scooby-Doo* (2005). Carrere has recorded songs she wrote and can be heard singing on different movie soundtracks, in particular *Wayne's World* and *Batman: Mask of the Phantasm* (1993).

Carroll, Eddie (1933–2010) A character actor, impersonator, and writer with television credits spread over four decades, he provided the voice of Jiminy Cricket in Disney videos and television programs from 1971 to 2007. He was born Edward Eleniak in Edmonton, Canada, and moved to Hollywood in the 1950s, eventually getting cast in such television series as *Gomer Pyle U.S.M.C., Mission: Impossible, The Andy Griffith Show, The Don Knotts Show,* and *Frasier*. When Cliff Edwards, the original voice of Jiminy Cricket, died in 1971, Carroll's impersonation of the voice was so effective that the studio hired him to provide the cricket's narration of the video *Bongo* (1971), a re-release of a segment from *Fun and Fancy Free* (1947). Carroll was the official voice of Jiminy Cricket for the next thirty-six years, heard in commercials, on the television shows *Walt Disney's Wonderful World of Color* and *House of Mouse*, in many Disney video games, as the Ghost of Christmas Past in *Mickey's Christmas Carol* (1983), and in such videos as *Jiminy Cricket's Christmas* (1986), *DTV Valentine* (1986), *DTV Doggone Valentine* (1987), *Mickey's Magical Christmas: Snowed in at the House of Mouse* (2001), and three *Disney Sing-Along Songs* videos. He toured for years in his one-man show in which he impersonated Jack Benny, even learning how to play the violin (poorly) for the role, and in the 1970s he wrote scripts for many Hanna-Barbera TV cartoon series.

Carroll, Pat (b. 1927) A plump, comic actress who excels at playing the villain or the best friend in stage and television comedies and musicals, she got one of her best roles late in her career: the scheming sea witch Ursula in *The Little Mermaid* (1989). She was born Patricia Angela Ann Bridget in Shreveport, Louisiana, and educated at Sacred Heart College and Catholic University of America before starting her career as a cabaret singer. By the early 1950s she had acted in dozens of stock productions across the country and started appearing regularly on television in variety shows. Carroll was featured on Broadway in the revues *Come What May* (1955) and *Catch a Star!* (1955), and the 1959 revival of *On the Town*, but most of her career was on the tube which best suited her performance style. She appeared in dozens of television shows, including the *Red Buttons Show, The Danny Thomas Show, The Red Skelton Hour, Getting Together, Busting Loose, Too Close for Comfort, She's the Sheriff,* and *ER*, but possibly her most memorable appearance on the small screen was as the stepsister Prunella in the 1965 TV remake of *Cinderella*. Starting in the 1970s, Carroll was in demand for doing voices for animated television series, among them *Legends of the Superheroes, Foofur, Pound Puppies,* and *Chip 'n Dale Rescue Rangers*, and for animated TV specials, such as *A Garfield Christmas Special* (1987), *A Pup Named Scooby-Doo* (1989), and *Garfield's Thanksgiving* (1989). By the 1980s Carroll returned to the theatre in serious roles and performed in everything from Shakespeare plays to new works, and was still active on stage and screen in 2009. The sea witch Ursula is one of the most fun of Disney villains. Because she is underwater, Ursula moves like no other villain, her tentacles becoming side-kick characters of their own. The look of the character was inspired by the drag performer Divine with Beatrice Arthur as the first choice to do the voice. Other actresses considered include Roseanne, Charlotte Rae, Nancy Marchand, Jennifer Saunders, and Elaine Stritch. Carroll was finally selected and her vocals are a delight, using a low register for some of the singing but then climbing the scales with her speaking voice. Carroll reprised her Ursula in the cartoon series *The Little Mermaid* as well as in the video movies *The Little Mermaid II: Return to the Sea* (2000), *Mickey's Magical Christmas* (2001), *Mickey's House of Villains* (2001), *Kingdom Hearts* (2002), and *House of Mouse* (2002).

Carson, Ken (1914–1994) An actor and cowboy singer who sang in some two dozen movies, he supplied the speaking and singing voice of the animated Wise Old Owl who gives advice to the live-action youth Jeremiah (Bobby Driscoll) in *So Dear to My Heart* (1948). He was born Hubert Paul Flatt in Coalgate, Oklahoma, and began singing on local radio in the 1930s. After playing bit roles in the films *It Happened One Night* (1934) and *In Old Monterey* (1939), he became a member of the famous western singing group Sons of the Pioneers and with them sang in such movies as *The Man from Music Mountain* (1943), *Cowboy and the Senorita* (1944), *Song of Nevada* (1944), *Lights of Old Santa Fe* (1944), *Bells of Rosarita* (1945), *Man from Oklahoma* (1945), *Sunset in El Dorado* (1945), and *Rainbow Over Texas* (1946). Carson also sang and/or played guitar in bit roles in other films, including *Hands Across the Border* (1944), *The Yellow Rose of Texas* (1944), *San Fernando Valley* (1944), *Don't Fence Me In* (1945), *Home on the Range* (1946), and *Bells of San Angelo* (1947). He was also a regular performer on the television program *The Garry Moore Show* in the early 1950s. Carson wrote several cowboy ballads which were heard in seven of his movies. The Wise Old Owl in *So Dear to My Heart* is a crusty, backwoods version of Jiminy Cricket in that he serves as a teacher and conscience for the young boy hero in the film. Yet Carson's rustic flavor in both his speaking and singing voice makes the Owl a distinctive character in his own right.

Casella, Max (b. 1967) A versatile actor of stage, television, and movies and also a singer in musicals, he voiced the wisecracking lemur Zini in *Dinosaur* (2000). He was born Max Deitch in Washington, D. C., the son of a newspaper columnist and a social worker, and grew up in Cambridge, Massachusetts. He was on national television by 1988 and soon was featured in the series *Doogie Howser, M.D.* Casella made his Broadway debut when he originated the role of Timon in the stage version of *The Lion King* (1997) and was featured in the Broadway revival of *The Music Man* (2000). He found wide recognition when he joined the cast of the cable TV series *The Sopranos* in 2001 playing Benny Fazio for five years. His film credits include *Newsies* (1992), *Ed Wood* (1994), *Sgt. Bilko* (1996), *Analyze This* (1999), *Leatherheads* (2008), and *Revolutionary Road* (2008). Casella can he heard in the cartoon series *Hey, Arnold!* and *The Legend of Tarzan*, as well as in the animated video *The Little Mermaid II: Return to the Sea* (2000). Many know him as the voice of Daxter on the video games *Jak and Daxter*.

Caselotti, Adriana (1916–1997) A trilling soprano with a disappointing career, she will always be remembered for providing the speaking and singing voice of the title heroine in *Snow White and the Seven Dwarfs* (1937). She was born in Bridgeport, Connecticut, into a family of opera singers and voice teachers who moved to Italy when Caselotti was a young girl. There she was educated at a convent school while her mother toured with an opera company. When the family returned to the States, young Caselotti didn't speak a word of English so she studied the new language even as she took singing lessons. As a teenager she worked as a soundtrack vocalist at MGM. Caselotti appeared in small roles in the movies *Naughty Marietta* (1935) and *The Bride Wore Red* (1937) then was hired by Walt Disney to voice his first feature film heroine. Originally teenage movie star Deanna Durbin was considered for voicing Snow White but, ironically, she sounded too mature and the much-older Caselotti was hired. She was the first person to audition for the part and Walt Disney couldn't believe that anyone would be better but he went and auditioned 149 other girls before deciding on Caselotti. He gave her a small role to voice in the short *The Tortoise and the Hare* (1935) so she would have some recording experience before making *Snow White and the Seven Dwarfs*. Her pay for the job was $960. Although playing Snow White made her somewhat famous, it hampered her career. Disney had Caselotti under contract and refused to let her work at any other studio while he kept her idle at his own studio. He strongly believed that having her sing or perform in anything else would destroy the illusion of Snow White that the movie had created. Caselotti reprised her Snow White on a 1938 broadcast of *Lux Radio Theatre*, was allowed to sing one line on the soundtrack of *The Wizard of Oz* (1939) as the voice of Juliet during the song "If I Only Had a Heart," and in 1946 she played the singer in Martini's Bar in *It's a Wonderful Life*. By the 1950s Disney let Caselotti appear at his theme park, on television, and in promotional events surrounding the various re-releases of *Snow White and the Seven Dwarfs*. She attempted an opera career but without success. For her whole life she was forced to be Snow White and no one else. Yet her personal life was very happy and she was always proud to be the first Disney princess. Much thought went into the creation of the character of Snow White, particularly her movements. The animators had brought motion to animals, trees, flowers, weather, and even inanimate objects in the Disney shorts but animating a human being who was not a grotesque caricature was a unique problem. Animator Art Babbitt suggested his wife, dancer Marge Belcher (later film performer Marge Champion), be filmed doing Snow White's moves, from running through the forest to dancing with the dwarfs. These live-action test films were copied by the animators and even by today's high-tech standards, the heroine's movements are graceful and lifelike. Her high-pitched speaking and singing voice may strike audiences today as too artificial but during the 1930s, when film operettas were very popular, high sopranos like Jeanette MacDonald were quite in vogue and audiences liked their operetta heroines to be naive, innocent, and gushing. Caselotti's performance is straightforward and not multi-layered; she is unblemished goodness and never displays the least bit of selfishness or vanity. Yet because Snow White is so "pure," the villains and comic characters in the movie are all the more potent. As with several later Disney heroines, she is the "straight man" for the more theatrical characters. Times have changed since *Snow White and* the Seven Dwarfs was released and both singing and acting styles have also changed; yet Snow White remains a favorite Disney heroine for young and old viewers.

Catlett, Walter (1889–1960) A favorite character actor who specialized in blustering, scatter-brained types, he was featured in a dozen Broadway musicals and in many movies, but his most remembered screen role was the voice of the conning fox J. Worthington Foulfellow, aka "Honest John," in *Pinocchio* (1940). He was born in San Francisco, educated at St. Ignatius College, started acting in 1906, and gained plenty of vaudeville and touring experience before he made his Broadway debut in the musical *The Prince of Pilsen* (1910). Catlett was soon featured in New York and London musicals, most notably in *Sally* (1920) and *Lady, be Good* (1924). He made his screen debut in 1924 and over the next thirty years played dozens of colorful character roles, including those in *The Front Page* (1931), *Every Night at Eight* (1935), *Cain and Mabel* (1936), *On the Avenue* (1937), *Going Places* (1939), *My Gal Sal* (1942), *Yankee Doodle Dandy* (1942), *Up in Arms* (1944), *Look for the Silver Lining* (1949), *The Inspector General* (1949), *Here Comes the Groom* (1951), *Friendly Persuasion* (1956), and *Beau James* (1957). Aside from *Pinocchio*, his other Disney credits are the television drama *Davy Crockett and the River Pirates* (1955) and the series *Disneyland*. The character of "Honest John" in *Pinocchio* is an unusual Disney villain in that he succeeds in his conniving ploys and is never punished. Seven years later, early storyboards of the "Mickey and the Beanstalk" segment of *Fun and Fancy Free* had the fox Foufellow and his cat sidekick Gideon sell the "magic" beans to Mickey, another con that works; but the characters were later dropped when the writers tightened up the story.

Cesar, Darko An animator who worked on several Disney features, his only acting credit is providing the voice of the Croatian Bear in *Brother Bear* (2003). In addition to *Brother Bear*, Cesar also served as an animator on *Mulan* (1998), *Fantasia/2000* (1999), *Lilo & Stitch* (2002), and *Robots* (2005).

Chabert, Lacey (b. 1982) A child singer-dancer who has matured into a popular television and movie actress, she provided the voice of the sassy Little Red in the animated short *Redux Riding Hood* (1997). She was born in Purvis, Mississippi, where she sang and danced as a young child and found recognition on television's *Star Search*. After doing some commercials and appearing on Broadway as the girl Cosette in *Les Misérables*, Chabert was a regular in the television series *Party of Five* for six years. She also shone as Baby June in the TV-movie *Gypsy* (1993) and played teens in such films and made-for-television movies as *When Secrets Kill* (1997), *Lost in Space* (1998), *Tart* (2001), and *Not Another Teen Movie* (2001). Among her films as an adult are *The Scoundrel's Wife* (2002), *Daddy Day Care* (2003), *Mean Girls* (2004), *Dirty Deeds* (2005), *High Hopes* (2006), *Black Christmas* (2006), *Being Michael Madsen* (2007), *Sherman's Way* (2008), and *In My Sleep* (2009). Chabert started doing voice work at the age of five with a series of children's story and song videos and over the years has sung and acted for dozens of animated movies and videos, including *Babes in Toyland* (1997), *Journey Beneath the Sea* (1997), *Anastasia* (1997), *The Lion King II: Simba's Pride* (1998), *An American Tail: The Treasure of Manhattan Island* (1998), *We Wish You a Merry Christmas* (1999), *The Wild Thornberrys: The Origin of Donnie* (2001), *Balto: Wolf Quest* (2002), *The Wild Thornberrys Movie* (2002), *Rugrats Go Wild!* (2003), *Choose Your Own Adventure: The Abominable Snowman* (2006), and *Bratz: Passion 4 Fashion* (2006). She can also be heard on the TV cartoon series *Gargoyles, Aaahh!!! Real Monsters, Hercules, Family Guy, The Wild Thornberrys, American Dragon: Jake Long, Bratz, The Spectacular Spider-Man*, and *Hey, Arnold!*

Chase, Daveigh (b. 1990) A child actress-singer with several film and television credits already to her name, she provided the voice of the young Hawaiian orphan Lilo in *Lilo & Stitch* (2002). She was born Daveigh Elizabeth Chase-Schwallier in Las Vegas, Nevada, raised in Albany, Oregon, and made her first television commercial at the age of seven. The next year she made her TV debut in an episode of *Sabrina, the Teenage Witch*, followed by appearances in such series as *The Practice, ER, Touched by an Angel, That's Life, CSI: Crime Scene Investigation, Oliver Beene, Big Love*, and *Without a Trace*. Chase's first movie was *Her Married Lover* (1999) and she has also appeared in *Robbers* (2000), *Donnie Darko* (2001), *The Ring* (2002), *Haunted Lighthouse* (2003), *Carolina* (2003), *S. Darko* (2009), and *In Between Days* (2010), and in the videos *The Rats* (2002) and *Beethoven's 5th* (2003). "Lilo" in Hawaiian can mean "generous one" but it also means "lost" which applies to the character in the film. Lilo is one of the more realistic Disney child heroines, full of life and adventure yet underneath it all a troubled and needy girl. Daveigh was nine years old when she started recording the vocals for Lilo who is six years old in the script. She reprised her Lilo in the videos *Stitch! The Movie* (2003) and *Leroy & Stitch* (2006), as well as in the TV cartoon series *Lilo & Stitch*. She can also be heard in the animated series *Fillmore!* and *Betsy's*

Kindergarten Adventures, and in the film *Spirited Away* (2001). Chase is also a singer who has performed in concert as an opening act for Reba McIntire and on a Christmas recording featuring young television performers. She can be heard singing "God Bless America" in the film *Artificial Intelligence: AI* (2001).

Chesney, Diana (1927–2004) An English stage actress who found a home in American television, she provided the voice of Basil's good-hearted mouse landlady Mrs. Judson in *The Great Mouse Detective* (1986). She was born in Mandalay, Burma, where her father, a major in the British army, was stationed, and she grew up in England where she attended London's Royal Academy of Dramatic Art. After entertaining American and British troops during World War II, Chesney appeared in English movies and on television while she continued acting on the stage. Moving to the States in 1961, she played matronly characters in several television shows, including *The Farmer's Daughter*, *The Monkees*, *It Takes a Thief*, *Nanny and the Professor*, *Hogan's Heroes*, *Bewitched*, *Ellery Queen*, and *Fantasy Island*. Among Chesney's film credits are *Shadow of a Man* (1956), *A Woman of Mystery* (1958), *Saturday Night and Sunday Morning* (1960), *Munster, Go Home!* (1966), *Airport 1975* (1974), *Swashbuckler* (1976), and *Robin Hood: Men in Tights* (1993). The character of Mrs. Judson in *The Great Mouse Detective* parallels that of Mrs. Hudson, Sherlock Holmes' landlady in the Arthur Conan Doyle stories. Both are matronly, understanding, caring, and never seem to be much perplexed by her boarder's strange habits.

Chevalier, Maurice (1888–1972) Perhaps the greatest of all French entertainers, the roguish *bon vivant* song-and-dance man captivated audiences on both sides of the Atlantic, never straying far from his bow tie, straw hat *boulevardier* persona; his final film credit was singing the title song over the opening credits of *The Aristocats* (1970). Maurice Auguste Chevalier was born in poverty in Paris and worked in a factory as a child, later becoming an acrobat in variety. He served in the French army during World War I and learned his broken English from British soldiers while in a German prisoner-of-war camp. Chevalier first became popular in Paris cafes, then was the star of the famous Folies Bergere. He made some films in France but it was his Hollywood debut in *Innocents of Paris* (1929) that made him an international star. His other notable films before World War II include *The Love Parade* (1929), *Paramount on Parade* (1930), *One Hour with You* (1932), *Love Me Tonight* (1932), *The Merry Widow* (1934), and *Folies Bergere* (1935). Chevalier left films in the 1940s and concentrated on concerts, nightclubs, and later television specials. He made a triumphal return to the musical screen as the charming Honore in *Gigi* (1958) and was featured in such movies as *Love in the Afternoon* (1957), *Can-Can* (1960), *Fanny* (1961), *In Search of the Castaways* (1962), and *I'd Rather Be Rich* (1964). After making the live-action film *Monkeys, Go Home!* (1967) for Disney, Chevalier retired from the screen. He was persuaded to record the title song for *The Aristocats* in Paris. His reasons, he said, were in tribute to the recently deceased Walt Disney and to Al Sherman (1897–1973), the father of the film's songwriters Richard M. and Robert B. Sherman, who had written one of the French entertainer's hit songs decades before. Chevalier was a unique talent in that he always played himself in every role he undertook and the audience would have it no other way. Autobiographies: *The Man in the Straw Hat* (1949), *With Love* (1960), *I Remember It Well* (1970); biographies: *Maurice Chevalier*, David Bret (2003); *The Good Frenchman: The True Story of the Life and Times of Maurice Chevalier*, Edward Behr (1993).

Christian, Claudia (b. 1965) A successful film and television actress who has played a variety of roles since her teen years, she voiced Helga Katrina Sinclair, Commander Rourke's second-in-command, in *Atlantis: The Lost Empire* (2001). Claudia Ann Christian was born in Glendale, California, grew up in Connecticut, then was back on the West Coast as a teenager where she started acting professionally in the television series *T. J. Hooker*, *Dallas*, *Falcon Crest*, and others. She first received wide recognition in the cult film *The Hidden* (1987) and went on to make dozens of films, yet she is best known for her recurring character of Commander Susan Ivanova in the sci-fi television series *Babylon 5*. Among her film credits are *Clean and Sober* (1988), *Mad About You* (1990), *Hexed* (1993), *The Chase* (1994), *Never on Tuesday* (1988), *The Haunting of Hell House* (1999), and *Half Past Dead* (2002), and her many TV series include *Berrenger's*, *L.A. Law*, *Freaks and Geeks*, *NYPD Blue*, *Broken News*, and *Starhyke*. Christian has provided voices for such animated videos and movies as *The Itsy Bitsy Spider* (1992), *Journey Beneath the Sea* (1997), *Earth and Beyond* (2002), *Shrek 2* (2004), and *Geppetto's Secret* (2005).

Christie, Paul A voice actor who has narrated television specials and voiced commercials, he provided the voice for one of the two Rams in *Brother Bear* (2003). He can also be heard on the television series *Square One TV*, *Stroker and Hoop*, and *Click and Clack's As the Wrench Turns*.

Clark, Blake (b. 1946) A heavy-set, raspy-voiced stand-up comic and character actor who usually plays rednecks in his many film and television shows, he supplied the voice of the toy Slinky Dog in *Toy Story 3* (2010). He was born in Macon, Georgia, served as Captain in the 101st Airborne Division in Viet Nam, and studied theatre at LaGrange College. Clark made his television debut on an episode of *The Greatest American Hero* in 1981, followed by dozens of other series, including *M*A*S*H*, *Newhart*, *The Facts of Life*, *Remington Steele*, *Gimme a Break!*, *Women in Prison*, *Designing Women*, *Roseanne*, *Grace Under Fire*, *The Drew Carey Show*, *Murphy Brown*, *Coach*, *Home Improvement*, *The Jamie Foxx Show*, *Boy Meets World*, *Lucky*, *My Name Is Earl*, *Everybody Hates Chris*, *Good Luck Charlie*, and *Sabrina, the Teenage Witch*. As a stand-up comic, he has appeared on talk shows, quiz programs, and comedy specials. Among Clark's many movie credits are *St. Elmo's Fire* (1985), *Fast Food* (1989), *Wired* (1989), *Shakes the Clown* (1991), *Toys* (1992), *Fatal Instinct* (1993), *The Mask* (1994), *Nothing to Lose* (1997), *The Waterboy* (1998), *Critical Mass* (2000), *Little Nicky* (2000), *Joe Dirt* (2001), *50 First Dates* (2004), *The Benchwarmers* (2006), *I Now Pronounce You Chuck & Larry* (2007), *Get Smart* (2008), and *Grown Ups* (2010). When Jim Varney, who voiced Slinky Dog in *Toy Story* (1995) and *Toy Story 2* (1999), died in 2000, the filmmakers considered dropping the character from the 2010 version. But once they heard some vocals by Clark, who was a close friend of Varney's, the character was reinstated with Clark's voice.

Clark, Buddy (1912–1949) A popular crooner of the late 1930s and 1940s who sang in a handful of films, he was the Master of Ceremonies and sang the title song on the soundtrack of *Melody Time* (1948). He was born Samuel Goldberg in Dorchester, Massachusetts, and attended Northeastern University in Boston to pursue a law career but left college to sing professionally. Clark first gained attention as the vocalist for Benny Goodman's band on the radio and then became a regular on the airwaves' *Your Hit Parade*. His recordings quickly caught on and several of his discs were best-sellers. Clark dubbed the singing for non-singing stars in the movies *Rawhide* (1938), *I Wonder Who's Kissing Her Now* (1947), and *Father Is a Bachelor* (1950), and audiences got to see and hear him in the films *Wake Up and Live* (1937), *Seven Days' Leave* (1942), *Musical Merry-Go-Round* (1948), and *Song of Surrender* (1949). He was at the peak of his popularity when he died in an airplane crash at the age of thirty-eight.

Clark, Dean As a child, he voiced the saucy Parisian kitten Berlioz in *The Aristocats* (1970) and sang "Scales and Arpeggios" with the rest of his feline family. He has no other film credits.

Clark, Kimberly Adair An employee at Pixar who voiced Lucius Best/Frozone's unseen but opinionated wife Honey in *The Incredibles* (2004), she has no other movie or television credits.

Clark, Sarah A radio commentator in San Francisco with a popular program titled *Morning Show with Sarah and NoName*, she provided the voice of the nosey reporter car Kori Turbowitz in *Cars* (2006). Clark's radio show was the inspiration for the television series *Sarah and NoName After Dark* in which she appeared.

Clemmons, Larry (1906–1988) A scriptwriter for animated films and sometimes an animator as well, his only acting credit is doing the voice of the aged, complaining turtle Gramps in *The Rescuers* (1977). The Chicago native worked on the stories for two early Disney shorts, *The Tortoise and the Hare* (1935) and *The Practical Pig* (1939), and the feature *The Reluctant Dragon* (1941), then helped animate a half dozen other cartoons, including *Sea Scouts* (1939), *The Autograph Hound* (1939), *Mr. Duck Steps Out* (1940), and *Put-Put Troubles* (1940). In the 1950s Clemmons wrote scripts for various Disney television specials and episodes of *Walt Disney's Wonderful World of Color*, then returned to animated films, contributing to the scripts for such features and shorts as *Winnie the Pooh and the Honey Tree* (1966), *The Jungle Book* (1967), *Winnie the Pooh and the Blustery Day* (1968), *The Aristocats* (1970), *Robin Hood* (1973), *Winnie the Pooh and Tigger Too* (1974), *The Many Adventures of Winnie the Pooh* (1977), *The Rescuers*, and *The Fox and the Hound* (1981).

Clifford, Ruth (1900–1998) A leading lady in silent films who found less notoriety once sound came in, she voiced Minnie Mouse in eight cartoon shorts between 1944 and 1952. She was born in Pawtucket, Rhode Island, and as a teenager went to Hollywood to live with an aunt who was an actress. By the age of fifteen, Clifford was on screen as ingenues and played major roles in such silents as *Polly Put the Kettle On* (1917), *Hungry Eyes* (1918), *The Cabaret Girl* (1918), *The Black Gate* (1919), *Daughters of the Rich* (1923), *The Dramatic Life of Abraham Lincoln* (1924), and *The Thrill Seekers* (1927). She continued to work in talkies but usually in minor character parts in such movies as *The Constant Woman* (1933), *Stand Up and Cheer!* (1934), *The Farmer Takes a Wife* (1935), *Safety in Numbers* (1938), *Keep Smiling* (1938), *Along the Rio Grande* (1941), *It Happened in Flatbush* (1942), *The Keys to the Kingdom* (1944), *The Spider* (1945), *Not Wanted* (1949), *Wagon Master* (1950), *Sunset Blvd.* (1950), *Give a Girl a Break* (1953), *Designing Woman* (1957), and *The Last Hurrah* (1958). Clifford acted in television for the last decade of her career, appearing in such series as *The Millionaire, Jungle Jim, Playhouse 90, Highway Patrol, Hazel,* and *Dr. Kildare*. When she retired in 1966, Clifford had over 140 movies to her credit. She first voiced Minnie Mouse in the short *First Aiders* (1944) and reprised the role in such classic cartoons as *Bath Day* (1946), *Pluto's Sweater* (1949), and *Pluto's Christmas Tree* (1952). She also voiced Daisy Duck in the shorts *Sleepy Time Donald* (1947) and *Donald's Dream Voice* (1948).

Close, Glenn (b. 1947) The regal star of Broadway and Hollywood who can play crazed *femme fatales* as easily as classy ladies of quality, she provided the voice for the tender mother gorilla Kala in *Tarzan* (1999) and introduced the Oscar-winning song "You'll Be in My Heart" with Phil Collins. Close was born in Greenwich, Connecticut, the daughter of a surgeon who took her with him on his missionary work in Africa. After graduating from the College of William and Mary, she toured as a folk singer before going to New York and making her legit debut in 1974. Close has been featured in plays and musicals on and Off Broadway over the years, giving highly-praised performances in *Rex* (1976), *Barnum* (1980), *The Real Thing* (1984), *Death and the Maiden* (1992), and *Sunset Boulevard* (1994). She made an impressive screen debut in *The World According to Garp* (1982), followed by a variety of popular films such as *The Natural* (1984), *Fatal Attraction* (1987), *Dangerous Liaisons* (1988), *Cookie's Fortune* (1999), and *The Stepford Wives* (2004). Her most flamboyant screen role has been bringing the animated villainess Cruella de Vil to life in the Disney live-action movies *101 Dalmatians* (1996) and *102 Dalmatians* (2000). She reprised her Kala in the video sequel *Tarzan II* (2005) and also provided voices for the animated TV show *The Simpsons*, and the films *Baby* (2000), *Hoodwinked!* (2005), and *Hoodwinked Too!* (2010). Close has appeared in several television series, such as *The Shield, The West Wing,* and *Damages,* and in many TV-movies, as in *Sarah Plain and Tall* (1991) and its sequels, *Serving in Silence: The Margarethe Cammermeyer Story* (1995), *South Pacific* (2001), *The Ballad of Lucy Whipple* (2001), and *The Lion in Winter* (2003). The character of Kala is truly the heart of the movie *Tarzan*; although she is a gorilla, she seems to be the most human character in terms of understanding and compassion.

Coburn, James (1928–2002) The grinning leading man of movies and television with a pleasing growl of a voice, he provided the voice of the monster crab Mr. Henry J. Waternoose III in *Monsters, Inc.* (2001). James Harrison Coburn, Jr., was born in Laurel, Nebraska, and studied at UCLA and under actress Stella Adler in New York before he was cast in minor roles in such television series as *Studio One in Hollywood, Wagon Train, The Restless Gun, State Trooper, Johnny Ringo, Death Valley Days, Wanted: Dead or Alive, Peter Gunn, Bat Masterson,* and *Richard Diamond, Private Detective*. He was first noticed as the deadly gunslinger Britt in the landmark western film *The Magnificent Seven* (1960), followed by featured roles in many movies, including *Hell Is for Heroes* (1962), *The Great Escape* (1963), *Charade* (1963), *The Americanization of Emily* (1964), *Major Dundee* (1965) *A High Wind in Jamaica* (1965), *Our Man Flint* (1966), *What Did You Do in the War, Daddy?* (1966), *In Like Flint* (1967), *The President's Analyst* (1967), *The Carey Treatment* (1972), *Pat Garrett & Billy the Kid* (1973), *The Last of Sheila* (1973), *Hard Times* (1975), *Midway* (1976), *Loving Couples* (1980), *Death of a Soldier* (1986), *Call from Space* (1989), *Sister Act 2: Back in the Habit* (1993), *Maverick* (1994), *Eraser* (1996), *The Nutty Professor* (1996), *Affliction* (1997), *The Good Doctor* (2000), *The Man from Elysian Fields* (2001), and *Snow Dogs* (2002). Throughout his career, Coburn frequently returned to television, appearing in dozens of series such as *Klondike, Alcapulco, Laramie, The Untouchables, Perry Mason, Bonanza, Route 66, The Defenders, Picket Fences, Profiler,* and *Murder, She Wrote*. He can be heard in the TV cartoon series *Captain Planet and the Planeteers*.

Cody, Jennifer An actress-singer-dancer of the stage with a funny, quirky voice, she provided the voice of the spoiled southern debutante Charlotte La Bouff in *The Princess and the Frog* (2009). Born in Henrietta, New York, and educated at the University of New York College at Fredonia, Cody toured with a production of *Gypsy* before making her Broadway debut as a replacement in *Cats,* followed by roles in *Beauty and the Beast* (1994), *Grease* (1994), *Seussical* (2000), *Urinetown* (2001), *Taboo* (2003), *The Pajama Game* (2006), and *Shrek* (2008), as well as the Off Broadway productions *The Wild Party* (2000), *Debbie Does Dallas* (2002), *Henry and Mudge* (2006), and *Junie P. Jones* (2008). She has also been in many touring and regional theatre productions, particularly at the Sacramento Music Circus. Cody appears in the videos *Damnation of Souls* (2006) and *Untitled Paul Reider Project* (2006), and has been on the television series *Law & Order*.

Collins, Eddie (1883–1940) A comic actor and singer mostly on the stage, he provided the sneezing of the Chipmunk and the Squirrel and he voiced Dopey's one line in *Snow White and the Seven Dwarfs* (1937). Edward Bernard Collins was born in Atlantic City, New Jersey, and was on the vaudeville stage for over thirty years until the Depression killed off the genre and he started making movies at the age of fifty-two. He played character parts in two dozen films over a period of only five years, including *Diamond Jim* (1935), *In Old Chicago* (1937), *Ali Baba Goes to Town* (1937), *Sally, Irene and Mary* (1938), *Kentucky Moonshine* (1938), *Alexander's Ragtime Band* (1938), *Down on the Farm* (1938), *Young Mr. Lincoln* (1939), *Quick Millions* (1939), *Drums Along the Mohawk* (1939), *The Blue Bird* (1940), and *The Return of Frank James* (1940). In the original storyboard for *Snow White and the Seven Dwarfs*, the character of Dopey was to be a non-stop talking chatterbox. Someone suggested going the opposite way with the character and Dopey was turned into an expressive mute much along the lines of Harpo Marx. The interesting thing about Dopey is that he is not mute; as one of the dwarfs says, he just never tried to talk. So when necessity forces him to speak (Dopey tells the other dwarfs which direction the old hag went), he does. Mel Blanc was considered for the voice of Dopey when he was talkative but the animators did not like the result and went with a mute dwarf.

Collins, Lindsey A production manager at Disney and later a producer at Pixar, she provided the voice of the red Mazda racing fan Mia in *Cars* (2006). She worked as a production assistant on *Pocahontas* (1995) and *The Hunchback of Notre Dame* (1996) before serving as production manager for *Hercules* (1997), *Finding Nemo* (2003), and *Ratatouille* (2007). Collins was co-producer of *WALL-E* (2008).

Collins, Paul (b. 1937) A British actor busy on the American stage, in movies, and on television since he was a child, he provided the voice of the top-hatted elder brother John Darling in *Peter Pan* (1953). He was born in London and made his first film in England at the age of nine. Collins' first Hollywood movie was *Challenge to Lassie* (1949) followed by children's roles in *Rogues of Sherwood Forest* (1950) and *Lorna Doone* (1951). By 1954 he was appearing on American television as well and over the decades would act in dozens of TV series, including *You Are There, Surfside 6, Another World, Matlock, Murphy Brown, L.A. Law, Night Court, Growing Pains, Quantum Leap, The Golden Girls, Star Trek: Deep Space Nine, Law & Order, Beverly Hills 90210, ER, Ally McBeal, Profiler, The Drew Carey Show, Chicago Hope, Scrubs, The West Wing, JAG, Las Vegas, Without a Trace*, and *Boston Legal*. Among Collins' other film credits are *Midnight Lace* (1960), *Funny About Love* (1990), *Guilty by Suspicion* (1991), *The Marrying Man* (1991), *Dave* (1993), *Mother* (1996), *Dead Man on Campus* (1998), *Instinct* (1999), *Art School Confidential* (2006), and *Evan Almighty* (2007), as well as many made-for-TV movies. He has frequently acted on stage throughout his career, appearing in many regional and Off Broadway productions, as well as on Broadway in *Generation* (1965), *The Royal Hunt of the Sun* (1965), *A Minor Adjustment* (1967), *A Meeting by the River* (1979), and *Eminent Domain* (1982).

Colonna, Jerry (1904–1986) A broad comic who rolled his eyes, bristled his bushy mustache, and bellowed through clenched teeth, he was an audience favorite in nightclubs, on radio, on television, and in twenty movies, including the voice of the raucous March Hare in *Alice in Wonderland* (1951), as well as the Narrator for the Disney cartoon short *The Brave Engineer* (1950). He was born Gerardo Luigi Colonna in Boston and started as a trombone player in the Columbia Orchestra in the 1930s but soon found he could make audiences laugh with his wild facial expressions. He was a hit in nightclubs and on the radio with Bob Hope who traded barbs with him for decades. Colonna went to Hollywood in 1937 and was featured in such movies as *Rosalie* (1937), *Little Miss Broadway* (1938), *College Swing* (1938), *Road to Singapore* (1940), *Sis Hopkins* (1941), *True to the Army* (1942), *Star-Spangled Rhythm* (1942), *Atlantic City* (1944), *Road to Rio* (1947), *Meet Me in Las Vegas* (1956), and *The Road to Hong Kong* (1962). He first worked with Disney when he provided the narration and character voices for the "Casey at the Bat" sequence in the animated anthology *Make Mine Music* (1946). Although his voice was well known from radio broadcasts, Walt Disney broke his policy of using only unknown voices for his animated features and cast Colonna as the March Hare in *Alice in Wonderland*, thereby starting the studio's use of celebrity voices in its productions. Colonna made many television appearances in the 1950s and 1960s and was also a respected composer of popular songs, including "At Dusk," "Sleighbells in the Sky," and "I Came to Say Goodbye." Biography: *Greetings, Gate! The Story of Professor Colonna*, Bob Colonna, John Williams (2007).

Colvig, Pinto (1892–1967) A master voice artist who worked with Disney for nearly forty years, he voiced the dwarfs Sleepy and Grumpy in *Snow White and the Seven Dwarfs* (1937), Maleficent's Goon in *Sleeping Beauty* (1959), and is fondly remembered as the man who provided the voice for Goofy and the barks for Pluto in dozens of cartoon shorts and some feature films as well. He was born Vance DeBar Colvig in Jacksonville, Oregon, and as a child in the summers he performed as a singing, clarinet-playing clown in the circus and in vaudeville. After studying at the Oregon Agricultural

College, he got a job as cartoonist for a Reno, Nevada, newspaper and played in the circus band in the summer months. Colvig created some silent cartoon shorts on his own and gained the attention of filmmaker Walter Lantz who hired him to create stories and voice characters for his studio. By 1930 he was writing stories for Disney and voiced his first cartoon for the studio in 1930. Colvig created the character of the good-natured but bumbling Goofy and first voiced him in the short *Mickey's Revue* (1932) when he was identified as Dippy Dawg. He was first called Goofy in *The Whoopee Party* (1932) and the hound character was soon as popular as Mickey Mouse and the rest of the gang. Colvig voiced him in forty-eight Goofy cartoons, in dozens of cartoons with others, and in the feature film *Fun and Fancy Free* (1947). Before he was even called Pluto, Colvig did the barks of Mickey's pet dog in a handful of shorts before he was identified as Pluto in *The Moose Hunt* (1931). Pluto was also featured in forty-eight cartoons of his own, as well as many others with Mickey and friends, and Colvig did all his barks until 1964. Other characters Colvig voiced for Disney shorts and features include the Practical Pig in *Three Little Pigs* (1933) and its sequels, the lazy Grasshopper in *The Grasshopper and the Ants* (1934), the Thin Mouse in *The Three Mouseketeers* (1936), Hortense the Ostrich in *Donald's Ostrich* (1937), and the insistent Aracuan Bird in three movies: *The Three Caballeros* (1944), the short *Clown of the Jungle* (1947), and the anthology feature *Melody Time* (1948). For Paramount he voiced the bully Bluto in a series of *Popeye* cartoons, as well as the excitable Gabby in the feature *Gulliver's Travels* (1939) and in a series of shorts. His live character "Bozo the Clown" was featured on several children's records in the 1940s and the character appeared on early television. Colvig was the only actor to voice more than one dwarf in *Snow White and the Seven Dwarfs*. His Sleepy is a delightful series of yawns and words (Disney favorite Sterling Holloway was first considered for the role) but it is his Grumpy that gets the most attention. Grumpy is the only dwarf who changes during the course of the movie; he is the most resistant to Snow White but slowly develops into her most fervent admirer and his weeping at her supposed death is one of the film's most telling moments. Perhaps Colvig's most vocally demanding character was the red-mopped Aracuan Bird with its weird, high-pitched squawks that seem to come out of a pipe organ. Few actors have contributed so much to the art of voicing animated films as Colvig did in his remarkable career.

Colyar, Michael An African American comedian who manages to inject inspirational thoughts into his routines, he voiced the New Orleans restaurant cook Buford who bosses Tiana around in *The Princess and the Frog* (2009). Colyar found fame doing stand-up comedy on the television talent show *Star Search*, followed by many TV appearances and such movies as *Hollywood Shuffle* (1987), *Johnny Be Good* (1988), *The Closer* (1990), *What's Love Got to Do with It* (1993), *Poetic Justice* (1993), *House Party 3* (1994), *High Frequency* (1998), *Rising to the Top* (1999), *The Beat* (2003), *Mean Jadine* (2004), *A Get2Gether* (2005), *Clean Up Men* (2005), *Norbit* (2007), *The Longshots* (2008), and *Church* (2010). He has also appeared in the television series *Dragnet*, *227*, *The John Larroquette Show*, *Martin*, *The Hugleys*, *In the House*, *The Parkers*, *Barbershop*, and *Everybody Hates Chris*. He was later host of the television show *BET Live in L.A.*

Compton, Dorothy A singer-dancer from the stage, she provided the speaking and singing voice of the Little Pig who plays the fife in the classic short *The Three Little Pigs* (1933) where she introduced "Who's Afraid of the Big Bad Wolf?" with her sibling pigs. Compton appeared on Broadway in the musicals *Between the Devil* (1937), *You Never Know* (1938), and *Leave It to Me!* (1938), and on screen in *It's Great to Be Alive* (1933), *When Do We Eat?* (1934), and *I Married an Angel* (1942). She reprised her Fifer Pig in the cartoon sequels *The Big Bad Wolf* (1934), *Three Little Wolves* (1936), and *The Practical Pig* (1939).

Connolly, Billy (b. 1942) A rough, foul-mouthed, and highly-popular comedian in Great Britain who is also a songwriter, singer, and author, he supplied the voice of Ben, the Scottish member of Ratcliffe's expedition, in *Pocahontas* (1995). William Connolly was born in Glasgow, Scotland, and quit school to work in the shipyards. His talent for writing and singing folk songs got him into the Scottish group Humblebums but it was Connolly's joking and commentary between songs that made him a comic favorite in Scotland. By the 1970s he was famous throughout the British Isles, appearing in concerts, on records, on the radio, and on television. Connolly took up acting later in his career and proved to be very successful in character parts, as in the films *Absolution* (1978), *Bullshot Crummond* (1983), *The Return of the Musketeers* (1989), *Crossing the Line* (1990), *Indecent Proposal* (1993), *Muppets Treasure Island* (1996), *Beverly Hills Ninja* (1997), *Her Majesty, Mrs. Brown* (1997), *The Impostors* (1998), *Still Crazy* (1998), *The Boondock Saints* (1999), *Beautiful Joe* (2000), *Gabriel & Me* (2001), *White Oleander* (2002), *The Last Samurai* (2003), *Lemony Snicket's a Series of Unfortunate Events* (2004), *The X Files: I Want to Believe* (2008), and *The Boondock Saints II: All Saints Day* (2009).

Connolly also appeared in such television series as *Head of the Class, Billy, Pearl, Tracey Takes On, 3rd Rock from the Sun*, and *Columbo*, and he can be heard in the animated movies *Open Season* (2006) and *Open Season 2* (2008). Memoir: *Bravemouth: Living with Billy Connolly*, Pamela Stephenson (his wife) (2004).

Conried, Hans (1917–1982)   A versatile character actor who played a variety of foreign types, from snarling Nazis to finicky Brits, the thin and beady-eyed comic added a dash of spice to several radio and television shows, as well as many films, including *Peter Pan* (1953) for which he provided the voices for the dastardly Captain Hook and the frustrated father Mr. Darling. Born Hans Georg Conried, Jr., in Baltimore to Jewish immigrants from Austria and educated at Columbia University, he began his acting career on the radio with Orson Welles' Mercury Theatre Company. Conried made his film debut in 1938 and was quickly typecast as eccentric supporting characters, though he was also exceptional in the leading role of the diabolical piano teacher Terwilliger in *The 5,000 Fingers of Dr. T* (1953). Among his other movie credits are *Bitter Sweet* (1940), *Sabateur* (1942), *Passage to Marsaille* (1944), *Mrs. Parkington* (1944), *On the Town* (1949), *The Barkleys of Broadway* (1949), *My Friend Irma* (1949), *Summer Stock* (1950), *I'll See You in My Dreams* (1951), *Texas Carnival* (1951), *Rich, Young and Pretty* (1951), *Rock-a-Bye Baby* (1958), *The Patsy* (1964), *Robin and the Seven Hoods* (1964), and *The Cat from Outer Space* (1978). He also shone on many radio shows and on Broadway in *Can-Can* (1953), but Conried was most active on television, appearing in dozens of programs and playing recurring characters on such series as *Meet Mr. Nutley, The Danny Thomas Show/Make Room for Daddy, Lost in Space, Burke's Law*, and *The Tony Randall Show*. Because of his flexible and brittle voice, Conried was heard in many television cartoon series, such as *The Woody Woodpecker Show, Rocky and His Friends, Hoppity Hooper*, and *Spider-Man and His Amazing Friends*, but he was most remembered for his comic villain Snidley Whiplash on *The Bullwinkle Show* in the 1960s. He provided the voice of Wally Walrus in a series of cartoons in the 1940s and voiced Thomas Jefferson in the Disney short *Ben and Me* (1953). Among his many non–Disney animated films and TV-movies are *The Emperor's New Clothes* (1953), *Hansel and Gretel* (1958), *1001 Arabian Nights* (1959), *The Magic Fountain* (1961), *Cricket on the Hearth* (1967), *Horton Hears a Who!* (1970), *The Phantom Tollbooth* (1970), *Dr. Seuss on the Loose* (1973), *The Magic Pony* (1977), *The Hobbit* (1977), *Tom Thumb* (1978), *The Furious Flycycle* (1980), *The Trolls and the Christmas Express* (1981), *Faeries* (1981), and *The Great Bear Scare* (1983). Conreid was still performing on television within a few weeks of his death. In preparation for animating *Peter Pan*, Conreid was put in costume and filmed doing some of the major scenes, his flourishes and gestures retained for the final product. It is a marvelous vocal performance as well, his Captain Hook being a satire of a proper English gentleman and his evil being something one laughs at rather than fears. Hook also resembles and behaves a lot like his animator Frank Thomas; not that Thomas was villainous but his comic frustration was used effectively in the characterization. In J. M. Barrie's original version of *Peter Pan*, Captain Hook has lost his right hand to the crocodile. The filmmakers found this too limiting and made for awkward gestures by the right-handed actor so they placed the hook on the pirate's left hand. Biography: *Hans Conreid: A Biography*, Suzanne Gargiulo (2002).

Conway, Tom (1904–1967)   A debonair, smooth-voiced British actor who had an up-and-down career in films and television, he was the narrator for *Peter Pan* (1953) and did the voices of the helpful Collie and the Quizmaster on the TV show "What's My Crime?" in *One Hundred and One Dalmatians* (1961). He was born Thomas Charles Sanders in St. Petersburg, Russia, the son of a wealthy manufacturer. His family fled to England when the Russian Revolution broke out. Conway and his younger brother, actor George Sanders, were educated at Brighton College then the elder sibling went to Rhodesia to work in mining but the venture failed. Returning to Britain, he began acting with the Manchester Repertory Theatre and on tour, eventually becoming a broadcaster on BBC radio. George Sanders encouraged his brother to join him in Hollywood so Conway made his screen debut in 1940, playing insignificant roles until he found success as Tom Lawrence the Falcon in *The Falcon's Brother* (1942) and eight sequels. His other movie credits include *Mr. and Mrs. North* (1942), *Cat People* (1942), *I Walked with a Zombie* (1943), *The Seventh Victim* (1943), *One Touch of Venus* (1948), *Painting the Clouds with Sunshine* (1951), *Tarzan and the She-Devil* (1953), *Prince Valiant* (1954), *Murder on Approval* (1955), *12 to the Moon* (1960), and *What a Way to Go!* (1964). Conway also appeared in a handful of television series, including *Mark Saber, Cheyenne, Suspicion, Tightrope, The Betty Hutton Show, Have Gun—Will Travel, Adventures in Paradise*, and *Perry Mason*. He sometimes also acted on American radio where he played the hero Simon Templar on *The Saint* in 1951.

Coogan, Keith (b. 1970)   A child performer. mostly in television, who graduated to adult roles in films, he provided the voice of Young Tod, the fox hero of *The Fox and the Hound* (1981). He was born Keith Eric Mitchell in Palm Springs, California, into a show business family (his grandfather is actor Jackie Coogan), and was appearing in television commercials at the age of five. Coogan made his first TV sit-com in 1978 and played kids in such series as *Eight Is Enough, The MacKenzies of Paradise Cove, The Waltons, Fantasy Island, Laverne & Shirley, Little House on the Prairie, Mork & Mindy, Gun Shy, CHiPs,* and *Growing Pains*. As an adult he worked more in films, appearing in *Adventures in Babysitting* (1987), *Under the Boardwalk* (1989), *Toy Soldiers* (1991), *Don't Tell Mom the Babysitter's Dead* (1991), *Downhill Willie* (1995), and *Spring Broke* (2010).

Cook, Carole (b. 1928)   A stage character actress and singer who has also been successful in nightclubs and on television, she supplied the voice for Pearl Gesner, the proud owner of the impoverished Little Patch of Heaven ranch, in *Home on the Range* (2004). She was born Mildred Frances Cook in Abilene, Texas, and made her television debut in *The Many Loves of Dobie Gillis* in 1963, the same year she made her first film, *Palm Springs Weekend* (1963). Cook appeared in such movies as *The Incredible Mr. Limpet* (1964), *The Gauntlet* (1977), *American Gigolo* (1980), *Summer Lovers* (1982), *Sixteen Candles* (1984), and *Fast Money* (1996), but she was busier on the small screen acting in many series, including *The Lucy Show, McMillan & Wife, Here's Lucy, Chico and the Man, Charlie's Angels, Kojak, Laverne & Shirley, Quincy M.E., Dynasty, Cagney & Lacey, Grey's Anatomy,* and *Murder, She Wrote*. Throughout her career Cook often turned to the stage, acting in many productions in Los Angeles and on Broadway in *Romantic Comedy* (1979) and *42nd Street* (1980).

Cooley, Josh   A storyboard artist at Pixar since 2006, he provided the voice of the pilot dog Omega who goes by the code name Grey 3 in *Up* (2009). Cooley worked on the storyboards for *Cars* (2006), *Ratatouille* (2007), and *Up*, as well as the shorts *Calendar Confloption* (2009) and *George & A. J.* (2009), writing and directing the last. Omega is his only voice credit to date.

Copeland, Joan (b. 1922)   A dramatic stage actress who has appeared in the New York theatre for nearly sixty years, she voiced the Native American shaman Tanana in *Brother Bear* (2003). She was born Joan Maxine Miller in New York, the sister of playwright Arthur Miller, and was educated at Brooklyn College before studying acting at the American Academy of Dramatic Arts and the Actors Studio. Copeland's first acting jobs were in classics Off Broadway then she made her Broadway debut in 1948. Two of her best performances were in her brother's plays, *The American Clock* (1980) and *The Price* (1982), but she also shone in such stage productions as *Detective Story* (1949), *The Diary of Anne Frank* (1955), *Tovarich* (1963), *Two by Two* (1970), *Pal Joey* (1976), *Isn't It Romantic* (1985), *The American Plan* (1990), *A Dybbuk* (1997), and *Over the River and Through the Woods* (1998). Copeland has made few films but has appeared in many television series, dramatic specials, and soap operas.

Corcoran, Kevin (b. 1949)   One of the most popular child actors in Disney live-action films, he provided voices for two animated shorts: the young title elephant in *Goliath II* (1960) and Goofy Jr., in *Aquamania* (1961). Kevin Anthony Corcoran was born in Santa Monica, California, the son of a police officer who later worked at the MGM studios, and one of a large family of child actors. He made his screen debut in *The Glenn Miller Story* (1954) and played kids in *Untamed* (1955), *Violent Saturday* (1955), *The Birds and the Bees* (1956), *Written on the Wind* (1956), and *Gun for a Coward* (1957) before finding success with the Disney studios. His nickname Moochie was used for the characters he played on television on *Mickey Mouse Club House* and *The Further Adventures of Spin and Marty* and in the film *The Shaggy Dog* (1959). Corcoran was also featured in other Disney movies, including *Old Yeller* (1957), *Toby Tyler, or Ten Weeks with a Circus* (1960), *Pollyanna* (1960), *Swiss Family Robinson* (1960), *Babes in Toyland* (1961), *Bon Voyage!* (1962), and *Savage Sam* (1963). His non–Disney film credits include *The Rabbit Trap* (1959), *A Tiger Walks* (1964), and *Blue* (1968), as well as the television series *The Ford Television Theatre* and *Wagon Train*. Corcoran gave up acting as an adult and has worked as a second unit director, assistant director, production manager, and producer for many television shows and a handful of films.

Corti, Jesse (b. 1955)   A character actor with several credits voicing animated films and television shows, he provided the voice of Gaston's foolish sidekick Lefou in *Beauty and the Beast* (1991). He was born José Juan Corti in Venezuela and was raised in Paterson, New Jersey, where his father was a Baptist minister. He has worked in the professional theatre for many years, appearing in the original Broadway cast of *Les Misérables* (1987), and acted in several television commercials and series, such as *Kate and Allie, Law and Order, The West Wing, CSI: Miami,* and *Desperate Housewives*. Among his film credits are *Heart* (1987), *High Stakes* (1989), *Love & Basketball* (2000), *Gone in Sixty Seconds* (2000), *Hulk* (2003), *Bringing Down* the House (2003), *Choker* (2005), *Stiletto* (2008), and *Night of the Living Dead: Origins* (2011). Much of Corti's career has been voicing characters for such animated TV series as *Tom and Jerry Kids Show, Gargoyles, The Wild Thornberrys, The Angry Beavers,* and *Batman,* as well as the movies and videos as *Bird in the Window* (1996), *The Undercover Kid* (1996), *All Dogs Go to Heaven 2* (1996), *The Christmas Lamb* (2000), *Kids' Ten Commandments* (2003), *Metal Gear Solid 3: Snake Eater* (2004), *Metal Gear Solid 3: Subsistence* (2005), and *Lost Odyssey* (2007). The character of Lefou in *Beauty and the Beast* is one of the sillier Disney sidekicks. He is a stooge to Gaston who often abuses him verbally and physically, yet the foolishly cheerful Lefou remains faithful for no apparent reason. Corti's vocals for the character are as energetic as the animators' movements for Lefou and his singing of the song tribute "Gaston" is a musical treat in the movie.

Costa, Mary (b. 1930) An internationally successful opera singer with some film and television credits scattered over four decades, she provided the speaking and singing voice of the heroine Princess Aurora (disguised as "Briar Rose" in the forest) in *Sleeping Beauty* (1959). She was born in Knoxville, Tennessee, and in her teens her family moved to Los Angeles where she studied voice at the Los Angeles Conservatory of Music. Costa was only eighteen when she was heard on national radio with Edgar Bergen and his dummies and in commercials. After doing the vocals for *Sleeping Beauty,* she made a sensational opera debut at the Hollywood Bowl and began her notable career singing opera roles around the world for the next three decades. Costa sang on television specials, variety shows, and gala occasions, such as the Academy Awards and the inauguration of the Kennedy Center. She can be seen and heard in the films *Marry Me Again* (1953), *The Big Caper* (1957), and *The Great Waltz* (1972). Costa appeared in the television programs *Shower of Stars, Climax!,* and *The Voice of Firestone,* and in the TV version of *The Merry Widow* (1972). The actress-dancer Helene Stanley, who had posed for the live-action test footage for Cinderella's moves, returned to the Disney studio to model the movements for Aurora in *Sleeping Beauty* and the character is very fluid on screen. Yet it is Costa's vocals that make Sleeping Beauty so alluring.

Costas, Bob (b. 1952) A well-respected sportscaster known for his wit as much as his wide knowledge of sports, he provided the voice of the race track announcer Bob Cutlass in *Cars* (2006). Robert Quinlan Costas was born in Queens, New York, educated at Syracuse University, and was a professional sportscaster in St. Louis at the age of twenty-two. Over the years he has appeared on hundreds of television programs, ranging from comedy and variety shows to such sports programs as *Later with Bob Costas, On the Record with Bob Costas, ESPN Sports Century, Costas Now, NBC Saturday Night Football,* and *Inside the NFL.* He has also written books about sports. Costas' name and announcer persona were the inspiration for the car character Bob Cutlass who comments on the races in *Cars.*

Crenshaw, Randy A singer and composer who also turns to acting on occasion, he provided the voices of the top-hatted Mr. Hyde and the Behemoth with a hatchet in his head in *The Nightmare Before Christmas* (1993). Crenshaw studied music at Williamete University in Oregon and Berklee College of Music in Boston before playing trombone in various orchestras and period instruments at Renaissance fairs. As a singer he performed with a cappella groups and jazz choirs. Crenshaw first started singing for films in 1988, sometimes on screen as in *The Adventures of Ford Fairlane* (1991), *Mr. Saturday Night* (1992), and *Death Becomes Her* (1992); other times in the soundtrack chorus, as in *Heartbreak Hotel* (1988), *Only You* (1992), *Robin Hood: Men in Tights* (1993), and *Blades of Glory* (2007). He can be heard singing in many animated movies, including *The Princess and the Cobbler* (1993), *The Swan Princess* (1994), *The Pebble and the Penguin* (1995), *The Tigger Movie* (2000), *Recess: School's Out* (2001), *Brother Bear* (2003), *Thumbelina* (1994), *The SpongeBob SquarePants Movie* (2004), *Pooh's Heffalump Movie* (2005), and *Ice Age: The Meltdown* (2006), as well as the animated videos *An All Dogs Christmas Carol* (1998), *The Little Mermaid II: Return to the Sea* (2000), *It's the Pied Piper, Charlie Brown* (2000), *Mickey's Magical Christmas: Snowed in at the House of Mouse* (2001), *Mickey's House of Villains* (2001), *The Jungle Book 2* (2003), *Mulan II* (2004), *The Fox and the Hound 2* (2006), *Pooh's Super Sleuth Christmas Movie* (2007), and *The Little Mermaid: Ariel's Beginning* (2008). Crenshaw's singing voice has also been heard on the television series *The Ren & Stimpy Show, Married with Children, Freakazoid!, Dexter's Laboratory, House of Mouse, Family Guy,* and *Phineas and Ferb.* He is a composer of jazz vocal compositions and has worked as a vocal arranger for different media.

Crosby, Bing (1903–1977) Arguably America's favorite singer, who recorded more songs and had more hits than any other entertainer, he played an easy-going, affable, and unconventional romantic figure in over sixty Hollywood musicals, appeared on many television specials over the years, and was the singing and speaking narrator of the "Ichabod Crane" section of the animated double feature *The Adventures of Ichabod and Mr. Toad* (1949). He was born Harry Lillis Crosby in Tacoma, Washington, and educated at Gonzaga University where he started singing with a campus band. He was not singing professionally very long before conductor Paul Whiteman teamed him with two other singers, billed them as the Rhythm Boys, and featured them in his concerts and in the film *King of Jazz* (1930). Crosby soon went solo, got his own radio show, started his phenomenal recording career, and was given specialty bits in some early 1930s movie musicals. He graduated to leading roles in *Going Hollywood* (1933) and *We're Not Dressing* (1934), followed by dozens of movies in which he usually sang at least a song or two. Among his many memorable films over the decades are *She Loves Me Not* (1934), *Anything Goes* (1936 and 1956), *Rhythm on the Range* (1936), *Pennies from Heaven* (1936), *Waikiki Wedding* (1937), *Birth of The Blues* (1941), *Holiday Inn* (1942), *Going My Way* (1944), *Here Come the Waves* (1944), *The Bells of St. Mary's* (1945), *Blue Skies* (1946), *Here Comes the Groom* (1951), *White Christmas* (1954), *The Country Girl* (1954), *High Society* (1956), and *Robin and the Seven Hoods* (1964), as well as *Road to Singapore* (1940) and six other "Road" pictures with Bob Hope. Autobiography: *Call Me Lucky*, with Gary Giddins, Pete Martin (1953); memoirs: *Bing and Other Things*, Kathryn Crosby (1967); *Going My Own Way*, Gary Crosby (1983); biographies: *Going My Way: Bing Crosby and American Culture*, Ruth Prigozy, Walter Raubicheck (2007); *Bing Crosby: The Hollow Man*, Donald Shepherd, Robert F. Slatzer (1981).

Crothers, Scatman (1910–1986)   The popular African American singer, songwriter, and actor who appeared in many movies and television shows, he was famous for his jubilant scat singing, as heard when he provided the voice for the hip Parisian feline Scat Cat in *The Aristocats* (1970). He was born Benjamin Sherman Crothers in Terre Haute, Indiana, and worked as a guitarist and singer in nightclubs before his songs started to catch on. Crothers made his movie debut in 1951 and appeared in bit parts (often as a singer or musician) in such films as *Meet Me at the Fair* (1953), *Walking My Baby Back Home* (1953), *Between Heaven and Hell* (1956), and *The Gift of Love* (1958). By the 1960s he started appearing on television and over the years he would be one of the most frequently seen African Americans on the small screen, acting in series that ranged from *Bonanza* and *Dragnet* to *Chico and the Man* and *Morningstar/Eveningstar*. Among Crothers' other movies are *The Great White Hope* (1970), *The King of Marvin Gardens* (1971), *Lady Sings the Blues* (1972), *One Flew Over the Cuckoo's Nest* (1975), *The Shootist* (1976), *Silver Streak* (1976), *The Shining* (1980), *Bronco Billy* (1980), *Twilight Zone: The Movie* (1983), and *The Journey of Natty Gann* (1985). His speaking and/or singing voice can be heard in the animated television special *Banjo the Woodpile Cat* (1979) and the film *The Transformers: The Movie* (1986), as well as the TV series *The Famous Adventures of Mr. Magoo*, *Hong Kong Phooey*, *Scooby-Doo*, *C B Bears*, and *Transformers*. The role of the swinging Scat Cat in *The Aristocats* was written with Louis Armstrong in mind and the studio tried to enlist the services of the great Satchmo but he was very ill at the time (he died soon after the movie was released) and unavailable. Crothers made no attempt to imitate Armstrong but used his own distinct sound and persona in voicing the character. Biography: *Scatman: An Authorized Biography*, James Haskins, Helen Crothers (1991).

Crow, Sheryl (b. 1962)   The singer-songwriter whose music mixes pop with rock and folk, she voiced the character of the hip auto Elvis in *Cars* (2006) and sang "Real Gone" on the film's soundtrack. She was born in Kennett, Missouri, the daughter of musicians, and studied music at the University of Missouri at Columbia before becoming a music teacher in an elementary school. Crow wrote songs for children at first and then found success writing jingles for commercials on network television. After touring with Michael Jackson, her singing career took off and her records and songs on movie soundtracks became very popular. In addition to many appearances on television talk shows and variety specials, she has played characters in the series *Cop Rock* and *Cougar Town*, and in such films as *The Minus Man* (1999) and *De-Lovely* (2004). Crow can be heard singing on over fifty film and television soundtracks.

Crystal, Billy (b. 1948)   The versatile comic actor of television and movies who also writes much of his material, he voiced the green monster hero Mike Wazowski in *Monsters, Inc.* (2001). William Jacob Crystal was born in Long Beach, Long Island, New York, the son of a concert promoter–record producer, and went to Marshall University in West Virginia on a baseball scholarship. He left to continue his studies at Nassau Community College and New York University for a theatre career but after graduation turned to stand-up comedy in clubs and formed a comedy improv group called 3's Company. Crystal was cast in roles in some television sit-coms and was featured in the movie *Rabbit Test* (1978) but he did not get wide recognition until he played the flamboyant Jodie Dallas on the sit-com *Soap*. His appearances on *Saturday Night Live* and other television shows secured his popularity, as did his performances in such movies as *The Princess Bride* (1987), *Throw Mama from the Train* (1987), *When Harry Met Sally* (1989), *City Slickers* (1991), *Mr. Saturday Night* (1992), *Forget Paris* (1995), *Hamlet* (1996), *Deconstructing Harry* (1997), *My Giant* (1998), *Analyze This* (1999), *America's Sweethearts* (2001), *Analyze That* (2002), and *Tooth Fairy* (2010). Crystal reprised his Mike Wazowski as Mike Car in *Cars* (2006) and in the short *Mike's New Car* (2002). He can also be heard in the animated videos *Horton Hatches the Egg* (1992), *In Search of Dr. Seuss* (1994), and the film *Howl's Moving Castle* (2004). He returned to the stage with his very successful one-man show *700 Sundays* which toured and was a hit on Broadway in 2004. Originally the character of Mike in *Monsters, Inc.* was to be armless but with his single eye such a character would have very limited movement possibilities so Mike was given arms. Crystal's stand-up comedy persona played a big part in developing the character of Mike who constantly cracks jokes and has a line for everyone he meets. Although he is neither human nor animal, Mike is a favorite Disney character with audiences.

Cullen, Peter (b. 1941)   A prolific voice artist with a low and raspy sound that made him ideal for villains, he has voiced the gloomy donkey Eeyore in the *Winnie the Pooh* films, videos, and television series since 1988. Peter Claver Cullen was born in Montreal, Canada, and educated at Regiopolios College and the National Theatre School of Canada. He began his career as an announcer and actor on television shows such as *The Smothers Brothers Comedy Hour* in the 1960s and *The Sonny and Cher Comedy Hour* in the 1970s. In 1979 he voiced characters in the cartoon series *Scooby-Doo and Scrappy-Doo*, followed by hundreds of episodes of such shows as *Spider-Man, The Smurfs, Knight Rider, The Dukes, G.I. Joe: A Real American Hero, Voltron: Defender of the Universe, Muppet Babies, Challenge of the GoBots, The Chipmunks, Dungeons & Dragons, Rainbow Brite, Jonny Quest, Foofur, Visionaries: Knights of the Magical Light, DuckTales, Chip 'n Dale Rescue Rangers, Adventures of the Gummi Bears, Bonkers,* and *The Pirates of Dark Water*, but he is best known as Optimus Prime in the original *The Transformers* and its many sequels, videos, and video games. Cullen first voiced Eeyore in the series *The New Adventures of Winnie the Pooh* and reprised the role in the series *My Friends Tigger and Pooh, House of Mouse*, and *The Book of Pooh*, and in such films and videos as *Winnie the Pooh and Christmas Too* (1991), *Boo to You Too! Winnie the Pooh* (1996), *Pooh's Grand Adventure: The Search for Christopher Robin* (1997), *A Winnie the Pooh Thanksgiving* (1998), *Winnie the Pooh: Seasons of Giving* (1999), *The Tigger Movie* (2000), *Piglet's Big Movie* (2003), *Winnie the Pooh: Springtime with Roo* (2004), *Pooh's Heffalump Movie* (2005), *Pooh's Super Sleuth Christmas Movie* (2007), and *Tigger & Pooh and a Musical Too!* (2009). Among his other animated films and videos are *Heidi's Song* (1982), *Christmas Comes to PacLand* (1982), *Voyage of the Rock Aliens* (1984), *Robotix* (1985), *Rainbow Brite and the Star Stealer* (1985), *Heathcliff: The Movie* (1986), *My Little Pony: The Movie* (1986), *G.I. Joe: The Movie* (1987), *Hagar the Horrible* (1989), and *The Little Engine That Could* (1991).

Cummings, Brian (b. 1948)   A busy voice actor of television cartoons and animated films, he provided the voice of the enchanted Stove in *Beauty and the Beast* (1991). He was born in Youngstown, Ohio, and began his career voicing characters on television in the 1970s. For over thirty years he has provided voices for hundreds of episodes of such animated series as *G.I. Joe, DuckTales, Midnight Patrol: Adventures in the Dream Zone, Adventures of the Gummi Bears, Where's Waldo?, Garfield and Friends, 2 Stupid Dogs, Timon and Pumbaa, The Grim Adventures of Bill and Mandy*, and *The Emperor's New School*. Cummings' many films and videos include *Stanley, The Ugly Duckling* (1982), *TRON Solar Sailor* (1983), *G.I. Joe: Arise, Serpentor, Arise* (1986), *G.I. Joe: The Movie* (1987), *Christmas Every Day* (1987), *Little Nemo: Adventures in Slumberland* (1989), *Jetsons: The Movie* (1990), *Ferngully: The Last Rainforest* (1992), *A Flintstone Christmas Carol* (1994), *The Story Keepers: Roar in the Night* (1996) and its eight sequels, *The Mark of Kri* (2002), *The Jungle Book 2* (2003), *EverQuest II* (2004), *The Emperor's New Grove 2: Kronk's New Grove* (2005), and *Super Capers* (2009). He is the elder brother of voice actor Jim Cummings.

Cummings, Jim (b. 1952)   One of the most versatile of all voice actors working in animation since the 1980s, the singer-performer has played characters ranging from the high-voiced innocent Winnie the Pooh to the deep-voiced bully Pete for Disney and other studios. James Jonah Cummings was born in Youngstown, Ohio, the younger brother of voice artist Brian Cummings, and worked at a variety of jobs in New Orleans before going to California where he was eventually selected to take over the vocals for Winnie the Pooh from the ailing actor Sterling Holloway. Cummings has been the voice of the perplexed little bear since 1985, heard in dozens of television specials, feature films, and made-for video movies. Also in 1985, Cummings created the character of the friendly Lionel the Lion in the Disney television series *Dumbo's Circus*, his first of dozens of television voices. When actor Paul Winchell, the voice of the tiger Tigger in the *Winnie the Pooh* films, retired in 1990, Cummings took over that role as well, often voicing both Winnie and Tigger in the same projects. Being an accomplished singer, Cummings did some of the song vocals for the lion villain Scar when actor Jeremy Irons suffered from a strained voice during the recording of *The Lion King* (1994). Soon Cummings was one of Disney's busiest and most flexible voice artists, creating such memorable characters as the laughing Hyena Ed in *The Lion King*, Razoul, Captain of the Guards, in *Aladdin* (1992), Nessus the river centaur in *Hercules* (1997), and the big-hearted cajun firefly Ray in *The Princess and the Frog* (2009), as well as the title role in the TV series *Darkwing Duck* and the creature Dingo in the series *Gargoyles*. Cummings is expert at imitating the voices of other actors. In addition to Holloway and Winchell, he successfully mimicked Louis Prima as King Louie in the television series *TaleSpin*, Billy Bletcher as Pete in many Goofy cartoons and the features *A Goofy Movie* (1995) and *An Extremely Goofy Movie* (2000), and Kenneth Mars as King Triton in the made-for-video feature *The Little Mermaid: Ariel's Beginning* (2008). Cummings was also able to provide the singing voice for non-singing actors, such as imitating Christopher Lloyd's voice when he did the songs for the evil Rasputin in *Anastasia* (1997). Because of his versatility, it is not uncommon for Cummings to voice five or more voices in one feature film. He can be heard as multiple supporting characters in such Disney features as *Who Framed Roger Rabbit* (1988), *Aladdin* (1992), *Pocahontas* (1995), *The Hunchback of Notre Dame* (1996), *Tarzan* (1999), and *Atlantis: The Lost Empire* (2001). Cummings has voiced recurring characters in Disney television series such as *Chip 'n Dale Rescue Rangers*, *Adventures of the Gummi Bears*, *Teenage Mutant Ninja Turtles*, *The New Adventures of Winnie the Pooh*, *TaleSpin*, *Goof Troop*, *The Little Mermaid*, *Aladdin*, *Timon and Pumba*, *The Legend of Tarzan*, *The Replacements*, and *Mickey Mouse Clubhouse*. Among the non-Disney films he provided voices for are *The Pagemaster* (1994), *Balto* (1995), *All Dogs Go to Heaven 2* (1996), *Antz* (1998), *Babe: Pig in the City* (1998), *The Road to El Dorado* (2000), and *Shrek* (2001), as well as the non-Disney television series *Tiny Tune Adventures*, *Sonic the Hedgehog*, *The Powerpuff Girls*, *CatDog*, *The Adventures of Jimmy Neutron: Boy Genius*, and *Star Wars: The Clone Wars*. All in all, Cummings has voiced over 500 films and series episodes since 1990. Although he did not start his voice artist career until he was in his mid-forties, Cummings prolific record is matched only by his versatility. He is called the "Mel Blanc of Disney" for good reason. His characterization and singing of the funny, touching firefly Ray in *The Princess and the Frog* is perhaps his finest performance to date, proving the man with so many voices is also an outstanding actor as well.

Cummings, Todd A voice artist heard on video games, he provided the voice for the very New Yorkese pigeon Joey in *Bolt* (2008). Cummings can also be heard in the films *American Splendor* (2003) and *Slap Back Jack: High Five Master* (2010), and the video *Little Spirit: Christmas in New York* (2008).

Curtis, Ken (1916–1991) A Big Band singer who later became a character actor specializing in thick-headed hillbillies, he provided the voice of the lame-brained vulture guard Nutsy in *Robin Hood* (1973). He was born Curtis Wain Gates in Lamar, Colorado, the son of the local sheriff, and began his career singing cowboy ballads. He eventually became a member of the singing Sons of the Pioneers on radio and in movies. By the mid–1940s he was featured on screen and sang many cowboy songs, introducing the hit song "Tumbling Tumbleweeds" in *Rhythm Round-Up* (1945). Curtis also sang in such musical westerns as *Song of the Prairie* (1945), *Throw a Saddle on a Star* (1946), *That Texas Jamboree* (1946), *Cowboy Blues* (1946), *Singing on the Trail* (1946), *Lone Star Moonlight* (1946), *Over the Santa Fe Trail* (1947), and *Call of the Forest* (1949). By 1949 Curtis temporarily replaced Frank Sinatra as the lead vocalist with Tommy Dorsey's Orchestra, then sang with Shep Fields and His New Music. With the waning of the Big Band era, Curtis turned to acting and was soon cast in colorful supporting roles, usually in westerns and often as rural hicks. Among his other films are *Rio Grande* (1950), *The Quiet Man* (1952), *Mister Roberts* (1955), *The Searchers* (1956), *The Last Hurrah* (1958), *The Horse Soldiers* (1959), *The Killer Shrews* (1959), *The Alamo* (1960), *How the West Was Won* (1962), *Cheyenne Autumn* (1964), and *Pony Express Rider* (1976). Curtis found his greatest success on television, particularly as the cranky deputy Festus Haggen on *Gunsmoke* for eleven years. He also appeared on such series as *Perry Mason*, *Wagon Train*, *Rawhide*, *Sea Hunt*, *Have Gun—Will Travel*, *Ripcord*, *Death Valley Days*, *The Life and Times of Grizzly Adams*, *Vega$*, *The Yellow Rose*, and *In the Heat of the Night*.

Cusack, Joan (b. 1962) The distinctive comic actress of film and television who excels at playing the feisty, outspoken friend of the star, she provided the voices for the yodeling cowgirl doll Jessie in *Toy Story 2* (1999) and *Toy Story 3* (2010) and the buck-toothed ugly duckling Abby Mallard in *Chicken*

Little (2005). Joan Mary Cusak was born in New York City, the daughter of an actor and a math teacher, and grew up in Evanston, Illinois. After graduating from the University of Wisconsin—Madison, she worked with comedy improv groups and eventually became a cast member of the television program *Saturday Night Live*. Cusack had her own television show, *What About Joan*, and made other appearances on the small screen but much of her career has been in the movies, giving memorable performances in such films as *My Bodyguard* (1980), *Broadcast News* (1987), *Married to the Mob* (1988), *Working Girl* (1988), *Addams Family Values* (1993), *Corrina, Corrina* (1994), *Nine Months* (1995), *In & Out* (1997), *Runaway Bride* (1999), *High Fidelity* (2000), *Ice Princess* (2005), and *Confessions of a Shopaholic* (2009). She is the sister of actor John Cusack with whom she has made ten movies. Among the actresses considered for the role of Abby in *Chicken Little* were Jamie Lee Curtis, Holly Hunter, Sarah Jessica Parker, Jodie Foster, Geena Davis, and Madonna, but Cusak's naturally comic voice won out and her performance in the movie is splendid. Similarly, her cowgirl Jessie in the *Toy Story* movies is a raucous delight, adding sass to the ensemble even as she is one of the more complex characters in the series of films.

Cygan, John A leading man in television shows and a popular voice artist, he supplied the voice of the toy insect-like creature Twitch who is one of Lotso's henchmen in *Toy Story 3* (2010). The native New Yorker made his television debut in an episode of *Babes* in 1990 and soon was a featured regular on the series *Bob* and *The Commish*. Cygan also appeared in such television shows as *The X-Files, Frasier, Diagnosis Murder, NYPD Blue, Becker, Judging Amy*, and *A Good Knight's Quest*. He can be heard doing voices for the TV cartoon series *The Grim Adventures of Billy & Mandy* and *Ben 10*, as well as the animated films and videos *Treasure Planet* (2002), *Ice Age: The Meltdown* (2006), *Cars* (2006), *Happily N'Ever After* (2007), *Surf's Up* (2007), *Horton Hears a Who!* (2008), *WALL-E* (2008), *Ponyo* (2008), *Up* (2009), and *Cloudy with a Chance of Meatballs* (2009). Cygan has also voiced many video games.

Cyrus, Miley (b. 1992) A young and highly-popular pop singer-songwriter who came to fame on television, she voiced the child actress Penny in *Bolt* (2008). She was born Destiny Hope Cyrus in Franklin, Tennessee, the daughter of singer-actor Billy Ray Cyrus, and made her television debut in her father's series *Doc* in 2001. Cyrus became a teen idol on the TV series *Hannah Montana*, singing songs on the show and selling many records. She has also appeared on the television series *The Suite Life of Zack and Cody* and *The Suite Life on Deck*, on movie videos involving her *Hannah Montana* character, and in the films *Big Fish* (2003) and *The Last Song* (2010). Cyrus's voice can be heard in the TV series *The Replacements* and *The Emperor's New School*. She and co-star John Travolta sing "I Thought I Lost You" over the end credits of *Bolt*, a song they also wrote together. Memoir: *Miles to Go* (2009); biography: *Miley Cyrus: This Is Her Life*, Brittany Kent (2008).

Dafoe, Willem (b. 1955) The dramatic leading man of stage and film who possesses a deep-voiced intensity in most of his work, he supplied the voice of the moody Moorish idol Gill, the leader of the aquarium fish, in *Finding Nemo* (2003). He was born William J. Dafoe in Appleton, Wisconsin, the son of a surgeon and a nurse, and studied drama for a time at the University of Wisconsin—Milwaukee. As a member of the experimental theatre group Theatre X, Dafoe toured the States and Europe, then he became a member of the New York–based Performance Group in which he played a variety of roles in experimental productions. In 1977 he co-founded the Off Broadway theatre troupe The Wooster Group where he often performs between movie work. Dafoe made his screen debut in 1980 and since then has appeared in over seventy films, most memorably *To Live and Die in L.A.* (1985), *Platoon* (1986), *The Last Temptation of Christ* (1988), *Mississippi Burning* (1988), *Born on the Fourth of July* (1989), *Cry-Baby* (1990), *Tom & Viv* (1994), *Clear and Present Danger* (1994), *The English Patient* (1996), *Speed 2: Cruise Control* (1997), *American Psycho* (2000), *Shadow of the Vampire* (2000), *Spider-Man* (2002), *Once Upon a Time in Mexico* (2003), *Spider-Man 2* (2004), *The Life Aquatic with Steve Zissou* (2004), *The Aviator* (2004), *Mr. Bean's Vacation* (2007), *Spider-Man 3* (2007), and *Daybreakers* (2009). He can be heard in the TV cartoon series *The Simpsons* and in the animated films *Tales from Earthsea* (2006) and *Fantastic Mr. Fox* (2009). The character of Gill in *Finding Nemo* is unusual in that he comes across as menacing and deadly but is really a helpful fish who is determined to save Nemo. The craggy-looking, bass-sounding Dafoe was ideal for the role and the animators created Gill with deep lines around the mouth which echo those on the actor's face.

Dalton, Timothy (b. 1944) A dashing, classically-trained British actor who has played everything from Shakespearean characters to James Bond, he provided the voice of the toy hedgehog Mr. Pricklepants who considers himself a classical thespian in *Toy Story 3* (2010). He was born in Colwyn Bay, Wales, the grandson of actors, and grew up in Manchester, England, later getting his acting training as a member of the National Youth Theatre and at the Royal Academy of Dramatic Art. Dalton made his professional stage debut with the Birmingham Repertory Theatre and throughout his subsequent career he performed with the Royal Shakespeare Company and other prestigious theatre organizations. He made his television debut in 1967 on the British series *Sat'day While Sunday* and the next year made an impressive film debut as Prince Philip in *The Lion in Winter* (1968). Often playing brooding and romantic characters, Dalton continues to move easily back and forth between British and American television and films. His screen credits include *Wuthering Heights* (1970), *Cromwell* (1970), *Mary, Queen of Scotland* (1971), *The Executioner* (1975), *Sextette* (1978), *Agatha* (1979), *Flash Gordon* (1980), *The Doctor and the Devils* (1985), *Brenda Starr* (1989), *The Rocketeer* (1991), *Naked in New York* (1993), *The Beautician and the Beast* (1997), *Time Share* (2000), *Hot Fuzz* (2007), and *The Tourist* (2010), but he is most remembered as James Bond in *The Living Daylights* (1987) and *Licence to Kill* (1989). Among the British and American television series he has acted in are *Charlie's Angels, Framed, Tales from the Crypt, Stories from My Childhood, Unknown Sender, Doctor Who,* and *Chuck*, and he was featured in the mini-series and TV-movies *The Three Princes* (1968), *Centennial* (1978), *Antony and Cleopatra* (1983), *Jane Eyre* (1983), *Mistral's Daughter* (1984), *Scarlett* (1994), *Cleopatra* (1999), and *Possessed* (2000). Biography: *Timothy Dalton*, Lambert M. Surhone, Miriam T. Timpledon, Susan F. Marseken (2010).

Dampier, Elizabeth The young African American actress who voiced the New Orleans heroine Tiana as a child in *The Princess and the Frog* (2009) has no other film or television credits so far.

Darby, Ken *see* **The Kings Men**

Darlington, Marion Practically nothing is known about this performer who worked at Disney except that she was an expert at making bird sounds and supplied the tweeting of the feathered ones in *Snow White and the Seven Dwarfs* (1937), *Pinocchio* (1940), *Bambi* (1942), and *Cinderella* (1950). Darlington was also an accomplished whistler and provided the whistling sound effects in *Pinocchio* (during the song "Give a Little Whistle") and *So Dear to My Dear* (1948).

Darro, Frankie (1917–1976) A short, husky-voiced character actor who played children, teenagers, and jockeys in many films going back to the silents, he is most remembered as the voice of the tough-talking kid Lampwick who turns into a donkey in *Pinocchio* (1940). He was born Frank Johnson in Chicago into a show business family (his parents were circus aerialists) and was on stage at the age of six. The next year he made his first of 140 films, among which are *So Big* (1924), *Kiki* (1926), *Tom's Gang* (1927), *The Public Enemy* (1931), *Wild Boys of the Road* (1933), *The Big Race* (1934), *Broadway Bill* (1934), *Charlie Chan at the Race Track* (1936), *A Day at the Races* (1937), *The Gang's All Here* (1941), *Junior Prom* (1946), *Sons of New Mexico* (1949), *The Lawless Rider* (1954), *Operation Petticoat* (1959), *Hook, Line and Sinker* (1969), and *Fugitive Lovers* (1975), as well as the sci-fi movie *Forbidden Planet* (1956) in which he supplied the voice of Robby the Robot. Darro was also active in television from its earliest days up until his death, appearing in such series as *The Adventures of Wild Bill Hickok, G.E. True Theatre, I Married Joan, The Public Defender, Have Gun—Will Travel, December Bride, Peter Gunn, The Untouchables, Bat Masterson, Checkmate, The Hathaways, Mister Ed, Perry Mason, The Addams Family, Batman,* and *The Red Skelton Hour*. Darro's performance in *Pinocchio* is one of the most memorable in animated films even though it is not a very large role. His snide, condescending voice is that of a streetwise bully and braggart. Yet all this dissolves when Lampwick realizes that he is turning into a donkey and his cries dissolve into a pathetic call for "Mama!" The look of the redheaded tough was patterned after Disney animator Fred Moore.

David, Keith (b. 1956) A deep-voiced African American actor-singer who can play heavies as easily as likable characters, he voiced the sun god Apollo in *Hercules* (1997) and the mesmerizing voodoo villain Dr. Facilier, sometimes called The Shadow Man, in *The Princess and the Frog* (2009). He was born Keith David Williams in New York City and studied acting at the New York High School for the Performing Arts and at Juilliard. He appeared in both new and classic plays Off Broadway, and on Broadway was featured in *The Lady from Dubuque* (1980), *Jelly's Last Jam* (1992), *Hedda Gabler* (1994), *Seven Guitars* (1996), and *Hot Feet* (2006). David made his screen debut in 1979 but was not noticed until his powerful performance in *Platoon* (1986), followed by over seventy films such as *Hot Pursuit* (1987), *Bird* (1988), *Always* (1989), *Reality Bites* (1994), *Clockers* (1995), *Eye for an Eye* (1996), *Armageddon* (1998), *Novocaine* (2001), *Barbershop* (2002), *Crash* (2004), *Superhero Movie* (2008), and *Chain Letter* (2010). He has appeared on many television series, including *Mister Rogers' Neighborhood, The Equalizer, The Young Indiana Jones Chronicle, New York Undercover, Law & Order, The Job, The Big House, ER,* and *7th Heaven,* but more frequently he can be heard on cartoon series such as *Aladdin, Gargoyles, Spawn, The Legend* of *Tarzan*, *Spider-Man*, and *Justice League*. David can also be heard in the animated movies and videos *Christmas in Tattertown* (1988), *Gargoyles: the Heroes Awaken* (1995) and several of its sequels, *Princess Mononoke* (1997), *The Chronicles of Riddick: Dark Fury* (2004), *The Proud Family Movie* (2005), *Justice League: The New Frontier* (2008), and *Coraline* (2009). Dr. Facilier in *The Princess and the Frog* is one of Disney's most visually hypnotic villains. The animators aimed for a cross between Captain Hook and Cruella de Vil and ended up with a unique con man who is dryly humorous and yet deadly earnest. While the actor David is a powerfully built man and The Shadow Man is as thin as a rail, both have a gap in their front teeth.

Davis, Cherry An actress with a handful of credits in the 1970s and 1980s, she provided the voice of the famous feathered cartoon character Woody Woodpecker in a cameo in *Who Framed Roger Rabbit* (1988). Davis has appeared on the television series *Cannon*, *L.A. Law*, and *Quantum Leap*, as well as the films *I Never Promised You a Rose Garden* (1977) and *The Return of the Living Dead* (1985), and the TV-movie *Eleanor and Franklin* (1976).

Davis, Dane A. A sound editor who has worked on over one hundred movies since 1981, he provided the vocals for John Silver's pet Morph, which is forever changing its shape, in *Treasure Planet* (2002). Davis has been a sound mixer, sound effects editor, and/or supervising sound designer for mostly science fiction and horror films. Among his screen sound credits are *Jason Lives: Friday the 13th Part VI* (1986), *Back to the Beach* (1987), *It's Alive III: Island of the Alive* (1987), *Friday the 13th Part VII: The New Blood* (1988), *Drugstore Cowboy* (1989), *The Hand That Rocks the Cradle* (1992), *Phantasm III: Lord of the Dead* (1994), *Don Juan DeMarco* (1994), *The Matrix* (1999), *Playing Mona Lisa* (2000), *They* (2002), *Treasure Planet*, *The Matrix Reloaded* (2003), *Ghost Rider* (2007), *The Day the Earth Stood Still* (2008), and *Prep & Landing* (2009). Davis can be heard doing voices in the animated movies *The Second Renaissance Part I* (2003), *The Animatrix* (2003), and *The Second Renaissance II* (2003).

Davis, Lisa (b. 1936) A British actress on American television and movies, she supplied the voice of the pretty and pert Londoner Anita who weds Roger Radcliff in *One Hundred and One Dalmatians* (1961). She was born Cherry Davis in London and as a teenager appeared in the English movie *Temptations* (1949). She made her first Hollywood film six years later and remained in the States for the rest of her career. Among her movie credits are *The Long Gray Line* (1955), *The Virgin Queen* (1955), *The Dalton Girls* (1957), *Baby Face Nelson* (1957), *Queen of Outer Space* (1958), and *Don't Give Up the Ship* (1959). Davis was kept busier in television, appearing in such series as *The Bob Cummings Show*, *The George Burns Show*, *77 Sunset Strip*, *Bachelor Father*, *The Beverly Hillbillies*, and *Perry Mason*. Anita is Disney's first contemporary human heroine and she manages to come across as modern without losing her classic stature. Actress Helene Stanley was the live-action model for the character (she had previously modeled for Cinderella and for Princess Aurora in *Sleeping Beauty*) yet it was Davis who managed to make Anita sound practical and prim yet still warm and loving. In some ways Anita is an early version of Mary Poppins.

Davis, Ossie (1917–2005) A ground-breaking African American actor, playwright, and director who had to play servants and minor roles early in his career, he eventually essayed powerful black characters on stage and screen, and near the end of his long career provided the voice for Yar, the gruff patriarch of the lemur clan, in *Dinosaur* (2000). He was born Raifors Chatman Davis in Cogdell, Georgia, the son of a railroad engineer, and was educated at Howard University before going to New York to be a writer. Instead he worked as a janitor, store clerk, and at other jobs before entering the army in World War II and getting involved in military theatrical activities. Davis made his Broadway debut in 1941 but did not find recognition until two decades later as the author and star of *Purlie Victorious* (1961). He also wrote and acted (with his wife Ruby Dee) in its film version titled *Gone Are the Days!* (1963). Over the years he has appeared in hundreds of episodes on television programs, including *The Defenders*, *Run for Your Life*, *The Name of the Game*, *B. L. Stryker*, *Evening Shade*, *The Client*, *Promised Land*, *City of Angels*, *Touched by an Angel*, and *The L Word*, as well as his own series *Ossie and Ruby!* Davis acted in many TV-movies and miniseries, such as *The Emperor Jones* (1955), *King* (1978), *Roots* (1979), and *The Stand* (1994). Among his film credits are *The Cardinal* (1963), *Slaves* (1969), *Let's Do It Again* (1975), *Do the Right Thing* (1989), *Gladiator* (1992), *Grumpy Old Men* (1993), *The Client* (1994), *Get on the Bus* (1996), *I'm Not Rappaport* (1996), and *Doctor Dolittle* (1998). Davis wrote a handful of other plays which are still potent and often produced. Memoir: *With Ossie and Ruby: In This Life Together*, Ossie Davis and Ruby Dee (2000).

Davis, Tim A child actor in a handful of movies in the late 1930s and early 1940s, he voiced both the Adolescent Flower the Skunk and (with Sam Edwards) the Adult Thumper the Rabbit in *Bambi*

(1942). Davis made his screen debut as a boy in *Riders of the Dawn* (1937) and was featured as a kid in such films as *Tex Rides with the Boy Scouts* (1937), *Gambling Ship* (1938), *Feathered Pests* (1939), *Our Town* (1940), and *Citizen Kane* (1941). He was not seen on the screen again until *Birdie* (1984) and played bit parts in subsequent films such as *Savage Beach* (1989), *Invader* (1992), and *Gentlemen* (1997). He is also a professional producer and photographer.

Day, Dennis (1916–1988) A boyish high tenor who usually played lame-brained sidekicks, he was featured on television and in Hollywood musicals, including the animated anthology *Melody Time* (1948) for which he provided the speaking and singing voices for the Narrator, Johnny Appleseed, the Old Settler, and Johnny's Angel in the "Johnny Appleseed" sequence. Born Owen Patrick Eugene McNulty in the Bronx, Day was a boy singer in the choir of St. Patrick's Cathedral before going to Manhattan College. He was discovered by Jack Benny, who first featured the young singer on his radio show in 1939; the two would become comic foils for each other on film and in Benny's successful television show in the 1950s. Day sang in such movie musicals as *Buck Benny Rides Again* (1940), *The Powers Girl* (1942), *Sleepy Lagoon* (1943), *Music in Manhattan* (1944), *I'll Get By* (1950), *The Golden Girl* (1951), and *The Girl Next Door* (1953). He appeared on many different television shows but continued to perform with Benny until the comic's death in 1974.

Days, Bill (1911–2002) A singer who found recognition as a member of the Sportsmen Quartet on screen and television, he voiced one of the singing vaudevillians in the Disney short *The Nifty Nineties* (1941). He was born in St. Louis, Missouri, and made his film debut as one of the chorus singers in *A Night at the Opera* (1935). Days sang solo or in a quartet in such movies as *The Great Ziegfeld* (1936), *This Is My Affair* (1937), *Rebecca of Sunnybrook Farm* (1938), and *Ziegfeld Girl* (1941), then as a member of the Sportsmen Quartet he appeared in *Puddin' Head* (1941), *Jingle Belles* (1941), *For Me and My Gal* (1942), *Lost Canyon* (1942), *Footlight Varieties* (1951), *Walking My Baby Back Home* (1953), and *Paris Follies of 1956* (1955). The quartet made records, toured, and were often featured on the television's *The Jack Benny Program*.

De Castro Sisters The Hispanic singing trio dubbed "The Cuban Andrews Sisters" for their zesty harmony singing, they voiced the singing Birds in the animated sections of *Song of the South* (1946). Peggy De Castro (1921–2004) was born in the Dominican Republic while her sisters Cherie (1922–2010) and Babette (1925–1992) were born in New York City, the daughters of a Ziegfeld Girl and a successful Cuban manufacturer who owned a sugar plantation in the Dominican Republic. Movie performer Carmen Miranda discovered the trio singing at the Club Brazil and promoted them, beginning a fifty-year career in nightclubs, concerts, films, television, and records. The De Castro Sisters made their screen debut singing in *Stairway for a Star* (1947), followed by such movies as *Over the Santa Fe Trail* (1947), *Copacabana* (1947), *Rhythms with Rusty* (1956), *Riot in Rhythm* (1957), and *The Helen Morgan Story* (1957). They also appeared on the television programs *Cavalcade of Stars*, *The Colgate Comedy Hour*, and *The Ed Sullivan Show*. When Babette retired in 1958, her cousin Olgita De Castro Marino replaced her, and for a while Peggy performed solo, later acting in an episode of *Chico and the Man* in 1977. Their billing was sometimes spelled DeCastro Sisters.

DeGault, Lance (b. 1935) A tall, thin character actor-singer with a surprisingly deep voice who often played stern authority types, he supplied the voice of the tough-talking buffalo guard Junior in *Home on the Range* (2004). He was born William Kance DeGault in Chicago, grew up in Chillicothe, Illinois, and was educated at the University of Kansas in Wichita. DeGault began his career as a stunt double for Elvis Presley in such films as *Girls! Girls! Girls!* (1962), *Kissin' Cousins* (1964), and *Viva Las Vegas* (1964), playing small roles in them as well. He got his first recognition singing the role of Iago in the rock musical movie *Catch My Soul* (1974) and was soon in demand as villains, hard-nosed cops, and humorless military officers. Among his many film credits are *Coma* (1978), *French Quarter* (1978), *Stripes* (1981), *Iron Eagle* (1986), *Shadow Force* (1992), *The Silencers* (1996), *Scorpio One* (1998), and *Stuntmen* (2009). DeGault was even busier on television where he has appeared in several TV-movies and on dozens of series, including *Barbary Coast*, *The Rockford Files*, *Battlestar Galactica*, *Walking Tall*, *Dynasty*, *Knight Rider*, *Simon & Simon*, *Airwolf*, *Magnum P.I.*, *Quantum Leap*, *Star Trek: The Next Generation*, *Dallas*, *Renegade*, and *L.A. Heat*, though he is best known as Col. Roderick Decker in *The A-Team*. He has voiced video games and commercials, done narration for various films and television shows, and can be heard on the audio tour of Presley's mansion Graceland.

DeGeneres, Ellen (b. 1958) The innovative comedienne and television talk show host, she voiced the hilarious blue tang fish Dory with short-term memory loss in *Finding Nemo* (2003). She was born in Metairie, Louisiana, the daughter of an insurance agent and a speech therapist, and grew up in New Orleans and Atlanta, Texas. After briefly attending the University of New Orleans and working at several different odd jobs, she started to do stand-up comedy in clubs, in concert, then on cable television. Soon DeGeneres' distinctive kind of humor caught on and she was featured in several television shows and had two series of her own, *Ellen* and *The Ellen Show*. She found even greater popularity as the host of *Ellen: The Ellen DeGeneres Show* and as a judge on *American Idol*. DeGeneres has appeared in a handful of movies, including *Coneheads* (1993), *Mr. Wrong* (1996), *Goodbye Lover* (1998), *The Love Letter* (1999), *Reaching Normal* (2001), and the comedy short *My Short Film* (2005). She has written comic nonfiction and is featured in the Universe of Energy presentation at the Disney theme parks. The character of Dory in *Finding Nemo* is one of the funniest of all Disney sidekicks, a wonderful combination of innocence, cheerfulness, curiosity, and warmth. The blue tang was named after Dory Lane, a street not far from Pixar's headquarters in San Francisco. The role was written specifically for DeGeneres whose lively performance is comparable to Robin Williams' hilarious Genie in *Aladdin* (1992). Memoir: *Love, Ellen: A Mother/Daughter Journey*, Betty DeGeneres (her mother) (2000); biographies: *Ellen DeGeneres*, Lisa Iannucci (2008); *Female Force: Ellen Degeneres*, Sandra Ruckdeschel, Pedro Ponzo, Vinnie Tartamella (2010).

Dehner, John (1915–1992)   A tall, deep-voiced character actor on radio, in over one hundred movies, and on hundreds of episodes of television programs, he was the tongue-in-cheek Narrator of the Disney shorts *The Litterbug* (1961) and *Aquamania* (1961). He was born John Forkum in New York City and worked as a disc jockey, radio actor, and professional pianist before turning to acting. Dehner was an animator at the Disney Studios in the early 1940s and appeared as himself in the live-action section of *The Reluctant Dragon* (1941). By 1944 he was playing characters on screen, usually villains and often in westerns. Among his many films are *Thirty Seconds Over Tokyo* (1944), *Christmas in Connecticut* (1945), *The Last Crooked Mile* (1946), *Big Town* (1947), *Riders of the Pony Express* (1949), *Horsemen of the Sierras* (1949), *Last of the Buccaneers* (1950), *Lorna Doone* (1951), *The Texas Rangers* (1951), *Plymouth Adventure* (1952), *Apache* (1954), *The Prodigal* (1955), *Carousel* (1956), *The Iron Sheriff* (1957), *The Left Handed Gun* (1958), *Cast a Long Shadow* (1959), *The Canadians* (1961), *The Chapman Report* (1962), *Youngblood Hawke* (1964), *Tiger by the Tail* (1968), *Stiletto* (1969), *The Cheyenne Social Club* (1970), *Dirty Dingus Magee* (1970), *Support Your Local Gunfighter* (1971), *Slaughterhouse-Five* (1972), *The Day of the Dolphin* (1973), *Fun with Dick and Jane* (1977), *The Boys from Brazil* (1978), *Airplane II: The Sequel* (1982), *The Right Stuff* (1983), and *Jagged Edge* (1985). Dehner's many television credits include the series *Schlitz Playhouse, The Millionaire, Four Star Playhouse, Zorro, Have Gun—Will Travel, Cimarron City, Wagon Train, Laramie, Wanted: Dead or Alive, Zane Grey Theatre, Bat Masterson, The Rifleman, The Roaring 20's, Maverick, Surfside 6, The Andy Griffith Show, 77 Sunset Strip, Rawhide, The Baileys of Balboa, The Wild Wild West, Hogan's Heroes, Gunsmoke, Walt Disney's Wonderful World of Color, Mission: Impossible, Judd for the Defense, The Virginian, The Doris Day Show, The New Temperatures Rising Show, Columbo, Big Hawaii, Enos, Bare Essence, The Colbys*, and the mini-series *War and Remembrance* (1988). Because of his rich resounding voice, Dehner narrated many movies and television shows and often played radio announcers and sportscasters in films.

DeLisle, Grey (b. 1972)   A singer and in-demand voice actress in television, she provided the voice for Penny's concerned Mother in *Bolt* (2008). She was born Erin Grey Van Oosbree in Fort Ord, California, and sang gospel music as a teenager. She started her professional career as a stand-up comic and her ability to impersonate speaking and singing voices led to work in television cartoons. DeLisle's over–300 television credits include the animated series *Buzz Lightyear of Star Command, Batman Beyond, House of Mouse, The Zeta Project, Rugrats, Clifford the Big Red Dog, Johnny Bravo, The Mummy: Secrets of Medjai, ChalkZone, Lilo & Stitch, The Weekenders, Samurai Jack, Evil Con Carne, Justice League, Duck Dodgers, Star Wars: Clone Wars, The Powerpuff Girls, Curious George, The Emperor's New School, Clifford's Puppy Days, The Fairly OddParents, What's New, Scooby-Doo?, Danny Phantom, Codename: Kids Next Door, Avatar: The Last Airbender, The Replacements, The Super Hero Squad Show, WordGirl*, and *The Penguins of Madagascar*, but is mostly recognized as the evil Mandy in *The Grim Adventures of Billy and Mandy*. She can also be heard in such videos and movies as *Baldur's Gate* (1998), *Star Wars: Episode I—The Phantom Menace* (1999), *Escape from Monkey Island* (2000), *Star Wars: Galactic Battlegrounds* (2001), *The Flintstones: On the Rocks* (2001), *The Powerpuff Girls* (2002), *Tarzan and Jane* (2002), *A Scooby-Doo Christmas* (2004), *Legend of Frosty the Snowman* (2005), *The Fox and the Hound 2* (2006), *The Little Mermaid: Ariel's Beginning* (2008), and *Tinker Bell and the Lost Treasure* (2009). She continues her singing career and has released a handful of albums.

Dell, Charlie (b. 1943) A balding, smiling character actor mostly active in television since the late 1970s, he provided the voice of the pig Ollie, the father of three mischievous piggies, in *Home on the Range* (2004). He was born in Nueces County, Texas, and made his screen debut in 1970, but even after several films his career seemed stalled until he played Professor Parsafoot in the sci-fi television series *Jason of Star Command*. Dell went on to featured roles in such series as *The Dukes of Hazzard, Faerie Tale Theatre, Silver Spoons, Chicago Hope, ER, Grace Under Fire, Evening Shade, Married with Children, Days of Our Lives, Desperate Housewives,* and *Two and a Half Men*. He reprised his Ollie the Pig in the animated short *A Dairy Tale* (2004).

DeLuise, Dom (1933–2009) A rotund, cheerful comic actor who usually played the hero's hapless sidekick in films, he lent his voice to many animated features, such as *Oliver & Company* (1988) for which he played the friendly, small-time thief Fagin. DeLuise was born in Brooklyn, New York, and educated at Tufts University before acting in stock companies and appearing in nightclubs. After getting roles in a handful of New York stage musicals and working in summer theatre, he gained recognition for his television appearances on *The Dean Martin Summer Show* and other television variety programs and eventually had his own shows in 1968 and 1987. DeLuise made his screen debut in 1964 and went on to make many films, including *The Glass Bottom Boat* (1966), *Who Is Harry Kellerman and Why Is He Saying Those Terrible Things About Me?* (1971), *The Adventure of Sherlock Holmes' Smarter Brother* (1975), *The End* (1978), *The Muppet Movie* (1979), *The Best Little Whorehouse in Texas* (1982), *Fatso* (1980), *The Princess and the Dwarf* (1989), as well as six Mel Brooks movies, including *The Twelve Chairs* (1970), *Silent Movie* (1976), *Spaceballs* (1987), and *Robin Hood: Men in Tights* (1993). After he provided the voice for the docile cat Tiger in the animated feature *An American Tail* (1986), DeLuise became one of the busiest voices in movies and on television. Among his animation credits are *All Dogs Go to Heaven* (1989), *An American Tail: Fievel Goes West* (1991), *The Skateboard Kid* (1993), *Happily Ever After* (1993), *A Troll in Central Park* (1994), *All Dogs Go to Heaven 2* (1996), *An All Dogs Christmas Carol* (1998), *An American Tail: The Treasure of Manhattan Island* (1998), and *The Secret of Nimh 2* (1998), as well as many television cartoons, such as *Fievel's American Tails, All Dogs Go to Heaven: The Series, Cow and Chicken, The Wild Thornberrys, Hercules, Dexter's Laboratory,* and *Duck Dodgers*. Unlike the calculating Fagin in Charles Dickens' *Oliver Twist* who exploits this gang of boys, the Fagin in *Oliver & Company* truly likes the members of his animal gang, perhaps because they are the only friends he has. DeLuise's giggles and nervous laughter keep Fagin from becoming too much the heavy in the film, making him more a genial bungler rather than an outright villain.

DeLyon, Leo A pop songwriter who is also a voice artist, he supplied the voice for Flunkey the Baboon in *The Jungle Book* (1967). DeLyon wrote songs and was musical director for the singing team of Saddler and Young as well as other performers. He also provided oddball sounds and ad-libs on some popular 1960s records. DeLyon appeared in the television series *My Mother the Car, Bewitched, Arrest and Trial, Spotlight,* and *The Incredible Hulk,* but he was better known for his voices for cartoons. He can be heard on *The Flintstones, The Smurfs,* and *Top Cat,* as well as the videos *Top Cat and the Beverly Hills Cats* (1987), *Adventures in Odyssey: The Knight Travellers* (1991), and *Adventures in Odyssey: A Flight to the Finish* (1991).

Dempsey, Taylor The child performer who voiced the nervous young elephant Tantor in *Tarzan* (1999) has also done voices for the animated video *Mickey's Once Upon a Christmas* (1999) and the television cartoon series *The Legend of Tarzan*.

Dench, Judi (b. 1934) The distinguished British actress of the stage and television who found a second career on screen in her late middle age, she supplied the voice of the very prim and proper cow Mrs. Caloway in *Home on the Range* (2004). Judith Olivia Dench was born in York, England, studied theatre at the Central School of Speech and Drama in London, and began her career in classical roles for such acclaimed organizations as the Royal Shakespeare Company, Old Vic, and Royal National Theatre. She appeared in plays and musicals in the West End as well, most memorably as Sally Bowles in the first London production of *Cabaret* (1968), and was popular on British television in sitcoms such as *Hilda Lessways, A Fine Romance,* and (years later) *As Time Goes By*. Although Dench made her film debut in 1964, she would not become an international screen star until the 1980s thanks to movies such as *A Room with a View* (1985), *Golden Eye* (1995), *Mrs. Brown* (1997), *Shakespeare in Love* (1998), *Tea with Mussolini* (1999), *Chocolat* (2000), *Iris* (2000), *The Shipping News* (2001), *Ladies in Lavender* (2004), *Pride and Prejudice* (2005), *Mrs. Henderson Presents* (2005), *Casino Royale* (2006), *Notes on a Scandal* (2006), *Quantum of Solace* (2008), *Nine* (2009), and *Jane Eyre* (2010). The very British, very reserved Mrs. Caloway in *Home on the Range* seems to be out of place in the Old West so she makes for a delicious contrast to the rural American characters that fill the movie, especially the crass bovine Maggie, played by Roseanne. Similarly, the acting styles of Dench and Roseanne are so different that the juxtaposition of the two voices is one of the delights of the film. Dench reprised her Mrs. Caloway in the animated film short *A Dairy Tale* (2004).

Denison, Leslie (1905–1992)   A British stage actor who played various Englishmen in over ninety movies, he provided voices for three Donald Duck shorts: Donald's look-alike in *Donald's Double Trouble* (1946), the Suave Donald in *Donald's Dream Voice* (1948), and the Narrator and the voice of Donald's Internal Thoughts in *Donald's Diary* (1954). He was born in the Warwickshire region of England and acted on the stage in his homeland and in the States, appearing on Broadway in such plays as *The Barretts of Wimpole Street* (1931), *The Passionate Pilgrim* (1932), *As Husbands Go* (1933), *On Location* (1937), and *Gloriana* (1938). He made his Hollywood debut in *Escape to Glory* (1940). Over the next three decades Denison portrayed British military types, aristocrats, police officers, and butlers in a variety of films, including *A Yank in the R.A.F.* (1941), *My Favorite Blonde* (1942), *Bombs Over Burma* (1942), *They Raid by Night* (1942), *Five Graves to Cairo* (1943), *Frenchman's Creek* (1944), *The House of Fear* (1945), *The Bandit of Sherwood Forest* (1946), *Bulldog Drummond Strikes Back* (1947), *Green Dolphin Street* (1947), *The Black Arrow* (1948), *Brave Warrior* (1952), *The Black Castle* (1952), *Rogue's March* (1953), *Bengal Brigade* (1954), *The Seventh Sin* (1957), and *Signpost to Murder* (1964). Before he retired in 1965, Denison appeared on some television series as well, including *The Great Gildersleeve*, *Studio 57*, *Four Star Playhouse*, *You Are There*, *Telephone Time*, *Peter Gunn*, *The Dick Powell Theatre*, and *The Eleventh Hour*.

Dennehy, Brian (b. 1938)   A large, powerful character actor who has shone in all media with his natural style of acting, he supplied the voice of the rat Django, Remy and Emile's well-meaning father, in *Ratatouille* (2007). Brian Manion Dennehy was born in Bridgeport, Connecticut, and was educated at Columbia and Yale Universities before beginning his career on television in 1977, appearing in such series as *Kojak*, *Serpico*, *M*A*S*H*, *Lou Grant*, *Dallas*, and *Pearl*. Dennehy acted in the films *Looking for Mr. Goodbar* (1977), *Semi-Tough* (1977), *F.I.S.T.* (1978), *Foul Play* (1978), *10* (1979), and *Little Miss Marker* (1980) before gaining wide attention in *First Blood* (1982). Among his subsequent movies are *Never Cry Wolf* (1983), *Gorky Park* (1983), *Cocoon* (1985), *Silverado* (1985), *Legal Eagles* (1986), *Return to Snowy Mountain* (1988), *Cocoon: The Return* (1988), *Presumed Innocent* (1990), *Gladiator* (1992), *Romeo + Juliet* (1996), *Silicon Towers* (1999), *Summer Catch* (2001), *Assault on a Precinct* (2005), *Welcome to Paradise* (2007), *Righteous Kill* (2008), and *Alleged* (2010), as well as many made-for-TV movies. Dennehy was also featured in such television series as *Dynasty*, *Star of the Family*, *The Last Place on Earth*, *Miami Vice*, *Birdland*, *The Fighting Fitzgeralds*, *Just Shoot Me!*, *The West Wing*, *30 Rock*, *Rules of Engagement*, and *Rizzoli & Isles*. He acted Off Broadway in the 1970s then returned to the stage two decades later to star in the Broadway productions of *Translations* (1995), *Death of a Salesman* (1999), *Long Day's Journey into Night* (2003), *Inherit the Wind* (2007), and *Desire Under the Elms* (2009). The character of Django in *Ratatouille* was named after the Belgian jazz guitarist Django Reinhardt who was very popular throughout Europe in the 1930s and 1940s.

Dennis, Charles (b. 1946)   An acclaimed Canadian author and actor who is heard on many video games, he voiced the stern bounty hunter Rico in *Home on the Range* (2004). He was born in Toronto and began his acting career at the age of eight as a regular on the Canadian radio series *Peter and the Dwarf*. Dennis pursued theatre as a teenager, was educated at the University of Toronto, and then became a film and theatre critic for the *Toronto Telegram*. In addition to writing several novels, plays, screenplays, and television scripts, he continued his acting career in both American and Canadian movies and television. Dennis has appeared in such U.S. series as *Star Trek: The Next Generation*, *Jake and the Fatman*, *Star Trek: Enterprise*, and *American Dad*. He can be heard in the animated film *Shrek* (2001). The character of Rico in *Home on the Range* is a comic homage to Clint Eastwood and the cold cowboy characters he played early in his career. Dennis imitates Eastwood's dry, no-nonsense voice and is supported by music that recalls the echoing theme songs of *The Good, the Bad and the Ugly* (1966) and other Eastwood westerns.

Derryberry, Debi (b. 1967)   A busy voice artist who usually plays young boy heroes in animated television shows, she provided the voices for the Troll Doll and the Aliens in *Toy Story* (1995), the Baby Maggots in *A Bug's Life* (1998), and various minor characters in *Aladdin* (1992), *The Hunchback of Notre Dame* (1996), *Hercules* (1997), *Tarzan* (1999), *Toy Story 2* (1999), *Brother Bear* (2003), and *Home on the Range* (2004). She was born in Indio, California, and began voicing Japanese animated films in 1986. Among her many animated movie and video credits are *Kiki's Delivery Service* (1989), *Life with Louie: A Christmas Surprise for Mrs. Stillman*

(1994), *Dot and Spot's Magical Christmas Adventure* (1996), *The Dog of Flanders* (1997), *Princess Mononoke* (1997), *Pocahontas II: Journey to a New World* (1998), *The Nuttiest Nutcracker* (1999), *Lady and the Tramp II: Scamp's Adventure* (2001), *Ice Age: The Meltdown* (2006), *Casper's Scare School* (2006), *Happily N'Ever After* (2006), *Horton Hears a Who!* (2008), and *The Legend of Secret Pass* (2010). Derryberry can be heard in such television cartoon series as *Peter Pan and the Pirates*, *TaleSpin*, *The Addams Family*, *Timon and Pumbaa*, *King of the Hill*, *Life with Louie*, *Jumanji*, *Clifford the Big Red Dog*, *ChalkZone*, *Fillmore!*, *Zatch Bell!*, *The Grim Adventures of Billy & Mandy*, and *Stitch!*, but she is most known as the voice of Jimmy Neutron in the TV series *The Adventures of Jimmy Neuton: Boy Genius* and its many videos.

Deutsch, Patti (b. 1945) The red-headed comedienne and character actress known for her television appearances and her voicing of cartoons, she provided the voice for the elephant Tantor's Mother in *Tarzan* (1999) and the put-upon Waitress in *The Emperor's New Groove* (2000). She was born in Pittsburgh, Pennsylvania, and began her professional career as a member of the comedy group The Ace Trucking Company. Deutsch made her television debut in 1968 as a stand-up comic on variety shows then became a member of the cast of *Rowan & Martin's Laugh-In*. Yet she received more notoriety as a regular on the quiz show *Match Game* where her bizarre and funny answers made her a favorite for five years. Her other television credits include the cartoon series as *As Told by Ginger*, *The Smurfs*, *Life with Louie*, *Darkwing Duck*, *Capitol Critters*, *Casper*, and *The Angry Beavers*. Deutsch can be heard in the animated movies and videos *Jetsons: The Movie* (1990), *The Land Before Time VII: The Stone of Cold Fire* (2000), *Monsters, Inc.* (2001), *The Emperor's New Groove 2: Kronk's New Groove* (2005), and *Happily N'Ever After* (2006).

Devine, Andy (1905–1977) One of the most easily identified of all Hollywood character actors because of his oddly-pitched, raspy voice, he supplied the voice for the badger Friar Tuck in *Robin Hood* (1973). Andrew Vabre Devine was born in Flagstaff, Arizona, the son of a hotel proprietor, and raised in nearby Kingman. He was a successful athlete in school, playing football at St. Mary and St. Benedict College, Arizona State Teachers College, and Santa Clara University. Devine first appeared on screen in the silents playing rugged, athletic types, but his high-pitched voice eliminated him from leading-man roles once talkies came in so he became a roly-poly character actor and usually played crusty, rural sidekicks in over 150 movies, including *Around the Bases* (1927), *We Americans* (1928), *The Spirit of Notre Dame* (1931), *The All-American* (1932), *Gift of Gab* (1934), *Wake Up and Dream* (1934), *The Farmer Takes a Wife* (1935), *Coronado* (1935), *Romeo and Juliet* (1936), *In Old Chicago* (1937), *A Star Is Born* (1937), *Stagecoach* (1939), *Little Old New York* (1940), *Top Sergeant* (1942), *Ali Baba and the Forty Thieves* (1944), *Frisco Sal* (1945), *The Eyes of Texas* (1948), *The Red Badge of Courage* (1951), *Pete Kelly's Blues* (1955), *The Man Who Shot Liberty Valance* (1962), *How the West Was Won* (1962), *The Ballad of Josie* (1967), *Myra Breckinridge* (1970), and *A Whale of a Tale* (1977). Devine is probably best remembered as Deputy Marshal Jingles P. Jones, Guy Madison's sidekick on the radio and television series *The Adventures of Wild Bill Hickok*. His other television credits include the series *Wagon Train*, *The Barbara Stanwyck Show*, *Twilight Zone*, *Burke's Law*, *Flipper*, *The Rounders*, *Batman*, *Bonanza*, *Gunsmoke*, *The Virginian*, *Alias Smith and Jones*, and his own children's show *Andy's Gang* in the late 1950s. Surprisingly, Devine has only one other voice credit: the animated film *The Mouse and His Child* (1977). The character of Friar Tuck in Disney's *Robin Hood* was originally going to be a pig but it was feared that having a porcine clergy member might be offensive to moviegoers so Tuck was turned into a badger. Devine's vocals for the character are not as thick-headed or as hayseed as many of the actor's live-action roles, but rather wise and authoritative.

DeVito, Danny (b. 1944) The short, round character actor who excels at playing lovably nasty types on screen and on television, he supplied the speaking and singing voice of the satyr Philoctetes who trains Hercules in *Hercules* (1997). Daniel Michael DeVito, Jr., was born in Neptune, New Jersey, and raised in nearby Asbury Park before studying at the American Academy of Dramatic Arts. He began his career in the theatre, getting noticed for his performance Off Broadway in *One Flew Over the Cuckoo's Nest* (1971) which he reprised on film in 1975. DeVito made his screen debut in 1970 and appeared in such movies as *Lady Liberty* (1971), *Car Wash* (1976), and *Goin' South* (1978), but it was as the obnoxious Louie De Palma in the TV sit-com *Taxi* that brought him fame and better screen roles, as in *Terms of Endearment* (1983), *Romancing the Stone* (1984), *The Jewel of the Nile* (1985), *Wise Guys* (1986), *Ruthless People* (1986), *Tin Men* (1987), *Throw Momma from the Train* (1987), *Twins* (1988), *War of the Roses* (1989), *Other People's Money* (1991), *Batman Returns* (1992), *Hoffa* (1992), *Get Shorty* (1995), *L.A. Confidential* (1997), *Man on the Moon* (1999), *Death to Smoochy* (2002), *Deck the Halls* (2006), and *Solitary Man* (2009).

He has also appeared in the television series *Angie, Starsky & Hutch, Friends,* and *It's Always Raining in Philadelphia,* can be heard on the cartoon series *The Simpsons,* and voiced the movies and videos *Happily Ever After* (1985), *My Little Pony: The Movie* (1986), *Look Who's Talking Now* (1993), *Little Red Riding Hood* (1995), and *Space Jam* (1996). DeVito is also a successful producer of films and comedy shows on television and he has directed a handful of movies over the years. While recording the vocals for Philoctetes in *Hercules,* DeVito was filmed and the animators noticed that the comic actor's mouth took various shapes when he talked so they incorporated it into the character's facial expressions.

Diller, Phyllis (b. 1917)   The veteran cackling comedienne whose career spans half a century, she turned to voice work in her later years and voiced the Queen of the ant colony in *A Bug's Life* (1998). She was born Phyllis Ada Driver in Lima, Ohio, and worked as a secretary, advertising copywriter, and (during World War II) in an airplane factory before turning to comedy at the age of thirty-seven. Her stand-up comedy routines in nightclubs led to hundreds of television appearances on talk shows, variety programs, quiz shows, sit-coms, and eventually her own series *The Phyllis Diller Show* in 1966. Diller's movie credits include *Splendor in the Grass* (1961), *Boy, Did I Get a Wrong Number!* (1966), *Eight on the Lam* (1967), *The Private Navy of Sgt. O'Farrell* (1968), *A Pleasure Doing Business* (1979), *Pink Motel* (1982), *The Boneyard* (1991), *The Silence of the Hams* (1994), *The Last Place on Earth* (2002), *Motorcross Kids* (2004), and *Unbeatable Harold* (2006). Her distinctive voice can be heard on many TV cartoon series, such as *Animaniacs, King of the Hill, The Wild Thornberrys, The Adventures of Jimmy Neutron: Boy Genius, The Powerpuff Girls,* and *Hey, Arnold!,* as well as in the animated films and videos *Alice Through the Looking Glass* (1987), *The Nutcracker Prince* (1990), *Happily Ever After* (1993), *The Nuttiest Nutcracker* (1999), *Casper's Scare School* (2006), and *Blaze of Glory* (2008). Autobiography: *Like a Lampshade in a Whorehouse* (2005).

Di Maggio, John (b. 1968)   A television voice actor who specializes in comic characters, he voiced the New York City pigeon Saul in *Bolt* (2008). He was born in North Plainfield, New Jersey, and began his career as a stand-up comic. Di Maggio made his first television appearances in such shows as *Law & Order, Chicago Hope,* and *N.Y.P.D. Blue,* but soon was concentrating on voicing animated series. Among his many TV cartoon credits are *Johnny Bravo, The Legend of Tarzan, The Mummy: Secrets of the Medjai, Samurai Jack, Teen Titans, What's New Scooby-Doo?, Kim Possible, The Simpsons, Lilo & Stitch, Duck Dodgers, Where My Dogs At?, El Tigre: The Adventures of Manny Rivera, American Dragon: Jake Long, American Dad, Ben 10: Alien Force,* and *Chowder,* but he is most known for voicing Bender Bending Rodriguez in the *Futurama* series, videos, and video games.

Dindal, Mark   A visual effects artist for animated films who became a director as well, he provided the voice of the hip Morkupine Porcupine in *Chicken Little* (2005). The Columbus, Ohio, native studied animation at the California Institute of the Arts and worked on the visual effects in such Disney animated movies as *Mickey's Christmas Carol* (1983), *The Black Cauldron* (1985), *The Great Mouse Detective* (1986), *Oliver & Company* (1988), *The Little Mermaid* (1989), *The Rescuers Down Under* (1990), and *Aladdin* (1992). Eventually he was both writer and director for *Cats Don't Dance* (1997), *The Emperor's New Groove* (2000), and *Chicken Little.*

The Dinning Sisters   A singing trio of siblings who specialized in country-flavored songs in the 1940s and 1950s, they performed the title song on the soundtrack of *Fun and Fancy Free* (1947) and "Blame It on the Samba" in *Melody Time* (1948). Twins Jean and Ginger Dinning and their elder sister Lou came from a large family in rural Kansas near Wichita and sang at state fairs, local radio stations, and in concerts throughout the midwest before becoming nationally known through their records. As members of the trio left to get married, they were replaced by sister Dolores and the unrelated Jayne Bundesen. The trio can be heard on the soundtracks of the movies *Strictly in the Groove* (1942), *National Barn Dance* (1944), *Throw a Saddle on a Star* (1946), and *Takin' the Breaks* (1946), and can be seen as well as heard in the movie *That Texas Jamboree* (1946). Records by the Dinning Sister continued to sell throughout the 1950s, none more successfully than their version of "Buttons and Bows."

DiSalvo, Lino   A film and video animator, he voiced the New York pigeon Vinnie in *Bolt* (2008). DiSalvo worked on the animation for *102 Dalmatians* (2000), *Reign of Fire* (2002), *Kangaroo Jack* (2003), *Chicken Little* (2005), *Meet the Robinsons* (2007), and *Tangled* (2010). As supervising animator for *Bolt,* his thick Italian–New Yorkese was deemed ideal for the character of Vinnie. DiSalvo's only other voice credit was Gristletoe Joe in the video *Prep & Landing* (2009).

Disney, Walt (1901–1966)   The one-man dynamo behind cartoon shorts, animated features, live-action adventure films, television programs, nature documentaries, big-budget screen musicals, and theme parks, he also was the first actor for Disney animated movies, providing the voice for Mickey Mouse for twenty years. Walter Elias Disney was born in Chicago and grew up in Marceline, Missouri, and Kansas City. After serving in World War I, he studied at the Kansas City Art Institute and in the early 1920s he set up his own animation studio to provide cartoons for a chain of movie theatres. After several failures, the young animator found success with the creation of Mickey Mouse and other beloved cartoon characters. With the arrival of sound, Disney experimented with ways to coordinate not only sound but music to the moving images. He provided the voice for Mickey in his first sound cartoon *Steamboat Willie* (1928), as well as that of Minnie Mouse and the Parrot. Many of Disney's early cartoon shorts were mini-musicals using classical music as well as original songs and did not need dialogue, but when Mickey needed to speak, Disney provided the squeaking falsetto voice for the character. He voiced the famous mouse for the last time in the "Mickey and the Beanstalk" segment of the anthology feature *Fun and Fancy Free* (1947). After that Disney let James MacDonald, Wayne Allwine, and other actors take over and provide Mickey's voice on screen and on television. Disney's creation of the feature-length animated movie with *Snow White and the Seven Dwarfs* (1937) raised the art of animation far beyond the existing cartoons and his experimentation with mixing live action and animation in movies such as *Song of the South* (1946) and *Mary Poppins* (1964) also opened up new possibilities for the medium. The creative and executive power of Disney was so great that the Walt Disney Company took years to recover from his death from lung cancer at the age of sixty-five. Mickey Mouse is the most famous animated character in the world and the reasons for his wide appeal are hard to pin down. The mouse is unflaggingly optimistic, playfully curious, loyal to others, and always ready to enjoy life. Like Charlie Chaplin's Little Tramp, he is a put-upon everyman who is rarely the champion or the success figure so audiences identify with him. Mickey Mouse became so famous and beloved that Disney soon realized he could not develop the character in new directions. Audiences wanted Mickey to stay the same so it was left to characters like Donald Duck to be irascible, Pluto to be mischievous, Goofy to be ridiculous, and Minnie Mouse to be parental. Since mice squeak, Disney's vocals for Mickey in *Steamboat Willie* and other early cartoons were more squeaking sounds than words. When the mouse had to talk, Disney chose a high-pitched falsetto even though the character is male. The high register seemed more appropriate for the merry rodent and Mickey has been voiced in that manner ever since. Memoir: *The Disney Story*, Diane Disney Miller [his daughter] (1957); biographies: *The Animated Man: A Life of Walt Disney*, Michael Barrier (2008); *Walt Disney: The Triumph of the American Imagination*, Neal Gabler (2006); *Walt Disney: An American Original*, Bob Thomas (1994); *Walt Disney: Hollywood's Dark Prince*, Marc Eliot (1993).

Docter, Pete (b. 1968) A Pixar writer and director who occasionally does voices for his projects, he voiced the Campmaster of the Wilderness Explorers in *Up* (2009) and made the bird sounds for Kevin, the tall, colorful exotic bird that Charles Muntz tries to capture in that movie. Peter Hans Docter was born in Bloomington, Minnesota, into a family of musicians and music teachers, and studied at the University of Minnesota and the California Institute of the Arts. He wrote and directed the animated short *Winter* (1988) then at the age of twenty-one he was hired by the new Pixar Company, writing scripts for *Toy Story* (1995) and *Toy Story 2* (1999) before becoming both writer and director of *Monsters, Inc.* (2001), the short *Mike's New Car* (2002), and *Up*. Docter also contributed to the script for *WALL-E* (2008). He can he heard doing various voices in *Monsters, Inc., The Incredibles* (2004), and the video *Mr. Incredible and Pals* (2005). His daughter **Elie Docter** supplied the voice of the young Tomboy Ellie in the prologue of *Up*.

Dodson, Jon *see* **The Kings Men**

Donnellan, Sean A television host and actor, he provided the voice of Penny's television Dad in *Bolt* (2008). He is most known as the host of the television programs *How to Boil Water* and *Faux Pause*, as well as the voice on many computer video games. Donnellan has appeared on such TV series as *Nip/Tuck, Without a Trace, Las Vegas*, and *Monk*, and he can be heard on animated cartoon shows, including *Batman Beyond, Justice League, Batman, Ben 10: Ultimate Alien*, and *Batman: The Brave and the Bold*. He reprised Penny's TV Dad in the film short *Super Rhino* (2009) and voiced the animated movie *The Ant Bully* (2006) and the video *Justice League: The New Frontier* (2008).

Donovan, Tate (b. 1963) A solid movie and television leading man, he provided the voice of Adult Hercules in *Hercules* (1997). Tate Buckley Donovan was born in Tenafly, New Jersey, and began his career as a teenager in TV-movies and series. After high school he moved to Los Angeles and attended the University of Southern California as he continued to work in films, later appearing in such movies as *Space Camp* (1986), *Clean and Sober* (1988), *Memphis Belle* (1990), *Love Potion No. 9*

(1992), *Ethan Frome* (1993), *Murder at 1600* (1997), *The Thin Pink Line* (1998), *Swordfish* (2001), *Good Night and Good Luck* (2005), *Nancy Drew* (2007), and *Below the Beltway* (2010). Donovan has been featured in a number of television series, including *Partners, Ally McBeal, Friends, The O.C.*, and *Damages*. The animators for *Hercules* wished to emphasize the title character's oversized muscles and athletic movements but Donovan voiced the character as a normal human with doubts, dreams, and personal issues. The Hercules of mythology is a mass of complexities and filled with many noble and ignoble qualities; he is both cursed and gifted by the gods. The Disney animated hero is more contemporary and accessible to moviegoers but he is never reduced to a thick-headed jock or a muscular stereotype. Donovan reprised his Hercules in the videos *Hercules: Zero to Hero* (1999) and *Kingdom Hearts II* (2005), and in the cartoon series *Hercules* and *House of Mouse*.

Dooley, Paul (b. 1928) A paunchy character actor busy in films and on television usually playing fathers and later grandfathers, he provided the voice for Sarge, the military jeep, in *Cars* (2006). He was born Paul Brown in Parkersburg, West Virginia, and educated at West Virginia University — Morgantown where he took up acting. He was cast in a variety of plays in New York City, including the famous Off Broadway production of *The Threepenny Opera* (1954) and the original Broadway version of *The Odd Couple* (1965), and started acting on television in 1963 and in films the following year. Dooley's screen credits include *Slap Shot* (1977), *A Wedding* (1978), *Breaking Away* (1979), *Popeye* (1980), *Paternity* (1981), *The Adventures of Bob & Doug McKenzie: Strange Brew* (1983), *Sixteen Candles* (1984), *Shakes the Clown* (1991), *My Boyfriend's Back* (1993), *Runaway Bride* (1999), *Come Away Home* (2005), *For Your Consideration* (2006), and *Hairspray* (2007). He has appeared in many TV-movies and was a regular on such series as *Coming of Age, Alf, Dream On, Grace Under Fire, Star Trek: Deep Space Nine, Once and Again, The Practice, ER*, and *Curb Your Enthusiasm*. Dooley reprised his Sarge in the video *Mater and the Ghostlight* (2006) and can be heard in the animated series *Duckman: Private Dick/Family Man*, the video *The Night the Animals Talked* (1970), and the film *Raggedy Ann & Andy: A Musical Adventure* (1977).

Dorn, Patrick (b. 1991) A child performer who began his performing career in 2000, he supplied the voice of the Boy on the beach who plays fetch with his dog in *Teacher's Pet* (2004). He was born in West Covina, California, the son of a child actors' advocate who runs BizParents. At the age of nine he was performing in live shows at Disney's California Adventure, the youngest "cast member" in the theme park. Dorn made his acting debut the next year in the video *Scooter Kidz* (2001) and had small parts in the films *First Days* (2001), *Little Dreams* (2002), *The Santa Clause 2* (2002), and *Outta Sync* (2006). He appeared in the television series *Oliver Beane* and *Over There* but is better known as Thomas Hamilton Forrester on *The Bold and the Beautiful* which he played for two years.

Dotrice, Roy (b. 1923) A distinguished British stage actor who was discovered by Americans late in his career, he was the Narrator of the Mickey Mouse featurette *The Prince and the Pauper* (1990). He was born in Guernsey in the Channel Islands and did not become interested in acting until he was a prisoner of war in Germany during World War II and got involved in amateur theatricals. After he returned to England, Dotrice studied at the Royal Academy of Dramatic Art and acted with various theatre companies, in particular the Royal Shakespeare Company for which he played many classical roles. In 1957 he also started acting on British television, appearing both in series and in dramatizations of the classics. Dotrice was forty-four years old before he made his Broadway debut in his one-person show *Brief Lives* in 1967, returning in it again in 1974, and going on to play featured roles on Broadway in *Mr. Lincoln* (1980), *A Life* (1980), *Kingdoms* (1981), *Hay Fever* (1985), *The Homecoming* (1991), and *A Moon for the Misbegotten* (2000). In the 1980s he started acting on American television series, such as *The Equalizer, Beauty and The Beast, Picket Fences, Mr. & Mrs. Smith, Wings, Touched by an Angel, Madigan Men*, and *Murder, She Wrote*, as well as providing voices for the cartoon series *Batman* and *Spider-Man*. Among his film credits are *The Heroes of Telemark* (1965), *The Buttercup Chain* (1970), *Nicholas and Alexandra* (1971), *Hide and Seek* (1972), *Cheech & Chong's The Corsican Brothers* (1984), *Amadeus* (1984), *Shaka Zulu* (1987), *The Cutting Edge* (1992), *Swimming with Sharks* (1994), *The Scarlet Letter* (1995), *Alien Hunter* (2003), *These Foolish Things* (2006), and *Go Go Tales* (2007).

Douglas, Mike (1925–2006) A well-known singer who hosted a popular talk show on television for many years, he provided the singing voice for Prince Charming in *Cinderella* (1950). He was born Michael Delaney Dowd in Chicago and started singing professionally in his teens. In the late 1940s he moved to California and was hired as a vocalist for Kay Kyser's band and sang on Kyser's television musical quiz show *Kollege of Musical Knowledge*. After appearing on many television variety shows, Douglas got his own syndicated program *The Mike Douglas Show* which started broadcasting from

Cleveland in 1961 then later moved to Philadelphia and continued until 1980. He sometimes sang on his show and recorded many records. Because the Prince in *Cinderella* has few spoken likes, much of the character is revealed through the singing. Douglas' voice is not the operatic one of, say, the Prince in *Snow White and the Seven Dwarfs*; instead it is a more casual, comfortable one which allows the audience to warm up to the character. Autobiographies: *Mike Douglas, My Story* (1978); *I'll Be Right Back: Memories of TV's Greatest Talk Show* (1999); biography: *Mike Douglas: When the Going Gets Tough*, Mel White (1983).

Dreyfuss, Richard (b. 1947) The hyperactive film actor who retains a boyish quality even in his mature roles, he provided the voice of the Brooklyn-accented Commodore Centipede in *James and the Giant Peach* (1996). The Brooklyn native moved with his family to Los Angeles when he was nine and he later studied at San Fernando State College. Dreyfuss made his New York acting debut Off Broadway in 1969 and appeared in classic stage roles until he found fame in the movies with *American Graffiti* (1973), followed by such hits as *Jaws* (1975), *The Goodbye Girl* (1977), *Close Encounters of the Third Kind* (1977), *Down and Out in Beverly Hills* (1986), *Tin Men* (1987), *Mr. Holland's Opus* (1995), and *W.* (2008). He returned to the New York stage with *Death and the Maiden* (1992) and *The Exonerated* (2002) even as he continued his film career and acted in many television series and specials. Dreyfuss also lent his voice to the animated video *Rudolph the Red-Nosed Reindeer & the Island of Misfit Toys* (2001) and the series *Family Guy*.

Driscoll, Bobby (1937–1968) The popular child star of Disney movies who had a tragic life as an adult, he shone in both musical and adventure films during his brief career but is probably most remembered as the voice of the adventurous young hero Peter in *Peter Pan* (1953). Robert Cletus Driscoll was born in Cedar Rapids, Iowa, and made his feature film debut in *Lost Angel* (1943) when he was six years old. He appeared in several films in the 1940s and 1950s, including the live-action sections of Disney's *Song of the South* (1946), *So Dear to My Heart* (1948), and *Melody Time* (1948), although his best screen role was Jim Hawkins in *Treasure Island* (1950). His non–Disney movies include *The Big Bonanza* (1944), *From This Day Forward* (1946), *The Window* (1949), and *The Happy Time* (1952). Driscoll first voiced Peter Pan in the 1951 TV broadcast *The Walt Disney Christmas Show* and after the movie was released he and some other original cast members recreated the tale on *Lux Radio Theatre* in 1953. He also voiced Goofy Jr. in the shorts *Fathers Are People* (1951), *Father's Lion* (1952), and *Father's Week End* (1953). Driscoll made several television appearances in the 1950s but when he stopped getting cast in the 1960s he took to drink and became a drug addict, dying of an overdose at the age of thirty-one. In preparing *Peter Pan* for the screen, the dancer Roland Dupree was filmed doing some of Peter's stunts and leaps and these were used by the animators, giving Peter's movements some of the most fluid of any Disney animated character. Driscoll was also filmed doing some of Peter's scenes but it was his vocal work that was so impressive. No longer was he the cute but sniveling kid actor of the screen but a robust, exciting pre-teen bursting with joyous abandon. Although there had been many stage and film versions of J. M. Barrie's classic tale before 1953, Disney's was the first to have the hero played by a male actor.

Driver, Minnie (b. 1970) A petite, versatile British actress effective in both period pieces and contemporary works, she voiced the English botanist Jane Porter who falls in love with the ape man in *Tarzan* (1999). She was born Amelia Fiona J. Driver in London, the daughter of a businessman and a fashion designer, was raised in Barbados and educated in Paris and Grenoble before training at the Webber Douglas Academy of Dramatic Arts in London. She made her television debut in the British TV-movie *God on the Rocks* in 1990 and has since appeared on many series in England and the States, including *My Good Friend, The X Files, Will & Grace, The Riches*, and *The Deep*. Driver's first film was *The Zebra Man* (1992), followed by such notable movies as *Circle of Friends* (1995), *Golden Eye* (1995), *Big Night* (1996), *Sleepers* (1996), *Grosse Pointe Blank* (1997), *Good Will Hunting* (1997), *The Governess* (1998), *An Ideal Husband* (1999), *Return to Me* (2000), *Beautiful* (2000), *Hope Springs* (2003), *Ella Enchanted* (2004), *The Phantom of the Opera* (2004), *Delirious* (2006), *Motherhood* (2009), and *Barney's Version* (2010). She can also be heard in the animated films *Princess Mononoke* (1997) and *South Park: Bigger Longer & Uncut* (1999). Unlike the Jane of most live-action movies about Tarzan, the Jane in the Disney version is a scholar first, a passionate woman second. She seems more interested in botany than love until she meets Tarzan and he arouses her intellectual curiosity long before he stirs her romantic feelings. Driver's vocals for Jane are very British, prim, and dispassionate at first, but slowly warming as the story progresses.

Dubin, Gary (b. 1959) A former child actor who moved into adult roles on television and in movies, he voiced the pugnacious Parisian kitten Toulouse in *The Aristocats* (1970). He was born in Edinburgh, Scotland, and by the age of eight was acting in American television. After bit parts in some films and TV shows, the pre-teen Dubin was a regular on the series *Bracken's World* and later *The Partridge Family*. As an adult he acted in such series as *The Paper Chase* and *Beverly Hills 90210*, as well as in the films *Jaws 2* (1978), *Time Walker* (1982), *King's Highway* (2002), *Little Black Book* (2004), *The Lodger* (2009), and others. *The Aristocats* was his first job voicing animated characters, followed by several videos including *Outlanders* (1986) and *Giant Robo: The Day the Earth Stood Still* (1991).

Dunagan, Donnie (b. 1935) A child actor who appeared in a handful of 1930s movies, his last screen credit was providing the voice of Young Bambi in *Bambi* (1942). He was born Donald Roan Dunagan in San Antonio, Texas, and grew up in Memphis where he took dance lessons and won a talent contest which brought him to the attention of a Hollywood talent scout. He made his screen debut as one of the Carey children in *Mother Carey's Chickens* (1938) and was subsequently seen in *Son of Frankenstein* (1939), *The Forgotten Woman* (1939), *Tower of London* (1939), *Vigil in the Night* (1940), and *Meet the Chump* (1941). It was usual practice to have adults impersonate children's voices in animated movies but Walt Disney insisted on kid actors for voicing the young animals in *Bambi*. The animators studied two fawns over the course of their first year of life and modeled Bambi after the real animals. For facial expressions, they used film footage of Dunagan recording the lines in the studio, After schooling, Dunagan joined the U.S. Marines and later worked in counter intelligence in Viet Nam. He told none of his fellow Marines that he had voiced Bambi, afraid it would undermine his ability to command fellow soldiers, Dunagan remained in the military until his retirement.

Duncan, Michael Clarke (b. 1957) A large, deep-voiced African American actor of movies and television, he provided the voice for the wise old bear Tug in *Brother Bear* (2003). He was born in Chicago and hoped for a career in sports but was forced to quit college to help support his family. After working at menial jobs in Chicago, Duncan went to Los Angeles where he was hired as a body guard for various film stars. His acting career began with a role in a television episode in 1995 and soon he was acting in such series as *The Fresh Prince of Bel-Air, Married with Children*, and *The Jaime Foxx Show*. Duncan made his screen debut in *Friday* (1995) and was noticed in such movies as *Bulworth* (1998), *Armageddon* (1998), *Breakfast of Champions* (1999), *The Green Mile* (1999), *The Whole Nine Yards* (2000), *Planet of the Apes* (2001), *Pursued* (2004), *School for Scoundrels* (2006), *American Crude* (2008), and *Slammin' Salmon* (2009). He reprised his Tug in the sequel *Brother Bear 2* (2006) and can be heard in other animated videos and movies such as *George of the Jungle 2* (2003), *Kim Possible: A Stitch in Time* (2003), *Land Before Time XI: Invasion of the Tinysauruses* (2004), *Dinotopia: Quest for the Ruby Sunstone* (2005), and *Kung Fu Panda* (2008), as well as the cartoon series *King of the Hill, Spider-Man, The Proud Family, Teen Titans, The Adventures of Jimmy Neutron: Boy Genius*, and *Family Guy*.

Duncan, Sandy (b. 1946) A tiny, perky singer-actress with a wide smile, she possesses a squeaky but pleasant little voice that has often limited her to lightweight roles but made her ideal for voicing animated characters, such as the very feminine fox Vixey in *The Fox and the Hound* (1981). Sandra Kay Duncan was born in Henderson, Texas, educated at Lon Morris College, and soon was performing in musicals in her home state. She made her Broadway debut in the 1965 revival of *The Music Man*, followed by featured roles in the musical revivals *Carousel* (1966), *Finian's Rainbow* (1967), *The Sound of Music* (1967), and *The Boy Friend* (1970). Duncan had her biggest stage hit as *Peter Pan* (1979) in the longest-running Broadway production of that musical on record. She made her film debut in Disney's *Million Dollar Duck* (1971) and has appeared in a handful of movies but is more famous for her many televisions appearances, from commercials and variety shows to serious dramas. Among her TV credits are *Bonanza, The Six Million Dollar Man, The Bionic Woman, Valerie's Family, Omnibus, Law & Order*, and her own series *Funny Face* and *The Sandy Duncan Show*, as well as the television movies and miniseries *Pinocchio* (1976), *Roots* (1977), and *My Boyfriend's Back* (1989). Duncan's other movies include *Star-Spangled Girl* (1971), *The Cat from Outer Space* (1978), *Survivor* (1987), and *Never Again* (2001). She has appeared on Disney specials such as *Sandy in Disneyland* (1974) and *Christmas in Disneyland* (1976) but, aside from *The Fox and the Hound*, her voices for animated films and television shows have been for other companies. She can he heard in *My Little Pony* (1984) and its TV series, *Rock-a-Doodle* (1991), and *The Swan Princess* (1994). Biography: *The Sandy Duncan Story*, Rochelle Reed (1973).

Dunn, Evan A child television actor, he was one of the three boys who voiced the young alien Kirby in *Chicken Little* (2005). Dunn also appeared on four episodes of the television series *Sleeper Cell* in 2006.

Dunn, Teala A teenage television actress on the small screen since 2002, she provided the voice of Bunny in the animated section of *Enchanted* (2007). Dunn has played recurring characters on such television sitcoms as *The Wonder Pets, The Naked Brothers Band,* and *Are We There Yet?*

Durst, Debi (b. 1953) A stand-up comedienne who appears in comedy clubs in the San Francisco area, she provided the voices of tubby little Corpse Kid, his Corpse Mom, and the Small Witch who all pop in and out of *The Nightmare Before Christmas* (1993). A native of San Francisco, she often performs with her husband Will Durst, the nationally-known political comic, in clubs, on television, and on the Internet. She appeared on the television program *Whose Line Is It Anyway?* and can be heard in the animated film *Monkeybone* (2001).

Dworsky, Sally A singer-songwriter heard on albums, television, and on the soundtracks for movies, she supplied the singing voice for the adult lioness Nala in *The Lion King* (1994), introducing the Oscar-winning song "Can You Feel the Love Tonight?" Growing up in St. Paul, Minnesota, Dworsky began singing with various groups and eventually worked her way to Los Angeles where she harmonized in the recording studio with top singers. She made her television debut as a singer in the musical specials *The Marvelous Land of Oz* (1981) and *Puss in Boots* (1982). Dworsky reprised her singing Nala in the video *Mickey's Magical Christmas: Snowed in at the House of Mouse* (2001) and can also be heard singing in the animated films *Mulan* (1998) and *Prince of Egypt* (1998). She occasionally sings on the radio program *A Prairie Home Companion* and has recorded albums of her own composition.

Earnhardt, Dale, Jr. (b. 1974) A professional race car driver known from the NASCAR Sprint Cup and other competitions, he provided the voice of the JR Motorsports #8 racer Junior in *Cars* (2006). He was born Ralph Dale Earnhardt, Jr., in Kannapolis, North Carolina, the son of race car driver Dale Earnhardt, Sr., and was a professional racer by the age of seventeen. He would go on to win eighteen Sprint Cup races and twenty-three Nationwide Series championships. Earnhardt also provided a voice for an episode of the television cartoon series *Handy Manny*.

Ebeling, Lulu A child performer who voiced the dentist's sadistic niece Darla in *Finding Nemo* (2003), she has no other film or television credits. Like the toy-torturer Sid Phillips in *Toy Story* (1995), Darla is a particularly gruesome Disney villain because she is so young yet fully formed in her sense of sadism. The character was named after Pixar producer Darla K. Anderson.

Eddy, Nelson (1901–1967) The stiff but lyrical king of Hollywood operettas who is most remembered for his films with Jeanette MacDonald, he gave a tour de force performance in "The Whale Who Wanted to Sing at the Met" section of *Make Mine Music* (1946) in which he did the speaking and singing voices for the narrator and all the characters, including the operatic Willie the Whale, the Italian impresario Professor Tetti Tatti, the scruffy seagull Whitey, the ancient Mephistopheles, and the heroine Isolde. Nelson Ackerman Eddy was born in Providence, Rhode Island, and was a boy soprano in church choirs until he was old enough to get jobs as a telephone operator and a news reporter. He grew up in Philadelphia where he joined the local Civic Opera, then toured in operettas until he was signed to a Hollywood contract in 1933, the year he made his screen debut. After the movie musicals *Broadway to Hollywood* (1933), *Dancing Lady* (1933), and *Student Tour* (1924), Eddy was teamed with MacDonald in *Naughty Marietta* (1935); the duo was an immediate hit and the two were paired in seven more musicals: *Rose Marie* (1936), *Maytime* (1937), *Sweethearts* (1938), *The Girl of the Golden West* (1938), *New Moon* (1940), *I Married an Angel* (1942), and *Bitter Sweet* (1940). He also starred with different leading ladies in *Rosalie* (1937), *Let Freedom Ring* (1939), *Balalaika* (1939), *The Chocolate Soldier* (1941), *The Phantom of the Opera* (1943), *Knickerbocker Holiday* (1944) and *Northwest Outpost* (1947). In the 1950s he concentrated on radio, concerts, nightclubs, recordings, and television where he had his own show. The baby-faced, wavy-haired baritone may seem the stuff of parody today but he was considered a dashing romantic figure in his day and he and MacDonald were the most famous singing team in Hollywood history. Eddy's performance in *Make Mine Music* is important because it reveals a playful side of the singer rarely captured in his live-action movies. His various voices for the Willie the Whale sequence are musically impressive and his sense of comedy is refreshingly sportive. Biographies: *Nelson Eddy: America's Favorite Baritone*, Gail Lulay (2000); *Nelson Eddy: The Opera Years*, Sharon Rich (2001).

Edmiston, Walker (1925–2007) A prolific character actor who was busy in radio, television, and films for fifty years, he voiced one of Ratigan's mouse Thugs in *The Great Mouse Detective* (1986). He was born in St. Louis, Missouri, and trained for an acting career at the Pasadena Playhouse. His ability to do many different voices brought him to the attention of filmmaker Walter Lantz who cast Edmiston as Wally the Walrus and other characters in cartoon shorts. By the 1950s he was doing voice work for *Time for Beany* and other television series and he had his own children's program, *The Walker*

Edminston Show, in which he created and voiced a variety of puppet characters. Working with puppeteers Sid and Marty Croft, he supplied voices for many of their puppet creations as well. Among his many cartoon series credits over the years are *H. R. Pufnstuf, The Bugaloos, Lidsville, Sigmund and the Sea Monsters, Yogi's Gang, The Smurfs, The Chipmunks, The Transformers, Adventures of the Gummi Bears, Spider-Man,* and *Avatar: The Last Airbender.* Edmiston frequently appeared on the big and little screen as well, acting in such television series as *Maverick, Green Acres, Star Trek, The Wild Wild West, The Big Valley, Mission: Impossible, Gunsmoke, Land of the Lost, Barnaby Jones, The Waltons, Little House on the Prairie, Dallas,* and *Knots Landing,* and in several movies, including *Stagecoach* (1966), *The Green Berets* (1968), *One More Train to Rob* (1971), *Scared to Death* (1981), *The Bear* (1984), *Fat Man and Little Boy* (1989), and *Diner* (1992).

Edwards, Cliff (1895–1971) The high-pitched singer, known as Ukulele Ike for his strumming on the ukulele as he sang, who was one of the most popular singers of his day, he is mostly remembered today as the voice of Jiminy Cricket in *Pinocchio* (1940) and other Disney features, shorts, and television shows. Clifton A. Edwards was born in Hannibal, Missouri, and left school at the age of fourteen to go to St. Louis to sing in saloons. His recording of "Ja Da" was a hit and he became a headliner in vaudeville and was featured in the Broadway musicals *The Mimic World* (1921), *Lady, Be Good!* (1924), and *Ziegfeld Follies* (1927). Edwards introduced "Singin' in the Rain" in his first film, *Hollywood Revue of 1929,* and was also featured (often playing himself) in a handful of movies in the 1930s and 1940s, including *Lord Byron of Broadway* (1930), *Shipmates* (1931), *Sidewalks of New York* (1931), *Take a Chance* (1933), *The Girl of the Golden West* (1938), *Gone with the Wind* (1939), *His Girl Friday* (1940), *Overland to Deadwood* (1942), *Sagebrush Law* (1943), and *The Avenging Rider* (1943). In *Pinocchio,* Edwards got to introduce what is perhaps the most famous of all Disney songs, "When You Wish Upon a Star." The character of Jiminy was so popular that he returned as the host of the anthology feature *Fun and Fancy Free* (1946). The nameless cricket in the original Collodi story *Pinocchio* is a very minor character but Walt Disney suggested the character be enlarged into a narrator, commentator, and sidekick to the hero. His instinct was right and Jiminy Cricket remains one of the most beloved Disney creations. Edwards' other notable Disney credit is *Dumbo* (1941) in which he did the speaking and singing voice of Jim (or Dandy) Crow. Edwards had his own television show in 1949, appeared on many other programs, and continued to voice Jiminy in dozens of Disney programs on the small screen until 1960. When Edwards died penniless in 1971, the Disney company paid for his funeral.

Edwards, Paddi (1931–1999) A character actress often seen in TV-movies, she did the voices of Ursula's sinister eel henchmen Flotsam and Jetsam in *The Little Mermaid* (1989) and the creepy Atropos, one of the Fates, in *Hercules* (1997). Edwards made her television debut in 1962 and over the years she appeared on many series, including *Laverne & Shirley, CHiPs, Newhart, Remington Steele, Cheers, Murphy Brown, Star Trek: The Next Generation, Night Court, Married with Children,* and *Ellen,* but she often got better roles in made-for-TV movies, such as *Rape and Marriage: The Rideout Cast* (1980), *Wait Till Your Mother Gets Home* (1983), *The Murder of Sherlock Holmes* (1984), *Under the Influence* (1986), and *Casualties of Love: The Long Island Lolita Story* (1993). Among her film credits are *Corvette Summer* (1978), *Halloween III: Season of the Witch* (1982), *To Be or Not to Be* (1983), and *Surrender* (1987). Flotsam and Jetsam (named after bits of ship wreckage that float on the sea) are electric eels and the directors of *The Little Mermaid* wanted them to have an eery and electrical sound. Edwards recorded the vocals then they were electronically processed to sound less human. Edwards reprised her Flotsam and Jetsam in the TV series *The Little Mermaid* and her Atropos in the video sequel *Hercules: Zero to Hero* (1999) and the *Hercules* television series. She can also be heard in the cartoon series *Batman* and *Timon and Pumbaa,* and in the animated videos *Edith Ann: Homeless Go Home* (1994), and *An Extremely Goofy Movie* (2000).

Edwards, Sam (1915–2004) A character actor whose long career included theatre, radio, film, and television, he provided (with Tim Davis) the voice of Adult Thumper in *Bambi* (1942). He was born in Macon, Georgia, into a family of actors and was carried onto the stage as a baby. During the Depression the family found success in radio with such shows as *The Adventures of Sunny and Buddy* and *The Edwards Family.* After entertaining the troops around the globe during World War II, Edwards concentrated on film and played rural, down-to-earth characters in several movies, including *Larceny* (1948), *The Street with No Name* (1948), *Twelve O'Clock High* (1949), *The Sun Sets at Dawn* (1950), *Witness to Murder* (1954), *Revolt in the Big House* (1958), *The Absent-Minded Professor* (1961), *Three Guns for Texas* (1968), *The Cheyenne Social Club* (1970), *Escape to Witch Mountain* (1975), and *The Postman Always Rings Twice* (1981). From the 1950s on he was kept busy in television, appearing on dozens of TV series including *I Love Lucy,*

Dragnet, Peter Gunn, Wagon Train, Hazel, The Andy Griffith Show, Green Acres, The Virginian, Gunsmoke, Barnaby Jones, and *Little House on the Prairie.* Edwards was heard in the animated television series *The Flintstones* and *Jonny Quest.*

Efron, Marshall (b. 1938) A roly-poly character actor, author, and radio favorite who has also voiced many TV cartoons, movies, and videos, he provided the voice for Larry the Duck in *Home on the Range* (2004). Efron first found success as a humorous commentator on radio stations in New York, Los Angeles, and on PBS radio, then made his screen debut in 1967, going on to make appearances in such movies as *THX 1138* (1971), *Bang the Drum Slowly* (1973), *California Dreaming* (1979), *Growing Pains* (1984), *The Road to Wellville* (1994), and *City Island* (2009). He found more success on television as a member of the cast of *The Great American Dream Machine* in 1971 and as a voice actor for such cartoon series as *The Smurfs, Pink Panther and Sons, The Transformers, The Kwicky Koala Show,* and *The 13 Ghosts of Scooby-Doo.* Efron can also be heard in the animated movies and videos *It's an O.K. Life* (1980), *Twice Upon a Time* (1983), *Fluppy Dogs* (1986), *The Big Bang* (1987), *Robots* (2005), *Ice Age: The Meltdown* (2006), and *Horton Hears a Who!* (2008). He is the author of several children's books and he hosted the children's television program *Marshall Efron's Illustrated, Simplified, and Painless Sunday School* in the 1970s.

Egan, Susan (b. 1970) A lively actress-singer of the stage who occasionally voices animated characters, she played the smart and worldly-wise Megara who is forced to work for Hades in *Hercules* (1997). Susan Farrell Egan was born in Seal Beach, California, and attended the University of Southern California before getting cast in major roles in the touring productions of *Bye Bye Birdie* and *State Fair.* She made an auspicious Broadway debut as Belle in the original stage production of *Beauty and the Beast* (1994) and also appeared on Broadway in *Triumph of Love* (1997), *Cabaret* (1999), and *Thoroughly Modern Millie* (2004). Egan has acted on such television series as *Almost Perfect, Party of Five, The Drew Carey Show, Nikki, NYPD Blue, Numb3rs,* and *House.* The character of "Meg" in *Hercules* is a unique Disney heroine because she is forced to be a helper to Hades, thereby making her a villain's sidekick. Also, having been burnt by a faithless lover, she is not interested in love. Despite the mythological setting of the movie, Meg is a very contemporary female in that she is a woman with a lot of emotional baggage. Her romance with Hercules is unconventional and very rocky, though it does end up traditionally. Egan's vocals for the character are playfully sarcastic and have a smart and cynical tone to them, making her all the more appealing. She reprised her Megara in the TV cartoon series *Hercules* and *House of Mouse,* and in the video *Hercules: Zero to Hero* (1999). Egan can also be heard in the animated video *Lady and the Tramp II: Scamp's Adventure* (2001) and the film *Spirited Away* (2001)

Eggar, Samantha (b. 1939) An English actress who often worked in American films and television, she voiced the goddess Hera, Hercules mother, in *Hercules* (1997). She was born Victoria Louise Samantha Marie Elizabeth Therese Eggar in London, the daughter of a British Army Major, and began her career playing classic roles on the stage. She made her television debut in 1961 and her first movie the following year, going on to act in such films as *The Collector* (1965), *Walk Don't Run* (1966), *Doctor Dolittle* (1967), *A Name for Evil* (1973), *The Exterminator* (1980), *Dark Horse* (1992), and *The Astronaut's Wife* (1999). Eggar was featured in many made-for-TV dramas on both sides of the Atlantic and appeared in such American series as *Columbo, Starsky and Hutch, Family, Fantasy Island, The Love Boat, Falcon Crest, Santa Barbara, Matlock, Star Trek: The Next Generation,* and *All My Children.* She can be heard in the television cartoon series *The Legend of Prince Valiant* and *Hercules,* as well as in the animated videos *P. J. Sparkles* (1992), *The Magic Voyage* (1992), and *Siegfried & Roy: Masters of the Impossible* (1996).

Eggleston, Ralph (b. 1965) A storyboard artist, character designer, and animator, he voiced the large and awkward Bird who upsets the smaller ones on a wire in the Pixar short *For the Birds* (2000) which he also directed. He was born in Baton Rouge, Louisiana, and by the time he was twenty years old was animating television cartoon specials such as *The Pound Puppies* (1985), *Garfield: His 9 Lives* (1988), and *Garfield's Thanksgiving* (1989). Eggleston designed characters and/or backgrounds for such movies as *FernGully: The Last Rainforest* (1992), *Toy Story* (1995), *Monsters, Inc.* (2001), *Finding Nemo* (2003), *The Incredibles* (2004), *WALL-E* (2008), and *Up* (2009). He has also designed the title sequences for the films *Hollywood Harry* (1986) and *Christmas Vacation* (1989).

Elfman, Danny (b. 1953) An innovative and in-demand film and television composer who often works with director Tim Burton, he provided the singing voice of the "Pumpkin King" Jack Skellington in *The Nightmare Before Christmas* (1993), as well as the malicious child Barrel and the Clown with the tear-away face. Daniel Robert Elfman was born in Los Angeles, the son of two teachers, and dropped out of high school to sing and play in various bands as he traveled the world. He and his brother Richard founded the band The Mystic Knights of the Oingo Boingo in Paris and it was featured in the film *Forbidden Zone* (1980) as was Elfman's score. While the band continued on for two decades, he found success composing the songs and/or soundtrack scores for such movies as *Pee-wee's Big Adventure* (1985), *Back to School* (1986), *Summer School* (1987), *Beetlejuice* (1988), *Scrooged* (1988), *Batman* (1989), *Dick Tracy* (1990), *Edward Scissorhands* (1990), *Batman Returns* (1992), *The Nightmare Before Christmas, Mission: Impossible* (1996), *Men in Black* (1997), *Flubber* (1997), *Spider-Man* (2002) and its sequels, *Charlie and the Chocolate Factory* (2005), *Corpse Bride* (2005), *Meet the Robinsons* (2007), *Milk* (2008), and *Alice in Wonderland* (2010). Elfman has also composed the theme music for several television series, including *Pee-wee's Playhouse, Tales from the Crypt, Beetlejuice, The Simpsons, Batman: The Animated Series, Dilbert, Desperate Housewives*, and *Point Pleasant*. He has appeared in the films *Hot Tomorrows* (1977), *I Never Promised You a Rose Garden* (1977), *Forbidden Zone* (1980), *Back to School*, and *The Gift* (2000), did the voice of an Oompa Loompa in *Charlie and the Chocolate Factory*, and voiced Bonejangles in the animated movie *The Corpse Bride*.

Ellis, Robert (1933–1973) A youthful-looking actor who was able to play kids and teenagers well into his twenties, he voiced Cubby, the Lost Boy in a bearskin, in *Peter Pan* (1953). He was born in Chicago and performed on the radio as a teenager, eventually playing the juvenile hero Henry Aldrich in the radio show *The Aldrich Family* in the early 1950s. Ellis made his screen debut in *April Showers* (1948), followed by such films as *The Babe Ruth Story* (1948), *Mexican Hayride* (1948), *The Green Promise* (1949), *El Paso* (1949), *A Kiss for Corliss* (1949), *Call Me Mister* (1951), *Niagara* (1953), *Prisoner of War* (1954), *The Long Gray Line* (1955), *The McConnell Story* (1955), *Pillars of the Sky* (1956), *Space Master X-7* (1958), *Gidget* (1959), and *Don't Give Up the Ship* (1959). Among the many television series he appeared on are *Meet Corliss Archer, I Love Lucy, Big Town, Schlitz Playhouse, The Loretta Young Show, The Lone Ranger, The Bob Cummings Show, The Adventures of Jim Bowie, The Life and Legend of Wyatt Earp, The George Burns and Gracie Allen Show, Death Valley Days*, and *M Squad*. Ellis retired from acting at the age of twenty-seven, returning to television only once for a Jackie Gleason special in 1973 before his premature death at forty.

Elmore, Sean A child performer, he was one of the three kids who voiced the young alien Kirby in *Chicken Little* (2005). He has no other film or television credits.

English, Liz As a child, she voiced the haughty Parisian kitten Marie in *The Aristocats* (1970) and can be heard singing "Scales and Arpeggios" and "Everybody Wants to Be a Cat" with the rest of the felines in that movie. She has no other film or television credits.

Epstein, Alvin (b. 1925) A versatile stage actor who has enjoyed one of the most diverse theatre careers on record, acting around the world in productions ranging from absurdist drama to Broadway musicals, one of his rare movies is *Beauty and the Beast* (1991) for which he provided the voice of the friendly Bookseller. He was born in the Bronx, New York City, the son of a doctor, and was educated at the High School of the Performing Arts and Fordham University before studying dance with Martha Graham, mime with Etienne Decroux, and acting with Sanford Meisner. Epstein made his Off Broadway debut in 1946, then traveled the world and performed in Europe and the Middle East. His Broadway debut in 1956 was with mime Marcel Marceau, the same year he acted with Orson Welles in *King Lear* and played Lucky in the American premiere of the Theatre of the Absurd classic *Waiting for Godot*. Epstein's other New York stage credits include *Endgame* (1958 and 1984), *No Strings* (1962), *A Midsummer Night's Dream* (1967), *A Kurt Weill Cabaret* (1979), *The Waltz of the Toreadors* (1985), *3 Penny Opera* (1989), and *Tuesdays with Morrie* (2002). He has acted in a handful of television dramas and such movies as *Never Met Picasso* (1996), *Beacon Hill* (2003), and *We Pedal Uphill* (2008). Epstein founded the Berkshire Theatre Festival in Massachusetts and ran the Yale Repertory Theatre and the Guthrie Theatre in the 1970s.

Ermey, R. Lee (b. 1944) A military career-man who often played military characters and acted as consultant on war movies. he provided the voice of the efficient toy soldier Army Sarge who leads the troops in *Toy Story* (1995) and its two sequels. Ronald Lee Ermey was born in Emporia, Kansas, and enlisted in the U.S. Marines, serving in Viet Nam and Japan and reaching the rank of Gunnery Sergeant. When he had to retire from the military due to health reasons, he moved to the Philippines and studied criminology and theatre at the University of Manila. He made his screen debut as a sergeant in *The Boys in Company C* (1978), also acting as military advisor on the film as he did for other movies as well. Ermey soon developed into a notable character actor in a variety of films, including *Apocalypse Now* (1979), *Purple Hearts* (1984), *Full Metal Jacket* (1987), *Mississippi Burning* (1988), *Demonstone* (1989), *The Siege of Firebase Gloria* (1989), *Fletch Lives* (1989), *The Rift* (1990), *Kid*

(1990), *Toy Soldiers* (1991), *Chain of Command* (1994), *Love Is a Gun* (1994), *Se7en* (1995), *Dead Man Walking* (1995), *The Frighteners* (1996), *Dead Men Can't Dance* (1997), *Gunshy* (1998), *The Sender* (1998), *Avalanche* (1999), *The Chaos Factor* (2000), *Jericho* (2000), *Saving Silverman* (2001), *Taking Sides* (2001), *On the Borderline* (2001), *The Salton Sea* (2002), *Birdseye* (2002), *The Texas Chainsaw Massacre* (2003) and its 2006 sequel, *Man of the House* (2005), and *Solstice* (2008), as well as several made-for-TV movies. Among the television series he has appeared in are *Miami Vice, China Beach, The Adventures of Brisco County Jr., The X-Files, JAG, Promised Land, Cracker: Mind Over Murder, Action, The District, Scrubs,* and *House*. Ermey can be heard doing voices for the TV cartoon series *The Simpsons, The Angry Beavers, Roughnecks: The Starship Troopers Chronicles, Family Guy, Fillmore!, Kim Possible, The Grim Adventures of Billy & Mandy, Father of the Pride, SpongeBob SquarePants,* and *Batman: The Brave and the Bold*. The character of Sarge in the *Toy Story* films was based on countless war movies featuring a fearless, dedicated commander who barks rather than talks. Originally the Sergeant was going to be a G.I. Joe toy but Hasbro, the company that manufactured the soldier doll, denied permission because one of the dolls gets blown up by the neighbor Sid. Instead, the familiar green plastic military toys were used. The animators had no difficulty creating the look of the toy soldiers but, because the feet were always fastened to a base, the challenge was how to have them move. So the animators glued their shoes to boards and hobbled around the studio, developing the unique movements for Sarge and his men.

Essman, Susie (b. 1955) A comedienne and character actress with a provocative, funny voice, she found recognition on television and has made a few films, including *Bolt* (2008) for which she provided the voice of the bossy alley cat Mittens. She was born in the Bronx, New York City, grew up in Mt. Vernon, New York, and was educated at the State University of New York at Purchase. Essman began her career as a stand-up comic, touring the country and eventually getting seen on television on such series as *Kate & Allie, Baby Boom, Hardcore TV,* and *Law and Order,* but she is most known for her shrewish wife Susie Greene on *Curb Your Enthusiasm*. Her film credits include *Crocodile Dundee II* (1988), *Volcano* (1997), *Keeping the Faith* (2000), *The Secret Lives of Dentists* (2002), and *Cop Out* (2010), and she can be heard on the animated TV series *Kim Possible, Crank Yankers,* and *American Dad*. The character of the cynical cat Mittens in *Bolt* is very modern in temperament and attitude. She is domineering and even cruel, yet her painful past sometimes slips out and she loses her tough exterior. Essman's vocals for the role are masterful, filled with sarcasm but still vulnerable. She reprised her Mittens in the animated short *Super Rhino* (2009). Biography: *What Would Susie Say* (2009).

Evans, Monica (b. 1940) A British actress with a handful of American credits, she voiced the English spinster goose Abigail Gabble in *The Aristocats* (1970) and the vixen heroine Maid Marian in *Robin Hood* (1973). Evans trained at the Royal Academy of Dramatic Art and had London stage experience when in 1962 she was cast as the recurring character of Sally Henderson on *Compact,* one of the first British television soap operas. She went to New York to play the character of the English "bird" Cecily Pigeon in the original Broadway cast of *The Odd Couple* (1965). Evans reprised her performance in the 1968 film version and also in the TV series, then returned to England for the rest of her stage career.

Everhart, Rex (1920–2000) A character actor primarily from the stage, he played a variety of types on television specials and series as well as in a handful of films, including *Beauty and the Beast* (1991) for which he provided the voice of Belle's father, the crackpot inventor Maurice. He was born in Watseka, Illinois, and by 1955 he was appearing on Broadway in the comedy *No Time for Sergeants*. Among his many other Broadway credits are *Tall Story* (1959), *Peer Gynt* (1960), *Tenderloin* (1960), *Skyscraper* (1965), *How Now Dow Jones* (1967), *The Iceman Cometh* (1973), *Chicago* (1977), *Working* (1978), and *Anything Goes* (1987), but he is most remembered for his many performances as Benjamin Franklin in *1776* in the original 1969 production, on tour, and in the 1997 revival. Everhart made his television debut in 1951 but did not perform on the small screen regularly until the 1960s. He made a few films, including *The Seven-Ups* (1973), *The Rosary Murders* (1987), and *Family Business* (1989), then became famous as Enos the tow-truck driver in *Friday the 13th* (1980) and *Friday the 13th Part 2* (1981). The character of Maurice in *Beauty and the Beast* is one in a long line of bumbling fathers in Disney films. Yet because he is an inventor who is out of touch with the real world, Maurice is more endearing than most such ineffectual fathers. Everhart's vocals are sportive yet sincere, keeping Maurice from becoming a clown and being inconsequential.

Eyster, Tim (b. 1978) A child performer mostly on television until he retired at the age of twenty, he provided the voice of one of the two street Kids in the Mickey Mouse featurette *The Prince and the*

Pauper (1990). Timothy Richard Eyster was born in Tarzana, California, and made his television debut at the age of nine on an episode of *Santa Barbara*. He played children in such series as *Family Ties, Hard Time on Planet Earth, Matlock, Married with Children, Get a Life, Dallas, Life Goes On*, and *Babylon 5*, though he is probably best known as Sponge on *Salute Your Shorts*. Eyster can be seen in the films and TV-movies *The Night Train to Kathmandu* (1988), *Prayer for the Rollerboys* (1990), *The Dreamer of Oz* (1990), and *Alligator II: The Mutation* (1991).

Fabio (b. 1959) The long-haired, hunky international model and author who later turned to acting, he supplied the voice of the Woodsman who has perfect hair in the short *Redux Riding Hood* (1997). He was born Fabio Lanzoni in Milan, Italy, and began modeling in his homeland before moving to New York City where he became a sensation in magazines and posed for the covers of romance paperbacks. Fabio retired from modeling in 1991 and concentrated on writing romantic fiction and appearing in commercials, on television talk shows, and in such movies as *Death Becomes Her* (1992), *Bubble Boy* (2001), and *Al's Brain in 3-D* (2009). He has also acted in the TV series *Dangerous Curves, Acapulco H.E.A.T., Boogies Diner, Rachel Gunn R.N., Arli$$*, and *Comedy Gumbo*. Fabio often pokes fun at his own macho image in his roles, as with *Redux Riding Hood* and the TV cartoon series *Stripperella*.

Fagerbakke, Bill (b. 1957) A busy voice artist and television actor, he supplied the voice of the Oafish Guard in *The Hunchback of Notre Dame* (1996). William Mark Fagerbakke was born in Fontana, California, and was educated at the University of Idaho and Southern Methodist University before making his film debut in *Perfect Strangers* (1984). A handful of movies followed but he would find much more work voicing such TV cartoon series as *Gargoyles, Jumanji, The Wild Thornberrys, Batman Beyond, Roughnecks: The Starship Troopers Chronicles, The Legend of Tarzan, The Grim Adventures of Billy & Mandy, W.I.T.C.H., Heroes, Kim Possible, Transformers: Animated, Batman: The Brave and the Bold*, and *SpongeBob SquarePants* in which he voices Patrick Starfish. Fagerbakke has provided voices for many animated videos, including *3×3 Eyes* (1991), *Gargoyles: the Heroes Awaken* (1995) and several of its sequels, *Hercules: Zero to Hero* (1999), *Lady and the Tramp II: Scamp's Adventure* (2001), *Atlantis: Milo's Return* (2003), *Jimmy Neutron's Nicktoon Blast* (2003), *Balto III: Wings of Change* (2004), *The SpongeBob SquarePants Movie* (2004), *Family Guy Presents Stewie Griffin: The Untold Story* (2005), *The Madagascar Penguins in a Christmas Caper* (2005), and *Legend of Frosty the Snowman* (2005), He has appeared on such television series as *The Stand, Burke's Law, Oz, Grey's Anatomy, How I Met Your Mother*, and *'Til Death*, although he is probably best known as Dauber Dybinski on *Coach*.

Fall, James Apaumut The Native American actor-singer who voiced Kocoum, the brave warrior who is betrothed to Pocahontas, in *Pocahontas* (1995) has only one other film credit: the Interpreter in the movie *Crazy for Love* (2005).

Farmer, Bill (b. 1952) A voice artist with an impeccable ability to impersonate celebrities, he has been the voice of Goofy and Pluto since 1987. William Farmer was born in Pratt, Kansas, and as a child copied the voices of his favorite cartoon characters. He began his career as a stand-up comic in Dallas, Texas, using some of these voices in his act. After he moved to California he performed on local television and radio and came to the attention of the Disney studio. Farmer first voiced Goofy in the television holiday special *DTV "Doggone" Valentine* (1987) and continued to provide the voice for Disney shorts and videos, the animated TV series *Goof Troop, Mickey Mouse Works, Raw Toonage, Bonkers, House of Mouse*, and *Mickey Mouse Clubhouse*, and in the features *A Goofy Movie* (1995) and *An Extremely Goofy Movie* (2000). For the film short *The Prince and the Pauper* (1990), Farmer also did the barks for Pluto and often reprised that character as well. Because of his vocal versatility, he has been used to voice many minor characters is such Disney features as *Beauty and the Beast* (1991), *Toy Story* (1995), *The Hunchback of Notre Dame* (1996), *Hercules* (1997), *A Bug's Life* (1998), *Toy Story 2* (1999), *Monsters, Inc.* (2001), *Brother Bear* (2003), *Home on the Range* (2004), *Cars* (2006), and *Meet the Robinsons* (2007), as well as many Disney videos, including *A Goof Troop Christmas* (1993), *Pocahontas 2: Journey to a New World* (1998), *Mickey's Once Upon a Christmas* (1999), *Kingdom Hearts* (2002), *The Lion King 1½* (2004), *Mickey's Great Clubhouse Hunt* (2007), and *Mickey's Adventures in Wonderland* (2009). Among Farmer's non–Disney credits are the TV cartoon series *Harvey Birdman: Attorney at Law, Robot Chicken, The Grim Adventures of Billy & Mandy, Jonah Hex: Motion Comics*, and *Mighty Mouse, the New Adventures*, as well as the movies and videos *Betty Boop's Hollywood Mystery* (1989), *Space Jam* (1996), *Casper: A Spirited Beginning* (1997), *The Iron Giant* (1999), *The Wacky Adventures of Ronald McDonald: Have Time, Will Travel* (2002), *Ice Age II: The Meltdown* (2006), *Happily N'Ever After* (2006), *Surf's Up* (2007), and *Horton Hears a Who!* (2008).

Farrow, Mia (b. 1945) A petite movie and television star who often plays frail or introspective characters, she provided the voice for the Wolf's disapproving wife Doris in the animated short *Redux Riding Hood* (1997). She was born Maria de Lourdes Villiers Farrow in Los Angeles, the daughter of director John Farrow (1904–1963) and film actress Maureen O'Sullivan (1911–1998), and did some modeling before getting cast in minor roles in the films *John Paul Jones* (1959) and *Guns at Batasi* (1964). Farrow first found recognition on the television series *Peyton Place* in the 1960s then became a movie star with the film *Rosemary's Baby* (1968). She was featured in such movies as *Secret Ceremony* (1968), *John and Mary* (1969), *See No Evil* (1971), *The Great Gatsby* (1974), *A Wedding* (1978), *Death on the Nile* (1978), and *Hurricane* (1979), then her career took a turn as she acted in thirteen films for director-actor Woody Allen and proved to be very versatile. Farrow portrayed very different characters in these Allen movies, in particular *A Midsummer Night's Sex Comedy* (1982), *Zelig* (1983), *Broadway Danny Rose* (1984), *The Purple Rose of Cairo* (1985), *Hannah and Her Sisters* (1986), *Alice* (1990), and *Husbands and Wives* (1992). Her subsequent films include *Coming Soon* (1999), *The Omen* (2006), *Arthur and the Invisibles* (2006) and its two sequels, and *Be Kind Rewind* (2008). Farrow has also starred in some TV-movies, most memorably *Johnny Belinda* (1967), *Peter Pan* (1976), *Forget Me Never* (1999), and *The Secret Life of Zoey* (2002), and did voices for the animated film *The Last Unicorn* (1982). Autobiography: *What Falls Away* (1997); biographies: *Mia Farrow: Flower Child, Madonna, Muse*, Sam Rubin, Richard Taylor (1989); *Mia: The Life of Mia Farrow*, Edward Z. Epstein (1992).

Feldman, Corey (b. 1971) A child performer in film and television who continues to work as an adult, he supplied the voice of Young Copper, the dog hero of *The Fox and the Hound* (1981). Corey Scott Feldman was born in Chatsworth, California, and made his first television commercial at the age of three. He appeared in his first sit-com in 1978 and was featured in kid roles in such series as *The Bad News Bears*, *Mork & Mindy*, *Madame's Place*, *The New Leave It to Beaver*, and *One Day at a Time*. Feldman made his screen debut in *Time After Time* (1979) and went on to make over seventy movies as a child and an adult, among them *Gremlins* (1984), *The Goonies* (1984), *Stand by Me* (1986), *The Lost Boys* (1987), *License to Drive* (1988), *Meatballs 4* (1992), *Maverick* (1994), *Storm Trooper* (1998), *My Life as a Troll* (2001), and *Lucky Fritz* (2009). He has appeared as an adult in such TV series as *Married with Children*, *Burke's Law*, *Dweebs*, *Sliders*, and *The Guardian*, and he can be heard in the animated series *Super Robot Monkey Team Hyperforce Go!*, as well as the movie *Teenage Mutant Ninja Turtles* (1990).

Felton, Verna (1890–1966) A versatile character actress with a husky, no-nonsense voice, she could play both warm and chilling characters, as evidenced in her variety of Disney roles that range from the temperamental Queen of Hearts in *Alice in Wonderland* (1951) to the caring Fairy Godmother in *Cinderella* (1950). She was born in Salinas, California, and acted in the theatre and on the radio before making her screen debut in 1939. Two years later she worked for Disney for the first time in *Dumbo*, providing voices for the loving mother Mrs. Jumbo and the stern Elephant Matriarch. Felton's other Disney credits are the uncaring Aunt Sarah in *Lady and the Tramp* (1955), the good fairy Flora in *Sleeping Beauty* (1959), and the elephant wife to Colonel Hathi in *The Jungle Book* (1967), as well as the short *Goliath II* (1960) in which she played yet another elephant, Eloise. After appearing in such movies as *The Gunfighter* (1950), *Belles on Their Toes* (1952), *Don't Bother to Knock* (1952), and *Picnic* (1955), she concentrated on television and acted in several series, most memorably *December Bribe* in which she played Hilda Crocker, a role she played in the spinoff *Pete and Gladys*. In some ways Felton's first Disney assignment, Mrs. Jumbo in *Dumbo*, was the most difficult. Dumbo's mother has only one word to speak: "Jumbo," when the stork asks the baby's name. Yet the animators built on Felton's warm tone of voice and made Mrs. Jumbo a deeply engaging character who, when she turns violent to protect her child, is one with whom anyone can empathize. Her Flora is the most mature and rational of the three fairies in *Sleeping Beauty*, as heard in her no-nonsense vocals. On the other hand her Aunt Sarah in *Lady and the Tramp* and elephant wife in *The Jungle Book* are formidable characters whose vocals do not tolerate any disagreement. Looking over her catalog of voices, it is clear that Felton was a masterful voice artist. She died one day before Walt Disney passed away.

Ferrer, Miguel (b. 1955) A character actor who usually plays villains on television and in movies, he voiced the ruthless Hun invader Shan Yu in *Mulan* (1998). He was born Miguel José Ferrer in Santa Monica, California, the son of actor-director José Ferrer (1912–1992) and singer Rosemary Clooney (1928–2002), and grew up in Hollywood. As a teenager he pursued music rather than acting and was a drummer in various bands, in particular the Jenerators, before studying acting at the Beverly Hills Playhouse. Ferrer made his television debut on an episode of *Magnum, P.I.* in 1981, going on to roles in such series as *Cagney & Lacey, Hill Street Blues, Miami Vice, Twin Peaks, Shannon's Deal, On the Air, The Stand, LateLine, Will & Grace, Bionic Woman, Law & Order: Criminal Intent*, and *Crossing Jordan* which he also directed on occasion. Among his film credits are *Heartbreaker* (1983), *Star Trek III: The Search for Spock* (1984), *RoboCop* (1987), *Deep Star Six* (1989), *The Guardian* (1990), *Twin Peaks: Fire Walk with Me* (1992), *Hot Shots! Part Deux* (1993), *Another Stakeout* (1993), *The Night Flier* (1997), *Mr. Magoo* (1997), *Traffic* (2000), *Sunshine State* (2002), *The Manchurian Candidate* (2004), and *Wrong Turn at Tahoe* (2009). Ferrer has provided voices for several TV cartoon series, including *Hercules, Superman, Jackie Chan Adventures, Robot Chicken, American Dad, The Batman*, and *The Spectacular Spider-Man*.

Fiedler, John (1925–2005) A diminutive but memorable character actor of stage, movies, and television known for his high-pitched voice and nervous demeanor, he was the voice of Piglet for many years and voiced other Disney characters such as the church mouse Father Sexton who plays the organ in *Robin Hood* (1973), Deacon the Owl in *The Rescuers* (1977), the Porcupine in *The Fox and the Hound* (1981), and the Old Man in *The Emperor's New Groove* (2000). John Donald Fiedler was born in Platteville, Wisconsin, the son of a beer salesman, and after serving in the Navy during World War II began his career in radio. Fiedler played major roles in such popular radio shows as *The Aldrich Family* and *Tom Corbett, Space Cadet* even as he was acting on the New York stage, performing on Broadway in *One Eye Closed* (1954), *Howie* (1958), *The Odd Couple* (1965), *Our Town* (1969), *The Crucible* (1991), *A Little Hotel on the Side* (1992), and other plays. His most memorable stage role was the white neighborhood representative Karl Lindner in *A Raisin in the Sun* (1959), a character he reprised in the 1961 film and the 1989 television versions of the play. Fiedler made a noteworthy screen debut as one of the jurors in *Twelve Angry Men* (1957) followed by such movies as *Sweet Smell of Success* (1957), *Stage Struck* (1958), *That Touch of Mink* (1962), *Kiss Me, Stupid* (1964), *A Fine Madness* (1966), *The Odd Couple* (1968), *True Grit* (1969), *The Fortune* (1975), *The Shaggy D.A.* (1976), *Harper Valley P.T.A.* (1978), *The Cannonball Run* (1981), and *Seize the Day* (1986). He appeared in dozens of television series, including *Armstrong Circle Theatre, Studio One in Hollywood, Peter Gunn, Dennis the Menace, The Many Loves of Dobie Gillis, Alfred Hitchcock Presents, Dr. Kildare, The Munsters, Star Trek, Bewitched, McMillan & Wife, The Odd Couple, Alice, Quincy M. E., Lobo, Buffalo Bill*, and *L.A. Law*, but he is perhaps best known as the reticent patient Mr. Emil Peterson on *The Bob Newhart Show*. The character of Piglet has long been one of the favorites in the menagerie of animals created by A. A. Milne but when Fiedler first voiced the nervous pig in the short *Winnie the Pooh and the Blustery Day* (1968), his popularity soared. Fiedler played Piglet for nearly forty years in feature films, shorts, and videos, such as *Winnie the Pooh and Tigger Too* (1974), *The Many Adventures of Winnie the Pooh* (1977), *Winnie the Pooh Discovers the Seasons* (1981), *Winnie the Pooh and a Day for Eyeore* (1983), *Winnie the Pooh and Christmas Too* (1991), *Pooh's Grand Adventure: The Search for Christopher Robin* (1997), *Winnie the Pooh: A Valentine for You* (1999), *The Tigger Movie* (2000), *Kingdom Hearts* (2002), *Piglet's Big Movie* (2003), and *Pooh's Heffalump Movie* (2005), and in the TV series *The New Adventures of Winnie the Pooh, The Book of Pooh*, and *House of Mouse*. Fiedler's last acting credit was voicing the video *The Emperor's New Groove 2: Kronk's New Groove* (2005).

Fierstein, Harvey (b. 1954) The sometimes outrageous and always fascinating writer and character actor with a raspy voice, he lent his unusual vocals to a handful of animated projects, including the scrappy Chinese recruit Yao in *Mulan* (1998). A native of Brooklyn, New York, Fierstein worked as a female impersonator at the age of fifteen then attended Pratt Institute before making his professional acting debut Off Off Broadway in 1971. He saw his first plays produced Off Off Broadway and in 1982 three of his one-acts were combined to make the Off Broadway and then Broadway hit *Torch Song Trilogy* in which he played the leading role of the drag queen Arnold. He has written other plays but has concentrated mostly on musicals since the 1980s, writing the librettos for the Broadway musicals *La Cage aux Folles* (1983), *Legs Diamond* (1988), and *A Catered Affair* (2008), also appearing in the last. He was busy in the 1990s acting on television and in films, then returned to his drag queen roots when he played the Baltimore housewife Edna Turnblad in the original Broadway cast of *Hairspray* (2002). Fierstein then shone in one of his few non-gay stage performances when he was a replacement on Broadway for Tevye in *Fiddler on the Roof* in 2004. Among his movie credits are *Garbo Talks* (1984), *Torch Song Trilogy* (1988), *Mrs. Doubtfire* (1993), *Independence Day* (1996), *Playing Mona Lisa* (2000), and *Death to Smoochy* (2002). Fierstein reprised his Yao in the videos *Mulan II* (2004) and *Kingdom Hearts II* (2005), provided voices for the non–Disney videos *The Sissy Duckling* (1999)—based on a children's book that he wrote—and *Farce of the Penguins* (2006), as well as the feature film *Foodfight!* (2009), and can be heard in the animated TV series *The Simpsons* and *Family Guy*.

Finn, Will An animator who worked on character designs and storyboards before becoming a writer and director of animated films, he voiced Hollywood Fish in *Chicken Little* (2005). Finn did character designs for such animated movies as *The Secret of Nimh* (1982), *Oliver & Company* (1988), *The Little Mermaid* (1989), *The Rescuers Down Under* (1990), *Beauty and the Beast* (1991), *Aladdin* (1992), *Happily Ever After* (19923), *A Goofy Movie* (1995), *Pocahontas* (1995), *The Hunchback of Notre Dame* (1996), and *Madagascar: Escape 2 Africa* (2008), sometimes contributing to the scripts as well. He directed *The Road to El Dorado* (2000), *Home on the Range* (2004), and the video shorts *A Dairy Tale* (2004) and *Hammy's Boomerang Adventure* (2006).

Firth, Peter (b. 1953) An English actor who found success on the stage early in his career then went on to act in many films and televisions shows on both sides of the Atlantic, he provided the voice of the doubting kangaroo Red in *The Rescuers Down Under* (1990). He was born in Bradford, England, the son of a pub owner, and was on the stage as a child. Firth left school at the age of sixteen and was featured in several British television programs before finding fame as the troubled youth Alan Strang in the play *Equus* (1973), first in London, then on Broadway, and in the 1977 film version. He matured from teenage roles to adult ones on stage and screen, and also appeared frequently in both British and American television, including the series *The Adventures of Black Beauty, The Flaxton Boys, Here Come the Double Deckers!, Walt Disney's Wonderful World of Color, Tales of the Unexpected, The Young Indiana Jones Chronicles, Highlander, Heartbeat, Resort to Murder, Total Recall: The Series, That's Life, Law & Order: Special Victims Unit,* and *MI-5*. Among his many notable films are *Brother Sun, Sister Moon* (1972), *King Arthur, the Young Warlord* (1975), *Aces High* (1976), *Joseph Andrews* (1977), *Tess* (1979), *Born of Fire* (1983), *Lifeforce* (1985), *Letter to Brezhnev* (1985), *The Hunt for Red October* (1990), *Shadowlands* (1993), *Amistad* (1997), *Mighty Joe Young* (1998), *Chill Factor* (1999), *Pearl Harbor* (2001), and *The Greatest Game Ever Played* (2005). Firth has often returned to the stage and he appeared on Broadway again in *Amadeus* (1980).

Fitzhugh, Ellen A musical theatre lyricist who performs on occasion, she voiced the saucy Bar Maid mouse in *The Great Mouse Detective* (1986). Fitzhugh has written the lyrics for the Off Broadway musicals *Herringbone* (1982), *Diamonds* (1984), and others, and her lyrics were heard on Broadway in *Grind* (1985).

Flaherty, Joe (b. 1941) The ingenious comic actor and writer with a seemingly endless supply of wacky characters, he voiced Jeb, the grouchy goat, in *Home on the Range* (2004). He was born in Pittsburgh, Pennsylvania, and began his career in Chicago with the comic improv group Second City. Moving to Toronto, Flaherty co-founded a Canadian version called Toronto Second City which became known first in clubs then on television in both Canada and in the States as *SCTV*. Like the other members of the troupe, Flaherty excelled at impersonations of celebrities and he also created original characterizations, some of which became popular favorites in both countries. Among his other television credits are the series *The David Steinberg Show, Maniac Mansion, Police Academy: The Series, Freaks and Geeks,* and *The King of Queens*, as well as voicing such cartoon series as *The Completely Mental Misadventures of Ed Grimley, Dinosaurs, The Legend of Tarzan,* and *Family Guy*. Flaherty appeared in several movies, including *Tunnel Vision* (1976), *1941* (1979), *Used Cars* (1980), *Johnny Dangerously* (1984), *Sesame Street Presents: Follow That Bird* (1985), *Club Paradise* (1986), *Innerspace* (1987), *Back to the Future Part II* (1989), *Snowboard Academy* (1996), *Happy Gilmore* (1996), *Freddie Got Fingered* (2001), *Slackers* (2002), and *Summerhood* (2008). He reprised his goat Jeb in the cartoon short *A Dairy Tale* (2004).

Fleischer, Charles (b. 1950) A stand-up comic and actor who has done a multitude of voices for animated movies and television series, he supplied the voices of the clownish "toon" Roger Rabbit, the reckless Benny the Cab, and Judge Doom's henchmen Greasy and Psycho in *Who Framed Roger Rabbit* (1988). He was born in Washington, D. C., and began to do stand-up comedy as a kid in summer camp. After studying at Southampton College of Long Island University and the Goodman Theatre School in Chicago, he performed in comedy clubs and played roles in the television series *Barney Miller, Keep on Truckin', The Richard Pryor Show,* and *Sugar Time* before finding recognition as Carvelli on *Welcome Back, Kotter*. Among his many subsequent TV credits are the series *Hill Street Blues, Aloha Paradise, Laverne & Shirley, The Paper Chase, Simon & Simon, Night Shift, Making a Living, Beverly Hills 90210, Tales from the Crypt, Kirk, Bone Chillers, The Weird Al Show, The Drew Carey Show,* and *Freddie*. Fleischer has appeared in many films and TV-movies, including *The Death of Ritchie* (1977), *Die Laughing* (1980), *A Nightmare on Elm Street* (1984), *Bad Dreams* (1988), *Back to the Future Part II* (1989), *Straight Talk* (1992), *Carry on*

Columbus (1992), *My Girl 2* (1994), *Ground Patrol* (1998), *Rusty: A Dog's Tale* (1998), *Genius* (1999), *Bel Air* (2000), *Big Monster on Campus* (2000), *G-Men from Hell* (2000), *Brain Juice* (2002), *The 4th Tenor* (2002), *Big Kiss* (2004), and *Zodiac* (2007). Roger Rabbit is not a typical Disney character but closer in spirit and animation to the Warner Brothers cartoon critters. Yet Roger is surely not like Warners' most famous rabbit, Bugs Bunny. The way Roger continually fails makes him more akin to the silent Wile E. Coyote. Fleischer's vocals for Roger are as exuberant and manic as the rabbit's movements, making him a hyper-clown driven to desperation yet still cracking jokes along the way. In order to stay in character during the recording sessions, Fleischer wore a complete rabbit outfit with rabbit ears. This led to rumors outside of the studio that Roger was to be a live-action character. Animator Richard Williams described Roger as having a Warner Brothers face but a Disney body. He also chose the red, white, and blue hues from the American flag for Roger's colors. Fleischer reprised his Roger Rabbit in the shorts *Tummy Trouble* (1989), *Roller Coaster Rabbit* (1990), and *Trail Mix-Up* (1993), and in the videos *Mickey's 60th Birthday* (1988), *Disney Sing-Along-Songs: Disneyland Fun* (1990), and *The Best of Roger Rabbit* (1996); and he reprised Benny the Cab on the TV series *House of Mouse*. The other cartoon series he has voiced include *Hard Times on Planet Earth*, *Weird Science*, *Buzz Lightyear of Star Command*, *100 Deeds for Eddie McDowd*, and *God, the Devil and Bob*, and the animated movies *Balto: Wolf Quest* (2002), *Balto III: Wings of Change* (2004), and *The Polar Express* (2004).

Fleming, Shaun (b. 1987) A teenage actor who grew up to become a busy voice artist, he provided the singing and speaking voice of the fourth grader Leonard Amadeus Helperman who has a smart dog in *Teacher's Pet* (2004). He was born in Westlake Village, California, and made his television debut at the age of nine in an episode of *Cyberkidz*. Fleming also appeared in the films *Operation Splitsville* (1999) and *Jeepers Creepers II* (2003), but the rest of his credits would be voicing such cartoon series as *Teacher's Pet*, *The Legend of Tarzan*, *Fillmore!*, *Kim Possible*, and *Lilo & Stitch*. He can also be heard in the animated videos *Mickey's Once Upon a Christmas* (1999), *Spot's Musical Adventures* (2000), *Kim Possible: A Stitch in Time* (2003), *The Lion King 1½* (2004), *Mickey's Twice Upon a Christmas* (2004), and *Kim Possible: So the Drama* (2005).

Flint, Shelby (b. 1939) A clear-voiced singer with some chart hits in the 1960s, she performed "The Journey" (aka "Who Will Rescue Me?") during the opening credits of *The Rescuers* (1977) as the bottle with Penny's note floats at sea. She was born in North Hollywood, California, and in 1961 had great success with her single "Angel on My Shoulder." Flint's other hit was "Cast Your Fate to the Wind" in 1966. She can be heard singing on the soundtracks for the films and videos *Snoopy Come Home* (1972), *Breezy* (1973), *The Borrowers* (1973), and *Hercules and Xena: The Battle for Mount Olympus* (1998). Flint voiced characters in the animated TV specials *The Stingiest Man in Town* (1978) and *Rudolph and Frosty's Christmas in July* (1979). The song that opens *The Rescuers* is very unusual, the lyric taking the point of view of the floating bottle, not the message inside. So the bottle and Flint's vocals become a character of sorts.

Flower, Jessie A young but experienced voice artist, she supplied the voice for Young Franny, the student who loses her frogs at the science fair, in *Meet the Robinsons* (2007). Flower has voiced children's roles in the feature films and videos *Finding Nemo* (2003), *The Emperor's New Groove 2: Kronk's New Groove* (2005), *Curious George* (2006), *Over the Hedge* (2006), *The Ant Bully* (2006), and *Brother Bear 2* (2006). She can also be heard in the TV cartoon series *The Emperor's New School*, *Avatar: The Last Airbender*, and *Random! Cartoons*.

Flynn, Dessie An actress with only one animated voice character, she provided the voice of the mischievous chipmunk Dale in a dozen Disney shorts between 1943 and 1956. Flynn was the first to voice Dale when the rodent team of Chip and Dale made its debut in *Private Pluto* (1943). She reprised her performance in such beloved shorts as *Chip an' Dale* (1947), *All in a Nutshell* (1949), *Pluto's Christmas Tree* (1952), *Corn Chips* (1951), and *Chips Ahoy* (1956), as well as on two television episodes of *Walt Disney's Wonderful World of Color*. When Chip and Dale were revived in new TV cartoons in the 1980s, Dale was usually voiced by Cory Burton or Tress MacNeille. The characters of Chip (with the black nose) and Dale (with the red nose) were created by the Disney animators as foils for Donald Duck. The excitable duck was at his best when annoyed or tormented by others and it wasn't in the personality of Mickey, Minnie, Pluto, or Goofy to harass Donald. His nephews Hewey, Dewey, and Louie often frustrated Donald but they were more playful than mean spirited. So the two little kleptomaniacs Chip and Dale were developed to keep Donald hassled. They often had the same effect on Pluto as well and before long the two chipmunks were among the most popular of Disney characters, appearing in over two dozen shorts and featured in many TV cartoon series.

Flynn, Joe (1924–1974) A nasal-voiced comic character actor who excelled at playing annoying and ineffective authority figures, his final role was voicing Mr. Snoops, Medusa's bumbling partner in crime, in *The Rescuers* (1977). Joseph A. Flynn was born in Youngstown, Ohio, and educated at Northwestern University before starting his career as a ventriloquist. He turned to comedy while serving in the Army's Special Services Branch during World War II and after he was discharged went to Hollywood, making his screen debut in 1948. Flynn had better luck in television, appearing in many series, including *Highway Patrol, Flight, Rescue 8, The George Gobel Show, Twilight Zone, M Squad, Wagon Train, Bachelor Father, The Danny Thomas Show, Hawaiian Eye, The Joey Bishop Show, The Jack Benny Program, Gunsmoke, The Adventures of Ozzie & Harriet, Batman, Laredo, I Dream of Jeannie, Family Affair, The Ghost and Mrs. Muir, The Tim Conway Show, That Girl, Alias Smith and Jones, The Girl Most Likely To*, and *Love, American Style*, but he is most remembered as the hectoring Capt. Binghamton in *McHale's Navy*, a role he played for four years and in the movies *McHale's Navy* (1964) and *McHale's Navy Joins the Air Force* (1965). Among his other films are *The Seven Little Foys* (1955), *The Desperate Hours* (1955), *The Boss* (1956), *Panama Sal* (1957), *This Happy Feeling* (1958), *The Last Time I Saw Archie* (1961), *Lover Come Back* (1961), *Son of Flubber* (1963), *Divorce American Style* (1967), *The Love Bug* (1968), *The Computer Wore Tennis Shoes* (1969), *The Barefoot Executive* (1971), *The Million Dollar Duck* (1971), *Now You See Him, Now You Don't* (1972), *Superdad* (1973), and *The Strongest Man in the World* (1975). The character of Mr. Snoops in *The Rescuers* was based on the film critic and historian John Culhane who was visiting the Disney studios for an interview and found the animators sketching him as he asked his questions. When the film was released, Culhane was proud to have served as the model for Snoops even though the character is a fat, balding, and clumsy stooge of Madame Medussa. Flynn's nasal vocals make the character even more unappealing but he turns out to be one of the funniest of Disney sidekicks. Flynn drowned in his backyard swimming pool soon after completing work on *The Rescuers*.

Fogelman, Dan A movie scriptwriter and occasional producer, his only voice credit is that of the New York City pigeon Billy in *Bolt* (2008). In addition to co-writing the screenplays for *Bolt* and *Cars* (2006), he has scripted the film *Fred Claus* (2007) and the television series *Like Family*.

Foley, Dave (b. 1963) The popular improv comic, writer, and actor well known in both his native Canada and the States, he voiced the ant hero Flik in *A Bug's Life* (1998). David Scott Foley was born in Toronto, Canada, and dropped out of school to pursue a career as a stand-up comic. Soon he was working with the improv group The Kids in the Hall which led to a successful television show from 1988 to 1995, followed by sequels and spinoffs. Foley was also featured in the TV series *NewsRadio, Will & Grace, Scrubs, Robson Arms*, and *The New Adventures of Old Christine*. The ant Flik in *A Bug's Life* is one of the new breed of Disney heroes. He is small, inconsequential, ignored or laughed at by others, and not very impressive. Yet he has a vivid imagination, plenty of brains, a lot of heart, and when push comes to shove is indeed a hero. In many ways, Flik is a cousin to Lewis in *Meet the Robinsons* (2007), Linguini in *Ratatouille* (2007), and the title character in *Chicken Little* (2005). Foley reprised his Flik in cameos in *Toy Story 2* (1999) and *Cars* (2006), and in the short *It's Tough to Be a Bug* (1998). Foley can also be heard in the movie *South Park: Bigger Longer & Uncut* (1999).

Fondacaro, Phil (b. 1958) A multi-talented three-foot-six-inch actor who has found plenty of good roles on television and in the movies, he voiced the nasty, incompetent, but comic bat-like creature Creeper in *The Black Caldron* (1985) and Lil Wolf in the short *Redux Riding Hood* (1997). He was born in New Orleans, Louisiana, and began his screen career when a casting call went out for "little people" for the film *Under the Rainbow* (1981). Fondacaro's minor role in that comedy led to acting jobs in such movies as *Something Wicked This Way Comes* (1983), *Star Wars Episode VI: Return of the Jedi* (1983), *Troll* (1986), *Invaders from Mars* (1986) *Willow* (1988), *Ghoulies II* (1988), *Night Angel* (1990), *The Creeps* (1997), *Sideshow* (2000), *The Polar Express* (2004), and *Land of the Dead* (2005). He has appeared in several television series, including *Faerie Tale Theatre, Star Trek: The Next Generation, Northern Exposure, thirtysomething, Married with Children, Touched by an Angel, CSI: Crime Scene Investigation*, and *Sabrina, the Teenage Witch*, and he provided voices for such animated series as *Timon and Pumbaa* and *Hercules*. The critter Creeper in *The Black Cauldron* is the only character not in Lloyd Alexander's original books but he is major in the film. With his fumbling ways, his fear as well as delight in evil, and the splendid vocals by Fondacaro, Creepy is one of Disney's finest villain sidekicks.

Foray, June (b. 1917) Dubbed the "Queen of Cartoons," she has voiced hundreds of episodes of animated TV series over a period of sixty years and for Disney voiced such characters as the deadly cat Lucifer in *Cinderella* (1950), one of the Mermaids and one of the Squaws in *Peter Pan* (1953), the laughing henchman Wheezy and the nymphomaniac Lena Hyena in *Who Framed Roger Rabbit* (1988), Scrooge McDuck's matronly secretary Mrs. Featherby in *DuckTales the Movie: The Treasure of the Lost Lamp* (1990), the Grandma in the short *Redux Red Riding Hood* (1997), the speaking voice for the ditzy Grandmother Fa in *Mulan* (1998), and various minor characters in *Beauty and the Beast* (1991). She was born in Springfield, Massachusetts, and by the age of twelve was doing various voices for local radio stations. As a teenager she moved to California and by the time Foray was fifteen she wrote and performed all the characters in her own radio show, *Lady Make Believe*. Her first movie credit was supplying the voice of a honey bee in the cartoon short *Eatin' Off the Cuff or The Moth Who Came to Dinner* (1942) and, after working for Disney on *Cinderella*, she played the comic Witch Hazel in a series of cartoon shorts for Warner Brothers. Foray's career really took off in the 1950s when television cartoons started to be made. Even as she continued to voice theatrical shorts for different studios, she worked on dozens of TV series. Her most fondly remembered voice was that of Rocky the Flying Squirrel on *Rocky and His Friends* and its many sequels and spinoffs. Foray's other cartoon series credits include The *Woody Woodpecker Show, Mister Magoo, The Yogi Bear Show, The Bugs Bunny Show, The Jetsons, Beetle Bailey, The Flintstones, The Road Runner Show, The Pink Panther Show, Heathcliff, Spider-Man and His Amazing Friends, The Incredible Hulk, The Chipmunks, Teen Wolf, DuckTales, Tiny Toon Adventures, Adventures of the Gummi Bears, Garfield and Friends, Baby Looney Tunes, Duck Dodgers*, and *The Marvelous Misadventures of Flapjack*. Audiences got to see what she looked like from her many appearances on sit-coms, such as *I Love Lucy, Father Knows Best, Gilligan's Island, Bewitched, Get Smart*, and *Married with Children*. Foray appeared in few movies but was heard in many animated films and videos, among them *Gay-Purr-ee* (1962), *How the Grinch Stole Christmas* (1966), *Mouse on the Mayflower* (1968), *The Little Drummer Boy* (1968), *Frosty the Snowman* (1969), *The Phantom Tollbooth* (1970), *Rikki-Tikki-Tavi* (1975), *Daffy Duck's Movie: Fantastic Island* (1983), *Happily Ever After* (1985), *Little Nemo: Adventures in Slumberland* (1989), *Thumbelina* (1994), and *Mulan II* (2004). She founded the Annie Awards, the Oscars for animal performers, and has served on the boards for many organizations involving children and film. Autobiography: *Did You Grow Up with Me Too?*, with Mark Evanier and Earl Kress (2009).

Ford, John H. H. The actor who voiced Mr. Harrington, the prospective father with a peanut allergy, in *Meet the Robinsons* (2007), his only other film credit is *Long Day's Nightmare* (2005).

Fox, Bernard (b. 1927) A British character actor who performed in hundreds of episodes of television in England and the States, he supplied the voice of the mouse Mr. Chairman of the Rescue Aid Society in *The Rescuers* (1977). He was born Bernard Lawson in Port Talbot, Wales, into a family of stage actors and began his career in the theatre. He made his British television debut in 1955 and the next year made his first film, *Spin a Dark Web* (1956), followed by the English films *Home and Away* (1956), *The Counterfeit Plan* (1957), *Inside Information* (1957), *The Safecracker* (1958), *A Night to Remember* (1958), and *The Two-Headed Spy* (1958). By the 1960s Fox was in America and appeared in dozens of television series, including *Combat!, Ensign O'Toole, The Danny Thomas Show, McHale's Navy, The Dick Van Dyke Show, Perry Mason, O. K. Crackerby!, F Troop, I Spy, Burke's Law, Tammy, I Dream of Jeannie, 12 O'Clock High, The Girl from U.N.C.L.E., The Monkees, The Wild Wild West, Here Come the Brides, It Takes a Thief, Ironside, Arnie, Columbo, Emergency!, Soap, M*A*S*H, Fantasy Island, Lou Grant, The Jeffersons, Simon & Simon, Riptide, Punky Brewster, Pee-wee's Playhouse*, and *Dharma & Greg*, yet he is better remembered as Sir Charles Chittery on several episodes of *Hogan's Heroes*, the gentle Malcolm Merriweather on three episodes of *The Andy Griffith Show*, and the witch doctor Dr. Bombay in three different series: *Bewitched, Tabitha*, and *Passions*. Among his notable Hollywood movies are *The Longest Day* (1962), *The List of Adrian Messenger* (1963), *Munster, Go Home!* (1966), *The Million Dollar Duck* (1971), *Herbie Goes to Monte Carlo* (1977), *Alien Zone* (1978), *Yellowbeard* (1983), *18 Again!* (1988), *Titanic* (1997), and *The Mummy* (1999). He reprised his Chairman in the sequel *The Rescuers Down Under* (1990) and also provided voices for the cartoon TV series *The Flintstones, The New Adventures of Huckleberry Finn*, and *The ABC Saturday Superstar Movie*.

Fox, Michael J. (b. 1961) The likable television and movie actor who found fame as a teenager and then secured a career as an adult, he voiced the young explorer Milo James Thatch in *Atlantis: The Lost Empire* (2001). Michael Andrew Fox was born in Edmonton, Alberta, Canada, the son of a military family who moved frequently, finally settling in Vancouver where he began acting as a young teen. After performing in the Canadian television series *Leo and Me* in 1981, Fox went to Hollywood where he appeared in small roles on film and in television before getting cast as a regular on *Palmerstown, USA*, then found fame as the conservative teenager Alex Keaton in the long-running series *Family Ties*. He secured his celebrity as the adventurous teen Marty McFly in the movie *Back to the Future* (1985), a role he reprised in the two hit sequels. Fox's other films include *Teen Wolf* (1985), *Bright Lights, Big City* (1988), *Doc Hollywood* (1991), *Life with Mikey* (1993), and *Mars Attack!* (1996), and he is also known for his appearances on such television programs as *Saturday Night Live*, *Spin City*, *Scrubs*, *Boston Legal*, and *Rescue Me*. Fox voiced the mischievous dog Chance in the live-action feature *Homeward Bound: The Incredible Journey* (1993) and its sequel *Homeward Bound II: Lost in San Francisco* (1996), and provided the voice for the title mouse in *Stuart Little* (1999) and its two sequels. Although Fox was diagnosed with Parkinson's disease in 2000, he continues to perform and wrote about his medical battle in three memoirs: *Lucky Me* (2002); *Always Looking Up: The Adventures of an Incurable Optimist* (2009); *A Funny Thing Happened on the Way to the Future: Twists and Turns and Lessons Learned* (2010). Biographies: *Michael J. Fox: A Real-Life Reader Biography*, John Bankston (2002); *Michael J. Fox: Courage for Life*, Barbara Kramer (2005).

Fox, Spencer (b. 1993) A child performer of television and movies, he provided the voice for the young and speedy super-hero Robert Dashiell "Dash" Parr in *The Incredibles* (2004). He was born in New York City, the son of an actor, and *The Incredibles* was his first voice artist job. Spencer can also be heard in the animated video *Kim Possible: So the Drama* (2005) and the cartoon series *Kim Possible*. He was seen in the films *The Groomsmen* (2006) and *Neal Cassady* (2007) and supplied the voice of Mudbud in the video *Air Buddies* (2006). The inspiration for the character of Dash in *The Incredibles* came from the comic strip super-hero The Flash.

Francis, Genie (b. 1962) A blonde teenage actress who grew up on television as she appeared year after year on the daytime series *General Hospital*, she provided the voices of the TV soap opera heroines Marcia and Marsha in *Teacher's Pet* (2004). She was born Eugenie Anne Francis in Englewood, New Jersey, the daughter of actor Ivor Francis, and made her television debut at the age of fourteen on two episodes of *Family*. The next year she played teenager Laura on *General Hospital* and remained with the soap opera for thirty-one years. During that time both Francis and the character of Laura became so popular that the fictional wedding of Luke (Anthony Geary) and Laura was one of the most watched television programs of its era. She also acted in such series as *Bare Essence*, *Hotel*, *Days of Our Lives*, *Loving*, *Roseanne*, *All My Children*, and *Murder, She Wrote*, as well as in the mini-series *North and South* (1985), *North and South, Book II* (1986), and *Heaven and Hell: North and South, Book III* (1994). Among Francis' film credits are *Camp Nowhere* (1994) and *Thunderbirds* (2004), as well as a handful of made-for-TV movies. She was reunited with Geary when they voiced the vapid soap opera characters seen on the television set in *Teacher's Pet*, one of the many inside jokes in that satirical animated movie.

Frankham, David (b. 1926) A British actor appearing in American films and television from 1957 to 2002, he supplied the voice of Sergeant Tibs, the earnest barnyard cat who finds and rescues the lost puppies, in *One Hundred and One Dalmatians* (1961). He was born in Kent, England, and served in India and Malaya during World War II. After the war he was a writer and news broadcaster for the BBC until moving to the States in the mid–1950s. Frankham made a handful of American films, including *Return of the Fly* (1959), *Ten Who Dared* (1960), *Master of the World* (1961), *Tales of Terror* (1962), *King Rat* (1965), and *The Great Santini* (1979), but he was kept busier on television where he acted in many series, such as *Studio 57*, *Death Valley Days*, *77 Sunset Strip*, *Maverick*, *Surfside 6*, *Alfred Hitchcock Presents*, *The Many Loves of Dobie Gillis*, *Thriller*, *The Outer Limits*, *The Beverly Hillbillies*, *12 O'Clock High*, *Star Trek*, *The F.B.I.*, *McCloud*, *Cannon*, *The Waltons*, *The Six Million Dollar Man*, and *The Bold and the Beautiful*. The efficient and brave cat Tibs in *One Hundred and One Dalmatians* is a secondary character but in many ways is the hero of the movie, rarely flinching even when trying to do the impossible. Frankham's vocals are those of a stiff-upper-lip military man who asks for no thanks for doing his duty.

Freberg, Stan (b. 1926) One of the few voice artists who was widely known by the public because of his comedy records and radio broadcasts, he supplied the voice of the lisping Beaver who removes Lady's muzzle in *Lady and the Tramp* (1955). Stanley Victor Freberg was born in Los Angeles, the son of a Baptist minister, and started doing voices for Warner Brothers cartoons right after he graduated from high school. He was soon in demand and provided dozens of "Looney Tunes" voices, sometimes pairing with Warner's other top voice artist Mel Blanc. In the 1950s, Freberg began making comedy records that often parodied popular music of the time but also made fun of soap operas, politics, American history, and TV commercials. He had his own radio show and later his own television show though Freberg, a religious man who disdained alcohol and smoking, had trouble finding sponsors. Ironically, he was the man who revolutionized television advertising by writing funny commercials and introducing satire to the field. Freberg voiced dozens of television cartoon series from the 1960s into the new century, including *The Bugs Bunny Show*, *The Famous Adventures of Mr. Magoo*, *Wuzzles*, *Tiny Toon Adventures*, *The Ren & Stimpy Show*, *Garfield and Friends*, *The Weird Al Show*, and *Duck Dodgers*. *Lady and the Tramp* was his only Disney feature film but he voiced several other animated movies and videos, such as *The First Easter Rabbit* (1976), *I Go Pogo: The Movie* (1980), *The Looney, Looney, Looney Bugs Bunny Movie* (1981), *The Jackie Bison Show* (1990), *Pullet Surprise* (1997), *Tweety's High-Flying Adventures* (2000), *Little Go Beep* (2000), and *Looney Tunes: Back in Action* (2003). In addition to his many appearances on television variety and talk shows, Freberg acted in a number of series, including *The Monkees*, *The Girl from U.N.C.L.E.*, and *Roseanne*. Although the role of the beaver is a small one in *Lady and the Tramp*, it is one of the comic highlights of the movie. Freberg came up with the lisp that whistled through his teeth, the actor sometimes speaking his lines with a whistle in his mouth to get the effect. Years later when Disney added the character of the gopher to the *Winnie the Pooh* shorts, the same kind of lisp-whistle was used, though Freberg did not do them this time. Autobiography: *It Only Hurts When I Laugh* (1988).

Freeman, Cheryl An African American stage actress and singer known for stopping the show with her powerful voice, she provided the singing for the Muse Melpomene in *Hercules* (1997). Freeman has sung on Broadway in *Show Boat* (1983), *Amen Corner* (1983), *The Who's Tommy* (1993), *Play On!* (1997), and *The Civil War* (1999), and Off Broadway in *Fame on 42nd Street* (2003). She reprised her Melpomene in the video sequel *Hercules: Zero to Hero* (1999) and in the television cartoon series *Hercules*. She has acted on such series as *New York Undercover* and *Law & Order: Criminal Intent*, and in a handful of films.

Freeman, Jonathan (b. 1950) A tall, deep-voiced character actor, he has often been singled out for his comic performances in supporting roles in musicals but is most known to the public as the voice of the villain Jafar in *Aladdin* (1992) and its sequels. Freeman was born in Bay Village, Ohio, and educated at Ohio University. He made his New York debut in *Sherlock Holmes* (1974) then was featured in the musicals *Platinum* (1978), *She Loves Me* (1993), *Beauty and the Beast* (1994), *How to Succeed in Business Without Really Trying* (1995), *Peter Pan* (1998), *On the Town* (1998), *A Class Act* (2001), *42nd Street* (2001), *The Producers* (2003), and *The Little Mermaid* (2007), playing the seasick Grimsby in the last. Freeman's distinctive and versatile voice has been used for Bil Baird Marionette Theatre productions and he has acted on a handful of television shows, including *The Days and Nights of Molly Dodd*, *Mathnet*, *Law & Order: Criminal Intent*, *Gossip Girl*, and *Law & Order: Special Victims Unit*, although he is most remembered as Rollie Pruitt in *Remember WENN*. Among his film credits are *Forever, Lulu* (1987), *A Shock to the System* (1990), *The Ice Storm* (1997), *The Producers* (2005), and some TV-movies. Freeman's performance as the evil wizard Jafar is one of the highlights of his career. The role was conceived as a male counterpart to the evil Maleficent in *Sleeping Beauty* (1959). Both are tall and thin, wear a long cape, carry a staff, and have a pet henchman on their shoulder: Maleficent a crow, Jafar a parrot. Also, both turn themselves into giant creatures near the end of the film: a dragon and a snake. Yet Freeman makes Jafar a comic villain in a way Maleficent never was. He based his vocals on the voices of Boris Karloff and Vincent Price, coming up with a variety of vocal tones for the character. Freeman reprised his Jafar in the videos *The Return of Jafar* (1994), *Aladdin in Nasira's Revenge* (2001), *Mickey's Magical Christmas* (2001), *Mickey's House of Villains* (2001), *Kingdom Hearts* (2002), *Kingdom Hearts II* (2005), and in the television series *Hercules* and *House of Mouse*. Freeman can also be heard in the Disney animated series *American Dragon: Jake Long*.

Freeman, Sarah (b. 1986) A child performer who found work as a teenage actress on television, she supplied the voice of Sid's put-upon little sister Hannah in *Toy Story* (1995). She was born in Los Angeles and made her television debut at the age of six in an episode of *Camp Wilder*, followed by such series as *Roseanne*, *Diagnosis Murder*, *Star Trek: Voyager*, *The Pretender*, *Promised Land*, *Teen Angel*, *ER*, *Legacy*, *Providence*, *Family Law*, *The Practice*, *7th Heaven*, *The Guardian*, and *Without a Trace*. Freeman has also appeared in the TV-movies *Dying to Love You* (1993), *One Woman's Courage* (1994), *A Time to Heal* (1994), *Someone She Knows* (1994), *No Greater Love* (1996), and *Alone* (1997). She can be heard in the animated films *Quest for Camelot* (1998) and *Recess: School's Out* (2001).

Frees, Paul (1920–1986) The prolific and versatile actor dubbed "Man of a Thousand Voices" for his hundreds of cartoons and voiceovers for live-action films, he can be heard in a handful of Disney animated features, such as the cowboy villain Dirty Dawson on the television show enjoyed by the dalmatian pups in *One Hundred and One Dalmatians* (1961), the barnyard horse in the animated section of *Mary Poppins* (1964), and in cartoon shorts, such as the voice of both Noah and God in *Noah's Ark* (1959), the Mouse in *Goliath II* (1960), the narrator of *Donald in Mathmagic Land* (1959) and *Goofy's Freeway Troubles* (1965), and the voice of Professor Ludwig Von Drake on television's *Walt Disney's Wonderful World of Color*. He was born Solomon Hersh Frees in Chicago and he began his career in radio where his four-octave voice range allowed him to play a very wide variety of characters. After serving in World War II he added film to his voice jobs, working with all the major animation studios and acting in over 300 cartoon shorts and features. Frees was also one of the most in-demand narrators and announcers for all kinds of movies and television shows, heard in dozens of productions as a radio announcer or providing the narration for everything from wildlife pieces to sci-fi commentary. Among the many television series he voiced are *The Woody Woodpecker Show, Steve Canyon, Mister Magoo, The Dick Tracy Show, Bozo: The World's Most Famous Clown, The Flintstones, Top Cat, Calvin and the Colonel, Krazy Kat, Snuffy Smith and Barney Google, Hoppity Hooper, George of the Jungle, Fantastic 4, The Banana Splits Adventure Hour, The Pink Panther Show*, and *Knight Rider*, but he is perhaps most famous for his various characters on *The Bullwinkle Show* and *Rocky and His Friends*, in particular Boris Badenov. Frees can be heard in such animated movies and videos as *The Sword and the Dragon* (1956), *The Snow Queen* (1957), *Gay Purr-ee* (1962), *Mr. Magoo's Christmas Carol* (1962), *Cricket on the Hearth* (1967), *Frosty the Snowman* (1969), *Santa Claus Is Comin' to Town* (1970), *Here Comes Peter Cottontail* (1971), *Rudolph's Shiny New Year* (1976), *The Hobbit* (1977), *The Stingiest Man in Town* (1978), *Jack Frost* (1979), *The Return of the King* (1980), and *The Wind in the Willows* (1987). He was not always unseen, playing roles in the live-action movies *The Thing from Another World* (1951), *A Place in the Sun* (1951), *The Las Vegas Story* (1952), *Prince of Players* (1955), *Son of Sinbad* (1955), *The Shaggy Dog* (1959), *Some Like It Hot* (1959), and *Mother's Little Helper* (1962), as well as the television series *The Adventures of Jim Bowie, Dragnet, The Millionaire*, and *Alias Smith and Jones*. Frees was a successful composer and singer who supplied singing voices for non-singing film actors, and he can still be heard as the voice of several "animatronics" at the Disney theme parks and as the voice of the "Ghost Host" in the Haunted Mansion. Biography: *Welcome, Foolish Mortals: The Life and Voices of Paul Frees*, Ben Ohmart (2004).

Frewer, Matt (b. 1958)   A lean, sallow-looking television actor and voice artist with an odd presence which makes him ideal for fantasy and science fiction characters, he supplied the voice of Hades' bumbling sidekick Panic in *Hercules* (1997). He was born in Washington D.C., grew up in Canada, and trained for an acting career in England at the Bristol Old Vic Drama School. He appeared in a handful of theatre productions in Great Britain and a few movies as well, but fame came when he played the title character in the television series *Max Headroom*. Frewer's other TV credits include *Star Trek: The Next Generation, Shaky Ground, PSI Factor: Chronicles of the Paramount, Taken, Eureka: Hide and Seek*, and *Intelligence*. He reprised his Panic in the videos *Hercules: Zero to Hero* (1999) and *Mickey's House of Villains* (2001), and in the cartoon series *Hercules* and *House of Mouse*, and he can also be heard in the animated series *Tiny Toon Adventures, Batman, Bonkers, Iron Man, Gargoyles, The Mighty Ducks, The Magic School Bus, The Incredible Hulk*, and *Mickey Mouse Works*. Frewer voiced characters for a number of animated videos and movies, including *In Search of Dr. Seuss* (1994), *Driving Mr. Pink* (1995), *Gargoyles: Brothers Betrayed* (1998), and *Gargoyles: The Hunted* (1998).

Fry, Jordan (b. 1993)   A child performer with few but impressive credits, he was one of two actors who provided the voice for the young orphaned hero Lewis in *Meet the Robinsons* (2007). Jordan Paul Fry was born in Spokane, Washington, and was raised in nearby Selah. He has had featured roles in the movies *Charlie and the Chocolate Factory* (2005), *Raising Flagg* (2006), and *The Journey* (2010). The role of the science geek Lewis was originally voiced by Daniel Hansen. When the producers were not happy with the first cut of *Meet the Robinsons*, the movie went back into production for ten months, by which time Hansen's voice had changed so Fry was hired to do the new dialogue.

Fry, Stephen (b. 1957)   A British actor and author who is most adept at dry, understated comedy, he voiced Chessur, the sly Cheshire Cat, in the 2010 version of *Alice in Wonderland*. Stephen John Fry was born in London, the son of a physicist, grew up in Norfolk, and was educated at Cambridge University where he wrote and performed in satirical revues. Although he scripted plays and screenplays, it was his acting and writing for television that made him famous in Great Britain and then in the States. Among the series he contributed to and/or performed are *Alfresco, Happy Families, A Bit of Fry and Laurie, Baddiel's Syndrome, Absolute Power, Kingdom*, and *Bones*, but he is most remembered for his various characters on the *Blackadder* series and for the impeccable gentleman's gentleman Jeeves in *Jeeves and Wooster*. Fry has acted on the London stage as well as in several movies, including *A Fish Called Wanda* (1988), *Peter's Friends* (1992), *I.Q.* (1994), *Wilde* (1997), *Gosford Park*

(2001), and *V for Vendetta* (2006). He has also written fiction, essays, and travel nonfiction. Fry has a professed aversion to cats so in playing the Cheshire Cat in *Alice in Wonderland* he was able to use his disgust for the species in his characterization. Autobiography: *Moab Is My Wapshot* (2003).

Fucile, Eli One of the two children who voiced the baby super hero Jack-Jack Parr in *The Incredibles* (2004), he reprised the character in the cartoon short *Jack-Jack Attack* (2005). He is the son of animator Tony Fucile. Jack-Jack's ability to turn into a flame of fire was inspired by the comic book super-hero The Human Torch.

Fucile, Tony An animator and character designer since the 1980s who has voiced a few characters, he provided the voices of Pompidou, the *patissier chef* at Gusteau's Restaurant, and the Health Inspector in *Ratatouille* (2007), as well as the sound of Peck the Stork and Gus the Cloud in the short *Partly Cloudy* (2009). Fucile has worked as an animator and/or designer on such Disney features as *Oliver & Company* (1988), *The Little Mermaid* (1989), *Aladdin* (1992), *The Lion King* (1994), *The Hunchback of Notre Dame* (1996), *Finding Nemo* (2003), *The Incredibles* (2004), *Ratatouille*, and *Up* (2009), as well as the shorts *Sport Goofy in Soccermania* (1987) and *Jack-Jack Attack* (2005). His other animation credits include *Blondie and Dagwood* (1987), *Christmas in Tattertown* (1988), *Box-Office Bunny* (1990), *FernGully: The Last Rainforest* (1992), *Tom and Jerry: The Movie* (1992), *The Iron Giant* (1999), and *Osmosis Jones* (2001), as well as the television cartoon series *The Bugs Bunny and Tweety Show* and *The Ren & Stimpy Show*. Fucile can also be heard doing voices in *Up*.

Fullilove, Donald An African American actor-singer and voice artist active since the early 1970s, he supplied the voice of the male nurse George from the Shady Oaks Retirement Village in *Up* (2009). Fullilove did the singing and speaking voice of Michael Jackson in the television cartoon series *Jackson 5ive*, followed by such series as *Kid Power, Emergency +4,* and *American Dad!* He appeared in the television series *Hill Street Blues, The Fall Guy, What's Happening Now!, Major Dad, Johnny Bago, Martin,* and *All of Us*, as well as the films *Tuff Turf* (1985), *Back to the Future* (1985), *Basic Training* (1985), *Cadillac Dreams* (1988), *Back to the Future Part II* (1989), *Penny Ante: The Motion Picture* (1990), *White Men Can't Jump* (1992), *Domestic Import* (2006), and *The Hustle* (2008), as well as some TV-movies. Fullilove can be heard in the animated films *Mulan* (1998), *Osmosis Jones* (2001), *Spirit: Stallion of the Cimarron* (2002), *Curious George* (2006), and *WALL-E* (2008).

Gabor, Eva (1910–1995) The glamorous, heavily-accented beauty from Hungary who specialized in playing classy ladies on television and in films, she provided the voices for the Parisian feline Duchess in *The Aristocats* (1970) and the chic and adventurous diplomat Miss Bianca in *The Rescuers* (1977) and *The Rescuers Down Under* (1990). Gabor was born in Budapest where she and her sisters Zsa Zsa (b. 1917) and Magda (1914–1997) became famous celebrities before coming to America. All three were as known for their many marriages and society column headlines as for their performances in films, yet Eva Gabor was the most accomplished actress of the sisters, beginning her career as a cafe singer and ice skating performer in her native country. She came to the States in the late 1930s and made many Hollywood films, including *A Royal Scandal* (1945), *Song of Summer* (1949), *Paris Model* (1953), *The Last Time I Saw Paris* (1954), *Artists and Models* (1955), *The Truth About Women* (1957), *Gigi* (1958), and *A New Kind of Love* (1963). Gabor also appeared on dozens of television programs starting as far back as 1949 but she is most remembered as the ditzy New Yorker Lisa living on a farm in the comedy series *Green Acres* (1965–1971). Both of Gabor's Disney characters, the Duchess and Miss Bianca, are very genteel, feminine characters who manage to keep their sophistication even during treacherous times. Both characters were physically modeled after Gabor's gestures and her alluring way of turning her head and using her eyes. The character of Bianca was so closely identified with Gabor that plans for another sequel to *The Rescuers* were cancelled when the actress died. Autobiography: *Orchids and Salamis* (1951); biographies: *Such Devoted Sisters: Those Fabulous Gabors,* Peter Harry Brown (1985); *Eva Gabor: An Amazing Woman,* Camyl Sosa Belanger (2005).

Gainey, M. C. (b. 1948) A tall, mustachioed character actor with a mean and threatening look and Southern accent that makes him ideal for hillbilly villains, he voiced the snarling Captain of the Guard who forever pursues Flynn Ryder in *Tangled* (2010). He was born Michael Connor Gainey in Jackson, Mississippi, and made his screen debut in *Pennies from Heaven* (1981), followed by fifty films in which he usually played rednecks, toughs, criminals, and corrupt cops. Among his movie credits are *Ratboy* (1986), *Two Idiots in Hollywood* (1988), *The Mighty Ducks* (1992), *Leap of Faith* (1992), *The Breakdown* (1997), *Con Air* (1997), *Terminator 3* (2003), *Sideways* (2004), *Are We There Yet?* (2005), *The Dukes of Hazzard* (2005), *All About Steve* (2009), and *Love Ranch* (2010). Gainey has been just as busy on television, appearing on such series as *Father Murphy, T. J. Hooker, Night Partners, Hart* to Hart, Cheers, Street Hawk, Knight Rider, Simon & Simon, The Young Riders, Against the Law, Designing Women, Days of Our Lives, Bones, The Young and the Restless, Justified, and Happy Town, but he is most remembered as Tom Friendly on eighteen episodes of Lost.

Gallant, Jim An actor with a few scattered credits over two decades, he provided the voice of the hardened cowboy Bullet #3 in Who Framed Roger Rabbit (1988). Gallant also voiced characters in the television cartoon series Burn-Up Excess and Geneshaft, and can he seen in the films Real Bullets (1990) and Hangman (2000), and on television in Oblivion: The Series.

Gammill, Noreen (1898–1988) A radio actress who later did a few television shows, her only movie was Dumbo (1941) in which she provided the voice of the snide Catty the Elephant. Noreen Ellers Gammill was born in rural Missouri and was busy on the radio in the 1940s, most memorably as Mrs. Martha Conklin on Our Miss Brooks. Her television acting credits include The Andy Griffith Show, Sanford and Son, and Maude.

Garay, Joaquin (b. 1921) A Mexican actor-singer who entertained on the radio and in a few films in the 1940s, he voiced the gun-toting Mexican rooster Panchito in The Three Caballeros (1944). He was born in El Oro, Mexico, and came to the States as a one-year-old baby. Garay performed in vaudeville and in nightclubs before finding popularity on the radio and on records. He appeared in the films Crisis (1950), Saddle Tramp (1950), Lightning Strikes Twice (1951), Fast Company (1953), Latin Lovers (1953), and Red Sky at Morning (1971), and can be heard as the Narrator and various characters in the Goofy animated short For Whom the Bulls Toil (1953). In 1941 Garay opened his own nightclub, the Copacabana in San Francisco, which was a popular hangout for Hollywood stars and enlisted men during World War II. Over one hundred actors were tested for the voice of the fiery Panchito before Garay was selected. His vocal pyrotechnics match the furious action on the screen as Panchito plays practical jokes, fires off his pistols, and is more frenetic than possibly any other Disney character. Although audiences loved the feathered trio of Donald Duck, Joe Carioca, and Panchito, the rooster was possibly too sadistic for some tastes. Perhaps that is why Disney never put Panchito in any other feature or cartoon short.

Garlin, Jeff (b. 1962) A chubby comic actor who is also a successful producer, he did the voices for the bloated Captain B. McCrea of the spaceship Axiom in WALL-E (2008) and the stuffed toy unicorn Buttercup in Toy Story 3 (2010). He was born in Chicago and raised in Florida where he started to do stand-up comedy while a student at the University of Miami. Garlin eventually returned to Chicago and became a member of the famed Second City improv group. He appeared on various television talk shows, had his own HBO comedy special, and played characters on such series as Roseanne, Baywatch, Mad About You, Three Sisters, What About Joan, Everybody Loves Raymond, Arrested Development, Law & Order: Criminal Intent, Wizards of Waverly Place, and Entourage, but he is mostly know as Jeff Greene on Curb Your Enthusiasm which he also produced. Among his film credits are Spring Break (1983), RoboCop 3 (1993), Senseless (1998), Austin Powers: The Spy Who Shagged Me (1999), Bounce (2000), Daddy Day Care (2003), Sleepover (2004), Fat Albert (2004), Fun with Dick and Jane (2005), Strange Wilderness (2008), The Rocker (2008), and The Bounty Hunter (2010). Garlin can be heard in the cartoon series King of the Hill, Crank Yankers, Tom Goes to the Mayor, Duck Dodgers, Shorty McShort's Shorts, and The Life & Times of Tim. The character of Captain McCrea in WALL-E, like the other humans aboard the space city Axion, is overweight, round, and balloon-like. Originally the humans were going to be green blobs but it was later decided that making them all look like bloated babies was more agreeable. Garlin reprised his Captain McCrea in the animated short BURN-E (2008). Memoir: My Footprint: Carrying the Weight of the World (2010).

Garner, James (b. 1928) The tall, handsome leading man of films and television who manages to find humor even in action roles, he voiced the cruel submarine captain Commander Lyle Tiberius Rourke in Atlantis: The Lost Empire (2001). He was born James Scott Bumgarner in Norman, Oklahoma, where he dropped out of school to join the merchant marines at the age of sixteen. After serving in the Korean War, Garner worked at many odd jobs before turning to acting and getting a bit part in the Broadway drama The Caine Mutiny Court-Martial (1954). He made his screen debut in 1956 but found his first success on television with the series Maverick in the late 1950s. By the 1960s Garner was a leading man in Hollywood with such hits as The Great Escape (1963), The Americanization of Emily (1964), Grand Prix (1966), and Support Your Local Sheriff (1969). He returned to television with the popular series The Rockford Files in the 1970s, followed by recurring characters in Bret Maverick, Man of the People, Chicago Hope, First Monday, 8 Simple Rules, and God, the Devil and Bob. Among his other notable movies are Sayonara (1957), Up Periscope (1959), Move Over, Darling (1963), Victor Victoria (1982), Murphy's Romance

(1985), *Twilight* (1998), *Divine Secrets of the Ya-Ya Sisterhood* (2002), *The Notebook* (2004), and *First Night* (2007). Garner voiced the character of Pat in the animated video *Land Before Time X: The Great Longneck Migration* (2003). Kurt Russell, Tommy Lee Jones, and Jack Davenport were considered for the role of Rourke in *Atlantis* but it was felt the older, more confident Garner would suit the character best. Biography: *James Garner*, Raymond Strait (1985).

Garner, Marcellite (1910–1993) The first actress to voice Minnie Mouse, she played the character in over fifty cartoon shorts before retiring from acting. Walt Disney himself voiced both Mickey and Minnie in some early sound cartoons. Garner was a cartoon artist at the Disney studio and first voiced Minnie in *The Barn Dance* (1929), continuing in the job for the next ten years. Among the classic cartoons she voiced are *Mickey's Follies* (1929), *The Fire Fighters* (1930), *The Shindig* (1930), *The Barnyard Broadcast* (1931), *Mickey's Orphans* (1931), *Mickey's Nightmare* (1932), *Puppy Love* (1933), *Camping Out* (1934), *Mickey's Steamroller* (1934), *Mickey's Rival* (1936), *Brave Little Tailor* (1938), and *Mickey's Surprise Party* (1939). The only time Garner voiced a character other than Minnie was in *King Neptune* (1932) in which she supplied the voices for the Mermaids. The character of Minnie Mouse goes back almost as far as Mickey Mouse himself, She is often the maiden in distress in the early cartoons but she becomes more independent with time and, while rarely in conflict with Mickey, she has her own ideas about how to do things. Another important aspect of Minnie is that she allows the audience to see Mickey in a romantic light. The mouse by himself may not strike moviegoers as a great lover but, because Minnie sees him that way, he actually becomes a romantic figure. The character of Minnie Mouse has appeared in seventy cartoon shorts over the years, playing opposite Mickey and/or Pluto in most of them. Minnie is rarely featured alone in a cartoon. She is an international movie star whose appeal is uncomplicated and comforting, and it is her relationship with other characters on the screen that makes her so.

Garofalo, Janeane (b. 1964) A bright-eyed, deadpan comedienne and actress with many television and movie credits, she provided the voice of the strong-willed Colette Tatou, the only female chef at Gusteau's Restaurant, in *Ratatouille* (2007). She was born Jane Anne Garofalo in Newton, New Jersey, was educated at Providence College, and began her career as a stand-up comic. She first gained attention as a writer and cast member of *The Ben Stiller Show* on television in 1992, followed by appearances on *Saturday Night Live* and such series as *The Adventures of Pete & Pete, NewsRadio, Ellen, Seinfeld, Home Improvement, The Larry Sanders Show, Law & Order, The Chris Rock Show, Mad About You, The King of Queens, The West Wing,* and *24*. Among her many movie credits are *That's What Women Want* (1992), *Reality Bites* (1994), *Bye Bye Love* (1995), *Sweethearts* (1996), *The Truth About Cats and Dogs* (1996), *The Cable Guy* (1996), *Romy and Michele's High School Reunion* (1997), *Cop Land* (1997), *The Thin Pink Line* (1997), *Clay Pigeons* (1998), *Can't Stop Dancing* (1999), *Dogma* (1999), *Steal This Movie* (2000), *Big Trouble* (2002), *Wonderland* (2003), *Jiminy Glick in Lalawood* (2004), *Southland Tales* (2006), *The Guitar* (2008), and *Love Hurts* (2009). Garofalo can be heard in the cartoon TV series *Duckman: Private Dick/Family Man, Freak-Show,* and *Dr. Katz, Professional Therapist,* as well as in the animated movies *Kiki's Delivery Service* (1989), *Titan A.E.* (2000), and *The Wild* (2006). The character of Colette in *Ratatouille* is one of the more hardened females in the Disney canon. She is succeeding in a male-dominated profession by hard work and grim determination. Colette feels she has to be tough to survive. No wonder she is at first disgusted with the weakling Linguini who hopes to be a chef like her. Garofalo captures Colette's many sides in her witty and revealing performance.

Garrett, Brad (b. 1960) The deep-voiced comedian and television favorite who plays likable if slow-witted characters, he provided the voices for the childlike rhinoceros beetle Dim in *A Bug's Life* (1998), the puffer fish Bloat in *Finding Nemo* (2003), the deceased chef Gusteau in *Ratatouille* (2007), and the one-handed pub thug Hook-Hand who dreams of becoming a concert pianist in *Tangled* (2010). He was born Brad H. Gerstenfeld in Los Angeles and dropped out of UCLA to do stand-up comedy in clubs. His big break came when he was featured on the talent program *Star Search* on national television and won, leading to guest spots on various TV shows and concerts. Garrett was cast in many sit-coms, including *First Impressions, The Pursuit of Happiness, Seinfeld, Murphy Brown, The King of Queens,* and *'Til Death,* but he is most remembered as the lovable lug Robert Barone in *Everybody Loves Raymond.* He has been even busier providing voices for television cartoons shows such as *The Transformers, Where's Waldo?, Bonkers, Batman, 2 Stupid Dogs, Mighty Ducks, Timon and Pumbaa, 101 Dalmatians, Hercules, Superman, Buzz Lightyear of Star Command, House of Mouse,* and *Justice League.* Garrett can also be heard in many animated movies and videos, including *Jetsons: The Movie* (1990), *Hollyrock-a-Bye Baby* (1993), *Spy Hard* (1996), *Superman: The Last Son of Krypton*

(1996), *Mighty Ducks the Movie: The First Face-Off* (1997), *Pocahontas II: Journey to a New World* (1998), *The Batman Superman Movie: World's Finest* (1998), *Hercules: Zero to Hero* (1999), *Hooves of Fire* (1999), *An Extremely Goofy Movie* (2000), *The Country Bears* (2002), *Robbie the Reindeer in the Legend of the Lost Tribe* (2002), *Garfield* (2004), *Mickey's Around the World in 80 Days* (2005), *Tom and Jerry Blast Off to Mars!* (2005), *Tarzan II* (2005), *Asterix and the Vikings* (2006), *Finding Nemo Submarine Voyage* (2007), *Underdog* (2007), *Unstable Fables: 3 Pigs & a Baby* (2008), and *Hoodwinked Too! Hood vs. Evil* (2010). The character of Gusteau was alive and still cooking in the early versions of *Ratatouille*. When Brad Bird took over the direction of the film, he revised the story and had Gusteau dead from the start with his ghost appearing to his illegitimate son Linguini.

Geary, Anthony (b. 1947) A dashing actor who was a heartthrob favorite on television for a time, he supplied the voices of the soap opera heroes John and Juan on television in *Teacher's Pet* (2004). He was born in Coalville, Utah, and educated at the University of Utah before beginning his career in regional theatre. Geary acted in classical and modern plays on tour and in resident companies in major cities even as he appeared on various television series such as *Room 222, All in the Family, The Mod Squad, The Partridge Family, Mannix, The Young and the Restless, Marcus Welby M.D., The Streets of San Francisco, Barnaby Jones, Starsky and Hutch, Hotel,* and *Murder, She Wrote,* but he is most famous as Luke Spencer in the soap opera *General Hospital* and its spinoffs *Port Charles* and *General Hospital: Night Shift.* Luke Spencer's romance with the character Laura (Genie Francis) was the most popular fictional courtship of its day and the episode of *General Hospital* in which they wed was one of the most watched programs of the era. Geary and Francis were reunited to voice the inane soap opera characters heard in *Teacher's Pet*. His film credits include *Johnny Got His Gun* (1971), *Blood Sabbath* (1972), *P.I. Private Investigations* (1987), *Disorderlies* (1987), *Penitentiary III* (1987), *You Can't Hurry Love* (1988), *Dangerous Love* (1988), *Night Life* (1989), *Night of the Warrior* (1991), *Whistlestop Girl* (1993), and *Carpool Guy* (2005), as well as several made-for-TV movies. Biography: *Anthony Geary*, John Blumenthal (1982).

Gerber, Joan (b. 1935) A very active television voice artist for over forty years, she supplied the voice for Scrooge McDuck's matronly cook and housekeeper Mrs. Betina Beakley in *DuckTales the Movie: The Treasure of the Lost Lamp* (1990). She was born in Detroit, Michigan, and began voicing TV cartoons in 1959 with the series *Matty's Funnies with Beany and Cecil*. Over the decades Gerber acted in live-action children's shows such as *H. R. Pufnstuf, The Bugaloos,* and *Lidsville,* and voiced dozens of animated series, including *Roger Ramjet, The Pink Panther Show, The Fantastic Four, The Dukes, The Chipmunks, Teenage Mutant Ninja Turtles, Midnight Patrol: Adventures in the Dream Zone, Tiny Toon Adventures, Sonic the Hedgehog,* and *Duck Dodgers,* as well as *DuckTales* where she first voiced Mrs. Beakley. Among her many animated movies and videos are *Corn on the Cob* (1965), *The Tales of Washington Irving* (1970), *Shinbone Alley* (1971), *The Boa Friend* (1973), *Charlotte's Web* (1973), *The Nine Lives of Fritz the Cat* (1974), *The Mouse and His Child* (1977), *Nutcracker Fantasy* (1979), *The World of Strawberry Shortcake* (1980), *Heidi's Song* (1982), *Peter and the Magic Egg* (1983), *DuckTales: Treasure of the Golden Suns* (1987), *Super DuckTales* (1989), and *A Flintstones Christmas Carol* (1994).

Germann, Greg (b. 1958) A stage, screen, and television actor who is also a writer, he provided the voice for the obnoxious talent Agent in *Bolt* (2008). Gregory Andrew Germann was born in Houston, Texas, the son of a playwright and theatre professor, and grew up in Colorado where he studied drama at the University of Northern Colorado. He made his New York stage debut Off Broadway with such companies as the Circle Repertory Company and The Ensemble Studio Theatre and was featured in such Manhattan productions as *Found a Peanut* (1984), *Biloxi Blues* (1985), *Assassins* (1990), *Dearly Departed* (1991), *Born Guilty* (1993), and *Boeing-Boeing* (2008). Germann made his movie bow in 1985 and appeared in such films as *Miss Firecracker* (1989), *The Night We Never Met* (1993), *Clear and Present Danger* (1994), *Joe Somebody* (2001), *Special Ed* (2005), and *Quarantine* (2008). He has acted on such television series as *Miami Vice, Tour of Duty, L.A. Law, Ellen, Ned and Stacey, Desperate Housewives, In Case of Emergency,* and *CSI: Crime Scene Investigation,* but he is most known as Richard Fish on the series *Ally McBeal*.

Gerson, Betty Lou (1914–1999) A radio actress who also made some memorable film and television appearances, she voiced one of Disney's greatest villains, Cruella de Vil, in *One Hundred and One Dalmatians* (1961) as well as providing the voice for the television panelist Miss Birdwell in the same film. She was born in Chattanooga, Tennessee, and grew up in Birmingham, Alabama. Gerson started her radio career in Chicago but soon moved on to New York City where she voiced such soap operas as *Arnold Grimm's Daughter, The Guiding Light,* and *Road of Life*. In Hollywood she made her film debut in 1949 and the next year worked for Disney for the first time, providing the narration for *Cinderella*

(1950). As the golden age of radio waned, Gerson took up television and appeared in such series as *Gang Busters, I Married Joan, Four Star Playhouse, Father Knows Best, Death Valley Days, Perry Mason, The Dick Van Dyke Show, The Farmer's Daughter,* and *Hazel.* Her film credits were few but she was noticed in *Undercover Girl* (1950), *An Annapolis Story* (1955), *The Green-Eyed Blonde* (1957), *The Fly* (1957), and *Mary Poppins* (1964). Gerson retired in 1966 but returned to the recording studio one last time in 1997 to do a voice for the animated movie *Cats Don't Dance.* The character of Cruella De Vil is a triumph of villainy and comedy. The animators patterned the character after the flamboyant actress Tallulah Bankhead and Gerson gave her an upper-crust British accent that kept Cruella vocally sophisticated even as her movements were erratic and bombastic. It is a dazzling vocal performance for an unforgettable Disney villain.

Gerson, Daniel A scriptwriter for television series and animated films, his only acting credit is voicing the silly monster janitors geeky Needleman and clumsy Smitty in *Monsters, Inc.* (2001) which he co-wrote. Gerson also contributed to the screenplays for *Chicken Little* (2005), *Cars* (2006), and the animated short *Prep & Landing* (2009). He has written scripts for the television series *Something So Right, The New Addams Family, Big Wolf on Campus,* and *Misguided Angels,* as well as the cartoon series *Duckman: Private Dick/Family Man.*

Gibbs, Mary (b. 1996) A child performer with limited credits so far, at the age of two and a half she voiced the two-year-old human girl "Boo" who mistakenly enters the monster world in *Monsters, Inc.* (2001). Mary Jessica Gibbs, the daughter of animator Rob Gibbs, was born in Pasadena, California, and can also be heard in the animated videos *The Lion King II: Simba's Pride* (1998) and *Mulan II* (2004). The real name of the character of Boo is Mary Gibbs but it is never spoken, only seen on one of the girl's crayon drawings. The character was not named for the voice artist but, coincidentally, was the name of the girl in the short story "There's a Boy in My Closet" which has some similarities with the movie. Originally Boo was to be six years old but during production it was deemed more effective if she was much younger and more dependent on Sulley. Gibbs was so young and antsy when the film was made that she wouldn't sit still during recording sessions. The crew ended up following her around the studio with a microphone and cleaned up the recording later.

Gibson, Mel (b. 1956) The rugged, romantic movie star who often plays persecuted individuals who seek justice, he supplied the voice for the hero Captain John Smith in *Pocahontas* (1995). Mel Columcille Gerard Gibson was born in Peekskill, New York, and grew up in Australia where he was educated at the University of New South Wales in Sydney. He began his career acting at the National Institute of Dramatic Arts then made a few movies before finding international recognition as the title character in the low-budget cult film hit *Mad Max* (1979). Among his many subsequent movies are *Gallipoli* (1981), *Mad Max 2: The Road Warrior* (1981), *The Year of Living Dangerously* (1982), *The Bounty* (1984), *The River* (1984), *Mad Max Beyond Thunderdome* (1985), *Lethal Weapon* (1987) and its three sequels, *Tequila Sunrise* (1988), *Hamlet* (1990), *Braveheart* (1995), *Ransom* (1996), *The Patriot* (2000), *What Women Want* (2000), *Signs* (2002), and *Edge of Darkness* (2010), as well as the stop-motion movie *Chicken Run* (2000) for which he voiced the hero Rocky. Gibson has produced many films and television shows and has directed as well, most memorably *Braveheart, The Passion of the Christ* (2004), and *Apocalypto* (2006). While two actresses did the speaking and singing vocals for the character of Pocahontas, Gibson sang his own songs in *Pocahontas,* the first time he had ever sung in the movies. The animators studied several Erroll Flynn movies to capture the movement they wanted for John Smith. Yet as much as the character moves like a romantic hero, Gibson's performance keeps Smith pretty down to earth and avoids the vocal flourishes that might trivialize the captain. Biographies: *Mel Gibson: Man on a Mission,* Wensley Clarkson (2005); *The Unofficial Mel Gibson,* Sandy Noble (1996).

Gibson, Mimi (b. 1948) A prolific child performer on the screen since the age of three and retired by the time she was eighteen, she provided the voice of the dalmatian pup Lucky who is addicted to television in *One Hundred and One Dalmatians* (1961). She was born in Renton, Washington, where her father died when she was an infant so her mother moved to California and supported them by the toddler's screen appearances. Gibson made over forty movies before she was thirteen years old, playing toddlers and children in such films as *Corky of Gasoline Alley* (1951), *I'll See You in My Dreams* (1951), *A Slight Case of Larceny* (1953), *There's No Business Like Show Business* (1954), *The Egyptian* (1954), *The Ten Commandments* (1956), *Courage of Black Beauty* (1957), *The Oklahoman* (1957), *The Three Faces of Eve* (1957), *Houseboat* (1958), *The Remarkable Mr. Pennypacker* (1959), and *The Children's Hour* (1961). She also appeared in over one hundred episodes of television series, including *Four Star Playhouse, The Loretta Young Show, The Adventures of Dr. Fu Manchu,*

Zane Grey Theatre, Highway Patrol, Playhouse 90, The Rebel, The Ann Sothern Show, Westinghouse Playhouse, Leave It to Beaver, and *My Three Sons.* When Gibson turned eighteen and found that the $100,000 she had earned had been squandered by others, she quit show business and became an advocate for revisions in the Coogan Law to protect child actors.

Gilbert, Billy (1894–1971)   A huge character actor who specialized in small but very noticeable roles in over 200 feature films from the silents to the 1960s, the rotund giant provided the voice (and sneezes) for Sneezy in *Snow White and the Seven Dwarfs* (1938) and Willie the Giant in the "Mickey and the Beanstalk" sequence in *Fun and Fancy Free* (1947). He was born William Gilbert Barron in Louisville, Kentucky, the son of Metropolitan Opera singers, and at the age of twelve he was doing comedy on the vaudeville circuits. He made his film debut in 1916 and clowned opposite Charles Chaplin and Laurel and Hardy in the silent movie days. When sound came in, Gilbert often played heavily-accented comic characters who always caught the audience's attention. Among his many screen credits are *Chinatown After Dark* (1931), *The Merry Widow* (1934), *Curly Top* (1935), *A Night at the Opera* (1935), *On the Avenue* (1937), *Captains Courageous* (1937), *Broadway Melody of 1938* (1937), *One Hundred Men and a Girl* (1937), *Rosalie* (1937), *No, No, Nanette* (1940), *The Great Dictator* (1940), *Anchors Aweigh* (1945), *Down Among the Sheltering Pines* (1953), and *Five Weeks in a Balloon* (1962). He appeared in a handful of Broadway musicals in the 1940s and was featured in several television programs in the 1950s. In vaudeville, Gilbert was famous for his sneezing routine and it was utilized in several of his screen appearances. When he read that Disney was making *Snow White and the Seven Dwarfs* and that one of the dwarfs was named Sneezy, he insisted on auditioning his sneezes for Walt Disney. He was hired on the spot. The animators not only used his voice and sneezing but modeled the character of Sneezy after Gilbert's looks and gestures. Originally Sneezy was going to be Deefy, a deaf dwarf, but Disney was afraid it would prove to be offensive and dropped the idea. Gilbert's Willy the Giant in *Fun and Fancy Free* is a roguish characterization. Despite his great size and bellowing voice, the giant seems a gentle and childlike character (he likes to sing and listen to the Singing Harp perform more than anything else) and Gilbert's vocals are more comic than menacing. Willie remains one of Disney's least frightening villains.

Gilbert, Ed (1931–1999)   A versatile character actor and voice artist with many television credits, he supplied the voice for the haughty cockroach maître d' Francois at the New York mouse restaurant in *The Rescuers Down Under* (1990). Gilbert made his television debut in a 1963 episode of *The Gallant Men* and, using his talent for different accents, played Americans and foreigners in such series as *Combat!, Ben Casey, The Wild Wild West, The Rogues, The Name of the Game, Here Come the Brides, Mannix, The Mod Squad, The Interns, Mission: Impossible, The F.B.I., Cannon, The Six Million Dollar Man, S.W.A.T., Police Story, The New Adventures of Wonder Woman, The Hardy Boys/Nancy Drew Mysteries, Nero Wolfe, Dallas, The A-Team,* and *Married with Children.* In the 1980s Gilbert turned to voice work and was kept busy for the next two decades voicing many TV cartoon series, including *Jem, InHumanoids, Rambo, G.I. Joe, The Transformers, DuckTales, BraveStarr, Adventures of the Gummi Bears, Peter Pan and the Pirates, Tale-Spin, The Pirates of Dark Water, Batman, Animaniacs, The Little Mermaid, Capitol Critters, Aladdin, Iron Man, Gargoyles, Dexter's Laboratory, The Tick, The Real Adventures of Jonny Quest, Duckman: Private Dick/Family Man, Superman,* and *The New Batman Adventures.* He can also be heard in such animated films and videos as *InHumanoids: The Movie* (1986), *The Transformers: The Movie* (1986), *G.I. Joe: The Movie* (1987), *Scooby-Doo and the Reluctant Werewolf* (1988), *BraveStarr: The Legend* (1988), *The Little Mermaid* (1989), *Tom and Jerry: The Movie* (1992), *Jonny's Golden Quest* (1993), *Yogi the Easter Bear* (1994), *The Pagemaster* (1994), *Gargoyles: The Heroes Awaken* (1995), *Baldur's Gate* (1998), and *Aladdin and the Adventure of All Time* (2000). When Phil Harris, who had voiced Baloo the Bear in *The Jungle Book* (1967), started doing the same character for the TV cartoon series *TaleSpin* two decades later, it was clear his voice had changed too much to be recognizable. Gilbert studied old recordings of Harris and impersonated the voice for Baloo in the cartoon series.

Gill, Florence (1877–1965)   A British voice actress who worked with Disney in the 1930s and 1940s, she was the speaking and singing voice of the prima donna hen Clara Cluck in a half dozen animated shorts. The London-born actress made her screen debut as a singer in the Hollywood live-action short *Dora's Dunking Doughnuts* (1933) then voiced her first cartoon the next year as the title character in *The Wise Little Hen* which became famous for introducing the character of Donald Duck. Gill first voiced Clara Cluck in *Orphan's Benefit* (1934) and reprised the role in such cartoons as *Mickey's Grand Opera* (1936), *Mickey's Amateurs* (1937), *Mickey's Birthday Party* (1942), and *Symphony Hour* (1942), in each short singing in her grand opera manner. She played hens and humans in several other Disney shorts, including *Mother Pluto* (1936), *Self-Control* (1938), *Golden Eggs* (1941), *The Nifty Nineties* (1941), *Chicken Little* (1943), and *Contrary Condor* (1944). Gill appeared as herself in the live-action section of *The Reluctant Dragon* (1941) and played small roles, usually as singers, in such movies as *Every Night at Eight* (1935), *Welcome Home* (1935), *Here Comes the Band* (1935), *Way Down East* (1935), *Larceny on the Air* (1937), *She Had to Eat* (1937), *Mr. Dodd Takes the Air* (1937), *Eagle Squadron* (1942), and *I Married a Witch* (1942).

Gillis, Ann (b. 1927) An actress on the screen as a child who successfully graduated to adult roles, she provided the voice of the adult deer Faline in *Bambi* (1942). She was born Alma Mabel Conner in Little Rock, Arkansas, and as a child was playing bit parts in such movies as *Men in White* (1934), *The Great Ziegfeld* (1936), *The Garden of Allah* (1936), and *Off to the Races* (1937) before being featured in *King of Hockey* (1936). Gillis had leading juvenile roles in *The Adventures of Tom Sawyer* (1938) and *Little Orphan Annie* (1938) but in most of her films she played supporting roles, usually spoiled brats. Among her other screen credits are *Little Men* (1940), *All This and Heaven Too* (1940), *Since You Went Away* (1944), *Sweetheart of Sigma Chi* (1946), and *The Time of Their Lives* (1946). Gillis left the movies after World War II and lived in England where she appeared on some British television shows in the 1960s. She returned to the screen one last time to play the astronaut Poole's mother in *2001: A Space Odyssey* (1968).

Gilmore, Art (b. 1912) A popular radio announcer who also narrated movie trailers, television shows, documentary films, and commercials, he provided the voice of President Franklin D. Roosevelt in the "Baby Weems" section of *The Reluctant Dragon* (1941). Raised in Tacoma, Washington, and educated at Washington State University, he began his career on the Warner Brothers radio station in Hollywood where he later narrated over fifty film shorts. After serving in World War II, he went on national radio, announcing many CBS shows, including *Amos 'n Andy, Dr. Christian, Stars Over Hollywood, The Sears Radio Theatre*, and *The Adventures of Frank Race*. With the coming of television in the 1950s, Gilmore became the announcer for such programs as *Climax!, The Red Skelton Show, The George Gobel Show, Highway Patrol, Mackenzie's Raiders*, and *Men of Annapolis*. He made some appearances on television, such as in *Dragnet, Emergency!, The Mary Tyler Moore Show, The Waltons*, and *Adam-12*. Gilmore's impersonation of FDR was so accurate he also provided the voice in the film *Yankee Doodle Dandy* (1942) and the documentary *The Gallant Hours* (1960). He wrote a book on radio announcing and recorded several books for children.

Givot, George (1903–1984) A round, full-voiced actor-singer from the stage who later appeared in many movies and television series, he provided the speaking and singing voice for Tony the Italian restaurant proprietor in *Lady and the Tramp* (1955). He was born in Omaha, Nebraska, and was on the vaudeville stage before getting featured parts on Broadway in *Earl Carroll's Sketchbook* (1929), *The Constant Sinner* (1931), *Americana* (1932), *Pardon My English* (1933), *Mexican Hayride* (1944), and *Do Re Mi* (1960). Givot was on the radio as a dialect comedian and made a series of movie shorts in which he played a Greek immigrant who destroyed the English language in every sentence. He graduated to features in the mid-1930s and eventually got straight dramatic roles as well as comic supporting characters. Among his films are *Paddy O'Day* (1935), *Wake Up and Live* (1937), *Thin Ice* (1937), *Hollywood Cavalcade* (1939), *Road to Morocco* (1942), *Du Barry Was a Lady* (1943), *Captain Pirate* (1952), *April in Paris* (1952), *Three Sailors and a Girl* (1953), *The Benny Goodman Story* (1956), *The Girl Can't Help It* (1956), and *China Gate* (1957). Givot also appeared in some television series in the 1950s, including *My Little Margie, Mr. and Mrs. North, Fireside Theatre, Damon Runyon Theatre, Blondie*, and *Mike Hammer*. In *Lady and the Tramp*, he sings the Italian serenade "Bella Notte" during Tramp and Lady's spaghetti dinner, one of the most memorable and beloved scenes in all of Disney animation.

Glover, William A British character actor on American television between 1968 and 1991, he provided the voice of little Jenny's caring chauffeur Winston in *Oliver & Company* (1988). Among the television series he appeared on are *The Monkees, Kung Fu, Fantasy Island, WKRP in Cincinnati, Bring 'Em Back Alive, General Hospital, St. Elsewhere, Punky Brewster, Dear John, Newhart, Santa Barbara, Star Trek: The Next Generation*, and *The Fresh Prince of Bel-Air*. Glover also acted in the films as *To Be or Not to Be* (1983), as well as a handful of made-for-TV movies.

Goldberg, Whoopi (b. 1955) The distinctive African American comic, actress, producer, writer, and TV hostess who has enjoyed a varied career on the stage, in movies, and on television, she provided the voices for Scar's sidekick hyena Shenzi in *The Lion King* (1994) and the purple toy octopus Stretch in *Toy Story 3* (2010). She was born Caryn Elaine Johnson in New York City and worked in comic improv groups in California before she was discovered by director-producer Mike Nichols. He presented the unknown performer-writer in the one-woman show *Whoopi Goldberg* on Broadway in 1984 and its HBO special made Goldberg instantly famous. She secured her movie career the next year with her performance in *The Color Purple* (1985), followed by such films as *Jumpin' Jack Flash* (1986), *Clara's Heart* (1988), *Ghost* (1990), *Soapdish* (1991), *The Player* (1992), *Sister Act* (1992), *Sarafina!* (1992), *Sister Act 2: Back in the Habit* (1993), *Made in America* (1993), *Corrina, Corrina* (1994), *Boys on the Side* (1995), *Ghosts of Mississippi* (1996), *How Stella Got Her Groove Back* (1998), *Girl, Interrupted* (1999), *Rat Race* (2001), *Star Trek: Nemesis* (2002), *The Last Guy on Earth* (2006), and *Stream* (2009). Goldberg has produced, written, and performed in many television specials, including a series of *Comic Relief* concerts for charity, has made many appearances on talk shows and *Saturday Night Live*, has been one of the hosts of *The View* since 2005, and acted in the television series *A Different World*, *Bagdad Cafe*, *Star Trek: The Next Generation*, *Strong Medicine*, *Freedom: A History of Us*, *Everybody Hates Chris*, *The Cleaner*, and her own show *Whoopi*. She has supplied voices for the TV cartoon series *Captain Planet and the Planeteers* and *Happily Ever After: Fairy Tales for Every Child*, as well as the animated videos and movies *The Pagemaster* (1994), *A Christmas Carol* (1997), *Rudolph the Red-Nosed Reindeer: The Movie* (1998), *The Rugrats Movie* (1998), *Our Friend Martin* (1999), *The Adventures of Rocky & Bullwinkle* (2000), *Madeline: My Fair Madeline* (2002), *The Lion King 1½* (2004), *Pinocchio 3000* (2004), *Farce of the Penguins* (2006), *Doogal* (2006), and *Everyone's Hero* (2006), Goldberg has returned to the stage on occasion, appearing on Broadway in *A Funny Thing Happened on the Way to the Forum* (1996), *Ma Rainey's Black Bottom* (2003), *Whoopi* (2004), and *Xanadu* (2007), starring in *Sister Act* in London in 2010, and produced the Broadway musical *Thoroughly Modern Millie* (2002) as well as several television programs. Memoir: *Book* (2004); biography: *Whoopi Goldberg: Her Journey from Poverty to Megastardom*, James Robert Parrish (1997).

Goldthwait, Bobcat (b. 1962) The hyperactive comic whose lively, high-pitched voice is ideal for animated characters, he voiced Hades' incompetent henchman Pain in *Hercules* (1997). He was born Robert Francis Goldthwait in Syracuse, New York, and started doing stand-up comedy while still in high school. His appearances in clubs and in concert, as well as his comedy albums, eventually put him on television where he appeared on many programs and had his own comedy specials. Goldthwait played characters in such films as *Police Academy 2: Their First Assignment* (1985) and two of its sequels, *Scrooged* (1988), *Shakes the Clown* (1991), *Radioland Murders* (1994), *Mrs. Winterbourne* (1996), *Grind* (2003), and *Sleeping Dogs Lie* (2006), as well as the television series *Married with Children*, *The John Larroquette Show*, *Unhappily Ever After*, and *Sabrina, the Teenage Witch*. Goldthwait reprised his Pain in the videos *Hercules: Zero to Hero* (1999) and *Mickey's House of Villains* (2001), and in the cartoon series *Hercules* and *House of Mouse*. He can also be heard in the animated television series *Capitol Critters*, *The Moxy & Flea Show*, *Duckman: Private Dick/Family Man*, *Beavis and Butt-Head*, *Buzz Lightyear of Star Command*, *Lilo & Stitch*, and *Back at the Barnyard*, and the videos and films *Rusty: A Dog's Tale* (1998), *Lion of Oz* (2000), *Hansel and Gretel* (2002), and *Leroy and Stitch* (2006).

Goldwyn, Tony (b. 1960) A recognized actor and director with many stage, film, and television credits, he voiced the title ape man hero of *Tarzan* (1999) as an adult. Anthony Howard Goldwyn was born in Los Angeles into a show business family (his grandfathers were playwright Sidney Howard and producer Samuel Goldwyn), was educated at Hamilton College and Brandeis University, and studied acting at the Herbert Berghof Studio in New York City and the London Academy of Music and Dramatic Art. He made his Off Broadway debut in *Digby* (1985), followed by praised performances in *The Sum of Us* (1990), *Spike Heels* (1992), *The Dying Gaul* (1998), *Exonerated* (2002), and *The Water's Edge* (2006), and on Broadway in *Holiday* (1995) and *Promises Promises* (2010). Goldwyn made his screen debut in *Jason Lives: Friday the 13th Part VI* (1986) and found notoriety as the villain in *Ghost* (1990). Among his many other movies are *Gaby: A True Story* (1987), *The Pelican Brief* (1993), *Pocahontas: The Legend* (1995), *Nixon* (1995), *The Substance of Fire* (1996), *Bounce* (2000), *An American Rhapsody* (2001), *Joshua* (2002), *The Last Samurai* (2003), *The Sisters* (2005), and *The Last House on the Left* (2009), as well as several made-for-TV movies. He has also acted in such television series as *St. Elsewhere*, *Matlock*, *Designing Women*, *L.A. Law*, *Hunter*, *Tales from the Crypt*, *Frasier*, *Without a Trace*, *The L Word*, *Dexter*, *Law & Order: Criminal Intent*, and *The Good Wife*. Except for Dracula, the character of Tarzan has appeared in more films than any other literary figure. The Disney version attempts to be true to the original Edgar Rice Burroughs book but details were changed. To animate Tarzan's movements, the studio filmed skateboard professional Tony Hawk in action. For the voice of Tarzan, Goldwyn did not imitate the most famous Tarzan of all, Johnny Weissmuller, but came up with his own sound for the famous Ape Man.

Gooding, Cuba, Jr. (b. 1968) The dynamic African American film and television actor who became a star in the 1990s, he supplied the voice of the over-eager, vain-glorious horse Buck in *Home on the Range* (2004). He was born in the Bronx, New York, the son of professional singers, and grew up in Los Angeles where he did some classical theatre after graduating from high school. Gooding made his television debut in 1986 and his screen bow the following year but he was not noticed until his performance in the movie *Boyz n the Hood* (1991). Solid performances in *A Few Good Men* (1992), *Judgement Night* (1993), *Outbreak* (1995), and *Losing Isaiah* (1995) followed, but it was his sports star Rod Todwell in *Jerry Maguire* (1996) that made Gooding famous. His other movie credits include *Instinct* (1999), *Men of Honor* (2000), *Pearl Harbor* (2001), *American Gangster* (2007), *Norbit* (2007), and *Hardwired* (2009), and he also appeared in such television series as *Nasty Boys* and *MacGyver*. The character of Buck in *Home on the Range* has much in common with the funny dragon sidekick Mushu in *Mulan* (1998). Both are hyperactive, fast-talking, and filled with visions of themselves as dashing heroes. Just as Eddie Murphy's bombastic vocals made Mushu a comic favorite, so too Gooding displays a first-rate sense of comedy in his performance of the over-active Buck. Gooding reprised his Buck in the cartoon short *A Dairy Tale* (2004) and can also be heard in the animated video *The Land Before Time XIII: The Wisdom of Friends* (2007).

Goodman, John (b. 1952) The paunchy, likable character actor with a deep voice and a down-home persona, he provided the voices for the honest peasant Pacha in *The Emperor's New Groove* (2000), the kind-hearted blue monster James P. "Sulley" Sullivan in *Monsters Inc.* (2001), and the New Orleans millionaire Eli "Big Daddy" La Bouff in *The Princess and the Frog* (2009). John Stephen Goodman was born in St. Louis, Missouri, the son of a postal worker, and educated at Southwest Missouri State before working in summer stock theatres, eventually finding jobs in New York City and appearing on Broadway in *Big River* (1985). He acted in several television sit-coms before he found wide recognition as the put-upon husband Dan Conner in *Roseanne* which ran nine years. Goodman's other television credits include *Now and Again*, *The West Wing*, *Center of the Universe*, and *Treme*. He has acted in over fifty movies, including *Revenge of the Nerds* (1984), *The Big Easy* (1986), *Raising Arizona* (1987), *Arachnophobia* (1990), *King Ralph* (1991), *The Babe* (1992), *The Flintstones* (1994), *The Borrowers* (1997), *The Big Lebowski* (1998), *O Brother, Where Art Thou?* (2000), *Beyond the Sea* (2004), and *Alabama Moon* (2009). The character of Sulley in *Monsters, Inc.* was originally a janitor named Johnson who had a lowly job at the factory because he proved to be incompetent as a Scarer. He was also planned as having tentacles rather than legs but it was felt the moving appendages would be too distracting. Bill Murray was the first choice to voice Sulley but a foul-up in communication lost him the part. Goodman, who had already voiced Disney's *The Emperor's New Groove*, stepped in and he and Billy Crystal, who voiced Mike, had an effective rapport during the recording. Goodman reprised his Sully in the short *Mike's New Car* (2002) and as Sullivan Truck in *Cars* (2006), and returned to Pacha in the video *The Emperor's New Groove 2: Kronk's New Groove* (2005) and the TV cartoon series *The Emperor's New School*. He can also be heard in the animated movies and videos *We're Back! A Dinosaur's Story* (1993), *Rudolph the Red-Nosed Reindeer: The Movie* (1998), *The Jungle Book 2* (2003), *Clifford's Really Big Movie* (2004), and *Bee Movie* (2007) as well as the cartoon series *The Simpsons* and *Father of the Pride*. He returned to the stage for the revival of *Waiting for Godot* on Broadway in 2009.

Gordon, Anita (1914–2006) A singer-actress heard more often than she was seen in the movies, she provided the voice of the Singing Harp in the "Mickey and the Beanstalk" segment of *Fun and Fancy Free* (1947). The New Orleans native was a vocalist for Ray Noble's Orchestra and made many recording with the band. Gordon dubbed the singing for movie actors, such as Pamela Tiffin in *State Fair* (1962) and Jean Seberg in *Paint Your Wagon* (1969), and appeared in a handful of television shows, singing on *The Ken Murray Show*, *The George Gobel Show*, and *The Tennessee Ernie Ford Show*, and acting in such series as *The Millionaire*, *Sugarfoot*, *Death Valley Days*, *Bachelor Father*, and *My Mother the Car*.

Gordon-Levitt, Joseph (b. 1981) A child performer who has developed into a busy actor on screen and television, he supplied the voice of the 15-year-old hero Jim Hawkins in *Treasure Planet* (2002). He was born in Los Angeles, the son of political activist Jane Gordon and politician Dennis Levitt, and made his television debut at the age of seven. His performance as David Collins in the TV-movie *Dark Shadows* (1990) led to a recurring role in the television series when he was ten. Gordon-Levitt went on to act in such series as *Family Ties*, *China Beach*, *Quantum Leap*, *L.A. Law*, *The Powers That Be*, *Roseanne*, and *The Outer Limits*, but he was most known as Tommy Solomon on the sit-com *3rd Rock from the Sun*. His film credits include *A River Runs Through It* (1992), *The Road Killers* (1994), *Angels in the Outfield* (1994), *The Juror* (1996), *10 Things I Hate About You* (1999), *Picking Up the Pieces* (2000), *Manic* (2001), *Brick* (2005), *The Lookout* (2007), *(500) Days of Summer* (2009), *Women in Trouble* (2009), *G.I. Joe: The Rise of Cobra* (2009), *Morgan M. Morgansen's Date with Destiny* (2010) and its sequel *Morgan and Destiny's Eleventeenth Date: The Zepplin Zoo* (2010), and *Inception* (2010). Gordon-Levitt left Hollywood for a time and attended Columbia University and performed Off Broadway in *Uncle Bob* (2001). He wrote, produced, and directed the short *Sparks* (2009) and directed his two Morgan M. Morgansen films. Although the youth Jim Hawkins in *Treasure Planet* enjoys "solar surfing" on his rocket-powered surf board, he is pretty much the same character as in Robert Louis Stevenson's *Treasure Island*. Gordan-Levitt plays Jim as a modern teenager but he retains the classic spirit of adventure in his vocals.

Gottfried, Gilbert (b. 1955) A comic actor with a distinctively loud and raspy voice, he has appeared in many films and television shows but is most known for the grating voice of the parrot Iago in *Aladdin* (1992). The Brooklyn native started doing stand-up comedy at the age of fifteen and soon developed a following in comedy clubs. He found a wider audience on television where he was a regular on *Saturday Night Live* and appeared in TV specials and series, such as *The Cosby Show, Totally Hidden Video, The Adventures of Superboy, Night Court, A Different World, Silk Stalkings, Wings, 30 Rock, Son of the Beach, 'Til Death, Greg the Bunny*, and *M'larky*. Gottfried's popularity was further enhanced by his appearances in small but scene-stealing roles in films, such as *Beverly Hills Cop II* (1987), *Hot to Trot* (1988), *The Adventures of Ford Fairlane* (1990), and *Problem Child* (1990) and its sequels. Yet none of his screen credits was as memorable as his squawking Iago. The parrot was originally conceived as a very polite but sarcastic bird with a thick British accent. But the entire concept was changed when Gottfried was considered for the role. The animators utilized Gottfried's large teeth and facial expressions in developing Iago. He is one of the funniest sidekicks in the Disney canon and much of Iago's effectiveness is due to Gottfried's hilariously barking vocals. He reprised the voice of Iago in the made-for-video films *The Return of Jafar* (1994), *Aladdin and the King of Thieves* (1995), *Mickey's House of Villains* (2001), *Aladdin in Nasira's Revenge* (2001), and *Disney Princess Enchanted Tales: Follow Your Dreams* (2007), and others, as well as in the Disney television series *Aladdin* and *House of Mouse*. When the Disney theme park attraction The Enchanted Tiki Room was redesigned in 1998, the parrot Iago was added and Gottfried again provided the voice. After *Aladdin*, Gottfried was called on to do the voices for many commercials and such movies as *Thumbelina* (1994), *Doctor Doolittle* (1998), *Lemony Snickett's A Series of Unfortunate Events* (2004), and *Farce of the Penguins* (2006), as well as the television series *Timon and Pumba, Duckman: Private Dick/Family Man, Dilbert, The Fairly OddParents, Crank Yankers, Family Guy, Cyberchase*, and *Hercules*.

Gough, Michael (1917–2011) A tall, lean British actor with years of stage, film, and television credits who became famous late in his career for playing stuffy Englishmen in American movies, he provided the voice of the Dodo bird Uilleam in the 2010 version of *Alice in Wonderland*. He was born in Kuala Lumpur, Malaysia, the son of British parents, and educated in Tunbridge Wells, England, before enrolling at London's Old Vic Theatre School in 1936. That same year he made his London stage debut and a year later was on Broadway, though much of his career was in England where he acted in both the classics and in new works. Gough made his film debut in *Anna Karenina* (1948), followed by over a hundred movies first in Great Britain then eventually in Hollywood. But it was his portrayal of the villain Councillor Hedin in the cult TV series *Doctor Who* between 1966 and 1983 that made him famous on both sides of the Atlantic. Gough secured his celebrity as the butler Alfred Pennyworth in the movie *Batman* (1989) and three of its sequels. Among his many film credits are *Androcles and the Lion* (1951), *Richard III* (1955), *The Horse's Mouth* (1958), *The Phantom of the Opera* (1962), *Women in Love* (1969), *The Go-Between* (1970), *The Boys from Brazil* (1978), *The Dresser* (1983), *Out of Africa* (1985), *The Age of Innocence* (1993), and *Sleepy Hollow* (1999). His deep, precise voice can be heard in the animated film *Corpse Bride* (2005).

Gould, Alexander (b. 1994) A teenage television actor who has several voice credits, he provided the voice of the curious young clown fish Nemo in *Finding Nemo* (2003). He was born in Los Angeles and began his acting career at the age of two and made his first movie when he was four. Gould has appeared on such TV series as *Malcolm in the Middle, Ally McBean, 7th Heaven, American Dreams, Criminal Minds, Law & Order: Special Victims Unit, Pushing Daisies*, and *Weeds*. His movie credits include *Mexico City* (2000), *Wheelmen* (2002), *They* (2002), and *How to Eat Fried Worms* (2006), and he has voiced the animated films and videos

Diary of a Worm (2005), *Bambi II* (2006), *Curious George* (2006), and *The Librarian from the Black Lagoon* (2007). The character of Nemo was first introduced in the previous Pixar film *Monsters, Inc.* (2001) when the little girl Boo plays with a clown fish doll. Nemo is Latin for "nobody" or "no one," an appropriate name for the young and naive fish who must be rescued by others.

Gould, Harold (1923–2010) A veteran character actor with stage and film credits who appeared in hundreds of television episodes over a period of fifty years, he voiced the Native American Old Denahi in *Brother Bear* (2003). He was born Harold V. Goldstein in Schenectady, New York, and studied at Albany Teacher's College and Cornell University before becoming a theatre teacher at Randolph-Macon Woman's College in Virginia and the University of California at Riverside. Although he had acted in many summer stock productions and a few movies, he did not give up teaching to become a full-time actor until he was thirty-seven years old. Gould appeared in many Off Broadway productions and on Broadway in such plays as *Fools* (1981), *Grown Ups* (1981), *Artist Descending a Staircase* (1989), and *Mixed Emotions* (1993). His many film credits include *Inside Daisy Clover* (1965), *Harper* (1966), *The Arrangement* (1969), *The Sting* (1973), *The Front Page* (1974), *Love and Death* (1975), *Gus* (1976), *Seems Like Old Times* (1980), *Patch Adams* (1998), *Stuart Little* (1999), *Freaky Friday* (2003), and *Nobody's Perfect* (2004). Gould was better known for his fathers, grandfathers, uncles, and elderly types in dozens of television series, including *The Donna Reed Show*, *Twilight Zone*, *Hazel*, *The Virginian*, *The Farmer's Daughter*, *The Fugitive*, *Hogan's Heroes*, *Mary Tyler Moore Show*, *Gunsmoke*, *Soap*, *Rhoda*, *Spencer*, *The Golden Girls*, *Touched by an Angel*, and *Nip/Tuck*.

Goulet, Robert (1933–2007) A rich-voiced baritone recording star who was a favorite in nightclubs and on television, he began his career on Broadway and ended it doing voices for animated videos and films, such as *Toy Story 2* (1999) in which he mocked his lounge-style crooning while providing the singing voice for Wheezy the Penguin. Robert Gerald Goulet was born in Lawrence, Massachusetts, but grew up in Edmonton, Canada, and later studied voice at the Royal Conservatory of Music in Toronto. After playing in musicals across Canada, he made a sensational Broadway debut as Lancelot in *Camelot* (1960), later returning to New York and receiving plaudits for his performance in *The Happy Time* (1968). Goulet's film debut was providing the speaking and singing voice of the feline Jaune-Tom in the animated feature *Gay Purr-ee* (1962). He made a handful of movies over the years but much of his career was on television where he appeared in sit-coms, musical specials, and dramatic series. Goulet's final credits were the singing vocals for the character Mikey Blumberg in the TV cartoon series *Recess* and the video sequels *Recess: School's Out* (2001) and *Recess Christmas: Miracle on Third Street* (2001). Autobiography: *Quebec Boy: An Autobiography* (2001).

Graae, Jason (b. 1958) A singer-actor with many musical theatre and recording credits who has appeared on television series, he was the singing voice of one of the thick-headed Willie Brothers in *Home on the Range* (2004). He was born in Chicago, grew up in Tulsa, Oklahoma, and began his career in New York City appearing in such Off Broadway musicals as *Forbidden Broadway* (1982), *Snoopy* (1982), *Just So* (1985), *Olympus on My Mind* (1986), *Forever Plaid* (1990), and *Hello Muddah, Hello Fadduh* (1992), as well as on Broadway in *Do Patent Leather Shoes Really Reflect Up?* (1982), *Stardust* (1987), *Falsettos* (1992), and *A Grand Night for Singing* (1993). Graae made his television debut in 1988 and has been on such series as *Friends*, *Caroline in the City*, *Coach*, *Frasier*, *Rude Awakening*, and *Six Feet Under*, as well as the TV musical *Geppetto* (2000). He can be heard on the cartoon series *The Angry Beavers* and the animated video *Sunshine Barry & the Disco Worms* (2008).

Graham, Frank (1914–1950) A multitalented radio actor who voiced over forty animated shorts before his untimely death, he provided the voices of Chicken Little, Turkey Lurkey, Foxy Loxy, and others in the Disney short *Chicken Little* (1943) and some of the narration in *The Three Caballeros* (1944). He was born in Michigan, the son of an operetta singer, and began working in radio in the 1930s. By the next decade he was voicing a variety of characters on such series as *Cosmos Jones*, *Jeff Regan*, and *Satin's Waitin'*. Graham made his movie debut narrating the animated short *Horton Hatches an Egg* (1942) and that same year voiced the lumberjack Fox in the cartoon *Woodman, Spare That Tree*; he reprised the character in over two dozen other Columbia Pictures shorts. He did voices for other characters, such as the Wolves in *Red Hot Riding Hood* (1943) and *Swing Shift Cinderella* (1945), but many of his credits were as a narrator for cartoons, as with *Coming! Snafu* (1943), *Sleepy Lagoon* (1943), *Going Home* (1944), *The Lady and the Monster* (1944), *The Eager Beaver* (1946), and *Each Dawn I Crow* (1949). He was still in great demand in Hollywood and on radio when he committed suicide at the age of thirty-six.

Grammer, Kelsey (b. 1955) The popular television comic actor who excels at snide and haughty types, he provided the voices for the sinister Dr. Frankenollie in the Mickey Mouse short *Runaway Brain* (1995), the friendly prospector toy Stinky Pete who turns evil in *Toy Story 2* (1999), and the crackpot scientist-villain Dr. Ivan Krank in *Teacher's Pet* (2004). He was born Allen Kelsey Grammer on St. Thomas in the Virgin Islands and was raised in New Jersey and Florida before studying acting at Juilliard. He began his career in classic plays at the Guthrie Theatre and other regional theatres, performed Off Broadway in *Plenty* (1982) and *Quatermaine's Terms* (1983), and on Broadway in *Macbeth* (1981 and 2000), *Othello* (1982), and *La Cage aux Folles* (2010). Grammer made his television debut in an episode of the soap opera *Ryan's Hope* in 1979 and four years later became famous for his portrayal of the pompous Dr. Frasier Crane in *Frasier*, a role for which he has forever since been identified. He first played Frasier on the series *Cheers*, made a guest appearance on *Wings*, then starred in his own long-running show, all in all playing the character for twenty years. Among the other TV series he acted in are *Another World, Star Trek: The Next Generation, Roc, Fired Up, Becker, Back to You*, and *Hank*. Grammer can be seen in such movies as *Galaxies Are Colliding* (1992), *Down Periscope* (1996), *The Real Howard Spitz* (1998), *The Big Empty* (2003), *X-Men: The Last Stand* (2006), *Swing Vote* (2008), *Fame* (2009), and *Crazy on the Outside* (2010), as well as the TV-movies and miniseries *Kennedy* (1983), *George Washington* (1984), *The Innocent* (1994), *London Suite* (1996), *Mr. St. Nick* (2002), *Benedict Arnold: A Question of Honor* (2003), and *A Christmas Carol: The Musical* (2004). He had done voices for the television cartoon series *Gary the Rat* and *The Simpsons*, and for such animated films and videos as *Anastasia* (1997), *Bartok the Magnificent* (1999), *Mickey's Once Upon a Christmas* (1999), *Gary the Rat* (2000), *Barbie of Swan Lake* (2003), and *The Simpsons Ride* (2008). Grammer is a very successful producer as well, presenting many of his own shows and several other series and television specials. Autobiography: *So Far...* (1995); biography: *Kelsey Grammer: The True Story*, Jeff Rovin, Kathleen Tracy, David Perrell (1995).

Grant, Campbell A Disney animator and writer, he was heard in one animated film, as the voice of the nervous badger accountant Angus MacBadger in "The Wind in the Willows" portion of *The Adventures of Ichabod and Mr. Toad* (1949). Grant was one of the many animators who worked on *Snow White and the Seven Dwarfs* (1937) and he helped with the character animation for *Pinocchio* (1940). He was also a freelance writer who helped script the "Night on Bald Mountain" and the "Ave Maria" segments of *Fantasia* (1940). Grant later wrote illustrated children's books, some of them based on Disney films.

Greenspan, Melissa A television actress who has voiced animated characters on occasion, she supplied the voice of the student Briar Langolier in *Doug's 1st Movie* (1999). Her television credits include the series *Boston Common, Party of Five, Beverly Hills 90210, 3rd Rock from the Sun*, and *Providence*, as well as the cartoon series *Doug* and *Disney's Doug* where she first played Briar. Greenspan can also be heard in the animated films *The Wild Thornberrys Movie* (2002) and *Curious George 2: Follow that Monkey!* (2009).

Greenwood, Peter (b. 1962) An Australian-born jack of all trades who has acted, designed costumes, created special effects for films, and painted backgrounds for cartoons, he supplied the voices of the airplane Captain and the Australian Radio Announcer who says that the search for Cody has failed in *The Rescuers Down Under* (1990). He was born in Sydney and as a teenager painted cells for Hanna Barbera Australia even as he performed on local radio. Greenwood acted in Australian television shows and commercials, and designed and marketed merchandise related to *Star Wars, Raiders of the Lost Ark, Star Trek*, and other popular films and television shows. He began doing voice work with the cartoon series *Gumby Adventures* in 1988, followed by such Australian series as *Big Bad Beetleborgs, Power Rangers Turbo, Crocadoo II*, and *Power Rangers Light Speed Rescue*, and he can be seen in the American TV series *The King of Queens* and *Lucky Louie*. Greenwood did the special effects for the movies *F/X2* (1991), *Curse III: Blood Sacrifice* (1991), and *The Flunky* (2000), as well as the television series *Star Trek: The Next Generation*. He designed costumes for the movie *Teenage Mutant Ninja Turtles III* (1993) and episodes of the series *Star Trek: Deep Space Nine*. Perhaps Greenwood's most offbeat credit is as operator of the Energizer Bunny on television commercials for three years.

Gregory, Natalie (b. 1975) A child performer on television and in movies who left show business at the age of fifteen, she provided the speaking and singing voice of the wealthy but neglected little New Yorker Jenny Foxworth in *Oliver & Company* (1988). Gregory made her television debut when she was eight years old, appearing in episodes of *Matt Houston, Cagney & Lacey, Magnum P.I., Amazing Stories, Fathers and Sons, Mr. Belvedere, Highway to Heaven*, and *Trapper John, M.D.*, but made the biggest impression as Alice in the live-action TV-movie musical *Alice in Wonderland* (1985). She acted in a half dozen other television films, most memorably *Robert Kennedy & His Times* (1985). If the character of Jenny in *Oliver & Company* is reminiscent of Penny in *The Rescuers*, it is no accident. *Oliver & Company* was first developed as a sequel to *The Rescuers*, showing Penny's life in New York City. The idea was eventually dropped and the little girl's name changed to Jenny but the similarities between the two characters remains.

Greno, Nathan An animator and script writer who has recently turned to directing, he supplied the voice of the Robinson family's octopus butler Lefty in *Meet the Robinsons* (2007). Greno worked on the story and animation for *Mulan* (1998), *Brother Bear* (2003), *Chicken Little* (2005), *Meet the Robinsons*, and *Bolt* (2008). Having directed the shorts *Super Rhino* (2009) and *Let It Begin* (2009), he helmed the animated feature *Tangled* (2010). Greno can also be heard doing voices in *Bolt*, the short *Prep & Landing* (2009), and *Tangled*.

Grey, Larry A stage actor whose few film credits span from 1941 to 1997, he voiced the chimney sweep lizard Bill in *Alice in Wonderland* (1951). Grey's career has been in regional theatre but he appeared in the films *Mr. Celebrity* (1941) and *Private Parts* (1997), and he was in New Jersey's Paper Mill Playhouse stage production of *Show Boat* which was broadcast on PBS-TV in 1972.

Guillaume, Robert (b. 1927) The much-respected and popular African American actor-singer who has shone on stage, in movies, and on television, he supplied the voice of the wise baboon Rafiki in *The Lion King* (1994). He was born Robert Peter Williams in St. Louis, Missouri, and attended the local schools St. Louis University and Washington University before beginning his stage career in Cleveland. After appearing in the international tour of the musical *Free and Easy*, he made his Broadway debut in *Finian's Rainbow* (1960) then played a featured role in *Kwamina* (1961), followed by such Broadway musicals as *Tambourines to Glory* (1963), *Purlie* (1970), *Guys and Dolls* (1976), and *Cyrano—The Musical* (1993), as well as the title role during part of the long run of *The Phantom of the Opera*. Guillaume made his television debut in 1966 and after making appearances in such series as *Julia*, *Sanford and Son*, *All in the Family*, *The Jeffersons*, and *Good Times*, he found recognition as the sarcastic butler Benson DuBois in *Soap*. He reprised the character in the even-more-popular spin-off series *Benson*, followed by featured roles in other series, including *The Love Boat*, *Pacific Station*, *A Different World*, *Sports Night*, and his own series *The Robert Guillaume Show*. Among his film credits are *Seems Like Old Times* (1980), *Prince Jack* (1985), *Wanted: Dead or Alive* (1986), *Lean on Me* (1989), *The Meteor Man* (1993), *Silicon Towers* (1999), *Big Fish* (2003), and *Satin* (2010), and the TV-movies *The Kid with the Broken Halo* (1982), *North and South* (1985), *Alchemy* (1996), and *Run for the Dream: The Gail Devers Story* (1996). The character of Rafiki in *The Lion King* is that of a wise old shaman, yet he can be playful at times and has a sense of humor. What is most impressive about the character, as animated and voiced, is the dignity that Rafiki carries at all time. One does not think of a funny-looking baboon as a creature of stature and wisdom, but Rafiki is both. Guillaume reprised his Rafiki in the videos *The Lion King II: Simba's Pride* (1998) and *The Lion King 1½* (2004), as well as in the cartoon series *Timon and Pumbaa*. He can also be heard in the television series *Captain Planet and the Planeteers*, *Fish Police*, and *Happily Ever After: Fairy Tales for Every Child*, and the animated videos *Snow White* (1996), *The Land Before Time VIII: The Big Freeze* (2001), and *The Adventures of Tom Thumb and Thumbelina* (2002). Biography: *Guillaume: A Life*, David Ritz (2002).

Hackett, Buddy (1924–2003) A short, pudgy comic with a twisted smile and a spitting voice, he was noticed in all media for his energetic and farcical performances, such as the goofy sea gull Scuttle in *The Little Mermaid* (1989). He was born Leonard Hacker in Brooklyn and left his father's upholstery business to do comedy in the Borscht Belt resorts and nightclubs. His routines, which always bordered on the obscene, made him a favorite at Las Vegas for decades and television audiences enjoyed his many (and much milder) appearances over the years. Hackett occasionally left stand-up comedy to appear on Broadway, as with a few comedies in the 1950s and the musical *I Had a Ball* (1964), and to act in movies, including *Walking My Baby Back Home* (1953), *God's Little Acre* (1958), *The Wonderful World of the Brothers Grimm* (1962), *The Music Man* (1962), *It's a Mad Mad Mad Mad World* (1963), *Muscle Beach Party* (1964), and *The Love Bug* (1968). The animators for *The Little Mermaid* developed the character of the sea gull Scuttle from the live-action film footage of Hackett's recording session. The comic tends to be crossed eyed and to speak out of the side of his mouth, and both of these characteristics were used in animating the character. Vocally, Hackett's performance is superb; a bit stand-up comic, a touch of vaudeville, and tons of sputtering energy. He reprised his Scuttle in the video sequel *The Little Mermaid II: Return to the Sea* (2000), provided voices for the animated television series *Dinosaurs*, *Fish Police*, and *Garfield and Friends*, and can be heard in the television special *Jack Frost* (1979) and the film *Mouse Soup* (1992).

Hadley, Guy A television production assistant, he provided the voice of Doug's rival, the snobby upperclassman Guy Graham, in *Doug's 1st Movie* (1999). Hadley first played Guy in the cartoon series *Disney's Doug* in 1996. He appeared in the movies *Baby's Day Out* (1994) and *Wild Girls Gone* (2007).

Hahn, Emily A child actress with only a few credits so far, she provided the voice of the little girl Bonnie who inherits Andy's toys in *Toy Story 3* (2010). Hahn appeared on the television series *Hawthorne* and *Brothers & Sisters*, and played as small role in the film *The Green Hornet* (2011).

Haid, Charles (b. 1943) A prolific television actor and director remembered mostly for cop shows, he voiced the rip-roaring, peg-legged jack rabbit Lucky Jack in *Home on the Range* (2004). Charles Maurice Haid III was born in San Francisco and educated at the Carnegie Institute of Technology in Pittsburgh. He began his career on the stage but turned more and more to television in the 1970s, appearing in such TV series as *Gunsmoke*, *Barney Miller*, *The Waltons*, *Police Woman*, *Delvecchio*, and *B. J. and the Bear* before finding success as Officer Andrew Renko on *Hill Street Blues*. Haid went on to featured television roles in *NYPD Blue*, *Third Watch*, *Criminal Minds*, *Nip/Tuck*, and *Murder, She Wrote*, as well as many made-for-TV movies. Among his film credits are *The Choir Boys* (1977), *Who'll Stop the Rain* (1978), *Oliver's Story* (1978), *Altered States* (1980), *The Twilight Zone* (1989), *Storyville* (1992), and *The Third Miracle* (1999). In the 1990s Haid turned to directing and has helmed episodes of the television series *L.A. Law*, *NYPD Blue*, *Boston Legal*, *Third Watch*, *Nip/Tuck*, *ER*, *Criminal Minds*, *In Plain Sight*, and *Doogie Howser, M.D.*

Hall, Don A Disney animator and script writer, he did voices on some of the projects he worked on, such as the thick-headed Coach and the French-accented relative Gaston in *Meet the Robinsons* (2007) and the big, dim-witted frog hunter Darnell in *The Princess and the Frog* (2009). Hall first worked for Disney on the screenplay for *Tarzan* (1999) and also contributed to the scripts for *Brother Bear* (2003) and *Home on the Range* (2004). He both wrote and animated *The Emperor's New Groove* (2000), *Meet the Robinsons*, and *The Princess and the Frog*. Hall's non–Disney credit is as storyboard artist for *Spirit: Stallion of the Cimarron* (2002).

Hamlin, Bob A tenor member of the singing group The Mellomen, he was heard on and off screen in a few films, such as *Alice in Wonderland* (1951) in which the quartet voiced the singing Cards painting the roses red. Hamlin was a member of the Norman Luboff Chorale and other singing groups but it was with The Mellomen he was seen and heard in the movie *The Glenn Miller Story* (1954) and heard in the Disney animated shorts *The Nifty Nineties* (1941), *Trick or Treat* (1952), *Toot Whistle Plunk and Boom* (1953), and *Pigs Is Pigs* (1954).

Hanks, Tom (b. 1956) A hugely popular movie star who has found success in everything from silly comedies to sobering dramas, one of his most beloved roles is that of the cowboy doll Woody in *Toy Story* (1995). Thomas Jeffrey Hanks was born in Concord, California, and was educated at Chabot College and California State University at Sacramento before doing amateur theatricals. He first gained attention as Kip Wilson on the television sit-com *Bosom Buddies* but wide renown came with his performance in the movie *Splash* (1984). What followed was one of the most remarkable film careers of his generation, filled with variety and many hits. Among his many notable movies are *Big* (1988), *A League of Their Own* (1992), *Sleepless in Seattle* (1993), *Philadelphia* (1993), *Forrest Gump* (1994), *Apollo 13* (1995), *That Thing You Do!* (1996), *Saving Private Ryan* (1998), *You've Got Mail* (1998), *The Green Mile* (1999), *Road to Perdition* (2002), *Catch Me If You Can* (2002), *The Polar Express* (2004), *The Da Vinci Code* (2006), and *Angels and Demons* (2009), as well as such celebrated TV mini-series as *Band of Brothers* (2001) and *The Pacific* (2010). Hanks reprised his Woody in *Toy Story 2* (1999), *Toy Story 3* (2010), and briefly as Woody Car in *Cars* (2006). The character of Woody was originally going to be a ventriloquist's dummy named Larry who spoke when you pulled his string. When the character was changed to a cowboy, Woody was very sarcastic and a bit too power hungry. The studio ordered production to shut down while a better script was written with a more likable Woody. (The character was named after Western character actor Woody Strode.) From the beginning, director John Lasseter wanted Tom Hanks to voice Woody. Hanks was attracted to the project because as a child he had always wondered if his toys moved and talked when no one was in the room. The very busy Hanks agreed to record Woody's voice during breaks while filming the light-weight movies *A League of Their Own* and *Sleepless in Seattle*; but he would not record while making the serious dramas *Philadelphia* and *Forrest Gump*. Although television Westerns and cowboy dolls have not been the fashion for decades, Woody was immediately popular with audiences and Woody dolls were in great demand. Moviegoers have maintained their affection for Woody and his friends through two sequels and the cowboy has become one of the most beloved of all Disney characters. There is no question much of this is due to Hanks' funny, sincere, and touching vocals. Biographies: *The Tom Hanks Enigma*, David Gardner (2007); *Tom Hanks: Actor*, James Robert Parish (2004).

Hansen, Bernice A voice artist who was heard in over seventy cartoon shorts in the 1930s and 1940s, she provided the voice for the sweet feline Tillie Tiger, the heartthrob of young Elmer, in the Silly Symphony short *Elmer Elephant* (1936). Hansen began her career as the voice of Cookie in *Buddy's Day Out* (1933), a role she reprised in thirteen other Buddy cartoons for Warner Brothers. For the same studio she supplied the voices of Little Kitty and Petunia Pig in many Porky Pig shorts. In the 1940s, Hansen was one of the voice artists to voice Andy Panda in a series of Walter Lantz cartoons and she played a variety of other characters in such shorts as *Jolly Little Elves* (1934), *Country Boy* (1935), *Three Lazy Mice* (1935), *The Merry Old Soul* (1935), *The Phantom Ship* (1936), *I Love to Singa* (1936), *Uncle Tom's Bungalow* (1937), *Dog Daze* (1937), *A Sunbonnet Blue* (1937), *The Sneezing Weasel* (1938), *A Star Is Hatched* (1938), *The Mice Will Play* (1938), *Kittens' Mittens* (1940), *A Gander at Mother Goose* (1940), *Pantry Panic* (1941), and *Lost and Foundling* (1944).

Hansen, Daniel A young actor with television and movie credits since 1997, he was one of the two actors who supplied the voice of the young scientist Lewis in *Meet the Robinsons* (2007). Hansen has appeared on such television series as *Everybody Loves Raymond, The Pretender, Roswell, ER,* and *Judging Amy,* and had minor roles in the films *6½* (1998), *Being John Malkovich* (1999), *Trust Me* (2000), *The Big Day* (2001), *Buying the Cow* (2002), and *Stuart Little 2* (2002). He can be heard in the television cartoon series *Avatar: The Last Airbender* and the animated video *Lucy Must Be Traded, Charlie Brown* (2003). The character of Lewis in *Meet the Robinsons* is very contemporary, though the situation of an orphan searching for his identity is far from new. Lewis is a bit of a geek, widely imaginative, and very driven. He is smart enough to invent things but he is immature in many ways and the film is about his journey to maturity and understanding. Hansen did all the voice work for Lewis but the first cut of the movie was deemed unsatisfactory by the studio so the movie went back into production for ten months with many changes made in plot and characters. By the time it came to voice the new footage, Hansen's voice had changed so Jordan Fry was hired to do Lewis' new lines. The difference between the two boys' voices can be detected in the final print.

Harlan, Otis (1865–1940) A busy character actor in silent movies and during the first dozen years of talkies, he voiced the dwarf Happy in *Snow White and the Seven Dwarfs* (1937) and his last film credit before he died was providing the voice for Mr. Mole *in Bambi* (1942). He was born in Zanesville, Ohio, and was on the vaudeville stage before making his Broadway debut in 1894. Harlan was featured in several musicals in the early years of the twentieth century, including *Broadway to Tokio* (1900), *Star and Garter* (1900), *The Girl from Up There* (1901), *Dream City* (1906), *A Parisian Model* (1908), *Little Boy Blue* (1911), *The Dancing Duchess* (1914), and *90 in the Shade* (1915). He made his screen debut in 1915 and stayed in Hollywood for the rest of his life, appearing in over one hundred movies in the next twenty-five years. Among his silent film credits are *A Stranger in New York* (1916), *The World's a Stage* (1922), *Captain Blood* (1924), *Lightnin'* (1925), *The Prince of Pilsen* (1926), and *The Student Prince in Old Heidelberg* (1927). Harlan played Captain Andy in the partial-sound movie *Show Boat* (1927) and was featured in such talkies as *The Mississippi Gambler* (1929), *King of Jazz* (1930), *Ride Him, Cowboy* (1932), *Music in the Air* (1934), *A Midsummer Night's Dream* (1935), and *Mr. Boggs Steps Out* (1938). The dwarf Happy is one of the least distinctive of the seven little men in *Snow White and the Seven Dwarfs*. Like his name, his chief characteristic is that he is cheerful. Yet all the dwarfs (except Grouchy) are pretty happy most of the time so poor Happy rarely stands out.

Harnell, Jess (b. 1963) A prolific voice artist and singer who has voiced over 400 episodes of television cartoons, he supplied the voice of the male nurse A. J. from the Shady Oaks Retirement Village in *Up* (2009). He was born in Teaneck, New Jersey, the son of film and television composer Joe Harnell, and began voicing animated cartoons in 1989 with the series *Camp Candy*. Over the next two decades he provided voices for such series as *Bonkers, 2 Stupid Dogs, Superhuman Samurai Syber-Squad, Biker Mice from Mars, Freakazoid!, The Tick, The Mask, Casper, Pinky and the Brain, Buzz Lightyear of Star Command, Horrible Histories, House of Mouse, The Powerpuff Girls, ChalkZone, Totally Spies, Duck Dodgers, Clifford's Puppy Days, Codename: Kids Next Door, The Grim Adventures of Billy and Mandy, Kim Possible, Drawn Together, Chowder, Atom TV, The Replacements,* and *The Super Hero Squad Show,* but he is best known as Wakko Warner in *Animaniacs*. Among the dozens of animated movies and videos he has voiced are *Yakko's World: An Animaniacs Singalong* (1994), *A Hollywood Hounds Christmas* (1994), *The Raccoon War* (1994), *Aladdin and the King of Thieves* (1995), *Casper* (1995), *Casper: A*

Spirited Beginning (1997), *A Bug's Life* (1998), *We Wish You a Merry Christmas* (1999), *Jingle Bells* (1999), *Wakko's Wish* (1999), *Toy Story 2* (1999), *Joseph: King of Dreams* (2000), *The Life and Adventures of Santa Claus* (2000), *Little Nicky* (2000), *The Emperor's New Groove* (2000), *Lady and the Tramp II: Scamp's Adventure* (2001), *Tom and Jerry: The Magic Ring* (2002), *Lilo & Stitch* (2002), *The Jungle Book 2* (2003), *Finding Nemo* (2003), *Comic Book: The Movie* (2004), *Clifford's Really Big Movie* (2004), *Mickey, Donald, Goofy: The Three Musketeers* (2004), *Racing Stripes* (2005), *Tom and Jerry Blast Off to Mars!* (2005), *Ice Age 2: The Meltdown* (2006), *Asterix and the Viking* (2006), *Cars* (2006), *The Wild* (2006), *Surf's Up* (2007), *Transformers* (2007), *Underdog* (2007), *Horton Hears a Who!* (2008), *WALL-E* (2008), *Ponyo* (2008), *Igor* (2008), *Transformers: Revenge of the Fallen* (2009), *The Haunted World of El Superbeasto* (2009), *Cloudy with a Chance of Meatballs* (2009), and *The Drawn Together Movie: The Movie* (2010). Harnell has sung on the soundtrack of both live-action and animated films and is the lead vocalist in the pop-rock band Rock Sugar.

Harris, Estelle (b. 1932) An active television character actress with a shrill and grating voice, she has played several minor roles in Disney animated films, most memorably as Mrs. Potato Head in *Toy Story 2* (1999) and *Toy Story 3* (2010). She was born Estelle Nussbaum in New York City, the daughter of a candy store owner, and made her screen debut in 1977, later appearing in such movies as *Once Upon a Time in America* (1984), *Stand and Deliver* (1988), *This Is My Life* (1992), *Perfect Alibi* (1995), *The Odd Couple II* (1998), *Playing Mona Lisa* (2000), and *The Grand* (2007). Harris has appeared on many television series since 1985, including *Night Court*, *Married with Children*, *Law & Order*, *Chicago Hope*, *ER*, *The Suite Life of Zack and Cody*, *American Dad*, and *Sabrina, the Teenage Witch*, but she is most remembered as Mrs. Costanza on *Seinfeld* for six years. Her other Disney animated characters include the Old Lady Bear in *Brother Bear* (2003), the far-sighted pet sitter Mrs. Boogin in *Teacher's Pet* (2004), and the hysterical chicken Audrey in *Home on the Range* (2004) and in the cartoon short *A Dairy Tale* (2004). Harris supplied voices for the animated videos *Tarzan II* (2005) and *Queer Duck: The Movie* (2006), and in such TV cartoon series as *Aladdin*, *Timon and Pumbaa*, *Hercules*, *The Wild Thornberrys*, *Mickey Mouse Works*, *Family Guy*, *House of Mouse*, *Kim Possible*, and *Dave the Barbarian*.

Harris, Jonathan (1914–2002) The veteran character actor with a crisp, affected voice who found fame on television playing villains, he provided the voices for the British-accented praying mantis Manny in *A Bug's Life* (1998) and Geri the Cleaner who repairs toys in *Toy Story 2* (1999). He was born Jonathan Charasuchin in the Bronx, New York, to Russian-Jewish immigrants and was educated at Fordham University for a career as a pharmacist. After acting in many theatre productions in stock and summer theatre he made his Broadway debut in *Heart of a City* (1942), followed by roles in *A Flag Is Born* (1946), *The Madwoman of Chaillot* (1948), *The Grass Harp* (1952), *Hazel Flagg* (1953), and *The Teahouse of the August Moon* (1953). Harris made his first television appearance in 1949 on *The Chevrolet Tele-Theatre* then went on to act in many TV series, including *Zorro*, *Twilight Zone*, *Bonanza*, *The Bill Dana Show*, *The Third Man*, *Bewitched*, *Space Academy*, *Battlestar Galactica*, and *Love, American Style*, but he is best remembered as the conniving Dr. Zachary Smith on *Lost in Space*. His voice can be heard on many cartoon series, including *My Favorite Martians*, *Rainbow Brite*, *Visionaries: Knights of the Magical Light*, *Darkwing Duck*, *The Mask*, *Mighty Ducks*, *Freakazoid!*, *Extreme Ghostbusters*, *Spider-Man*, *The Angry Beavers*, and *Buzz Lightyear of Star Command*, as well as the movies and videos *Rainbow Brite and the Star Stealer* (1985), *Pinocchio and the Emperor of the Night* (1987), *Happily Ever After* (1993), *Hubert's Brain* (2001), and *The Bolt Who Screwed Christmas* (2009), the last not released until seven years after his death.

Harris, Phil (1904–1995) The gravel-voiced character actor with a Southern flavor who was expert at playing con men, shady businessmen, and overconfident Romeos in many films, television shows, and on the radio, he is best known to audiences today as the speaking and singing voice of the freewheeling Baloo the Bear in *The Jungle Book* (1967). Harris was born in Linton, Indiana, the son of a musician, and grew up in Nashville, Tennessee, where he played drums at an early age. He started his own band in 1931, playing the drums and singing, and became popular enough to interest Hollywood. Harris was featured in such movie musicals as *Melody Cruise* (1933), *Turn Off the Moon* (1937), *Man About Town* (1939), *Buck Benny Rides Again* (1940), *Wabash Avenue* (1950), *Starlift* (1951), *Here Comes the Groom* (1951), and *Anything Goes* (1956). Harris was very popular on the radio, first as the music director and sidekick on Jack Benny's show and then later on his own show with his wife Alice Faye. He also appeared in dozens of television programs as a singer and a musician. In *The Jungle Book*, Harris introduced the hit song "The Bare Necessities" and was soon featured in two other Disney animated features: as the cool cat J. Thomas O'Malley in *The Aristocats* (1970) and the cheerful bear Little John in *Robin Hood* (1973). He also voiced the fowl Patou in the non-Disney film *Rock-a-Doodle* (1991). The character of Baloo in *The Jungle Book*, who is patterned after the blustering actor Wallace Beery, is one of the most enjoyable in the Disney canon. Originally the bear was to be a minor character who was in only one scene. In Rudyard Kipling's book, Baloo is serious and practical and that was how he was to be portrayed in the movie. But once Harris was in the recording studio, his speaking and singing vocals were so exciting that the role was enlarged. Although he returned to do voices for other Disney films, his subsequent characters were pretty much copies of his Baloo. With reissues of *The Jungle Book*, Baloo has remained a favorite and was eventually featured in the TV cartoon series *TaleSpin* and the video *Jungle Book 2* (2003), though not with Harris' voice.

Hawthorne, Nigel (1929–2001) The distinguished British character actor of stage, screen, and television, he found movie fame late in his career and can be heard in two Disney animated features: as the wandering minstrel and flamboyant poet Fflewddur Fflam in *The Black Cauldron* (1985) and Jane's exuberant father, biologist Professor Archimedes J. Porter, in *Tarzan* (1999). Nigel Barnard Hawthorne was born in Coventry, England, but grew up in South Africa where he studied at the University of Cape Town and started acting in local theatres. He made his London stage debut in 1951 and was soon a seasoned professional working with such British companies as the Royal Court, National Theatre, and the Young Vic. Hawthorne rarely was on the American stage, though he was highly praised for his New York City performances in *Shadowlands* (1990) and *The Madness of George III* (1993), and he became known to many Americans through the 1994 film version of the later play and the British television series *Yes, Minister* shown in the States. Hawthorne's notable films include *Young Winston* (1972), *Ghandi* (1982), *Turtle Diary* (1985), *Richard III* (1995), *Amistad* (1997), and *The Winslow Boy* (1999), and he can be heard in the animated features *Watership Down* (1978) and *The Plague Dogs* (1982) and in the video *Tarzan Untamed* (2001). Autobiography: *Straight Face* (2001); biography: *Nigel Hawthorne on Stage*, Kathleen Riley (2005).

Haydn, Richard (1905–1985) A nasal-sounding British song-and-dance man from the variety stage, he appeared in many Hollywood films and provided the voice for the hookah-smoking Caterpillar who turns into a haughty butterfly in *Alice in Wonderland* (1951). George Richard Hayden was born in London and found fame in the 1930s for his comic singing in revues and on the radio. He made his Hollywood debut as Charley Wyckham in *Charley's Aunt* (1941), followed by dozens of films in which he played stuffy Brits or crusty Europeans, including *Ball of Fire* (1941), *Tonight and Every Night* (1945), *And Then There Were None* (1945), *The Late George Apley* (1947), *Forever Amber* (1947), *Sitting Pretty* (1948), *The Emperor Waltz* (1948), *The Merry Widow* (1952), *Jupiter's Darling* (1955), *The Lost World* (1960), *Please Don't Eat the Daisies* (1960), *The Lost World* (1960), *Mutiny on the Bounty* (1962), *The Adventures of Bullwhip Griffin* (1967), and *Young Frankenstein* (1974), although he is probably best remembered as the impresario Max in *The Sound of Music* (1964). Haydn also appeared in many American television shows in the 1950s and 1960s, such as *Playhouse 90, The Man from U.N.C.L.E., Bewitched, Bonanza, Laredo, It Takes a Thief,* and *Love, American Style*. His vocal performance as the Caterpillar in *Alice in Wonderland* is humorously dry and lethargic. He acts very superior to Alice yet is so fey and unenthusiastic that he is never a threat, just a curiosity.

Hayes, Billie (b. 1932) A comic character actress who has spent most of her career in television, she voiced Orgoch, the crabbiest and most vindictive of the three witches of Morva, in *The Black Caldron* (1985). She was born in DuQuoin, Illinois, and trained as a dancer. She did musical revues across the country, eventually performing in New York where she was one of the featured newcomers in the Broadway revue *New Faces of 1956*. Hayes played Mammie Yokum in *Li'l Abner* on Broadway, in the 1959 film version, and in a 1971 television presentation. Although she started acting in television in 1963, it was her performance as the delightful Witchiepoo in the TV series *H. R. Pufnstuf* in 1969 that brought her national recognition. Her other television series include *General Hospital, The Monkees, Lidsville, Bewitched,* and *Murder, She Wrote*, as well as providing voices for the animated series *TaleSpin, Darkwing Duck, Johnny Bravo, Teen Titans, The Grim Adventures of Billy and Mandy,* and *Batman*. Hayes can also be heard in the video *My Freaky Family* (2001) and the movie *Shrek Forever After* (2010).

Hegarty, Susan A renowned Hollywood dialect coach who has acted on occasion, she provided the voice for the lifeguard who calls herself the Rescue Lady in *Lilo and Stitch* (2002). Hegarty coached the British actors in *Dead Again* (1991) on their American dialects, then went on to coach actors in over fifty other movies, including the Disney films *The Lion King* (1994), *Pocahontas* (1995), *Mulan* (1998), *The Parent Trap* (1998), *The Emperor's New Groove* (2000), *Atlantis: The Lost Empire* (2001), and *Ratatouille* (2007). Her other dialect credits include *Surviving Picasso* (1996), *Titanic* (1997), *High Fidelity* (2000), *Almost Famous* (2000), *Vanilla Sky* (2001), *Munich* (2005), and *Revolutionary Road* (2008). Hegarty appeared in the television series *Hunter* and *Mancuso, FBI*, as well as in the films *Police Academy 6: City Under Siege* (1989) and *The Chumscrubber* (2005).

Helmond, Katherine (b. 1928) A comic actress with a distinctive and quirky manner who found great success on television, she voiced Lizzie, the elderly Model T Ford, in *Cars* (2006). She was born in Galveston, Texas, where she did amateur theatricals before going to New York City and appearing in several plays, including the Broadway productions of *Private Lives* (1969), *The Great God Brown* (1972), and *Don Juan* (1972), Helmond appeared in a handful of television shows before she found recognition as the ditzy Jessica Tate in *Soap*, a role she reprised in the spinoff series *Benson*. Her other television credits include several TV-movies and the series *The Love Boat*, *Coach*, and *Everybody Loves Raymond*, though she is probably best remembered as Mona Robinson in *Who's the Boss?* Helmond has acted in many films, including *The Hospital* (1971), *The Hindenburg* (1975), *Family Plot* (1976), *Time Bandits* (1981), *Brazil* (1985), *The Flight of the Dove* (1994), and *Longfellow* (2010).

Henriksen, Lance (b. 1940) A thin, intense actor with a surprisingly low and growly voice, he supplied the voice of the stern gorilla leader Kerchak in *Tarzan* (1999). He was born in New York City and studied at the Actors Studio before making his stage debut Off Broadway and eventually appearing on Broadway in *The Basic Training of Pavlo Hummel* (1977). Henriksen started playing bit parts in films in 1972 and was noticed in *Dog Day Afternoon* (1975), going on to play a variety of characters in such movies as *Network* (1976), *Close Encounters of the Third Kind* (1977), *Prince of the City* (1981), *The Right Stuff* (1983), *The Terminator* (1984), *Jagged Edge* (1985), *The Last Samurai* (1990), *Stone Cold* (1991), *Delta Heat* (1992), *Super Mario Bros.* (1993), *The Outfit* (1993), *Spitfire* (1995), *The Quick and the Dead* (1995), *Profile for Murder* (1996), *Scream 3* (2000), *Dream Warrior* (2003), *Pirates of Treasure Island* (2006), *Bone Dry* (2007), *Appaloosa* (2008), *The Seamstress* (2009), and *The Genesis Code* (2010), as well as featured roles in such TV-movies as *The Day Lincoln Was Shot* (1998), *Lost Voyage* (2001), *The Last Cowboy* (2003), and *Evel Knievel* (2004). Among the many television series he has acted in are *Ryan's Hope*, *Cagney & Lacey*, *Hardcastle and McCormick*, *Tales from the Crypt*, *Millennium*, *The X-Files*, and *NCIS*. Henriksen reprised his Kerchak in the video *Tarzan II* (2005) and the TV cartoon series *The Legend of Tarzan*. He also voiced the animated series *Static Shock*, *Super Robot Monkey Team Hyperforce Go!*, *Transformers: Animated*, and *IGPX: Immortal Grand Prix*, and the animated videos and films *Superman: Brainiac Attacks* (2006), *The Chosen One* (2007), and *Godkiller* (2010).

Heston, Charlton (1923–2008) The bigger-than-life Hollywood leading man who often played legendary heroes for over sixty years, he provided the tongue-in-cheek opening narration for *Hercules* (1997). He was born John Charles Carter in a suburb of Chicago, Illinois, and was educated at Northwestern University. After serving in World War II, he performed in regional theatres and appeared on Broadway in *Julius Caesar* (1947), *Leaf and Bough* (1949), *Design for a Stained Glass Window* (1950), and *The Tumbler* (1960). Heston made his screen debut in 1941 but was not noticed until his Antony in *Julius Caesar* (1950). Over seventy movies followed, most memorably *The Greatest Show on Earth* (1952), *The Ten Commandments* (1956), *Touch of Evil* (1958), *Ben-Hur* (1959), *El Cid* (1961), *The Greatest Story Ever Told* (1965), *The Agony and the Ecstasy* (1965), *Khartom* (1966), *Planet of the Apes* (1968), *Beneath the Planet of the Apes* (1968), *Julius Caesar* (1970), *The Three Musketeers* (1973), *Airport 1975* (1974), *Earthquake* (1974), *Gray Lady Down* (1978), *Tombstone* (1993), *Hamlet* (1996), and *Any Given Sunday* (1999). He acted in many television drama series in the 1950s and in the 1980s he returned to the small screen and appeared in several TV movies and on such series as *Chiefs*, *Dynasty*, *The Colbys*, and *The Bold and the Beautiful*. Autobiography: *Into the Arena* (1995); biographies: *Charlton Heston: An Incredible Life*, Michelle Bernier (2009); *Charlton Heston: A Biography*, Michael Munn (1986).

Hickey, William (1928–1997) The growly-voiced, odd-looking character actor who worked in all media, he supplied the voice of the evil scientist Dr. Finklestein in *The Nightmare Before Christmas* (1993). He was born in Brooklyn, New York, and at the age of ten was acting on the radio. As an adult Hickey first pursued a stage career and throughout his life he often returned to the theatre, appearing in such Broadway productions as *Tovarich* (1952), *Miss Lonelyhearts* (1957), *The Body Beautiful* (1958), *Make a Million* (1958), *Happy Birthday, Wanda June* (1970), *Mourning Becomes Electra* (1972), *Thieves* (1974), and *Arsenic and Old Lace* (1986). Hickey was active in early television, acting in such 1950s series as *Studio One in Hollywood*, *Decoy*, *Lamp Unto My Feet*, and *The DuPont Show of the Month*; later he was featured in a variety of TV series, including *The Defenders*, *N.Y.P.D.*, *One Life to Life*, *Ryan's Hope*, *Moonlighting*, *The*

Tracey Ullman Show, Miami Vice, Baby Talk, L.A. Law, The Adventures of Pete & Pete, and *Wings*. Among his movie credits are *A Hatful of Rain* (1957), *Operation Mad Ball* (1957), *Invitation to a Gunfighter* (1964), *The Boston Strangler* (1968), *Little Big Man* (1970), *The Sentinel* (1977), *Wise Blood* (1979), *Seize the Day* (1986), *The Name of the Rose* (1986), *Bright Lights, Big City* (1988), *Sea of Love* (1989), *Christmas Vacation* (1989), *Tales from the Darkside: The Movie* (1990), *My Blue Heaven* (1990), *Forget Paris* (1995), *Sandman* (1995), *Mousehunt* (1997), and *Knocking on Death's Door* (1999), but he is most remembered as the Mafia don in *Prizzi's Honor* (1985). Hickey was an influential acting teacher, working as an instructor at the Herbert Berghof Studio for several years and coaching many future stars.

Higgins, Joe (1925–1998) A television character actor who played a variety of roles but was mostly known as a sheriff, he supplied the voice of the belligerent Guard in the short *The Small One* (1978). Joseph H. Higgins was born in Logansport, Indiana, and was on the stage at the age of nine. He began doing radio as a student at the University of Dayton then made his television debut in an episode of *Shirley Temple Theatre* in 1961. For the next three decades he acted in such TV series as *My Three Sons, The Hathaways, The Detectives Starring Robert Taylor, The Dick Powell Theatre, Twilight Zone, Ensign O'Toole, Bonanza, The Rifleman, Arrest and Trial, Burke's Law, Voyage to the Bottom of the Sea, I Dream of Jeannie, Petticoat Junction, Daktari, The Monkees, The Big Valley, Judd for the Defense, Ironside, Green Acres, Sigmund and the Sea Monsters, The Dukes of Hazzard,* and *Hill Street Blues*. Higgins also appeared in a handful of movies, including *Geronimo* (1962), *Flipper* (1963), *Flipper's New Adventure* (1964), *Namu, the Killer Whale* (1966), *The Perils of Pauline* (1967), *The Man from Clover Grove* (1975), *Sixpack Annie* (1975), and *Record City* (1978). In his later years he was often cast as a crusty old sheriff. When he played one in a popular 1969 car commercial, Higgins became nationally famous as a sheriff and repeated the role in many commercials, print ads, and personal appearances.

Hill, Amy (b. 1953) An Asian-American character actress who has extensive credits in all media, she provided the voice of the Hawaiian Mrs. Hasagawa who owns the fruit stand in *Lilo & Stitch* (2002). She was born in Deadwood, South Dakota, and found recognition in the theatre world for her performances at San Francisco's Asian American Theatre Company, eventually appearing on Broadway in *Twelfth Night* in 1998. Hill made her television debut in 1984 and went on to featured roles in such series as *Night Court, All-American Girl, Pauly, Strip Mall, Hot Properties, General Hospital,* and *Two and a Half Men,* but she is most remembered as Mrs. DePaulo in *That's So Raven*. Among her film credits are *Dim Sum: A Little Bit of Heart* (1985), *Judgement* (1992), *Rising Sun* (1993), *Yellow* (1998), *Pavilion of Women* (2001), *Big Fat Liar* (2002), *The Cat in the Hat* (2003), *Cheaper by the Dozen* (2003), *50 First Dates* (2004), and *Couples Retreat* (2009). Hill reprised her Mrs. Hasagawa in the TV cartoon series *Lilo & Stitch* and can be heard in other series, such as *Spider-Man, Happily Ever After: Fairy Tales for Every Child, The Proud Family, King of the Hill, American Dad, Kim Possible, Jackie Chan Adventures, Avatar: The Last Airbender, American Dragon: Jake Long, The Goode Family,* and *Kung Fu Panda: Legends of Awesomeness,* as well as the animated video *The Magic Pearl* (1997) and movie *Curious George 2: Follow That Monkey!* (2009). Hill is also a performance artist who writes and acts in her own theatre pieces.

Hill, Ramsay (1890–1976) A British actor working in American movies and television for three decades, he supplied the voices of the Labrador who assists the fleeing dalmatians and the Television Announcer in *One Hundred and One Dalmatians* (1961). He was born in Georgetown, in what was British Guyana at the time, and was in Hollywood by 1931 usually playing British types in such movies as *Riptide* (1934), *The Crusades* (1935), *Folies-Bergere* (1936), *Old Louisiana* (1937), *Parnell* (1937), *Conquest* (1937), *Letter from an Unknown Woman* (1948), *When Worlds Collide* (1951), *Battles of Chief Pontiac* (1952), *The Ten Commandments* (1956), *Midnight Lace* (1960), *Susan Slade* (1961), *The Three Stooges Go Around the World in a Daze* (1963), *The Unsinkable Molly Brown* (1964), and *Do Not Disturb* (1965). Hill appeared in some television series as well, including *The Whistler, Damon Runyon Theatre, I Love Lucy, The Gale Storm Show, Ensign O'Toole,* and *Karen*.

Hilton, Connie An actress who voiced one of the Mermaids in *Peter Pan* (1953), she has no other film or television credits.

Hirsch, Lou An American actor who often plays American characters in the British theatre and on television shows, he provided the growly, complaining adult actor Baby Herman in *Who Framed Roger Rabbit* (1988). He was born in Brooklyn, New York, and educated at the University of Miami and the Guildhall School of Music and Drama in London. Hirsch joined the Cambridge Theatre Company in 1979 and throughout his career has often returned to Great Britain to act in the West End and for various theatre companies, as well as in British television series such as *We'll Meet Again, The Kenny Everett Television Shows, London Embassy, The Tomorrow People*, and *My Hero*. Among his film credits are *Superman III* (1983), *Insignificance* (1985), *The American Way* (1986), *Haunted Honeymoon* (1986), *Wild West* (1992), *Tom & Viv* (1994), *Thunderbirds* (2004), and *Death Doesn't Live Here Anymore* (2006). Hirsch's hoarse vocals for Baby Herman are a buffoonish contrast to the gurgling high-pitched sounds of the "baby" on screen (voiced by April Winchell). He reprised his Baby Herman in the shorts *Tummy Trouble* (1989), *Roller Coaster Rabbit* (1990), and *Trail Mix-Up* (1993), and in the video *The Best of Roger Rabbit* (1996).

Holbrook, Hal (b. 1925) An accomplished actor who has appeared in dozens of plays, films, and television programs but will always be most remembered for his vivid impersonation of Mark Twain in his one-man show *Mark Twain Tonight!*, he provided the voice of the hero's adoptive father Amphitryon in *Hercules* (1997). Harold Rowe Holbrook was born in Cleveland and educated at Denison University where he studied theatre before training with Uta Hagen at the Herbert Berghof studio in New York. His first jobs were in television soap operas and in nightclubs where he first developed his Twain characterization. When the program was a hit in a San Francisco cabaret, he transferred *Mark Twain Tonight!* to Off Broadway in 1955, followed by Broadway and touring productions for several years. Holbrook returned to the character in the early 2000s; it is estimated he has performed Twain well over 2,000 times. His other notable New York stage credits include *Abe Lincoln in Illinois* (1963) *After the Fall* (1964), *I Never Sang for My Father* (1968), *Does a Tiger Wear a Necktie?* (1969) *The Country Girl* (1984), *King Lear* (1990), and *An American Daughter* (1997). Holbrook has been acting on television since 1953 and on film since 1966, rarely playing leading roles but he is usually memorable, as in the movies *The Group* (1966), *All the President's Men* (1976), *Midway* (1976), *Wall Street* (1987), and *The Firm* (1993). His many television credits include *The F.B.I., The Name of the Game, The Bold Ones: The Senator, Designing Women, Evening Shade, The West Wing, ER, The Event*, and *Sons of Anarchy*, as well as such made-for-TV movies and mini-series as *The Glass Menagerie* (1966), *Lincoln* (1974), *Our Town* (1977), *George Washington* (1984), *North and South* (1985 and 1986), *My Own Country* (1998), and *Captain Cook's Extraordinary Atlas* (2009). Holbrook can be heard in the feature films *Jonathan Livingston Seagull* (1973) and *Cats Don't Dance* (1997) and on the video *The Life and Adventures of Santa Claus* (2000).

Holden, Eddie An actor who appeared in only a few movies, he provided the voices of one of the Clowns in *Dumbo* (1941) and the Chipmunk in *Bambi* (1942), his last film credit. Holden's other movies include *The Fighting Deputy* (1937), *The Battle of Broadway* (1938), *Torture Ship* (1939), and *The Mad Monster* (1942).

Holloway, Sterling (1905–1992) An easily recognizable character actor with his lanky frame and raspy voice, the unusual song-and-dance man played country bumpkins, telegram boys, clerks, and soda jerks in over one hundred films but is mostly known as the voice of Winnie the Pooh. Sterling Price Holloway, Jr., was born in Cedartown, Georgia, and was a juvenile actor on the regional stage. He trained at the American Academy of Dramatic Arts, made his Broadway debut in 1923 in a drama, and two years later got to introduce the first Rodgers and Hart song hit "Manhattan" in the revue *The Garrick Gaieties* (1925). Holloway was featured in the 1926 and 1930 editions of the *Gaieties* but rarely returned to Broadway because of his busy film and television schedule. He appeared in a few silent films but with the coming of sound his high-pitched drawl was an asset and he was frequently cast in comedies, dramas, and musicals, including *Blonde Venus* (1932), *Gold Diggers of 1933* (1933), *Dancing Lady* (1933), *The Merry Widow* (1935), *Palm Springs* (1936), *Varsity Show* (1937), *Doctor Rhythm* (1938), *Remember the Night* (1940), *Meet John Doe* (1941), *Iceland* (1942), *Hit Parade of 1941* (1940), and *The Beautiful Blonde from Bashful Bend* (1949). Holloway's best performances were in Disney animated films where he provided the voices of Mr. Stork in *Dumbo* (1940) and again in the short *Lambert, the Sheepish Lion* (1952), the Adult Flower the skunk in *Bambi* (1942), the mysterious Cheshire Cat in *Alice in Wonderland* (1951), the hissing snake Kaa in *The Jungle Book* (1967), and the faithful mouse Roquefort in *The Aristocats* (1970), as well as roles in Disney shorts, such as the mouse Amos in *Ben and Me* (1953). He was Walt Disney's favorite narrator and Holloway can be heard narrating sections of the anthology features *The Three Caballeros* (1945) and *Make Mine Music* (1946) as well as many shorts, from *The Penguin and the Snipe* (1944) to *Goliath II* (1960). Yet Holloway's true claim to fame came late in his career when he voiced Winnie the Pooh in the bear's first movie short *Winnie the Pooh and the Honey Tree* (1966). This was followed by *Winnie the Pooh and the Blustery Day* (1968), *Winnie the Pooh and Tigger Too* (1974), and *The Many Adventures of Winnie the Pooh* (1977). Holloway appeared in dozens of television shows, including many Disney programs, and had his own series in the mid–1950s. He was one of Disney's finest animation actors and his warm, distinctive voice is still familiar to audiences. The messenger stork in *Dumbo* was Holloway's first Disney credit and in many ways it is his best performance. The bird is both fumbling and yet a stickler for doing things correctly. His brief scene near the beginning of *Dumbo* is a marvelous piece of vocal and physical comedy. No wonder Disney brought Holloway and the stork back for the short *Lambert, the Sheepish Lion*. Another Holloway performance that stands out is his Cheshire Cat in *Alice in Wonderland*. While most of the characters in the film are running around screaming at each other, this cat is quiet, cool, and disturbingly calm. The character's sometimes-nonsensical dialogue is uttered by Holloway is such sibilant sounds that he is mesmerizing. Finally, mention must be made of Holloway's delightful snake Kaa in *The Jungle Book*, one of the few times he got to voice a villain. With his lines and lyrics filled with "s" words, Holloway got to hiss away with abandon, being more silly than threatening. (In the original Kipling stories, the snake is Mowgli's friend, not an antagonist.) More than perhaps any other actor, Holloway was the consummate Disney voice.

Holm, Ian (b. 1931) The distinguished British actor of stage, films, and television who was never a traditional leading man yet always found fascinating leading roles, he voiced the short and greedy Skinner who manages Gusteau's Restaurant and food franchise in *Ratatouille* (2007). He was born Ian Holm Cuthbert in Goodmayes, England, the son of a psychiatrist and a nurse, and raised in London. He studied at the Royal Academy of Dramatic Art before becoming a member of the Royal Shakespeare Company where he played dozens of classical roles. Holm also appeared in many modern plays and performed on Broadway in *The Homecoming* when the London cast went to New York in 1967. Most of his early television and film work was in screen versions of classic plays, then he was noticed in such movies as *The Fixer* (1968), *The Bofors Gun* (1968), *Oh! What a Lovely War* (1969), *A Severed Head* (1970), *Nicholas and Alexandra* (1971), *Young Winston* (1972), *Juggernaut* (1974), *Robin and Marian* (1976), *Alien* (1979), *Chariots of Fire* (1981), *Time Bandits* (1981), *Brazil* (1985), *Wetherby* (1985), *Naked Lunch* (1991), *The Madness of King George* (1994), *Big Night* (1996), *The Fifth Element* (1997), *The Emperor's New Clothes* (2001), *The Lord of the Rings: The Fellowship of the Rings* (2001) and its two sequels, *Garden State* (2004), *The Day After Tomorrow* (2004), *The Aviator* (2004), and *O Jerusalem* (2006). Holm has also acted in many British television series and original TV-movies. The character of Skinner in *Ratatouille* is named after behavioral psychologist B. F. Skinner who placed rats in a "Skinner box" and studied their learning patterns. The scientist's work is evoked in the movie when the villain Skinner captures Remy and puts him in a box. Autobiography: *Acting My Life* (2004).

Holmes, Taylor (1878–1959) A durable and busy character actor of stage and screen for over fifty years, he voiced Princess Aurora's gushing father King Stefan in *Sleeping Beauty* (1959), his last acting credit. Born in Newark, New Jersey, and educated in Chicago, Holmes started in vaudeville and played in British music halls before making his Broadway debut in 1901. He appeared in supporting roles in stage comedies, dramas, and musicals through 1946, including *Trilby* (1915), *The Hotel Mouse* (1922), *Joy of Living* (1931), *I'd Rather Be Right* (1937), *Marinka* (1945), and *Woman Bites Dog* (1946). Holmes worked in films starting as early as 1917, going on to act in over seventy movies including *Fools for Luck* (1917). *Nothing but the Truth* (1920), *Before Morning* (1933), *The Crime of Dr. Forbes* (1936), *Nightmare Alley* (1947), *Joan of Arc* (1948), *Mr. Belvedere Goes to College* (1949), *Father of the Bride* (1950), *Gentlemen Prefer Blondes* (1953), *The Outcast* (1954), and *The Maverick Queen* (1956). He made his television debut in 1949 as Ebenezer Scrooge in a short version of *A Christmas Carol*, then went on to appear in such TV series as *Ford Television Theatre*, *Big Town*, *Damon Runyon Theatre*, *The Millionaire*, *The Life of Riley*, *Dragnet*, *Lassie*, and *The Loretta Young Show*.

Holowicki, E. J. A sound engineer for Pixar since 2002, he provided the voice of the blue hot rod gang member D. J. in *Cars* (2006). He has designed the sound and served as sound mixer for such films as *Finding Nemo* (2003), *The Incredibles* (2004), *Cars, Ratatouille* (2007), *WALL-E* (2008), *Up* (2009), and *Toy Story 3* (2010).

Holt, Bob (1928–1985) A general utility actor who quickly became a busy voice artist, he supplied the voice of the urbane British Codfish in the animated section of *Bedknobs and Broomsticks* (1971). He was born Robert John Holthaus in St. Louis, Missouri, and made an impressive film debut in *Julius Caesar* (1950) but dropped out of movies and did stage work regionally until taking up voicing cartoons in the 1970s. Holt provided all the voices in the animated short *Johnny Learns His Manners* (1968) and so impressed the networks that he soon became an in-demand artist, working on dozens of TV series and specials. He voiced the title character in the series *Doctor Dolittle*, followed by *The Houndcats*, *Bailey's Comets*, *The New Tom & Jerry Show*, *Challenge of the SuperFriends*, *Flash Gordon*,

The Smurfs, Dungeons & Dragons, The Incredible Hulk, The Dukes, Challenge of the GoBots, and *Adventures of the Gummi Bears.* Holt also voiced the Old West lawyer Hoot Kloot is seventeen cartoon shorts, the canine Dogfather in eleven cartoons, and was heard in such animated movies and videos as *The Lorax* (1972), *Charlotte's Web* (1973), *Dr. Seuss on the Loose* (1973), *The Bear Who Slept Through Christmas* (1973), *Oliver Twist* (1974), *The Nine Lives of Fritz the Cat* (1974), *Wizards* (1977), *The Mouse and His Child* (1977), *The World of Strawberry Shortcake* (1980), *Puff and the Incredible Mr. Nobody* (1982), *The Grinch Grinches the Cat in the Hat* (1982), *Flash Gordon: The Greatest Adventure of All* (1982), *Peter and the Magic Egg* (1983), and *The Adventures of the American Rabbit* (1986).

Hong, James (b. 1929) An Asian American actor who has appeared on over 400 episodes of television series as well as many movies, he supplied the voice of the Emperor's begrudging advisor Chi-Fu in *Mulan* (1998). He was born in Minneapolis, Minnesota, and studied civil engineering at the University of Minnesota and the University of Southern California. While working as a road engineer for the County of Los Angeles, Hong took up acting, co-founding the celebrated Asian American theatre company East-West Players and performing in and directing many productions over the years. He made his screen debut in *Soldier of Fortune* (1955), followed by such films as *Love Is a Many Splendored Thing* (1955), *Battle Hymn* (1957), *Never So Few* (1959), *Flower Drum Song* (1961), *The Satan Bug* (1965), *Destination Inner Space* (1966), *The Sand Pebbles* (1966), *Colossus: The Forbin Project* (1970), *The Hawaiians* (1970), *The Carey Treatment* (1972), *Chinatown* (1974), *No Deposit, No Return* (1976), *The In-Laws* (1979), *Airplane!* (1980), *Blade Runner* (1982), *Missing in Action* (1984), *The Golden Child* (1986), *Revenge of the Nerds II: Nerds in Paradise* (1987), *Tango & Cash* (1989), *Dragonfight* (1990), *Merlin* (1992), *Wayne's World 2* (1993), *Operation Dumbo Drop* (1995), *Gladiator Cop* (1995), *Red Corner* (1997), *The Art of War* (2000), *American Fusion* (2005), *Adventures of Johnny Tao* (2007), *Shanghai Kiss* (2007), *The Day the Earth Stood Still* (2008), and *How to Make Love to a Woman* (2010), as well as many TV-movies. Hong has had an even more prolific television career, appearing on dozens of series over a period of fifty-five years, such as *Sky King, The Millionaire, The New Adventures of Charlie Chan, Death Valley Days, Peter Gunn, Bachelor Father, Bonanza, Hawaiian Eye, Adventures in Paradise, Wagon Train, Ensign O'Toole, Perry Mason, Slattery's People, The Wackiest Ship in the Army, The Man from U.N.C.L.E., The Iron Horse, I Spy, Days of Our Lives, Family Affair, Here's Lucy, Ironside, Barnaby Jones, Hawaii Five-O, Kung-Fu, Jigsaw John, The Streets of San Francisco, Switch, Soap, Dallas, Marco Polo, Dynasty, Falcon Crest, Santa Barbara, The A-Team, Miami Vice, Hunter, Tour of Duty, Seinfeld, MacGyver, Diagnosis Murder, Chicago Hope, Home Improvement, Ellen, Friends, The Practice, Martial Law, The West Wing, Malcolm in the Middle, Las Vegas, Bones, Zoey 101,* and *The Big Bang Theory.* He can be heard in the TV cartoon series *Dexter's Laboratory, Spawn, Jackie Chan Adventures, Teen Titans, Avatar: The Last Airbender, Super Robot Monkey Team Hyperforce Go!, Chowder,* and *Kung Fu Panda: Legends of Awesomeness,* as well as the animated videos and movies *Spawn 3: Ultimate Battle* (1999), *Choose Your Own Adventure: The Abominable Snowman* (2006), *Chill Out, Scooby-Doo!* (2007), *Kung Fu Panda* (2008), and *Kung Fu Panda: The Kaboom of Doom* (2011).

Hoover, Kelly An assistant production manager at the Disney studios, she worked on *Lilo & Stitch* (2002) and *Brother Bear* (2003) before providing voices for minor characters. She played the scolding pig Mama Runt in *Chicken Little* (2005), the daffy Aunt Billie in *Meet the Robinsons* (2007), the no-nonsense animal shelter guard Ester in *Bolt* (2008), and the dog Stella in *The Princess and the Frog* (2009). The last character was a farcical reference to Stella Kowalski from Tennessee Williams' 1947 play *A Streetcar Named Desire* set in New Orleans, also the setting for *The Princess and the Frog.* In the famous 1951 film version of the play, Marlon Brando uttered an anguished cry of "Stella!" and that cry was echoed by Big Daddy (another Williams character reference) at the masquerade party when the dog Stella chases the frogs Tiana and Prince Naveen.

Hopkins, Nikita A child performer who did voice work for six years early in the new century, he supplied the singing and speaking voice of the young kangaroo Roo in six *Winnie the Pooh* movies and videos. Hopkins hails from Santa Clarita, California, and began his career voicing Roo in the video-movie *Winnie the Pooh: Seasons of Giving* (1999), reprising the character in *The Tigger Movie* (2000), *Mickey's Magical Christmas: Snowed in at the House of Mouse* (2001), *Piglet's Big Movie* (2003), *Pooh's Heffalump Movie* (2005), and *Pooh's Heffalump Halloween Movie* (2005), as well as in the TV cartoon series *The Book of Pooh.* He can also be heard in the series *House of Mouse, The Zeta Project, Power Rangers Wild Force,* and *Lilo and Stitch,* and in the animated video *101 Dalmatians II: Patch's London Adventure* (2003). Hopkins stopped performing in 2006 and studied motion pictures and television at the Academy of San Francisco.

Howard, Clint (b. 1959) A child performer who grew up to become a prolific character actor usually playing unlikable types, he provided the voices for Colonel Hathi's son, Junior the Elephant, in *The Jungle Book* (1967) and the baby kangaroo Roo in *Winnie the Pooh and the Honey Tree* (1966), *Winnie the Pooh and the Blustery Day* (1968), *Winnie the Pooh and Tigger Too* (1974), and *The Many Adventures of Winnie the Pooh* (1977). Clinton E. Howard was born in Burbank, California, the younger brother of actor-turned-director Ron Howard, and as a child appeared on television episodes of such series as *The Courtship of Eddie's Father, Ben Casey, Bonanza, Please Don't Eat the Daisies, The Andy Griffith Show, The Baileys of Balboa, Star Trek, Gentle Ben, The Virginian, Nanny and the Professor,* and *The Streets of San Francisco*. He also appeared in child roles in a handful of movies, including *An Eye for an Eye* (1966), *Gentle Giant* (1967), *The Wild Country* (1970), and *Salty* (1973), as well as the TV-movies *The Red Pony* (1973) and *Huckleberry Finn* (1975). Howard made the transition to teenage characters and then into adult roles with little difficulty, going on to act in hundreds of episodes of television and over eighty movies, among them *Grand Theft Auto* (1977), *Harper Valley P.T.A.* (1978), *Cocoon* (1985), *Parenthood* (1989), *Backdraft* (1991), *The Rocketeer* (1991), *The Paper* (1994), *Apollo 13* (1995), *The Waterboy* (1998), *Austin Powers: The Spy Who Shagged Me* (1999), *How the Grinch Stole Christmas* (2000), *Austin Powers in Goldmember* (2002), *The Cat in the Hat* (2003), *Fun with Dick and Jane* (2005), *Frost/Nixon* (2008), *Halloween* (2007), *Night at the Museum: Battle of the Smithsonian* (2009), and *Alabama Moon* (2009). His adult television credits include *Gung-Ho, Hunter, Space Rangers, Star Trek: Deep Space Nine, Married with Children, The Pretender, Star Trek: Enterprise,* and *My Name Is Earl*. Howard can be heard in the animated movies and videos *Rapsittie Street Kids: Believe in Santa* (2002), *Fur on the Asphalt: The Greg the Bunny Reunion Show* (2005), *Curious George* (2006), *Curious George 2: Follow That Monkey!* (2009), and *The Haunted World of El Superbeasto* (2009).

Howard, Terrence (b. 1969) An African American actor, singer, and musician who has shone on television and in the movies, he provided the voice of Tiana's hard-working father James in *The Princess and the Frog* (2009). Terrence Dashon Howard was born in Chicago and raised in Cleveland, Ohio, the great-grandson of the stage actress-singer Minnie Gentry. He made his television debut as Jackie Jackson in the TV-movie *The Jacksons: An American Dream* (1992) then acted in the series *Tall Hopes, Living Single, Coach, Family Matters, Getting By,* and *Picket Fences* before finding recognition as Louis Russ in the film *Mr. Holland's Opus* (1995). Among Howard's other notable movies are *Lotto Land* (1995), *Dead Presidents* (1995), *Sunset Park* (1996), *Johns* (1996), *Double Tap* (1997), *Spark* (1998), *The Players Club* (1998), *Butter* (1998), *The Best Man* (1999), *Big Momma's House* 2000), *Angel Eyes* (2001), *Glitter* (2001), *Hart's War* (2002), *Biker Boyz* (2003), *Love Chronicles* (2003), *Crash* (2004), *Ray* (2004), *Four Brothers* (2005), *Idlewild* (2006), *The Brave One* (2007), *Awake* (2007), *Iron Man* (2008), and *Fighting* (2009). He has returned to television in several made-for-TV movies, most memorably as Cassius Clay in *King of the Whole World* (2000), and the series *Sparks, NYPD Blue, Fastlane, Soul Food, Street Time,* and *Law & Order: Los Angeles*. Howard is also a singer and plays guitar and piano, and has recorded with others and on his own.

Høybye, Laus (b. 1978) A singer-actor who has made movies and appeared on television in his native Denmark, he provided the singing voice of teenager Max in *A Goofy Movie* (1995). Laus Rottbøoll Høoybye was born in Farum, Denmark, and as a teenager became famous for his acting and singing the title role in the Danish film *Krummerne* (1991) and its sequel *Krummerne 2* (1992). Høoybye found an audience in American with his animated series *Camp Lazlo* and some of his songs got on the American charts.

Hubbard, Thelma She voiced three characters in *Bambi* (1942): the Mother Quail, the Girl Bunny, and the Female Pheasant. There is no record of her working on any other Disney or non–Disney film.

Hudson, Lord Tim (b. 1941) A British music promoter who started as a DJ in the States, he voiced the singing Liverpool-accented vulture Dizzy in *The Jungle Book* (1967) and the English guitar player Hit Cat in *The Aristocats* (1970). Timothy Hudson was born in Prestbury, England, and came to America in the early 1960s to manage such music groups as The Seeds and The Lollipop Shoppe. He became a popular radio DJ in Los Angeles and, claiming that he knew the Beatles from his Great Britain days, he was assigned to follow the famous Fab Four during their first U.S. concert tour and report on their doings for his radio station. Because Hudson did a very accurate Liverpool dialect, Disney hired him for *The Jungle Book* to voice one of the vultures who were obviously a spoof of the Beatles. After providing the "scat cat" Hit Cat for *The Aristocats*, Hudson returned to management, promoting singers and sports teams. Brian Epstein, the manager of the Beatles, approached Disney about having the Fab Four do the voices of the vultures in *The Jungle Book* but he didn't tell his clients. The quartet found out and vetoed the idea.

Hulce, Tom (b. 1953) A compelling television and movie actor who later moved into theatrical producing, he provided the speaking and singing voice of the hunchbacked hero Quasimodo in *The Hunchback of Notre Dame* (1996). Thomas Edward Hulce was born in Whitewater, Wisconsin, grew up in Plymouth, Michigan, and studied theatre at the North Carolina School of the Arts. He made his New York stage debut in 1974 as a replacement for the lead in *Equus* and played the role on tour as well. His other New York theatre credits include *Twelve Dreams* (1981) and other plays Off Broadway, and *A Memory of Two Mondays* (1976) and *A Few Good Men* (1989) on Broadway. Hulce found greater success in films, getting noticed in *Animal House* (1978) and winning high acclaim for his performance as Mozart in *Amadeus* (1984). His other films include *September 30, 1955* (1977), *Those Lips, Those Eyes* (1980), *Dominick and Eugene* (1988), *Parenthood* (1989), *The Inner Circle* (1991), and *Frankenstein* (1994), as well as the TV-movies *The Rise and Rise of Daniel Rocket* (1986), *Murder in Mississippi* (1990), and *The Heidi Chronicles* (1995). Hulce retired from acting in the late 1990s to concentrate on stage directing and producing, presenting some Off Broadway plays and the rock musicals *Spring Awakening* (2006) and *American Idiot* (2010) on Broadway. The character of Quasimodo is such a revered one in world literature that any film version of *The Hunchback of Notre Dame* is open to many criticisms. The Disney artists wanted to make a deformed, ugly creature yet didn't want to disgust or turn off moviegoers. The compromise on screen is a worthy one, with outsized features, distorted muscles, and yet a warm glow coming from the pathetic Quasimodo. Hulce's vocals in the film are masterful. Quasimodo may be deformed but his voice is full and honest. The childlike nature of the character can be heard in Hulce's performance, but the hunchback's emerging sense of self-worth is also there. Hulce reprised his Quasimodo in the video sequel *The Hunchback of Notre Dame II* (2002).

Humphries, Barry (b. 1934) The Australian actor and female impersonator known on three continents for his character of the flamboyant Dame Edna Evridge, he provided the voice of the great white shark Bruce who tries to control his carnivorous appetite in *Finding Nemo* (2003). He was born John Barry Humphries in Melbourne, Australia, the son of a construction manager, and attended Melbourne University where he performed in revues and plays. He relocated to London in 1960 and found success on television playing variations of the Edna character on variety programs, talk shows, and TV series. By the late 1970s Humphries and Edna were well known in the States as well from many television appearances. He even brought his Dame Edna to Broadway in 1999, 2004, and 2010. Humphries also appeared on Broadway in the original cast of *Oliver!* (1963) and played non–Edna characters (male and female) in the movies *The Getting of Wisdom* (1978), *Shock Treatment* (1981), *Immortal Beloved* (1994), *Spice World* (1997), *Nicholas Nickleby* (2002), and *Moll Flanders* (2010). The character of the shark Bruce is unusual for a Disney villain in that he does not want to be evil and tries to psyche himself into going against his carnivorous nature. The character is an homage to the shark in the film *Jaws* (1975), the mechanical model that was nicknamed Bruce by the crew. Autobiography: *My Life as Me: A Memoir* (2004).

Hunt, Bonnie (b. 1961) A successful actress, writer, and producer who has had two television shows of her own, she voiced the maternal black widow spider Rosie in *A Bug's Life* (1998). the snake-like monster teacher Ms. Flint in *Monsters, Inc.* (2001), the Porsche lawyer Sally Carrera in *Cars* (2006), and little Bonnie's toy Dolly in *Toy Story 3* (2010). Bonnie Lynn Hunt was born in Chicago where she co-founded the comedy improv troupe An Impulsive Thing. After doing comedy with the Second City troupe, she worked in television, writing for various comedy shows and later producing series in which she starred. Her TV acting credits include *Grand, Davis Rules, The Building, Bonnie, Life with Bonnie*, and *The Life and Times of Tim*. Hunt has also appeared in several films, among them *Beethoven* (1992), *Dave* (1993), *Beethoven's 2nd* (1993), *Jumanji* (1995), *Jerry Maguire* (1996), *Random Hearts* (1999), *The Green Mile* (1999), *Cheaper by the Dozen* (2003), *Cheaper by the Dozen 2* (2005), and *I Want Someone to Eat Cheese With* (2006). The character of the legal auto Sally Carrera in *Cars* is a Porsche which is a pun on Shakespeare's Portia, today the nickname for female lawyers.

Hunt, Linda (b. 1945) A very short but commanding character actress whose quizzical facial expressions and hypnotic, husky voice make her unique, she supplied the voice for the wise tree ancestor Grandmother Willow in *Pocahontas* (1995). She was born Lydia Susanna Hunter in Morristown, New Jersey, educated at the Interlochen Arts Academy and the Goodman Theatre School in Chicago, and made her New York stage debut in 1972, though she spent much of her theatre career in regional theatre. The four-foot, nine-inch actress shone in New York in such plays as *Top Girls* (1983),

End of the World (1984), *Aunt Dan and Lemon* (1985), and *The Cherry Orchard* (1988), as well as in the films *Popeye* (1980), *The Year of Living Dangerously* (1983), *The Bostonians* (1984), *Ready to Wear* (1994), and *Stranger Than Fiction* (2006). In the original plans for the movie *Pocahontas*, the spirit of the ancestors was to be a male character called Old Man River and Gregory Peck was cast to voice it. But Peck realized that the character ought to be a maternal figure and the filmmakers agreed so Grandmother Willow was developed and Hunt was hired to voice her. She reprised her Grandmother Willow in the video *Pocahontas II: Journey to a New World* (1998).

Hunter, Bill (b. 1940) A leading film actor in Australian cinema for four decades, he provided the voice of the oblivious Sydney dentist Dr. Philip Sherman in *Finding Nemo* (2003). He was born in Ballarat, Australia, and began his career in 1960s Australian television. Soon he was featured in such notable films as *Gallipoli* (1981), *An Indecent Obsession* (1985), *Strictly Ballroom* (1992), *The Adventures of Priscilla, Queen of the Desert* (1994), *Muriel's Wedding* (1994), and *Australia* (2008).

Hunter, Holly (b. 1958) A small but fiery movie star who excels at playing outspoken and sometimes outrageous women, she voiced the super-hero mom Helen Parr/Elastigirl in *The Incredibles* (2004). Hunter was born in Conyers, Georgia, worked in summer stock as a teenager, and trained at Carnegie Mellon University in Pittsburgh before making her New York stage debut in 1981. Most of her theatre credits are in plays by Beth Henley, such as *Crimes of the Heart* (1982), *The Wake of Jamey Foster* (1982), *Miss Firecracker Contest* (1984), and *Impossible Marriage* (1998). Hunter also made her screen debut in 1981 and found wide acclaim for such movies as *Raising Arizona* (1987), *Broadcast News* (1987), *Miss Firecracker* (1989), *The Piano* (1993), *Home for the Holidays* (1995), *Crash* (1997), and *O Brother, Where Art Thou?* (2000). The idea for the character of Elastigirl in *The Incredibles* was based on three comic strip super-heroes: Elongated Man, Mr. Fantastic, and Elasti-Girl.

Hurt, John (b. 1940) A magnetic British actor of the stage, movies, and television whose lean look works equally well for villainous as well as sympathetic characters, he provided the voice of the grotesque and evil Horned King in *The Black Caldron* (1985) and narrated *The Tigger Movie* (2000). John Vincent Hurt was born in Shirebrook, England, the son of a parish vicar and a former actress, and studied at the Grimsby Art School and St. Martin's School of Art for a career as a painter. He turned to acting and enrolled at the Royal Academy of Dramatic Art for a time, making his London stage debut in 1962, the same year he made his first movie. Hurt found wide recognition on both sides of the Atlantic when he played the perverted Caligula in the BBC-TV series *I, Claudius* (1976) and secured his reputation with such popular films as *Midnight Express* (1978), *Alien* (1979), and *The Elephant Man* (1980). His other notable movies over the decades include *10 Rillington Place* (1971), *Little Malcolm* (1974), *The Shout* (1978), *Heaven's Gate* (1980), *History of the World: Part I* (1981), *The Osterman Weekend* (1983), *The Field* (1990), *Even Cowgirls Get the Blues* (1993), *Contact* (1997), *Harry Potter and the Sorcerer's Stone* (2001), *Miranda* (2002), *V Is for Vendetta* (2005), *Indiana Jones and the Kingdom of the Crystal Skull* (2008), *Outlander* (2008), and *Harry Potter and the Deathly Hallows* (2011). He has acted in dozens of television programs, including the British series *Crime and Punishment, The Storyteller,* and *The Alan Clark Diaries,* as well as the animated series *Watership Down* and *Merlin*, and provided voices for such animated movies and videos as *Watership Down* (1978), *The Lord of the Rings* (1978), *Thumbelina* (1994), and *Hellboy Animated: Blood and Iron* (2007). The Horned King in *The Black Cauldron* is a villain not unlike Darth Vader in *Star Wars*, though Lloyd Alexander's books (the basis for the animated film) predate that space character. He is a humorless, deadly character with a skeleton face and shroud-like robes, but it is Hurt's deep yet hollow vocals that give the Horned King his true villainy.

Huston, John (1906–1987) The distinguished Hollywood director, actor, writer, and producer whose career spanned six decades, one of his last acting performances was providing the narration for *The Black Caldron* (1985). John Marcellus Huston was born in Nevada, Missouri, the son of the renowned stage and screen actor Walter Huston (1884–1950) and international journalist Rhea Gore, and began performing in vaudeville at the age of three. As an adult he took up boxing professionally then turned to acting, making his Broadway debut in 1925. The restless Huston got tired of acting, turned to writing and stage directing, then returned to the movies where he wrote and acted in *The Storm* (1930). As the writer and director of *The Maltese Falcon* (1941), Huston became a much-in-demand talent in Hollywood and for the next forty-six years wrote, directed, produced and occasionally acted in film projects of his choice. Among the outstanding films he directed are *The Treasure of Sierra Madre* (1948), *Key Largo* (1948), *The Asphalt Jungle* (1950), *The Red Badge of Courage* (1951), *The African Queen* (1951), *Moby*

Dick (1956), *The Bible: In the Beginning* (1966), *The Man Who Would Be King* (1975), *Prizzi's Honor* (1985), and *The Dead* (1987). Huston sometimes played minor roles in his own movies and gave notable performances in films by others, including *The Cardinal* (1963), *Chinatown* (1974), *The Wind and the Lion* (1975), *Wise Blood* (1979), and *A Minor Miracle* (1983). His deep, gravelly voice could be heard in the animated TV-movies *The Hobbit* (1977) and *The Return of the King* (1980) and he narrated several television and film projects. Autobiography: *An Open Book* (1981); biographies: *John Huston*, Axel Marsden (1978); *King Rebel*, W. F. Nolan (1990); *The Hustons: The Life and Times of a Hollywood Dynasty*, Lawrence Grobel (2000).

Hutton, Malcolm   A child actor with only a few screen credits, his last film was *Dumbo* (1941) in which he voiced Skinny, the red-headed boy who taunts baby Dumbo at the circus and is spanked by Mrs. Jumbo. Hutton played similarly unruly boys in the films *Peck's Bad Boy with the Circus* (1938) and *Reg'lar Fellers* (1941).

Ingham, Barrie (b. 1934)   An English stage actor who also found popularity on British and American television, he provided the voices for the mouse sleuth Basil of Baker Street and the drunken mouse Bartholomew in *The Great Mouse Detective* (1986). He was born in Halifax, England, and began his career with the Manchester Library Theatre Company. Ingham went on to act with all the major British stage companies, including the Old Vic, The Royal Shakespeare Company, the Mermaid Theatre Company, and the Royal National Theatre. Touring productions brought him to the States on several occasions and he was seen on Broadway in *Much Ado About Nothing* (1959), *Copperfield* (1981), *Camelot* (1981), *Aspects of Love* (1990), and *Jekyll & Hyde* (1997). Ingham made his television debut in 1960 and acted in many British series and TV dramas but he found more fame for his appearances in the series *Doctor Who* in the late 1960s. He also appeared on many American television shows, such as *The Jeffersons*, *Hart to Hart*, *Days of Our Lives*, *Matlock*, *Webster*, *Star Trek: The Next Generation*, and *Murder, She Wrote*. The character of the Sherlock Holmes–like Basil in *The Great Mouse Detective* is obviously a nod to Basil Rathbone who played Holmes on screen many times. Ingham doesn't so much imitate Rathbone as capture the dry enthusiasm and intellectual tone of the actor when he voiced Holmes. Comic actor John Cleese was the original choice to voice Basil but he was in great demand at the time because of the *Monty Python* television shows and films and was unavailable.

Irons, Jeremy (1948)   The highly-acclaimed British actor who has found major success in all media, he supplied the voice for the power-hungry lion Scar in *The Lion King* (1994). Jeremy John Irons was born on the Isle of Wight, England, the son of a tax accountant, and trained at the Bristol Old Vic School before becoming a member of the company. He excelled in classical roles on the stage but he found more recognition when he played John the Baptist in the first British production of *Godspell*. Irons' performances in the BBC-TV mini-series *The Pallisers* and *Love for Lydia* made him well known in Great Britain but it was his portrayal of Charles Ryder in the series *Brideshead Revisited* that made him famous in the States as well. Among his many notable screen credits are *Nijinsky* (1980), *The French Lieutenant's Woman* (1981), *Dead Ringers* (1988), *Reversal of Fortune* (1990), *M. Butterfly* (1993), *Stealing Beauty* (1996), *Lolita* (1997), *The Merchant of Venice* (2004), *Being Julia* (2004), *Kingdom of Heaven* (2005), and *The Color of Magic* (2008). Irons frequently returns to the stage in England and on Broadway appeared in *The Real Thing* (1984) and *Impressionism* (2009). British actors Tim Curry and Malcolm McDowell were seriously considered for the role of Scar in *The Lion King* but the directors cast Irons because of his classical theatre training, wanting the villain to come across as a Shakespearean character. Scar is indeed a classic villain yet there is a sense of comedy in Irons' performance that is sportive without diminishing the character's villainy. During the recording of Scar's song "Be Prepared," Irons hurt his voice shouting one line and voice artist Jim Cummings had to fill in and sing some of the high notes for him.

Irving, Amy (b. 1953)   A multi-talented stage, television, and screen star, she provided the singing voice of the *femme fatale* "toon" Jessica Rabbit in *Who Framed Roger Rabbit* (1988). Amy Davis Irving was born in Palo Alto, California, the daughter of theatre producer and director Jules Irving and actress Priscilla Pointer, and trained at the American Conservatory Theatre in San Francisco and the London Academy of Music and Dramatic Art. Although she made her New York stage debut Off Broadway in 1970, she would spend much of that decade on television in such series as *The Rookies*, *Police Woman*, and *Happy Days*, and in the TV-movies *James Dean* (1976), *Dynasty* (1976), *Panache* (1976), and *I'm a Fool* (1977). Irving made a noticeable film bow in *Carrie* (1976) and over the years has been featured in such movies as *The Fury* (1978), *Honeysuckle Rose* (1980), *The Competition* (1980), *Yentl* (1983), *Micki + Maude* (1984), *Rumpelstiltskin* (1987), *Crossing Delancey* (1988), *Carried Away* (1996), *I'm Not Rappaport* (1996), *Deconstructing*

Harry (1997), *The Confession* (1999), *Blue Ridge Fall* (1999), *Traffic* (2000), *Bossa Nova* (2000), *Thirteen Conversations About One Thing* (2001), *Tuck Everlasting* (2002), *Hide and Seek* (2005), and *Adam* (2009). She also acted in the later made-for-TV movies and mini-series *Once an Eagle* (1976), *The Far Pavillions* (1984), and *Anastasia: The Mystery of Anna* (1986), and in the series *Spin City, Law & Order: Special Victims Unit*, and *Alias*. Irving has returned to the theatre throughout her career, featured on the New York stage in *Amadeus* (1981), *Heartbreak House* (1983), *The Road to Mecca* (1988), *Broken Glass* (1994), *Three Sisters* (1996), *The Guys* (2002), *Ghosts* (2002), and *The Coast of Utopia* (2006). She can be heard in the animated film *An American Tail: Fievel Goes West* (1991). Kathleen Turner, who did the speaking voice for Jessica Rabbit, was not a singer so Irving imitated Turner's husky voice when she sang "Why Didn't You Do Right?" on the soundtrack; she did it without pay as a favor to director Robert Zemeckis.

Ivory, Edward Little is known about the actor who voiced the not-so-jolly Santa Claus in *The Nightmare Before Christmas* (1993). His only other film credits are minor roles in *Rampage* (1987), *Blood Red* (1989), and *Nine Months* (1995), and he appeared in the TV-movies *Eye on the Sparrow* (1987) and *Long Road Home* (1991), in one episode of *Midnight Caller*, and in the video *Quest of the Delta Knights* (1995). Vincent Price was originally cast as Santa in *The Nightmare Before Christmas* and he completed the vocals but the actor was very ill and weak at the time (he died a week after the film was released) and the recording was unusable so Ivory re-recorded Santa's lines for the final print.

Jackson, Samuel L. (b. 1949) A magnetic African American movie star known for his quiet, smoldering characterizations, he got to display a lighter vein as the voice of the super-hero Frozone in the disguise of Lucius Best in *The Incredibles* (2004). Samuel Leroy Jackson was born in Washington, D.C., grew up in Chattanooga, Tennessee, and was educated at Morehouse College before becoming a social worker and then a security officer. He started acting in the 1970s and made his Off Broadway debut in 1979, appearing in various dramas for the next decade, most memorably *A Soldier's Play* (1981) and *Home* (1981). Jackson appeared on the screen for the first time in 1972 and on television five years later, keeping busy in both media and playing a variety of characters once they stopped typecasting him as heavies. Among his notable movies are *Ragtime* (1981), *Do the Right Thing* (1989), *Goodfellas* (1990), *Jurassic Park* (1993), *Pulp Fiction* (1994), *A Time to Kill* (1996), *Star Wars: The Phantom Menace* (1999), *Unbreakable* (2000), *Star Wars: Attack of the Clones* (2002), *Star Wars: Revenge of the Sith* (2005), *Iron Man* (2008), and *Iron Man 2* (2010). He has appeared in dozens of television programs, as well as voicing such animated series as *Afro Samurai* and *Star Wars: The Clone Wars*. Jackson can also be heard in the animated films *Astro Boy* (2009), *Quantum Quest: A Cassini Space Odyssey* (2010), and *The RRF in New Recruit* (2010), and reprised his Frozone in the video *Mr. Incredible and Pals* (2005). The character of Frozone swings his arms in an unusual manner when he skates, a move copied from the Olympic gold medalist skater Shani Davis. Biographies: *Samuel L. Jackson*, Stacie Deutsch and Rhody Cohon (2009); *Samuel L. Jackson: The Unauthorized Biography*, Jeff Hudson (2004).

Janney, Allison (b. 1959) The acclaimed television, stage, and film actress with a distinct no-nonsense persona, she voiced the starfish Peach in *Finding Nemo* (2003). Allison Brooks Janney was born in Dayton, Ohio, and studied theatre at Kenyon College, New York's Neighborhood Playhouse School, and London's Royal Academy of Dramatic Art. She appeared in several New York productions, including the Off Broadway plays *Five Women Wearing the Same Dress* (1993), *New England* (1995), *Blue Window* (1996), and *The Taming of the Shrew* (1999), and on Broadway in *Present Laughter* (1996), *A View from the Bridge* (1997), and *9 to 5* (2009). Janney made her screen debut in 1989 and was soon cast in many films, such as *Big Night* (1996), *The Ice Storm* (1997), *Primary Colors* (1998), *The Object of My Affection* (1998), *Celebrity* (1998), *10 Things I Hate About You* (1999), *American Beauty* (1999), *Nurse Betty* (2000), *The Hours* (2002), *Hairspray* (2007), *Juno* (2007), *Away We Go* (2009), and *Life During Wartime* (2009), but she got more recognition on television where she shone as C. J. Cregg on *The West Wing* for seven years. She has also appeared on the series *Weeds, Two and a Half Men, In Plain Sight, Lost*, and *Shameless*, and provided voices for the TV cartoon series *Phineas and Ferb* and *Family Guy*.

Jay, Tony (1933–2006) A commanding character actor with a sinister basso voice, he had an extensive career on the stage, on television, and in the movies, providing the voices for the lunatic asylum proprietor Monsieur D'Arque in *Beauty and the Beast* (1991)), the complicated villain Judge Claude Frollo in *The Hunchback of Notre Dame* (1996), and the Narrator of *Treasure Planet* (2002). He was born in London and started his career as a radio announcer in South Africa. Back in England, Jay acted with the Royal Shakespeare Company before coming to the States where he eventually became a U.S. citizen. As a member of the RSC he was on Broadway in *The Life and Adventures of Nicholas Nickleby* (1986) but he soon left the stage and concentrated on television and film work. His movie credits include *Love and Death* (1975), *The Greek Tycoon* (1978), *Time Bandits* (1981), *Little Dorrit* (1988), and *My Stepmother Is an Alien* (1988), but much of his career has been on the small screen. Although he acted in such series as *The Golden Girls, Mr. Belvedere, Newhart, The New Lassie, Twin Peaks, Murphy Brown, Star Trek: The Next Generation*, and *Lois and Clark: The New Adventures of Superman*, he was busier voicing cartoon series, such as *TaleSpin, 2 Stupid Dogs, Rugrats, Mighty Max, Fantastic Four, Mighty Ducks, Spider-Man, ReBoot, House of Mouse, Miss Spider's Sunny Patch Friends*, and *Hey, Arnold!* Jay also provided voices for many animated movies and videos, including *The Easter Story* (1990), *Adventures in Odyssey: The Knight Travellers* (1991), *Tom and Jerry: The Movie* (1992), *Thumbelina* (1994), *Scooby-Doo in Arabian Nights* (1994), *Bruno the Kid: The Animated Movie* (1996), *All Dogs Go to Heaven 2* (1996), *Mighty Ducks the Movie: The First Face-Off* (1997), *The Rugrats Movie* (1998), *An American Tail: The Treasure of Manhattan Island* (1998), *Recess: School's Out* (2001), *The Jungle Book 2* (2003), *Lionheart* (2003), *X-Men Legends* (2004), and *Mickey's Around the World in 80 Days* (2005). The role of the creepy asylum owner D'Arque consists of one scene and Jay recorded the whole scene for his audition. The directors were so pleased that they used the audition tape for the movie. They were also so impressed with Jay that from the start the directors of *The Hunchback of Notre Dame* had him in mind for Judge Frollo, one of the most complex of all Disney villains. Among Frollo's sinister characteristics is lust for Esmeralda, the first Disney animated villain to be overtly sexual in character. His song "Hellfire," in which he conjures up the image of a nearly-naked Esmeralda in the flames of a fire, remains the most erotic scene in any Disney animated feature.

Jbara, Gregory (b. 1961) A durable stage, screen, and television actor-singer who usually plays likable characters, he provided the singing voice for one of the dense Willie Brothers in *Home on the Range* (2004). He was born in Westland, Michigan, and educated at the University of Michigan School of Music and Juilliard before beginning his career in regional and New York City theatres. Jbara was in the Off Broadway productions of *Have I Got a Girl for You* (1986), *Serious Money* (1987), and *Privates on Parade* (1989), then was featured on Broadway in *Born Yesterday* (1989), *Damn Yankees* (1994), *Victor/Victoria* (1995), *Chicago* (1996), *Dirty Rotten Scoundrels* (2005), and *Billy Elliot* (2008). He made his television debut on an episode of *Newhart* in 1987, followed by appearances in such series as *Frasier, That's Life, Malcolm in the Middle, Ally McBeal, Providence, The West Wing, Without a Trace, Friends, Grounded for Life, Monk*, and *Law & Order*. Among Jbara's movie credits are *Crocodile Dundee II* (1988), *Jeffrey* (1995), *In & Out* (1997), *The Out-of-Towners* (1999), *The Sure Hand of God* (2004), *World Trade Center* (2006), *Epic Movie* (2007), and *Remember Me* (2010). He can be heard on the cartoon series *Rocket Power, Higglytown Heroes, American Dad*, and *Family Guy*.

Jillette, Penn (b. 1955) The tongue-in-cheek comic and magician who often works with his silent partner Teller, he supplied the voice of the television Announcer in *Toy Story* (1995). Penn Fraser Gillette was born in Greenfield, Massachusetts, and in high school worked up a magic and juggling act which he perfected when he studied at the Ringling Brothers and Barnum & Bailey Clown College. Unhappy with conventional magic performance, Jillette teamed with Raymond Joseph Teller and created an act in which the illusions of stage magic were destroyed and comedy replaced mysticism. Billed as Penn & Teller, the duo found recognition in clubs, in concert, on television, in films, and Off Broadway. Jillette has had a career outside of the twosome, serving as an announcer on cable-TV's Comedy Channel, hosting and guesting on television talk shows, and acting on occasion. He has appeared in the television series *Miami Vice, Lois & Clark: The New Adventures of Superman, The Drew Carey Show, Friends, Dharma & Greg, Home Improvement, Just Shoot Me!, Girlfriends*, and *Sabrina, the Teenage Witch*, as well as the movies *Savage Island* (1985), *My Chauffeur* (1986), *Off Beat* (1986), *Tough Guys Don't Dance* (1987), *Penn & Teller Get Killed* (1989), *Car 54, Where Are You?* (1994), *Burnzy's Last Call* (1995), *Hackers* (1995), *Life Sold Separately* (1997), *Nothing Sacred* (1997), *Fear and Loathing in Las Vegas* (1998), and *Fear of Fiction* (2000). Jillette can be heard doing voices for the TV cartoon series *The Moxy & Flea Show, Mickey Mouse Works, House of Mouse*, and *Handy Manny*.

Joel, Billy (b. 1949) The durable and individual pop singer-songwriter-musician known as The Piano Man, his only acting credit is providing the speaking and singing voice of the street-smart Manhattan canine Dodger in *Oliver & Company* (1988). He was born William Martin Joel in the Bronx, New York, and raised in nearby Hicksville where he left high school to perform in clubs and with various bands. Joel recorded his first solo album in 1971 and two years later he had a chart hit with "Piano Man," followed by three decades of best-selling songs and albums. He remains a top-selling concert performer and his songs and/or recordings have been used in over fifty movies and television shows. The character of Dodger is the largest one in *Oliver & Company* and he holds the movie together. He is a variation on the hero Tramp from *Lady and the Tramp*, although Dodger is pure New York and less a lady killer than a cool and cocky street survivor. Both Steve Martin and Burt Reynolds were considered for the role before it went not to an actor but a singer. Billy Joel's rendition of Dodger's theme song "Why Should I Worry?" is the musical highlight of the movie but it is Joel the actor who surprises. It is curious that the singer has not embarked on other acting projects, his performance in *Oliver & Company* being so effective. Biography: *Billy Joel: The Life and Times of an Angry Young Man*, Hank Bordowitz (2006).

Johnson, Bruce Bayley A television voice artist who has also made many commercials, he provided the voice for the neighbor Mr. Swirly in *Doug's 1st Movie* (1999). He first voiced Mr. Swirly on the television cartoon series *Doug* and *Disney's Doug*, and can also be heard on the series *PB&J Otter* and *Jo Jo's Circus*, as well as on the videos *Harry the Dirty Dog* (1997) and *Legend of Kay* (2005).

Johnson, George An actor who provided the voice of Goofy in a dozen Disney shorts, he took over for voice artist Pinto Colvig for the years 1939 to 1943. Johnson first played Goofy in *Goofy and Wilbur* (1939) then reprised the role in a series of sports shorts, including *The Art of Skiing* (1941), *How to Play Baseball* (1942), *The Olympic Champ* (1942), and *How to Swim* (1942). His only other screen acting credit is an episode of the television series *Rawhide* in 1960.

Jones, Dickie (b. 1927) A child performer who grew up to become a successful actor in westerns, his most famous role is the wooden puppet-hero of *Pinocchio* (1940). He was born in Snyder, Texas, grew up on a ranch, and by the age of six was an expert horseman and lariat handler. Spotted by western star Hoot Gibson at a rodeo, Jones was encouraged to go to Hollywood and appear in westerns himself. He made his screen debut in 1934 and played children in a variety of movies for the rest of the decade, including *Kid Millions* (1934), *Little Men* (1934), *Queen of the Jungle* (1935), *The Pecos Kid* (1935), *The Hawk* (1935), *The Adventures of Frank Merriwell* (1936), *Little Lord Fauntleroy* (1936), *Daniel Boone* (1936), *Black Legion* (1937), *Stella Dallas* (1937), *A Man to Remember* (1938), *The Frontiersmen* (1938), *Young Mr. Lincoln* (1939), *On Borrowed Time* (1939), and *Destry Rides Again* (1939). Jones was able to continue working as a teenager, appearing in such films as *Virginia City* (1940), *The Howards of Virginia* (1940), *Mountain Rhythm* (1943), *Heaven Can Wait* (1943), and *The Adventures of Mark Twain* (1944). At the age of fifteen he played the teen hero Henry Aldrich in the popular radio series *The Aldrich Family* and was old enough to serve during the final year of World War II. As an adult billing himself as Dick Jones, he made more films after the war, including *Battleground* (1949), *Sands of Imo Jima* (1949), *Redwood Forest Trail* (1950), *Fort Worth* (1951), *Wagon Team* (1952), *Last of the Pony Riders* (1953), *The Bamboo Prison* (1954), *The Wild Dakotas* (1956), *The Cool and the Crazy* (1958), *Shadow of the Boomerang* (1960), and *Requiem for a Gunfighter* (1965). Many of his westerns were Gene Autry films and Jones was featured on television's *The Gene Autry Show* from 1950 to 1954, then he got his own series, *Buffalo Bill, Jr.* Jones' other TV credits include *The Lone Ranger*, *The Range Rider*, *Annie Oakley*, *The Gray Ghost*, *Pony Express*, *The Blue Angels*, and *Wagon Train*. He retired from acting in 1965 and went into business. Jones was first heard as Pinocchio on a 1939 broadcast of the *Lux Radio Theatre* while the film version was being completed. The character of Pinocchio was a difficult one to animate because he must move like a puppet yet have freedom of movement like a human boy. Instead of using a human model, the animators studied films of marionettes in action then decided at which point Pinocchio could behave with "no strings attached." The experienced, twelve-year-old actor Jones had little difficulty voicing the wooden hero except for the underwater sequence in which various methods were tried to give him a gurgling sound. One attempt of trying to talk in an underwater tank nearly drowned the boy actor. Originally Pinocchio was going to be a wisecracking puppet like the very popular Charlie McCarthy who was on the radio and in films at the time. But Walt Disney thought the audience would have little sympathy for such a smart-aleck character and Pinocchio was rethought as more like an adventurous little boy.

Jones, Freddie (b. 1927) A frenetic, highly-mannered British character actor with many stage, screen, and television credits over a period of fifty years, he voiced the aged and wise wizard Dalben in *The Black Caldron* (1985). He was born in Stoke-on-Trent in England and, after working for ten years as a lab assistant, trained for the theatre at Rose Buford College of Speech and Drama. Jones later became a member of the Royal Shakespeare Company and played a variety of roles but recognition came when he played Claudius in the British TV mini-series *The Caesars* in 1968. Among his many film credits are *Marat/Sade* (1967), *Far from the Madding Crowd* (1967), *The Bliss of Mrs. Blossom* (1968), *Otley* (1968), *Frankenstein Must Be Destroyed* (1969), *Kidnapped* (1971), *Son of Dracula* (1974), *Krull* (1983), *The Elephant Man* (1980), *Firestarter* (1984), *Dune* (1984), *The Neverending Story III* (1994), *Ladies in Lavender* (2004), and *Caught in the Act* (2008). Jones has acted in over one hundred British TV-movies and series ranging from adaptations of classics, such as *Nana* (1968), *Nicholas Nickleby* (1977), *The Mayor of Casterbridge* (1978), *Silas Marner* (1985), *Vanity Fair* (1987), and *David Copperfield* (2000), to such unusual or innovative series as *Jackanory, Love and Mr. Lewisham, Children of the Stones, The Duchess of Duke Street,* and *Pennies from Heaven.*

Jones, James Earl (b. 1931) The sturdy, rich-voiced African American actor who has given indelible performances in both the classics and new works, he has lent his voice to many film projects including *The Lion King* (1994) for which he played the wise, understanding King Mufasa. Jones was born in Arkabutla, Mississippi, the son of prize fighter-turned-actor Robert Earl Jones, and attended the University of Michigan to study medicine. But he was soon attracted to his father's profession and trained at the American Theatre Wing and with Lee Strasberg before getting his first acting jobs Off Broadway in 1958. Jones first gained wide attention playing classical roles for the New York Shakespeare Festival and became a Broadway star with his performance in *The Great White Hope* (1968). His other notable stage credits include *Mister Johnson* (1963), *The Blood Knot* (1964), *Othello* (1964 and 1982), *Boesman and Lena* (1970), *The Cherry Orchard* (1972), *The Iceman Cometh* (1973) *Paul Robeson* (1978), *Fences* (1987), *On Golden Pond* (2005), *Cat on a Hot Tin Roof* (2008), and *Driving Miss Daisy* (2010). Jones made his film debut in *Dr. Strangelove* (1964), followed by dozens of movies over the years, including *Claudine* (1974), *Matewan* (1987), *Field of Dreams* (1989), *The Sandlot* (1993), and *Cry the Beloved Country* (1995); but his greatest screen role remains the voice of Darth Vadar in four of the *Star Wars* films. He has also appeared in many television dramas, series, and specials. Because of his deep, resounding voice, Jones has narrated many documentary films and television programs; he was one of the hosts of *Fantasia/2000* (1999). Jones voiced characters in the movie *Pinocchio and the Emperor of the Night* (1987), the video films *Caspar: A Spirited Beginning* (1997), *Merlin* (1998), *Our Friend Martin* (1999), *Recess Christmas: Miracle on Third Street* (2001), *The Magic 7* (2009), *Jack and the Beanstalk* (2010), and *Quantum Quest: A Cassini Space Odyssey* (2010), the TV series *Garfield and Friends, The Simpsons,* and *Recess*. The character of Mufasa in *The Lion King* is one of the most regal and awe-inspiring of all Disney creations. He is powerful yet gentle, wise but human, stern but understanding. With Jones' vocals, the character carries a mythic quality about him. Jones reprised his Mufasa in the video *The Lion King II: Simba's Pride* (1998). Autobiography: *Voices and Silences* (1993) with Penelope Niven; biography: *James Earl Jones: Overcoming Adversity*, Judy L. Hasday (1999).

Jones, Tom (b. 1940) The popular Welsh singer who was the heartthrob of American and British females in the 1960s and 1970s, he provided the singing and speaking voice of the lounge lizard Theme Song Guy in *The Emperor's New Groove* (2000). He was born Thomas John Woodward in Pontypridd, Wales, the son of a coal miner, and sang in churches, schools, and pubs before getting his first record contract in 1964. The next year he had his first of many hit songs, mostly swinging ballads ("It's Not Unusual") and novelty numbers ("What's New Pussycat") that emphasized his full throttle baritone voice. In addition to numerous television appearances on variety shows, Jones also appeared as characters in some British TV programs and the American series *Fantasy Island*. He continues to sing in Las Vegas and concert arenas on both sides of the Atlantic. Biography: *Tom Jones: From the Valleys to Vegas*, Gwen Russell (2010).

Jordan, Jim (1896–1988) A radio actor remembered for playing the husband Fibber McGee on the air for twenty-four years, he voiced the scatter-brained but enthusiastic albatross Orville who flies Bernard and Bianca down to the Devil's Bayou in *The Rescuers* (1977). Jordan first played the character of McGee on the radio series *Fibber McGee and Molly* in 1935 with his wife Marian Jordan as Molly. He took some time off to serve in World War II then returned to the role until the show went off the air in 1959. Jordan also played McGee in the movies *This Way Please* (1937), *Look Who's Laughing* (1941), *Here We Go Again* (1942), *Heavenly Days* (1944), and *Popular Science* (1946), as well as in the documentary shorts *The All-Star Bond Rally* (1945), *Is Everybody Listening?* (1947), and *Behind Your Radio Dial* (1948). Jordan's rare non–McGee portrayals were in an episode of the television series *Chico and the Man* in 1976 and voicing Orville for *The Rescuers* before he retired in 1977.

Josten, Matthew (b. 1997) A child performer in commercials and on television since the age of four, he was one of the three boys who voiced the young alien Kirby in *Chicken Little* (2005) and played Lewis' weary roommate Michael "Goob"

Yagoobian in *Meet the Robinsons* (2007). The Santa Clarita, California, native has been featured in recurring roles in the television series *Birds of Prey*, *JAG*, *The Drew Carey Show*, *October Road*, and *Rodney*.

Judels, Charles (1882–1969) A balding, rough-voiced character actor who appeared in 137 movies from the silent era up to the end of the 1940s, he voiced two memorable villains in *Pinocchio* (1940): the hot-tempered Italian puppet master Stromboli and the smiling, sinister Coachman who lures the boys to Pleasure Island. He was born in Amsterdam, Netherlands, and by 1902 he was on the New York stage. Judels was featured in two dozen Broadway productions, mostly musicals, including *A Trip to Buffalo* (1902), *The Knickerbocker Girl* (1903), *Old Dutch* (1909), *Ziegfeld Follies of 1912*, *Twin Beds* (1914), *Nobody Home* (1915), *My Lady's Glove* (1917), *Mary* (1920), *For Goodness Sake* (1922), *Wildflower* (1923), *Gay Paree* (1925), *The Merry World* (1926), *A Night in Spain* (1927), *Artists and Models* (1927), and *Louisiana Lady* (1947). By 1915 he was in Hollywood making silent movies, among them *Old Dutch* (1915), *The Commuters* (1915), *Under the Red Robe* (1923), and *Little Old New York* (1923). With the coming of sound, Judels was often cast as foreign types in a wide variety of films, including *Cheer Up and Smile* (1930), *The Life of the Party* (1930), *50 Million Frenchmen* (1931), *Close Relations* (1933), *The Night Is Young* (1935), *Enchanted April* (1935), *San Francisco* (1936), *The Great Ziegfeld* (1936), *Swing High, Swing Low* (1937), *Song of the City* (1937), *Love and Hisses* (1937), *Idiot's Delight* (1939), *Ninotchka* (1939), *Balallaika* (1939), *Strange Cargo* (1940), *Down Argentine Way* (1940), *Bitter Sweet* (1940), *Sweetheart of the Campus* (1941), *Tortilla Flat* (1942), *Broadway Rhythm* (1944), *Knickerbocker Holiday* (1944), *A Bell for Adano* (1945), *In Old Sacramento* (1946), *I Wonder Who's Kissing Her Now* (1947), *Panhandle* (1948), and *Samson and Delilah* (1949). Judels' double performance in *Pinocchio* is noteworthy. His Stromboli is an obvious, hot-tempered villain yet his Coachman is frightening in his duplicity. He looks and sounds like a gentle Santa Claus at first but once the boys start turning into donkeys he looks and sound like the devil himself. This kind of reversal would occur on and off in Disney animated movies over the decades, right up to the lovable but despicable Lots-O-Lovin' Bear in *Toy Story 3* (2010).

Jump, Gordon (1932–2003) A portly character actor who specialized in bumbling or incompetent types, he provided the voice of the gentle Joseph who buys the donkey from the Boy for his wife Mary to ride on in the short *The Small One* (1978). He was born in Dayton, Ohio, educated at Kansas State University, and began his career working behind the scenes on local radio and television stations in the Midwest. Moving to Los Angeles in 1963, he worked as an actor in regional theatre before making his television debut in an episode of *Daniel Boone* in 1965. After appearing in small roles in many series, including *Run for Your Life*, *Get Smart*, *Here Come the Brides*, *Green Acres*, *Mannix*, *The Brady Bunch*, *Mary Tyler Moore*, *The Partridge Family*, *McCloud*, *That's My Mama*, *The Rockford Files*, *McMillan & Wife*, and *Lou Grant*, he found wide recognition as Chief of Police Tinker in *Soap*. Jump's later series include *Diff-rent Strokes*, *Night Court*, *The Golden Girls*, *The Love Boat*, *Growing Pains*, *Baywatch*, *Empty Nest*, *Seinfeld*, *Married with Children*, and *Mike Hammer*, and *Private Eye*, but he is best remembered as the radio station manager Arthur Carlson on the series *WKRP in Cincinnati* and *The New WKRP in Cincinnati*. Among his film and TV-movie credits are *Anatomy of a Crime* (1969), *Ransom Money* (1970), *Conquest of the Planet of the Apes* (1972), *Trouble Man* (1972), *A Cry for Help* (1975), *Sybil* (1976), *Ruby and Oswald* (1978), *The Fury* (1978), *House Calls* (1978), *Midnight Offerings* (1981), *For Lovers Only* (1982), *Making the Grade* (1984), *On Fire* (1987), *Moving* (1988), *Honeymoon Academy* (1990), *Bitter Vengeance* (1994), and *A Dog's Tale* (1999). Voicing the Biblical Joseph in *The Small One* is perhaps Jump's most atypical performance, but it is an effective one all the same.

Kahl, Milt (1909–1987) A renowned film animator who worked at the Disney studio for forty years, his only acting credit was voicing the friendly bovine Ferdinand in the animated short *Ferdinand the Bull* (1938). Milton Irwin Kahl was born in San Francisco and dropped out of school to become a magazine illustrator. After seeing the animated short *The Three Little Pigs* (1933), he sought out Walt Disney and began working for the studio in 1934, eventually becoming one of the company's leading animators and years later earning recognition as "The Animation Michelangelo." Kahl not only animated major characters in the Disney features and shorts, he was mostly responsible for giving the studio its artistic look. Among the many Disney features he animated are *Snow White and the Seven Dwarfs* (1937), *Pinocchio* (1940), *Bambi* (1942), *Saludos Amigos* (1942), *The Three Caballeros* (1944), *Make Mine Music* (1946), *Song of the South* (1946), *Melody Time* (1948), *Cinderella* (1950), *Alice in Wonderland* (1951), *Peter Pan* (1953), *Lady and the Tramp* (1955), *Sleeping Beauty* (1959), *One Hundred and One Dalmatians* (1961), *The Sword in the Stone* (1963), *Mary Poppins* (1964), *The Jungle Book* (1967), *The Aristocats* (1970), *Robin Hood* (1973), and *The Rescuers* (1977). Kahl also helped animate such animated short favorites as *Mickey's Fire Brigade* (1935), *Elmer Elephant* (1936), *Ferdinand the Bull*, *Ugly Duckling* (1939), *Chicken Little* (1943), *Hockey Homicide* (1945), *The Brave Engineer* (1950), *Winnie the Pooh and the Blustery Day* (1968), and six cartoons on the television program *Walt Disney's Wonderful World of Color*. He returned to the Disney studio for the last time in 1983 to help design some of the characters in *The Black Cauldron* (1985). Kahl also served as the mentor for Brad Bird, Andreas Deja, and other young artists who would comprise the next generation of animators. Biography: *Walt Disney's Nine Old Men and the Art of Animation*, John Canemaker (2001).

Kahn, Madeline (1942–1999) A bold, offbeat comedienne who had a multi-range singing voice, she also had dozens of funny character voices which she sometimes used in animated features, such as the magician's gypsy moth assistant Gypsy in *A Bug's Life* (1998). Born Madeline Gail Wolfson in Boston, she was educated at Hofstra University as a speech therapist but she also trained for an opera career. After singing in nightclubs and honing her skills in a series of Off Broadway musical revues, Kahn gained attention on Broadway in *New Faces of 1968*. She also shone in the musicals *Promenade* (1969) and *Two by Two* (1970) but did not achieve stardom until such 1970s movies as *Paper Moon* (1973), *Blazing Saddles* (1974), *Young Frankenstein* (1974), and *The Cheap Detective* (1978), followed by *Happy Birthday, Gemini* (1980), *City Heat* (1984), *Clue* (1985), *Betsy's Wedding* (1990), and *Nixon* (1995). Kahn then returned to Broadway and gave stellar performances in *On the Twentieth Century* (1978), *Born Yesterday* (1989), and *The Sisters Rosensweig* (1992). *A Bug's Life* was her only Disney credit but she also provided distinctive voices for the animated features *My Little Pony: The Movie* (1986) and *An American Tail* (1986). Kahn had her own television series, *Oh Madeline*, in the 1980s and appeared on many other programs, ranging from *Sesame Street* to *Cosby* to *Saturday Night Live*, before her premature death from cancer at the age of fifty-seven.

Kandel, Paul (b. 1951) A singer-actor whose career has mostly been on the stage, he provided the voice for the singing narrator Clopin in *The Hunchback of Notre Dame* (1996). He was born in Queens, New York, and by the 1970s was acting Off Broadway in such productions as *Nightclub Cantata* (1977), *Ta-Dah!* (1981), *Lucky Stiff* (1988), *One Flea Spare* (1997), and *Shockheaded Peter* (2005). Kandel's Broadway credits include *The Who's Tommy* (1993), *Titanic* (1997), *Jesus Christ Superstar* (2000), and *The Drowsy Chaperone* (2004). He appeared on the television series *The Client* and *Law and Order*, and can be heard on the animated videos *Aladdin and the King of Thieves* (1995), *Buster & Chauncey's Silent Night* (1998), and *The Hunchback of Notre Dame II* (2002) in which he reprised Clopin. The opening sequence of *The Hunchback of Notre Dame* was originally all narration and the result was deemed too lifeless so the song "The Bells of Notre Dame" was written and Kandel sang it as Clopin, resulting in one of the most potent musical openings for any Disney film.

Kane, Brad (b. 1973) An actor since childhood in television commercials and films, he provided the singing voice of Aladdin in the 1992 feature film and, with Lea Salonga, introduced the Oscar-winning song "A Whole New World." Born Bradley Caleb Kane in New York City, he was featured in national television commercials and was on Broadway before he was nine. He was originally hired to do both the singing and speaking voice for Aladdin but at the last minute Scott Weinger was brought in to do the non-singing Aladdin. Kane provided the singing for Aladdin in the videos *The Return of Jafar* (1994), *Aladdin and the King of Thieves* (1995), and *Aladdin in Nasira's Revenge* (2001). His singing can also be heard in the animated video *Christmas in Cartoontown* (1996) and in the film *Tom Thumb & Thumbelina* (2002). He has acted and sung on the New York stage, including the Broadway revivals of *She Loves Me* (1993) and *Grease* (1994). Most recently Kane has turned to television producing, presenting the series *Crash* and *Fringe*, and sings with his own band Misconceptions.

Kassir, John (b. 1957) A comedian and actor who has become a busy voice artist, he provided the sounds of the fun-loving raccoon Meeko in *Pocahontas* (1995). He was born in Baltimore, Maryland, and educated at Towson State University before beginning his career as a stand-up comic in clubs. Winning the Grand Prize on the TV show *Star Search* in 1983 gave his career a boost and Kassir was soon playing Las Vegas casinos and appearing on television. Among the TV series in which he has played characters are *Moonlighting*, *The Facts of Life*, *1st & Ten: The Championship*, *FM*, *Lenny*, *The Single Guy*, *Boston Common*, *Early Edition*, *Friends*, *The Amanda Show*, *Grounded for Life*, *CSI: Crime Scene Investigation*, *My Life as a Teenage Robot*, *Bones*, and his own show *Johnytime*, but he is most known as the voice of the Crypt Keeper in the live-action *Tales from the Crypt* and the animated series *Tales from the Cryptkeeper*. In the 1990s Kassir concentrated more and more on voice work, doing characters for such cartoon series as *Tiny Toon Adventures, Animaniacs, Sonic the Hedgehog, Duckman: Private Dick/Family Man, Earthworm*

Jim, Team Knight Rider, CatDog, Buzz Lightyear of Star Command, Time Squad, The Simpsons, Rocket Power, Johnny Bravo, Danger Rangers, As Told by Ginger, The Grim Adventures of Billy & Mandy, Kung Fu Panda: Legends of Awesomeness, and *Random! Cartoons.* He reprised his Meeko in the video *Pocahontas II: Journey to a New World* (1998) and can also be heard in other animated movies and videos, including *Tiny Toons Spring Break* (1994), *Justice League of America* (1997), *An American Tail: The Treasure of Manhattan Island* (1998), *The Flintstones: On the Rocks* (2001), *Casper's Scare School* (2006), *Curious George 2: Follow That Monkey!* (2009), and *The Princess and the Frog* (2009). Kassir has appeared Off Broadway in the musicals *3 Guys Naked from the Waist Down* (1985), *Reefer Madness* (2001), and *The Glorious Ones* (2007), and can be seen as well as heard in the films *Monster Mash: The Movie* (1995), *Spy Hard* (1996), *The Glass Jar* (1999), *Who Slew Simon Thaddeus Mulberry Pew* (2002), *The Midget Stays in the Picture* (2003), *Soccer Dog: European Cup* (2004), *Dr. Rage* (2005), *Reefer Madness: The Movie Musical* (2005), *Channels* (2008), *Race to Witch Mountain* (2009), and *Monster Mutt* (2010), as well as the TV-movie *The Three Stooges* (2000).

Katz, Kerry A singer-actor who has sung on the soundtrack of the animated films *The Princess and the Cobbler* (1993) and *The Swan Princess* (1994), he provided the voices for the snake-fingered Man Under the Stairs, the Corpse Dad, and one of the quartet of Vampires in *The Nightmare Before Christmas* (1993). Katz also sang on the soundtrack for the live-action movie *Robin Hood: Men in Tights* (1993).

Kawagley, Angayuqaq Oscar (b. 1934) A Native American educator and spokesman for the Inuit people, he provided the narration for *Brother Bear* (2003). He was born in Bethel, Alaska, and educated in the Bureau of Indian Affairs and Territorial Schools, becoming a teacher himself. Kawagley has served on many committees and councils regarding the Inuit tribes in North America. He currently is a Professor of Education at the University of Alaska Fairbanks College of Liberal Arts.

Kaye, David (b. 1964) A voice artist since 1986 with over 150 films, television shows, and video games to his credit, he provided the announcer's voice in the 1930's newsreel in the prologue of *Up* (2009). He was born David V. Hope in Peterborough in Ontario, Canada, and was working professionally on the radio by the time he was sixteen years old. After voicing some very popular radio programs in Canada, he started voicing cartoons in the States, although he often returned to his homeland to do theatre. Among the many American and Canadian cartoon series he voiced are *Ranma ½, The Jungle Book: The Adventures of Mowgli, Prince Mackaroo, Exosquad, G.I. Joe Extreme, Street Sharks, Kleo the Misfit Unicorn, Dragon Ball Z, Beast Wars: Transformers, Beast Machines: Transformers, Monster Rancher, Jackie Chan Adventures, X-Men: Evolution, Transformers: Energon, Kog: The Animated Series, Fantastic Four, Transformers: Animated,* and *The Avengers: Earth's Mightiest Heroes.* Kaye can also be heard in many animated videos and movies, including *Fortune Quest* (1991), *Ranma ½: The Movie* (1991) and its sequels, *Green Legend Ran* (1992), *Fatal Fury: Legend of the Hungry Wolf* (1992) and its sequels, *Walter Melon* (1993), *Dazzle the Dinosaur* (1994), *Key: The Metal Idol* (1996), *Jin Roh: The Wolf Brigade* (1998), *Brainium* (1998), *Mummies Alive! The Legend Begins* (1998), *Rudolph the Red-Nosed Reindeer: The Movie* (1998), *Casper's Haunted Christmas* (2000), *Barbie as Rapunzel* (2002), *Ratchet: Deadlocked* (2005) and its sequels, *Barbie in the 12 Dancing Princesses* (2006), and *Planet Hulk* (2010). He can be seen as well as heard in such films as *The Occultist* (1989), *Opening Night* (1992), *Downhill Willie* (1995), *The Love Charm* (1996), *Carpool* (1996), *Excess Baggage* (1997), and *Martian Child* (2007), as well as many TV-movies.

Kearns, Joseph (1907–1962) A former radio actor who had a long and busy career in television, he supplied the voice of the punning Doorknob in *Alice in Wonderland* (1951). He was born in Salt Lake City, Utah, and began his career as a pipe organ musician playing in movie palaces during the silent film era. In the 1930s he turned to radio and found fame as the voice of Professor Moriarty opposite Basil Rathbone's Sherlock Holmes. Kearns made his television debut on *The George Burns and Gracie Allen Show* in 1951, followed by many TV series, including recurring characters in *Professional Father, Our Miss Brooks, December Bride, The Adventures of Ozzie and Harriet, Gunsmoke, How to Marry a Millionaire,* and *The Jack Benny Program.* His most famous television role was the frustrated Mr. Wilson on *Dennis the Menace,* a role he played for the last four years of his life. The Doorknob in *Alice in Wonderland* is the only character in the movie not found in Lewis Carroll's original story. He is one of the few characters in the film who tries to assist Alice, though he isn't much help in the end. Still, Kearns' friendly yet silly vocals make the secondary role memorable.

Keaton, Josh (b. 1979) A television and screen actor and singer who has voiced many video games and cartoons, he provided the speaking voice of Young Hercules in *Hercules* (1997). He was born

Joshua Luis Wiener in Hacienda Heights, California, and at the age of three was doing television commercials. As a teenager he was in the boy band No Authority and began his recording career with the group and then as a solo vocalist. Keaton began voicing TV cartoons when he was eleven and over the years has been heard in such series as *Peter Pan and the Pirates*, *Back to the Future*, *Batman*, *The Grim Adventures of Billy & Mandy*, *Ben 10*, *The Spectacular Spider-Man*, *King of the Hill*, and *Transformers: Prime*, as well as in the animated videos and films *Snoopy's Reunion* (1991), *Recycle Rex* (1993), *The Wild* (2006), and *Doctor Strange* (2007). He has appeared on many series as well, most notably *Boy Meets World*, *The Secret World of Alex Mack*, *The Young and the Restless*, and *Will & Grace*. Among Keaton's film credits are *All I Want for Christmas* (1991), *Newsies* (1992), *Infinity* (1996), *Chimera House* (1999), and *Up-in-Down Town* (2007).

Keaton, Michael (b. 1951)   A very popular comic actor of television and films who can also portray the dark side of his characters, he provided the voices for the vain celebrity stock car Chick Hicks in *Cars* (2006) and the clothes-conscious Ken doll in *Toy Story 3* (2010). He was born Michael John Douglas in Coraopolis, Pennsylvania, and studied for a time at Kent State University in Ohio before going into stand-up comedy. He appeared on a handful of television sit-coms in the 1970s but his big break came with his hilarious performance in the movie *Night Shift* (1982). From that point on, Keaton easily moved back and forth between the small and the big screen, having hits in both media. His notable movies include *Mr. Mom* (1983), *Johnny Dangerously* (1984), *Beetlejuice* (1988), *Batman* (1989), *Batman Returns* (1992), *The Paper* (1994), *Jack Frost* (1998), *Quicksand* (2003), *Herbie Fully Loaded* (2005), *The Last Time* (2006), and *The Other Guys* (2010). Of the dozens of television series he has appeared in, he played recurring characters in *All's Fair*, *Working Stiffs*, *Report to Murphy*, and *The Company*. Keaton can be heard on the cartoon series *The Simpsons* and *King of the Hill*. The character of Ken in *Toy Story 3* was modeled after the "Animal Loving" Ken doll manufactured in 1988. In the film, Ken sports no less than twenty-one different outfits.

Keen, Earl   Little is known about this performer who had a talent for impersonating dog sounds, something he did in *Cinderella* (1950) when he and James MacDonald voiced the lazy dog Bruno. Keen played dog impersonators in the movies *On Stage Everybody* (1945) and *The Swindler* (1946). His only other film credit is a bit part in *It Should Happen to You* (1954).

Keever, Douglas (b. 1958)   A North Carolina construction supervisor who is an avid fan of auto racing, he provided the voice of the gas-guzzling motor home Albert Hinkley who is a big racing fan in *Cars* (2006). Film director John Lasseter met Keever, who goes by the nickname Mater, at Lowe's Speedway in 2001 and was impressed with his knowledge of racing. Consequently, Keever served as a consultant on *Cars*, the name Mater was given to the redneck tow truck in the film, while Keever voiced the fan Hinkley.

Keillor, Garrison (b. 1942)   The popular writer and radio commentator whose cracker barrel-like wisdom has been heard on radio's *A Prairie Home Companion* for over thirty-five years, he was the wry Narrator for the Disney short *Redux Riding Hood* (1997). He was born Gary Edward Keillor in Anoka, Minnesota, and was educated at the University of Minnesota where he started his career on the student radio station. In 1974 he created *A Prairie Home Companion* and the fictional town of Lake Wobegon as a stage production in St. Paul, later broadcasting it locally and then eventually nationally. Many of these broadcasts have been recorded and/or shown on television so Keillor's popularity extends far beyond just radio. He is also a prolific author of short stories, essays, novels, and children's books. Keillor played himself in the fiction film *A Prairie Home Companion* (2007) and can be heard on the animated short *Afraid So* (2006) and an episode of the TV cartoon series *Hercules*. Memoir: *Life Among the Lutherans*, with Holly Harden (2010).

Kelly, Moira (b. 1968)   An expressive actress, and sometime director, who can play slightly edgy characters, she provided the voice for the lioness Nala as an adult in *The Lion King* (1994). She was born in Queens, New York, the daughter of a professional violinist and a nurse, and was educated at Marymount Manhattan College before making her television debut in 1991. That same year she made her first movie, going on to appear in *Billy Bathgate* (1991), *The Cutting Edge* (1992), *Twin Peaks: Fire Walk with Me* (1992), *Chaplin* (1992), *Little Odessa* (1994), *The Tie That Binds* (1995), *Dangerous Beauty* (1998), *The Safety of Objects* (2001), and *Remember the Daze* (2007), as well as the TV movies *Entertaining Angels: The Dorothy Day Story* (1996) and *Monday After the Miracle* (1998). Kelly is better known for her television appearances in various series, such as Mandy Hampton in *The West Wing* and Karen Roe in *One Tree Hill*. She can also be seen in the series *To Have & to Hold*, *Law and Order*, and *Numb3rs*. The character of Nala in *The Lion King* is a strong one, both as a cub and as an adult lioness. She is not afraid of adventure when she is young and she doesn't fear adversity as an adult. Nala stands up to Scar and confronts Simba, proving that she is more mature than either of them. Kelly's vocals for adult Nala are warm yet determined, helping to make the character stand out from the other lions. She reprised her Nala in the videos *The Lion King II: Simba's Pride* (1998) and *The Lion King 1½* (2004).

Kelso, Kellyann A child actress who voiced Pacha's young daughter Chaca in *The Emperor's New Groove* (2000), she has no other film or television credits.

Kennedy, Mark An animator who worked on storyboards before becoming a writer of animated films, he voiced Hollywood Runt in *Chicken Little* (2005). Kennedy served as story artist on such movies as *The Rescuers Down Under* (1990), *Beauty and the Beast* (1991), *Aladdin* (1992), *Treasure Planet* (2002), and *Bolt* (2008), as well as the television cartoon series *Animaniacs*. He contributed to the scripts for *Hercules* (1997), *Tarzan* (1999), *Home on the Range* (2004), and *Chicken Little*.

Kenny, Tom (b. 1962) The lively, bespectacled stand-up comic who has developed into a prolific voice artist, he supplied the voice of the nerdy science teacher Mr. Willerstein in *Meet the Robinsons* (2007). Thomas James Kenny was born in East Syracuse, New York, and began his career doing stand-up comedy in clubs in Boston and San Francisco. After appearances on cable stations then network talk shows, Kenny became a regular on the series *The Edge*, followed by such shows as *Brotherly Love*, *Mr. Show with Bob and David*, and *Just Shoot Me*. He found even more success in animation, heard in over 500 cartoon episodes and voicing the title character of *SpongeBob SquarePants* on the television series since 1999 as well as on many videos and video games. Among Kenny's dozens of other cartoon series are *2 Stupid Dogs*, *Rocko's Modern Life*, *Hercules*, *I Am Weasel*, *Cow and Chicken*, *Family Guy*, *CatDog*, *Godzilla: The Series*, *Dilbert*, *Mission Hill*, *Futurama*, *Gotham Girls*, *The Mummy: Secrets of the Medjai*, *Dexter's Laboratory*, *Samurai Jack*, *Stripperella*, *Johnny Bravo*, *The Powerpuff Girls*, *The Adventures of Jimmy Neutron: Boy Genius*, *Duck Dodgers*, *Brandy & Mr. Whiskers*, *Xiaolin Showdown*, *Shorty McShorts' Shorts*, *Super Robot Monkey Team Hyperforce Go!*, *Kim Possible*, *Handy Manny*, *Squirrel Boy*, *The Grim Adventures of Billy & Mandy*, *Codename: Kids Next Door*, *The Fairly OddParents*, *Camp Lazlo*, *Out of Jimmy's Head*, *My Gym Partner's a Monkey*, *Back at the Barnyard*, *Foster's Home for Imaginary Friends*, *Transformers: Animated*, *Sit Down Shut Up*, *Batman: The Brave and the Bold*, *Chowder*, *The Super Hero Squad Show*, and *WordGirl*. He can also be heard on many animated videos based on these characters as well as on several video games.

Kernion, Jerry A chubby character actor with many television credits, he supplied the voice of the crooked real estate dealer Henry Fenner in *The Princess and the Frog* (2009). Kernion made his film debut in 1990 and appeared in such movies as *Baby Face Nelson* (1995), *True Friends* (1998), *Flamingo Dreams* (2000), *King for a Day* (2003), *Come as You Are* (2005), and *Dating in the Middle Ages: The Movie* (2010). He has been more successful on television, acting in several made-for-TV movies and in many series, including *Campus Cops*, *Smart Guy*, *Beverly Hills 90210*, *Maggie*, *Joan of Arcadia*, *Without a Trace*, *Gilmore Girls*, *Crossing Jordan*, *Monk*, *Cold Case*, *The West Wing*, *Scrubs*, *Ugly Betty*, *Mad Men*, *The Suite Life of Zack and Cody*, *Zoey 101*, *Knight Rider*, *ER*, *Castle*, *Better Off Ted*, *Grey's Anatomy*, and *Weeds*.

Kerry, Margaret (b. 1929) A singing-dancing child performer on screen since the age of six, she voiced one of the Mermaids in *Peter Pan* (1953). The native of Los Angeles made her movie debut in *Teacher's Beau* (1935) using the name Peggy Lynch. After appearing in *The Pinch Singer* (1936) and *Aladdin's Lantern* (1938), she returned to her birth name and was featured in the movie musical *If You Knew Susie* (1948), followed by the films *Canon City* (1948) and *The Sickle or the Cross* (1949). Kerry also acted in the television series *The Ruggles*, *Ethel and Albert*, *The Lone Ranger*, *The Andy Griffith Show*, and *Space Angel*. It was Kerry, and not Marilyn Monroe (as rumors persist), who served as the model for the fairy Tinker Bell. The studio filmed her doing various leaps and poses and then the animators created the weightless "Tink" for the screen. Also, legend has it that the boy actor Tommy Luske, who was voicing Wendy's younger brother Michael, experienced a vocal change during the long production process for *Peter Pan* and that Kerry was used to re-record some of his lines.

Kiel, Richard (b. 1939) A huge, fierce-looking character actor who has played henchmen, killers, monsters, and giants in the movies and on television, he voiced the ugly pub thug Vlad, who secretly collects little ceramic unicorns, in *Tangled* (2010). Richard Dawson Kiel was born in Detroit, Michigan, and suffered from a hormonal condition that gave him an adult height of seven feet and one and a half inches. Kiel worked as a nightclub bouncer and other jobs utilizing his bulky frame before making his television debut in an episode of *Laramie* in 1960. He was obviously noticed even in small roles in such series as *The Phantom*, *The*

Twilight Zone, The Man from U.N.C.L.E., I Dream of Jeannie, The Wild Wild West, I Spy, The Monkees, Starsky and Hutch, Barbary Coast, Simon & Simon, and *Superboy.* Kiel started appearing in movies in 1961 and acted in twenty films before he became famous as Jaws, the metal-tooth villain in the James Bond thriller *The Spy Who Loved Me* (1977), a role so memorable he reprised it in the films *Moonraker* (1979) and *Inspector Gadget* (1999). His other movies include *Skidoo* (1968), *The Longest Yard* (1974), *Gus* (1976), *Force 10 from Navarone* (1978), *Cannonball Run II* (1984), *Think Big* (1989), and *The Giant of Thunder Mountain* (1991). Autobiography: *Making It Big in the Movies* (2002).

Kimball, Ward (1914–2002) A revered animator, producer, writer, and director of Disney films, his only voice credit is the vaudeville tap-dancer Ward in the short *The Nifty Nineties* (1941). Ward Walrath Kimball was born in Minneapolis, Minnesota, and left art school to work with Disney in 1934. For the next four decades he worked on just about every animation project at the studio, animating such famous characters as Jiminy Cricket and Lucifer the Cat, writing and directing shorts such as *Adventures in Music: Melody* (1953), *Toot Whistle Plunk and Boom* (1953), and *It's Tough to Be a Bird* (1969), and producing episodes of the television series *Walt Disney's Wonderful World of Color.* Kimball was an accomplished jazz trombonist and formed a Dixieland band with other Disney employees called the Firehouse Five Plus Two. The group toured, made several records, appeared in the film *Hit Parade of 1951* (1950) and the movie short *Teresa Brewer and the Firehouse Five Plus Two* (1951), and were heard in the Disney animated cartoon *How to Dance* (1953). Kimball was one of the distinguished "nine old men" at the Disney studio and his specialty was comic supporting characters rather than the heroes or princesses. The characters of the vaudevillian team of Fred and Ward in *The Nifty Nineties* were based on Kimball and his fellow animator Fred Moore who he often worked with at the studio. Biography: *Walt Disney's Nine Old Men and the Art of Animation,* John Canemaker (2001).

Kimbrough, Charles (b. 1936) An affable, all-purpose actor who has played both leading men and comic character roles, he voiced the understanding gargoyle Victor in *The Hunchback of Notre Dame* (1996). He was born in St. Paul, Minnesota, and educated at Indiana University and Yale, then gained acting experience at the Milwaukee Repertory Theatre before making his New York stage debut in 1961. Among his notable stage credits are *Company* (1970), *Candide* (1975), *The Dining Room* (1982), *Sunday in the Park with George* (1984), *Later Life* (1993), *Sylvia* (1995), and *Tartuffe* (1999). Kimbrough made his television debut in 1975 and his first film the following year, finding national recognition later as a regular on the TV series *Murphy Brown.* He reprised his gargoyle Victor for the video *The Hunchback of Notre Dame II* (2002) and provided other voices for the animated videos *The Land Before Time VII: The Stone of Cold Fire* (2000), *Buzz Lightyear of Star Command: The Adventure Begins* (2000), and *Recess: School's Out* (2001), as well as the television series *Dinosaurs* and *Family Guy.*

Kind, Richard (b. 1956) A smiling character actor and comic who has been very successful on television, he voiced the loudmouth grasshopper Molt in *A Bug's Life* (1998), the lost tourist Van in *Cars* (2006), and the toy librarian Bookworm in *Toy Story 3* (2010). He was born in Trenton, New Jersey, the son of a jeweler, and educated at Northwestern University before working with a comedy improv group in Chicago. Kind did regional theatre for ten years and eventually replaced stars in the Broadway productions of *The Tale of the Allergist's Wife* (2000), *The Producers* (2001), *Sly Fox* (2004), and *Dirty Rotten Scoundrels* (2005). He made his television debut in 1985 and over the decades appeared in hundreds of episodes of TV series, including *Unsub, Carol & Company, The Nanny, Blue Skies, The Commish, A Whole New Ballgame, Scrubs,* and *Curb Your Enthusiasm,* but he is most remembered for his roles in *Mad About You* and *Spin City.* Among Kind's movie credits are *Nothing in Common* (1986), *Mr. Saturday Night* (1992), *Stargate* (1994), *Quicksand* (2002), *Shrink Rap* (2003), *Bewitched* (2005), *For Your Consideration* (2006), and *A Serious Man* (2009). His voice can be heard in such TV cartoon series as *Kim Possible, Chowder, American Dad,* and *The Penguins of Madagascar,* as well as in the animated videos and movies *Ghoulies III: Ghoulies Go to College* (1991), *Tom and Jerry: The Movie* (1992), *Quest of the Delta Knights* (1993), *Our Friend, Martin* (1999), *Tom Sawyer* (2000), *Stitch's Great Escape* (2004), *Garfield* (2004), *Hermie & Friends: Milo the Mantis Who Wouldn't Pray* (2007), *Dr. Dolittle: Tail to the Chief* (2008), and *Santa Buddies* (2009).

King, Cammie (1934–2010) A child actress who retired from films at the age of five, she provided the voice of the doe Young Faline in *Bambi* (1942). She was born Eleanore Cammack King in Los Angeles, the stepdaughter of Herbert T. Kalmus who founded the Technicolor Corporation. She made two films in 1939, *Blondie Meets the Boss* and *Gone with the Wind* in which she played the role of the daughter Bonnie Blue Butler. After working on *Bambi,* King began her schooling and never returned to show business, working as a marketing coordinator until her retirement.

The Kings Men A singing quartet heard and seen in several movies and popular on radio and records, they did the singing narration for "The Martins and the Coys" section of *Make Mine Music* (1946) and sang "The Ballad of Casey Jones" on the soundtrack of the animated short *The Brave Engineer* (1950). Ken Darby (1909–1992) was the bass singer and did the vocal arrangements for baritone Rad Robinson (1910–1988), lead tenor Jon Dodson (1907–1963), and top tenor Bud Linn (1909–1968). The quartet found fame singing with Paul Whiteman's Orchestra on radio and records and they were regularly featured on Rudy Vallee's radio program and the popular radio sit-com *Fibber McGee and Molly*. The Kings Men made their screen debut in *Sweetie* (1929) followed by appearances in two-dozen movies, including *Let's Go Native* (1930), *Going Hollywood* (1933), *We're Not Dressing* (1934), *Hollywood Party* (1934), *Thanks a Million* (1935), *The Roundup* (1941), *Call Out the Marines* (1942), *For Me and My Gal* (1942), *Song of the Range* (1949), and *With a Song in My Heart* (1952). Their most famous film credit was an unseen one: the voices of some of the Muchkins in *The Wizard of Oz* (1939). The quartet was also heard on the television series *The Adventures of Jim Bowie* and *Walt Disney's Wonderful World of Color*. Ken Darby became a much-awarded music arranger and conductor in Hollywood and his Ken Darby Singers were also favorites on the radio and made many successful recordings, none more popular than "White Christmas" with Bing Crosby.

Kitt, Eartha (1927–2008) The durable African American singer-actress, a longtime favorite in cabarets and swank supper clubs, she possessed a feline demeanor and a unique, resonating voice which was used to great effect as the conniving sorceress Yzma in *The Emperor's New Groove* (2001). Born Eartha May Keith in the town of North in South Carolina, she grew up in Harlem and attended the High School of the Performing Arts. She joined Katherine Dunham's dance company and toured Europe before making her Broadway bow in two of Dunham's dance concerts in the 1940s. It was in *New Faces of 1952* that Kitt gained wide attention for her smoldering singing style as she delivered the song "Monotonous." Kitt returned to the New York stage for such musicals as *Shinbone Alley* (1957), *Timbuktu!* (1978), *The Wild Party* (2000), *Nine* (2003), and *Mimi le Duck* (2006). On screen she danced in *Casbah* (1948), reprised her performance in the film version of *New Faces of 1952* called *New Faces of 1954*, and was featured in such films as *St. Louis Blues* (1958), *Anna Lucasta* (1959), *Friday Foster* (1975), *Ernest Scared Stupid* (1991), *Harriet the Spy* (1996), and *Holes* (2003). Kitt appeared in hundreds of television shows, from drama and comedy series to quiz programs and musical specials, but she is best remembered as Cat Woman on the live-action series *Batman* in the 1960s. The character of Yzma in *The Emperor's New Groove* is surely one of the most distinctive Disney villains due to Kitts' amazing speaking and singing voice. She reprised her funny Yzma in the video movie *The Emperor's New Groove 2: Kronk's New Groove* (2005) and the TV series *The Emperor's New School*, and voiced the panther Bagheera in the video *The Jungle Book: Mowgli's Story* (1998). Kitt was a long-time outspoken activist for civil rights and against war, causing her to be blacklisted at times, so she often returned to Europe to perform, especially in Paris where she was a particular favorite. Autobiographies: *Thursday's Child* (1956); *A Tart Is Not a Sweet* (1976); *I'm Still Here: Confessions of a Sex Kitten* (1992).

Kline, Kevin (b. 1947) A high-energy leading man with a dynamic presence on stage and screen, he has excelled at playing everything from farce to *King Lear* and provided the voice of the dashing captain of the guard Phoebus in *The Hunchback of Notre Dame* (1996). Kevin Delaney Kline was born in St. Louis, Missouri, the son of a record store owner, and educated at Indiana University and Juilliard, then toured the country as a member of John Houseman's Acting Company. His first acting jobs in Manhattan were in 1970 with the New York Shakespeare Festival, an organization with which he would long be associated, playing (and sometimes directing) many classical roles including Hamlet twice. It was through the Acting Company that Kline appeared in the New York musicals *The Beggar's Opera* (1973) and *The Robber Bridegroom* (1975), then he received many plaudits for his performance in *On the Twentieth Century* (1978). Among his other notable stage credits are *The Three Sisters* (1973), *Loose Ends* (1979), *The Pirates of Penzance* (1980), *Richard III* (1983) *Arms and the Man* (1985), *Much Ado About Nothing* (1988), *Ivanov* (1997), *Henry IV* (2003), and *Cyrano de Bergerac* (2007). Kline made an impressive screen debut in *Sophie's Choice* (1982) followed by many movies, including *The Big Chill* (1983), *A Fish Called Wanda* (1988), *Dave* (1993), *In and Out* (1997), *A Midsummer Night's Dream* (1999), and *De-Lovely* (2004). He reprised his Phoebus in the video sequel *The Hunchback of Notre Dame II* (2002) and for non–Disney animated features he provided voices for *The Road to El Dorado* (2000) and *The Tale of Despereaux* (2008). On the small screen, Kline has shone in everything from soap operas to historical dramas.

Knight, Elissa (b. 1975) An assistant producer at Pixar since 2004, she sometimes provides voices for characters in the films, such as the red Mazda racing fan Tia in *Cars* (2006) and the robot probe EVE (Extra-terrestrial Vegetation Evaluator) in *WALL-E* (2008). She can also be heard in the animated video shorts *BURN-E* (2008) and *Tokyo Mater* (2008). The look of the robot character of EVE resembles an iPod which is not surprising since EVE and the first iPod were both designed by Apple senior vice president Johnny Ive. Although the name EVE is an acronym for her job, it also refers to Biblical Eve who also was the only female on Earth for a time.

Knight, Wayne (b. 1955) The corpulent, bespectacled character actor who can play jolly as well as threatening characters, he voiced Demetrius the Pot Maker in *Hercules* (1997), the paranoid elephant Tantor as an adult in *Tarzan* (1999), and Al the Toy Collector in *Toy Story 2* (1999). Wayne Eliot Knight was born in Cartersville, Georgia, and briefly attended the University of Georgia before leaving to become an actor. He acted in regional theatres and in New York in various Off Broadway plays as well as on Broadway in *Gemini* (1977), *Mastergate* (1989), *Art* (1998), and *Sweet Charity* (2005). Knight made his television debut in 1990 and two years later found fame as the mailman Newman on the series *Seinfeld*. His other television series include *The Edge*, *The Second Half*, *3rd Rock from the Sun*, *Catscratch*, *Woke Up Dead*, and *Hot in Cleveland*. Knight has appeared in several movies, among them *Dirty Dancing* (1987), *Born on the Fourth of July* (1989), *Dead Again* (1991), *JFK* (1991), *Basic Instinct* (1992), *Jurassic Park* (1993), *Space Jam* (1996), and *Rat Race* (2001). He can be heard in such TV cartoon series as *Hercules*, *Dilbert*, *Buzz Lightyear of Star Command*, *The Grim Adventures of Billy & Mandy*, *Justice League*, *Xiaolin Showdown*, *The Penguins of Madagascar*, and *Kung Fu Pandas: Legends of Awesomeness*, as well as in the animated movies and videos *The Brave Little Toaster Goes to Mars* (1998), *Hercules: Zero to Hero* (1999), *Buzz Lightyear of Star Command: The Adventure Begins* (2000), *Dinotopia: Quest for the Ruby Sunstone* (2005), *Kung Fu Panda* (2008), *Scooby-Doo and the Goblin King* (2008), and *Cat Tale* (2010).

Knotts, Don (1924–2006) The thin, nervous, beloved comic actor who played the hapless Barney Fife on television's *The Andy Griffith Show* for eight years, he voiced the mayor Turkey Lurkey in *Chicken Little* (2005), his last film role. He was born Jesse Donald Knotts in Morgantown, West Virginia, and was educated at West Virginia University. He began his career as a ventriloquist but, after serving in the Special Services Branch entertaining the troops in World War II, he took up acting and got jobs on the radio and in television soap operas. While playing a small role in the comedy *No Time for Sergeants* on Broadway in 1955, he impressed the star Andy Griffith so much that Griffith cast him as his deputy Barney. Knotts also made an impression with audiences for his comic turns on *The Steve Allen Plymouth Show*, *The Red Skelton Hour*, and *The Tonight Show* with Jack Paar. His many movie credits include *No Time for Sergeants* (1958), *The Incredible Mr. Limpet* (1964), *The Ghost and Mr. Chicken* (1966), *The Reluctant Astronaut* (1967), *The Shakiest Gun in the West* (1968), *The Apple Dumpling Gang* (1975), *Gus* (1976), *Herbie Goes to Monte Carlo* (1977), *Hot Lead and Cold Feet* (1978), and *Pleasantville* (1998). Knotts played Ralph Furley on *Three's Company* for five years, appeared in guest roles in several other TV series, and he voiced such cartoon series as *Garfield and Friends* and *101 Dalmatians*. His nervous, halting voice can also be heard in the movies and videos *Pinocchio and the Emperor of the Night* (1987), *The Little Troll Prince* (1987), *Cats Don't Dance* (1997), *Jingle Bells* (1999), *Tom Sawyer* (2000), and *Hermie: A Common Caterpillar* (2003) and its many sequels. Memoir: *Barney Fife and Other Characters I Have Known* (1999); biography: *The Incredible Mr. Don Knotts*, Stephen Cox (2008).

Kopf, Kim A film actress with scattered credits on television, she supplied the voice of the overfed Mother in the Hooverchair in *WALL-E* (2008). Kopf appeared in such films as *Prison Planet* (1992), *Midnight Tease II* (1995), *Stormswept* (1995), *Secret Places* (1996), *Between Somewhere and Salinas* (1996), *Zigzag* (1997), *The Theory of the Leisure Class* (2001), *Big Time* (2001), and *Searching for Ron Ficus* (2009), as well as the TV-movie *Witchcraft 8: Salem's Ghost* (1996). She can also be seen on the television series *Love Street*, *Hollywood Espectacular*, and *Fat Actress*.

Korbich, Eddie (b. 1960) An actor-singer who has played character parts in the theatre and on television, he voiced the brainy schoolboy twins Al and Moo Sleech in *Doug's 1st Movie* (1999) as well as the small role of the Robocrusher in the same film. He was born in Shamokin, Pennsylvania, and educated at the Boston Conservatory before going to New York where he was featured in many Off Broadway plays and musicals, including *Godspell* (1988), *Assassins* (1990), *Eating Raoul* (1992), and *Taking a Chance on Love* (2000), as well as on Broadway in *Sweeney Todd* (1989), *Carousel* (1994), *Seussical* (2000), *Wicked* (2003), *The Drowsy Chaperone* (2006), and as the sea gull Scuttle in *The Little Mermaid* (2008). Korbich made his television debut on an episode of *Law & Order* in 1992, followed by other series but most of his work on TV has been voicing cartoon series such as *Doug, Disney's Doug*, and *PB&J Otter*. He also supplied the voices for minor characters in the film *The Hunchback of Notre Dame* (1996).

Krakoff, Rocky A child actor who was in show business for only seven years, he provided the voice of one of the two street Kids in the Mickey Mouse featurette *The Prince and the Pauper* (1990). Krakoff appeared in the television series *Simon & Simon, Mathnet*, and *Square One TV*, and played kids in the films and TV-movies *Testament* (1983), *Rocky IV* (1985), *Poltergeist II: The Other Side* (1986), *SpaceCamp* (1986), *When the Bough Breaks* (1986), *Welcome Home, Roxy Carmichael* (1990), and *Ghost Dad* (1990). He can also be heard voicing minor roles in *Oliver & Company* (1988).

Kroner, Amber The child actress who provided the voice for Peatrice, one of the three plush peas-in-a-pod toy, in *Toy Story 3* (2010), she has no other film or television credits so far.

Kuhn, Judy (b. 1958) The slim, dark-haired leading lady of Broadway musical hits and flops who has a sparkling clear soprano voice, she provided the singing voice for the title character in *Pocahontas* (1995) and introduced the Oscar-winning song "Colors of the Wind." The native New Yorker was educated at Oberlin College's Conservatory of Music before making her Broadway debut in the short-lived *Oh, Brother!* (1981), then appeared in *The Mystery of Edwin Drood* (1985) before giving a powerful performance as the tragic immigrant Bella in the short-lived *Rags* (1986). Kuhn was also featured in the original Broadway productions of *Les Misérables* (1987), *Chess* (1988), and *Two Shakespearean Actors* (1992), as well as the 1993 revival of *She Loves Me*. She reprised her singing Pocahontas in the video sequel *Pocahontas II: Journey to a New World* (1998) and also sang in *Mulan II* (2004). Among her television credits are the series *Hope & Faith, Law & Order, Law & Order: Criminal Intent*, and *Law & Order: Special Victims Unit*, and she has appeared in the films *What's Your Sign?* (1997), *Day on Fire* (2006), and *Enchanted* (2007). Kuhn has recorded several CDs of Broadway songs and has sung with renowned orchestras in concert and on television. In 2007, twenty years after playing the orphaned Cosette on Broadway, she returned to play her mother Fantine during the revival of *Les Misérables*.

Kulp, Nancy (1921–1991) A thin, homely-looking character actress who found her greatest success on television, she voiced the friendly horse Frou-Frou in *The Aristocats* (1970). Nancy Jane Kulp was born in Harrisburg, Pennsylvania, and educated at Florida State University and the University of Miami before serving as a WAVE during World War II. She went to Hollywood as a publicist but was encouraged by director George Cukor to pursue acting; within a few weeks of her arrival in California she made her screen debut in *The Model and the Marriage Broker* (1951). Kulp played character types in such movies as *Shane* (1953), *Sabrina* (1954), *A Star Is Born* (1954), and *The Shrike* (1955) before getting work in television where she would appear in many series, most memorably as the bird-loving spinster Pamela Livingstone in *The Bob Cummings Show* in the 1950s and as the bank secretary Jane Hathaway in *The Beverly Hillbillies* in the 1960s. She also acted on the stage, was active in politics, and taught acting in her later years.

LaChanze (b. 1961) The wide-eyed African American singer-actress who has been featured in several Broadway musicals, she provided the voice of the Muse Terpsichore in *Hercules* (1997). She was born Rhonda LaChanze Sapp in St. Augustine, Florida, grew up in Connecticut, and attended the University of the Arts in Philadelphia. She made her Broadway debut in the revue *Uptown... It's Hot!* (1986) and played various roles in the 1987 revival of *Dreamgirls*, but wide recognition came with her performance in *Once on This Island* first Off Broadway and then on Broadway in 1990. LaChanze has won much acclaim for her subsequent performances on Broadway in *Company* (1995), *Ragtime* (1998), and *The Color Purple* (2005). She reprised her Terpsichore in the video sequel *Hercules: Zero to Hero* (1999) and in the TV cartoon series *Hercules*. LaChanze has appeared on such television series as *The Cosby Show, New York Undercover, Sex and the City*, and *Law & Order: Special Victims Unit*, as well as in a few films, including *Leap of Faith* (1992), *Heartbreak Hospital* (2002), and *Breaking Upwards* (2009).

Lagasse, Emeril (b. 1959) The celebrated chef made famous by his television shows, restaurants, and cookbooks, he voiced the bayou crocodile Marlon who tries to eat the frogs Tiana and Prince Naveen in *The Princess and the Frog* (2009). Emeril John Lagasse was born in Fall River, Massachusetts, the son of French-Canadian and Portuguese parents, and studied at Johnson & Wales University's College of Culinary Arts and in Paris and Lyon, France. Lagasse became famous as the executive chef at New Orleans' famed Commander's Palace restaurant. His culinary talents were written about in magazines and his appearances on cooking shows furthered his popularity. He has had two cooking shows of his own, *The Essence of Emeril* and *Emeril Live*. In addition to his best-selling cookbooks, he has owned and operated Emeril Restaurants in New

Orleans and other cities. Lagasse's likable stage presence led to his acting on the television series *Cosby* and his own sit-com *Emeril*, as well as doing voices in the cartoon series *Hercules* and *Family Guy*. The character of the alligator Marlon in *The Princess and the Frog* is named after Marlon Brando, famous for his New Orleans–set *A Streetcar Named Desire* performance, but is more a reference to chef Lagasse, even including his trademark "Bam" in the dialogue. Biography: *Emeril!*, Marcia Layton Turner (2004).

Lander, David L. (b. 1947) A comic and actor who has a cartoon-like character voice, he supplied the voices of Judge Doom's henchman Smart Ass in *Who Framed Roger Rabbit* (1988) and the snarling attack grasshopper Thumper in *A Bug's Life* (1998). David Leonard Lander was born in Brooklyn, New York, the son of schoolteachers, and educated at Carnegie Mellon University in Pittsburgh. He and fellow student Michael McKean developed the comic characters of Lenny and Squiggy there and made it part of their repertoire when the two joined the comedy troupe The Credibility Gap in Los Angeles. Lander started appearing on television series in 1969 and revived his sketch character as Andrew "Squiggy" Squiggman on an episode of *Happy Days* with McKean in 1979. The characters of Lenny and Squiggy were then featured on *Laverne & Shirley* for seven years. His other television credits include *Rhoda, Barney Miller, The Love Boat, Highway to Heaven, Simon & Simon, Father Dowling Mysteries, Married with Children, Star Trek: The Next Generation, Head of the Class, Twin Peaks, On the Air, Family Album, The Nanny, Pacific Blue, The Bold and the Beautiful, Mad About You*, and *Sabrina, the Teenage Witch*. Lander appeared in such movies as *1941* (1979), *Used Cars* (1980), *Pandemonium* (1982), *The Man with One Red Shoe* (1985), *Masters of Menace* (1990), *A League of Their Own* (1992), *The Modern Adventures of Tom Sawyer* (1998), *Scary Movie* (2000), *Say It Isn't So* (2001), *Christmas with the Kranks* (2004), and *Imps* (2009). He has voiced many TV cartoon series, including *Galaxy High School, Camp Candy, TaleSpin, Midnight Patrol: Adventures in the Dream Zone, The Little Mermaid, Superman, Johnny Bravo, Jungle Cubs, 101 Dalmatians, Recess, 100 Deeds for Eddie McDowd, Oswald, The Simpsons*, and *The Grim Adventures of Billy & Mandy*, and can be heard on the animated movies or videos *The Big Bang* (1987), *A Garfield Christmas Special* (1987), *Tom and Jerry: The Movie* (1992), *Titan A.E.* (2000), *The Tangerine Bear: Home in Time for Christmas* (2000), and *Jimmy Neutron: Boy Genius* (2001). Lander has suffered from multiple sclerosis for many years and became a spokesman for the National M.S. Society. He still performs on occasion but is more active as a professional baseball talent scout. The weasel henchman Smart Ass in *Who Framed Roger Rabbit* is one of five cronies of Judge Doom. Originally there were to be seven weasels (Greasy, Sleazy, Smart Ass, Psycho, Stupid, Slimy, and Wheezy) in order to parody the seven dwarfs from Disney's first animated film. Memoir: *Fall Down, Laughing*, with Lee Montgomery (2000).

Landor, Rosalyn (b. 1958) A British child actress who continued her career as an adult in America, she voiced the dream Blue Fairy in the *Pinocchio* spoof in *Teacher's Pet* (2004). She was born in London and made her screen debut at the age of ten in the film *The Devil's Bride* (1968). After being featured in a British television version of *Jane Eyre* (1970), Landor was in demand for both movies and television first in England and then in the States. She acted in the TV series and mini-series *The Edwardians, Z Cars, Divorce His—Divorce Hers, The King of Argos, Love in a Cold Climate, Little Gloria ... Happy at Last, Rumpole of the Bailey, The Adventures of Sherlock Holmes, Arthur the King, C.A.T.S. Eyes, Matlock, Star Trek: The Next Generation*, and *Hunter*. Landor also appeared in the films *The Amazing Mr. Blunden* (1972) and *Bad Influence* (1990), and provided voices for the cartoon series *House of Mouse* and for several video games. She has acted in West End theatre productions and has recorded many audio books.

Lane, Charles (1905–2007) An instantly recognized character actor of hundreds of films and television shows whose thin, scowling face was the figure of authority and miserliness, he voiced the aged lawyer Georges Hautecourt in *The Aristocats* (1970). He was born Charles Gerstle Levison in San Francisco, survived that city's famous earthquake in 1906, and began a career as an insurance salesman. Encouraged by a local theatre director to take up acting, Lane studied at the Pasadena Playhouse then made his film debut in 1931. For the next sixty years he portrayed mean-spirited bankers, judges, politicians, rent collectors, clerks, and misers on screen and later in television, rarely playing a major role but always getting noticed, such as his performance as the Internal Revenue agent in *You Can't Take It with You* (1938). In addition to over 200 movies, Lane acted in over one hundred television episodes, playing recurring characters on such series as *Dear Phoebe, I Love Lucy, Dennis the Menace, The Lucy Show, The Many Loves of Dobie Gillis, The Phyllis Diller Show, Petticoat Junction, The Beverly Hillbillies*, and *Soap*. His last credit was at the age of ninety when he narrated the movie short *The Night Before Christmas* (2006).

Lane, Nathan (b. 1956) The pudgy, smirking comic actor-singer has the qualities and talents of the great Broadway clowns, yet has successfully appeared in serious and classic plays as well, he is most known to moviegoers as the voice of the wisecracking meerkat Timon in *The Lion King* (1994) and its sequels, and he also voiced the dog Spot Helperman who disguises himself as the human boy Scott Leadready II in *Teacher's Pet* (2004). He was born Joseph Lane in Jersey City, New Jersey, the son of a policeman, and worked as a telemarketer, pollster, singing telegram delivery boy, and stand-up comic before he began acting in dinner theatres and stock. He was on the New York stage by 1978 and was first noticed for his comic shenanigans in a Broadway revival of the comedy *Present Laughter* (1982). Lane appeared in a variety of productions on and Off Broadway before he became a full-fledged star as Nathan Detroit in the popular 1992 revival of *Guys and Dolls*. He also shone on the New York stage in *Laughter on the 23rd Floor* (1993), *Love! Valour! Compassion!* (1994), *A Funny Thing Happened on the Way to the Forum* (1996), *The Man Who Came to Dinner* (2000), *The Producers* (2001), *The Frogs* (2004), *Butley* (2007), *November* (2008), and *The Addams Family* (2010). Lane has appeared in a number of films, most memorably *The Birdcage* (1996), *Mousehunt* (1997), and *Nicholas Nickleby* (2002), but perhaps his greatest screen performances have been in animated movies and videos. Originally Lane and Ernie Sabella, who had worked together so well on Broadway in *Guys and Dolls*, were hired to voice the hyenas Banzai and Shenzi but during the first recording session the two comics were so funny the directors decided to have them play the larger roles of Timon and Pumbaa. Lane did several ad-libs in the recording studio, many of which were retained in the final film. The wisecracking Timon has become one of the most popular Disney characters and much of that popularity is due to Lane's lively vocals. He reprised his Timon in the videos *Timon and Pumbaa's Wild Adventure* (1997), *The Lion King II: Simba's Pride* (1998), *The Lion King 1½* (2004), and *Behind the Legend: Timon* (2004), as well as in the TV series *Timon and Pumbaa*. He also voiced Spot in the cartoon series *Teacher's Pet* for two years. Lane's expressive voice can also be heard on the large and small screen in *Stuart Little* (1999), *Titan A.E.* (2000), *Stuart Little 2* (2002), *Stuart Little 3: Call of the Wild* (2005), and *Astro Boy* (2009). He has appeared in many television programs, including two series of his own, *Encore! Encore!* and *George and Martha*.

Langford, Frances (1913–2005) A radio singer with a smooth and creamy voice and a small, round face who appeared in many movie musicals, she was the vocalist for the "Once Upon a Wintertime" section of *Melody Time* (1948). She was born Frances Newbern in Lakeland, Florida, and began singing in public at an early age. Her caressing voice made her a radio favorite, particularly when she teamed up with Bob Hope on a series of broadcasts. Langford was featured in the Broadway musical *Here Goes the Bride* (1931) then made her screen debut in the musical *Every Night at Eight* (1935). She gained moviegoers' attention when she sang "Broadway Rhythm" in *Broadway Melody of 1936* (1935). Among her subsequent musicals are *Born to Dance* (1936), *Too Many Girls* (1940), *Swing It, Soldier* (1941), *Yankee Doodle Dandy* (1942), *Follow the Band* (1943), *This Is the Army* (1943), *Never a Dull Moment* (1943), *The Girl Rush* (1944), *People Are Funny* (1946), *Bamboo Blonde* (1946), *Beat the Band* (1947), and *The Glenn Miller Story* (1954). Langford was also a very successful recording star and made several appearances on television variety shows.

Lansbury, Angela (b. 1925) The very popular, many-sided actress-singer who has conquered every medium, she provided the speaking and singing voice for the wise and motherly enchanted teapot Mrs. Potts in *Beauty and the Beast* (1991) in which she introduced the Oscar-winning title song. The native Londoner, the daughter of a Labour Party leader and an actress, took singing and dancing lessons as a child, then continued her studies in New York City when she was evacuated during the Blitz. Lansbury was still a teenager when she made a noticeable film debut in *Gaslight* (1944), followed by many films over the next five decades, including *National Velvet* (1944), *The Picture of Dorian Gray* (1945), *State of the Union* (1948), *The Three Musketeers* (1948), *Kind Lady* (1951), *Remains to Be Seen* (1953), *The Court Jester* (1955), *The Manchurian Candidate* (1962), *The World of Henry Orient* (1964), *Death on the Nile* (1978), *The Company of Wolves* (1984), and *Nanny McPhee* (2005). Some of her movies were musicals, such as *The Harvey Girls* (1946), *Till the Clouds Roll By* (1946), and *Blue Hawaii* (1961), though often her singing was dubbed. It was not until Lansbury appeared on Broadway in *Mame* (1966) that she was considered a singer and she got to do her own vocals when she played the friendly witch Eglantine Price in the Disney movie musical *Bedknobs and Broomsticks* (1971). Also for Disney, she was one of the on-screen hosts of *Fantasia/2000* (1999) and she reprised her Mrs. Potts for the made-for-video animated sequel *Beauty and the Beast: The Enchanted Christmas* (1997). Her other New York stage credits include *Hotel Paradiso* (1957), *A Taste of Honey* (1960), *Anyone Can Whistle*

(1964), *Dear World* (1969), *Gypsy* (1974), *The King and I* (1978), *Sweeney Todd* (1979), *Deuce* (2007), *Blithe Spirit* (2009), and *A Little Night Music* (2009). Lansbury found a whole new audience on television with the long-running series *Murder, She Wrote* in the 1980s and 1990s. She also appeared on many TV specials and in 1997 she provided the voice for the Dowager Empress Marie in the animated musical *Anastasia*. From the start of her film career, Lansbury often played characters much older than herself so she has always been more a character actress than a leading lady, bringing a sparkling presence to her work and mixing humor and subtle nuance as she shifts from lovable to chilling in the blink of an eye. Lansbury was not the first choice to voice Mrs. Potts in *Beauty and the Beast*. Julie Andrews was approached but without success. Casting Lansbury in the role made the character older, more mature, and at the same time very practical and efficient. During the recording of *Beauty and the Beast*, Lansbury questioned the character of Mrs. Potts singing the title song and was hesitant to do so. The directors asked her to record it as a backup in case they couldn't find another character appropriate to sing it. Lansbury's rendition of "Beauty and the Beast" not only was used but it was so effective that her rendition of it helped the ballad win the Academy Award. Biographies: *Balancing Act: The Authorized Biography of Angela Lansbury*, Martin Gottfried (1999); *Angela Lansbury: A Life on Stage and Screen*, Rob Edelman and Audrey E. Kupferberg (1999).

Lansing, Mary (1911–1988)   A radio and television actress who made only a few movies in her long career, she voiced Aunt Ena and Mrs. Possum in *Bambi* (1942). She was born in rural Louisiana and began her career on the radio, later featured as one of the Georgia Fifield Players. Lansing made her screen debut in 1929 but only appeared in two films before working on *Bambi*. She left show business to pursue a career as an architect, not returning to acting until the 1960s when she appeared on such television series as *The Real McCoys*, *The Jack Benny Program*, *The Patty Duke Show*, *Gomer Pyle U.S.M.C.*, *Bewitched*, and *Apple's Way*, but she is most remembered for playing Martha Clarke on *The Andy Griffith Show* and its spinoff *Mayberry R.F.D.*

Larkin, Linda (b. 1970)   A very active television and movie actress since 1990, she is best known as the speaking voice for Princess Jasmine in *Aladdin* (1992) and its many sequels. The Los Angeles native got her first acting jobs in television in such series as *Almost Home*, *Wings*, *Doogie Howser M.D.*, *Trinity*, *Law & Order: Criminal Intent*, and *Murder, She Wrote*. She has appeared in a handful of movies, including *Childhood's End* (1997), *My Girlfriend's Boyfriend* (1999), *Runaway Bride* (1999), *Two Ninas* (1999), *Final Rinse* (1999), *Fear of Fiction* (2000), *The Next Best Thing* (2000), and *You Belong to Me* (2007). Originally Jasmine in *Aladdin* was to be a spoiled princess who cared only for clothes and jewelry. In the development of the movie she was turned into a stronger, more mature woman who wants to escape from her gilded cage. Although she was five years older than Scott Weinger who voiced Aladdin, Larkin's voice sounded too young for Jasmine so she was instructed to lower her pitch for the character. Jasmine ended up being one of Disney's most self-reliant princesses and one of the most beloved as well. Larkin reprised her Jasmine in the videos *The Return of Jafar* (1994), *Aladdin and the King of Thieves* (1995), *Aladdin's Arabian Adventures* (1998), *Aladdin's Math Quest* (1998), *Jasmine's Wish* (1999), *True Hearts* (1999), *Aladdin in Nasira's Revenge* (2001), *Mickey's House of Villains* (2001), *Kingdom Hearts I* and *II* (2002 and 2005), *Disney Princess Party Volume Two* (2005), *Jasmine's Enchanted Tales: Journey of a Princess* (2005), and *Disney Princess Enchanted Tales: Follow Your Dreams* (2007), as well as the animated TV series *Aladdin* and *House of Mouse*.

Larry the Cable Guy (b. 1963)   The "redneck" comic with a thick rural accent who has appeared as himself on many television shows and a handful of movies, he voiced the big-hearted tow-truck Mater in *Cars* (2006). He was born Daniel Lawrence Whitney in Pawnee City, Nebraska, and worked as a disc jockey in Missouri and Florida before joining the comedy troupe Blue Collar Comedy Tour. He found recognition with the group's concerts, recordings, and television appearances, most memorably on the series *Blue Collar TV*. Larry the Cable Guy was in such movies and videos as *Larry the Cable Guy: Health Inspector* (2006), *Larry the Cable Guy's Christmas Spectacular* (2007), *Delta Farce* (2007), and *Larry the Cable Guy's Hula-Palooza Christmas Luau* (2009), and he reprised the character of Mater in the videos *Mater and the Ghostlight* (2006), *Toyko Mater* (2008), and the animated TV series *Mater's Tall Tales*. Mater has quickly become one of Disney's most endearing sidekicks, a selfless friend and supporter even though his new pal Lightning McQueen is sometimes arrogant and difficult. The dialogue for Mater was drawn from Larry the Cable Guy's comedy routines, including the catch phrase "Git-R-Done!"

Lasseter, John (b. 1957)   The innovative writer, director, and producer of animated movies and the creator and CEO of Pixar, he voiced the barman Harry the Mosquito in *A Bug's Life* (1998) and the blue Rock 'Em Sock 'Em Robot in *Toy Story 2* (1999). John Alan Lasseter was born in Hollywood,

California, the son of a car salesman and an art teacher, and educated at Pepperdine University and the California Institute of the Arts. He began working for Disney as an animator and writer but eventually started his own studio to experiment more with computer animation. After some of his short films received notice, Lasseter and Pixar created (under the supervision of Disney) the first fully-computerized feature film, *Toy Story* (1995), which he wrote, directed, and produced. The subsequent Pixar movies he produced, some of which Lasseter also wrote and directed, include *Toy Story 2* (1999), *Monsters, Inc.* (2001), *Finding Nemo* (2003), *The Incredibles* (2004), *Cars* (2006), *Meet the Robinsons* (2007), *Ratatouille* (2007), *WALL-E* (2008), *Bolt* (2008), and *Toy Story 3* (2010). Lasseter is perhaps the most important and creative influence on film animation since Walt Disney. Biography: *John Lasseter: Pixar Animator*, Adam Woog (2009).

Laurita, Dana (b. 1964) A child performer from the 1970s with a handful of credits, she provided the voice of the young rabbit Sis in *Robin Hood* (1973). The Los Angeles native made her television debut on an episode of *Gunsmoke* when she was seven years old, followed by the series *Escape*, *CHiPs*, and *Lewis & Clark*. Laurita also appeared in the films *Demon Seed* (1977) and *The Goodbye Girl* (1977), as well as the TV-movies *The Couple Takes a Wife* (1972) and *Devil Dog: The Hound of Hell* (1978). She retired from acting at the age of eighteen.

LaVerne, Lucille (1872–1945) A versatile and notable stage actress, director, and producer who also made many films, she provided the voice for the first Disney feature villain: the jealous Queen who turns herself into the ugly old Witch in *Snow White and the Seven Dwarfs* (1937). She was born Lucille Mitchum in Nashville, Tennessee, and was on the stage as a child and in summer stock as a teenager. After years of touring in professional productions, LaVerne managed the Empire Theatre in Richmond, Virginia, and directed and acted in both classical and modern plays. Among her Broadway credits are *Pudd'n-Head Wilson* (1895), *Clarice* (1906), *Uncle Tom's Cabin* (1907), *The Blue Mouse* (1908), *Ann Boyd* (1913), *The House of Bondage* (1914), *The Goldfish* (1922), *Hot Water* (1929), and *Black Widow* (1936), but her most famous role was the North Carolina mountain woman Widow Cagle in *Sun-Up* (1923) which she also played on tour in the States, in Europe, in the 1925 film version, and on Broadway again in 1928; all in all, over 3,000 performances. She also produced and directed Broadway productions and for a time a New York theatre was named for her. LaVerne made her screen debut in 1915 and was featured in such memorable silents as *Sweet Kitty Bellairs* (1916), *Polly of the Circus* (1917), *Orphans of the Storm* (1921), *The White Rose* (1923), *Zaza* (1923), and *His Darker Self* (1924). She matured into a flexible character actress and appeared in over two dozen movies after the advent of sound, including *Abraham Lincoln* (1930), *Sinners' Holiday* (1930), *Little Caesar* (1931), *An American Tragedy* (1931), *While Paris Sleeps* (1932), *Beloved* (1934), *The Mighty Barnum* (1934), and *A Tale of Two Cities* (1935). The character of the Queen in *Snow White and the Seven Dwarfs* is the first great Disney villainess yet, contrary to tradition, the evil female is beautiful, not ugly. The animators had to make the Queen technically attractive yet appear cold and haughty enough so that her beauty was not becoming. Disney legend has it that Walt Disney thought the sixty-five-year-old LaVerne possessed the cool, regal voice of the wicked Queen but he told her he wanted another actress who sounded older to voice the Witch. LaVerne promptly removed her dentures and went into the cackling words of the Witch and won both parts. After voicing *Snow White and the Seven Dwarfs*, LaVerne retired and became co-owner of a nightclub. (Note: throughout her long career, her name was spelled both La Verne and LaVerne.)

Lawrence, Joseph (b. 1976) A child performer in movies and television who became a teen idol and continues to find acting work as an adult, he provided the voices for the orphaned kitten Oliver in *Oliver & Company* (1988) and Chad, the high schooler caught kissing his girlfriend Lisa, in *A Goofy Movie* (1995), He was born Joseph Lawrence Mignogna, Jr., in Philadelphia, the son of an insurance broker, and was educated at the University of Southern California. He made his first television commercial at the age of five and his first sit-com appearance on *Diff'rent Strokes* a year later. Lawrence found national recognition as Joey Donovan on the series *Gimme a Break!*, a role he played for four years, then became a teenage heartthrob as Joey Russo on the series *Blossom* for five years. His other television credits include *Empty Nest*, *Brotherly Love*, *Touched by an Angel*, *American Dreams*, *Run of the House*, *Half & Half*, and *Melissa & Joey*. Lawrence has appeared in a handful of movies, including *Summer Rental* (1985), *Pulse* (1988), *Chains of Gold* (1991), *Radioland Murders* (1994), *Tequila Body Shots* (1999), and *Killer Pad* (2008). The character of Oliver originally was to be a teenage cat who was a bit surly and rambunctious but in development the cat was turned into a kitten and played as an innocent waif adrift in New York City. Lawrence was less than twelve when he recorded the vocals for Oliver, old enough to sound young but not so young as to be too cute or naive.

Leader, Zoe (b. 1949) The actress who voiced Nala's mother, the lioness Sarafina, in *The Lion King* (1994), her only other credits are the video sequel *The Lion King II: Simba's Pride* (1998) and an episode of the television series *Ironside* in 1968.

Leary, Denis (b. 1957) A provocative stage, television, and movie actor and writer whose work is usually controversial, he voiced the aggressive male ladybug Frances in *A Bug's Life* (1998). Denis Colin Leary was born in Worcester. Massachusetts, and educated at Emerson College where he later taught for five years. He did stand-up comedy and wrote comic pieces for magazines, then found recognition with a theatre piece he wrote and performed called *No Cure for Cancer*. After it was a hit at the Edinburgh Festival in Scotland, the show played in the States, was filmed for television, and led to a book, a recording, and a video. Leary became popular with the television series *Rescue Me*, which he also wrote and produced, and has been seen in such movies as *Strictly Business* (1991), *The Sandlot* (1993), *Operation Dumbo Drop* (1995), *Wag the Dog* (1997), *The Thomas Crown Affair* (1999), *Bad Boy* (2002), and *The Secret Lives of Dentists* (2002). He provided the voice for Diego in *Ice Age* (2002) and reprised the character in *Ice Age: The Meltdown* (2006), *Ice Age: Dawn of Dinosaurs* (2006), *Lost Historical Films of the Ice Age Period* (2006), and *Ice Age: Continental Drift* (2011).

Leary, Jeremy The young actor who supplied the voice of the dreamy boy Carl Fredrickson in the prologue of *Up* (2009), he has no other film or television credits so far.

Le Doux, Leone The actress who, with Raymond Severn, provided the voice for the infant prodigy Baby Herbert Weems in the "Baby Weems" segment of *The Reluctant Dragon* (1941), has only one other credit: the voice of Christopher Hapgood Day in the 1960 television cartoon series *Happy*.

Lee, Bill (1916–1980) A baritone singer who was heard more than seen on screen, he often dubbed the singing for movie stars and voiced animated films, such as *One Hundred and One Dalmatians* (1961) in which he provided the singing voice for the songwriter Roger Radcliff. He was born in Johnson, Nebraska, and found success as a member of the singing quartet The Mellomen. Lee made his film debut when The Mellomen were hired to voice the singing Cards painting the roses red in *Alice in Wonderland* (1951). The quartet also provided the singing for the pound dogs in *Lady and the Tramp* (1955), can be heard in such Disney shorts as *Trick or Treat* (1952), *Toot Whistle Plunk and Boom* (1953), *Paul Bunyan* (1958), *Noah's Ark* (1959), and were seen as well as heard in the live-action films *The Glenn Miller Story* (1954) and *It Happened at the World's Fair* (1963). Lee played singers in such movies as *Take the High Ground* (1953), *Love Me or Leave Me* (1955), *The Sea Chase* (1955) *State Fair* (1962), and the TV musical *Cinderella* (1965), but his most heard performances were dubbing the singing for others. He sang for Matt Mattox as Caleb in *Seven Brides for Seven Brothers* (1954), for George Nader as Matt Davis in *The Second Greatest Sex* (1955), for Joseph Buloff as Commisar Ivanov in *Silk Stockings* (1957), for John Kerr as Lt. Joe Cable in *South Pacific* (1958), for Christopher Plummer as Captain Von Trapp in *The Sound of Music* (1965), and for John Gavin as Trevor Grayden in *Thoroughly Modern Millie* (1967). Lee's other animated film and video credits include *Pigs Is Pigs* (1954), *Hey There, It's Yogi Bear* (1964), *Tom and Jerry* (1965), *Babar Comes to America* (1971), and *Charlotte's Web* (1973). In the animated sequence in *Mary Poppins* (1964), he voiced the singing Ram. Along with Marnie Nixon, Lee has perhaps sung more famous songs on screen unseen than anyone else.

Lee, Billy (1929–1989) A child singer, actor, and dancer who made many movies before retiring at the age of thirteen, he voiced the Boy who sets up the battle between Sir Giles and the Dragon in *The Reluctant Dragon* (1941). He was born William Lee Schlenaker in Nelson, Indiana, and his family moved to California when he was a toddler so by the age of four he was appearing on screen in a "Little Rascals" short *Mike Fright* (1934) in which he got to tap dance. Lee also sang in many of his movies, which include *Wagon Wheels* (1934), *Two-Fisted* (1935), *Sky Parade* (1936), *Easy to Take* (1936), *Make a Wish* (1937), *Sons of the Legion* (1938), *Sudden Money* (1939), *In Old Monterey* (1939), *Jeepers Creepers* (1939), *Parole Fixer* (1940), *The Biscuit Eater* (1940), *Nevada City* (1941), *Reg'lar Fellers* (1941), *Road to Happiness* (1942), *Eyes of the Underworld* (1942), *Mrs. Wiggs of the Cabbage Patch* (1942), and *War Dogs* (1942).

Lee, Christopher (b. 1922) A popular British character actor most remembered for his sinister portrayals in many horror movies, he provided the voice of the angry Jabberwocky in the 2010 version of *Alice in Wonderland*. Christopher Frank Carandini Lee was born in London, attended Wellington College, and served in the Royal Air Force during World War II before embarking on an acting career. He appeared in several British films but didn't find success until he was featured in *The Curse of Frankenstein* (1957) and other horror movies made by Hammer Film Productions, often teaming with Peter Cushing. By the 1970s he was in Hollywood where he appeared in over eighty movies, including such hits as *The Three Musketeers* (1973), *The Four Musketeers* (1974), *The Man with the Golden Gun* (1974), *House of Long Shadows* (1983), *Gremlins 2: The New Batch* (1990), *The Lord of the Rings* (2001) and its two sequels, and *Charlie and the Chocolate Factory* (2005). Lee's deep, penetrating voice can be heard in the animated movies and videos *The Last Unicorn* (1982), *Conquest: Frontier Wars* (2001), *Star Wars: Attack of the Clones* (2002), *EverQuest II* (2004), *GoldenEye: Rogue Agent* (2004), *Corpse Bride* (2005), *Kingdom Hearts II* (2005), and *Monstermania!* (2010). Autobiographies: *Lord of Misrule: The Autobiography of Christopher Lee*, with Peter Jackson (2004); *Christopher Lee: Tall, Dark and Gruesome* (1999); biography: *Christopher Lee: The Authorized Screen History*, Jonathan Rigby, George Lucas (2010).

Lee, Greg (b. 1962) A television announcer and host who also voiced characters in cartoons, he played the self-patronizing school principal Mr. "Bob" White in *Doug's 1st Movie* (1999). He was born in Hebron, Nebraska, and educated at York College in Nebraska and Oklahoma Christian University in Oklahoma City, before making his television debut as the co-host of the Nickelodeon kids' show *Total Panic* in 1989. As an actor, he appeared in the television series *Ghostwriter*, *Mad About You*, *The Drew Carey Show*, *The District*, and *George Lopez*, but he is most remembered as the host of the children's game show *Where in the World Is Carmen Sandiego?* Lee can be heard in the TV cartoon series *Doug* and *Disney's Doug* where he first voiced Principal White and other characters.

Lee, Jason (b. 1970) A film and television actor usually involved with experimental or offbeat projects, he provided the voice of the eager super-hero-wanna-be Buddy Pine who turns into the arch-villain Syndrome in *The Incredibles* (2004). Jason Michael Lee was born in Orange, California, and was a professional skateboarding athlete before turning to acting. He was first noticed in the movie *Mallrats* (1995) then went on to featured roles in such films as *Chasing Amy* (1997), *Kissing a Fool* (1998), *Dogma* (1999), *Mumford* (1999), *Almost Famous* (2000), *Vanilla Sky* (2001), *Jay and Silent Bob Strike Back* (2001), *A Guy Thing* (2003), *Clerks II* (2006), *Alvin and the Chipmunks* (2007), *Alvin and the Chipmunks: The Squeakquel* (2009), and *Cop Out* (2010). Lee found wider recognition as the title character in the television sit-com *My Name Is Earl* which he also produced. The character of Syndrome in *The Incredibles* is, like much of the movie, a spoof on comic books. In the first version of the movie, Syndrome was a minor character and the real villain of the piece was a character named Xerek. But the animators were so fascinated with Buddy/Syndrome that he replaced the other villain. The character's facial features are based on those of director Brad Bird. Lee, who did all his vocals for the film in four days, reprised his Buddy/Syndrome in the Pixar film short *Jack-Jack Attack* (2005) and can be heard in the animated movies *Monster House* (2006), *Underdog* (2007), and *Noah's Ark: The New Beginning* (2010).

Lee, Jason Scott (b. 1966) A handsome Asian-American actor with varied credits on television and in movies, he supplied the voice for Nani's surfing boy friend David Kawena in *Lilo & Stitch* (2002). He was born in Los Angeles and grew up in Hawaii before studying acting at Fullerton College. Lee also studied martial arts which he demonstrated when cast in the title role of the film *Dragon: The Bruce Lee Story* (1993) and other movies, and he played Mowgli in the live-action screen version of *The Jungle Book* (1994). His other film credits include *Back to the Future Part II* (1989), *Murder in Mind* (1997), *Tale of the Mummy* (1998), *Only the Brave* (2006), *Balls of Fury* (2007), and *Dance of the Dragon* (2008), as well as the TV-movies *Arabian Nights* (2000), *Dracula II: Ascension* (2003), and *Dracula III: Legacy* (2005). Lee reprised his David Kawena in the video *Lilo & Stitch 2: Stitch Has a Glitch* (2005). Because of his personal knowledge of Hawaii, Lee contributed ideas to the dialogue and coached other actors on the authentic Hawaiian dialect during the making of *Lilo & Stitch*, which was the first animated feature to be set in Hawaii.

Lee, Johnny (1898–1965) An African American character actor, singer, and voice artist with a distinctive cackle, he supplied the speaking and singing voice of the laughing Brer Rabbit in the animated sequences in *Song of the South* (1946). John Dotson Lee, Jr., was born in Los Angeles and began his career as a dancer before making his screen debut in *The Black King* (1932). Among his subsequent films are *The Green Pastures* (1936), *Tales of Manhattan* (1942), *Stormy Weather* (1943), *Come on, Cowboy!* (1948), *My Forbidden Past* (1951), *The Narrow Man* (1952), *The First Traveling Saleslady* (1956), *The Spirit of St. Louis* (1957), *The Rat Race* (1960), *High Time* (1960), and *North to Alaska* (1960). Lee was more successful in television, appearing on such series as *Ramar of the Jungle*, *Screen Director's Playhouse*, *Soldiers of Fortune*, *The Adventures of Jim Bowie*, and *Dennis the Menace*, but most viewers knew him as the shyster lawyer Algonquin J. Calhoun in the sit-com *Amos 'n' Andy* for two years. Lee's characterization of the bouncing Brer Rabbit in *Song of the South* is a masterwork of being both foolish and clever. The rabbit is not very smart but when put into a sticky situation he manages to outwit Brer Fox and Brer Bear. The character of Brer Rabbit, taken from the Uncle Remus stories by Joel Chandler Harris, is an audience favorite and Lee's contagious laugh is, once heard, not to be forgotten. The actor Lee is not to be confused with the "urban cowboy" songwriter-singer Johnny Lee (b. 1946).

Lee, Margaret (1909–1989)   A screen actress who appeared in a dozen films around the time sound came in, she voiced the rabbit Thumper's Mother in *Bambi* (1942), her last movie credit. She was born Margaret Lightfoot in Fairfield, Idaho, and made her screen debut in *Man, Woman and Sin* (1927), followed by such films as *Love* (1927), *Rose-Marie* (1928), *Bringing Up Father* (1928), *Confessions of a Chorus Girl* (1929), *Follow Thru* (1930), *Old Lace* (1931), and *Keep Laughing* (1932).

Lee, Peggy (1920–2002)   The unique recording star known for her smoky and precise way with a song, the classy blonde also acted in films, wrote songs, and provided the speaking and singing voices for the Siamese cats Si and Am, the human mother Darling, and the sexy canine Peg in *Lady and the Tramp* (1953). She was born Norma Deloris Egstrom in Jamestown, North Dakota, the daughter of a railway station agent, and began her career singing on the local radio station. Her big break came when Benny Goodman heard her and hired Lee as a vocalist for his band. Soon she was known nationally for her recordings and was a favorite for decades in nightclubs and in concerts. Lee did specialty spots in the movie musicals *The Powers Girl* (1942), *Stage Door Canteen* (1942), and *Mr. Music* (1950), then got to play leading character roles in *The Jazz Singer* (1953) and *Pete Kelly's Blues* (1955). Lee performed on dozens of television variety shows over the years and made her Broadway debut at the age of sixty-two in the autobiographical musical *Peg* (1983) for which she sang old favorites and new songs that she wrote for the short-lived show. Lee's many contributions to *Lady and the Tramp* cannot be underestimated. Collaborating with composer Sonny Burke, Lee wrote the lyrics for the songs and sang "The Siamese Cat Song" and "He's a Tramp" on the soundtrack. Her vocals for four different characters are distinct (though the Siamese cats sound similar) and masterful. Her streetwise vamp Peg is particularly vivid, not only in singing but in her dialogue in the dog pound. Originally the character was named Mame but the creators thought the character might be thought of as a satire of Mamie Eisenhower (as if the First Lady was anything like this sultry canine). Lee suggested they use her own name and the animators even copied some of Lee's singing mannerisms while animating the character. For the voices of the pampered Si and Am (originally named Nip and Tuck), Lee recorded two tracks and they were played simultaneously for both speaking and singing. *Lady and the Tramp* was Lee's only Disney film; it is surprising her songwriting and vocal talents were never used by Disney again. Autobiography: *Miss Peggy Lee* (2002); biography: *Fever: The Life and Music of Miss Peggy Lee*, Peter Richmond (2007).

Leeves, Jane (b. 1961)   A lithe, striking English actress very active in American television and movies, she provided the voice of the motherly Ladybug in *James and the Giant Peach* (1996). She was born Amanda Jane Leeves in Ilford, England, and trained to be a ballerina until a leg injury made her pursue a modeling career. Leeves made her screen debut dancing in *The Meaning of Life* (1983) but recognition came with the British television series *Benny Hill*. Moving to Hollywood, she was featured on the series *Murphy Brown* then became better known as Daphne Crane on *Frasier* during its eleven-year run. Leeves' other television credits include the series *Throb, Who's the Boss?, Caroline in the City, Seinfeld, Misconceptions, The Starter Wife,* and *Desperate Housewives*, although she might best be remembered as Joy Scroggs in *Hot in Cleveland*. She also voiced such cartoon series as *Hercules, The Simpsons, Phineas and Ferb,* and *The Penguins of Madagascar*. Leeves has appeared in a handful of films, including *To Live and Die in L.A.* (1985), *Miracle on 34th Street* (1994), *Don't Go Breaking My Heart* (1999), *Music of the Heart* (1999), *The Event* (2003), and *Endless Bummer* (2009), and supplied voices for the animated videos *The Adventures of Tom Thumb & Thumbelina* (2002) and *Garfield: A Tale of Two Kitties* (2006).

LeGault, Lance (b. 1935)   A tall, deep-voiced character actor-singer often cast as hardened authority types, he provided the voice of Junior the Buffalo in *Home on the Range* (2004). He was born William Lance LeGault in Chicago, educated at the University of Wichita, Kansas, and began his career as a stunt double for Elvis Presley in such movies as *Girls! Girls! Girls!* (1962), *Kissing Cousins* (1964), *Viva Las Vegas* (1964), and *Roustabout* (1964), also playing small roles in the Presley films. His other movie credits include *Sweet Charity* (1969), *Catch My Soul* (1974), *Coma* (1978), *Stripes* (1981), *Fast-Walking* (1982), *Werewolf* (1987), *Nightmare Beach* (1988), *The Silencers* (1996), *Scorpio One* (1998), and *Stuntmen* (2009). LeGault made his television bow in 1968 and went on to appear in episodes of *Gunsmoke, Black Sheep Squadron, The Rockford Files, Battlestar Galactica, Buck Rogers in the 25th Century, Dynasty, Knight Rider, Airwolf, The A-Team, Magnum P.I., Werewolf, Dallas,* and *Renegade*. He can be heard in the animated videos

Bigfoot and the Muscle Machines (1985), *Tugger: The Jeep 4×4 Who Wanted to Fly* (2005), and *The Legend of Sasquatch* (2006). DeGault narrates the audio portion of the tour of Elvis Presley's mansion Graceland in Memphis.

Leno, Jay (b. 1950) The popular and durable talk show host who started as a stand-up comic, he provided the voice of the limousine Jay Limo in *Cars* (2006). He was born James Douglas Muir Leno in New Rochelle, New York, and educated at Emerson College in Boston before going on the circuit of clubs doing stand-up comedy. He made his national television debut in 1976, followed by hundreds of appearances on talk shows, variety programs, and sit-coms. After being the guest host for *The Tonight Show Starring Johnny Carson* for several years, in 1992 he took over as permanent host. Leno has played characters in such television series as *Good Times, One Day at a Time, Laverne & Shirley, Frasier, Home Improvement,* and *The Drew Carey Show*, and has appeared in a handful of movies, including *American Hot Wax* (1978), *Americathon* (1979), *Collision Course* (1989), and *The Flintstones* (1994). He has voiced such TV cartoon series as *South Park*, and *The Fairly OddParents*, as well as the animated videos and films *We're Back! A Dinosaur's Story* (1993), *Robots* (2005), *Ice Age: The Meltdown* (2006), *Unstable Fables: Tortoise vs. Hare* (2008), *Igor* (2008), and *Scooby-Doo and the Goblin King* (2008). Autobiography: *Leading with My Chin* (1997).

Leonard, Queenie (1905–2002) A British character actress who played both English maids and aristocrats in over two dozen Hollywood films and on television, she voiced the indignant Nesting Mother Bird in *Alice in Wonderland* (1951) and the generous cow Princess in *One Hundred and One Dalmatians* (1961). She was born Pearl Walker in London and performed in cabarets and in British films before making her first Hollywood movie in 1941 in *Ladies in Retirement*. After such films as *The Lodger* (1944), *Our Hearts Were Young and Gay* (1944), *And Then There Were None* (1945), *Cluny Brown* (1946), *Life with Father* (1947), *Million Dollar Mermaid* (1952), and *Les Misérables* (1952), Leonard started appearing in television dramas and series ranging from *General Electric Theatre* and *Schiltz Playhouse of Stars* to *Hazel* and *Bewitched*. Her later movies include *Gaby* (1956), *23 Paces to Baker Street* (1956), *All the Fine Young Cannibals* (1960), *The Notorious Landlady* (1962), *My Fair Lady* (1964), and *Doctor Dolittle* (1967). Leonard often returned to the stage, performing in nightclubs and touring in her one-woman show before her retirement in 1970.

Lester, Robie (1925–2005) A busy actress-singer whose voice was heard in many television commercials in the 1960s, she provided the singing voice for Eva Gabor on three occasions: the Parisian cat Duchess in *The Aristocats* (1970) and the very feminine mouse Miss Bianca in both *The Rescuers* (1977) and *The Rescuers Down Under* (1990). She was born Roberta Lester in Detroit, Michigan, grew up in Ontario, Canada, and served in the U.S. Army Air Corps before studying music at UCLA. Lester sang in commercials, as a backup vocalist in films, and on many children's records for Disney and other companies. Her singing and speaking voice was featured in the animated television specials *The Sword of Ali Baba* (1965), *Santa Claus Is Comin' to Town* (1970), and *The City That Forgot About Christmas* (1974), as well as the television series *The Funny Company, The Famous Adventures of Mr. Magoo,* and *Devlin*.

Levi, Zachary (1980) An appealing television actor who found wide fame early in the new century, he provided the singing and speaking voice of the dashing yet comic bandit Flynn Rider in *Tangled* (2010). He was born Zachary Levi Pugh in Lake Charles, Louisiana, and his family moved about the country before settling in Ventura, California, for his high school years. He was acting and singing on the stage in school and community theatre productions starting at the age of six, then after high school performed in regional theatres in California while he worked as a bus boy, at a car wash, and in other such jobs. Levi made his screen debut in *Big Shot: Confessions of a Campus Bookie* (2002) then found wide recognition that same year as Kipp Steadman in the television series *Less Than Perfect* which he stayed with for four years. His other TV credits include *Curb Your Enthusiasm* and *The Division,* but he is best known as the geeky Chuck Bartowski in the spy sit-com *Chuck*. Zevi has made a handful of other films, including *Big Momma's House 2* (2006), *Spiral* (2007), *Wieners* (2008), *Stuntmen* (2009), and *Alvin and the Chipmunks: The Squeakquel* (2009), and acted in a few made-for-TV movies. The character of Flynn Rider in *Tangled* was originally to be a British swashbuckler named Bastian and actor Dan Fogler and singer Clay Aiken were seriously considered for the role before Levi was cast. Levi did his audition and later some of the vocals with a British dialect until the creative staff on the film changed and Bastian was turned into an Errol Flynn–like character named Flynn Ryder who looks like both Levi and Flynn. Levi re-recorded the funny bandit without the English accent, allowing the wise-cracking character to surface.

Levine, Sam J. (b. 1973) A writer and Disney animator since 1996, he provided the speaking voices for the three empty-headed Willie Brothers in *Home on the Range* (2004), each sibling more stupid than the other. The New York City native worked on the animation for *Hercules* (1997), *Tarzan* (1999), *Treasure Planet* (2002), and *Bolt* (2008). Levine contributed to the script and helped animate *Home on the Range* and the related cartoon short *A Dairy Tale* (2004).

Lewis, Jenifer (b. 1957) A vivacious African American actress and singer of the stage, television and movies, she provided the voice of Flo, owner of Flo's Cafe and Gas Station in Radiator Springs, in *Cars* (2006) and the gospel-singing voodoo priestess Mama Odie in *The Princess and the Frog* (2009). Jenifer Jeanette Lewis was born in Kinloch, Missouri, where she sang in the church choir before studying theatre at Webster College in St. Louis. After appearing in several plays and musicals, including the Broadway productions of *Eubie!* (1978) and *Comin' Uptown* (1979), she went to California where she was one of the back-up singing Harlettes for Bette Midler. Lewis appeared in such movies as *Beaches* (1988), *Sister Act* (1992), *What's Love Got to Do with It?* (1993), *Corrina, Corrina* (1994), *The Preacher's Wife* (1996), and *The Cookout* (2004), but she was mostly seen on television where she was a regular on such series as *A Different World*, *Courthouse*, *The Fresh Prince of Bel-Air*, *Strong Medicine*, *Girlfriends*, and *Meet the Browns*. She can be heard on the TV cartoon series *Happily Ever After: Fairy Tales for Every Child* and *The PJs*, as well as the animated video *Shark Tale* (2004). Lewis returned to Broadway and was featured in the musical *Hairspray* (2002). The character of Mama Odie in *The Princess and the Frog* is inspired by the New Orleans storyteller and author Coleen Salley and Lewis imitated her deep-throated voice. Salley served as a consultant on the film and the writers even used her famous catch-phrase "You ain't got the sense you was born with!" The author died before the movie was released.

Lewis, Jenny (b. 1976) A television actress who played children in the 1980s before graduating to adult roles, she voiced the Assistant Director of the TV show in *Bolt* (2008). She was born in Las Vegas, Nevada, made television commercials as a child, then sang professionally in a rock band in Los Angeles. Lewis made her television debut at the age of nine and soon was featured on the series *Life with Lucy*. Her other television credits include the series *The Golden Girls*, *Mr. Belvedere*, *Baywatch*, *Shannon's Deal*, *Brooklyn Bridge*, and *Murder, She Wrote*. Lewis has appeared in many TV-movies as well as such feature films as *Trading Hearts* (1988), *Troop Beverly Hills* (1989), *Foxfire* (1996), *Little Boy Blue* (1997), *Pleasantville* (1998), and *Don's Plum* (2001). She continues to sing and record and can be heard on the soundtracks of several television shows and movies, including *Bolt*.

Lewis, Vicki (b. 1960) A livewire red-headed character actress and singer of stage and television, she supplied the voice of the ditzy damsel fish Deb, who thinks her reflection in the aquarium glass is her sister Flo, in *Finding Nemo* (2003). She was born in Cincinnati, Ohio, the daughter of an air traffic supervisor and a nursing administrator, and educated at the Cincinnati College Conservatory of Music before pursuing a theatre career. She performed in musicals and plays in Los Angeles and New York, including the Broadway productions of *Do Black Patent Leather Shoes Really Reflect Up?* (1982), *Wind in the Willows* (1985), *Damn Yankees* (1994), and *Chicago* (1996). Lewis made her television debut in 1985, then appeared in such series as *Home Improvement*, *Seinfeld*, *Caroline in the City*, *Grace Under Fire*, *Three Sisters*, *Mission Hill*, *Til Death*, *Surviving Suburbia*, *Curb Your Enthusiasm*, and *Sonny with a Chance*, but she is most remembered as Beth in *NewsRadio*. She has provided voices for several TV cartoon series, including *Hercules*, *The Wild Thornberrys*, *King of the Hill*, *Rugrats*, *The Penguins of Madagascar*, and *Phineas and Ferb*, as well as the animated films and videos *An Extremely Goofy Movie* (2000), *Justice League: The New Frontier* (2008), *Wonder Woman* (2009), and *Ben 10: Alien Swarm* (2009). Lewis' live-action film credits include *I'll Do Anything* (1994), *Mousehunt* (1997), *Godzilla* (1998), *Breakfast of Champions* (1999), *Pushing Tin* (1999), and *The Ugly Truth* (2009). The character of Deb in *Finding Nemo* and her reflection Flo make for a pun on the nautical expression "ebb and flow."

Libertini, Richard (b. 1933) The prolific character actor of stage, movies, and television who can do a wide variety of foreign accents, he voiced the sorcerer Merlock's dog-assistant Dijon in *DuckTales the Movie: The Treasure of the Lost Lamp* (1990). He was born in Cambridge, Massachusetts, was educated at Emerson College, and began his career as a trumpet player. Taking up acting and moving to New York City, he performed in satiric revues Off Broadway and was seen on Broadway in such plays as *Don't Drink the Water* (1969), *Paul Sills' Story Theatre* (1971), and *Bad Habits* (1974). Libertini made his screen debut in 1968 and was featured in comic supporting roles in several movies, including *The Night They Raided Minsky's* (1968), *The Out of Towners* (1970), *Catch-22* (1970), *Fire Sale* (1977), *Days of Heaven* (1978), *The In-Laws* (1979), *Popeye* (1980), *Best Friends* (1982), *All of Me* (1984), *Fletch* (1985), *Awakenings* (1990), *The Bonfire of the Vanities* (1990), *Nell* (1994), and *The 4th Tenor* (2002).

Among the many television series he has appeared on are *Mary Tyler Moore, The Tony Randall Show, Soap, The Bob Newhart Show, Laverne & Shirley, Mork & Mindy, Family Man, The Fanelli Boys, Pacific Station, Murphy Brown, Jenny, Law & Order, The District,* and *Numb3rs,* as well as voicing such cartoon series as *DuckTales, Animaniacs, Duckman: Private Dick/Family Man,* and *The Zeta Project.*

Lima, Kevin (b. 1962) An animator-turned-director, he voiced the trailer park proprietor Lester and the Possum Park Emcee in *A Goofy Movie* (1995) and the chipmunk Pip in the live-action section of *Enchanted* (2007), directing both movies as well. Lima was educated at Emerson College and studied film and animation at the California Institute of the Arts before working as an animator in Taiwan. He first worked for Disney animating *Sport Goofy in Soccermania* (1987) then went on to work on *Oliver & Company* (1988), *The Little Mermaid* (1989), *Beauty and the Beast* (1991), and *The Rescuers Down Under* (1990), as well as contributing to the script for *Oliver & Company* and *Aladdin* (1992). Lima also directed the animated feature *Tarzan* (1999), the live-action film *102 Dalmatians* (2000), and the TV-movies *Eloise at the Plaza* (2003) and *Eloise at Christmastime* (2003). His young daughter **Emma Rose Lima** voiced the Bluebird, the Fawn, and Rapunzel in the animated section of *Enchanted* (2007) and was heard in the animated video *Bambi II* (2006).

Lindo, Delroy (b. 1952) A powerful-looking African American actor of stage and film who usually plays heavies, he provided the voice of the rottweiller henchman Beta in *Up* (2009). He was born in Eltham, England, to Jamaican immigrants, and grew up in Toronto, Canada, and San Francisco where he trained at the American Conservatory Theatre. Although he made his first film in 1976, Lindo concentrated on theatre, performing regionally and in New York City where he was in *The Heliotrope Bouquet by Scott Joplin & Louis Chauvin* (1993) and *Things of Dry Hours* (2009) Off Broadway and *Master Harold ... and the Boys* (1982) and *Joe Turner's Come and Gone* (1988) on Broadway. He acted in such films as *More American Graffiti* (1979), *The Blood of Heroes* (1989), *Mountains of the Moon* (1990), *Bright Angel* (1990), and *The Hard Way* (1991) before getting noticed in *Malcolm X* (1992). Lindo's subsequent movies include *Crooklyn* (1994), *Clockers* (1995), *Get Shorty* (1995), *Broken Arrow* (1996), *Ransom* (1996), *The Devil's Advocate* (1997), *The Cider House Rules* (1999), *Romeo Must Die* (2000), *Gone in Sixty Seconds* (2000), *The Core* (2003), *Domino* (2005), and *This Christmas* (2007), as well as several made-for-TV movies. He reprised his Beta in the short *Dug's Special Mission* (2009).

Lindsey, George (b. 1935) A comic character actor who specialized in playing dim-witted but cheerful hicks on television, he provided the voice of three colorful Disney characters: the defensive farm dog Lafayette in *The Aristocats* (1970), the cross-bow armed vulture Trigger, a guard of the Sheriff of Nottingham, in *Robin Hood* (1973), and the fighting critter Deadeye the Rabbit in *The Rescuers* (1977). He was born in Jasper, Alabama, attended military school, and majored in Bioscience at the University of North Alabama before becoming a high school science teacher. Lindsey began his acting career as a stand-up comic then, after appearing in some stage productions, made his television debut on an episode of *The Rifleman* in 1963. Although he acted in some films, such as *Ensign Pulver* (1964), *Charley and the Angel* (1973), *Treasure of Matecumbe* (1976), and *Cannonball Run II* (1984), he was busiest on the small screen where he appeared in dozens of TV series and became famous as the genial hayseed Goober Pyle first on *Gomer Pyle, U.S.M.C.* then on *The Andy Griffith Show* and its sequel *Mayberry R.F.D.* Lindsey can be heard on the animated video *The New Misadventures of Ichabod Crane* (1979). Memoir: *Goober in a Nutshell*, Lindsey, Ken Beck, Jim Clark (1995).

Linn, Bud *see* **The Kings Men**

Linnetz, Eli Russell (b. 1990) A child actor with a handful of movie and television credits, he provided the voice of the peasant Pacha's son Tipo in *The Emperor's New Groove* (2000) as well as in the video sequel *The Emperor's New Groove 2: Kronk's New Groove* (2005). Linnetz appeared in the films *On Edge* (2001), *Tortilla Soup* (2001), and *A Black Widow* (2009), and the television series *Bull* and *ER*. He can be heard in the animated videos *Kingdom Hearts* (2002) and *101 Dalmatians II: Patch's London Adventure* (2003).

Linz, Alex D. (b. 1989) A child performer with many credits in his young career, he supplied the voice of the title ape man hero as a boy in *Tarzan* (1999). Alexander David Linz was born in Santa Barbara, California, the son of a college professor, and made his television debut at the age of six in an episode of *Cybill*. His subsequent television credits include *Lois & Clark: The New Adventures of Superman, Step by Step, Touched by an Angel, Boy Meets World, ER,* and *Jack & Bobby,* but he is most recognized as Pete Calcatera on *Providence*. Linz's first film was *The Cable Guy* (1996), followed by such movies as *One Fine Day* (1996), *Home Alone 3* (1997), *My Brother the Pig* (1999), *Bruno* (2000), *Bounce* (2000), *Max Keeble's Big Movie* (2001), *Race to Space* (2001), *The Moguls* (2005), and *Choose Connor* (2007), as well as several made-for-TV movies. He has provided voices for the TV cartoon series *Hey, Arnold!* and the animated films and videos *The Wacky Adventures of Ronald McDonald: Scared Silly* (1998) and two of its sequels, *Titan A. E.* (2000), *Nicktoons Racing* (2001), and *Red Dragon* (2002).

Lipton, James (b. 1926)   A well-known celebrity who wears many hats, including writer, producer, educator, choreographer, and interviewer, he has also acted on several occasions, including providing the voice of the irascible television Director in *Bolt* (2008). He was born in Detroit, Michigan, the son of a beatnik poet and a teacher-librarian, and studied at Wayne State University for a law career but took up acting to help finance his schooling. After studying acting with Stella Adler in New York City, he appeared in some Broadway plays and television soap operas, eventually becoming a writer for several of the episodes. Lipton wrote the book and lyrics for the Broadway musicals *Nowhere to Go but Up* (1962) and *Sherry!* (1967), choreographed other shows, and produced a few as well. His writings on language and theatre led to teaching and administrative positions at New York's New School University and the Actors Studio. One of his courses at the latter developed into the popular television interview series *Inside the Actors Studio* which he hosted. Lipton became such a familiar face from the show that he has appeared many times on the small screen in such shows as *Saturday Night Live*, *Arrested Development*, *Cold Squad*, *Late Night with Conan O'Brie*n, and *Jimmy Kimmel Live!*, as well as some television commercials. Memoir: *Inside Inside* (2008).

Lish, Becca (b. 1959)   A voice artist in television since 1991, she played Mrs. Theda Funnie, her daughter Judy, and the gossiping Connie Benge in *Doug's 1st Movie* (1999). She was born in San Francisco and educated at Yale University before making her television debut in 1983. Although she has been seen in such movies as *The Witches of Eastwick* (1987) and *Complex World* (1992), Lish is mostly known for her voicing of Judy Funnie in the cartoon series *Doug* and then *Disney's Doug*. She can also be heard in the animated videos *Is It College Yet?* (2002) and *The Easter Egg Adventure* (2004).

Lloyd, Christopher (b. 1938)   A popular stage, film, and television actor who specializes in off beat or downright whacked-out characters, he voiced the evil sorcerer Merlock in *DuckTales: The Movie: Treasure of the Lost Lamp* (1990) and the villainous Judge Doom in *Who Framed Roger Rabbit?* (1988), a live-action character who is revealed to be a "toon" at the end of the film. Christopher Allen Lloyd was born in Stamford, Connecticut, studied acting at the Neighborhood Playhouse in New York, and made his Off Broadway debut in 1969. For ten years he appeared in experimental and absurdist plays in New York while appearing in a handful of films and television programs, first getting noticed in the movie *One Flew Over the Cuckoo's Nest* (1975). Lloyd gained national attention with his recurring role of the spaced-out Rev. Jim Ignatowski in the television series *Taxi*. He then became a screen star with his performance in *Back to the Future* (1985) and its sequels, followed by such film hits as *The Addams Family* (1991), *Angels in the Outfield* (1994), and *My Favorite Martian* (1999). Because of Lloyd's unusual and expressive voice, he has been in demand for animated videos and films. He can be heard in the movies *Anastasia* (1997), *Hey, Arnold! The Movie* (2002), and *The Tale of Despereaux* (2008), and the videos *The Animated Adventures of Tom Sawyer* (1998), *Here Comes Peter Cottontail: The Movie* (2005), *The Simpsons Ride* (2008), and *Jack and the Beanstalk* (2010). The character of Judge Doom was unique in that he was portrayed by both a live-action actor and as a toon. (This was later done in *Enchanted* as well.) Originally Roddy McDowell, Tim Curry, John Cleese, and Christopher Lee were each approached to play the Judge but the director Robert Zemeckis opted for Lloyd because he had worked so well with him on *Back to the Future*.

Lloyd, Doris (1896–1968)   A British character actress who was busy on the radio, on television, and in over 150 films, she provided the voice of the haughty Rose, one of the flowers who speaks to Alice, in *Alice in Wonderland* (1951). She was born Hessy Doris Lloyd in Liverpool, England, and began her career on the stage, but by 1920 she was acting in silent British movies. By the time talkies came in, Lloyd was in Hollywood where she was in demand for character roles, usually of English or Irish flavor. Among her many screen credits are *Disraeli* (1930), *Charley's Aunt* (1930), *Oliver Twist* (1933), *Dangerous Corner* (1934), *Becky Sharp* (1935), *Tovarich* (1937), *The Old Maid* (1939), *The Great Lie* (1941), *Dr. Jekyll and Mr. Hyde* (1941), *The Lodger* (1944), *To Each His Own* (1946), *Devotion* (1946), *The Secret Life of Walter Mitty* (1947), *The Prisoner of Zenda* (1952), *The Swan* (1956), *The Time Machine* (1960), and *The Sound of Music* (1965). Lloyd also acted on the radio in the 1930s and 1940s and was busy in television in the 1950s and 1960s.

Loggia, Robert (b. 1930)   A gruff Italian-American character actor who usually plays the heavies in movies, on stage, and on television, he voiced the mobster boss Sykes in *Oliver & Company* (1988). He was born Salvatore Loggia in New York

City and studied journalism at Wagner College and the University of Missouri—Columbia before serving in the army. He made his film debut in *Somebody Up There Likes Me* (1956) and his television bow the next year, finding success as the title character in the series *Elfego Baca* on Walt Disney's *Wonderful World of Color*. Loggia went on to play mostly supporting roles in hundreds of television episodes, including the series *Wagon Train, Naked City, The Untouchables, The Defenders, Rawhide, Route 66, Ben Casey, Run for Your Life, T.H.E. Cat, The Big Valley, The High Chaparral, Search for Tomorrow, Kojak, Mannix, S.W.A.T., Police Woman, The Six Million Dollar Man, The Rockford Files, Hawaii Five-O, Charlie's Angels, Emerald Point N.A.S., Magnum P.I., Mancuso F.B.I., Sunday Dinner, Frasier, Touched by an Angel, The Sopranos, Queene Supreme*, and *Monk*. Among his many movies are *The Lost Missile* (1958), *The Greatest Story Ever Told* (1965), *Che!* (1969), *First Love* (1977), *Revenge of the Pink Panther* (1978), *An Officer and a Gentleman* (1982), *Trail of the Pink Panther* (1982), *Psycho II* (1983), *Curse of the Pink Panther* (1983), *Scarface* (1983), *Prizzi's Honor* (1985), *Big* (1988), *The Marrying Man* (1991), *Gladiator* (1992), *Innocent Blood* (1992), *Independence Day* (1996), *Forget About It* (2006), and *Harvest* (2010), as well as such TV-movies as *A Woman Named Golda* (1982), *Conspiracy: The Trial of the Chicago 8* (1987), and *Bonanno: A Godfather's Story* (1999). Loggia has appeared on the New York stage throughout his career, acting off Broadway in such plays as *The Man with the Golden Arm* (1956), *Passing Through from Exotic Places* (1969), *Wedding Band* (1972), and *Trumbo: Red White and Blacklisted* (2003), and on Broadway in *The Three Sisters* (1964) and *Boom Boom Room* (1973). The animators for *Oliver & Company* wanted the gangster Sykes to be more an evil presence than a fully realized character and they kept him in shadows or in his car for much of the movie. Disney CEO Michael Eisner himself approached Marlon Brando to voice the role but he was turned down, Brando believing that the movie sounded like a failure. Loggia's performance as Sykes brings all his experience in playing heavies to the role; he is one of Disney's coldest and most dispassionate of villains.

Lohr, Aaron (b. 1976) An actor-singer who started in show business as a child, he supplied the singing voice of teenager Max in *A Goofy Movie* (1995). Aaron Christopher Lohr, Jr., was born in Los Angeles and at the age of nine acted in an episode of *St. Elsewhere* on television. He also appeared on the series *Bustin' Loose, Baywatch, Family Matters, The Wonder Years, Blossom*, and *Sister, Sister* before going to UCLA to study film. After graduation, Lohr turned to the musical theatre, performing Off Broadway in *Radiant Baby* (2003), *Bare: A Pop Opera* (2004), and *See What I Wanna See* (2005). He has also sung in the movie musicals *Newsies* (1992) and *Rent* (2005). Lohr's other screen credits include *D2: The Mighty Ducks* (1994), *D3: The Mighty Ducks* (1996), *Trojan War* (1997), *Noise* (2007), and *The Wreck* (2008), as well as several TV-movies. He can be heard on the television cartoon series *Peter Pan and the Pirates* and the animated video *Cartoon All-Stars to the Rescue* (1990).

Louis, Dominique A background artist and animator who has worked mostly with Pixar, he provided the voice of the French mime saboteur Bomb Voyage in *The Incredibles* (2004). Louis first worked with Disney as an artist on *A Goofy Movie* (1995) and contributed to the Pixar films *Monsters, Inc.* (2001), *Finding Nemo* (2003), *Ratatouille* (2007), and *Up* (2009), as well as the shorts *Mr. Incredible and Pals* (2005) and *Mater and the Ghostlight* (2006). His other art department credits include *Quest for Camelot* (1998), *The Iron Giant* (1999), and the short *Lifted* (2006). The character of Bomb Voyage was originally called Bomb Perignon after the famous champagne Dom Perignon, but the French company would not allow the use of the name. Bomb Voyage is Louis' only voice credit.

Louis-Dreyfus, Julia (b. 1961) A popular comedienne and actress who has found wide recognition on television, she voiced the ant Princess Atta in *A Bug's Life* (1998). She was born Julia Elizabeth Scarlett Louis-Dreyfus in New York City, the daughter of a French attorney who was heir to the commodities trading firm Louis Dreyfus Group. She was educated at Northwestern University then quickly found fame on television as one of the cast members of *Saturday Night Live* from 1982 to 1985. Louis-Dreyfus found even greater celebrity as Elaine Benes for eight years on *Seinfeld*, followed by such television shows as *Watching Ellie, Arrested Development, Curb Your Enthusiasm*, and *The New Adventures of Old Christine*. She made her movie debut in 1986 and has appeared in such films as *Hannah and Her Sisters* (1986), *Christmas Vacation* (1994), *North* (1989), *Father's Day* (1997), and *Deconstructing Harry* (1997), as well as the television musical *Gepetto* (2000). Her voice can be heard on the TV cartoon series *Hey, Arnold!* and *The Simpsons*.

Luckey, Bud (b. 1934) An artist and animator who has worked on several Pixar movies, he supplied the voices of the agent Rick Dicker from the Super Relocation Program in *The Incredibles* (2004) and Chuckles the unsmiling toy clown in *Toy Story 3* (2010), both of which he animated. The Montana native first worked on television animation for *Sesame Street* in 1969 while he provided voices for the program as well. Luckey's first Pixar film was *Toy Story* (1995), followed by character designs and/or storyboards for *A Bug's Life* (1998), *Toy Story 2* (1999), *Monsters, Inc.* (2001), *Cars* (2006), and *Ratatouille* (2007). He reprised his Rick Dicker in the animated short *Jack-Jack Attack* (2005) and was the Narrator of the Pixar short *Boundin'* (2003) which he also designed, wrote, and directed.

Luddy, Barbara (1908–1979) A movie actress from the days of silent films and a popular radio artist, she is best remembered as the voice of some cherished Disney characters, including the canine heroine Lady in *Lady and the Tramp* (1955), the good fairy Merryweather in *Sleeping Beauty* (1959), the puppy Rover in *One Hundred and One Dalmatians* (1961), the church mouse Mother Sexton and the Mother Rabbit in *Robin Hood* (1973), and the mother kangaroo Kanga in the shorts *Winnie the Pooh and the Honey Tree* (1966), *Winnie the Pooh and the Blustery Day* (1968), and *Winnie the Pooh and Tigger Too!* (1974). She was born in Great Falls, Montana, and made her screen debut in *An Enemy of Men* (1925). After appearing in such movies as *Sealed Lips* (1925), *East Side, West Side* (1925), *Pawnshop Politics* (1926), *Bathing Suitor* (1927), and *Her Secret* (1933), Luddy went to Chicago where she became a favorite radio personality on *The Chicago Theatre of the Air*, later finding a national audience on the radio shows *Grand Hotel, Great Guns, Lonely Woman*, and *The Road of Life*. When she returned to films in the 1950s it was mostly as a voice artist but she made appearances on such television series as *The Donna Reed Show, Lawman, Hazel, Dragnet 1967, Adam-12*, and *Kolchak: The Night Stalker*. The character of the cocker spaniel Lady in *Lady and the Tramp* was based on a dog of the same name owned by animator Hamilton Luske and many of the adult Lady's moves and expressions were inspired by the real pet. Although she was nearly fifty years old when she recorded Lady, Luske's voice manages to convey the young innocence of Lady. Yet she can be determined and is not easily won over by the philandering mutt Tramp. Walt Disney had once given his wife the gift of a puppy in a hat box; years later he made sure it was included in *Lady and the Tramp*.

Luske, Tommy (b. 1941?) The child actor who voiced the younger brother Michael Darling in *Peter Pan* (1953) has fallen into obscurity, perhaps by choice. He made no other movies and appeared only once on television, in *The Walt Disney Christmas Show* (1951) in which he was introduced as the boy who was currently making *Peter Pan*. Legend has it that Luske's voice changed during the long period of making *Peter Pan* and that actress Margaret Kerry had to re-record some of Michael's lines.

Luz, Dora An attractive Mexican singer who had a few hit records in the States in the 1940s, she appeared in and sang "You Belong to My Heart" on the soundtrack of *The Three Caballeros* (1944) and was the soloist heard in the experimental animated short *Destino* (2003). In 1946 Walt Disney and surrealist artist Salvador Dali collaborated on a short animated film titled *Destino* and Luz recorded the title song for the soundtrack. The short was never completed and the two men parted ways, but six decades later Roy E. Disney had the footage restored and, retaining the Luz recording, had *Destino* completed and shown in 2003. Luz's only other screen credit was the Mexican film *Si Gran Ilusión* (1945).

MacDonald, James (1906–1991) A special effects artist who later took up voicing animated characters, he voiced several Disney character and was the voice of Mickey Mouse for thirty years. John James MacDonald was born in Dundee, Scotland, and began his career as a drummer. He collected various objects to add to his percussion performances and then became interested in sound effects, mixing music and non-musical sounds together. MacDonald's first job for Disney was supplying the yodeling for "The Dwarfs' Yodel Song" in *Snow White and the Seven Dwarfs* (1937). He remained at the Disney studio for the next forty years doing sound effects and voices. MacDonald first voiced the chipmunk Chip in the short *Private Pluto* (1943) and reprised the role in a dozen cartoons. In 1947 Walt Disney, who had provided the voice of Mickey Mouse since *Steamboat Willie* (1928), retired from voice work and assigned MacDonald to take over. After providing Mickey's voice one last time in *Fun and Fancy Free* (1947), Disney turned the reins over to MacDonald who voiced dozens of animated shorts and features over the years. His other voice credits include the dog Bruno and the two mice Gus and Jaq in *Cinderella* (1950), the sleepy Dormouse in *Alice in Wonderland* (1951), the Wolf in *The Sword in the Stone* (1963), the Bees in *Winnie the Pooh and the Honey Tree* (1966), and the out-of-breath dragonfly Evinrude in *The Rescuers* (1977), as well as Humphrey the Bear who was featured in six Disney cartoon shorts. The *Cinderella* mice Gus and Jaq are of particular interest. The two mice as distinct characters do not exist in the original tale yet are essential in the plotting and the humor of the Disney version. MacDonald's high-pitched voices for the two little heroes are barely understandable yet there is never any question about what they are feeling or talking about.

In many ways they are MacDonald's crowning achievement. Years later, MacDonald came out of retirement to voice *The Rescuers'* breathless dragonfly Evinrude who was named after the well-known manufacturing company that makes outboard boat motors.

Maga, Mickey (b. 1950) A child actor who retired from acting at the age of eleven, he voiced the feisty dalmatian pup Patch in *One Hundred and One Dalmatians* (1961). He was born Michael Maga in Los Angeles and at the age of six he made his screen debut in *Diane* (1956), followed by children's roles in *The Man in the Gray Flannel Suit* (1956), *The Eddy Duchin Story* (1956), *Lust for Life* (1956), and *Raintree County* (1957). He also appeared in the television series *Boots and Saddles*, *The Millionaire*, *Shirley Temple Theatre*, and *Twilight Zone*. As an adult, Maga became a music teacher.

Magliozzi, Tom (b. 1937) and **Ray** (b. 1949) The NPR-Radio commentators, known as "Click and Clack, the Tappet Brothers," who have hosted the program *Car Talk* for over twenty years, they provided two voices for *Cars* (2006): Tom as the Dodge Dart convertible Rusty Rust-eze and Ray as his brother the Dodge van Dusty Rust-eze. The Magliozzi brothers were born in East Cambridge, Massachusetts, and educated at Massachusetts Institute of Technology. Tom studied at Northwestern University before he took up teaching at various colleges while Ray taught science in Vermont. The two Magliozzis eventually opened a car repair shop, the two of them soon going on the local radio station and talking about cars. This led to their national radio show on NPR. The Magliozzis provided the voices for the television show *Click and Clack's as the Wrench Turns*. The characters of the sponsors Rusty and Dodge in *Cars* are taken directly from the Magliozzi brothers, even to the point of shouting their catch phrase, "Don't drive like my brother!"

Mahoney, John (b. 1940) The popular character actor of stage, screen and television who began his acting career late and found fame in his fifties, he provided the voice for the eccentric millionaire Preston B. Whitmore in *Atlantis: The Lost Empire* (2001). He was born in Blackpool, England, where his family was evacuated from their Manchester home during the Blitz. Mahoney emigrated to the States, served a term in the army, and became a U.S. citizen. He was educated at Quincy College and Western Illinois University then taught English at various colleges for several years, not turning to acting until the 1980s in Chicago. Performances with the Steppenwolf Theatre led to the New York stage where he shone in *The House of Blue Leaves* (1987). Mahoney's film credits include *The Manhattan Project* (1986), *Tin Men* (1987), *Moonstruck* (1987), *Eight Men Out* (1988), *The Russia House* (1990), *The Hudsucker Proxy* (1994), and *Almost Salinas* (2001), but he is better known as Martin Crane on the television series *Frasier* and for his many appearances in such programs as *Saturday Night Live*, *H.E.L.P.*, and *In Treatment*, as well as several TV-movies and specials. Mahoney reprised his Preston B. Whitmore in the sequel *Atlantis: Milo's Return* (2003) and his voice can be heard in the animated movies and videos *Antz* (1998), *The Iron Giant* (1999), and *The Emperor's New Groove 2: Kronk's New Groove* (2005). Actor Lloyd Bridges was originally cast as Whitmore in *Atlantis* but he died soon after production began. The much younger Mahoney was then cast and the character changed slightly, making the eccentric Whitmore more spry and comical.

Main, Laurie (b. 1929) An English actor mostly seen in American television and movies, he supplied the voice of the human Dr. Watson in *The Great Mouse Detective* (1986). The London-born Main acted in British television in the 1950s then moved to the States in the 1960s and remained, appearing in such series as *Shirley Temple Theatre*, *Bachelor Father*, *Maverick*, *Hawaiian Eye*, *The Jack Benny Program*, *The Girl from U.N.C.L.E.*, *That Girl*, *The Guns of Will Sonnett*, *Ironside*, *The Monkees*, *Hogan's Heroes*, *Family Affair*, *Bewitched*, *McMillan & Wife*, *Little House on the Prairie*, and *Murder, She Wrote*, but he is most remembered as the host and narrator for the series *Welcome to Pooh Corner* in the 1980s and the many *Winnie the Pooh* records and cassette tapes he recorded for Disney. Main's movie credits include *The Yellow Balloon* (1953), *The Master Plan* (1955), *The Phantom of the Opera* (1962), *The Three Stooges Go Around the World in a Daze* (1963), *My Fair Lady* (1964), *Munster, Go Home!* (1966), *On a Clear Day You Can See Forever* (1970), *Darling Lili* (1970), *The Strongest Man in the World* (1975), *Herbie Goes to Monte Carlo* (1977), *Time After Time* (1979), *The Competition* (1980), *Cheech & Chong's The Corsican Brothers* (1984), and *Robin Hood: Men in Tights* (1993).

Maiwand, Brianna A child actress who provided the voice for Peanelope, one of the three plush peas-in-a-pod toy, in *Toy Story 3* (2010), so far she has no other film or television credits but she has done some commercials and modeled for national retail ads.

Majors, Austin (b. 1995) A child actor with an impressive list of credits, he voiced the three-year-old Jim Hawkins in the prologue of *Treasure Planet* (2002). The California native began acting in commercials at the age of two and had a bit part in the film *Nevada* (1997) before gaining notice as a regular on the television series *NYPD Blue* for six years. Majors' other television credits include *Providence, ER, According to Jim, NCIS, Desperate Housewives*, and *How I Met Your Mother*. In addition to appearing in such films as *The Price of Air* (2000), *Volare* (2004), and *Bye Bye Benjamin* (2006), he has done voices for the live-action movies *Dead Silence* (2007) and *The Gray Man* (2007), the animated film *The Ant Bully* (2006), and the cartoon series *American Dad!*

Malet, Arthur (b. 1927)   The British character actor with a flowing Welsh accent, he often played characters much older than himself and frequently voiced animated characters, such as the jolly little King Eidilleg in *The Black Caldron* (1985). He was born in Lee-on-Solent, England, but grew up in Wales and emigrated to the States after World War II. Malet began his career on the stage and appeared in a few Broadway plays in the late 1950s, the same time he was acting on television in such dramatic programs as *Playwrights '56, Camera Three, The United States Steel Hour,, The DuPont Show of the Month*, and *Alfred Hitchcock Presents*. He alternated between films and the small screen after 1960, appearing in such television series as *The Donna Reed Show, Leave It to Beaver, The Untouchables, My Favorite Martian, The Andy Griffith Show, Bewitched, Bonanza, The Man from U.N.C.L.E., Charlie's Angels, Barney Miller, Dallas,* and *Picket Fences*. Malet's film credits include *The Man from Galveston* (1963), *Mary Poppins* (1964), *King Rat* (1965), *Lt. Robin Crusoe, U.S.N.* (1966), *In the Heat of the Night* (1967), *The Great White Hope* (1970), *Bedknobs and Broomsticks* (1971), *Young Frankenstein* (1974), *Heaven Can Wait* (1978), *Hook* (1991), and *A Little Princess* (1995). He also provided voices for such animated films and videos as *The Secret of Nimh* (1982), *Anastasia* (1997), and *The Secret of Nimh 2: Timmy to the Rescue* (1998).

Malick, Wendie (b. 1950)   A television actress who has often done voice work, she provided the voice of the peasant Chicha, the understanding wife of Pacha, in *The Emperor's New Groove* (2000). She was born in Buffalo, New York, and educated at Ohio Wesleyan University before working as a model and then as an assistant for a congressman in Washington. Malick turned to acting and made her television debut in 1978, appearing in such series as *Trauma Center, Kate & Allie, The Fanelli Boys, Anything but Love*, and *Baywatch*, but not getting noticed until her performance as Judith Tupper Stone in *Dream On*, a role she played for six years. She also appeared in *Good Behavior, The X Files, Fillmore!, Frasier, Jake in Progress*, and *Big Day*, but is most remembered for playing fashion editor Nina Van Horn in *Just Shoot Me!* and Victoria Chase in *Hot in Cleveland*. Malick's movie credits include *A Little Sex* (1982), *Scrooged* (1988). *Just Add Love* (1997), *Jerome* (1998), *Racing Stripes* (2005), *Waiting for Yvette* (2008), and *Confessions of a Shopaholic* (2009). The character of Chicha in *The Emperor's New Groove* is that of an ordinary loving wife and far from memorable except for one fact: Chicha is obviously expecting a child and she is the first pregnant character in a Disney animated movie. Malick reprised her Chicha in the video *The Emperor's New Groove 2: Kronk's New Groove* (2005) and in the animated series *The Emperor's New School*. She has done voices for such cartoon series as *Batman Beyond, Kim Possible, Father of the Pride, American Dragon: Jake Long, The Adventures of Jimmy Neutron: Boy Genius*, and *The X's*, as well as the video *Brother Bear 2* (2006) and the movie *Alvin and the Chipmunks: The Squeakquel* (2009).

Malis-Morey, Adele (1927–2000)   A stage actress with limited film and television credits, she voiced Orwen, the fattest of the three witches of Morva, in *The Black Caldron* (1985). Her movie credits include *Kingdom of the Spiders* (1977), *The Black Marble* (1980), *Critters* (1986), *Doc Hollywood* (1991), and *Saving Souls* (1995), and she acted in such series as *Hunter, The John Larroquette Show*, and *ER*.

Manchester, Melissa (b. 1951)   The popular songwriter-singer who also acts in films and on television, she supplied the voice of the pub entertainer Miss Kitty Mouse who sings the seductive "Let Me Be Good to You" in *The Great Mouse Detective* (1986). She was born in the Bronx, New York, the daughter of a musician for the Metropolitan Opera, and was singing professionally in commercials as a teenager. Manchester studied music at Manhattan's High School of the Performing Arts and under Paul Simon at New York University before becoming a back-up singer for Bette Midler and Barry Manilow. Her first album came out in 1973 and since then she has written and performed hit singles and albums and sung on television specials and in concert. Manchester can be heard singing on several movies and television series and appeared in *Fame* and *Blossom* on the small screen and in the movie *For the Boys* (1991). Originally the singer Madonna was slated to voice Miss Kitty (a nod to the character of the same name in the old television series *Gunsmoke*) but the directors decided she could not pass as a British performer. Manchester is also American but was deemed closer to what they had in mind.

Mann, Danny   A busy voice artist in television and animated movies since 1965, he provided the canine sounds of Ratcliffe's spoiled pug Percy in *Pocahontas* (1995), voiced the construction worker Steve in *Up* (2009), and played various minor roles in *The Emperor's New Groove* (2000), *Monsters, Inc.* (2001), *Finding Nemo* (2003), and *Cars* (2006). Mann's most recognized television cartoon characters are Hector in *Heathcliff & the Catillac Cats*, Freeway in *The Transformers*, and Bud in *Slimer! The Real Ghostbusters*. Among the many other series he has voiced are *Scooby-Doo and Scrappy-Doo*, *Galaxy High School*, *The Little Wizards*, *Hard Time on Planet Earth*, *Captain Planet and the Planeteers*, *TaleSpin*, *Bobby's World*, *Back to the Future*, *Darkwing Duck*, *Land of the Lost*, *Yo Yogi!*, *Batman*, *Family Dog*, *Sonic the Hedgehog*, *Aladdin*, *Quack Pack*, *The Tick*, *Duckman: Private Dick/Family Man*, *Space Goofs*, *Time Squad*, *Jackie Chan Adventures*, *Rugrats*, *Samurai Jack*, *W.I.T.C.H.*, *The Grim Adventures of Billy & Mandy*, and *Hey, Arnold!* Mann can be heard in such animated movies and videos as *Heathcliff: The Movie* (1986), *Little Nemo: Adventures in Slumberland* (1989), *Rover Dangerfield* (1991), *FernGully: The Last Rainforest* (1992), *Thumbelina* (1994), *Balto* (1995), *The Land Before Time VI: The Secret of Saurus Rock* (1998), *Bartok the Magnificent* (1999), *Aladdin and the Adventure of All Time* (2000), *Osmosis Jones* (2001), *The Nutcracker and the Mouseking* (2004), *Ice Age: The Meltdown* (2006), *The Wild* (2006), *Open Season* (2006), *Happy Feet* (2006), *Surf's Up* (2007), *Horton Hears a Who!* (2008), *Ponyo* (2008), *Open Season 2* (2008), and *Cloudy with a Chance of Meatballs* (2009), as well as voices for the live-action films *Babe* (1995), *Babe: Pig in the City* (1998), and *Cats & Dogs* (2001).

Manoux, J. P. (b. 1969) A comic actor mostly in television, he has voiced many cartoon series and some animated films, including *Bolt* (2008) in which he played the desperate pigeon Tom who wants to write for television. He was born Jean-Paul Christophe Manoux in Fresno, California, and was educated at Northwestern University, L.A. Theatresports, ACME Comedy Theatre, and the Groundlings School, making his television and movie debut in 1996. Manoux has appeared in such television series as *3rd Rock from the Sun*, *Just Shoot Me*, *Smallville*, *How I Met Your Mother*, *Caveman*, *Aaron Stone*, and *Sabrina, the Teenage Witch*, but he is most remembered as the effeminate principal Mr. Hackett in *Phil of the Future* and Dr. Dustin Crenshaw on *ER*. His film credits include *Fairfax Fandango* (1997), *Inspector Gadget* (1999), *Galaxy Quest* (1999), *Ocean's Eleven* (2001), *Meet the Fockers* (2004), and *Knocked Up* (2007). Among the many TV cartoon series that Manoux has voiced are *House of Mouse*, *Higglytown Heroes*, *The Emperor's New School*, *Family Guy*, and *The Replacements*, as well as the animated videos *Mickey's Magical Christmas: Snowed in at the House of Mouse* (2001), *Scooby-Doo* (2002), *Scooby-Doo 2: Monsters Unleashed* (2004), *Star Troopers 2: Hero of the Federation* (2004), *The Emperor's New Groove 2: Kronk's New Grove* (2005), and *Kingdom Hearts II* (2005).

Maples, David A television writer and producer with a few acting credits, he voiced the angry Beefeater in Buckingham Palace in *Teacher's Pet* (2004). Maples wrote episodes for the television cartoon series *Rugrats*, the sit-com *Home Improvement*, and the series *Huff*, becoming co-producer on the last. He has written and produced the series *In Plain Sight* and acted in one episode. Maples also appeared in the film *For Richer or Poorer* (1997).

Margolyes, Miriam (b. 1941) A round British character actress on the London stage who later found success in films on both sides of the Atlantic, she provided the voice of the Glowworm in the stop-action section of *James and the Giant Peach* (1996), as well as the horrid Aunt Sponge in the live-action portion of that movie; and voiced the blunt Chinese Matchmaker in *Mulan* (1998). She was born in Oxford, England, the daughter of a physician and a real estate investor, and educated at Cambridge University where she acted in campus theatre productions. Margolyes has appeared in dozens of new plays, classics, and musicals in Great Britain, the States, and Australia, with productions ranging from *Romeo and Juliet* and *The Importance of Being Earnest* to *Fiddler on the Roof* and *Wicked*. Her film career started with her doing voices for Japanese animated cartoons and she later received her first widespread recognition in the movie *Stand Up, Virgin Soldiers* (1977). Among her other notable films are *The Awakening* (1980), *Yentl* (1983), *Little Dorrit* (1988), *Dead Again* (1991), *As You Like It* (1992), *The Age of Innocence* (1993), *Immortal Beloved* (1994), *Romeo + Juliet* (1996), *Magnolia* (1999), *Cats and Dogs* (2001), *Harry Potter and the Chamber of Secrets* (2002), *The Life and Death of Peter Sellers* (2004), *Ladies in Lavender* (2004), *Being Julia* (2004), and *Harry Potter and the Deathly Hallows* (2010). Margolyes was featured on such British television series as *Jackanory*, *Take a Letter Mr. Jones*, *The Black Adder*, *Frannie's Turn*, *Supply and Demand*, and *Magic Grandad*, as well as on many American and English TV-movies and miniseries. She supplied voices for the films *Babe* (1995) and *Babe: Pig in the City* (1998) and can be heard in the animated movies and videos *The Fool of the World and the Flying Ship* (1990), *The Princess and the Cobbler* (1993), *Balto* (1995), *The First Snow of Winter* (1998), *Sir Billi the Vet* (2006), *Flushed Away* (2006), *Happy Feet* (2006), *Legend of the*

Guardians: The Owls of Ga'Hoole (2010), and *Sir Billi* (2010).

Margulies, Julianna (b. 1966) An attractive leading lady of movies and television, she provided the voice of the loving iguanodon Neera in *Dinosaur* (2000). Julianna Luisa Margulies was born in Spring Valley, New York, the daughter of an ad writer and a professional ballet dancer, and grew up in France, England, and various U.S. states before attending Sarah Lawrence College. She began her career in regional theatre and doing commercials and made her film debut in *Out for Justice* (1991), followed by such films as *Paradise Road* (1997), *The Man from Elysian Fields* (2001), *Snakes on a Plane* (2006), and *City Island* (2009). Margulies found wider recognition on television where she appeared in several series, including *Scrubs, The Sopranos, Canterbury's Law*, and *The Good Wife*, but she is most known as Nurse Carol Hathaway in *ER*.

Marin, Cheech (b. 1946) A durable stand-up comic and actor who sports a thick Mexican accent and exudes a crass, vulgar persona in his characters, he provided the voices for the sassy Chihuahua Alonzo Ignacio Julio Federico de Tito in *Oliver & Company* (1988), the excitable hyena Banzai in *The Lion King* (1994), and Ramone, the lady-killer Chevy Impala Lowrider, in *Cars* (2006). He was born Richard Anthony Marin in Los Angeles, the son of a policeman, and educated at California State University at Northridge before fleeing the draft and residing in Canada. In Vancouver he teamed up with comic Tommy Chong and, as Cheech and Chong, they found popularity through comedy records, television appearances, and in such movies as *Up in Smoke* (1978) and *Cheech & Chong's Next Movie* (1980), *Nice Dreams* (1981), *Still Smoking* (1983), and *Cheech & Chong's Corsican Brothers* (1984). After the team broke up, Marin was featured in several films, including *Ghostbusters II* (1989), *Rude Awakening* (1989), *Desperado* (1995), *Tin Cup* (1996), *Spy Kids* (2001) and its sequels, *Christmas with the Kranks* (2004), *Upperclassmen* (2005), and *The Perfect Game* (2009), but he was even more successful on television where he appeared in such series as *The Tracy Ullman Show, The Golden Palace, Married with Children, Nash Bridges, Judging Amy*, and *Lost*. Originally Marin and his comedy partner Tommy Chong were to voice the hyenas Banzai and Shenzi but when Chong wasn't available Whoopi Goldberg was cast as Shenzi. Marin reprised his Banzai in the videos *The Lion King 1½* (2004) and *Kingdom Hearts II* (2005) and his Ramone in *Mater and the Ghostlight* (2006). He can also be heard in the animated movies and videos *FernGully: The Last Rainforest* (1992), *It's Tough to Be a Bug* (1998), *The Nuttiest Nutcracker* (1999), and *Hoodwinked Too! Hood vs. Evil* (2010). Marin's wild, funny Tito in *Oliver & Company* was an immediate hit with the animators, not to mention audiences. Filmed during the recording session, Marin was an explosion of verbal and physical energy that inspired the animators to make Tito into an irresistible comic character. About a fourth of Tito's lines in the final cut were ad-libs by Marin. There was less flexibility in *The Lion King* and *Cars*, though his Ramone in the latter manages to be a car with very human lustiness. Biography: *Cheech Marin: A Real-Life Biography*, Valerie Menard (2001).

Marin, Jason (b. 1974) A teenage actor who was active only between 1985 and 1993, he supplied the voice of Ariel's fish pal Flounder in *The Little Mermaid* (1989). He was born in Brooklyn, New York, and made his film debut in a small role in *Back to the Future* (1985). After brief appearances in the television series *Newhart, Once a Hero, Highway to Heaven*, and *Trapper John, M.D.*, he was featured as a regular on the series *Starting from Scratch*. Marin did voice work on the animated movie *Rock-a-Doodle* (1991) then, after appearing in one episode of *Beverly Hills 90210*, he retired from show business.

Marr, Eddie (1900–1987) A beefy character actor who usually played thugs and other heavies on screen and later con men and city slickers on television, he supplied the voice of columnist Walter Winchell in the "Baby Weems" segment of *The Reluctant Dragon* (1941). He was born in Jersey City, New Jersey, and made his screen debut in *It Could Happen to You* (1937) as a henchman, the type of role he would play in over fifty movies. Marr can be seen in such films as *The Last Gangster* (1937), *Mr. Moto's Gamble* (1938), *Garden of the Moon* (1938), *King of Alcatraz* (1938), *Torchy Blane: Playing with Dynamite* (1939), *Parole Fixer* (1940), *The House Across the Bay* (1940), *Johnny Apollo* (1940), *Charlie Chan at the Wax Museum* (1940), *One Dangerous Night* (1943), *Rhapsody in Blue* (1945), *Tell It to a Star* (1945), *The Damned Don't Cry* (1950), *The Steel Trap* (1952), *Indestructible Man* (1956), *I Was a Teenage Werewolf* (1957), *How to Make a Monster* (1958), *The Lawbreakers* (1960), and *Roustabout* (1964). Among the television series he appeared in are *Gang Busters, The Life of Riley, My Little Margie, Mike Hammer, Circus Boy, Dragnet, Perry Mason, Maverick, The Real McCoys, Leave It to Beaver, Dennis the Menace, Bachelor Father, Twilight Zone, The Addams Family, The Munsters, The Bob Hope Show*, and *Land of the Giants*.

Mars, Kenneth (b. 1936) A deep-voiced character actor known for his different dialect characters in films and on television, he provided the voice of Ariel's father King Triton in *The Little Mermaid* (1989). The Chicago native began his television career in an episode of *Car 54, Where Are You?* in 1963, going on to play usually eccentric types in such series as *Get Smart, He & She, The Ghost & Mrs. Muir, McMillan & Wife, Police Woman, Columbo, Fernwood Tonight, America 2-Night, Barnaby Jones, Alice, The Twilight Zone, Hardcastle and McCormick, Star Trek: Deep Space Nine, Becker, Malcolm in the Middle,* and *Hannah Montana.* Since the 1980s Mars has concentrated on voicing cartoon characters and can be heard in over 300 episodes of such series as *The Dukes, Foofur, Teen Wolf, The Flintstone Kids, DuckTales, Midnight Patrol: Adventures in the Dream Zone, TaleSpin, Darkwing Duck, Fievel's American Tails, Bonkers, The Pirates of Dark Water, Life with Louie, The Angry Beavers, Mighty Max,* and *The Legend of Tarzan,* as well as the animated videos and films *The Adventures of the American Rabbit* (1986), *Top Cat and the Beverly Hills Cats* (1987), *We're Back! A Dinosaur's Story* (1993), *Thumbelina* (1994), *The Land Before Time II: The Great Valley Adventure* (1994) and ten of its sequels, and *Bruno the Kid: The Animated Movie* (1996). Among his film credits are *The April Fools* (1969), *Butch Cassidy and the Sundance Kid* (1969), *Viva Max* (1969), *What's Up, Doc?* (1972), *The Parallax View* (1974), *The Apple Dumpling Gang Rides Again* (1979), *Full Moon High* (1981), *Protocol* (1984), *Fletch* (1985), *Prince Jack* (1985), *Radio Days* (1987), *Police Academy 6: City Under Siege* (1989), *Shadows and Fog* (1991), *Rough Magic* (1995), and *Teddy Bears' Picnic* (2002), but he is best remembered for two Mel Brooks movies: as the Nazi Franz Liebkind in *The Producers* (1968) and Inspector Kemp in *Young Frankenstein* (1974). Actor Patrick Stewart was the first choice to voice King Triton in *The Little Mermaid* but his schedule did not allow it. So Mars, who excelled at comic roles, was given this rather serious role and he used his versatile voice to come up with the deep-voiced, authoritative sound for Ariel's father. Mars reprised his King Triton in the video *The Little Mermaid II: Return to the Sea* (2000) and in the TV cartoon series *The Little Mermaid.*

Marsden, James (b. 1973) The dashing leading man of films and television, he played the ardent Prince Edward in both the animated and live-action sections of *Enchanted* (2007). James Paul Marsden was born in Stillwater, Oklahoma, the son of a college professor and a nutritionist, and studied broadcast journalism at Oklahoma State University. He made his television debut in 1993 and soon appeared in such series as *The Nanny, Blossom, Touched by an Angel, Second Noah,* and *Ally McBeal.* Marsden's movie credits include *Disturbing Behavior* (1998), *X-Men* (2000), *Zoolander* (2001), *The Notebook* (2004), *X-Men: The Last Stand* (2006), *Superman Returns* (2006), *Hairspray* (2007), *27 Dresses* (2008), and *Cats and Dogs: The Revenge of Kitty Galore* (2010). He can also be heard on the TV cartoon series *Extreme Ghostbusters* and *Robot Chicken.* The character of Prince Edward in *Enchanted* is a delicious spoof of animated fairy tale princes, showing how little personality or depth they usually have. Marsden gives a sportive live-action performance that echoes the moves and poses of animated princes. His vocals in both sections are similarly bombastic and empty until the end of the movie when the cartoonish prince starts to become a real human being.

Marsden, Jason (b. 1975) A child actor on television who grew up to become a prolific voice artist, he supplied the speaking voice of Goofy's teenage son Max in *A Goofy Movie* (1995) and its video sequel *An Extremely Goofy Movie* (2000). Jason Christopher Marsden was born in Providence, Rhode Island, and grew up in Fullerton, California, where he began acting on television soap operas and sit-coms at the age of eleven. Among his early TV credits are *Webster, General Hospital, Murphy Brown, The Munsters Today, Star Trek: The Next Generation, Blossom, Almost Home, Tom, Full House, Boy Meets World,* and *Step by Step,* as well as such movies as *Almost an Angel* (1990), *Robot Jox* (1990), and *Mr. Saturday Night* (1992). As a teenager, Marsden started doing voice work on the series *Peter Pan and the Pirates* and *The Adventures of the Gummi Bears,* eventually doing more and more animated cartoons as he got older. He can he heard in over 300 episodes of series such as *Marsupilami, Sonic the Hedgehog, Extreme Ghostbusters, Jungle Cubs, Superman, Buzz Lightyear of Star Command, The Legend of Tarzan, Invader ZIM, House of Mouse, The Weekenders, Static Shock, Justice League, Codename: Kids Next Door, Teen Titans, Xiaolin Showdown, W.I.T.C.H., Kim Possible, The Fairly OddParents, American Dad, The Replacements,* and *Batman: The Brave and the Bold,* as well as in many animated videos and movies, including *Superman: The Last Son of Krypton* (1996), *The Lion King 2: Simba's Pride* (1998), *Tarzan* (1999), *Spirited Away* (2001), *The Jimmy Timmy Power Hour* (2004), *Felix the Cat Saves Christmas* (2004), *Mickey's Twice Upon a Christmas* (2004), *Brother Bear 2* (2006), and *Dragonlance: Dragons of Autumn Twilight* (2008). Marsden has appeared in adult roles in such television series as *Alley McBeal, Even Stevens, Will & Grace,* and *Just Shoot Me!*

Marshall, Garry (b. 1934) A high-powered television producer, writer, and director with many hit series to his credit, he is also a respected actor and voiced Chicken Little's ex-sports hero father Buck "Ace" Cluck in *Chicken Little* (2005). He was born Garry Kent Marsciarelli in New York City, the son of an industrial film producer and a dancing instructor. After graduating from Northwestern University, he wrote jokes for star comics and then teamed up with Jerry Belson and scripted such successful television shows as *The Dick Van Dyke Show, The Joey Bishop Show, The Lucy Show, The Danny Thomas Show*, and *The Odd Couple*. Marshall developed, wrote, produced, and/or directed a series of popular television shows, such as *Happy Days, Laverne & Shirley*, and *Mork & Mindy*, as well as such successful movies as *The Flamingo Kid* (1984), *Beaches* (1988), *Pretty Woman* (1990), *Dear God* (1996), *Runaway Bride* (1999), *The Princess Diaries* (2001) and its sequel *The Princess Diaries 2: Royal Engagement* (2004). He made his film acting debut in 1961 and was seen in such movies as *Grand Theft Auto* (1977), *A League of Their Own* (1992), *Call Him Sasquatch* (2003), *Keeping Up with the Steins* (2006), and *Race to Witch Mountain* (2009), but most of his acting has been on television where he was featured in many series, including *The Odd Couple, Laverne & Shirley*, and *Murphy Brown*. He is the brother of actress-director Penny Marshall.

Marshall, Sean (b. 1965) A child actor with a short but noteworthy career, he provided the speaking and singing voice of the Boy who sells his donkey to Joseph and Mary in the short *The Small One* (1978). He was born in Canoga Park, California, and made his television debut at the age of eight in an episode of the series *Kung Fu*. He made his screen bow the same year in *The Deadly Trackers* (1973) then won the coveted role of the youth Pete who befriends the dragon Elliott in the movie musical *Pete's Dragon* (1977). Marshall also appeared in the television series *Little House on the Prairie, The Fitzpatricks*, and *The MacKenzies of Paradise Cove*, as well as the TV-movies *Stickin' Together* (1978), *The New Adventures of Heidi* (1978), and *To Race the Wind* (1980) before retiring from acting at the age of fifteen.

Martin, Kellie (b. 1975) A child performer on television and films who continued her career as an adult, she provided the voice of Max's caring teenage sweetheart Roxanne in *A Goofy Movie* (1995). Kellie Noelle Martin was born in Riverside, California, and made her television debut at the age of seven in the series *Father Murphy* and her screen bow in 1986. She was on a few other series before finding wide recognition as Becca Thacher in *Life Goes On* and the title character in *Christy*. As an adult, Martin was featured on the small screen in *Crisis Center, ER*, and the *Mystery Woman* series of TV-movies, as well as in such films as *All You Need* (2001), *Malibu's Most Wanted* (2003), and *Open House* (2004). She started voicing television cartoons in 1988 and can be heard in the series *A Pup Named Scooby-Doo, Taz-Mania*, and *Aladdin*, and the video *Mickey's Twice Upon a Christmas* (2004).

Marwood, Linda The actress who voiced the concerned Mother of the infant prodigy Baby Herbert Weems in the "Baby Weems" section of *The Reluctant Dragon* (1941) has no other film or television credits.

Mastrogiorgio, Danny An Italian-American who has played ethnic types on the large and small screen, he voiced one of the two Rams in *Brother Bear* (2003). He was born in Mt. Vernon, New York, and trained at Marin Community College and Juilliard for a stage career. Mastrogiorgio has acted on the New York stage and in regional theatres, and has developed a one-man show *My Italy Story* which he has performed Off Broadway and on tour. He has appeared on such television series as *Spin City, The Book of Daniel, The Sopranos*, and *Law & Order* and its two spinoffs, as well as in films, including *Sleepers* (1996), *Dead Broke* (1998), *Friends and Family* (2001), *The Producers* (2005), *Enchanted* (2007), and *Fighting* (2009).

Mateo, Joseph An animator and artist for Disney since 1995, he provided the roaring sounds for T-Rex, the dinosaur conjured up by the Bowler Hat Man, in *Meet the Robinsons* (2007), a film he also co-wrote. Mateo has worked on the art and/or animation for *Pocahontas* (1995), *The Hunchback of Notre Dame* (2006), *Mulan* (1998), *Tarzan* (1999), *The Emperor's New Groove* (2000), *Atlantis: The Lost Empire* (2001), *Treasure Planet* (2002), *Home on the Range* (2004), and *Bolt* (2008), as well as the shorts *Super Rhino* (2009) and *Prep & Landing* (2009). He has also acted in the live-action movies *Vampire Hunter* (2004) and *No Pain, No Gain* (2004).

Matthews, Junius C. (1890–1978) A durable character actor with a long career in several media, he voiced the surly owl Archimedes in *The Sword in the Stone* (1963) and Rabbit in the shorts *Winnie the Pooh and the Honey Tree* (1966) and *Winnie the Pooh and the Blustery Day* (1968), as well as in the compilation feature *The Many Adventures of Winnie the Pooh* (1977). Junius Conyers Matthews was born in Chicago and began his career on the stage, appearing in such Broadway productions as *Young Wisdom* (1914), *The Phantom Legion* (1919), *Pot Luck* (1921), *The Green Ring* (1922), *The Grand Street Follies* (1924, 1925, 1927, and 1929), *The Little Clay Cart* (1924), *The Critic* (1924), *The Dybbuk* (1925), and *The Taming of the Shrew* (1927). He was a familiar voice on the radio from the late 1920s to the mid-1950s, voicing everything from soap operas to westerns. Although Matthews had acted in the silent film *The Silent Witness* (1917), he did not return to the screen until the 1940s, appearing in a variety of movies over the next twenty years, including *Without Reservations* (1946), *The Shocking Miss Pilgrim* (1947), *Chicken Every Sunday* (1949), *My Wife's Best Friend* (1952), *Good Morning, Miss Dove* (1955), *Jeanne Eagels* (1957), and *A Summer Place* (1959). Among his television credits are the series *I Led Three Lives, The Lineup, The Gene Autry Show, Dragnet, The Gale Storm Show, The Real McCoys,* and *Have Gun—Will Travel.* The disapproving owl Archimedes in *The Sword in the Stone* is a fine characterization by Matthews. (The animators copied Walt Disney's nose for the look of the character.) His vocals are constantly complaining yet it is clear that the owl has an affection for the boy Wart. This is very different from Matthews' Rabbit in the Winnie the Pooh shorts who is a take-charge, bossy organizer and the instigator of events, his squeaking voice used not to grumble but to take command.

Mattraw, Scotty (1880–1946) A rotund character actor whose two dozen movies stretch from the silent days to 1940, he supplied the voice of the dwarf Bashful in *Snow White and the Seven Dwarfs* (1937). He was born in Evans Mills, New York, and made his screen debut in 1924. Mattraw played pudgy bit parts in such films as *The Thief of Bagdad* (1924), *The Red Mill* (1927), *The Return of the Riddle Rider* (1927), *Two Lovers* (1928), *Arizona Cyclone* (1928), *The Merry Frinks* (1934), *Babes in Toyland* (1934), *George White's 1935 Scandals* (1935), *Escapade* (1935), *Under Your Spell* (1936), *In Old Chicago* (1937), *Wee Willie Winkie* (1937), and *The Grapes of Wrath* (1940).

Maude-Roxby, Roddy (b. 1930) An English character actor who spent most of his career in British television, he provided the voice of the scheming butler Edgar in *The Aristocats* (1970). The London-born actor trained at the Royal College of Art for a career as an artist but became interested in improv theatre and was an early "performance artist" long before the term was used. Maude-Roxby used his comic and improvisation skills at the Royal Court Theatre and in such British television comedy shows as *The Goodies, Snooze* and *Not Only but Also,* as well as in the American series *Rowan and Martin's Laugh-In.* Among his films made in England and the States are *Dangerous Afternoon* (1961), *The Party's Over* (1965), *Greystone: The Legend of Tarzan, Lord of the Apes* (1984), *Plenty* (1985), *White Hunter Black Heart* (1990), *Shadowlands* (1993), and *Unconditional Love* (2002). Although *The Aristocats* is set in France, the fumbling butler-villain Edgar is very British: a dapper dresser and, as voiced by Maude-Roxby, a dry and subtle character. To audiences, he seems to pose little threat because he is so pleasantly ineffective.

McBride, Susan A voice artist with limited credits, she voiced the Big Witch who pops up to give advice and commentary throughout *The Nightmare Before Christmas* (1993). She can also be heard voicing minor characters in the animated movies *The Swan Princess* (1994) and *Mulan* (1998), and in the video *Pocahontas II: Journey to a New World* (1998).

McCann, Chuck (b. 1934) A rotund comic and actor who often played sidekicks on television and in the movies, he voiced Scrooge McDuck's stuffy butler Duckworth in *DuckTales the Movie: The Treasure of the Lost Lamp* (1990). He was born in New York City, the son of a bandleader-singer, and was on the stage and on radio as a child. By the end of his teens, McCann was appearing on television variety shows and even created, wrote, and starred in his own children's shows, including *Far Out Space Nuts, Chuck McCann's Funstuff, Chuck McCann's Laurel and Hardy Show.* and *The Chuck McCann Show.* Among his many television appearances are those in *Bonanza, The Bob Newhart Show, Little House on the Prairie, The Rockford Files, A New Kind of Family, One Day at a Time, Santa Barbara, Knots Landing, Empty Nest, Boston Legal,* and *Sabrina, the Teenage Witch.* McCann's film credits include *The Heart Is a Lonely Hunter* (1968), *Play It as It Lays* (1972), *Herbie Rides Again* (1974), *Silent Movie* (1976), *Foul Play* (1978), *C.H.O.M.P.S.* (1979), *Robin Hood: Men in Tights* (1993), *Dracula: Dead and Loving It* (1995), and *They Call Him Sasquatch* (2003). He has provided voices for many TV cartoon series, such as *C B Bears, Scooby-Doo and Scrappy-Doo, The Get-Along Gang, G.I. Joe, Garfield and Friends, Adventures of the Gummi Bears, The New Adventures of Winnie the Pooh, DuckTales, TailSpin, Attack of the Killer Tomatoes, Where's Waldo?, Iron Man, Fantastic Four,* and *The Powerpuff Girls,* and can be heard in several animated videos and movies, including *Christmas Comes to PacLand* (1982), *G.I. Joe: The Movie* (1987), *DuckTales: Treasure of the Golden Suns* (1987), *Super DuckTales* (1989), and *Mickey's Twice Upon a Christmas* (2004).

McClory, Sean (1924–2003) An Irish character actor from the stage who went on to American films and television, he provided the voices of one of the hounds and some of the reporters in the animated section of *Mary Poppins* (1964). Sean Joseph McClory was born in Dublin, Ireland, and grew up in Galway but as an adult returned to the capital city where he acted with the famous Abbey Theatre for several years. Coming to America after the World War II, he was cast as Irish cops and other types in many Hollywood films, including *The Daughter of Rosie O'Grady* (1950), *Lorna Doone* (1951), *The Desert Fox: The Story of Rommel* (1951), *The Quiet Man* (1952), *What Price Glory* (1952), *Niagara* (1953), *Rogue's March* (1953), *Plunder of the Sun* (1953), *Them!* (1954), *Ring of Fear* (1954), *The Long Gray Line* (1955), *Valley of the Dragons* (1961), *Cheyenne Autumn* (1964), *Follow Me, Boys!* (1966), *The Gnome-Mobile* (1967), *The Happiest Millionaire* (1967), *The Day of the Wolves* (1973), *My Chauffeur* (1986), and *The Dead* (1987). McClory was also very busy on television, appearing in dozens of series such as *Four Star Playhouse*, *Broken Arrow*, *The Californians*, *Alfred Hitchcock Presents*, *Overland Trail*, *Surfside 6*, *Checkmate*, *The Untouchables*, *Bonanza*, *Perry Mason*, *My Favorite Martian*, *Daktari*, *The Monroes*, *Lost in Space*, *Daniel Boone*, *Death Valley Days*, *Little House on the Prairie*, *Battlestar Galactica*, *Simon & Simon*, *Falcon Crest*, and *Murder, She Wrote*.

McClurg, Edie (b. 1951) A child performer who returned to show business as an adult and has appeared in many films and television programs, she did the voices of the palace housekeeper Carlotta in *The Little Mermaid* (1989), the ant physician Doctor Flora in *A Bug's Life* (1998), and the lost mini-van tourist Minny in *Cars* (2006). She was born in Kansas City, Missouri, and at the age of five was singing and dancing professionally as one of the Kansas City Rhythm Kids. McClurg gave up performing to attend Syracuse University and then taught radio at the University of Missouri at Kansas City. While working as a disc jockey she began to do comic improvisations which led to appearances on various television shows such as *Late Night with David Letterman*, *The Richard Pryor Show*, *WKRP in Cincinnati*, *Harper Valley*, *Madame's Place*, *Diff'rent Strokes*, *The Jeffersons*, *Small Wonder*, *Valerie's Family* (aka *The Hogan Family*), *Drexell's Class*, *Melrose Place*, *Married with Children*, *Caroline in the City*, *CSI: Crime Scene Investigation*, *7th Heaven*, and *Days of Our Lives*. McClurg's many film credits include *Carrie* (1976), *Oh, God! Book II* (1980), *Eating Raoul* (1982), *Mr. Mom* (1983), *Ferris Bueller's Day Off* (1986), *Planes, Trains & Automobiles* (1987), *She's Having a Baby* (1988), *A River Runs Through It* (1992), *Natural Born Killers* (1994), and *Flubber* (1997). She can be heard in such TV cartoon series as *The Jetsons*, *The Smurfs*, *TaleSpin*, *Tiny Toon Adventures*, *Darkwing Duck*, *Goof Troop*, *The Addams Family*, *Life with Louie*, *Batman Beyond*, *Clifford the Big Red Dog*, *The Adventures of Jimmy Neutron: Boy Genius*, *American Dragon: Jake Long*, *Higglytown Heroes*, and *The Life & Times of Tim*, as well as in the animated movies and videos *The Secret of Nimh* (1982), *Christmas Every Day* (1987), *Kiki's Delivery Service* (1989), *Tiny Toons Spring Break* (1994), *Casper: A Spirited Beginning* (1997), *The Rugrats Movie* (1998), *The Little Mermaid II: Return to the Sea* (2000), *Home on the Range* (2004), *Scooby-Doo! Pirates Ahoy!* (2006), *Holidaze: The Christmas That Almost Didn't Happen* (2006), and *Toot & Puddle: I'll Be Home for Christmas* (2006).

McDonald, Kevin (b. 1961) A high-pitched voice artist for television cartoons who also writes several series, he supplied the voice of the Councilwoman's agent Pleakley in *Lilo & Stitch* (2002). Kevin Hamilton McDonald was born in Montreal, Canada, and briefly attended Humber College before becoming a stand-up comic. Teaming with actor-comic Dave Foley, the twosome found success as a comedy team and then as the comic improv group The Kids in the Hall which had its own television program as well as movies and videos. McDonald has appeared in a handful of films, most memorably *Brain Candy* (2002), but is busier doing voices for such animated series as *Johnny Bravo*, *The Angry Beavers*, *Invader ZIM*, *Catscratch*, *Back at the Barnyard*, *The Penguins of Madagascar*, and *WordGirl*. He reprised his Agent Pleakley in the videos *Stitch! The Movie!* (2003), *Stitch's Great Escape* (2004), *Lilo & Stitch 2: Stitch Has a Glitch* (2005), *Leroy & Stitch* (2006), and the TV series *Lilo & Stitch*. In addition to *The Kids in the Hall* and *The Kids in the Hall: Death Comes to Town*, McDonald has appeared on the television series *Friends*, *NewsRadio*, *Seinfeld*, *Ellen*, *The Drew Carey Show*, *That 70's Show*, *Grounded for Life*, *Arrested Development*, and *Less Than Kind*.

McDonough, Andrew (b. 1994) A child performer with a handful of voice credits, he provided the voice of Danny, grown-up Wendy's young son, in *Return to Never Land* (2002). A native of West Covina, California, he was five years old when he made his debut as the Poor Boy in the animated video *Mickey's Once Upon a Christmas* (1999), followed by small roles in the video sequel *Lady and the Tramp II: Scamps's Adventure* (2001) and the movie *Finding Nemo* (2003).

McDowall, Roddy (1928–1998) A British child star of Hollywood who grew up and found a variety of roles in theatre and films, he provided the voice of the stage-struck ant Mr. Soil in *A Bug's Life* (1998), his last of over one hundred movies. He was born Roderick Andrew Anthony Jude

McDowall in London, the son of a merchant mariner, and appeared in a few British films before he was evacuated to the States in 1940 to escape the London bombings. He became a child star with his sensitive performance in *How Green Was My Valley* (1941) and remained popular because of such hits as *My Friend Flicka* (1943), *Lassie Come Home* (1943), *The White Cliffs of Dover* (1944), and *Kidnapped* (1948). McDowall started his television career in 1951 and two years later did his first Broadway play, returning to the stage for such successes as *No Time for Sergeants* (1955), *Compulsion* (1957), and *Camelot* (1960). Although he rarely played leading roles, McDowall was consistently seen on the large and small screen. He voiced the friendly robot V.I.N.CENT (Vital Information Necessary CENTralized) in the live-action Disney film *The Black Hole* (1979), he can be heard in the animated television specials *Cricket on the Hearth* (1967) and *The Return of the King* (1980), and in the series *The Wizard, Camp Candy, The Pirates of Dark Water, Darkwing Duck, Swat Kats: The Radical Squadron, Batman, Gargoyles, Pinky and the Brain, The New Batman Adventures, Superman,* and *Godzilla: The Series*. McDowall was a highly respected photographer and published several books of his work.

McDowell, Malcolm (b. 1943)   The charismatic British film actor who can be frightfully mesmerizing on the screen, he provided the voice of the sinister villain Dr. Calico on the television show in *Bolt* (2008). He was born Malcolm John Taylor in Leeds, England, the son of a pub owner, and studied acting at the London Academy of Music and Art. After appearing in small roles in a handful of British films, McDowell became famous as the restless teenager Mick in *If...* (1968) and secured his fame as the futuristic gang leader Alex in *A Clockwork Orange* (1971). Among his over one hundred other movie credits are *O Lucky Man!* (1973), *Caligula* (1979), *Time After Time* (1979), *Cat People* (1982), *Night Train to Venice* (1993), *Dangerous Indiscretion* (1995), *Fatal Pursuit* (1998), *My Life So Far* (1999), *Love Lies Bleeding* (1999), *Between Strangers* (2002), *Bye Bye Benjamin* (2006), *Doomsday* (2008), and *Halloween II* (2009). He has acted in many American and British television series and specials and in the 1990s started voicing animated series such as *Spider-Man, Wing Commander Academy, The Magic School Bus, Superman, Teen Titans, The Grim Adventures of Billy and Mandy, Justice League, Phineas and Ferb, Metalocalypse,* and *South Park*. McDowell reprised his Dr. Calico in the movie short *Super Rhino* (2009) and voiced other animated videos, including *Superman: The Last Son of Krypton* (1996), *Dinotopia: Quest for the Ruby Sunstone* (2005), and *Robot Chicken: Star Wars* (2007). Biography: *Malcolm McDowell on Screen*, Chris Wade (2009).

McElroy, Niki   The actress who voiced the Mother lounging by the pool aboard the spaceship *Axiom* in *WALL-E* (2008), she has appeared in the films *The Hustle* (2008), *The Cellar* (2009), *Chain Letter* (2010), and *He Who Finds a Wife 2: Thou Shalt Not Covet* (2010).

McGarry, Dara (b. 1964)   A production assistant at Disney who is also an actress on occasion, she voiced Hollywood Abby in *Chicken Little* (2005) as well as the prospective adoptive mother Mrs. Harrington and the cool Receptionist at InventCo in *Meet the Robinsons* (2007). The Nashville, Tennessee, native made her television debut in the TV-movie *A Time to Triumph* (1986) and appeared as a continuing character in the series *7 Deadly Hollywood Sins* in 2006. McGarry can also be heard in *Bolt* (2008) and its video spinoff *Super Rhino* (2009).

McGoohan, Patrick (1928–2009)   A handsome Irish-British-American actor who found success in all media, his last acting job was providing the voice of the dying spaceship pilot Billy Bones in *Treasure Planet* (2002). He was born in Queens, New York, to Irish immigrants who returned to Ireland soon after he was born. McGoohan grew up in County Leitrim, Ireland, and Sheffield, England, making his professional acting debut at the Sheffield Repertory Company. After appearing in dozens of stage productions throughout England, he made his television debut as Parnell in the British series *You Are There* in 1954. Other series followed but wide recognition did not come until he played John Drake in *Danger Man*; he continued the character in the American television series *Secret Agent*, making him a popular favorite on both sides of the Atlantic. McGoohan's other television credits include *ITV Play of the Week, Walt Disney's Wonderful World of Color, Rafferty, Columbo,* and *Murder, She Wrote,* but he is perhaps best remembered as inmate Number Six in *The Prisoner*, a series he also produced and sometimes directed. McGoohan made many movies in both England and Hollywood, among them *The Dark Avenger* (1955), *I Am a Camera* (1955), *Zarak* (1956), *Hell Drivers* (1957), *High Tide at Noon* (1957), *The Gypsy and the Gentleman* (1958), *Two Living, One Dead* (1961), *Walk in the Shadow* (1962), *The Quare Fellow* (1962), *Dr. Syn, Alias the Scarecrow* (1963), *The Three Lives of Thomasina* (1964), *Ice Station Zebra* (1968), *Mary, Queen of Scots* (1971), *Silver Streak* (1976), *Escape from Alcatraz* (1979), *Baby: Secret of the Lost Legend* (1985), *Braveheart* (1995), *A Time to Kill* (1996), *The Phantom* (1996), and *Hysteria* (1998), as well as several made-for-TV movies. Biography: *Patrick McGoohan: Danger Man or Prisoner?*, Roger Langley (2007).

McGovern, Johnny (b. 1941) A child performer who worked for a decade in movies and television then retired from acting, he voiced one of the Raccoon Twins, members of the Lost Boys, in *Peter Pan* (1953). McGovern's film credits include *Tumbleweed Trail* (1946), *Night Unto Night* (1949), *Tea for Two* (1950), *When I Grow Up* (1951), *Room for One More* (1952), *Singin' in the Rain* (1952), and *The Pride of St. Louis* (1952). He also appeared on episodes of the television series *Waterfront*, *The Loretta Young Show*, and *Studio 57*.

McGovern, Terence (b. 1942) A busy television and movie actor who can also be heard on many video games and cartoons, he voiced the haphazard, featherbrained duck pilot Launchpad McQuack in *DuckTales the Movie: The Treasure of the Lost Lamp* (1990). He was born in Berkeley, California, the son of an actor, and grew up in Pittsburgh, Pennsylvania, where he attended Duquesne University and began his radio career on a local station. Moving to Los Angeles to work at another station, he started acting in films, making his voiceover debut with *THX 1138* (1971) and appearing in such movies as *American Graffiti* (1973), *Smile* (1975), *Americathon* (1979), *The Incredible Shrinking Woman* (1981), *Innerspace* (1987), and *Mrs. Doubtfire* (1993). McGovern also was seen in many television series, including *Fernwood Tonight*, *Happy Days*, *Lou Grant*, *Newhart*, *Silver Spoons*, *Charlie & Co.*, *Cagney & Lacey*, and *My Sister Sam*. He first voiced the buffoonish Launchpad in the TV cartoon series *DuckTales* and reprised the character in the series *Darkwing Duck* and *Raw Toonage*, and in the videos *DuckTales: The Treasure of the Golden Suns* (1987), *Super DuckTales* (1989), and *DuckTales: The Quest for Gold* (1990). McGovern can also be heard in other cartoon series, such as *Moondreamers*, *The Transformers*, and *Mighty Mouse, the New Adventures*, as well as in the animated videos *Daniel and the Lion's Den* (1986) and six subsequent Biblical videos.

McGowan, Mickie A voice artist who has provided many voices for minor characters in Disney and Pixar projects, she played Mrs. Phillips, the mother of the sadistic boy Sid, in *Toy Story* (1995), the Mom at the yard sale in *Toy Story 2* (1999), and the sympathetic police officer Edith in *Up* (2009). She was born Maryanne McGowan in Culver City, California, the daughter of Robert A. McGowan (1901–1955) who wrote and directed some of the *Our Gang* comedy shorts. She began voicing animated characters in 1983 for the TV cartoon series *The New Scooby and Scrappy-Doo Show*. By the late 1980s she was working for Disney and providing voices for such animated films as *The Little Mermaid* (1989), *Beauty and the Beast* (1991), *Aladdin* (1992), *The Hunchback of Notre Dame* (1996), *Hercules* (1997), *A Bug's Life* (1998), *The Emperor's New Groove* (2000), *Monsters, Inc.* (2001), *Lilo & Stitch* (2002), *Treasure Planet* (2002), *Brother Bear* (2003), *Home on the Range* (2004), *Cars* (2006), *WALL-E* (2008), and *Toy Story 3* (2010). Among her other animated film and video credits are *An American Tail: Fievel Goes West* (1991), *Porco Rosso* (1992), *Theodore Rex* (1995), *Pocahontas II: Journey to a New World* (1998), *The Iron Giant* (1999), *Spirited Away* (2001), *Osmosis Jones* (2001), *Ice Age: The Meltdown* (2006), *Happily N'Ever After* (2007), *Surf's Up* (2007), *Horton Hears a Who!* (2008), *Ponyo* (2008), *Tokyo Mater* (2008), and *Cloudy with a Chance of Meatballs* (2009).

McHugh, Thomas (b. 1966) A voice artist working mostly in television, he voiced the schoolboy hero Doug Funnie in *Doug's 1st Movie* (1999) as well as his imaginary super hero Quailman and the character of Lincoln. He was born in Chicago and attended the American Academy of Dramatic Arts in New York. After getting a role in the movie *Mad Dog Coll* (1992), McHugh was cast as the title character in the animated series *Disney's Doug*. He reprised the role in *Doug's 1st Movie* which was intended as a video but instead went to the big screen. McHugh can also be heard in the TV cartoon series *PB&J Otter* and appeared in an episode of *Law & Order*.

McIntire, John (1907–1991) A rough-looking, gruff-sounding character actor ideal for crusty characters in Westerns and crime melodramas, he voiced the elderly orphanage cat Rufus in *The Rescuers* (1977) and the Grumpy Badger in *The Fox and the Hound* (1981). John Herrick McIntire was born in Spokane, Washington, the son of a lawyer, and grew up in rural Montana where he rode horses, busted broncos, and did other cowboy activities that would later serve him well on the screen. He began his career on the radio, his deep, gravely voice useful for many characters and as an announcer for such programs as *March of Time*. Relocating to Hollywood in the late 1940s, he was cast in supporting roles in over sixty movies, including *Call Northside 777* (1948), *Scene of the Crime* (1949), *Winchester '73* (1950), *The Asphalt Jungle* (1950), *The Mississippi Gambler* (1953), *The Far Country* (1954), *The Kentuckian* (1955), *The Tin Star* (1957), *The Light in the Forest* (1958), *Psycho* (1960), *Elmer Gantry* (1960), *Summer and Smoke* (1961), *Herbie Rides Again* (1974), *Rooster Cogburn* (1975), and *Turner & Hooch* (1989). McIntire was kept just as busy on television where he appeared in dozens of series such as *G.E. True Theatre, Naked City, The Virginian, Peter Gunn, Alfred Hitchcock Presents, The Americans, Laramie, Wagon Train, Bonanza, The F.B.I., Young Maverick, Shirley, The Love Boat, St. Elsewhere,* and *Trapper John, M.D.* The character of the aged cat Rufus in *The Rescuers* was modeled after veteran Disney animator Ollie Johnson. McIntire's crusty but warm vocals make Rufus a wise and endearing character who gives hope to the sad orphan Penny. McIntire was married to actress Jeanette Nolan who also is heard in *The Rescuers*.

McKennon, Dal (1919–2009) A versatile character actor who acted in many television Westerns, he supplied the voices of the mongrel pound dog Toughy and the Professor in the park in *Lady and the Tramp* (1955), the Owl who dances with Princess Aurora in *Sleeping Beauty* (1959), a penguin, fox, reporter, and other minor roles in the animated sequence in *Mary Poppins* (1964), and the Fisherman Bear in the cartoon section of *Bedknobs and Broomsticks* (1971). He was born Dallas Raymond McKennon in La Grange, Oregon, and began voicing animated shorts in 1951, most memorably as Buzz in a series of Woody Woodpecker cartoons. In the early 1950s he also hosted the Los Angeles children's television show *Space Funnies/Capt. Jet* which brought him to the attention of the movie studios. McKennon appeared in such movies as *Son of Flubber* (1963), *House of the Damned* (1963), *The Misadventures of Merlin Jones* (1964), *7 Faces of Dr. Lao* (1964), *Daniel Boone: Frontier Rider* (1966), *The Cat from Outer Space* (1978), *Hot Lead and Cold Feet* (1978), *Mystery Mansion* (1983), and *Frozen Assets* (1992), and he acted in many television series, including *The Untouchables, 87th Precinct, Gunsmoke, The Virginian, Wagon Train, The Rifleman, Bonanza, The Andy Griffith Show, Daniel Boone,* and *Cannon*. Among the many TV cartoon series he voiced are *The Woody Woodpecker Show, Q. T. Hush, The Famous Adventures of Mr. Magoo, The Gumby Show,* and *Archie's Fun House,* and he can be heard in the animated movies *One Hundred and One Dalmatians* (1961), *Winnie the Pooh and the Honey Tree* (1966), *Treasure Island* (1973), *Oliver Twist* (1974), *Journey Back to Oz* (1974), *The Adventures of Mark Twain* (1986), and *The Puppetoon Movie* (1987). McKennon provided recorded voices for the Disney theme park attractions Big Thunder Mountain Railroad, Country Bears Jamboree, and The American Adventure in which he is heard as Ben Franklin.

McLeish, John (1916–1968) A Disney animator and writer who had such a serious voice that he was used to do the tongue-in-cheek narration for the "how to" Goofy cartoon shorts. McLeish first worked for Disney on the story development for the "Rite of Spring" segment of *Fantasia* (1940). That same year the animators were creating the short *Goofy's Glider* and thought McLeish's highly educated and dignified voice would contrast with Goofy's slapstick adventures. Without telling McLeish about the shenanigans, the animators had him record the narration straight. The effect was so successful that McLeish narrated the "How to Ride a Horse" section of *The Reluctant Dragon* (1941) and a dozen subsequent cartoon shorts including *The Art of Skiing* (1941), *The Art of Self Defense* (1941), *The Olympic Champ* (1942), *How to Swim* (1942), *How to Be a Sailor* (1944), and *Goofy Gymnastics* (1949). He voiced the Officer in *Donald Gets Drafted* (1942), Pegleg Pete in *Bellboy Donald* (1942), Professor Small in *Professor Small and Mr. Tall* (1943), and Jupiter and Vulcan in *Trombone Trouble* (1944). McLeish can also be heard narrating *Dumbo* (1941) and as the stern Prosecutor in "The Wind in the Willows" section of the animated double bill *The Adventures of Ichabod and Mr. Toad* (1949). McLeish sometimes used the name John Ployardt for his voice work.

McShane, Michael (b. 1955) An improv comic who has played wisecracking supporting characters in films and on television, he provided the voices of the Eastern European pill bugs Tuck and Roll in *A Bug's Life* (1998) and the shipmate Hands in *Treasure Planet* (2002). He was born in Boston and grew up in Kansas before attending San Joaquin College and the University of California Berkeley. When McShane went to England for part of his studies, he was accepted into London improv groups and ended up on the British television program *Whose Line Is It Anyway?* He also performed on stage in Great Britain before going to Hollywood and making such films as *Tucker: The Man and His Dream* (1988), *Robin Hood: Prince of Thieves* (1991), and *Tom and Huck* (1995). McShane has appeared in such American television series as *Brotherly Love, Seinfeld, Caroline in the City, 3rd Rock from the Sun, Malcolm in the Middle,* and *The Drew Carey Show,* and has voiced such cartoon series as *Avenger Penguins, Spawn, Clerks, King of the Hill,* and *Dave the Barbarian*. He can also be heard in the animated movies and videos *Balto* (1995), *Princess Mononoke* (1997), *Thunder Pig* (2001), *Thru the Moebius Strip* (2005), *Holly Hobbie and Friends: Christmas Wishes* (2006), *Happily N'Ever After* (2006), and *Holly Hobbie and Friends: Secret Adventures* (2007).

Means, Russell (b. 1939) A Native American actor, musician, and spokesman for his people, he supplied the voice of Powhatan, the tribal chief and

Pocahontas' father, in *Pocahontas* (1995). He was born on the Pine Ridge Indian Reservation in South Dakota, a member of the Oglala-Lakota Sioux tribe, and grew up in San Francisco. Starting in the 1960s, Means became an activist for Indian rights, participating in the takeover of Alcatraz Island in 1969, the demonstration at Mt. Rushmore and the seizing of the Mayflower II in 1970, and the famous occupation of Wounded Knee in 1973. Means has been one of the prominent leaders of the American Indian Movement (AIM) and has been involved in controversial politics and humanitarian causes all his life. He made his screen debut as Chief Chingachgook in *The Last of the Mohicans* (1992), followed by such films as *Natural Born Killers* (1994), *Wagons East* (1994), *Windrunner* (1995), *Song of Hiawatha* (1997), *Wild River* (1998), *Thomas and the Magic Railroad* (2000), *Cowboy Up* (2001), *29 Palms* (2002), *Black Cloud* (2004), *Looks Twice* (2005), *Pathfinder* (2007), *Unearthed* (2007), and *Rez Bomb* (2008), as well as the TV-movies *Buffalo Girls* (1995) and *Black Cat Run* (1998). Means also appeared in the television series *Touched by an Angel*, *Walker: Texas Ranger*, *Profiler*, *Remember WENN*, *Nash Bridges*, *Family Law*, *Curb Your Enthusiasm*, and *Into the West*. He reprised his Powhatan in the video *Pocahontas II: Journey to a New World* (1998) and voiced the animated video *Turok: Son of Stone* (2007). Means has also written and recorded songs about the history of Native Americans. Autobiography: *Where White Men Fear to Tread* (1996).

Mercer, Jack (1910–1984) A prolific cartoonist, scriptwriter, and voice artist who was the voice of Popeye for nearly fifty years, he supplied the voice for the talking Rough House Statue at Pleasure Island in *Pinocchio* (1940). He was born in New York City, the son of actors, and put on the stage as a child, but he later chose to become an artist. While working as an in-between artist at the Fleischer Studio, Mercer often imitated different workers in the office as well as the in-house actor Billy Costello who voiced Popeye. When Costello became too difficult to work with, producer Lou Fleischer replaced him with Mercer in 1935 and he continued to voice Popeye for hundreds of film shorts and television episodes. Mercer continued to write cartoon scripts and work on animation even as he also voiced Popeye's father Poopdeck Pappy, his nephews, his friend Wimpy, and many other characters. He was married for a time to actress Margie Hines who was the voice of Olive Oyl. Mercer's role in *Pinocchio* is small but easy to distinguish. As the runaway boys dash about Pleasure Island, a huge statue of a ruffian (looking not unlike Popeye) growls out words of invitation, urging the boys to enter the attraction where they can destroy things. The unmistakable voice of Mercer serves as both a welcome and a foreshadowing for the dark fate awaiting the boys.

Merin, Eda Reiss (1913–1998) A character actress whose career was mostly in television, she voiced the Orddu, the tallest of the three Witches of Morva, in *The Black Caldron* (1985). The native New Yorker made her Broadway debut in 1944 and her first movie in 1947, followed by such films as *Knock on Any Door* (1949) *Where the Sidewalk Ends* (1950), *Don't Bother to Knock* (1952), *The Shrike* (1955), *Hester Street* (1975), *To Be or Not to Be* (1983), *Ghostbusters* (1984), *Turner & Hooch* (1989), *Don't Tell Mom the Babysitter's Dead* (1991), and *For Better or Worse* (1995). Much of her career was in television appearing in drama specials and such series as *Schlitz Playhouse*, *The DuPont Show of the Month*, *East Side/West Side*, *Charlie's Angels*, *Baretta*, *The White Shadow*, *Family Ties*, *St. Elsewhere*, *Hill Street Blues*, *Mr. Belvedere*, *ER*, *Nurses*, and *Murder, She Wrote*. Merin often returned to the New York stage, acting in the Broadway productions of *A Far Country* (1961), *The Good Woman of Setzuan* (1970), *A Doll's House* (1971), and *Hedda Gabler* (1971).

Mertens, Tim A film editor and sound engineer, he provided the voice of the pigeon Bobby with the thick New York City accent in *Bolt* (2008). Mertens was sound editor on such animated television series as *The Ren & Stimpy Show*, *Darkwing Duck*, *Goof Troop*, and *Aladdin*. Among his editing credits are *Bolt* and *Brother Bear* (2009); his only other acting credit was providing voices for some minor characters in the latter and in *Tangled* (2010).

Metcalf, Laurie (b. 1955) A multi-talented actress who has won acclaim for her work on the stage, in movies, and on television, she supplied the voice of Andy's Mom in all three *Toy Story* films, Jim Hawkins' mother Sarah who runs the inn in *Treasure Planet* (2002), and the kooky science fair judge Dr. Lucille Krunklehorn in *Meet the Robinsons* (2007). Lauren Elizabeth Metcalf was born in Carbondale, Illinois, and raised in Edwardsville where her father worked at Southern Illinois University and her mother was a librarian. After attending Illinois State University, she co-founded Chicago's famous Steppenwolf Theatre Company and throughout her career often returned to act there. It was the Steppenwolf production of *Balm in Gilead* in 1984 that first brought her to the New York stage and she would later act is such Off Broadway plays as *Bodies, Rest and Motion* (1986), *Educating Rita* (1987), and *A Lie of the Mind* (2010), as well as on Broadway in *My Thing of Love* (1995),

November (2008), and *Brighton Beach Memoirs* (2009). Metcalf made her television debut on *Saturday Night Live* and went on to perform in many series, including *3rd Rock from the Sun*, *Norm*, *Frasier*, *Monk*, *Grey's Anatomy*, *Desperate Housewives*, and *Easy Money*, but she is most remembered as Roseanne's sister Jackie on *Roseanne*. Among her many film credits are *Desperately Seeking Susan* (1985), *Stars and Bars* (1988), *Uncle Buck* (1989), *Pacific Heights* (1990), *JFK* (1991), *Leaving Las Vegas* (1995), *Scream 2* (1997), *Bulworth* (1998), *Runaway Bride* (1999), *Fun with Dick and Jane* (2005), *Georgia Rule* (2007), and *Stop-Loss* (2008). Metcalf has done voices for the TV cartoon series *Duckman: Private Dick/Family Man*, *King of the Hill*, and *Life with Louie*.

Metchik, Aaron Michael (b. 1980) A child actor on television who continues as an adult to perform and is also an acting coach in California, he voiced the Greek youth Ithicles who taunts the teenage Hercules in *Hercules* (1997). Metchik made a notable television debut as Steven on the series *The Torkelsons*, then went on to appear on such shows as *Boy Meets World*, *Party of Five*, and *The Practice*. He was in a handful of movies, including *Trading Mom* (1994), *The Baby-Sitters Club* (1995), *Feeling Minnesota* (1996), *Pumpkin Hill* (1999), and *10 Years Later* (2010), and can be heard in the animated films and videos *The Magic Paintbrush* (1992), *Christmas in Oz* (1996), *Who Stole Santa?* (1996), *The Nome Prince and the Magic Belt* (1996). *Toto Lost in New York* (1996), *Virtual Oz* (1996), and *Journey Beneath the Sea* (1997).

Meyer, Carla A Hollywood dialect coach who has worked on over fifty films, she provided the voices of Cody's Mother and the kangaroo Faloo who alerts Cody and the animals about the eagle being captured in *The Rescuers Down Under* (1990). Among Meyer's dialect credits are *The Milagro Beanfield War* (1988), *Dead Again* (1991), *JFK* (1991), *A River Runs Through It* (1992), *The Piano* (1993), *Batman Forever* (1995), *Nixon* (1995), *Air Force One* (1997), *The Horse Whisperer* (1998), *Erin Brockovich* (2000), *Pearl Harbor* (2001), *The Road to Perdition* (2002), *Frida* (2002), *Pirates of the Caribbean: Dead Man's Chest* (2006), *Angels & Demons* (2009), *Avatar* (2009), and *Alice in Wonderland* (2010). Her only other acting credit is the TV-movie *Sister Margaret and the Saturday Night Ladies* (1987).

Midler, Bette (b. 1945) The sometimes outrageous, often bawdy, and always fascinating singer-actress with a big voice and even bigger emotions, she has frequently left the world of pop music to makes movies, as with *Oliver & Company* (1988) in which she provided the speaking and singing voice for the pampered poodle Georgette. Bette Davis Midler was born in Honolulu and educated at the University of Hawaii at Manoa before going to New York where she was cast as a replacement on Broadway in *Fiddler on the Roof* in 1967. She jump started her career by getting noticed singing in a gay bathhouse and a record contract followed, making her a nationally known pop singer by 1972. Midler made an auspicious film debut in *The Rose* (1979), followed by such films as *Down and Out in Beverly Hills* (1986), *Ruthless People* (1986), *Beaches* (1988), *For the Boys* (1991). *The First Wives Club* (1996), and *The Women* (2008). She was one of the hosts in Disney's *Fantasia/2000* (1999) and provided the voice for another feline, Kitty Galore, in *Cats & Dogs: The Revenge of Kitty Galore* (2010). In addition to many television appearances, including the television version of *Gypsy* (1993), she has given concerts across the country and on Broadway, and has made several popular recordings. The self-absorbed poodle Georgette in *Oliver & Company* is a highly satiric character that illustrates all the cliches of a spoiled pet. Yet Midler's vocals make the dog surprisingly likable. Georgette is something of a cousin to Peggy Lee's Peg in *Lady and the Tramp* and Midler's rendition of the lazy ballad "Perfect Isn't Easy" is a similarly comic treat. Autobiography: *Bette Midler: A View from a Broad* (1981); biographies: *Bette Midler: Still Divine*, Mark Bego (2002); *Bette: An Intimate Biography of Bette Midler*, George Mair (1996).

Millar, Lee (1888–1941) A radio actor who was seen in only two movies, he provided the barks, howls, and yelps of the canine Pluto in a dozen Disney cartoon shorts between 1939 and 1941. He was born in Oakland, California, and spent his career in radio doing voices and sound effects. Millar had a talent for imitating different animals and was cast as a Bird Imitator in the film *Make Way for Tomorrow* (1937). He first voiced Pluto in *Beach Picnic* (1939) and reprised the role in such cartoon favorites as *The Pointer* (1939), *Bone Trouble* (1940), *Pluto's Dream House* (1940), *Window Cleaners* (1940), and *Pluto's Playmate* (1941). Right before his death he played a minor role in the film *Nobody's Children* (1940). Millar's wife was voice actress Verna Felton and their son Lee Jr., also did voices for Disney.

Millar, Lee (Jr.) (1924–1980) A television actor of the 1950s and 1960s, he provided the voices of Lady's human master "Jim Dear" and the Dog Catcher in *Lady and the Tramp* (1955). Lee Carson Millar, Jr., was born in Vancouver, Canada, the son of a radio actor Lee Millar and voice artist Verna Felton, and made his television debut on *The*

George Burns and Gracie Allen Show in 1952. Among his other TV series are *I Love Lucy, December Bride, Father Knows Best, Dragnet, The Donna Reed Show, Dennis the Menace, Twilight Zone, The Jack Benny Program, Combat!, Voyage to the Bottom of the Sea,* and *The Mothers-in-Law*.

Miller, Beatrice A child actress with a variety of credits over a short period of time, she provided the voice of Andy's younger sister Molly in *Toy Story 3* (2010). Miller has appeared in the live-action shorts *Teddy Grams* (2008) and *Hens and Chicks* (2010), the films *Confessions of a Shopaholic* (2009) and *Tell Tale* (2009), the TV-movie *Yes, Virginia* (2009), and did voices for the cartoon series *The Wonder Pets* and the animated feature *Ice Age: Dawn of the Dinosaurs* (2009).

Miller, Marvin (1913–1985) An actor with a full-bodied, baritone voice who narrated dozens of films and television shows, he was the Narrator for *Sleeping Beauty* (1959). He was born Marvin Elliott Mueller in St. Louis, Missouri, and educated locally at Washington University before starting his career on local radio. Soon Miller was voicing national radio shows in Hollywood and appearing, usually as heavies and often as Asian characters, in movies such as *Blood on the Sun* (1945), *Johnny Angel* (1945), *The Phantom Thief* (1946), *Dead Reckoning* (1947), *Smuggler's Island* (1951), *The Golden Horde* (1951), *Off Limits* (1953), *The Shanghai Story* (1954), *The Story of Mankind* (1957), *When the Girls Take Over* (1962), *Where Does It Hurt?* (1972), *I Wonder Who's Killing Her Now* (1975), *Kiss Daddy Goodbye* (1981), *Swing Shift* (1984), and *Hell Squad* (1986). Yet in most of his seventy-plus movies he was the narrator or an offscreen voice, such as Robby the Robot in the cult film *Forbidden Planet* (1956). Miller narrated many television shows as well, and was also seen in such series as *Mysteries of Chinatown, Space Patrol, The Adventures of Ozzie and Harriet, Bat Masterson, Perry Mason, The Green Hornet, Insight, This Is the Life, The New Adventures of Wonder Woman,* and *Love, American Style,* yet he is mostly remembered as Michael Anthony, the man who handed out checks for $1 million on the series *The Millionaire* for five years. He can be heard doing voices for such TV cartoon series as *Jonny Quest, The Famous Adventures of Mr. Magoo, Here Comes the Grump,* and *The Pink Panther Laugh and a Half Hour and a Half Show,* as well as the animated shorts *Christopher Crumpet* (1953), *Gerald McBoing-Boing's Symphony* (1953), *Ballet-Oop* (1954), *Fudget's Budget* (1954), *How Now Boing Boing* (1954), *Christopher Crumpet's Playmate* (1955), *The Rise of Duton Lang* (1955), *Gerald McBoing! Boing! on Planet Moo* (1956), *Our Mr. Sun* (1956), *French Feud* (1969), *Pierre and the Cottage Cheese* (1969), *Scratch a Tiger* (1970), *The Froggy Froggy Duo* (1970), *Robin Goodhood* (1970), and *Fantastic Planet* (1973), as well as several *Inspector Clouseau* shorts. Miller also recorded many books for children, including some popular Dr. Seuss stories.

Miller, Roger (1936–1992) The unique songwriter-singer whose novelty songs mix country-western, scat-singing, and honky-tonk sounds in a laid-back manner, he supplied the voice of the red rooster Alan-a-Dale, the lute-strumming troubadour in *Robin Hood* (1973), for which he wrote and sang three songs. Roger Dean Miller was born in Fort Worth, Texas, grew up in Oklahoma, and served in the military before embarking on a career singing his own songs. By the late 1950s he was nationally known from recordings, concerts, and television appearances. In addition to his best-selling records such as "King of the Road," "Dang Me," and "England Swings," Miller also wrote hits songs for other artists, such as Jim Reeves' "Billy Bayou," Alan Jackson's "Tall, Tall Trees," Ricky Van Shelton's "Don't We All Have the Right," and Brooks & Dunn's "Husbands and Wives." He also wrote the country-flavored score for the Broadway musical *Big River* (1985). Miller acted in small roles in the television series *Daniel Boone; Quincy, M.E.; Love, American Style;* and *Murder, She Wrote,* and he can be heard in the animated videos *Nestor, the Long-Eared Christmas Donkey* (1977) and *The Trolls and the Christmas Express* (1981), and he narrated both the television series and movie *Lucky Luke* (1991). Miller's songs can be heard in over fifty movies and television shows. Biography: *Ain't Got No Cigarettes: Memories of Music Legend Roger Miller,* Lyle E. Style (2005).

Miller-Zarneke, Tracey A production manager with Disney Studios, she supplied the voice of Lizzy, the spooky elementary school student with the fire ants exhibit at the science fair, in *Meet the Robinsons* (2007), her only voice credit. She has worked on the films *The Emperor's New Groove* (2000), *Chicken Little* (2005), *Meet the Robinsons,* and *Happy Holidays* (2008).

Ming-Na (b. 1963) A strikingly beautiful Asian American actress of television and films, she provided the speaking voice of the warrior heroine Fa Mulan in *Mulan* (1998). She was born Ming-Na Wen on the Pacific island of Macau, lived briefly in Hong Kong, then at the age of four her family moved to Queens, New York, and then to Pittsburgh, Pennsylvania. There she studied theatre at Carnegie Mellon University before making her television debut on the locally-produced *Mr. Rogers Neighborhood* in 1985. Ming-Na made her first film in 1992 and found recognition the next year in *The Joy Luck Club* (1993), followed by such movies as *Terminal Voyage* (1994), *Street Fighter* (1994), *One Night Stand* (1997), *12 Bucks* (1998), *Teddy Bears' Picnic* (2002), *Push* (2009), and *BoyBand* (2010). Among her many television credits are the series *All-American Girl*, *The Single Guy*, *Law & Order: Special Victims Unit*, *ER*, *Vanished*, *George Lopez*, *Boston Legal*, *Two and a Half Men*, and *SGU Stargate Universe*. Mulan is not only the first Asian heroine for Disney animation but also one of the most independent and strong-willed of all Disney women. She has an undiminished sense of family pride, which is part of her Chinese heritage, but she also has a great deal of self-confidence and independent spirit, which is not typical for the character of traditional Chinese women. That makes Mulan very modern, even though she is based on a centuries-old legend. Ming-Na reprised her Mulan in the videos *Mulan II* (2004) and *The World of Mulan* (2005), and in the TV cartoon series *House of Mouse*. She can be heard in other animated series such as *Happily Ever After: Fairy Tales for Every Child*, *Spawn*, *The Adventures of Jimmy Neutron: Boy Genius*, *Robot Chicken*, and *The Batman*, as well as the videos *Spawn 3: Ultimate Battle* (1999), *Aki's Dream* (2001), and *Final Fantasy: The Spirits Within* (2001).

Moder, Mary (1905–1993) A singer who only appeared in one film, she provided the speaking and singing voice of the Little Pig who plays the fiddle in the classic short *The Three Little Pigs* (1933) where she helped introduce the hit song "Who's Afraid of the Big Bad Wolf?" She was born Mary Ellen Fritzlen in rural Nebraska and became a Hollywood studio singer heard on soundtracks, only appearing in the movie musical *The Harvey Girls* (1946). Moder reprised her Fiddler Pig in the cartoon sequels *The Big Bad Wolf* (1934), *Three Little Wolves* (1936), *The Practical Pig* (1939), and *The Thrifty Pig* (1941).

Mohr, Gerald (1914–1968) A prolific television actor with a smooth, appealing voice who appeared in over 300 episodes of television series between 1949 and his premature death in 1968, he narrated the "Baby Weems" section of *The Reluctant Dragon* (1941) and also voiced the Studio Security Guard in that movie. He was born in New York City and as a teenager was on the radio, getting the attention of Orson Welles who made Mohr a member of his Mercury Theatre on radio and on stage. After serving in World War II, Mohr found success on radio and then in the 1950s on television. Among the dozens of series he either narrated or acted in are *The Lone Ranger*, *My Friend Irma*, *I Love Lucy*, *Foreign Intrigue*, *Climax!*, *The Loretta Young Show*, *Schlitz Playhouse*, *Love That Jill*, *Wanted: Dead or Alive*, *Rawhide*, *Tightrope*, *Sugarfoot*, *Johnny Ringo*, *The Red Skelton Hour*, *The Deputy*, *Overland Trail*, *Harrigan and Son*, *Bat Masterson*, *Maverick*, *Outlaws*, *77 Sunset Strip*, *Ripcord*, *The Jack Benny Program*, *Bronco*, *Hawaiian Eye*, *The Man from U.N.C.L.E.*, *The Rogues*, *Burke's Law*. *Death Valley Days*, *Perry Mason*, *The Girl from U.N.C.L.E.*, *Laredo*, *Bonanza*, *The Big Valley*, and the voice of Mr. Fantastic on the cartoon series *Fantastic 4*. Mohr made several movies in the 1940s, including, *The Sea Hawk* (1940), *Jungle Girl* (1941), *Lady of Burlesque* (1943), *Redhead from Manhattan* (1943), *The Truth About Murder* (1946), *Gilda* (1946), and *Two Guys from Texas* (1948), then sporadically returned to the screen in such movies as *Detective Story* (1951), *Ten Tall Men* (1951), *The Eddie Cantor Story* (1953), *The Angry Red Planet* (1959), *West Side Story* (1964), and *Funny Girl* (1968).

Molina, Dan A sound designer and film editor for animated movies, he provided the voice of the gurgling goldfish Fish Out of Water in *Chicken Little* (2005). Molina supervised the sound for *An American Tail* (1986) and *The Land Before Time* (1988), and was also supervising editor for both movies, as well as for *Rock-a-Doodle* (1991), *The Pagemaster* (1994), *Cats Don't Dance* (1997), *The Road to El Dorado* (2000), *Chicken Little*, and *Meet the Robinsons* (2007). He also can be heard in the movie *All Dogs Go to Heaven* (1989). In order to get the sound he wanted for Fish Out of Water in *Chicken Little*, Molina spoke his lines through a tube into a cooler of water.

Mollenhauer, Heidi A New York actress and singer who has performed in nightclubs and in regional theatres, she provided the singing voice of the gypsy Esmeralda in *The Hunchback of Notre Dame* (1996), introducing the song "God Help the Outcasts." She has no other film or television credits.

Montgomery, Ritchie A character actor who has appeared in many television series and made-for-TV movies, he supplied the voice of the bayou frog hunter Reggie in *The Princess and the Frog* (2009). Montgomery made his television debut in 1979 and since then has acted in such series as *Beulah Land*, *Code Red*, *Simon & Simon*, *T. J. Hooker*, *Hill Street Blues*, *The Dukes of Hazzard*, *Designing Women*, *Evening Shade*, *Hearts Afire*, *Home Improvement*, *Married with Children*, *ER*, and *Days of Our Lives*. He has been in even more TV-movies, including *Old Man* (1997), *Sisters and Other Strangers* (1997), *Chasing Destiny* (2001), *How Can I Get You?* (2004), *Heart of the Storm* (2004), *Heartless* (2005), *Elvis* (2005), *Not Like Everyone Else*

(2006), and *Cirque du Freak: The Curse of the Judas Chalice* (2009). Among Montgomery's films are *Monster in the Closet* (1986), *Body Shot* (1994), *Cheyenne* (1996), *Hungry for You* (1996), *Yakima Wash* (1998), *Vice* (2000), *Malpractice* (2001), *Above & Beyond* (2001), *Monster's Ball* (2001), *Catch Me If You Can* (2002), *Knuckle Sandwich* (2004), *The Dukes of Hazzard* (2005), *Glorious Mail* (2005), *Glory Road* (2006), *Cleaner* (2007), *Blonde Ambition* (2007), *The Last Lullabye* (2008), *Soul Men* (2008), *Nine Dead* (2010), and *Two Gates of Sleep* (2010).

Moore, Demi (b. 1962) A popular leading lady with a sexy, husky voice who has starred in films and a few television shows, she supplied the speaking voice of the feisty gypsy Esmeralda in *The Hunchback of Notre Dame* (1996). She was born Demetria Gene Guynes in Roswell, New Mexico, dropped out of school to model as a pin-up girl, and worked as a bill collector before getting her first acting job in the movies in 1981. The next year she was cast in the television soap opera *General Hospital* which led to better roles in such films as *Blame It on Rio* (1984), *St. Elmo's Fire* (1985), and *About Last Night* (1986). Among Moore's many movies since then are *Ghost* (1990), *A Few Good Men* (1992), *Indecent Proposal* (1993), *Disclosure* (1994), *The Scarlet Letter* (1995), *Striptease* (1996), *G.I. Jane* (1997), *Charlie's Angels: Full Throttle* (2003), *Half Light* (2006), *Flawless* (2007), and *The Joneses* (2009). She has appeared in the television series *Moonlighting, Tales from the Crypt, Ellen,* and *Will & Grace*. Moore was chosen to voice Esmerelda in *The Hunchback of Notre Dame* because the directors wanted a non-traditional sound for the gypsy and Moore's lower, raspy vocals kept the character from sounding like other Disney heroines. She reprised her Esmeralda in the video sequel *The Hunchback of Notre Dame II* (2002) and can also be heard in the animated features *Beavis and Butt-Head Do America* (1996) and *The Magic 7* (2009). Biography: *Demi Moore: The Most Powerful Woman in Hollywood,* Nigel Goodall (2000).

Moore, Fred (1911–1952) One of the earliest and most respected Disney animators, his only acting credit was providing the voice of the vaudeville tap-dancer Fred in the short *The Nifty Nineties* (1941). Robert Fred Moore was born in Los Angeles and, with no formal art training, began working with the Disney studio at the age of nineteen. He animated such shorts as *Santa's Workshop* (1932), *The Three Little Pigs* (1933), *The Golden Touch* (1935), and *Three Little Wolves* (1936) before giving the character of Mickey Mouse a new design for the cartoon *Brave Little Tailor* (1938) and perfecting that look for the "Sorcerer's Apprentice" segment of *Fantasia* (1940). Among the feature films Moore helped animate are *Snow White and the Seven Dwarfs* (1937), *Pinocchio* (1940), *The Reluctant Dragon* (1941), *The Three Caballeros* (1944), *Make Mine Music* (1946), *The Adventures of Ichabod and Mr. Toad* (1949), *Cinderella* (1950), *Alice in Wonderland* (1951), and *Peter Pan* (1953). He also worked on several other shorts which later were shown on television on *Walt Disney's Wonderful World of Color*. Moore spent two years in the late 1940s working for Walter Lanz and was responsible for redesigning the cartoon character Woody Woodpecker. The characters of the vaudevillians Fred and Ward in *The Nifty Nineties* were based on Moore and his fellow animator Ward Kimball who were good friends and often clowned together while animating different projects. In addition to his many achievements, Moore is most responsible for creating the look of Mickey Mouse as we know him today. He died in a car accident at the age of forty-one.

Moore, Mandy (b. 1984) A teenage pop singer who later became an actress and fashion designer, she supplied the singing and speaking voice of the long-haired heroine Rapunzel in *Tangled* (2010). Amanda Leigh Moore was born in Nashua, New Hampshire, the daughter of an airline pilot and a journalist, and grew up near Orlando, Florida, where as a teen she became well known from singing the National Anthem at sporting events. Moore was signed by a record company when she was fifteen and soon she was touring with the Backstreet Boys and had albums on the charts. In 2000 she had her own talk show on MTV, was endorsing products on the air, modeling clothes, and raising money for various charities. Her acting debut was in the film *The Princess Diaries* (2001), followed by such movies as *Dr. Dolittle 2* (2001), *A Walk to Remember* (2002), *How to Deal* (2003), *Chasing Liberty* (2004), *Saved!* (2004), *Dedication* (2007), and *Swinging with the Finkels* (2010). Moore has also acted in the television series *Entourage, Scrubs, How I Met Your Mother,* and *Grey's Anatomy,* has been heard on the cartoon series *The Simpsons,* and did a voice in the animated video *Brother Bear 2*. For a time she designed her own line of clothes that were sold in hundreds of boutiques across the country. Rapunzel is the most recent in a long line of Disney princesses and, while spirited and determined at times, at other times she doubts herself and her decisions. Kristin Chenoweth was originally slated to voice Rapunzel until the directors on the project were replaced and the studio went with the singer Moore instead. The movie was titled *Rapunzel* until Disney's *The Princess and the Frog* failed to attract a young male audience so the film was retitled

Tangled and the character of the fun-loving bandit Errol Flynn was emphasized in the previews and the ads.

Moranis, Rick (b. 1953) The comic actor and writer who can play a wide variety of characters but is often cast as nerdy types, he provided the voice of the Canadian moose Rutt in *Brother Bear* (2003). He was born Frederick Alan Moranis in Toronto, Canada, where he later was a popular radio disc jockey. Moranis became famous in both Canada and the States with the television series *SCTV* which he helped write. The comedy show allowed him to do uncanny impersonations of celebrities and create dozens of original characters, most memorably the dense Canadian Bob McKenzie who with his brother Doug (Dave Thomas) was featured in skits titled "The Great White North." The popularity of *SCTV* launched Moranis' film career, making his screen debut in *The Adventures of Bob & Doug McKenzie: Strange Brew* (1983). His other notable movies include *Ghostbusters* (1984), *Brewster's Millions* (1985), *Club Paradise* (1986), *Little Shop of Horrors* (1986), *Spaceballs* (1987), *Ghostbusters II* (1989), *Honey, I Shrunk the Kids* (1989), *Parenthood* (1989), *Honey, I Blew Up the Kids* (1992), and *The Flintstones* (1994). Moranis reprised his moose Rutt in the video sequel *Brother Bear 2* (2006) and he also voiced *Rudolph the Red-Nosed Reindeer & the Island of Misfit Toys* (2001), *Miss Spider's Sunny Patch Kids* (2003), and the television series *The Animated Adventures of Bob & Doug McKenzie*.

Moretz, Chloe (b. 1997) A young actress with already considerable television and movie credits, she voiced Young Penny who picks out the puppy Bolt from the pet store in *Bolt* (2008). Chloe Grave Moretz was born in Atlanta, Georgia, and was a child model before making her television acting debut in the series *The Guardian* in 2004. The next year she was widely recognized as little Chelsea Lutz in the film *The Amityville Horror*, followed by such movies as *Big Momma's House 2* (2006), *Wicked Little Things* (2006), *The Poker House* (2008), *Kick-Ass* (2010), and *Diary of a Wimpy Kid* (2010). Moretz has appeared on the television series *Desperate Housewives*, *My Name Is Earl*, and *Dirty Sexy Money*, and provided voices for the animated series *The Emperor's New School*. In 2007 she voiced the new character of the little girl Darby in the video *Pooh's Super Sleuth Christmas Movie* and reprised Darby in *My Friends Tigger and Pooh's Friendly Tails* (2008), *My Friends Tigger and Pooh: The Hundred Acre Wood Haunt* (2008), and *Tigger and Pooh and a Musical Too!* (2009), as well as the television series *My Friends Tigger and Pooh*. Moretz was hired to voice the young heroine Penny throughout the movie *Bolt* and completed all the recording before it was decided to have the teen star Miley Cyrus play Penny. Only her cameo as Young Penny featured Moretz's voice in the final print.

Morita, Pat (1932–2005) One of the first and most beloved Asian-American actors to find recognition on the big and little screen, he supplied the voice of the grateful Emperor of China in *Mulan* (1998). He was born Noriyuki Morita in Isleton, California, and endured a childhood battling tuberculosis and his teen years in an internment camp for Japanese Americans during World War II. As an adult he worked in his family's restaurant in Sacramento and was a clerk in a state office before becoming a stand-up comic billed as the Hip Nip. Morita made his screen debut in *Thoroughly Modern Millie* (1967) and that same year made his television bow in an episode of *Gomer Pyle, U.S.M.C.* He was noticed for his quirky characters in such television series as *The Courtship of Eddie's Father*, *Nanny and the Professor*, *Room 222*, *M*A*S*H*, *Sanford and Son*, *Kung Fu*, and *Love, American Style*, but it was his cafe owner "Arnold" Takahaski on *Happy Days* that made him a national favorite. After appearing on the show for eight years, he became a movie star with his performance as Mr. Kesuke Miyagi in *The Karate Kid* (1984), a role he reprised in *The Karate Kid, Part II* (1986), *The Karate Kid, Part III* (1989), and *The Next Karate Kid* (1994). Morita's other film credits include *The Shakiest Gun in the West* (1968), *Every Little Crook and Nanny* (1972), *Cancel My Reservation* (1972), *Midway* (1976), *Collision Course* (1989), *Gengis Khan* (1992), *Honeymoon in Vegas* (1992), *Even Cowgirls Get the Blues* (1993), *Hammerlock* (2000), *Down and Derby* (2005), *Coming Attractions* (2006), *Only the Brave* (2006), and *Royal Kill* (2009), as well as many made-for-TV movies. He frequently returned to television, appearing in such later series as *Ohara*, *Harry and the Hendersons*, *The Fresh Prince of Bel-Air*, *Married with Children*, *Boy Meets World*, *The Mystery Files of Shelby Woo*, *Caroline in the City*, *Adventures with Kanga Roddy*, *The Hughleys*, and *Baywatch*. Morita reprised his voice of the Emperor in *Mulan II* (2004) and was heard in such television cartoon series as *Happily Ever After: Fairy Tales for Every Child*, *Adventures from the Book of Virtues*, and *SpongeBob SquarePants*.

Morris, Howard (1919–2005) The short-of-stature but giant-sized comic talent who was one of the delights of the early years of television, he supplied the voice of the incompetent Gopher in the shorts *Winnie the Pooh and the Honey Tree* (1966) and *Winnie the Pooh and the Blustery Day* (1968), and in the compilation feature *The Many Adventures of Winnie the Pooh* (1977), the only character in the series who does not exist in the original A. A. Milne stories. Howard Jerome Morris was born in New York City and teamed with comic Carl Reiner to entertain troops during World War II. He later appeared on Broadway in *Hamlet* (1945), *Gentlemen Prefer Blondes* (1949), and *Finian's Rainbow* (1960). Morris joined Reiner and other talented comics and writers as regulars on Sid Caesar's television program *Your Show of Shows*, playing a variety of hilarious characters for four years. He went on to appear in other TV series over the years, including *Kraft Theatre, Alfred Hitchcock Presents, The Danny Thomas Show, The Lucy Show, The Bob Newhart Show, Fantasy Island, Baywatch,* and *Trapper John, M.D.*, but he is most remembered as Ernest T. Bass on *The Andy Griffith Show*. In the 1960s he started voicing cartoon series and soon became one of the busiest voice artists in television, heard in such shows as *Beetle Bailey, The Flintstones, The Jetsons, Archie's Fun House, The Chipmunks, The 13 Ghosts of Scooby-Doo, Galaxy High School, Adventures of the Gummi Bears, DuckTales, Midnight Patrol: Adventures in the Dream Zone, TaleSpin, Yo Yogi!, Garfield and Friends,* and *Cow and Chicken*. Morris can also be heard as the title character in a series of *Beetle Bailey* cartoon shorts and in the animated movies and videos *Stop Driving Us Crazy* (1961), *Munro* (1961), *Habit Rabbit* (1963), *The Huffless, Puffless Dragon* (1964), *Alice in Wonderland in Paris* (1966), *Alice in Wonderland or What's a Nice Kid Like You Doing in a Place Like This?* (1966), *Deck the Halls with Wacky Walls* (1983), *Star Fairies* (1985), *The Adventures of Ronald McDonald: McTreasure Island* (1989), *Tom and Jerry: The Movie* (1992), and *A Flintstones Christmas Carol* (1994). He rarely played leading roles in films but often stood out as comic supporting characters, as in *Boys Night Out* (1962), *40 Pounds of Trouble* (1962), *The Nutty Professor* (1963), *Fluffy* (1965), *With Six You Get Eggroll* (1968), *10 from Your Show of Shows* (1973), *High Anxiety* (1977), *History of the World Part I* (1981), *Splash* (1984), *Transylvania Twist* (1989), *Life Stinks* (1991), and *The Wonderful Ice Cream Suit* (1998). Morris was also an adept director of television sit-coms, helming several episodes of such series as *The Bill Dana Show, Gomer Pyle U.S.M.C., The Andy Griffith Show, The Dick Van Dyke Show, The Patty Duke Show, Get Smart, Please Don't Eat the Daisies, Bewitched, Hogan's Heroes, One Day at a Time, Laverne & Shirley,* and *Private Benjamin*.

Morris, John (b. 1984) The young boy who provided the voice of the youth Andy Davis in *Toy Story* (1995), he only returned to film acting to voice the same character in *Toy Story 2* (1999) and *Toy Story 3* (2010). Morris was seven years old when he auditioned for the role of Andy and voiced the animated movies *The Little Engine That Could* (1991) and *The Nightmare Before Christmas* (1993) before actually doing the voice for Andy. He had to audition again in 1999 to see if his voice was still appropriate for the character in the first sequel. By the time Morris made *Toy Story 3*, he was a twenty-five-year-old graduate of the University of California, Los Angeles School of Theatre, Film and Television but was still able to voice the seventeen-year-old Andy effectively. Morris has pursued a career in regional theatre since he graduated from UCLA. The character of Andy is named after Andries "Andy" Van Dam, the Brown University professor of computer science and animation who taught several of the animators who made *Toy Story*.

Morris, Phil (b. 1959) An African-American character actor who has been seen or heard in many television series, he voiced the bi-racial medic Dr. Joshua Strongbear Sweet in *Atlantis: The Lost Empire* (2001). Philip Morris was born in Iowa City, Iowa, the son of television actor Greg Morris (1933–1996) and as a child acted in an episode of the original *Star Trek* television series. As an adult he made his film debut in *Star Trek III: The Search for Spock* (1984) and later appeared in episodes of *Star Trek: Deep Space Nine* and *Star Trek: Voyager*. Among the many other series Morris acted in are *The Young and the Restless, Making a Living, Marblehead Manor, Mission: Impossible, WIOU, Melrose Place, The Love Boat: The Next Wave, Wanda at Large,* and *Smallville*, but he is most known for his portrayal of the defense attorney Jackie Chiles in *Seinfeld*. He reprised his Dr. Sweet in the sequel *Atlantis: Milo's Return* (2003) and has provided voices for many TV cartoon series, including *Kim Possible, Justice League, Danny Phantom, The PJs, Legion of Super Heroes, Black Panther,* and *The Secret Saturdays*.

Moss, Ronn (b. 1952) A durable soap opera star with a handful of film credits, he voiced Dr. Forrester in *Bolt* (2008). Ronald Montague Moss was born in Los Angeles and educated at UCLA before starting his career as a singer with the rock band Player in the 1970s. He made his screen debut in 1983 and two years later was on television in an episode of *Trapper John, M.D.* Moss began playing the fashion designer Ridge Forrester in the daytime drama *The Bold and the Beautiful* in 1987 and remained with the series for over twenty-four years. He has often returned to music as a composer and a musician.

Mullally, Megan (b. 1958) A television comic actress-singer with stage experience who often plays ditzy or oddball types, she provided the voice of the mutant mosquito Adele, a failed experiment by Dr. Krank, in *Teacher's Pet* (2004). She was born in Los Angles, the daughter of an actor and a model, and attended Northwestern University for a time, did theatre in Chicago, and studied ballet at the School of American Ballet in New York City. Mullally made her television debut in the TV-movie *The Children Nobody Wanted* (1981), followed by such series as *The Ellen Burstyn Show*, *Wings*, *My Life and Times*, *Rachel Gunn R.N.*, *How I Met Your Mother*, *30 Rock*, *In the Motherhood*, *Party Down*, and *Children's Hospital*, but she is most remembered as the pill-popping Karen Walker in *Will & Grace*. She also had her own talk show in 2006 called *The Megan Mullally Show*. Her first film was *Risky Business* (1983), followed by such movies as *Last Resort* (1986), *About Last Night* (1986), *Queens Logic* (1991), *Best Man in Grass Creek* (1999), *Everything Put Together* (2000), *Speaking of Sex* (2001), *Stealing Harvard* (2002), *Rebound* (2005), and *Fame* (2009), as well as several TV-movies. Mullally's distinctive voice can be heard in the cartoon series *Fish Police*, *Extreme Ghostbusters*, *King of the Hill*, and *Peep and the Big Wide World*, as well as the animated films and videos *I Yabba-Dabba-Do!* (1993), *Hollyrock-a-Bye Baby* (1993), *A Flintstone Family Christmas* (1993), *The Flintstone Christmas in Bedrock* (1996), and *Bee Movie* (2007). She has returned to the stage on occasion and was featured on Broadway in *Grease* (1994), *How to Succeed in Business Without Really Trying* (1995), and *Young Frankenstein* (2007).

Mulligan, Richard (1932–2000) The expressive, broad comic actor of stage, screen, and television, he voiced Einstein, the slow-moving, dense Great Dane, in *Oliver & Company* (1988). He was born in New York City and studied playwriting at Columbia University before turning to acting, appearing on Broadway in *All the Way Home* (1960), *A Thousand Clowns* (1962), *Never Too Late* (1962), *Nobody Loves an Albatross* (1963), *Mating Dance* (1965), *How the Other Half Loves* (1971), *Ring Round the Bathtub* (1972), *Thieves* (1974), and *Special Occasions* (1982). Mulligan made his television debut on an episode of *Route 66* in 1963 and over the next thirty years appeared in many series, including *The Hero*, *Mannix*, *I Dream of Jeannie*, *Bonanza*, *The Partridge Family*, *Little House on the Prairie*, *Charlie's Angels*, *Switch*, *The Love Boat*, *Reggie*, *The Twilight Zone*, *The Golden Girls*, *Nurses*, and *The John Larroquette Show*, but he is better remembered as the hyper husband Burt Campbell in *Soap* and the widower Dr. Harry Weston in *Empty Nest*. Among his movie credits are *40 Pounds of Trouble* (1962), *One Potato, Two Potato* (1964), *The Group* (1966), *Little Big Man* (1970), *The Big Bus* (1976), *S.O.B.* (1981), *Trail of the Pink Panther* (1982), *Meatballs Part II* (1984), *Teachers* (1984), *Micki + Maude* (1984), and *A Fine Mess* (1986), as well as several TV-movies such as *Harvey* (1972), *Pueblo* (1973), *Babes in Toyland* (1986), *Lincoln* (1988), and *London Suite* (1996). Mulligan voiced characters for the cartoon series *The Angry Beavers* and *Hey, Arnold!*

Murphy, Donna (b. 1959) The acclaimed Broadway actress-singer with dark, exotic features and a compelling stage presence, she provided the speaking and singing voice of the deceptive Madame Gothel who pretends to be Rapunzel's mother in *Tangled* (2010). She was born in Corona, New York, grew up on Long Island and in Massachusetts, and was educated at New York University's Tisch School of the Arts and the Stella Adler Studio before making her professional stage debut as a replacement in the Broadway musical *They're Playing Our Song* in 1979. Although she has acted in both comedies and dramas, Murphy became best known for her sterling performances in musicals, such as *Birds of Paradise* (1987), *Song of Singapore* (1991), and *Hello Again* (1994) Off Broadway, and *Passion* (1994), *The King and I* (1996), *Wonderful Town* (2003), and *LoveMusik* (2007) on Broadway. She has acted in such television series as *Another World*, *Murder One*, *Remember WENN*, *Ally McBeal*, *Law & Order*, *Hack*, *Damages*, *Trust Me*, and *Ugly Betty*, and in several TV-movies and mini-series, including *Liberty! The American Revolution* (1997), *The Day Lincoln Was Shot* (1999), and *The Last Debate* (2000). Murphy made her screen debut in 1995 and has appeared in such films as *Star Trek: Insurrection* (1998), *The Astronaut's Wife* (1999), *Center Stage* (2001), *Spider-Man 2* (2004), *World Trade Center* (2006), and *The Nanny Diaries* (2007). Madame Gothel in *Tangled* is in the tradition of the first Disney villainess: the evil Queen in *Snow White and the Seven Dwarfs* (1937). Both of them are obsessed with physical appearance and are willing to lie and kill to preserve their beauty. Yet Gothel can rarely reveal her sinister nature, spending much of the film playing the loving mother in front of Rapunzel. Gothel's physical look resembles Murphy's striking facial features yet the animators found subtle ways to hint at the decrepit old crone that lurks beneath the surface. It is a tribute to Murphy's vivid performance in both dialogue and song that makes it clear this woman is filled with duplicity.

Murphy, Eddie (b. 1961) The most bankable movie star of his era, the African American comedian and actor possesses a variety of voices, one of which he used as the pint-sized, outspoken dragon Mushu in *Mulan* (1998). Edward Regan Murphy was born in Brooklyn, New York, and as a teenager started doing stand-up comedy in Manhattan clubs, eventually getting noticed at The Comic Strip. At the age of nineteen he was hired as a cast member for television's *Saturday Night Live* and by the end of the first season Murphy was a star. He was featured in his first movie *48 Hrs.* (1982), followed by several hits over the next three decades, many of which gave him the opportunity to play more than one role. Among his notable films are *Trading Places* (1983), *Beverly Hills Cop* (1984) and its two sequels, *The Golden Child* (1986), *Coming to America* (1988), *Harlem Nights* (1989), *Another 48 Hrs.* (1990), *The Nutty Professor* (1996) and its sequel, *Doctor Dolittle* (1998) and its sequel, *Bowfinger* (1999), *The Adventures of Pluto Nash* (2002), *The Haunted Mansion* (2003), *Dreamgirls* (2006), *Norbit* (2007), *Meet Dave* (2008), and *Imagine That* (2009). Murphy provided voices for the animated movies *Shrek* (2001) and its three sequels, as well as the TV cartoon series *The PJs* which he also wrote and produced. He created and produced the sit-com *The Royal Family*. In the planning of *Mulan*, it was thought that having a dragon companion for Mulan would make her seem small in comparison so the idea was dropped. Only when the animators learned that in Chinese folklore dragons come in all sizes, they restored the character of Mushu and even made jokes in the dialogue about his small size. While Mushu is a physically entertaining critter and his lines are very funny, it is Murphy's high-powered comic performance that makes the character so unforgettable. Memoir: *Growing Up Laughing with Eddie Murphy*, Harris Haith (2002); biographies: *Eddie Murphy: The Life and Times of a Comic on the Edge,* Frank Sanello (1997); *Eddie Murphy*, Hal Marcovitz (2011).

Murray, Brian (b. 1937) A British actor who has spent most of his career on the New York stage, he provided the voice of the sly and secretive cook John Silver who befriends young Jim Hawkins in *Treasure Planet* (2002). He was born Brian Bell in Johannesburg, South Africa, where he was educated and started acting in the theatre. By 1959 he appeared on the London stage and made his television debut on the British series *ITV Play of the Week*. Murray first came to the States as a member of the Royal Shakespeare Company production of *A Midsummer Night's Dream* which toured the country for several months in 1964. He returned three years later as Rosencrantz in the Broadway production of *Rosencrantz and Guildenstern Are Dead*, winning numerous plaudits. Murray continued to act on both sides of the Atlantic until the late 1970s when he settled in New York and did American theatre, television, and an occasional film. Among his many memorable New York stage credits are *Ashes* (1977), *Da* (1978), *Noises Off* (1983), *Hamlet* (1990), *A Small Family Business* (1992), *Black Comedy* (1993), *The Merry Wives of Windsor* (1994), *Racing Demon* (1995), *The Entertainer* (1996), *The Little Foxes* (1997), *Twelfth Night* (1998), *Uncle Vanya* (2000), *The Play About the Baby* (2001), *The Crucible* (2002), *The Rivals* (2004), and *Mary Stuart* (2009). Murray has acted in such television series as *Another World, Law & Order: Criminal Intent,* and *30 Rock*, was in the films *Bob Roberts* (1992) and *City Hall* (1996), and did voices for the animated movie *My Dog Tulip* (2009).

Nagai, Jordan (b. 2000) An Asian American child performer who made an auspicious film debut when he voiced the hyperactive, talkative Russell, the roly-poly Junior Wilderness Explorer, in *Up* (2009), he reprised his Russell in the animated short *Dug's Special Mission* (2009). A native of Los Angeles, he has also voiced one episode of the TV cartoon series *The Simpsons*. Nagai was only seven years old when he did the vocals for *Up* yet it is a performance that has various nuances throughout. He never pursued the role, but only accompanied his older brother Hunter Nagai when he went to audition for the role of Russell. About 400 boys were at the audition and little Jordan stood out because he would not stop talking. Director Pete Docter heard the non-stop chatter and knew what Russell should sound like. The character is the first Asian American male in a major role in a Disney animated movie.

Najimy, Kathy (b. 1957) A comic actress of stage, television, and film who excels at playing offbeat but likable characters, she provided the voice of the human resident Mary of the spaceship *Axiom* who discovers the joys of life in *WALL-E* (2008). She was born in San Diego, California, the daughter of Lebanese immigrants, and began her career in the theatre, writing and performing (with Mo Gaffney) Off Broadway in *The Kathy and Mo Show* in 1986. The team did new versions of the comic revue and then performed it on television in 1991. Najimy was cast in such films as *The Hard Way* (1991), *Soapdish* (1991), *The Fisher King* (1991), and *This Is My Life* (1992), but first received wide recognition in *Sister Act* (1992) and its sequel *Sister Act 2: Back in the Habit* (1993). Among her other movie credits are *Hocus Pocus* (1993), *Jeffrey* (1995), *Nevada* (1997), *Hope Floats* (1998), *Zack and Reba* (1998), *Attention Shoppers* (2000), *Leaving Peoria* (2000), *The Wedding Planner* (2001), *Rat Race* (2001), and *Step Up 3D* (2010), as well as some TV-movies. In addition to quiz programs, talk shows, and comedy specials, Najimy has appeared in several television series, including *Chicago Hope, Clueless, Early Edition, Ellen, That's So Raven,*

Numb3rs, The Suite Life of Zack and Cody, Privileged, Drop Dead Diva, Desperate Housewives, and *Ugly Betty*, but she is perhaps best known as Olive Massery on *Veronica's Closet*, She can be heard on such cartoon series as *Duckman: Private Dick/Family Man, Hercules, The Wild Thornberrys, Pepper Ann, The Legend of Tarzan, Higglytown Heroes*, and *Hey, Arnold!*, but her most recognized voice is that of Peggy Hill on *King of the Hill*. Najimy also did voices for the animated films and videos *Cats Don't Dance* (1997), *The Jungle Book: Mowgli's Story* (1998), *The Sissy Duckling* (1999), *Balto III: Wings of Change* (2004), *Brother Bear 2* (2006), *Tom and Jerry in Shiver Me Whiskers* (2006), *Scooby-Doo! Pirates Ahoy!* (2006), and *Tinker Bell* (2008). Najimy has returned to the stage on occasion, as when she starred in *Dirty Blonde* (2001) on Broadway.

Napier, Alan (1903–1988) A tall, thin British character actor who appeared in American movies and television from the 1950s through the 1970s, he provided the voices of the aging, dusty Sir Pelinore in *The Sword in the Stone* (1963) and a huntsman, a reporter, and one of the hounds in the animated sequence in *Mary Poppins* (1964). He was born Alan William Napier-Clavering in Birmingham, England, a cousin of Prime Minister Neville Chamberlain, and was educated at Clifton College and the Royal Academy of Dramatic Art before beginning his stage career. He appeared in several West End productions and acted in a handful of British films, including *Caste* (1930), *Bitter Sweet* (1933), *Loyalties* (1933), and *The Secret Four*, then he emigrated to the States in 1939. Napier acted on Broadway in *Lady in Waiting* (1940), *Gertie* (1952), and *Too Late the Phalarope* (1956), but most of his career in America was in movies, such as *A Yank at Oxford* (1942), *Cat People* (1942), *Lassie Come Home* (1943), *The Song of Bernadette* (1943), *Thirty Seconds Over Tokyo* (1944), *Hanover Square* (1945), *Sinbad the Sailor* (1947), *Forever Amber* (1947), *Johnny Belinda* (1948), *Joan of Arc* (1948), *The Adventure of the Speckled Band* (1949), *The Great Caruso* (1951), *Across the Wide Missouri* (1951), *Julius Caesar* (1953), *Desirée* (1954), *The Court Jester* (1955), *The Mole People* (1956), *Journey to the Center of the Earth* (1959), *Tender Is the Night* (1962), *Marnie* (1964), *36 Hours* (1965), and *The Loved One* (1965). Among his television credits are the series *Four Star Playhouse, The Loretta Young Show, Alfred Hitchcock Presents, Checkmate, Don't Call Me Charlie, Daniel Boone, Night Gallery, Ironside, Kojak*, and *The Paper Chase*, but he is probably most remembered as the butler Alfred on the live-action *Batman* series in the 1960s.

Nash, Clarence (1904–1985) One of the most famous (and easily recognized) of all voice actors, he was the voice of Donald Duck for thirty years. Clarence Charles Nash was born in Watonga, Oklahoma, and began his career in radio. There are two versions of how he came to the attention of Walt Disney: one was that Disney heard Nash do a talking goat on a Los Angles radio station and sought him out; the other version says that Nash was employed as a delivery man for the Adohr Milk Company and while whistling and doing funny voices as he passed the Disney studio he was asked to audition. What is known for certain is that Nash voiced the irascible duck in the character's first appearance in the short *The Wise Little Hen* (1934) and reprised his performance as Donald in over 175 features and shorts before retiring in 1965. It is difficult to explain or justify the international appeal of Donald Duck. He is not lovable, cute, admirable, good-natured, nor even remotely nice. Yet the duck's temper tantrums, stubbornness, and willingness to fight anyone or anything make him surprisingly appealing. He is the bad temper in each of us, escaping for the enjoyment of others. All these characteristics might make for an interesting character but it is Nash's vocals that make Donald Duck exceptional. Barely understandable as he moves back and forth between words and squawks, the duck makes sounds that defy language; no wonder he is so popular around the world. Nash also dubbed Donald's voice in the Spanish, Portuguese, French, German, Chinese, and Japanese versions of the cartoons, speaking the lines phonetically in what he called "Duckspeask." For a period in the 1940s the Duck was more popular than the Mouse, appearing on ads, merchandising, and war-effort promotions. Donald and Nash starred in 128 Donald Duck cartoons, more than Mickey Mouse himself, and was featured in the full-length anthology films *Saludos Amigos* (1943), *The Three Caballeros* (1945), *Fun and Fancy Free* (1947), and *Melody Time* (1948). (To this day the term scuba divers use to describe the result of helium gas on the human voice as the "Donald Duck effect.") Over the years Nash also provided the voices of Daisy Duck and Donald's nephews Huey, Dewey and Louie on occasion, as well as the kitten Figaro in some shorts and the Bullfrog in *Bambi* (1942). Nash returned to the studio one last time in 1983 to voice Donald as Nephew Fred in the short *Mickey's Christmas Carol*. Tony Anselmo took over the vocals for Donald Duck in 1986 and others will take his place in the future. Everyone knows how Donald sounds and how he will always sound. Nash did his job so well that his voice lives on.

Nelson, Craig T. (b. 1944) A durable character actor on television and in movies for the past forty years, he voiced the super-hero Mr. Incredible who must remain disguised as Bob Parr in *The Incredibles* (2004). Craig Theodore Nelson was born in Spokane, Washington, and educated at Central Washington University and the University of Arizona. He began his career as a stand-up comic and radio commentator before making his film debut in 1971. Supporting roles in ... *And Justice for All* (1979), *Private Benjamin* (1980), *Where the Buffalo Roam* (1980), and other films brought little recognition but his career took off when he played the father, Steve Freeling, in *Poltergeist* (1982). Never becoming a major star, Nelson instead was a familiar face seen in many movies and television series over the years. Among his other film credits are *All the Right Moves* (1983), *Silkwood* (1983), *The Killing Fields* (1984), *Poltergeist II: The Other Side* (1986), *Turner & Hooch* (1989), *Ghosts of Mississippi* (1996), *Wag the Dog* (1997), *Blades of Glory* (2007), and *The Proposal* (2009). In addition to many made-for-TV movies, Nelson was featured in such series as *Chicago Story, Private Benjamin, Call to Glory, The District, My Name Is Earl,* and *Parenthood,* but he is most known as the title character in the sit-com *Coach* for eight years. He reprised his Mr. Incredible in the animated short *Mr. Incredible and Pals* (2005). The character of Mr. Incredible is based on the super-heroes The Thing and the Incredible Hulk. He shares their superhuman strength but is much more agreeable-looking. Because of the complicated production schedule for the film, Nelson's voice work for *The Incredibles* was stretched over a two-year period.

Nelson, Mike (b. 1976) A radio and television personality whose irreverent commentary sometimes raises eyebrows, he voiced the short-tempered forklift Not Chuck in *Cars* (2006). He was born in the Bronx, New York, and educated at Fordham University and the Actors Studio for a theatre career. Instead he went into radio and for six years was heard on a San Francisco station. Nelson has appeared in the film *Head in the Sand* (2009) and on such television shows as *Ned's Declassified School Survival Guide, Sarah and No Name After Dark,* and HGTV's *House Detective* which he hosted.

Newhart, Bob (b. 1929) The low-key stand-up comic who became a favorite on television, he provided the voice of the timid janitor mouse Bernard who goes on adventures in *The Rescuers* (1977) and *The Rescuers Down Under* (1990). He was born George Robert Newhart in Oak Park, Illinois, and studied business at Loyola University of Chicago. After serving in World War II he worked as an accountant in Chicago then started doing comedy on local radio stations. This led to some best-selling comedy albums and appearances on all the major variety and talk shows on television, becoming famous for his telephone monologues and hesitant, self-conscious delivery. Although his 1961 variety show was not successful he had much better luck as psychiatrist Dr. Bob Hartley on *The Bob Newhart Show* which ran for six years in the 1970s and as lodge owner Dick Loudon on *Newhart* which ran for eight years in the 1980s. Newhart's other TV credits include the series *The Alfred Hitchcock Hour, The Don Rickles Show, Bob, Insight, George & Leo, Murphy Brown, ER,* and *Desperate Housewives.* He usually played small but funny roles in films, including *Hell Is for Heroes* (1962), *Hot Millions* (1968), *On a Clear Day You Can See Forever* (1970), *Catch-22* (1970), *Cold Turkey* (1971), *Little Miss Marker* (1980), *First Family* (1980), *In & Out* (1997), *Legally Blonde 2: Red, White & Blonde* (2003), and *Elf* (2003), as well as some TV-movies and the three-part television adventure *The Librarian* (2004, 2006, 2008). Newhart can also be heard in the animated film *Rudolph the Red-Nosed Reindeer* (1998). The comic actor's nervous, reticent delivery was used by the Disney animators as they developed the character of Bernard in *The Rescuers.* The little mouse is fearful and superstitious yet he serves as a hero in the two movies thanks to Newhart's warm and likable vocals. Memoir: *I Shouldn't Even Be Doing This* (2007); biography: *Bob Newhart,* Jeff Sorensen (1988).

Newman, Fred (b. 1952) A sound engineer who is also an actor, he provided the voices of Judge Doom's henchman Stupid who dies laughing in *Who Framed Roger Rabbit* (1988) and Doug's nervous pal Skeeter Valentine in *Doug's 1st Movie* (1999), as well as the roles of the neighbor Mr. Bud Dink, the critical gang member Ned Cauphee, and the dog Porkchop in that film. Frederick R. Newman was born in LaGrange, Georgia, and was educated at Harvard University for a career in business. Instead he turned to acting and working on sound effects, pursuing both vocations on the NPR-Radio program *Prairie Home Companion.* Newman made his screen debut providing voices for the film *Gremlins* (1984). He was the host for the TV series *The All-New Mickey Mouse Club* in 1989 and two years later started voicing Skeeter and other characters, first on the cartoon series *Doug* and then on *Disney's Doug.* Newman also composed the theme song for the two series and designed the sound as well. He voiced several characters in the animated videos *A Very Wompkee Christmas* (2003) and *Little Spirit: Christmas in New York* (2008), and played Fred the Conductor on the children's show *Lomax: The Hound of Music.*

Newman, Paul (1925–2008) Hollywood's perennial romantic leading man who lost none of his appeal as he grew older, the accomplished stage and screen actor's last film was *Cars* (2006) for which he provided the voice of the 1951 Hudson Hornet automobile judge and doctor Doc Hudson who was once a racing champ. He was born in Shaker Heights, Ohio, the son of a sporting goods store owner, and after serving in the Navy Air Corps in World War II he attended Kenyon College to study economics. Newman got involved in campus theatricals and after graduation went to the Yale Drama School and the Actors Studio to train for the theatre. After appearing in stock he made a notable Broadway debut in *Picnic* (1953), followed by lauded performances in *The Desperate Hours* (1955) and *Sweet Bird of Youth* (1959). Newman made his television debut in 1952 and his screen bow in 1954, getting noticed for *Somebody Up There Likes Me* (1956). For the next four decades he would star in a wide variety of films, though he specialized in unconventional and renegade characters. Among his many famous movies are *The Long Hot Summer* (1958), *Cat on a Hot Tin Roof* (1958), *Sweet Bird of Youth* (1962), *Hud* (1963), *Cool Hand Luke* (1967), *Butch Cassidy and the Sundance Kid* (1969), *The Sting* (1973), *Verdict* (1982), *The Color of Money* (1986), *Blaze* (1989), *The Hudsucker Proxy* (1994), *Nobody's Fool* (1994), and *The Road to Perdition* (2002). Newman returned to Broadway after a long absence to play the Stage Manager in the 2002 revival of *Our Town*. He was also a recognized film director and a noted humanitarian. The role of Doc Hudson in *Cars* was Newman's first animated film credit. He reprised the character in the video *Mater and the Ghostlight* (2006). The character of Doc Hudson was based on NASCAP racer Herb Thomas who was a champ in 1951 and 1953 but, after losing the title in 1954 and having crashes in 1955 and 1956, fell out of favor. Newman was drawn to the character and the movie because of his life-long interest in racing and his years as a race car driver. After the film was completed, the actor stated he thought his performance was his best since *Verdict*. *Cars* grossed more money than any other Newman film. Biography: *Paul Newman*, Lawrence J. Quick (1998); *Paul Newman: A Life*, Shawn Levy (2010).

Newman, Randy (b. 1943) The popular songwriter-singer and film composer who brings the flavor of folk, jazz, and rhythm and blues to his songs and scores, he sang the songs on the soundtrack for *Toy Story* (1995) and its sequels, and voiced the cameo role of the firefly Randy who is Ray's cousin in *The Princess and the Frog* (2009). Randall Stuart Newman was born in New Orleans, Louisiana, and grew up in Los Angeles as a member of a celebrated musical family. His uncles Alfred, Lionel and Emil Newman were all widely-recognized film composers, as were his cousins Thomas and David Newman. By the time he was attending UCLA he was already a professional pianist and songwriter. Newman's songs often were satiric and offbeat, yet surprisingly popular, and his growly, unpolished singing of them was reminiscent of Bob Dylan's style. Some of his songs were heard in movies before he turned to composing film scores with *Ragtime* (1981), followed by two dozen other films, including the animated movies *Toy Story* and its two sequels, *James and the Giant Peach* (1996), *Cats Don't Dance* (1997), *Monsters, Inc.* (2001), *Cars* (2006), and *The Princess and the Frog* (2009). Newman's acting credits include the voice of a singing bush in the film *Three Amigos* (1986), small roles in the movie *Leatherheads* (2008), and the television series *Private Schulz*. A stage musical revue of Newman's songs titled *Harps and Angels* was presented in Los Angeles in 2010. Biography: *Randy Newman's American Dreams*, Kevin Courrier (2005).

Newton, Teddy A Pixar animator and layout artist, he voiced the Newsreel Narrator in *The Incredibles* (2004), Skinner's conniving lawyer Talon Labarthe in *Ratatouille* (2007), and the toy Chatter Telephone on wheels who tries to help Woody in *Toy Story 3* (2010). He was born in Encino, California, and for a time attended the California Institute of the Arts before first working with Disney on sketches for *Pocahontas* (1995). Newton contributed to the storyboard and/or animation for the films *The Iron Giant* (1999), *Osmosis Jones* (2001), *The Incredibles*, *Ratatouille*, and *Up* (2009), as well as the shorts *Loose Tooth* (1997), *Your Friend the Rat* (2007), and *Presto* (2008), and the television cartoon series *2 Stupid Dogs* and *Dexter's Laboratory*. He also directed the animated shorts *Boys Night Out* (2003) and *Day & Night* (2010).

Nimoy, Leonard (b. 1931) A deep-voiced, hypnotic actor who will always be remembered as the Vulcan space traveler Mr. Spock on the original *Star Trek* television series, he has played many parts on stage, television, and screen, including the voice for Kashekim Nedakh, the King of Atlantis, in *Atlantis: The Lost Empire* (2001). Leonard Simon Nimoy was born in Boston, the son of a barber, and acted in local community theatres as a child. After an education at Antioch College and serving in the U.S. Army, he started getting bit roles in films and some television series but it was his appearance as Mr. Spock in 1966 that made him famous. Nimoy returned to the role in later series and film versions, some of which he wrote and directed. His many other television credits include the series *Dragnet, Sea Hunt, Wagon Train, The Outer Limits, The Virginian, Gunsmoke, Mission: Impossible*, and *Fringe*. Nimoy's deep, resonating voice can be heard in the animated movies and videos *The Transformers: The Movie* (1986), *The Halloween Tree* (1993), *The Pagemaster* (1994), *Rashi: A Light After the Dark Ages* (1999), *Sinbad: Beyond the Veil of Mists* (2000), *Land of the Lost* (2009), and *Kingdom Hearts: Birth by Sleep* (2010). He has returned to the stage on several occasions, most memorably in his one-man show *Vincent* about Vincent Van Gogh. Autobiographies: *I Am Not Spock* (1973); *I Am Spock* (1996).

Nixon, Marni (b. 1929)   One of the most famous singing voices in Hollywood, though only seen by movie audiences once, she sang the vocals for non-singing stars in some popular film musicals and provided the singing voice of the quixotic Grandmother Fa in *Mulan* (1998). A native of Altadena, California, she was born Marni McEathron and studied violin and singing as a child, then she and her sister formed a kiddie act for vaudeville. When she was a bit older she trained as an opera singer and became a soloist with the Roger Wagner Chorale. Nixon's clear, soprano voice allowed her to sing everything from opera to pop in nightclubs, in concerts, and on recordings, and by 1948 she was in Hollywood dubbing the vocals for Margaret O'Brien in *Big City*. Her most famous "unseen appearances" were singing for Deborah Kerr in *The King and I* (1955), for Natalie Wood in *West Side Story* (1961), and for Audrey Hepburn in *My Fair Lady* (1964), and she also dubbed for Jeanne Crain, Janet Leigh, Marilyn Monroe, and even some animated geese in *Mary Poppins* (1964). Nixon dubbed Kerr a second time when she provided her singing for the songs in *An Affair to Remember* (1957). Movie audiences finally got to see Nixon's face when she played Sister Sophia in the 1965 screen version of *The Sound of Music* where she joined in singing "(How Do You Solve a Problem Like) Maria?" Nixon provided the singing voice for Princess Serena in the animated-live action TV-movie *Jack and the Beanstalk* (1967). She has also performed on the New York stage in the musicals *The Girl in Pink Tights* (1954), *Taking My Turn* (1984), *James Joyce's The Dead* (2000), *Follies* (2001), and *Nine* (2003). She continues to sing in concerts and on soundtracks, and in 2007 played Mrs. Higgins in the national tour of *My Fair Lady*. Autobiography: *I Could Have Sung All Night*, with Stephen Cole (2006).

Nolan, Jeanette (1911–1998)   An all-purpose radio, film, and television actress who appeared in over 400 episodes of various TV series, she provided the voice for the take-charge muskrat Ellie Mae in *The Rescuers* (1977) and the kindly old Widow Tweed in *The Fox and the Hound* (1981). She was born in Los Angeles, educated at Los Angeles City College, and began her career on stage at the Pasadena Playhouse. Soon she was on the radio and was voicing a variety of characters on such programs as *Omar Khayyam*, *The March of Time*, *The Court of Missing Heirs*, *Life Begins*, and *Cavalcade of America*. Nolan made an auspicious screen debut as Lady Macbeth in Orson Welles' *Macbeth* (1948), followed by roles in such films as *Words and Music* (1948), *Kim* (1950), *The Happy Time* (1952), *The Big Heat* (1953), *Everything but the Truth* (1956), *April Love* (1957), *The Great Impostor* (1961), *The Man Who Shot Liberty Valance* (1962), *The Reluctant Astronaut* (1967), *The Sky's the Limit* (1975), *True Confessions* (1981), and *The Horse Whisperer* (1998). Yet she was busier in television, appearing in such early series as *Mr. & Mrs. North*, *The Adventures of Ozzie and Harriet*, *The Loretta Young Show* and *You Are There*, and ending her career with such series as *St. Elsewhere*, *Night Court*, *The Golden Girls*, *MacGyver*, and *Dear John*. While recording the vocals of the swamp dweller Ellie in *The Rescuers*, Nolan was asked by the directors to try a higher-pitched voice, so she used the voice she had come up with while providing the vocals for Norman Bates' "mother" in *Psycho* (1960). Nolan's husband John McIntire was also heard as one of the voices in *The Rescuers*. Biography: *Jeanette Nolan*, Frederic P. Miller (2010).

Norris, Daran (b. 1964)   A television voice artist with over 200 episodes to his credit, he voiced the pigeon Louie who is always picked on by the cat Mittens in *Bolt* (2008). He was born Daran Morrison Nordland in Ferndale, Washington, and made his television debut at the age of thirteen. Although he would later act in such films as *Hobgoblins* (1988), *Vice Academy* (1989), *Billy Frankenstein* (1998), and *In the Bedroom* (2001), he was busier in television where he began voicing characters in Japanese cartoons in 1979. Among the many animated TV series Norris voiced are *Cowboy Rebop*, *Time Squad*, *ChalkZone*, *Transformers: Robots in Disguise*, *Digimon: Digital Monsters*, *My Life as a Teenage Robot*, *What's New, Scooby-Doo?*, *Samurai Jack*, *Star Wars: Clone Wars*, *The Powerpuff Girls*, *The Adventures of Jimmy Neutron: Boy Genius*, *Duck Dodgers*, *Codename: Kids Next Door*, *The Fairly OddParents*, *The Replacements*, and *WordGirl*. He can also be heard in the animated videos and movies *Dinosaur* (2000), *Cowboy Rebop the Movie* (2001), *The Little Polar Bear* (2001), *Super Santa in South Pole Joe* (2002), *Super Santa in Vegetation* (2002), *Comic Book: The Movie* (2004), and *Ben 10: Race Against Time* (2007). Norris' voice is also featured on many computer video games.

Novello, Don (b. 1943)   The comic actor and writer who became famous for his portrayal of the worldly priest Father Guido Sarducci on the television program *Saturday Night Live*, he provided the voice of the Italian demolition expert Vincenzo "Vinny" Santorini in *Atlantis: The Lost Empire* (2001) as well as in the video sequel *Atlantis: Milo's Return* (2003). He was born in Lorain, Ohio, and educated at the University of Dayton before he started writing for television. He created the character of Fr. Sarducci in the early 1970s and portrayed him in stand-up comedy clubs, getting enough attention that Novello made an appearance as Sarducci on *The Smothers Brothers Show* in 1975. This led to his acting and writing for *Saturday Night Live* as well as appearances on various television sit-coms. Novello's film credits include *Tucker: The Man and His Dreams* (1988), *New York Stories* (1989), *The Godfather Part III* (1990), *Jack* (1996), *Just One Night* (2000), and *Factory Girl* (2006). He has also written comedy books about politics and government.

Novis, Donald (1906–1966) A British-born singer-actor on the Broadway stage and in several Hollywood films, he provided the singing narration for the cartoon short *The Night Before Christmas* (1933) and can be heard singing solo on the soundtracks for *Bambi* (1942) and *Lady and the Tramp* (1955). He was born in Hastings, England, but began his career in the States singing with big bands. In the 1930s he led his own orchestra, making some recordings, and he played leading roles in the Broadway musicals *Luana* (1930) and *Jumbo* (1935). The tenor sang solo in such films as *Kathleen Mavourneen* (1930), *Monte Carlo* (1930), *Love in the Rough* (1930), *Her Majesty, Love* (1931), *One Hour with You* (1932), *This Is the Night* (1932), *The Big Broadcast* (1932), and *Cut Out for Love* (1937), and played characters in other movies, including *Bulldog Drummond* (1929), *The Pajama Party* (1931), *Crooner* (1932), *The Policy Girl* (1934), *Sweethearts of the U.S.A.* (1944), and *Slightly Terrific* (1944), In 1955 Novis helped create the Golden Horseshoe Revue at Disneyland and often sang in the show during the next nine years.

Noyes, Betty (1912–1987) A singer who dubbed other actors' singing in movies, she sang the ballad "Baby Mine" on the soundtrack of *Dumbo* (1941) when Mrs. Jumbo is in a cage and comforts her baby Dumbo through the bars. Since most of Noyes' screen work was not credited, it is not possible to say exactly which films she can be heard in but it is confirmed that she dubbed some of Debbie Reynolds' singing in *Singin' in the Rain* (1952) and sang for secondary characters in the movie musicals *I Married an Angel* (1942) and *Seven Brides for Seven Brothers* (1954). Noyes can be seen as well as heard in an episode of the sit-com *I Love Lucy* in 1956 and in the TV musical *Cinderella* (1965).

Obradors, Jacqueline (b. 1966) An Hispanic television actress who has appeared on several popular series and occasionally in films, she voiced the Latina mechanic Audrey Rocio Ramirez in *Atlantis: The Lost Empire* (2001). Jacqueline Danell Obradors was born in the San Fernando Valley, California, to Argentine immigrants and made her television debut in 1992. Among the many series she has appeared on are *Diagnosis Murder*, *Live Shot*, *Jesse*, *Freddie*, *Cold Case*, *NCIS*, and *Murder, She Wrote*, but she is most known for playing Detective Rita Ortiz in *NYPD Blue*. Obradors' film credits include *Red Sun Rising* (1994), *Soldier Boyz* (1996), *Seven Days Seven Nights* (1998), *Tortilla Soup* (2001), *A Man Apart* (2003), and *Crossing Over* (2009). She reprised her mechanic Audrey in the video sequel *Atlantis: Milo's Return* (2003).

Ochoa, Adrian A production assistant for Pixar since 1996, he provided the voice of the troublemaking hot rod Wingo in *Cars* (2006). He worked on *A Bug's Life* (1998), *Toy Story 2* (1999), *Finding Nemo* (2003), *The Incredibles* (2004), *Cars*, and its video spinoffs *Mater and the Ghostlight* (2006) and *Tokyo Mater* (2008).

O'Donnell, Rosie (b. 1962) The popular comedienne, actress, and talk show hostess who is also a powerful producer, she voiced the wisecracking tomboy gorilla Terk in *Tarzan* (1999). Roseann O'Donnell was born in Commack, New York, and briefly attended Boston University and Dickinson College before beginning her career as a stand-up comic. After winning exposure on the television program *Star Search* at the age of twenty, she started appearing in supporting comic roles in such television series as *Gimme a Break!* and *Stand by Your Man*, as well as in such films as *A League of Their Own* (1992), *Sleepless in Seattle* (1993), *Another Stakeout* (1993), *Car 54, Where Are You?* (1994), and *The Flinstones* (1994). O'Donnell found her biggest success on television talk shows, such as *Rosie O'Donnell*, *The Rosie O'Donnell Show*, *Rosie Live*, and *The View*, most of which she produced as well. Among the other television series she acted in are *Murphy Brown*, *Ally McBeal*, *Spin City*, *Judging Amy*, *Queer as Folk*, *Nip/Tuck*, *Curb Your Enthusiasm*, and *Drop Dead Diva*. O'Donnell's other film credits include *Exit to Eden* (1994), *Now and Then* (1995), *Harriet the Spy* (1996), *The Twilight of the Golds* (1996), *Wide Awake* (1998), and some TV-movies such as *Riding the Bus with My Sister* (2005) and *America* (2009). She frequently promoted New York theatre on her shows, produced the London transfer *Taboo* (2003) on Broadway, and appeared in the Broadway musicals *Grease* (1994), *Seussical* (2001), and *Fiddler on the Roof* (2005). O'Donnell published her own magazine and has co-written works of nonfiction on various topics. The role of Turk in *Tarzan* was originally written to be a male gorilla but the animators were so impressed with O'Donnell's audition for another role that they changed Turk to a female. Memoir: *Celebrity Detox: The Fame Game* (2007); biographies: *Rosie O'Donnell: Her True Story*, George Mair (1998); *Rosie O'Donnell: Talk Show Host and Comedian*, Virginia Meachum (2000).

Oh, Soon-Tek (1943) A Japanese actor who has appeared on the American stage, in films, and on television since the 1960s, he supplied the voice of Mulan's sickly but proud father Fa Zhou in *Mulan* (1998). He was born in Japan, raised in Korea, and came to the States as a teenager, later studying at UCLA and the Neighborhood Playhouse School in New York. Oh acted in several Off Broadway productions and appeared on Broadway in *Pacific Overtures* (1976). His many television credits include the series *Mister Roberts*, *The Wild Wild West*, *It Takes a Thief*, *Death Valley Days*, *Kung Fu*, *Black Sheep Squadron*, *Hawaii Five-O*, *Charlie's Angels*, *M*A*S*H*, *Quincy M.E.*, *Marco Polo*, *Hart to Hart*, *Hill Street Blues*, *Cagney & Lacey*, *Dynasty*, *T. J. Hooker*, *MacGyver*, *Simon & Simon*, *Kung Fu: The Legend Continues*, *Seven Days*, and *Touched by an Angel*. Among his movies are *Murderers' Row* (1966), *The President's Analyst* (1967), *The Man with the Golden Gun* (1974), *The Final Countdown* (1980), *Missing Action 2: The Beginning* (1985), *Steele Justice* (1987), *Death Wish 4: The Crackdown* (1987), *Collision Course* (1989), *A Home of Our Own* (1993), *Red Sun Rising* (1994), *Beverly Hills Ninja* (1997), *Yellow* (1998), and *True Blue* (2001). Fa Zhou in *Mulan* is one of several ineffectual Disney fathers who rely on a son or daughter to save him. Mulan's father has more dignity than most and his failing is a physical one: he is old and sickly, rather than a matter of incompetence. Oh reprised his Fa Zhou in *Mulan II* (2004) and can be heard in the TV cartoon series *Jonny Quest*, *Sky Commanders*, *The Real Adventures of Jonny Quest*, *Life with Louie*, and *King of the Hill*.

O'Hara, Catherine (b. 1954) A comic actress with an uncanny ability to create different voices and impersonate celebrities, she provided the voices of the rag doll heroine Sally and the mischief-making imp Shock in *The Nightmare Before Christmas* (1993) and the alien mother Tina in *Chicken Little* (2005). She was born in Toronto, Canada, where she became a member of the comedy troupe Second City. She and other members of the company created, wrote, and performed the television series *SCTV* which made her a comedy favorite in both Canada and the States. Her subsequent television credits include *Saturday Night Live*, *Six Feet Under*, and *Curb Your Enthusiasm*, as well as many talk shows and comedy specials. O'Hara has been featured in many films, including *Heartburn* (1986), *Beetlejuice* (1988), *Dick Tracy* (1990), *Betsy's Wedding* (1990), *Home Alone* (1990), *Home Alone 2: Lost in New York* (1992), *The Paper* (1994), *Wyatt Earp* (1994), *Lemony Snicket's A Series of Unfortunate Events* (2004), and *Away We Go* (2009), as well as most of the "mockumentary" movies directed by Christopher Guest, such as *Waiting for Guffman* (1996), *Best in Show* (2000), *A Mighty Wind* (2003) and *For Your Consideration* (2006). Her versatility with voices can he heard in the TV cartoon series *The Completely Mental Misadventures of Ed Grimley*, as well as in the animated movies and videos *Witch's Night Out* (1978), *Rock & Rule* (1983), *Pippi Longstocking* (1997), *Bartok the Magnificent* (1999), *Over the Hedge* (2006), *Monster House* (2006), *Brother Bear 2* (2006), *Barbie in the 12 Dancing Princesses* (2006), *A Monster in Paris* (2010), and *Cat Tale* (2010).

O'Hara, Paige (b. 1956) A stage and concert singer with a crystal clear soprano voice, she is most known as the speaking and singing voice of the strong-willed heroine Belle in *Beauty and the Beast* (1991). She was born Donna Paige Helmintoller in Ft. Lauderdale, Florida, and appeared on stage in musicals as a child. She made her Broadway debut in the 1983 revival of *Show Boat* then went on to play leading roles in New York, on tour, and internationally in such musicals as *Les Misérables*, *The Mystery of Edwin Drood*, *Oklahoma!*, and *South Pacific*. O'Hara has made many recordings of vintage Broadway musicals and often performs in pops concerts. She can be seen on screen in the cameo role of the soap opera character Angela in the Disney film *Enchanted* (2007). The inspiration for the character of Belle in *Beauty and the Beast* did not come from the 1946 acclaimed French film by Jean Cocteau but from Katharine Hepburn's feisty performances as Jo March in *Little Women* (1933). Originally Jodi Benson, who had voiced Ariel in *The Little Mermaid*, was to record the vocals for Belle as well but it was felt she sounded too American. The directors settled on O'Hara because her vocals reminded them of the young Judy Garland, a sound that they had in mind for Belle from the start. While recording one of the songs for the soundtrack, a strand of O'Hara's hair got in her mouth and she tucked it aside as she kept singing. The animators like the simple gesture so much they used it in the movie. Sherri Stone served as the live-action model for Belle, just as she had for Ariel, and in the film the character moves like a ballet dancer at times. It is a tribute to the animators and to O'Hara that Belle is one of the strongest, most determined Disney heroines, yet she never loses her femininity or warmth. O'Hara reprised her Belle in the made-for-video movies *Beauty and the Beast: The Enchanted Christmas* (1997), *Beauty and the World of Music* (1999), *Mickey's Magical Christmas* (2001), *Disney Christmas Party: Volume Two* (2005), and *Kingdom Hearts II* (2005).

Oliveira, José A Brazilian actor and singer, he provided the voice of the dapper, straw-hatted, bow-tied parrot José Carioca in the feature anthology films *Saludos Amigos* (1942), *The Three Caballeros* (1944), and *Melody Time* (1948). The native of Rio de Janeiro appeared in only one Hollywood film, *Hell's Island* (1955), but in addition to his Joe Carioca voices he was heard singing "Aquarela do Brasil" on the soundtrack of *Saludos Amigos*. The character of José Carioca is based on a Brazilian comic type and a familiar favorite in South America. The parrot also appealed to North Americans so it is surprising that Disney did not feature "Joe" in cartoon shorts. He did appear on television in one episode of *Walt Disney's Wonderful World of Color* in 1962 and Oliveira again did the voice. The character of José Carioca makes for an interesting contrast with his American pal Donald Duck. Joe, described as a "Brazilian Jitterbug" by the animators, is lively, colorful, and hyperactive like Donald, yet the Portuguese-accented parrot is more debonair, more worldly-wise, and even sexy in his way. The humor comes from Donald's attempt to copy Joe and failing miserably each time. Some commentators have pointed out that the playful friendship between Donald and José was one of the more successful illustrations of the Good Neighbor policy between North and South America in the 1940s.

Olsen, Moroni (1889–1954) A tall, imposing character actor seen in over one hundred movies from the mid-1930s to the mid-1950s, he supplied the voice of the spirit (or is it slave?) in the Magic Mirror in *Snow White and the Seven Dwarfs* (1937). He was born John Willard Clawson, Jr., in Ogden, Utah, the son of portrait painter John Willard Clawson (1858–1936), and went on the stage as a young man, eventually forming his own professional touring company, the Moroni Olsen Players. He later appeared on Broadway in ten productions, including *Medea* (1920), *The Trial of Joan of Arc* (1921), *The Great Way* (1921), *Candida* (1922), *Mr. Faust* (1922), *Mary of Scotland* (1933), *Romeo and Juliet* (1934), and *The Barretts of Wimpole Street* (1935), and returned to the classical stage regionally throughout his career, particularly at the Pasadena Playhouse. Olsen made his screen debut in *The Three Musketeers* (1935) and was featured in such films as *Annie Oakley* (1935), *Seven Keys to Baldpate* (1935), *Yellow Dust* (1936), *The Farmer in the Dell* (1936), *Mary of Scotland* (1936), *The Plough and the Stars* (1936), *The Life of Emile Zola* (1937), and *The Last Gangster* (1937). Much of the rest of his career had him playing smaller and less significant roles in movies, though the tall, balding actor was usually noticed. Among his many other film credits are *Kidnapped* (1938), *Rose of Washington Square* (1939), *Sons of Liberty* (1939), *Allegheny Uprising* (1939), *Invisible Stripes* (1939), *Brigham Young* (1940), *Santa Fe Trail* (1940), *My Favorite Spy* (1942), *Air Force* (1943), *Mission to Moscow* (1943), *Ali Baba and the Forty Thieves* (1944), *Mildred Pierce* (1945), *Notorious* (1946), *Life with Father* (1947), *Possessed* (1947), *Up in Central Park* (1948), *Father of the Bride* (1950), *Father's Little Dividend* (1951), *So This Is Love* (1953), *The Long, Long Trailer* (1953), and *Sign of the Pagan* (1954). Olsen also appeared in episodes of the television series *I Love Lucy* and *G.E. True Theatre*. The role of the Magic Mirror in *Snow White and the Seven Dwarfs* is not a large one but an unforgettable one. Olsen's impersonal, detached vocals are chilling yet he is not the villain, just the messenger of truth. In order to get the right effect, Olsen placed his head inside a box with an opening for the microphone and delivered his lines within the mini-echo chamber.

O'Malley, J. Pat (1901–1985) A beloved character actor of movies and television with an Irish brogue and a twinkling smile, he voiced many animated characters in Disney films, often playing several roles in one movie, as in *Alice in Wonderland* (1951) in which he voiced the twins Tweedledum and Tweedledee, the Walrus, and the Carpenter. James Patrick O'Malley was born in Burnley, England, and performed in British music halls before coming to the States at the beginning of World War II. Although he acted on the Broadway stage a few times after the war, he was more successful in films, playing kindly relatives and colorful character types in dozens of films, including *Lassie Come Home* (1943), *The Long Hot Summer* (1958), *Star!* (1968), *Hello, Dolly!* (1969), and *Willard* (1971). O'Malley was also very popular on television, appearing over one hundred times on sit-coms, dramas, and specials. His versatility with different voices made him ideal for animated films and Disney used him frequently. Among his many Disney voices are Mr. Toad's singing horse Cyril Proudbottom in *The Adventures of Ichabod and Mr. Toad* (1949), the father elephant Goliath I in the short *Goliath II* (1960), the bumbling villain Jasper and the old English sheepdog the Colonel in *One Hundred and One Dalmatians* (1961), Mayor Crum in the short *The Saga of Windwagon Smith* (1961), the Master of the Hounds, the Pearly Drummer, and other characters in the animated sequence in *Mary Poppins* (1964), the military-minded elephant Colonel Hathi and the buzzard Buzzie in *The Jungle Book* (1967), and Otto the dog blacksmith in *Robin Hood* (1973). He can also be heard in the animated film *Hey There, It's Yogi Bear* (1964). In many ways O'Malley's first Disney assignment was his best. His Cyril Proudbottom in *The Adventures of Ichabod and Mr. Toad* is one of the highlights of "The Wind in the Willows" section and the character is not even in Kenneth Grahame's original book. Basing his performance on the beloved English music-hall performer George Formby, O'Malley sings with a bluster and, in harmony with Eric Blore's Mr. Toad, their duets are a highlight in the film.

Orbach, Jerry (1935–2004)   The likable, durable leading man of musicals and comedies, he became known to most Americans late in his career for his dramatic roles on television but perhaps his most recognized performance is the speaking and singing voice of the enchanted French candlestick Lumiere in *Beauty and the Beast* (1991) in which he introduced "Be Our Guest." Jerome Bernard Orbach was born in the Bronx, New York, the son of a vaudevillian and a radio singer, was educated at the University of Illinois and Northwestern University, and trained with Herbert Berghof and Lee Strasberg in New York. After dozens of productions in stock, he was cast Off Broadway as a replacement in *The Threepenny Opera*. Orbach originated the role of the bandit El Gallo in the record-breaking musical *The Fantasticks* (1960) then made his Broadway debut in *Carnival* (1961), followed by feature roles in such New York stage productions as *The Cradle Will Rock* (1964), *Guys and Dolls* (1965), *Carousel* (1965), *Annie Get Your Gun* (1966), *Scuba Duba* (1967), *Promises Promises* (1968), *6 Rms Riv Vu* (1972), *Chicago* (1975), and *42nd Street* (1980). Orbach left Broadway in the 1980s and concentrated on television, appearing in dozens of programs before finding fame on *Law and Order*. The character of Lumiere in *Beauty and the Beast* developed from songwriter Howard Ashman's idea that the people in the castle were changed into objects with some of their human characteristics remaining. Lumiere is obviously inspired by the great French entertainer Maurice Chevalier and the animators even had the candlestick character doff a hat in the Chevalier manner during "Be Our Guest." Yet Orbach made no attempt to copy Chevalier vocally and he created his own voice for the bon vivant Lumiere who is a bit of an adventurer, clearly a ladies' man, and a kind of French master of ceremonies. Orbach reprised his Lumiere in the video movies *Beauty and the Beast: The Enchanted Christmas* (1997) and *Belle's Magical World* (1998), and the television series *House of Mouse*. He also provided voices for the TV-movie *The Special Magic of Herself the Elf* (1983) and the video film *Aladdin and the King of Thieves* (1995). In 2007 an Off Broadway theatre was named after Orbach, a fitting tribute for the man who led the cast of Off Broadway's biggest hit, *The Fantasticks*. Memoir: *Remember How I Love You: Love Letters from an Extraordinary Marriage*, Jerry and Elaine Orbach, Ken Bloom (2009).

Osmond, Donny (b. 1957)   The boyish pop singer who has acted on occasion, he provided the singing voice of the Chinese Captain Li Shang in *Mulan* (1998). Donald Clark Osmond was born in Ogden, Utah, into a family of singers, later the popular Osmond Family of television and concert tours. His older brothers were hired to sing at Disneyland where they were discovered by Andy Williams who featured the whole family on his television show. Donny Osmond was only six when he began singing professionally and grew up on television, singing on many variety shows and specials. He and his sister Marie became teen idols in the 1970s with hit records and their own TV show, *Donny and Marie*, which ran four years. After that both siblings continued to sing and record together and separately. Donny has turned to the stage on occasion, performing in *Little Johnny Jones* on Broadway in 1982 and touring in *Joseph and the Amazing Technicolor Dreamcoat* throughout the 1990s; and in 2006 he played Gaston in the Broadway production of *Beauty and the Beast*. Autobiography: *Life Is Just What You Make It: My Story So Far* (2006).

Ossman, David (b. 1936)   A comedian and writer who works in theatre, radio, and television, he supplied the voice of the curmudgeonly old ant Cornelius in *A Bug's Life* (1998). He was born in Santa Monica, California, and found recognition as a member of the comedy group The Firesign Theatre on stage, records, radio, and television. Ossman wrote many of the sketches for the troupe and with them appeared in the films *Martian Space Party* (1972) and *Everything You Know Is Wrong* (1975), and the TV-movie *Firesign Theatre: Weirdly Cool* (2001). He has provided voices for the cartoon series *The Tick* and acted in the movie *Nowheresville* (2000). Ossman also writes and directs audio plays for children.

Oswalt, Patton (b. 1969)   A popular comedian in clubs and on television, as well as a successful comedy writer, he provided the voice of the rat Remy, who dreams of becoming a chef, in *Ratatouille* (2007). He was born in Portsmouth, Virginia, and educated at the College of William and Mary before beginning his career doing stand-up comedy. Oswalt had his own HBO comedy special in 1996 and was soon in demand for television series, movies, and voice work. He can be seen in such TV shows as *Seinfeld, MADtv, NewsRadio, Mr. Snow with Bob and David, The King of Queens, Reno 911!, Dollhouse, Caprica, United States of Tara,* and *Neighbors from Hell,* as well as several films, including *Desperate but Not Serious* (1999), *Magnolia* (1999), *Zoolander* (2001), *The Vinyl Battle* (2002), *ZigZag* (2002), *Calendar Girls* (2003), *Starsky & Hutch* (2004), *Blade: Trinity* (2004), *Failure to Launch* (2006), *Reno 911!: Miami* (2007), *Greetings from Earth* (2007), *Balls of Fury* (2007), *All Roads Lead Home* (2008), *Big Fan* (2009), *The Informant!* (2009), and *A Very Harold & Kumar Christmas* (2011). The character of Remy in *Ratatouille* is unusual for a Disney animal because his features are not exaggerated. He and the other rats in the movie look very much like real rats while the humans have the typical oversized noses, ears, and other features expected in an animated film. Oswalt was cast as Remy after director Brad Bird heard the comic do a stand-up routine about the menu at a steakhouse and thought he had the sound of a rat gourmet. Oswalt reprised his Remy in the animated short *Your Friend the Rat* (2007) and can be heard doing voices in such TV cartoon series as *Crank Yankers, The Fairly OddParents, Static Shock, Aqua Teen Hunger Force, Human Giant, SpongeBob SquarePants, Kim Possible, The Batman,* and *WordGirl.* He has recorded comedy albums, participated in national tours featuring various comics, and written for such television shows as *MADtv, Comedy Central Presents, The Comedians of Comedy, Human Giant, Small Doses,* and *Dr. Katz, Professional Therapist,* as well as comedy specials and videos.

O'Toole, Peter (b. 1932) The acclaimed Irish-born actor who played many dashing leading roles in films then excelled as eccentrics and colorful types in his later years, he supplied the voice for the stern, humorless Parisian food critic Anton Ego in *Ratatouille* (2007). Peter Seamus O'Toole was born in Connemara, Ireland, was raised in Leeds, England, and was on the professional stage by the age of seventeen. After training at the Royal Academy of Dramatic Art, he acted at the Bristol Old Vic for several seasons then made his British television debut in 1958. Two years later he made his first movie, *Kidnapped* (1960), but it was his performance in the title role in *Lawrence of Arabia* (1962) that made him an international star. Among O'Toole's many other notable films are *Becket* (1964), *Lord Jim* (1965), *What's New Pussycat* (1965), *How to Steal a Million* (1966), *The Night of the Generals* (1967), *The Lion in Winter* (1968), *Goodbye, Mr. Chips* (1969), *Murphy's War* (1971), *The Ruling Class* (1972), *Man of La Mancha* (1972), *Caligula* (1979), *The Stunt Man* (1980), *My Favorite Year* (1982), *Club Paradise* (1986), *The Last Emperor* (1987), *King Ralph* (1991), *Phantoms* (1998), *Bright Young Things* (2003), *Troy* (2004), *Venus* (2006), *Stardust* (2007), and *Dean Spanley* (2008). He also acted in many British television series and mini-series. O'Toole has returned to the London stage on occasion and starred in the Broadway production of *Pygmalion* in 1987. The character of Anton Ego in *Ratatouille* was designed to resemble a vulture even though he is human. His stooped shoulders and beak-like nose give the sense that he is perched and ready to attack. O'Toole's performance is quiet, subtle, and yet stinging. Ego's change from cynical critic to joyous food lover is unique for a secondary character. One taste of the plate of ratatouille and Ego is transformed before our eyes. Autobiographies: *Loitering with Intent: The Child* (1997); *Loitering with Intent: The Apprentice* (1997); memoir: *Public Places: My Life in the Theatre, with Peter O'Toole and Beyond,* Sian Phillips (his ex-wife) (2003); biographies: *Peter O'Toole,* Michael Freedland (1985); *Peter O'Toole,* Carolyn Soutar (2008).

Owen, Harriet An English actress who voiced Jane, Wendy's unbelieving daughter, in *Return to Never Land* (2002), her other acting credits are the British television series and mini-series *Gallowglass, Castles, Animal Ark,* and *Relative Strangers.*

Owen, Tudor (1898–1979) A Welsh actor who worked in the States after World War II, he provided the deep, howling voice of the hound Towser who is part of the "twilight bark" in *One Hundred and One Dalmatians* (1961). Owen often played Brits and Irishmen in his many Hollywood films, including *Top o' the Morning* (1949), *Lorna Doone* (1951), *Angels in the Outfield* (1951), *Talk About a Stranger* (1952), *When in Rome* (1952), *The Return of Gilbert & Sullivan* (1952), *My Cousin Rachel* (1952), *Botany Bay* (1953), *Dangerous When Wet* (1953), *How to Marry a Millionaire* (1953), *Brigadoon* (1954), *The Court Jester* (1955), *Congo Crossing* (1956), *Duel at Apache Wells* (1957), *Jet Over the Atlantic* (1959), *North to Alaska* (1960), *The Notorious Landlady* (1962), *How the West Was Won* (1962), and *Jack the Giant Killer* (1962). Among the many television series he appeared in are *Family Theatre, Schlitz Playhouse, Mayor of the Town, The Lone Wolf, Gang Busters, Topper, My Friend Flicka, The Adventures of Rin Tin Tin, The Lone Ranger, Mike Hammer, The Thin Man, Cheyenne, Captain David Grief, Shirley Temple Theatre, 77 Sunset Strip, Twilight Zone, Wagon Train, Perry Mason,* and *Voyage to the Bottom of the Sea.*

Oz, Frank (b. 1944) The puppeteer, actor, voice artist, and director mostly known for his many years of working with the Muppets, he provided the voice of the three-eyed, hard-hat monster Fungus in *Monsters, Inc.* (2001). He was born Richard Frank Oznowicz in Hereford, England, the son of refugees from Nazi Poland who were both puppeteers, and grew up in Oakland, California. He was with Muppet creator Jim Henson almost from the beginning, creating puppet characters and voices for television's *Sesame Street,* then later *The Muppet Show* and the various Muppet films. Among Oz's voices for *Sesame Street* are Bert, Grover, and Cookie Monster; for the Muppets gang he voiced Fozzie Bear, Miss Piggy, Animal, Sam the Eagle, the Swedish Chef, and others. He can be heard in the movies *The Muppet Movie* (1979), *The Great Muppet Caper* (1981), *The Dark Crystal* (1982), *The Muppets Take Manhattan* (1984), *Sesame Street Presents Follow That Bird* (1985), *Labyrinth* (1986), *The Muppet Christmas Carol* (1992), *Muppet Treasure Island* (1996), *Muppets from Space* (1999), *The Adventures of Elmo in Grouchland* (1999), and *Zathura: A Space Adventure* (2005), but perhaps his most famous voice role was Yoda in five of the *Star Wars* films. Oz can also be heard in dozens of *Sesame Street* and Muppet television specials and videos. He can be seen in minor roles in such live-action films as *The Blues Brothers* (1980), *An American Werewolf in London* (1981), *Trading Places* (1983), *Spies Like Us* (1985), *Innocent Blood* (1992), and *Blues Brothers 2000* (1998). Oz has directed or co-directed a dozen movies, including *The Dark Crystal, The Muppets Take Manhattan, Little Shop of Horrors* (1986), *Dirty Rotten Scoundrels* (1988), *What About Bob?* (1991), *The Indian in the Cupboard* (1995), *In & Out* (1997), *The Stepford Wives* (2004), and *Death at a Funeral* (2007).

Page, Geraldine (1924–1987) A highly mannered, eccentric stage actress who conveyed a nervous neurosis in most of her performances, her television and film credits are few but memorable, such as the voice of the wacky villainess Madame Medusa in *The Rescuers* (1977). Geraldine Sue Page was born in Kirksville, Missouri, the daughter of a physician, and was educated in Chicago where she later enrolled at the Goodman Theatre School. She studied acting with Uta Hagen in New York and became a strong advocate for Method acting. Page made her Off Broadway debut in 1945 then was lauded for her performance as the spinster Alma in *Summer and Smoke* (1952), an acclaimed Off Broadway revival that made both the play and its star famous. Concentrating on the New York stage over the next three decades, she shone in such productions as *The Rainmaker* (1954), *Sweet Bird of Youth* (1959), *Strange Interlude* (1963), *Absurd Person Singular* (1974), *Agnes of God* (1982), *Vivat! Vivat! Regina!* (1985), and *A Lie of the Mind* (1985). Page got to reprise two of her stage triumphs in the films *Summer and Smoke* (1961) and *Sweet Bird of Youth* (1962), and gave powerful performances in such movies as *Toys in the Attic* (1963), *Interiors* (1978), and *The Trip to Bountiful* (1985). She appeared in several television dramas throughout her career, most memorably *A Christmas Memory* (1966), and although *The Rescuers* was her only animated film, she appeared in the Disney movie musical *The Happiest Millionaire* (1967). Page died during the run of the 1987 Broadway revival of *Blithe Spirit* in which she played the zany medium Madame Arcati. The character of Madame Medussa in *The Rescuers* has been compared (usually unfavorably) to that of Cruella De Vil in *One Hundred and One Dalmatians* (1962); both are vain, ego-centric women with an obsession (for either dog fur coats or diamonds). Yet Page's performance reveals many levels of Medusa's tactics, ranging from gentle, pseudo-loving caresses to outright fury.

Page, Ken (b. 1954) A rotund, full-voiced African American actor-singer who has lit up several stage musicals in character roles, he provided the deep speaking and singing vocals for the monstrous Oogie Boogie in *The Nightmare Before Christmas* (1993). A native of St. Louis, Page studied theatre at the local Fontbonne College before performing in stock. He made a lively Broadway debut in *Guys and Dolls* (1976), stopping the show with his gospel number "Sit Down, You're Rockin' the Boat." Page found further acclaim in *Ain't Misbehavin'* (1978 and 1988), *The Wiz* (1979), and *Cats* (1982). He played the Lion in the Madison Square Garden Theatre version of the movie *The Wizard of Oz* (1997 and 1998), as well as the Ghost of Christmas Present in the same venue's musical *A Christmas Carol* (1997). He also starred as God in the London musical *Children of Eden* (1991) and has performed in many regional theatres, such as his hometown's St. Louis Municipal Opera. Page has appeared in a handful of movies, including *Torch Song Trilogy* (1988) and *Dreamgirls* (2006), and on television, as in the TV musicals *Polly* (1989) and *Polly—Comin' Home!* (1990). He reprised his Oogie Boogie in the video movies *Kingdom Hearts* (2002), *The Nightmare Before Christmas: Oogie's Revenge* (2004), and *Kingdom Hearts II* (2005), and played King Gator in the non–Disney animated feature *All Dogs Go to Heaven* (1989).

Palmer, Garrett (b. 1997) A child actor who began his career at the age of eight, he supplied the voice of the blond-headed Boy in the BnL (Buy-n-Large Corporation) commercial in *WALL-E* (2008). Born in San Ramon, California, Palmer appeared in the TV-movie *Out of the Woods* (2005) and on the series *Big Time Rush*.

Panettiere, Hayden (b. 1989) A young film and television actress with many years experience in soap opera, she provided the voices of the young ant Princess Dot in *A Bug's Life* (1998) and the young iguanodon Suri in *Dinosaur* (2000). Hayden Leslie Panettiere was born in Palisades, New York, the daughter of a soap opera actress, and before she was a year old was in television commercials. At the age of four she started acting in the daytime drama *One Life to Live* and remained with the series for three years, then acted in the soap opera *The Guiding Light* for four years. As a teenager, Panettiere appeared in such television series as *Ally McBeal*, *Law & Order: Special Victims Unit*, and *Malcolm in the Middle*, although is probably most remembered as Claire Bennet in *Heroes*. Her film credits include *The Object of My Affection* (1998), *Remember the Titans* (2000), *Raising Helen* (2004), *Racing Stripes* (2005), *Ice Princess* (2005), and *I Love You Beth Cooper* (2009). Panettiere provided voices for the animated videos *Kingdom Hearts* (2002), *Kingdom Hearts II* (2005), and *Scooby-Doo and the Goblin King* (2008), and the films *Hoodwinked Too! Hood vs. Evil* (2010) and *Alpha and Omega* (2010).

Parker, Barnett (1886–1941) The tall and very British character actor who played supporting roles in many Hollywood films of the 1930s, he voiced the genteel Dragon and the Boy's Father in *The Reluctant Dragon* (1941). He was born William Barnett Parker in Batley, England, and became a popular comic on the London stage in the 1910s and 1920s even as he acted in silent movies in Britain. Parker made his Hollywood screen debut in *Mr. Deeds Goes to Town* (1936) then went on to play mostly English types in such films as *Libeled Lady* (1936), *A Woman Rebels* (1936), *The Last of Mrs. Cheyney* (1937), *Ready, Willing and Able* (1937), *Married Before Breakfast* (1937), *Broadway Melody of 1938* (1937), *Wake Up and Live* (1937), *Sally, Irene and Mary* (1938), *Marie Antoinette* (1938), *She Married a Cop* (1939), *Babes in Arms* (1939), *At the Circus* (1939), *Hit Parade of 1941* (1940), *One Night in the Tropics* (1940), *Love Thy Neighbor* (1940), *A Man Betrayed* (1941), and *New Wine* (1941). The title character in *The Reluctant Dragon* is an atypical Disney character: low-key, very British, and mockingly aesthete. Parker's vocals are ideal for the role, his voice being lazy and slightly arrogant at the same time. The dragon made a cameo appearance decades later in *Who Framed Roger Rabbit* (1988).

Parker, Bret "Brook" (b. 1970) A Pixar animator who does voices on occasion, she supplied the voice of Kari McKeen, Jack-Jack's teenage babysitter, in *The Incredibes* (2004). Educated at Oberlin College and in the Netherlands, she first worked with Pixar on *A Bug's Life* (1998), followed by *Toy Story 2* (1999), *Monsters, Inc.* (2001), *Finding Nemo* (2003), *The Incredibles*, and *Ratatouille* (2007), as well as the short *Mike's New Car*. Parker reprised her Kari in the short *Jack-Jack Attack* (2005) and provided the voices for minor characters in *Monsters, Inc.* She is currently an Associate Professor of Animation at the California College of the Arts.

Parris, Patricia An actress and voice artist who works mostly in television, she supplied the voice of Daisy Duck as Belle in *Mickey's Christmas Carol* (1983). Parris began to voice TV cartoon series in the 1970s and played recurring characters on such shows as *The Littles*, *Meitantei Holmes*, and *The New Adventures of Winnie the Pooh*, as well as various characters in episodes of *Jabberjaw*, *Yogi's Space Race*, *The Smurfs*, *Buford and the Galloping Ghost*, *Scooby-Doo and Scappy-Doo*, *Dumbo's Circus*, *Adventures of the Gummi Bears*, *DuckTales*, *Tom & Jerry Kids Show*, and *Fievel's American Tails*. She can also be heard on many animated videos, including *Davy Crockett on the Mississippi* (1976), *The Flintstones' New Neighbors* (1980), *Here Come the Littles* (1985), *The GLO Friends Save Christmas* (1985), *DuckTales: Treasure of the Golden Suns* (1987), *Rover Dangerfield* (1991), and *Winnie the Pooh Friendship: Pooh Wishes* (1999).

Paulsen, Rob (b. 1956) A very busy voice artist who can be heard in over one thousand commercials and over 600 episodes of television cartoon series, he supplied the voice of Max's teenage friend P. J. Pete in *A Goofy Movie* (1995) and in its video sequel *An Extremely Goofy Movie* (2000), and the lisping class weirdo Ian "Weewan" Wazselewski in *Teacher's Pet* (2004). Robert Frederick Paulsen III was born in Detroit, Michigan, and began his career voicing characters for *The Smurfs* in 1981. He has made a handful of appearances on TV series and films but his forty years in animation make him one of the most prolific voice artists on record. Paulsen is mostly known as the voice of Raphael in *The Teenage Mutant Ninja Turtles*, Yakko Warner and Dr. Otto Scratchansniff in *Animaniacs*, Arthur in *The Tick*, and Pinky in *Pinky and the Brain*, and he has also been heard on dozens of other series, including *G.I. Joe*, *The Transformers*, *DuckTales*, *Midnight Patrol: Adventures in the Dream Zone*, *Adventures of the Gummi Bears*, *Where's Waldo?*, *Yo Yogi!*, *Darkwing Duck*, *Tiny Toon Adventures*, *Bonkers*, *The Addams Family*, *Goof Troop*, *Mighty Max*, *Sonic the Hedgehog*, *Biker Mice from Mars*, *Jungle Cubs*, *The Real Adventures of Johnny Quest*, *The Mask*, *Histeria!*, *Buzz Lightyear of Star Command*,

Dexter's Laboratory, The Powerpuff Girls, The Fairly OddParents, The Adventures of Jimmy Neutron: Boy Genius, Loonatics Unleashed, Danny Phantom, The Replacements, and *Back in the Barnyard*. Among Paulsen's many animated videos and movies are *Daniel in the Lion's Den* (1986) and several others in the Biblical series, *G.I. Joe: The Movie* (1987), *Top Cat and the Beverly Hills Cat* (1987), *The Little Troll Prince* (1987), *Jetsons: The Movie* (1990), *A Goof Troop Christmas* (1993), *The Land Before Time II: The Great Adventure* (1994) and several of its sequels, *Aladdin and the King of Thieves* (1995), *Belle's Magical World* (1998), *Pocahontas II: Journey to a New World* (1998), *The Little Mermaid II: Return to the Sea* (2000), *Lady and the Tramp II: Scamp's Adventure* (2001), *Return to Never Land* (2002), *Balto: Wolf Quest* (2002), *Cinderella II: Dreams Come True* (2002), *101 Dalmatians II: Patch's London Adventure* (2003), *Stitch! The Movie* (2003), *The Nightmare Before Christmas: Oogie's Revenge* (2004), *Mulan II* (2004), *The Ant Bully* (2006), *Barnyard* (2006), *The Fox and the Hound 2* (2006), *Happily N'Ever After* (2006), *Cinderella III: A Twist in Time* (2007), *The Little Mermaid: Ariel's Beginning* (2008), *Tinker Bell* (2008) and its four sequels, *The Haunted World of El Superbeasto* (2009), and *Hoodwinked Too! Hood vs. Evil* (2010).

Pelling, George (1914–2008) A character actor who usually played British types in American movies and television, he supplied the voices of Danny the Great Dane in *One Hundred and One Dalmatians* (1961) and a reporter and one of the hounds in the animated sequence in *Mary Poppins* (1964). He was born in Salisbury, South Rhodesia, and began his film career in England with such movies as *Bedelia* (1946) and *Green Fingers* (1947). By the 1950s he was in the States appearing on television series, including *Highway Patrol, The Loretta Young Show, Studio 57, Sergeant Preston of the Yukon, Alfred Hitchcock Presents, The Outer Limits*, and *The Farmer's Daughter*. Among Pelling's movie credits are *Les Girls* (1957), *Witness for the Prosecution* (1957), *Midnight Lace* (1960), *The Notorious Landlady* (1962), *Brainstorm* (1965), *King Rat* (1965), and *Not with My Wife, You Don't!* (1966).

Peña, Elizabeth (b. 1961) An Hispanic actress known for playing outspoken or rebellious characters in films and on television, she provided the sexy voice for Syndrome's seductive accomplice Mirage in *The Incredibles* (2004). She was born in Elizabeth, New Jersey, the daughter of actors who cofounded Off Broadway's Latin American Theatre Ensemble, and trained at the High School of the Performing Arts. After appearing in some stage productions and television commercials, Peña made her film debut in 1979 but was not widely recognized until her upstart maid Carmen in *Down and Out in Beverly Hills* (1986). Her other movies include *La Bamba* (1987), *Batteries Not Included* (1987), *Blue Steel* (1989), *The Waterdance* (1992), *Dead Funny* (1994), *Free Willy 2: The Adventure Home* (1995), *Lone Star* (1996), *Rush Hour* (1998), *Tortilla Soup* (2001), *Impostor* (2001), *How the Garcia Girls Spent Their Summer* (2005), *The Lost City* (2005), *Dragon Wars: D-War* (2007), *Nothing Like the Holidays* (2008), and *Down for Life* (2009). Among Peña's television credits are several made-for-TV movies and the series *Tough Cookies, I Married Dora, Shannon's Deal, L.A. Law, Boston Public*, and *Numb3rs*. She can be heard in the television cartoon series *Justice League*.

Peña, Javier Fernández An Hispanic actor-singer who has voiced commercials and video games, he provided the voice of Buzz Lightyear when he was switched into a Spanish-speaking mode in *Toy Story 3* (2010).

Pendleton, Austin (b. 1940) A lean, bespectacled, nasal character actor who turned to stage directing in the 1970s, he is still a familiar face performing in different media, including animated films such as *Finding Nemo* (2003) in which he voiced the germ-phobic aquarium fish Gurgle. Pendleton was born in Warren, Ohio, and educated at Yale University before making a noticeable Broadway debut in *Oh Dad, Poor Dad ...* (1962), followed by *Fiddler on the Roof* (1964) in which he originated the role of the tailor Motel. His other notable New York stage credits include *The Last Sweet Days of Isaac* (1970), *The Little Foxes* (1970), *The Three Sisters* (1977), *Julius Caesar* (1978), *Doubles* (1985), *Educating Rita* (1987), *Sophistry* (1993), and *The Diary of Anne Frank* (1997). Pendleton started directing in regional theatres in the 1970s and then in New York, helming such notable plays as the Elizabeth Taylor revival of *The Little Foxes* (1981) and the dramas *The Runner Stumbles* (1976) and *Spoils of War* (1988). He also turned to writing in the 1990s and scripted such Off Broadway plays as *Booth* (1994) and *Orson's Shadow* (2005). Since the late 1960s Pendleton has appeared in many films, often playing oddball supporting characters, as in *The Front Page* (1974), *The Muppet Movie* (1979), *My Cousin Vinny* (1992), *Guarding Tess* (1994) and *A Beautiful Mind* (2001), as well as dozens of television programs. He reprised his Gurgle in the animated short *Finding Nemo Submarine Voyage* (2007).

Perkins, Elizabeth (b. 1960) A stage, screen, and television actress with a bit of an edge to her characterizations, she supplied the voice of Nemo's mother, the clown fish Coral, in *Finding Nemo* (2003). She was born in Queens, New York, grew up in Vermont, and studied acting at the Goodman School of Drama and DePaul University. After performing in tours and in Chicago theatres, Perkins moved to New York where she appeared in many Off Broadway productions and on Broadway in *Brighton Beach Memoirs* in 1984. She made her screen debut in a major role in *About Last Night* (1986) followed by such notable movies as *Big* (1988), *Avalon* (1990), *He Said, She Said* (1991), *The Flintstones* (1994), *Crazy in Alabama* (1999), *Cats & Dogs* (2001), and *The Thing About My Folks* (2005). Perkins has appeared in the television series *From the Earth to the Moon, Battery Park,* and *Monk,* but she is most known as Celia Hodes in *Weeds.* She can be heard in the cartoon series *King of the Hill.*

Perl, Michael A television and film actor with stage experience, he provided the voice of the clueless Mungo, one of Tarzan's ape friends, in *Tarzan* (1999). He was born in Los Angeles and studied acting at UCLA's School of Theatre before performing in classical and modern roles in regional theatres. Perl played Winston Egbert on the television series *Sweet Valley High* for three years and has appeared in such films as *The Terrapin* (2002), *Porno* (2004), *The Five-Cent Curve* (2005), *War Torn* (2006), *Vagabond* (2006), *Surviving New Year's* (2008), and *Bittersweet Paradise* (2009).

Perlman, Ron (b. 1950) The tall, imposing actor of stage, films, and television with a deep musical voice, he provided the voices for the twin Stabbington brothers who seek revenge on Flynn Ryder in *Tangled* (2010). Ronald Francis Perlman was born in New York City, the son of a Big Band drummer, and was educated at Lehman College and the University of Minnesota. He attempted stand-up comedy for a while then found acting jobs in New York, eventually appearing on Broadway in *Teiblele and Her Demon* (1979), *A Few Good Men* (1989), and *Bus Stop* (1996). Perlman made his television debut on *Ryan's Hope* in 1979 and his screen bow in *Quest for Fire* (1981) but did not receive wide recognition until he played the lion-man Vincent in the television series *Beauty and the Beast* in 1987. His other film credits include *Sleepwalkers* (1992), *The Adventures of Huck Finn* (1993), *Cronos* (1993), *The City of Lost Children* (1995), *Alien: Resurrection* (1997), *Blade II* (2002), *Star Trek: Nemesis* (2002), *Hellboy* (2004), *Hellboy 2: The Golden Army* (2008), and *Acts of Violence* (2010). Perlman has appeared on other television series, such as *Family Law, The Magnificent Seven, The Tick,* and *Sons of Anarchy,* but he has been busier voicing TV cartoons, including *Batman, Animaniacs, Mighty Max, Aladdin, Fantastic Four, Wing Commander Academy, Mortal Kombat: Defenders of the Realm, Superman, Buzz Lightyear of Star Command, The Legend of Tarzan, Teen Titans, Justice League, Danny Phantom, Chowder,* and several others. He can also be heard on many video games, most based on his films or cartoons shows.

Perrette, Pauley (b. 1969) A widely recognized television actress who is also a writer and singer, she provided the voice of the Female Lover Bear in *Brother Bear* (2003). She was born in New Orleans, Louisiana, grew up in various states as her family moved about, and was educated at Valdosta State University in Georgia for a career in forensics. After singing in a rock band and working as a Spoken Word artist, Perette gained attention as a regular on the television series *Murder One* in 1996. Her other television series include *Frasier, That's Life, The Drew Carey Show, The Time of Your Life, Special Unit 2, CSI: Crime Scene Investigation,* and *Jag,* but she is best known as Abby Sciuto on *NCIS* and *NCIS: Los Angeles.* Perette is a published poet and has released CDs of her music.

Peterson, Bob (b. 1961) An animator and writer who later became a director, he often voiced minor characters in Pixar features, such as the frail senior citizen Geri who plays chess in the park in the short *Geri's Game* (1997); the slug-like monster Roz in *Monsters, Inc.* (2001); Mr. Ray, the spotted eagle ray science teacher, in *Finding Nemo* (2003); two very different dogs in *Up* (2009): the friendly tracker Dug and the vicious "Head Hound" doberman Alpha; and the Janitor in the day-care center in *Toy Story 3* (2010). He was born in Wooster, Ohio, and studied mechanical engineering at Ohio Northern University and Purdue University. Getting interested in animation, he started working on cartoon shorts then joined Pixar where he was a story artist for *Toy Story* (1995), *A Bug's Life* (1998), and *Toy Story 2* (1999). Peterson contributed to the scripts of *Finding Nemo* and *Ratatouille* (2007) then was co-director for *Up.* He can be heard in such films and videos as *The Incredibles* (2004), *Cars* (2006), *Finding Nemo Submarine Voyage* (2007), *Tokyo Mater* (2008), *Dug's Special Mission* (2009), and *George & A. J.* (2009). The canine Dug in *Up* bears some similarities to Pluto, particularly his color and his "point" pose in which head, back, and tail form a straight line. The sinister dog Alpha in the same movie has two voices: a deep, menacing sound and a high squeaky sound when his talking collar is not functioning properly; Peterson did both voices.

Petty, Richard (b. 1937) The record-breaking stock car racer who has been dubbed "The King," he provided the voice for Strip "The King" Weathers, the aging Plymouth Superbird race car, in *Cars* (2006). He was born in Level Cross, North Dakota, into a family of race car drivers and went on to become the most famous of them. Before his retirement in 1992, he won 200 Winston Cup races, seven Winston Cup Championships, and seven Daytona 500's. His wife **Lynda Petty** (b. 1942) provided the voice for Mrs. "The King" in *Cars*. Autobiography: *King Richard I* (1987); biography: *Richard Petty: Images of the King*, Ben Blake (2005).

Phillips, Chris A voice artist for television who can be heard on many video games, he provided the voices of the bully schoolboy Roger Klotz and his gang member Boomer Bledsoe in *Doug's 1st Movie* (1999), as well as the smaller roles of Larry and Mr. Chiminy in the same film. A graduate of Emerson College, he made his professional debut voicing the title character of the film *Felix the Cat: The Movie* (1988). Most of his subsequent credits are in animated television shows, such as *Where in the World Is Carmen Sandiego?*, *PB&J Otter*, *Between the Lions*, *Generation Jets*, *Doug*, and *Disney's Doug*. Phillips can be heard on the animated videos *A Very Wompkee Christmas* (2003) and *Davey & Goliath's Snowboard Christmas* (2004).

Phipps, William (b. 1922) A busy television and film actor, mostly in Westerns and science fiction movies, he provided the speaking voice of Prince Charming in *Cinderella* (1950). He was born in Vincennes, Indiana, grew up in St. Francisville, Illinois, and was educated at Eastern Illinois University. After appearing in a few regional stage productions, he went to Hollywood where he made his screen debut in 1947 but was not noticed until the early 1950s for his appearances in such sci-fi movies as *Five* (1951), *Invaders from Mars* (1953), *The War of the Worlds* (1953), *Cat-Woman of the Moon* (1953), and *The Snow Creature* (1954). Phipps turned to television as the decade progressed and was a particular favorite in many Western series such as *The Cisco Kid*, *The Adventures of Rin Tin Tin*, *Annie Oakley*, *The Adventures of McGraw*, *Broken Arrow*, *Colt .45*, *Cimarron City*, *Bat Masterson*, *The Rifleman*, *Tombstone Territory*, *Wanted: Dead or Alive*, *The Rebel*, *The Life and Legend of Wyatt Earp*, *Rawhide*, *Gunsmoke*, *The Virginian*, *The Guns of Will Sonnett*, and *Bonanza*. Even after the appeal of Westerns waned, he was kept busy acting in a variety of television series, including *Twilight Zone*, *Perry Mason*, *The Rockford Files*, *The Waltons*, *Little House on the Prairie*, *Santa Barbara*, and *Empty Nest*. Among Phipps' other film credits are *Executive Suite* (1954), *The Man in the Gray Flannel Suit* (1956), *Lust for Life* (1956), *The FBI Story* (1959), *Dead Heat on a Merry-Go-Round* (1966), and *Homeward Bound: The Incredible Journey* (1993). Like the Prince in *Snow White and the Seven Dwarfs*, Prince Charming in *Cinderella* is not a very complex character but more an idealized version of a handsome royal who figures in young ladies' dreams. In the original script the role was substantially larger but, just like Snow White's Prince, Prince Charming was reduced to a secondary character in the final cut. Dancer Ward Ellis was the live-action model for the Prince and it is clear that the character's movements in *Cinderella* are much more natural than those of Snow White's prince a dozen years earlier. Phipps has few lines in the script (he is more a visual creation than a talking one) but he makes every word count and the Prince comes across as romantic and charismatic even though he is far from an active character.

Phoenix, Joaquin (b. 1974) A dark and handsome film and television leading man, he voiced the Native American Kenai who is turned into a bear in *Brother Bear* (2003). He was born Joaquin Rafael Bottom in San Juan, Puerto Rico, the son of missionaries, and grew up in Los Angeles where he and his four siblings appeared in television commercials and series. (During these years he went by the name Lief Phoenix.) He made his television debut on the series *Seven Brides for Seven Brothers* in 1982 and was later featured in such shows as *Hill Street Blues*, *Morningstar/Eveningstar*, *The New Leave It to Beaver*, and *Murder, She Wrote*. After acting in a few TV-movies, Phoenix found more recognition on the big screen in *SpaceCamp* (1986) and *Parenthood* (1989), becoming a star with *Gladiator* (2000). Phoenix's other movies include *To Die For* (1995), *Inventing the Abbotts* (1997), *Return to Paradise* (1998), *Clay Pigeons* (1998), *Quills* (2000), *Buffalo Soldiers* (2001), *Signs* (2002), *The Village* (2004), *Walk the Line* (2005), and *Reservation Road* (2008). The late actor River Phoenix (1970–1993) is one of his acting siblings.

Pidgeon, Jeff A television and movie animator who has often supplied additional voices in animated feature films, he voiced the keyboard toy Mr. Spell, the plastic Robot, and the Aliens in *Toy Story* (1995) and its sequel *Toy Story 2* (1999), and the clumsy four-handed monster Thaddeus Bile in *Monsters, Inc.* (2001). Pidgeon has designed characters and layout for the TV cartoon series *Tiny Toon Adventures*, *The Simpsons*, *Taz-Mania*, and *Mighty Mouse, the New Adventures*, as well as the movies and videos *Christmas in Tattertown* (1988), *The Butter Battle Book* (1989), *FernGully: The Last Rainforest* (1992), *Toy Story, a Bug's Life* (1998), *Toy Story 2*, *Monsters, Inc.*, *WALL-E* (2008), and *Up* (2009). He can be heard voicing minor characters in the animated films and videos *Bring Me the Head* of *Charlie Brown* (1986), *Somewhere in the Arctic* (1988), *A Bug's Life*, *Finding Nemo* (2003), *The Incredibles* (2004), *WALL-E*, *and Up*. In order to get the squeaky quality in the voices of the Aliens in the *Toy Story* films, Pidgeon inhaled helium at the recording sessions.

Pierce, Bradley (b. 1982) A teenage actor of film and television whose career has continued successfully into adulthood, he provided the voices of the teacup Chip in *Beauty and the Beast* (1991) and the "Lost Boy" Nibs in *Return to Never Land* (2002). Pierce was appearing on national television by the age of eight, spent a year on the soap opera *Days of Our Lives*, and played Charlie Chaplin as a child in the movie *Chaplin* (1992). Among his other film credits are *Man's Best Friend* (1993), *Jumanji* (1995), *The Borrowers* (1997), and *Down to You* (2000), but he has been more frequently seen on television where he appeared in such series as *Life Goes On, Roseanne, Shaky Ground, Picket Fences, Touched by an Angel, Star Trek: Voyager,* and *Beverly Hills 90210*. Pierce has provided voices for such animated series as *The Little Mermaid, Sonic the Hedgehog, The Oz Kids,* and *The Wild Thornberrys*. Originally the character of Chip in *Beauty and the Beast* was a minor one with only one line of dialogue. When Pierce was recording the line, the directors were so impressed with him that the part was expanded and Chip became crucial to the plotting of the tale.

Pierce, David Hyde (b. 1959) The widely popular comic actor who found fame on television playing meek, deadpan characters, he voiced the put-upon walking stick insect Slim in *A Bug's Life* (1998) and faithful Dr. Delbert Doppler in *Treasure Planet* (2002). He was born in Saratoga Springs, New York, and went to Yale University to study music but ended up majoring in English and Drama. Pierce acted on the New York stage and was cast in television shows and movies without getting much recognition until he played Dr. Niles Crane on *Frasier* in 1993 and stayed with the show for nine years. His film credits include *Bright Lights, Big City* (1988), *Crossing Delancey* (1988), *Little Man Tate* (1991), *The Fisher King* (1991), *Sleepless in Seattle* (1993), *Addams Family Values* (1993), *Nixon* (1995), *Full Frontal* (2002), *Down with Love* (2003), and *The Perfect Host* (2010). Pierce returned to the stage after his television success and starred in the Broadway productions of *Spamalot* (2005), *Curtains* (2007), *Accent on Youth* (2009), and *La Bête* (2010). His voice can be heard in the television cartoon series *The Mighty Ducks, Happily Ever After: Fairy Tales for Every Child, Hercules, Gary the Rat,* and *The Simpsons*, as well as in the animated videos *The Tangerine Bear: Home in Time for Christmas!* (2000) and *The Amazing Screw-On Head* (2006). The character of Doppler in *Treasure Planet* was written with Pierce in mind.

Pinney, Patrick A television voice actor who began in the theatre and worked on minor characters in several Disney features, he provided the voice of the Cyclops in *Hercules* (1997). A graduate of the University of the Pacific in California, he voiced his first television cartoon series in 1978 and over the decades supplied voices for such shows as *Blackstar, The Dukes, G.I. Joe, Darkwing Duck, TaleSpin, Men in Black: The Series, SpongeBob SquarePants, Samurai Jack, Robot Chicken,* and *Mighty Mouse, The New Adventures*. Pinney first worked for Disney in the 1980s and voiced multiple minor characters in the films *The Little Mermaid* (1989), *Duck Tales: The Movie—Treasure of the Lost Lamp* (1990), *Beauty and the Beast* (1991), *Aladdin* (1992), *Toy Story* (1995), *The Hunchback of Notre Dame* (1996), *Mulan* (1998), *Atlantis: The Lost Empire* (2001), *Lilo & Stitch* (2002), *Treasure Planet* (2002), and *Brother Bear* (2003). He can also be heard in such animated movies and videos as *G.I. Joe: Arise, Serpentor, Arise!* (1986), *G.I. Joe: The Movie* (1987), *The Chipmunk Adventure* (1987), *Christmas in Tattertown* (1988), *Ghoulies III: Ghoulies Go to College* (1991), *An American Tail: Fievel Goes West* (1991), *Cool World* (1992), *Theodore Rex* (1995), and *The Wacky Adventures of Ronald McDonald: Scared Silly* (1998).

Piven, Jeremy (b. 1965) The television actor known for his smirking expression and deadpan delivery, he voiced the shallow, slick celebrity agent Harv in the U.S. version of *Cars* (2006). Jeremy Samuel Piven was born in New York City and raised in Evanston, Illinois, son of stage actors who ran a theatre school in Chicago where he trained. After further study at Drake University, he made his film debut in 1986 and his television bow four years later. Piven was featured in such television series as *Carol & Company, Pride & Joy, The Larry Sanders Show, Ellen,* and *Cupid*, but he is most known as Ari Gold on *Entourage*. His movie credits include *Say Anything* (1989), *Singles* (1992), *Car 54, Where Are You?* (1994), *Dr. Jekyll and Ms. Hyde* (1995), *Grosse Pointe Blank* (1997), *Red Letters* (2000), *The Family Man* (2000), *Rush Hour 2* (2001), *Runaway Jury* (2003), *Scary Movie 3* (2003), *Keeping Up with the Steins* (2006), and *The Kingdom* (2007). Piven has voiced such TV cartoon series as *Duckman: Private Dick/Family Man, Buzz Lightyear of Star Command, Rugrats, Spider-Man,* and *Justice League*. It is unusual for a character to be re-voiced for the British version of an animated film but Jeremy Clarkson, a well-known commentator on British television, did the voice of the lawyer Harv in the U.K. release.

Playten, Alice (b. 1947) A lively, wide-eyed actress of stage, television, and movies who excels at enthusiastic, loud-mouthed characters, she provided the voice of the rich school girl Beebe Bluff in *Doug's 1st Movie* (1999) as well as the minor character of Elmo in that film. She was born Alice Plotkin in New York City and was on Broadway as one of the youngsters in *Gypsy* (1959), *Oliver!* (1963), and *Hello, Dolly!* (1964). She stopped the show each night as the assertive teenager Kafritz singing "Nobody Steps on Kafritz" in the Broadway musical *Henry, Sweet Henry* (1967) then went on to appear in several Off Broadway plays and musicals, returning to Broadway in *Spoils of War* (1988), *Rumors* (1988), *Seussical* (2000), and *Caroline, or Change* (2004). Yet it was a 1970 Alka-Seltzer commercial on nationwide television that made her a recognized face. Playten's television credits include the series *The Lost Saucer, Disco Beavers from Outer Space, Remember WENN, Frasier, Law & Order, As the World Turns,* and *The Book of Daniel,* and she appeared in such movies as *Who Killed Mary What's 'Er Name?* (1971), *California Dreaming* (1979), *Legend* (1985), *For Love or Money* (1993), *I.Q.* (1994), *Pants on Fire* (1998), and *The Rebound* (2009). She can be heard in the TV cartoon series *Ghostwriter, Doug,* and *Disney's Doug,* as well as in the animated movies and videos *Really Rosie* (1975), *Isabella and the Magic Brush* (1976), *Petronella* (1978), *Heavy Metal* (1981), *My Little Pony: Escape from Catrina* (1985), *The Big Bang* (1987), *My Little Pony: The Movie* (1988), *Felix the Cat: The Movie* (1988), *The Amazing Feats of Young Hercules* (1997), and *A Very Wompkee Christmas* (2003).

Plowright, Joan (b. 1929) A renowned British stage actress of both the classics and daring new plays, she became famous in America late in her career from her supporting roles in films, such as *Dinosaur* (2000) in which she voiced the old but dignified brachiosaurus Baylene. Joan Ann Plowright was born in Brigg, England, and trained at the Old Vic School. By 1954 she was on the London stage and acted with such distinguished companies as the Old Vic, Royal Court, Chichester Festival, and the Royal National Theatre, sometimes working with her husband Laurence Olivier. Plowright reprised some of her stage performances on Broadway, such as in the drama *The Entertainer* (1958) which she filmed in 1960. Her other film credits include *The Three Sisters* (1970), *Equus* (1977), *Avalon* (1990), *Enchanted April* (1992), and *Tea with Mussolini* (1999), as well as many television dramas. Plowright played the housekeeper Nanny in the live-action movie version of *101 Dalmatians* (1996) and can be heard in the animated film *Curious George* (2006). Memoir: *And That's Not All* (2002).

Plummer, Amanda (b. 1957) A unique actress who specializes in callow, odd, and quiet characters, she has excelled on the stage but has also appeared in a variety of films, such as *Hercules* (1997) for which she provided the voice for Clotho, one of the creepy three Fates. She was born in New York City, the daughter of actors Christopher Plummer and Tammy Grimes, and was educated at Middlebury College before acting at the Neighborhood Playhouse School in Manhattan. Plummer made her professional New York stage debut in 1979 and was first acclaimed for her performance in *A Taste of Honey* (1981), followed by such Broadway successes as *Agnes of God* (1982), *A Lie of the Mind* (1985), and *Pygmalion* (1987), as well as *Killer Joe* (1998) Off Broadway. Her first movie was in 1981 and she has shone in such films as *The World According to Garp* (1982), *The Hotel New Hampshire* (1984), *The Fisher King* (1991), *Pulp Fiction* (1994), and *My Life Without Me* (2003). Plummer has appeared in several television series and original dramas and provided voices for such animated shows as *WordGirl* and *Phineas and Ferb*.

Plummer, Christopher (b. 1927) One of America's finest classical actors who has thrilled theatregoers on Broadway, Canadian, and British stages but is mostly known from his many movie appearances, he provided the voice of the maniac explorer Charles F. Muntz in *Up* (2009). He was born Arthur Christopher Orme Plummer in Toronto, Canada, and started working in stock companies in Ottawa in 1950. Four years later he was on Broadway but he did not receive recognition until *The Lark* (1955). Among his other notable New York stage credits are *J. B.* (1958), *The Royal Hunt of the Sun* (1965), *Cyrano* (1973), *The Good Doctor* (1973), *Othello* (1982), *Macbeth* (1994), *Barrymore* (1997). *King Lear* (2004), and *Inherit the Wind* (2007). Plummer has also performed with the finest classical companies in Canada and Great Britain. He first appeared on television in an original drama in 1953 and made his film debut in *Stage Struck* (1958), followed by such memorable movies as *The Sound of Music* (1965), *Battle of Britain* (1969), *The Return of the Pink Panther* (1975), *The Man Who Would Be King* (1975), *Murder by Decree* (1979), *Star Trek VI: The Undiscovered Country* (1991), *Twelve Monkeys* (1995), *A Beautiful Mind* (2001), *Nicholas Nickleby* (2002), *National Treasure* (2004), *The Last Station* (2009), and *The Imaginarium of Doctor Parnassus* (2009). Plummer's rich and musical voice has been used as the narrator of many movies and television programs and he can be heard in such animated videos and films as *The Happy Prince* (1974), *Rumplestiltskin* (1985), *The Velveteen Rabbit* (1985), *An American Tail*

(1986), *The Tin Soldier* (1986), *The Nightingale* (1987), *The Gnomes Great Adventure* (1987), *Madeline* (1989) and its many sequels, *The Little Crooked Christmas Tree* (1990), *Rock-a-Doodle* (1991), *Babes in Toyland* (1997), *The Dinosaur Hunter* (2000), and *My Dog Tulip* (2009). The character of Charles F. Muntz was somewhat based on aviation pioneers Charles Lindbergh and Howard Hughes and his airship *Spirit of Adventure* recalls Lindbergh's *Spirit of St. Louis*. Yet Muntz obsessively tracks the elusive bird "Kevin" and turns from a hero into a deadly villain. Plummer's performance captures the character's hero persona and sinister true self beautifully on the soundtrack. The character's name Muntz was taken from movie producer Charles B. Mince who battled Walt Disney in his early days in Hollywood. Autobiography: *In Spite of Myself: A Memoir*, 2008.

Pollatschek, Susanne (b. 1978) An eight-year-old performer from Glasgow, Scotland, who provided the voice of the toymaker's daughter Olivia Flaversham in *The Great Mouse Detective* (1986), she has no other movie or television credits. Although the character of Olivia is another in a line of cute, victimized little girls in Disney films, Olivia is more realistic and less helpless. She is determined to find and save her father and the young Scots actress Pollatschek gives her lines a practical and no-nonsense reading.

Pope, Tony (1947–2004) A voice artist who did the English voices for dozens of foreign cartoons, he supplied the voices of Goofy and the Big Bad Wolf in cameo performances in *Who Framed Roger Rabbit* (1988) and Goofy in the short *Sport Goofy in Soccermania* (1987). He was born in Cleveland, Ohio, and voiced his first of many Japanese cartoons in 1977. Pope can also be heard in the American cartoon series *Spider-Man, The New Scooby-Doo and Scrappy-Doo Show, The Dukes, Pole Position, The Transformers, TaleSpin, Tom & Jerry Kids Show, Tiny Toon Adventures, Swat Kats: The Radical Squadron, Superman*, and *House of Mouse*. Among his animated films and videos are *Akira* (1988), *The Cockpit* (1994), *Adventures in Odyssey: Go West Young Man* (1995), *George and Junior's Christmas Spectacular* (1995), *Black Jack* (1996), *The King and I* (1999), *Fake* (2000), *The Prince of Light* (2000), *Metropolis* (2001), *Marco Polo: Return to Xanadu* (2001), *Space Pirate Captain Harlock: The Endless Odyssey* (2002), *The Nutcracker and the Mouseking* (2004), and the English versions of many *anime* movies.

Potts, Annie (b. 1952) A pert, lively film and television actress who often shines in minor roles, she supplied the voice of the seductive doll Bo Peep who has a crush on Woody in *Toy Story* (1995) and *Toy Story 2* (1999). Anne Hampton Potts was born in Nashville, Tennessee, raised in Franklin, Kentucky, and studied theatre at Stephens College. She made her television debut in 1977 and the next year appeared in her first film, *Corvette Summer* (1978), followed by unnoticed roles in *King of the Gypsies* (1978), *Heartaches* (1981), and *Bayou Romance* (1982). Potts found wide recognition as Janine Melnitz in *Ghostbusters* (1984) and reprised the character in *Ghostbusters II* (1989). Among her other movies are *Pretty in Pink* (1986), *Who's Harry Crumb?* (1989), *Texasville* (1990), *Breaking the Rules* (1992), *Elvis Has Left the Building* (2004), *The Sunday Man* (2007), and many made-for-TV movies. Potts has acted in several television series, including *Busting Loose, Goodtime Girls, Remington Steele, Amazing Stories, Love & War, Over the Top, Any Day Now, Huff, Joan of Arcadia, Men in Trees, Ugly Betty, Law & Order: Special Victims Unit, Designing Women, Boston Legal*, and *Two and a Half Men*, but she is mostly remembered as Mary Jo Shively in *Designing Women* for six years. She can be heard doing voices on the TV cartoon series *Hercules* and *Johnny Bravo*. Potts has returned to the stage regionally and acted Off Broadway in *The Vagina Monologues* (1999) and on Broadway in *God of Carnage* (2009). The character of Bo Beep was a late addition to *Toy Story*. Originally Woody had a crush on a Barbie doll who helped rescue him in her Corvette during the final chase. But Mattel, the toy company that manufactures Barbie, thought the movie would be a failure and didn't want to jeopardize the popular doll's persona. When the movie was such a hit, Mattel allowed Barbie to be in the two sequels.

Preis, Doug (b. 1930) A veteran announcer and voice artist for commercials and television cartoons, he played the local water polluter Bill Bluff in *Doug's 1st Movie* (1999) as well as Doug's father Mr. Phil Funnie, the dense gang member Willie White, the super jock Chalky Studebaker, and Bill Bluff's corrupt Agent. Preis can be heard in the TV cartoon series *The Adventures of the Galaxy Rangers, Where in the World Is Carmen Sandiego?, Doug, Disney's Doug, PB&J Otter*, and *Harvey Birdman, Attorney at Law*, as well as the animated video *The Easter Egg Adventure* (2004).

Price, Vincent (1911–1993) The cultivated American film actor who many thought was British because of his distinguished voice and gentlemanly manners, he excelled at playing polite but deadly villains, such as the diabolical Professor Ratigan whom he voiced in *The Great Mouse Detective* (1986), and he provided the narration for the Tim Burton short *Vincent* (1982). Born Vincent Leonard

Price, Jr., in St. Louis, the son of a wealthy manufacturer, he developed a great appreciation for the arts as a boy and, after touring all the famous museums in Europe, he attended Yale University where he received degrees in art history and English. When Price decided to go on the stage, he found no work in New York so he went to England and studied art at the University of London where he got his first acting jobs. He was so heartily applauded as Prince Albert in the play *Victoria Regina* that he recreated the role on Broadway in 1935. Price made his film debut three years later and went on to make over sixty movies over the next half century. Although he shone in such screen favorites as *The Private Lives of Elizabeth and Essex* (1939), *Song of Bernadette* (1943), *Laura* (1944), *The Three Musketeers* (1948), *The Ten Commandments* (1956), *The Whales of August* (1987), and *Edward Scissorhands* (1990), Price was mostly known for his many horror flicks which ranged from classics like *House of Wax* (1953) to the campy *Dr. Goldfoot and the Bikini Machine* (1965). He returned to the stage on occasion, appeared in many television dramas and series, and he can he heard in such animated videos and movies as *Here Comes Peter Cottontail* (1971), *The Butterfly Ball* (1976), *The Sorcerer's Apprentice* (1980), *Pogo for President* (1980), *The 13 Ghosts of Scooby Doo* (1985), *Sparky's Magic Piano* (1987), *The Nativity* (1987), *The Little Troll Prince* (1987), and *The Princess and the Cobbler* (1993). The short *Vincent* concerned a young boy who wanted to be Vincent Price so it was more than appropriate that Price did the chilling narration. The Disney studio was so pleased with the stop-action piece that they backed Burton's later work, in particular *The Nightmare Before Christmas* (1993). Although Price played many villains on screen, his sewer rat Ratigan in *The Great Mouse Detective* is one of his most playful. He delights in his fiendish plots, enjoys the power he holds over his minions, and revels in his matching wits with the Sherlock Holmes–like Basil. The animators filmed Price in the recording session and used many of his gestures in making the film. Near the end of his life, Price said that Ratigan was his favorite screen role. Autobiography: *I Like What I Know*, 1959; memoir: *Vincent Price: A Daughter's Biography*, Victoria Price, 2000; biography: *Vincent Price: The Art of Fear*, Denis Meikle, 2006.

Prima, Louis (1910–1978)   The renowned jazz trumpeter, bandleader, composer, and singer, he provided the speaking and singing voice of the jumping and jiving King Louie of the Apes in *The Jungle Book* (1967). He was born in New Orleans, Louisiana, and studied violin as a child but eventually took up the trumpet and formed his own jazz band. Prima was soon famous, playing in nightclubs, in concerts, on television, and in such movies as *Rhythm on the Range* (1936), *Swing It* (1936), *Rose of Washington Square* (1939), *The Continental Twist* (1961), and *Rafferty and the Gold Dust Twins* (1975). Over the years his two main female vocalists were Keely Smith and Gia Maione, marrying and making many records with each of them. Prima can be heard on the soundtrack of over one hundred movies. *The Jungle Book* was the first Disney movie in which most of the voices were those of recognized stars. Prima's way of singing and his very physical way of delivering a song were used by the animators to create the ape king. The character is supposed to be something of a villain but Louie is so much fun that to audiences he poses no threat to Mowgli. Biographies: *Louis Prima*, Garry Boulard (2002); *That Old Black Magic: Louis Prima, Keely Smith, and the Golden Age of Las Vegas*, Tom Clavin (2010).

Proctor, Phil (b. 1940)   A flexible actor who has been providing voices for film and television since 1962 and often plays several small roles in one film, he supplied the voices of the Cave of Wonders in *Aladdin* (1992), the Pizza Planet Guard in *Toy Story* (1995), and the Japanese investor Mr. Konishi in *Toy Story 2* (1999). Philip G. Proctor was born in Goshen, Indiana, and began his career on the radio before making his television debut in an episode of *Run for Your Life* in 1968. He found recognition as one of the founders and continuing members of the comedy troupe called The Firesign Theatre with many recording and appearances on television, radio, and on stage. Proctor made several appearances in both films and TV shows but by the 1990s was in great demand in animated movies and cartoons. He can be heard playing minor characters and providing "additional voices" in such Disney features as *Beauty and the Beast* (1991), *The Lion King* (1994), *The Hunchback of Notre Dame* (1996), *Hercules* (1997), *A Bug's Life* (1998), *Tarzan* (1999), *Monsters, Inc.* (2001), *Treasure Planet* (2002), *Brother Bear* (2003), *Home on the Range* (2004), and *The Princess and the Frog* (2009). Proctor has also voiced many non–Disney movies and videos, including *The Town Santa Forgot* (1993), *Theodore Rex* (1995), *Doctor Dolittle* (1998) and its sequels, *The Rugrats Movie* (1998), *The Rugrats in Paris* (2000), *Recess: School's Out* (2001), *Lionheart* (2003), *Blue Dragon* (2006), and *Happily N'Ever After* (2006), as well as such cartoon series as *Scooby Doo*, *Smurfs*, *The Pirates of Dark Water*, *Spider-Man*, and *Rugrats*.

Proops, Greg (b. 1959)   An improv comic and voice actor who performs in England and the States, he provided the voices of the multi-toothed

Harlequin Demon, the skinny Devil, and the Sax Player in the skeleton band in *The Nightmare Before Christmas* (1993) and Male Lover Bear in *Brother Bear* (2003). Gregory Everett Proops was born in Phoenix, Arizona, and did stand-up comedy and worked with improv comedy groups before going to London where he appeared on the television program *Whose Line Is It Anyway?* for five years. His American television credits include *Space Cadets, The Daily Show with Jon Stewart, Hollywood Squares, Third Rock from the Sun, Just for Laughs, Head Games,* and *True Jackson, VP*. Proops can be heard in the animated movies and videos *Bagboy!* (2002), *Bob the Builder: Building Friendships* (2003), *Kaena: The Prophecy* (2003), *Asterix and the Vikings* (2006), and *Dr. Dolittle: Million Dollar Mutts* (2009), as well as the TV cartoon series *Bob the Builder, Stripperella,* and *Star Wars: The Clone Wars.*

Pullen, Purv (1909–1992) A voice artist and actor who made an entire movie career out of doing animal sounds, he created the bird chirps for *Snow White and the Seven Dwarfs* (1937). He was born A. Purves Pullen in Philadelphia but grew up on a farm where he learned to imitate various bird sounds. Starting as a disc jockey on a local radio station in Akron, Ohio, Pullen added his bird imitations to his chatter as he worked at various radio stations. By the 1930s he was providing bird and other animal sounds for movies, though he was rarely credited. Perhaps his most remembered animal vocals were those for the chimpanzee Cheetah in the Tarzan movies. Band leader Spike Jones heard Pullen perform and hired him for his famous novelty orchestra called the City Slickers, Pullen doing all kinds of animal sounds during the songs under the cockeyed stage name Dr. Horatio Q. Birdbath. He also was an accomplished ventriloquist and performed in nightclubs with his dummy Johnny.

Quaid, Randy (b. 1950) The veteran character actor of over ninety films who can play everything from goofy to menacing types, he supplied the speaking and singing voice for the fat, yodeling cattle rustler Alameda Slim in *Home on the Range* (2004). Randall Rudy Quaid was born in Houston, Texas, and attended the University of Houston before heading to California where he got a job as a janitor. He was noticed in small roles in three Peter Bogdonovich movies — *The Last Picture Show* (1971), *What's Up, Doc?* (1972), and *Paper Moon* (1973) — and was roundly applauded as the young recruit Meadows in *The Last Detail* (1973). Among his many other notable movies are *Bound for Glory* (1976), *The Choirboys* (1977), *Midnight Express* (1978), *The Long Riders* (1980), *National Lampoon's Vacation* (1983) and three of its sequels, *The Slugger's Wife* (1985), *Caddyshack II* (1988), *Texasville* (1990), *The Paper* (1994), *Last Dance* (1996), *Independence Day* (1996), *The Adventures of Pluto Nash* (2002), *Brokeback Mountain* (2005), and *Real Time* (2008), as well as such outstanding TV-movies as *Of Mice and Men* (1981), *A Streetcar Named Desire* (1984), *LBJ: The Early Years* (1987), and *Elvis* (2005). Quaid was a regular on the television show *Saturday Night Live* and has been featured in such series as *Davis Rules* and *The Brotherhood of Poland, New Hampshire*. He can be heard on the TV cartoon series *The Ren & Stimpy Show* and the video *Stanley's Dinosaur Round-Up* (2006). His brother is actor Dennis Quaid. The character of Alameda Slim in *Home on the Range,* modeled after country singer and yodeler Wilf Carter (known as Montana Slim), is one of Disney's more grotesque human villains, his size and facial features as outlandish as his voice. Like some of the other characters in that film, he is more reminiscent of Warner Brothers cartoon figures than Disney ones.

Quaroni, Guido A production artist for Pixar animated films, he supplied the voice of Guido the Italian forklift in *Cars* (2006). He worked on the modeling, computer software, and special effects on such movies as *Toy Story 2* (1999), *Monsters, Inc.* (2001), *Finding Nemo* (2003), *The Incredibles* (2004), and *Ratatouille* (2007). Quaroni also voiced minor characters in *Monsters, Inc.* and the short *Tokyo Mater* (2008). Guido, the actor and the character's first name, is Italian for "I drive."

Questel, Mae (1908–1998) A multi-voiced actress who made over 350 cartoon shorts between 1931 and 1962, she returned to the screen near the end of her life to voice the black-and-white flapper "toon" Betty Boop in *Who Framed Roger Rabbit* (1988). She was born Mae Kwestel in the Bronx, New York, and studied at the Theatre Guild School and Columbia University. At an early age she demonstrated a talent for impersonation, doing an act in vaudeville imitating current stars, and when she was seventeen Questel won a contest recreating the singing voice of the Broadway "Boop-Oop-a-Doop" girl Helen Kane. Film producer Max Fleischer heard Questel and hired her to voice the cartoon character Betty Boop in *Silly Scandals* (1931), followed by over seventy more animated shorts. She also provided the voice for Olive Oyl in over 200 *Popeye* cartoons on film and television, as well as the title character in many *Little Lulu* shorts in the 1940s. She voiced animals, babies, fairy tale characters, and modern adults in many other cartoon shorts until the early 1960s. Questel can be seen in such feature films as *Bubbles* (1930), *Wayward* (1932), *One Hour with You* (1932), *Take a Chance* (1933), *The Great Ziegfeld* (1936), *A Majority* *of One* (1961), *It'$ Only Money* (1962), *Funny Girl* (1968), *Move* (1970), *Hot Resort* (1985), *New York Stories* (1989), and *Christmas Vacation* (1989). She occasionally acted on the stage regionally as well as on Broadway in *Doctor Social* (1948), *A Majority of One* (1959), *Enter Laughing* (1963), and *Bajour* (1964).

Rabson, Jan (b. 1954) An actor who began voicing animated television series and movies in the 1990s, he provided the voice of the toy robot Sparks at Sunnyside Daycare Center in *Toy Story 3* (2010). He was born in East Meadow, New York, and began his acting career on television in 1982, appearing on such series as *One Day at a Time*, *The Facts of Life*, *Knight Rider*, *Cheers*, *Hunter*, *thirtysomething*, *Empty Nest*, *Tour of Duty*, *Night Court*, *Baywatch*, and *Beverly Hills 90210*. Rabson also played bit parts in a handful of movies before turning to animation work. Among the cartoon series he has voiced are *Where's Waldo?*, *The Pirates of Dark Water*, *Animaniacs*, *Babylon 5*, *The Real Adventures of Jonny Quest*, *Pinky and the Brain*, *Batman Beyond*, *Justice League*, and *Edgar & Ellen*. He can also be heard in several animated movies and videos, including *A Flintstones Christmas Carol* (1994), *Toy Story* (1995), *Theodore Rex* (1995), *The Hunchback of Notre Dame* (1996), *Hercules* (1997), *A Bug's Life* (1998), *Toy Story 2* (1999), *Monsters, Inc.* (2001), *Barbie as the Princess and the Pauper* (2004), *A Fairytale Christmas* (2005), *Ice Age: The Meltdown* (2006), *Cars* (2006), *Happily N'Ever After* (2007), *Surf's Up* (2007), *Bratz: Super Babyz* (2007), *Horton Hears a Who!* (2008), *WALL-E* (2008), *Ponyo* (2008), *Tokyo Mater* (2008), *Up* (2009), and *Cloudy with a Chance of Meatballs* (2009). Rapson has made hundreds of TV commercials and he sometimes uses the name Stanley Gurd, Jr., in voicing *anime* films.

Radford, Mary T. An assistant to movie producer Frank Marshall on some two dozen films, she provided the voice of Hyacinth Hippo in a cameo in *Who Framed Roger Rabbit* (1988). Radford worked on such diverse movies as *Indiana Jones and the Temple of Doom* (1984), *Back to the Future* (1985), *The Color Purple* (1985), *The Land Before Time* (1988), *Hook* (1991), *The Sixth Sense* (1999), *Seabiscuit* (2003), *Eight Below* (2006), and *The Curious Case of Benjamin Button* (2008). Although Hyacinth was featured as the dancing hippo in *Fantasia* (1940), she never spoke in that film; Radford's vocals for Hyacinth in *Who Framed Roger Rabbit* is her only acting credit.

Raize, Jason (1975–2004) An African American actor and singer on the stage, his only movie credit is the voice of the Native American Denahi who seeks to avenge his brother's death in *Brother Bear* (2003). He was born Jason Raize Rotherenberg in Oneonta, New York, and studied at the American Musical and Dramatic Academy in New York and the Perry-Mansfield School for Performance Art in Colorado. After performing in musicals in summer stock and on tour, Raize made his Broadway debut originating the role of Adult Simba in the stage version of *The Lion King* in 1994, playing the role for three years. He sang in concerts and on television specials and served as a Goodwill Ambassador for the United Nations Environment Program before his premature death by suicide.

Ralph, Sheryl Lee (1956) A strikingly elegant African American singer and actress of the stage and television, she supplied the speaking voice of the tough and sexy Afghan hound Rita in *Oliver & Company* (1988). She was born in Waterbury, Connecticut, raised in Jamaica and on Long Island, and at the age of seventeen was named Miss Black Teen-age New York. Ralph was educated at Rutgers University for a career in medicine but even as a student she was busy doing commercials and performing in college theatre productions. She made her Broadway debut in the musical *Reggae* (1980) then scored a triumph as Deena Jones in the original production of *Dreamgirls* (1981). In 1984 she recorded a chart album but most of her subsequent work has been as an actress rather than a singer. Ralph has appeared in such television series as *Black Sheep Squadron*, *Good Times*, *The Jeffersons*, *Search for Tomorrow*, *Code Name: Foxfire*, *L.A. Law*, *Falcon Crest*, *New Attitude*, *Designing Women*, *George*, *Street Gear*, *The District*, *Moesha*, *Las Vegas*, *Barbershop*, *ER*, and *Hannah Montana*, but she is most remembered as Vicki St. James on *It's a Living* for three years. Among her movie credits are *A Piece of the Action* (1977), *The Mighty Quinn* (1989), *Skin Deep* (1989), *The Distinguished Gentleman* (1992), *Sister Act 2: Back in the Habit* (1993), *The Flintstones* (1994), *White Man's Burden* (1995), *Unconditional Love* (1999), and *Blessed and Cursed* (2010). She can be heard in the TV cartoon series *The Wild Thornberrys*, *Recess*, *The Proud Family*, *Static Shock*, and *Justice League*. Ralph returned to the Broadway stage as Muzzy in *Thoroughly Modern Millie* (2002).

Randolph, Lillian (1898–1980) An African American character actress and singer on radio, in films, and on television, she supplied the voice of the harassed cook Mammy Two-Shoes in the Disney short *Pantry Pirate* (1940). She was born in Louisville, Kentucky, and began her career on the radio where she was heard on many programs, most memorably as the maid Birdie Lee in *The Great Gildersleeve*, a role she later reprised on film and in the television series. Randolph appeared in over fifty movies, usually playing cooks and maids who were memorable, as in *Life Goes On* (1938), *Way Down South* (1939), *Streets of New York* (1939), *Am I Guilty?* (1940), *Little Men* (1940), *West Point Widow* (1941), *Kiss the Boys Goodbye* (1941), *Gentleman from Dixie* (1941), *All-American Co-Ed* (1941), *Mexican Spitfire Sees a Ghost* (1942), *Hi, Neighbor* (1942), *The Great Gildersleeve* (1942) and its four sequels, *Happy Go Lucky* (1943), *Three Little Sisters* (1944), *Riverboat Rhythm* (1946), *It's a Wonderful Life* (1946), *The Bachelor and the Bobby-Soxer* (1947), *Once More, My Darling* (1949), *That's My Boy* (1951), *Hush ... Hush, Sweet Charlotte* (1964), *How to Seduce a Woman* (1974), *The Wild McCullochs* (1975), *The World Through the Eyes of Children* (1975), *Magic* (1978), and *The Onion Field* (1979). Although she was most known on television as Birdie Lee on *The Great Gildersleeve* and Madam Queen on *Amos 'n Andy*, Randolph appeared in many other series, including *Ben Casey, The Bill Cosby Show, Room 222, Mannix, That's My Mama, Sanford and Son, The Six Million Dollar Man, The Jeffersons, Sirota's Court, Nashville 99*, and the miniseries *Roots* (1977). She also had an extensive career in animation, providing the voice of Mammy Two-Shoes in twenty MGM cartoon shorts between 1940 and 1952. The character of the African American maid Mammy Two-Shoes was introduced in two Disney cartoons, *Three Orphan Kittens* (1935) and *More Kittens* (1936), but the voice for the character is unknown. MGM revived the character in the short *Puss Gets the Boot* (1940) with Randolph as the voice and that same year she did her only Disney cartoon, *Pantry Pirate*.

Ranft, Jerome An artist who has sculpted models for Pixar films, he supplied the voice of the bulldog henchman Gamma in *Up* (2009). Ranft created some of the models for *The Nightmare Before Christmas* (1993) before joining Pixar and working on the short *Geri's Game* (1997). He went on to sculpt figures for *A Bug's Life* (1998), *Toy Story 2* (1999), *Monsters, Inc.* (2001), *Finding Nemo* (2003), *Cars* (2006), and *Ratatouille* (2007). Ranft reprised his Gamma in the short *Dug's Special Mission* (2009) and can be heard in the animated movie *Coraline* (2009). He is the brother of Pixar writer-animator Joe Ranft.

Ranft, Joe (1960–2005) A writer for animated movies who often did voices in the films he worked on, he played the toy Lenny the Binoculars in *Toy Story* (1995), the German-accented green caterpillar Heimlich in *A Bug's Life* (1998), the speaking voice of Wheezy the toy penguin in *Toy Story 2* (1999), Jacques the clean-freak shrimp in *Finding Nemo* (2003), Red the oversensitive fire truck and the annoyed semi-hauler truck Jerry Recycled Batteries in *Cars* (2006), and various characters in *Monsters, Inc.* (2001) and *The Incredibles* (2004). Joseph Henry Ranft was born in Pasadena, California, and studied animation at the California Institute of the Arts before beginning to work for Disney in 1980. He contributed to the storyboards for *Oliver & Company* (1988), *The Rescuers Down Under* (1990), *Beauty and the Beast* (1991), *The Lion King* (1994), *Toy Story, A Bug's Life*, and *Cars*. Ranft's other voice credits include minor roles in *The Brave Little Toaster* (1987), *Buzz Lightyear of Star Command: The Adventure Begins* (2000), and *Monkeybone* (2001). He died in an automobile accident right after finishing *Cars* and that movie is dedicated to him. His son **Jordan Ranft** (b. 1991) voiced the long-nosed butterfly fish Tad in *Finding Nemo* (2003). The shrimp Jacques in that movie was based on the character actor Fritz Feld who often made a popping sound with his mouth then slapped his cheek for emphasis. Joe Ranft recreated the sound in his vocals for Jacques.

Rarig, John (1912–1991) A singer and choral arranger for records and movies, he voiced one of the singing vaudevillians in the short *The Nifty Nineties* (1941). He was born in Washington, D.C., and in 1938 he joined the popular choral group The Sportsmen Quartet, singing with them on tour, on screen, and on records, usually writing their vocal arrangements. Rarig can be seen and heard singing with the quartet in such movies as *Puddin' Head* (1941), *Ziegfeld Girl* (1941), *Jingle Belles* (1941), *For Me and My Gal* (1942), *Lost Canyon* (1942), *Footlight Varieties* (1951), and *Irish Eyes Are Smiling* (1944). The quartet was also featured on the television show *The Jack Benny Program* several times. Rarig was also a composer, writing the theme songs for the television series *Mr. & Mrs. North* and *The Files of Jeffrey Jones*, and did the choral arrangements for some movies, including the soundtrack chorus for *Lady and the Tramp* (1955) and *Sleeping Beauty* (1959).

Rathbone, Basil (1892–1967) The debonair British actor who was one of Hollywood's favorite villains and the screen's finest Sherlock Holmes, he lent his precise voice as the narrator of "The Wind in the Willows" section of the animated double feature *The Adventures of Ichabod and Mr. Toad* (1949). Philip St. John Basil Rathbone was born in Johannesburg, South Africa, and was educated in England, making his stage debut in 1911. After serving as a second lieutenant in intelligence during World War I, he came to the States to act on Broadway and in 1921 started making silent films. With the advent of sound the stern-faced, deep-voiced actor was in demand for playing dashing villains yet the same qualities served him well as Sherlock Holmes whom he portrayed first in 1939 and returned to in thirteen movies. Among Rathbone's other notable screen credits are *David Copperfield* (1935), *Anna Karenina* (1935), *Captain Blood* (1935), *Romeo and Juliet* (1936), *The Adventures of Robin Hood* (1938), *If I Were King* (1938), *The Mark of Zorro* (1940), *The Court Jester* (1955), *We're No Angels* (1955), and *The Last Hurrah* (1958). He appeared in many television dramas and occasionally returned to the stage, most memorably on Broadway in *Romeo and Juliet* (1934), *The Heiress* (1947), and *Jane* (1952). As a tribute to the late actor, the detective in Disney's *The Great Mouse Detective* (1986) was named Basil of Baker Street. Autobiography: *In and Out of Character* (1962); biography: *Basil Rathbone: His Life and His Films*, Michael B. Druxman (1972).

Ratzenberger, John (b. 1947) A distinctive character actor who found fame on television, the expressive-voiced comic actor has become the most-used voice in Pixar animated features, most memorably as Hamm the piggy bank in all three *Toy Story* movies. John Deszo Ratzenberger was born in Bridgeport, Connecticut, and educated at Sacred Heart University before turning to comedy in improv groups. He made his screen debut in *The Ritz* (1976) and was seen in minor roles in such movies as *Twilight's Last Gleaming* (1977), *A Bridge Too Far* (1977), *Yanks* (1979), *Star Wars: Episode V—The Empire Strikes Back* (1980), *Reds* (1981), *Gandhi* (1982), and *The Falcon and the Snowman* (1985). By the 1980s Ratzenberger was kept busy appearing in television series, including *Magnum P.I.*, *St. Elsewhere*, *Small World*, *Wings*, *Murphy Brown*, *Caroline in the City*, *Frasier*, *8 Simple Rules*, and *Sister, Sister*, but it was his role as the genial Cliff Clavin on *Cheers* that made him famous. He also had his own documentary series, *Made in America*. Ratzenberger has been heard in every Pixar film, playing such characters as the circus ringmaster P. T. Flea in *A Bug's Life* (1998). the banished yeti Abominable Snowman in *Monsters, Inc.* (2001), a school of Moonfish in *Finding Nemo* (2003), the mole-like monster The Underminer in *The Incredibles* (2004), the truck Mack and other characters in *Cars* (2006), the nervous head waiter Mustafa in *Ratatouille* (2007), the Axiom human resident John in *WALL-E* (2008), and Tom the construction foreman in *Up* (2009), Ratzenberger can also be heard on the TV cartoon series *Captain Planet and the Planeteers*, *The Simpsons*, *Happily Ever After: Fairy Tales for Every Child*, and *Pigs Next Door*. Pixar considers Ratzenberger its good luck charm and always finds at least one role for him in each film. During the final credits of *Cars*, a montage of car versions of his many Pixar characters is shown and Ratzenberger is heard making funny comments, finally concluding that all these characters have the same voice and the company is too cheap to hire more actors. Of all of Ratzenberger's animated characters, perhaps his most beloved is the fatalistic piggy bank Hamm who never looks on the bright side of things.

Ravenscroft, Thurl (1914–2005) A deep bass singer-actor long associated with Disney movies and theme parks, he rarely played a leading role but was distinctive all the same in cameo parts, such as the military-minded horse Captain in *One Hundred and One Dalmatians* (1961), the imposing knight Black Bart in *The Sword in the Stone* (1963), and the "Scat Cat" Russian musician Billy Bass in *The Aristocats* (1970). Thurl Arthur Ravenscroft was born in Norfolk, Nebraska, and, after serving in the Air Transport Command during World War II, found a career as a singer with such singing groups as The Sportsmen, The Johnny Mann Singers, and The Mellomen. This last quartet voiced the Cards painting the roses red in *Alice in Wonderland* (1951), the pound dogs in *Lady and the Tramp* (1955), and can be heard in some Disney shorts such as *Trick or Treat* (1952) and *Toot Whistle Plunk and Boom* (1953), *Paul Bunyan* (1958), and *Noah's Ark* (1959). Ravenscroft's deep singing and speaking voice was ideal for animated shorts and he voiced dozens of them for Disney and other companies. He was also a favorite voice for television commercials, none more popular than his Tony the Tiger for Frosted Flakes. Ravenscroft's other Disney feature film credits include the Hog in the animated sequence in *Mary Poppins* (1964), the singing voice for the tiger Shere Khan in *The Jungle Book* (1967), and various singing and speaking voices in *Dumbo* (1941), *Make Mine Music* (1946), *Cinderella* (1950), *Peter Pan* (1953), *Sleeping Beauty* (1959), and *The Many Adventures of Winnie the Pooh* (1977). He can also be heard in such Disney shorts as *The Nifty Nineties* (1941), *Springtime for Pluto* (1944), *Donald and the Wheel* (1961), and *The Small One* (1978). Ravenscroft had a very successful career outside of Disney, appearing and singing in such films as *Puddin' Head* (1941), *Because You're Mine* (1952), *The Glenn Miller Story* (1954), *South Pacific* (1958), and *It Happened at the World's Fair* (1963), and lending his singing-speaking voice to such animated movies and television specials as *Guy Purr ee* (1962), *Horton Hears a Who!* (1970), *The Cat in the Hat* (1971), *Snoopy Come Home* (1972), *The Lorax* (1972), *The Hobbit* (1977), and *The Brave Little Toaster* (1988) and its sequels, but his most beloved credit is singing "You're a Mean One, Mr. Grinch" in *How the Grinch Stole Christmas* (1968). He can be heard singing in the

Haunted House, the Pirates of the Caribbean, and other attractions at the Disney theme parks.

Redson, Aurian An animator and script writer for animated films, his only acting credit is doing the voice of the suave singing frog Frankie in *Meet the Robinsons* (2007), a film he also co-wrote and animated. Redson also worked on the script and/or storyboards for *Eight Crazy Nights* (2002), *Brother Bear* (2003), *In the Realm of the Unreal* (2004), and *Chicken Little* (2005), as well as the television series *Dilbert* and *The Proud Family*. He contributed to the animation for *Bolt* (2008) and the short *Prep & Landing* (2009). The character of Frankie in *Meet the Robinsons* is a spoof of singer Frank Sinatra, from his crooning styling to his Mafia connections.

Reed, Alan (1907–1977) A character actor of film and television who will always be remembered as the voice of Fred Flintstone, he voiced of the Russian wolfhound Boris in the dog pound in *Lady and the Tramp* (1955) and was the Narrator for the Disney short *Teachers Are People* (1952). He was born Edward Bergman in New York City and studied acting at the American Academy of Dramatic Arts and journalism at Columbia University before beginning his career as an actor Off Broadway and then on radio. With his variety of dialects and deep voice, Reed moved back and forth from the theatre to the air waves, heard in such radio shows as *The Shadow*, *The Fred Allen Show*, *My Friend Irma*, and *Life with Luigi*, and on stage in the Broadway productions of *Love's Old Sweet Song* (1940), *Hope for a Harvest* (1941), and *The Pirate* (1942). He made his screen debut in *Days of Glory* (1944) and appeared in a number of films, including *The Postman Always Rings Twice* (1946), *The Redhead and the Cowboy* (1951), *Here Comes the Groom* (1951), *Viva Zapata!* (1952), *The Far Horizons* (1955), *The Desperate Hours* (1955), *Peyton Place* (1957), *Marjorie Morningstar* (1958), *Breakfast at Tiffany's* (1961), and *A Dream of Kings* (1969). Reed acted in several television series, such as *The Life of Riley*, *Duffy's Tavern*, *Damon Runyon Theatre*, *The Gale Storm Show*, *Mr. Adams and Eve*, *The Bob Cummings Show*, *Have Gun—Will Travel*, *The Dick Powell Theatre*, *The Lucy Show*, *The Dick Van Dyke Show*, *The Addams Family*, *Dr. Kildare*, *The Mothers-in-Law*, *Petticoat Junction*, and *The Beverly Hillbillies*. In addition to *The Flintstones*, he voiced other cartoon series, including *The Jetsons*, *Where's Huddles?*, and *The Pebbles and Bamm-Bamm Show*, and can be heard in the animated movies and videos *1001 Arabian Nights* (1959), *Stop! Look! and Laugh!* (1960), *Alice in Wonderland or What's a Nice Kid Like You Doing in a Place Like This?* (1966), *The Man Called Flintstone* (1966), and *Shinbone Alley* (1971).

Rees, Roger (b. 1944) A classically-trained British stage actor who later found success in American television, he provided the voice of Edward, grown-up Wendy's soldier-husband, in *Return to Never Land* (2002). He was born in Aberystwyth, Wales, and grew up in London where he acted in school and church productions but studied art as his chosen vocation. Hired to paint scenery for professional productions, Rees got more interested in acting and was made a member of the prestigious Royal Shakespeare Company in 1968. He played many classic roles for the company but it was his performance as the title hero of the play *The Life and Adventures of Nicholas Nickleby* in London and then on Broadway that secured his fame. Rees appeared in such TV-movies as *The Three Sisters* (1981), *Imaginary Friends* (1983), *A Christmas Carol* (1984), *The Ebony Tower* (1984), *The Return of Sam McCloud* (1989), *Charles and Diana: Unhappily Ever After* (1992), *The Possession of Michael D.* (1995), *Titanic* (1996), and *The Crossing* (2000), and was featured in several television series, including *Singles*, *Cheers*, *M.A.N.T.I.S.*, *Liberty! The American Revolution*, *Oz*, *Law & Order*, *The West Wing*, *Related*, *Grey's Anatomy*, *The Cleveland Show*, and *Warehouse 13*. Among his film credits are *Star 80* (1983), *God's Outlaw* (1986), *If Looks Could Kill* (1991), *Robin Hood: Men in Tights* (1993), *Next Stop Wonderland* (1998), *A Midsummer Night's Dream* (1999), *The Scorpion King* (2002), *Frida* (2002), *Crazy Like a Fox* (2004), *The Pink Panther* (2006), *The Prestige* (2006), and *The Narrows* (2008). Rees frequently returns to the stage in England and the States, starring on Broadway in *Indiscretions* (1995) and *Uncle Vanya* (2000), and acting Off Broadway in the productions *The End of the Day* (1992), *The Rehearsal* (1996), *The Uneasy Chair* (1998), *A Man of No Importance* (2002), and *Trumbo: Red White and Blacklisted* (2003). He has also written for and directed theatre productions and for three years was the artistic director of the Williamstown Theatre Festival in Massachusetts.

Reese, Della (b. 1931) The award-winning African American singer of gospel and jazz, she has also had a successful career as a television actress and provided the voice of the old, wise, and slow-moving styracosaurus Eema in *Dinosaur* (2000). She was born Delloreese Patricia Early in Detroit, Michigan, the daughter of a steel worker and a cook, and began singing in public as a child. While she was still a teenager, she toured with gospel favorite Mahalia Jackson and by the time she was eighteen was performing in Las Vegas with her own group, the Meditation Singers. Reese's recordings of gospel, pop, and jazz became very popular, winning her many awards and making her a favorite in nightclubs, in concert, and on television variety shows. After playing a role in an episode of the TV series *Mod Squad* in 1968, she took up acting and appeared on such series as *McCloud, Chico and the Man, It Takes Two, Charlie & Co., The Royal Family, Promised Land,* and her own talk show *Della,* but she is most remembered for playing Tess on *Touched by an Angel* for nine years. Reese gave one of her finest performances in the TV-movie *Having Our Say: The Delaney Sisters' First 100 Years* (1999). She can be heard in the animated cartoon series *A Pup Named Scooby-Doo* and *Happily Ever After: Fairy Tales for Every Child.* Reese is an ordained minister and has written a few books of inspiration. Autobiography: *Angels Along the Way: My Life with Help from Above* (2001); biography: *Della Reese,* Tanya Dean (2001).

Reitherman, Bruce [Philip] (b. 1955) A child actor with only a few film credits, he provided the voices of the British boy Christopher Robin in *Winnie the Pooh and the Honey Tree* (1966) and the Indian youth Mowgli in *The Jungle Book* (1967). He was born in Burbank, California, the son of Disney animation director Wolfgang Reitherman who made both movies. After graduating from the University of California at Berkeley, Reitherman worked as a naturalist and a biologist which eventually brought him back to the movies as a cinematographer, producer, writer, and director of nature films and television programs, including *Nature* (1982), *The Living Edens* (1997–2002), *Wild Indonesia* (1999), *Alaska: Dances of the Caribou* (2000), and *Big Bear Week* (2006). He is the younger brother of child actors Robert and Richard Reitherman.

Reitherman, Richard (b. 1947) and **Robert Reitherman** (b. 1950) Two brothers who were not actors by profession, with actor Ricky Sorensen they provided the voice for the young English boy Wart (later King Arthur) in *The Sword in the Stone* (1963). Both were born in Burbank, California, the son of Disney animator Wolfgang Reitherman who directed *The Sword in the Stone*. The brothers did not sound exactly alike and neither matched Sorensen's voice so it is not difficult to hear the differences in Wart's voice throughout the movie. Also, none of the three boys has a British accent and their American delivery of the lines is one of the recurring criticism of the film. The two siblings' younger brother is Bruce Reitherman who was also an actor for a short time. All three brothers later took up professions in the sciences. Richard was later the Director of Women's Imaging at Newport Diagnostic Center in Newport, California, and Robert became Executive Director of the Consortium of Universities for Research in Earthquake Engineering (CUREE).

Remar, James (b. 1953) A prolific television and film character actor with everyday looks but an intense persona, he provided the voice of Larousse, the chef who prepares the food displays at Gusteau's restaurant, in *Ratatouille* (2007). He was born William James Remar in Boston and studied at the Neighborhood Playhouse in New York City before working on the stage, making an impressive Broadway debut in *Bent* (1979). After appearing in two movies, Remar was noticed in *The Warriors* (1979), followed by many other films, including *Cruising* (1980), *The Long Riders* (1980), *Windwalker* (1981), *48 Hrs.* (1982), *The Cotton Club* (1984), *Quiet Cool* (1986), *The Dream Team* (1989), *Drugstore Cowboy* (1989), *Tales from the Darkside: The Movie* (1990), *White Fang* (1991), *Fatal Instinct* (1993), *Renaissance Man* (1994), *Boys on the Side* (1995), *Wild Bill* (1995), *Robo Warriors* (1996), *Rites of Passage* (1999), *Guardian* (2001), *Betrayal* (2003), *The Girl Next Door* (2004), *Blade: Trinity* (2004), *Pineapple Express* (2008), *Endless Bummer* (2009), and *Red* (2010), as well as several TV-movies. Remar's television credits include such series as *The Incredible Hulk, Hill Street Blues, The Equalizer, Miami Vice, Total Security, 7th Heaven, The Huntress, The X-Files, Third Watch, Sex and the City, Battlestar Galactica, North Shore, CSI: Miami, Jericho, Criminal Minds, Numb3rs, Dexter,* and *The Vampire Diaries,* as well as voices for the cartoon series *Justice League, The Batman, The Spectacular Spider-Man, Batman: The Brave and the Bold, Ben 10: Alien Force,* and *Transformers Prime.*

Renaday, Pete (b. 1935) A character actor who has voiced over one hundred animated films and television shows, he provided the voice for many minor Disney animated characters and his deep, smooth voice can be heard throughout the Disney theme parks. He was born Pierre L. Renoudet in rural Louisiana and made his television acting debut in an episode of *Combat!* in 1965. After appearing in bit parts in such films as *The Love Bug* (1968), *The Computer Wore Tennis Shoes* (1969), *The Barefoot Executive* (1971), *The Shaggy D.A.* (1976), and *The Cat from Outer Space* (1978), he did some voices for the animated series *Scooby-Doo and Scappy-Doo* and his career from then on concentrated on voice work. Among his Disney credits are the French Milkman and the Le Petit Café cook in *The Aristocats* (1970), one of the Henchman in *The Black Cauldron* (1985), and various voices in *Mulan* (1998), *The Lion King II: Simba's Pride* (1998), and *The Princess and the Frog* (2009), as well as the Disney cartoon series *DuckTales, TaleSpin, Darkwing Duck, Animaniacs,* and *Gargoyles.* Renaday can also be heard in many other animated videos and in such non–Disney cartoon series as *Challenge of the*

GoBots, The Transformers, Defenders of the Earth, Teenage Mutant Ninja Turtles, The Pirates of Dark Water, The Real Adventures of Jonny Quest, Superman, Justice League*, and *The Grim Adventures of Billy and Mandy*. At the Disney theme parks, Renaday can be heard on several attractions, such as the voice of Abraham Lincoln in the Hall of presidents, Mark Twain on the *Mark Twain* riverboat, Henry the Bear in the Country Bear Jamboree, and as the host and narrator on the Tomorrow Transit Authority and the defunct attractions Mission to Mars and 20,000 Leagues Under the Sea.

Reubens, Paul (b. 1952) The hyperactive character actor mostly known for his geeky caricature Pee-wee Herman on television and in films, he has voiced many animated characters including the mean-spirited kid Lock in *The Nightmare Before Christmas* (1993) and the dumb alligator mutant Dennis in *Teacher's Pet* (2004). He was born Paul Rubenfeld in Peekskill, New York, and grew up in Sarasota, Florida, where he began his acting career at the Asolo Theatre. After attending Boston University and the California Institute of the Arts, he joined the comedy improv group The Groundlings in which he first started to develop the character of Pee-wee Herman. After Reubens performed the character in nightclubs and on an HBO special, he was given his own network television program *Pee-wee's Playhouse* which ran five years and inspired the movies and video *Pee-wee's Big Adventure* (1985), *Big Top Pee-wee* (1988), and *Pee-wee Gets an iPad* (2010). A sex scandal harmed Reubens' career and he turned to other character roles. He enjoyed another resurgence of popularity when he brought his *Pee-wee Herman Show* to Broadway in 2010. Among the television series Reubens has appeared on are *Working Stiffs, Mork & Mindy, Murphy Brown, Everybody Loves Raymond, Ally McBeal, 30 Rock, Dirt,* and *Pushing Daisies,* and he can be heard on the cartoon series *Rugrats, Tripping the Rift, Tom Goes to the Mayor, Chowder,* and *Batman: The Brave and the Bold*. Reubens played secondary roles in the films *Cheech & Chong's Next Movie* (1980), *Meatballs Part II* (1984), *Back to the Beach* (1987), *Batman Returns* (1992), *Buffy the Vampire Slayer* (1992), *Dunston Checks In* (1996), *Matilda* (1996), *Buddy* (1997), *Mystery Men* (1999), *Blow* (2001), and *Life During Wartime* (2009), as well as doing voices for such live-action movies as *Flight of the Navigator* (1986), *Moonwalker* (1988), and *Doctor Dolittle* (1998). He also voiced the animated films and videos *Beauty and the Beast: The Enchanted Christmas* (1997), *The Groovenians* (2002), *Re-Animated* (2006), and *The Smurfs* (2011).

Rhames, Ving (b. 1959) The muscular African American actor with a deep resounding voice, he provided the voice of the social worker Cobra Bubbles in *Lilo & Stitch* (2002). He was born Irving Rameses Rhames in New York City, the son of a mechanic, and studied acting at the High School of the Performing Arts, Juilliard, and the State University of New York at Purchase before beginning his career Off Broadway. He appeared in Shakespeare in the Park productions and on Broadway in *The Winter Boys* (1985) while performing in soap operas on television. Rhames was seen in such films as *Native Son* (1986), *Casualties of War* (1989), *Flight of the Intruder* (1991), and *Dave* (1993) before finding wide recognition in *Pulp Fiction* (1994). This was followed by featured parts in many other movies, including *Mission: Impossible* (1996) and its two sequels, *Striptease* (1996), *Con Air* (1997), *Dawn of the Dead* (2004), *I Now Pronounce You Chuck & Larry* (2007), *Day of the Dead* (2008), *Master Harold ... and the Boys* (2010), and *Piranha 3D* (2010), as well as the TV-movies *Don King: Only in America* (1997), *Holiday Heart* (2000), *RFK* (2002), and *Animal* (2005). He has also appeared on the television series *ER, UC: Undercover, The System, The District, Freedom: A History of Us, Kojak,* and *Gravity*. The character of Cobra Bubbles in *Lilo & Stitch* was based on the gangster Rhames played in the movie *Pulp Fiction*, right down to the earring that the character wore. Rhames reprised his Cobra in the video *Stitch! The Movie!* (2003).

Richards, Ann (1933–2006) A colorful politician who was known for her outspoken ways and unconventional behavior, she provided the voice of the saloon proprietor Annie in *Home on the Range* (2004). She was born Dorothy Ann Willis in Lakeview, Texas, educated at Baylor University and the University of Texas at Austin, and began her career as a teacher. Not until she was married with four children did she pursue a political career, getting national attention when she delivered the keynote address at the Democratic National Convention in 1988. Richards served as Governor of Texas from 1991 to 1995 then remained an active campaigner for Democratic candidates and causes. She made appearances as herself in the television series *Murphy Brown* and *The Roseanne Show* and voiced characters in the cartoon series *King of the Hill* and *Happily Ever After: Fairy Tales for Every Child*. Autobiographies: *Straight from the Heart: My Life in Politics and Other Places* (1990); *I'm Not Slowing Down*, with Richard M. Levine (2004); biography: *Ann Richards: A Woman's Place Is in the Dome*, April D. Stumpff, Patrick Messersmith (2008).

Richards, Michael (b. 1949) A tall, odd-looking comic and actor who found fame on television, he voiced the frustrated Wolf in the animated short *Redux Riding Hood* (1997). Michael Anthony

Richards was born in Los Angeles and educated at the California Institute of the Arts and Evergreen State College. He worked with a comedy improv group and in regional theatre before turning to stand-up comedy. Actor Billy Crystal discovered Richards and featured him in one of his television comedy specials which led to Richards becoming a regular on the comedy variety show *Fridays*. Richards also acted in such series as *St. Elsewhere*, *Cheers*, *Making a Living*, *Miami Vice*, *Hill Street Blues*, *Marblehead Manor*, and *Airheads*. He found wide fame as the convulsive neighbor Cosmo Kramer on the series *Seinfeld* but after playing the role for eight years he found difficulty getting cast in other roles. His sit-com *The Michael Richards Show* was short-lived but he has appeared in several movies, including *UHF* (1989), *Problem Child* (1990), *Coneheads* (1993), *So I Married an Axe Murderer* (1993), *Unstrung Heroes* (1995), and *Trial and Error* (1997), as well as the TV-movies *Camp MTV* (1989), *London Suite* (1996), and *David Copperfield* (2000). Richards can be heard in the animated film *Bee Movie* (2007).

Richards, Robyn (b. 1987)   A television actress who has grown up on the tube appearing in soap operas, she voiced Lester's Grinning Girl in *A Goofy Movie* (1995). The Los Angeles native started playing Maxie Jones on the daytime series *General Hospital* as a teenager then later reprised the character on the spinoff series *Port Charles*.

Richardson, Kevin Michael (b. 1964)   A deep-voiced, large-framed African American actor who turned to voicing animated television series and video games early in his career and has become one of the most prolific voice artists of his generation, he played the spaceship commander Captain Gantu in *Lilo & Stitch* (2002), the train Conductor in *Teacher's Pet* (2004), and Ian the Gator who tries to eat Tiana and Prince Naveen in *The Princess and the Frog* (2009). He was born in the Bronx, New York, and educated at Syracuse University before making his television debut in 1992. After appearing in various series and a handful of films, Richardson supplied some voices for the cartoon series *Sonic the Hedgehog* and his menacing bass voice proved to be ideal for animated characters. He has gone on to voice over 600 episodes of cartoon shows such as *Road Rovers*, *The Mask*, *The Real Adventures of Jonny Quest*, *Homeboys in Outer Space*, *Hercules*, *Spawn*, *Adventures from the Book of Virtues*, *Voltron: The Third Dimension*, *Buzz Lightyear of Star Command*, *Clerks*, *The Legend of Tarzan*, *The Ripping Friends*, *The Powerpuff Girls*, *The Mummy: Secrets of the Medjai*, *ChalkZone*, *Static Shock*, *Justice League*, *The Fairly OddParents*, *Samurai Jack*, *Higglytown Heroes*, *Megas XLR*, *Dave the Barbarian*, *The Proud Family*, *Duck Dodgers*, *Teen Titans*, *Danger Rangers*, *Super Robot Monkey Team Hyperforce Go!*, *Loonatics Unleashed*, *Kim Possible*, *The PJs*, *Codename: Kids Next Door*, *Pokémon*, *Wolverine and the X-Men*, *The Spectacular Spider-Man*, *Ben 10: Alien Force*, *The Marvelous Misadventures of Flapjack*, *Black Panther*, *Batman: The Brave and the Bold*, *The Boondocks*, *Family Guy*, *The Cleveland Show*, and *The Penguins of Madagascar*. Richardson can also be heard on dozens of animated videos and movies, including *All Dogs Go to Heaven 2* (1996), *The Wacky Adventures of Ronald McDonald: Scared Silly* (1998), *The Secret of Nimh 2: Timmy to the Rescue* (1998), *Tom Sawyer* (2000), *Whispers: An Elephant's Tale* (2000), *Buzz Lightyear of Star Command: The Adventure Begins* (2000), *Rugrats in Paris: The Movie — Rugrats II* (2000), *Recess: School's Out* (2001), *The Flintstones: On the Rocks* (2001), *The Powerpuff Girls* (2002), *Tarzan & Jane* (2002), *The Wild Thornberrys Movie* (2002), *George of the Jungle 2* (2003), *Comic Book: The Movie* (2004), *Mulan II* (2004), *Hoodwinked!* (2005), *The Happy Elf* (2005), *Queer Dick: The Movie* (2006), *Happily N'Ever After* (2006), *Doctor Strange* (2007), *Star Wars: The Clone Wars* (2008), *The Little Mermaid: Ariel's Beginning* (2008), *Planet Hulk* (2010), *Dante's Inferno: An Animated Epic* (2010), and *Batman: Under the Red Hood* (2010). He reprised his Captain Gantu in the videos *Stitch! The Movie* (2003), *Stitch's Great Escape* (2004), and *Leroy & Stitch* (2006), and in the TV cartoon series *Lilo & Stitch*.

Richardson, Lori   An assistant to directors and producers at Pixar who sometimes does voices as well, she supplied the sounds of the Female Cloud and the Human Mother in the short *Partly Cloudy* (2009). Richardson voiced various minor characters in the Pixar movies *The Incredibles* (2004), *Ratatouille* (2007), and *WALL-E* (2008), and can be seen in the films *Tracy* (2009) and *Real Men Go Hunting* (2009).

Rickles, Don (b. 1926)   A loud, forceful stand-up comic who fashioned a long career out of insulting members of his audiences in a good-natured way, he found his greatest success late in his career as the voice of the grouchy toy Mr. Potato Head in *Toy Story* (1995) and its two sequels. Donald Jay Rickles was born in New York City to Jewish immigrants from Lithuania and served in the U.S. Navy during World War II before attending the American Academy of Dramatic Arts to become an actor. When jobs were hard to come by, he turned to doing comedy in nightclubs and got noticed by the way he would insult celebrities in the audience. His success on television variety and talk shows opened up acting jobs and Rickles moved easily back and forth from stand-up comedy to film and television characters for fifty years. His movie credits include *Run Silent Run Deep* (1958), *The Rabbit Trap* (1959), *The Rat Race* (1960), *Muscle Beach Party* (1964), *Bikini Beach* (1964), *Pajama Party* (1964), *Beach Blanket Bingo* (1965), *Enter Laughing* (1967), *Kelly's Heroes* (1970), *Innocent Blood* (1992), *Casino* (1995), *Dirty Work* (1998), and some TV-movies. Rickles appeared in many television series, including *M Squad*, *Twilight Zone*, *Wagon Train*, *Hennesey*, *The Addams Family*, *The Dick Van Dyke Show*, *Burke's Law*, *The Munsters*, *The Beverly Hillbillies*, *The Andy Griffith Show*, *F Troop*, *The Wild Wild West*, *I Spy*, *I Dream of Jeannie*, *Run for Your Life*, *Get Smart*, *Sanford and Son*, *Archie Bunker's Place*, *Gimme a Break!*, *Newhart*, *Daddy Dearest*, *Murphy Brown*, and *The Single Guy*, as well as two shows of his own, the variety program *The Don Rickles Show* and the sit-com *C.P.O. Sharkey*. He provided the voice of the Wolf's boss Otis in the Disney short *Redux Riding Hood* (1997) and can also be heard in the animated feature *Quest for Camelot* (1998). The character of Mr. Potato Head in the *Toy Story* movies was inspired by the popular Hasbro toy from the past but was given its persona by Rickles' brash comedic style. Even some of the comic's familiar lines, such as referring to someone as a "hockey puck," were incorporated into the script. While Mattel and other toy manufacturers refused to let Pixar use their famous toys, Hasbro allowed the movie to use Mr. Potato Head. Sales of the toy skyrocketed after the film became such a hit. Autobiography: *Rickles' Book: A Memoir*, with David Ritz (2007).

Rickman, Alan (b. 1946) A deep-voiced English actor who has played moody romantic heroes but is most know for his sinister villains, he provided the voice for Absolem, the cryptic Blue Caterpillar, in the 2010 version of *Alice in Wonderland*. Alan Sidney Patrick Rickman was born in London and attended the Chelsea College of Art and Design and the Royal College of Art before starting his career as a graphics designer. At the age of twenty-six he changed careers, enrolling at the Royal Academy of Dramatics Art and soon after graduation getting noticed on the London stage. His performance in the hit drama *Les Liaisons Dangereuses* brought him to Broadway in 1987 but he achieved more fame with his first major movie role, the villain Hans Gruber in *Die Hard* (1988). Rickman's other notable films include *Robin Hood: Prince of Thieves* (1991), *Sense and Sensibility* (1995), *Michael Collins* (1996), *Love Actually* (2003), and *Sweeney Todd: The Demon Barber of Fleet Street* (2007), but he is best known for his mysterious Severus Snape in all the *Harry Potter* films. He often returns to the stage, as with his London and Broadway appearances in *Private Lives* (2001 and 2002). Rickman's distinctive, silky voice can also be heard in the movies *The Hitchhiker's Guide to the Galaxy* (2005) and *The Wildest Dream* (2010). Originally the character of Absolem in *Alice in Wonderland* was to be live action, using Rickman's face on an animated caterpillar. But director Tim Burton decided to completely animate the character and used only Rickman's haunting voice. Biography: *Alan Rickman: The Unauthorized Biography*, Maureen Paton (2003).

Riehle, Richard (b. 1948) The prolific character actor who has performed in theatres ranging from rural summer stock to Broadway, he has also appeared in many television shows and films, including *Home on the Range* (2004) where he voiced Sheriff Sam Brown. He was born in Menomonee Falls, Wisconsin, was educated at Notre Dame University and the Academy of Dramatic Art in Rochester, Michigan, and he acted in dozens of regional theatre productions before going to New York City. Riehle appeared in Off Broadway productions and on Broadway in *Execution of Justice* (1986), *The Iceman Cometh* (1999), and *The Man Who Had All the Luck* (2002). He made his film debut in 1977 and over the next thirty years acted in over fifty movies, including *Glory* (1989), *Fried Green Tomatoes* (1991), *Prelude to a Kiss* (1992), *Free Willy* (1993), *The Fugitive* (1993), *Ghosts of Mississippi* (1996), *The Odd Couple II* (1998), *Fear and Loathing in Las Vegas* (1998), *Lethal Weapon 4* (1998), *Joe Dirt* (2001), *The Memory Thief* (2007), *Necessary Evil* (2008), *Halloween II* (2009), and *Five Star Day* (2010). Riehle has been active on television since 1989 and has appeared in dozens of series such as *Dragnet*, *Quantum Leap*, *The Golden Girls*, *L.A. Law*, *Murder One*, *Kirk*, *Men Behaving Badly*, *Ally McBeal*, *Buffy the Vampire Slayer*, *Home Improvement*, *Diagnosis Murder*, *Star Trek: Voyager*, *The West Wing*, *Married to the Kellys*, *Star Trek: Enterprise*, *Grounded for Life*, *Boston Legal*, *7th Heaven*, *The Young and the Restless*, *Poor Paul*, and *BoyBand*. Throughout his movie and television career, Riehle has often returned to the stage as an actor, director, and acting coach.

Rivera, Jonas A Hollywood executive who served as production manager on a number of Pixar films, he provided the voice for Boost, the hotrod gang leader, in *Cars* (2006). He worked as art department manager and production manager for such movies as *A Bug's Life* (1998), *Toy Story 2* (1999), and *Monsters, Inc.* (2001), then turned to producing, presenting *Up* (2009) and the 82nd Annual Academy Awards in 2010.

Roberts, Larry (b. 1926–1988?) A stage actor-singer with an obscure career, he provided the voice of the street-smart mutt Tramp in *Lady and the Tramp* (1955). He was born Larry Saltzman in Cleveland, Ohio, and went to Los Angeles in the 1940s where he co-founded the Circle Theatre and acted on stage under the name Larry Salters. He also performed with the Hollywood theatre group called the Players Ring before serving under Gen. Patton during World War II. As a member of the USO, Roberts entertained troops during the Korean War then made some appearances as a singer on early television programs such as *The All Star Revue* and *Lights, Camera, Action; Bandstand Revue*. After making a few recordings and doing stand-up comedy in Las Vegas, he retired from show business and became a designer for clothing businesses in Cleveland and then New York. Roberts made no other films, fell into obscurity, and his death was never confirmed. His vocals for Tramp are very effective, capturing both the cynical, self-serving aspects of this slick Romeo and yet remaining likable enough that the romance with Lady is satisfying. During the long process of developing *Lady and the Tramp*, the male dog was named Homer, Rags, and even Bozo, until it was decided Tramp said it best.

Robertson, Kimmy (b. 1954) A television comic actress with a high-pitched voice who has played characters in several animated series and movies, she provided the voice for Ariel's sister Alana in *The Little Mermaid* (1989) and the enchanted Featherduster in *Beauty and the Beast* (1991). Kim Robertson was born in Hollywood, California, where she studied to become a ballet dancer but her comic talents were recognized by an agent and she took up acting. She made her screen debut in the movie *The Last American Virgin* (1982), followed by such features as *Growing Pains* (1984), *Honey, I Shrunk the Kids* (1989), *Don't Tell Mom the Babysitter Is Dead* (1991), *Speed 2: Cruise Control* (1997), *Stuart Little* (1999), and *Anderson's Cross* (2010). Robertson acted on such television series as *Webster, Married with Children, Tales from the Crypt, Perfect Strangers, The Louie Show, Ellen,* and *ER*, but she is most remembered as Lucy Moran on *Twin Peaks*. She has done voices for such cartoon series as *The Simpsons, Batman, The Little Mermaid, 2 Stupid Dogs, Pepper Ann,* and *House of Mouse,* and she reprised her Featherduster in the video *Belle's Magical World* (1998).

Robinson, Bumper (b. 1974) A busy actor who started as a child performer in television, he provided the voices of the Chipmunks in *Brother Bear* (2003). He was born Larry C. Robinson II in Cleveland, Ohio, and made his professional television debut at the age of four in a Jell-O commercial with Bill Cosby. He went on to act in such series as *The Jeffersons, Webster, Hill Street Blues, Cagney & Lacey, Night Court, Days of Our Lives,* and *Family Matters*. As an adult, Robinson appeared in many other series, including *A Different World, Star Trek: Deep Space Nine, Living Single, Guys Like Us, Grown Ups, Futurama,* and *Sister, Sister*. He did his first voice work for animated shows in 1986 as one of *The Flintstone Kids*, later supplying voices for such cartoon shows as *Teenage Mutant Ninja Turtles, Batman Beyond, What's with Andy?, Static Shock, Legion of Super Heroes, Transformers: Animated,* and *Batman: The Brave and the Bold*.

Robinson, Rad *see* **The Kings Men**

Robson, Wayne (b. 1946) A flexible Canadian character actor with many film and television credits in the States, he supplied the voice of the wacky frill-necked lizard Frank imprisoned with Cody in *The Rescuers Down Under* (1990). He was born in Vancouver, Canada, and acted on stage in his hometown and in Toronto before getting cast in American films such as *McCabe and Mrs. Miller* (1971), *Flashpoint* (1977), *Popeye* (1980), *The Grey Fox* (1982), *Finders Keepers* (1984), *Mrs. Soffel* (1984), *One Magic Christmas* (1985), *Goofballs* (1987), *Candy Mountain* (1988), *Bye Bye Blues* (1989), *Bingo* (1991), *Stand Off* (1993), *Dolores Claiborne* (1995), *Two If by Sea* (1996), *Affliction* (1997), *The Highwayman* (2000), *Cold Creek Manor* (2003), *Welcome to Mooseport* (2004), *In Between* (2007), *The Timekeeper* (2009), and *Survival of the Dead* (2009), as well as many made-for-TV movies. Robson has acted in dozens of television series, including *Seeing Things, Alfred Hitchcock Presents, Street Legal, Avonlea, RoboCop, Due South, Goosebumps, The Zach Files, Little Mosque on the Prairie, Kids in the Hall: Death Comes to Town,* and *Sea Wolf*, but he is most remembered as Mike Hamar in *The Red Green Show*, a role he played for eleven years and in the film *Duct Tape Forever* (2002). He can be heard on the TV cartoon series *The Adventures of Tin Tin, The NeverEnding Story, Rupert, Pippi Longstocking, Mythic Warriors: Guardians of the Legend, Franklin,* and *Miss Spider's Sunny Patch Friends,* as well as the animated films and videos *The Get-Along Gang* (1984), *Pippi Longstocking* (1997), and *Babar: King of the Elephants* (1999). Robson got the job of voicing the scatterbrained Frank when a Disney casting director saw him on an episode of *The Twilight Zone* in 1989.

Rocco, Alex (b. 1936) A character actor often cast as tough Italian types on television and in the movies, he voiced the gruff engineering ant Thorny in *A Bug's Life* (1998). He was born Alexander Federico Petricone, Jr., in Boston and worked as a bartender while trying to break into the movies in California. He made his screen debut in 1966 and his television bow the next year, but did not find recognition until he played the mobster Moe Green in *The Godfather* (1972). Rocco's other film credits include *Slither* (1973), *Freebie and the Bean* (1974), *Hearts of the West* (1975), *The Stunt Man* (1980), *Wired* (1989), *Boris and Natasha* (1992), *Get Shorty* (1995), *That Thing You Do!* (1996), *Dudley Do-Right* (1999), *The Wedding Planner* (2001), *The Country Bears* (2002), and *Ready or Not* (2009). He has appeared in dozens of television series, mostly as heavies at first but eventually in several sit-coms such as *The Facts of Life, Murphy Brown, The Famous Teddy Z, Can't Hurry Love, The George Carlin Show*, and *Sabrina, the Teenage Witch*. Rocco has also provided voices for the TV cartoon series *The Simpsons, The Angry Beavers*, and *Family Guy*.

Rogers, Roy (1911–1998) The genial singing cowboy who, with his wife Dale Evans, starred in movies and on television in westerns that always included a song or two, he and the Sons of the Pioneers sang the narrative "Pecos Bill" section of *Melody Time* (1948). He was born Leonard Franklin Slye in Cincinnati, Ohio, and went to California to pick fruit, remaining to form a singing group which he titled the Sons of the Pioneers. The singers were featured on the radio and in few films, such as *Tumbling Tumbleweeds* (1935), then Rogers was cast in B westerns where he sang cowboy ballads. Rogers and Evans married in 1947 and appeared together in *Apache Rose* (1947) but were not considered a singing team until 1951 when they started their popular television program *The Roy Rogers Show* which lasted, in one form or another, until 1962. Rogers sometimes returned to films as a solo, as with *The Gay Ranchero* (1948), *Twilight in the Sierras* (1950), *Son of Paleface* (1952), *Alias Jesse James* (1959), and *Mackintosh and T. J.* (1975). He was a shrewd businessman who promoted everything from cowboy wear to restaurants with his name on them. Biography: *The Cowboy and the Senorita: A Biography of Roy Rogers and Dale Evans*, Howard Kazanjian (2005).

Rogers, Tristan (b. 1946) One of the first Australian actors to find success in America without hiding his Aussie accent, he supplied the voice for the macho Outback mouse guide Jake who has a soft spot for Miss Bianca in *The Rescuers Down Under* (1990). He was born in Melbourne and appeared on some Australian television shows before coming to the States and finding success as the agent Robert Scorpio in the soap opera *General Hospital*, a role he played for nearly thirty years on daytime television and on the prime time spin-off *General Hospital: Night Shift*. Rogers has also appeared on the series *The Love Boat, Hotel, Tales from the Crypt, Super Force, Babylon 5, The Bold and the Beautiful, Fast Track*, and *Family Law*. He can be heard in the TV cartoon series *The Real Adventures of Jonny Quest, Batman Beyond*, and *The Wild Thornberrys*. Among his movie credits are *Soulmates* (1992), *Night Eyes Three* (1993), *A Piece of Eden* (2000), *Opportunity Knocks* (2007), *Jack Rio* (2008), *Raven* (2009), and *Sebastian* (2010). *The Rescuers Down Under* was made during the high popularity of the *Crocodile Dundee* movies and the animators took pains to make the character Jake different from that Outback hero. Jake is less cocky and countrified than Dundee but he is also an efficient and dashing hero who contrasts nicely with the timid mouse Bernard (Bob Newhart). Also, Rogers' smooth, confident vocals are very different from Newhart's reticent delivery.

Romano, Lou (b. 1972) An acclaimed artist and film animator who has also successfully provided voices on occasion, he can be heard as the paranoid fifth-grade teacher Bernie Kroop in *The Incredibles* (2004), the sneezing hotrod Snotrod in *Cars* (2006), and the hapless human hero Alfredo Linguini in *Ratatouille* (2007). He was born in San Diego, California, and studied animation at the California Institute of the Arts before working on such television cartoon series as *The Powerpuff Girls, Dexter's Laboratory*, and *The Iron Giant*. Romano contributed background designs and storyboards for the Pixar movies *Monsters, Inc.* (2001) and *Up* (2009), as well as the shorts *Boys Night Out* (2003) and *Jack-Jack Attack* (2005). Romano's artwork has been exhibited at the Museum of Modern Art and has appeared on magazine covers. The character of Linguini in *Ratatouille* is a Disney first: an illegitimate hero. He is the son of the chef Gusteau and a woman who was never married. Many Disney heroes and heroines have been orphans without parents but they were always the offspring of wedlock. (The parentage of Lewis in *Meet the Robinsons*, which came out the same year as *Ratouille*, is unclear; his mother abandoned him at an orphanage.) Linguini is also an unusual hero in that he is a oafish klutz with no clear dream or ambition in life until he discovers himself and his true parentage. Romano reprised his Linguini for the video *Your Friend the Rat* (2007) and the actor can also be heard in the animated shorts *Whoopass Stew!* (1992) and *Boys Night Out*.

Rooney, Mickey (b. 1920) The beloved and durable pint-sized actor-singer-dancer with a perennial adolescent glow about him, he has enjoyed one of the longest careers in show business, from playing toddlers to senior citizens on the screen, and providing voices for animated television shows and movies such as *The Fox and the Hound* (1981) in which he voiced the adult fox hero Tod. He was born Joe Yule in Brooklyn, New York, the son of vaudevillian Joe Yule, and was on the stage by the time he was fifteen months old, singing, dancing, and later telling jokes as part of the family act. Rooney made his first silent movie short in 1926 and as the comic strip character Mickey Maguire appeared in over fifty films before sound came in. (Some legends persist that Walt Disney named his famous mouse after Rooney and the character Mickey Maguire.) Cast in supporting roles in early talkies, he found further recognition as Puck in *A Midsummer Night's Dream* (1935) but true stardom did not come until he played adolescent Andy Hardy in the B picture *A Family Affair* (1937); it was so popular Rooney starred in fourteen more Hardy films. Even this series of hits would be overshadowed by the "let's put on a show" musicals with Judy Garland, including *Babes in Arms* (1939), *Strike Up the Band* (1940), *Babes on Broadway* (1941), *Girl Crazy* (1943), and *Thousands Cheer* (1943). At the same time, he also appeared in many notable nonmusical films, such as *Ah, Wilderness!* (1935), *Captains Courageous* (1937), *The Adventures of Huckleberry Finn* (1939), *Young Tom Edison* (1940), *The Human Comedy* (1943), and *National Velvet* (1944). After World War II, Rooney was forced to graduate to more mature roles and concentrated on nonmusical films which were not as popular as his earlier efforts. He was a frequent visitor to television, appearing in his own show in the 1950s and on hundreds of programs and specials. His chipper voice was ideal for animated characters and he voiced such animated movies, television specials, and videos as *Santa Claus Is Coming to Town* (1970), *Journey Back to Oz* (1974), *The Year Without a Santa Claus* (1974), *Rudolph and Frosty's Christmas in July* (1979), *The Care Bears Movie* (1985), *Little Nemo: Adventures in Slumberland* (1989), *Lady and the Tramp II: Scamp's Adventure* (2001), *The Happy Elf* (2005), and *A Miser Brothers' Christmas* (2008). At the age of fifty-nine Rooney made his Broadway debut in the revue *Sugar Babies* (1979) and was a hit, returning to the New York stage in *The Will Rogers Follies* (1993) and as Professor Marvel/Wizard in the Madison Square Garden Theatre musical version of *The Wizard of Oz* (1998). He was still acting in nightclubs and films in 2010. Rooney's unceasing energy and pixie charm seem to render him timeless and he has carried the showmanship from his vaudeville days into everything he has done for eighty years. Autobiographies: *i.e.* (1965); *Life Is Too Short* (1991); biography: *The Nine Lives of Mickey Rooney*, Arthur Marx (1988).

Root, Stephen (b. 1951) A prolific character actor mostly on television, he supplied the voice of the yellow tang fish Bubbles in *Finding Nemo* (2003). He was born in Sarasota, Florida, and studied theatre at the University of Florida before appearing Off Broadway and later acting on Broadway in *So Long on Lonely Street* (1986) and *All My Sons* (1987). Root made his screen debut in *Crocodile Dundee II* (1988) then went on to act in such films as *Monkey Shines* (1988), *Stanley & Iris* (1989), *Ghost* (1990), *Buffy the Vampire Slayer* (1992), *Dave* (1993), *Bicentennial Man* (1999), *Office Space* (1999), *O Brother, Where Art Thou?* (2000), *The Ladykillers* (2004), *No Country for Old Men* (2007), *Leatherheads* (2008), and *The Men Who Stared at Goats* (2009). He has been kept even busier in television where he has appeared on over fifty different series, among them *Roseanne*, *Golden Years*, *Star Trek: The Next Generation*, *Night Court*, *Murphy Brown*, *L.A. Law*, *Harts of the West*, *From the Earth to the Moon*, *Ladies Man*, *CSI: Crime Scene Investigation*, *Grounded for Life*, *The West Wing*, *Pushing Daisies*, *True Blood*, *24*, and *Glenn Martin DDS*, although he is most known as Jimmy James on *NewsRadio*. Root can be heard on such cartoon series as *Johnny Bravo*, *Superman*, *Buzz Lightyear of Star Command*, *The Legend of Tarzan*, *Justice League*, *American Dad!*, *Kim Possible*, *Teen Titans*, *The X's*, *Tripping the Rift*, *Batman: The Brave and the Bold*, *King of the Hill*, and *Kung Fu Pandas: Legends of Awesomeness*, as well as the animated videos and films *The Sissy Duckling* (1999), *Ice Age* (2002), *The Country Bears* (2002), *Ice Age: The Meltdown* (2006), *The Fox and the Hound 2* (2006), *Finding Nemo Submarine Voyage* (2007), and *Tripping the Rift: The Movie* (2008).

Rose, Anika Noni (b. 1972) The vivacious African American actress and singer who first found success on the New York stage, she provided the speaking and singing voice of the New Orleans waitress-heroine Tiana in *The Princess and the Frog* (2009). She was born in Bloomfield, Connecticut, and educated at Florida A & M University and the American Conservatory Theatre in San Francisco before making her Broadway debut as a replacement in *Footloose* in 1998. Rose appeared in the Off Broadway productions of *Eli's Coming* (2001) and *Caroline, or Change* (2003), winning high acclaim when the latter transferred to Broadway. She made her film debut with *King of the Bingo Game* (1999), followed by *From Justin to Kelly* (2003), *Temptation* (2004), *Surviving Christmas* (2004), *Dreamgirls* (2006), *Just Add Water* (2008), and *Skyler* (2011). Rose was also featured on the television series *100 Centre Street*, *Third Watch*, *Hack*, *The Starter Wife*, and *The No. 1 Ladies' Detective Agency*. She returned to Broadway as the leading lady in *Cat on a Hot Tin Roof* in 2008. Tiana in *The Princess and the Frog* is Disney's first African American "princess" and there was much concern over how she was to be presented. Originally a chambermaid named Maddy, she was changed to the waitress Tiana with dreams of owning her own restaurant. Among the actresses/singers considered for the role of Tiana were Jennifer Hudson, Tyra Banks, and Alicia Keys. Because of her musical theatre background, Rose was selected and provided the superb speaking and singing vocals for the character. The animators utilized many of the actress' gestures, including making Tiana a "lefty" because Rose is left-handed.

Roseanne (b. 1952)   The controversial television comedienne and writer known for her blunt sense of humor, she provided the voice of the outspoken, crude cow Maggie in *Home on the Range* (2004). She was born Roseanne Cherrie Barr in Salt Lake City, dropped out of high school, and was a married woman of thirty-two with children before she started doing stand-up comedy professionally. After appearing as a guest on talks shows and a brief, unsuccessful show of her own, she found success as star and writer of her own sit-com *Roseanne* which ran nine years. Roseanne has also appeared on the television series *General Hospital*, *A Different World*, *The Nanny*, *3rd Rock from the Sun*, and *My Name Is Earl*, and she has made a handful of movies, including *She-Devil* (1989), *Freddy's Dead: The Final Nightmare* (1991), *Even Cowgirls Get the Blues* (1993), *Blue in the Face* (1995), and the animated video short *A Dairy Tale* (2004) in which she reprised her Maggie. Throughout a tabloid life filled with marriages, children, divorces, mental breakdowns, and lawsuits, she has gone under various names — Roseanne Barr, Roseanne Arnold, Roseanne Thomas — and she was the subject of the TV-movie *Roseanne: An Unauthorized Biography* (1994) in which she was played by Denny Dillon. Autobiography: *Roseanne: My Life as a Woman* (1991); *My Lives* (1994); memoir: *My Sister Roseanne: The True Story of Roseanne Barr Arnold*, Geraldine Barr (1994).

Roux, Stéphane   A French actor on television and films in his native country, he provided the voice of the Narrator of the cooking channel on French television in *Ratatouille* (2007), his only Hollywood movie. Roux's film credits include *Cyrano de Bergerac* (1990), *Les Aphrorécits* (1992), *Africa Paradis* (2006), and *Sagan* (2008).

Rub, Christian (1886–1956)   A German-born character actor who played quiet, likable foreign types in over one hundred Hollywood films, he provided the voice of the gentle old toymaker Geppetto in *Pinocchio* (1940). He was born in Passau in the Bavarian state of Germany and after World War I he emigrated to the States where he appeared as Christian Rube in the silent movies *The Belle of New York* (1919), *In the Soup* (1902), and *Dog-Gone Clever* (1920). With the coming of sound he was in demand for foreign characters and was kept busy up into the 1950s. Among his movie credits are *The Trial of Vivienne Ware* (1932), *The Cat and the Fiddle* (1934), *Stamboul Quest* (1934), *Music in the Air* (1934), *A Dog of Flanders* (1935), *Stolen Harmony* (1935), *Peter Ibbetson* (1935), *Mr. Deeds Goes to Town* (1936), *Fury* (1936), *Captains Courageous* (1937), *One Hundred Men and a Girl* (1937), *You Can't Take It with You* (1938), *Haunted House* (1940), *Nazi Agent* (1942), *Leather Burners* (1943), *Jungle Woman* (1944), *Strange Confession* (1945), *Fall Guy* (1947), and *Something for the Birds* (1952). Rub was not the first actor hired to voice Geppetto. When Spencer Charters' vocals were deemed too abrasive and the character came across as more crude than kindly, Rub was hired and the animators redid the look of Geppeto, modeled on the gentler voice and facial expressions of Rub.

Ruggles, Charles (1886–1970)   One of Broadway and Hollywood's favorite character actors, he specialized in playing well-dressed but nervous types who were usually gullible and/or henpecked, and his distinctive voice was heard in many cartoons, including the Disney short *Ben and Me* (1953) in which he played Ben Franklin. Charles Sherman Ruggles was born in Los Angeles and in 1914 he made both his screen and Broadway debuts. On Broadway he was featured in such productions as *The Passing Show of 1918* (1918), *Tumble In* (1919), *The Demi-Virgin* (1922), *Queen High* (1926), *Rainbow* (1928), *Spring Is Here* (1929), *The Pleasure of His Company* (1958), and *Roar Like a Dove* (1964), and he was seen in over one hundred movies, including The *Battle of Paris* (1929), *Queen High* (1930), *Trouble in Paradise* (1932), *One Hour with You* (1932), *Love Me Tonight* (1932), *Big Broadcast of 1936* (1935), *Ruggles of Red Gap* (1935), *Anything Goes* (1936), *Bringing Up Baby* (1938), *Balalaika* (1939), *No Time for Comedy* (1940), *Give My Regards to Broadway* (1948), *Look for the Silver Lining* (1949), *The Parent Trap* (1961), *I'd Rather Be Rich* (1964), and *Follow Me, Boys!* (1966). Ruggles was also a familiar favorite on television, appearing on many shows, including *Playhouse 90*, *The Life of Riley*, *The Dinah Shore Chevy Show*, *The Real McCoys*, *The Red Skelton Hour*, *Ben Casey*, *Burke's Law*, *Bonanza*, and *The Beverly Hillbillies*. His distinctive voice was heard providing the wry narration as Aesop for the "Aesop's Fables" section of the TV cartoon series *The Bullwinkle Show* in the 1960s.

His brother was actor-director Wesley Ruggles (1889–1972).

Rupp, Debra Jo (b. 1951)   A busy television comic actress with theatre and film credits, she supplied the voice of the fourth-grade teacher who is Leonard's mom, the hyperactive Mrs. Mary Lou Moira Angela Darling Helperman in *Teacher's Pet* (2004). She was born in Glendale, California, raised in Boxford, Massachusetts, and was educated at the University of Rochester. Rupp made some commercials and acted in some Off Broadway plays before making her television debut on an episode of *Spenser for Hire* in 1987. Among the many TV series she has appeared in are *Kate & Allie, Newhart, Blossom, Davis Rules, Phenom, L.A. Law, Empty Nest, The Office, If Not for You, The Jeff Foxworthy Show, Seinfeld, Caroline in the City, 7th Heaven, Friends,* and *All My Children,* though she is best known as Kitty Forman on *That 70's Show*. Rupp's movie credits include *Big* (1988), *Death Becomes Her* (1992), *Reasons of the Heart* (1996), *Sgt. Bilko* (1996), *Clockwatchers* (1997), *Lucky 13* (2005), *Spymate* (2006), *Kickin It Old Skool* (2007), and *She's Out of My League* (2010), as well as many TV-movies. She originally voiced the frantically cheerful Mrs. Helperman on the television cartoon series *Teacher's Pet* and her voice can be heard in the animated film *Garfield* (2004) and the video *Air Buddies* (2006). Rupp has returned to the theatre on occasion and was featured on Broadway in *Cat on a Hot Tin Roof* (1990).

Rush, Geoffrey (b. 1951)   A versatile Australian actor who has found critical and popular success on three continents, he provided the voice of the friendly pelican Nigel in *Finding Nemo* (2003). Geoffrey Roy Rush was born in Toowoomba, Australia, and raised in Brisbane where he started doing theatre. After graduating from the University of Queensland, he played a variety of classical and modern roles for the Queensland Theatre Company and then the State Theatre Company of South Australia. Rush began making movies in Australia in the 1980s and won international recognition for his performance in *Shine* (1996), followed by many movies in Hollywood and Great Britain as well. Among his most notable films are *Children of the Revolution* (1996), *Oscar and Lucinda* (1997), *Elizabeth* (1998), *Shakespeare in Love* (1998), *Quills* (2000), *The Life and Death of Peter Sellers* (2004), *Munich* (2005), *Elizabeth: The Golden Age* (2007), *The Warrior's Way* (2010), and *The King's Speech* (2010), though he is best known as the wily Barbossa in *Pirates of the Caribbean: The Curse of the Black Pearl* (2003) and its three sequels. Rush has returned to the stage often, acting in Australian productions as well as those in England, and he made a belated but sensational Broadway debut in *Exit the King* in 2009.

Russell, Andy (1919–1992)   A popular crooner on records and radio in the 1940s, he sang "Without You" on the soundtrack of *Make Mine Music* (1946) during the "A Ballad in Blue" section illustrating the end of a relationship using raindrops, flower petals, and a love letter. He was born Andrés Rabago in Los Angeles, the son of Mexican immigrants, and at the age of thirteen was vocalist for Gus Arnheim's Orchestra. Singing songs in English and Spanish, Russell had many hit recordings, none more popular than "Besame Mucho." His Hollywood film credits include *The Stork Club* (1945), *Breakfast in Hollywood* (1946), *Copacabana* (1947), and *House Party* (1953). In the 1950s Russell moved to Mexico where he sang in a handful of Spanish-language movies but retained his U.S. citizenship and frequently returned to the States to sing in concerts and on television.

Russell, Kurt (b. 1951)   The long-time youthful-looking actor who grew up on the screen in several Disney movies, he provided the voice of Adult Copper, the canine hero of *The Fox and the Hound* (1981). Kurt Vogel Russell was born in Springfield, Massachusetts, the son of an actor and a dancer, and by the age of six was on television in six episodes of the series *Sugarfoot*, followed by several other series. He made his screen debut in *It Happened at the World's Fair* (1963) but fame did not come until he played the title role in the television series *The Travels of Jaimie McPheeters*. Russell first worked for Disney in the movie *Follow Me, Boys!* (1966) then went on to appear in thirteen more live-action features for the studio, including *The One and Only, Genuine, Original Family Band* (1968), *The Horse in the Gray Flannel Suit* (1968), *The Computer Wore Tennis Shoes* (1969), *The Barefoot Executive* (1971), *Charley and the Angel* (1973), and *The Strongest Man in the World* (1975). As he outgrew teenage roles, Russell made the transition to adult characters with little difficulty and has remained a familiar face on screen for decades. Among his other movie credits are *Used Cars* (1980), *Escape from New York* (1981), *The Thing* (1982), *Silkwood* (1983), *Swing Shift* (1984), *Tequila Sunrise* (1988), *Backdraft* (1991), *Escape from L.A.* (1996), *Vanilla Sky* (2001), *Poseidon* (2006), and *Death Proof* (2007). Russell gave a memorable performance as Elvis Presley in the TV-movie *Elvis* (1979) and as an adult appeared in such series as *The Virginian, Daniel Boone, Gunsmoke,* and *The Quest*.

Ryan, Roz (b. 1951)   An African American singer-actress on stage and television who has also done stand-up comedy, she provided the voice of the singing Muse Thalia in *Hercules* (1997). She was born Rosalyn Bowen in Detroit, Michigan, and started appearing in musicals in New York in the 1970s, being featured on Broadway in *Ain't Misbehavin'* (1978), *Dreamgirls* (1981), *Chicago* (1996), *One Mo' Time* (2002), and *The Pajama Game* (2006). She made a memorable television debut as Amelia Hetebrink in the series *Amen* and went on to act on other shows, including *The Good News*, *Danny*, *All About the Andersons*, and *Barbershop*. Ryan reprised her Thalia in the video sequel *Hercules: Zero to Hero* (1999) and in the TV cartoon series *Hercules*, and the actress can also be heard in the animated series *Kim Possible*, *Buzz Lightyear of Star Command*, *The Marvelous Adventures of Flapjack*, and *Kick Buttowski: Suburban Daredevil*.

Ryan, Will (b. 1939) A singer-actor-songwriter who has also been a busy voice artist in television since the 1960s, he supplied the voices of Willy the Giant who plays the Ghost of Christmas present in *Mickey's Christmas Carol* (1983) and the Seahorse who makes the announcements at the undersea palace in *The Little Mermaid* (1989). The San Francisco native began his career singing professionally with Phil Baron as the duo Willio & Phillio who were successful on radio, records, and television. After recording some children's records for Disney, Ryan started doing the voices of Rabbit, Tigger, and Eeyore in the popular TV cartoon series *Welcome to Pooh Corner*. Also for Disney he has voiced the bully Pete in the series *Mickey Mouse Works*. Ryan reprised his Willie the Giant in the video *Mickey's Great Clubhouse Hunt* (2007) and the cartoon series *House of Mouse* and *Mickey Mouse Clubhouse*. Among Ryan's many other cartoon credits are *Space Ghost*, *The Smurfs*, *G.I. Joe*, *Dumbo's Circus*, *The Adventures of Teddy Ruxpin*, *Teen Wolf*, *DuckTales*, *Adventures of the Gummi Bears*, and *Garfield and Friends*, as well as the animated movies and videos *Winnie the Pooh and a Day for Eeyore* (1983), *Frog and Toad Are Friends* (1985), *An American Tail* (1986), *Frog and Toad Together* (1987), *Down and Out with Donald Duck* (1987), *Sport Goofy in Soccermania* (1987), *The Land Before Time* (1988), *Stanley and the Dinosaur* (1989), *Adventures in Odyssey: The Knight Travellers* (1991) and over a dozen of its sequels, *Rock-a-Doodle* (1991), *Mouse Soup* (1992), *Thumbelina* (1994), *Stanley's Magic Garden* (1994), *A Flintstones Christmas Carol* (1994), *The Pebble and the Penguin* (1995), and *Looney Tunes: Back in Action* (2003). Ryan has written many songs, some of them recorded by name vocalists, and he has recorded several songs about the American West.

Ryen, Adam (b. 1980) A child actor from Norway who later became a popular television writer in his native country, he supplied the voice of the adventurous, eight-year-old Outback boy Cody in *The Rescuers Down Under* (1990). Adam Sebastian Ryen was born in Norway, the son of Norwegian writer-director Tom Ryen, and came to the States when he was five. At the age of ten he was on American television in *Star Trek: The Next Generation* and in the films *Child's Play 2* (1990), *Unbecoming Age* (1992), *Twenty Bucks* (1993), and *In the Living Years* (1994), as well as the TV-movies *Before the Storm* (1991) and *Stepfather III* (1992). Ryen returned to Norway as a teenager and wrote some successful Norwegian television series but gave up acting in 1994. Because of his slight Scandinavian accent, Ryen was able to make Cody foreign enough to sound Australian to American audiences.

Sabella, Ernie (1949) A roly-poly comic character actor of the stage, movies and television, he provided the singing and speaking voice of the good-hearted warthog Pumbaa in *The Lion King* (1994). He was born in Westchester, New York, and educated at the University of Miami before going on the stage in New York. After appearing on Broadway in *The Robber Bridegroom* (1976) and *Little Johnny Jones* (1982), Sabella made his television debut on an episode of *St. Elsewhere*, followed my many other series such as *Newhart*, *Knots Landing*, *Cagney & Lacey*, *It's Your Move*, *Cheers*, *Roxie*, *Perfect Strangers*, *Hill Street Blues*, *A Fine Romance*, *Saved by the Bell*, *The Practice*, and *That's So Raven*. Among his film credits are *City Heat* (1984), *Fright Night Part 2* (1988), *Quiz Show* (1994), *In & Out* (1997), *Mousehunt* (1997) *The Out-of-Towners* (1999), and *Listen to Your Heart* (2010). The character of Pumbaa would be an amiable enough creature on his own but, when teamed with the wise-cracking meerkat Timon (Nathan Lane), the twosome make for a sprightly vaudeville-like comedy duo. Pumbaa plays the dense, innocent stooge to Timon's more worldly-wise wheeler-dealer. Yet there is a bond of affection between the two and, unlike Laurel and Hardy or Abbott and Costello, one never derides the other. Voice artists usually work alone in the recording studio without the other performers present but Sabella and Lane did all their scenes together and it shows. The two actors worked together on Broadway in *Guys and Dolls* (1992) and the expert comic timing heard in *The Lion King* is not something that instantly happened in the recording studio. Sabella reprised his Pumbaa in the videos *Timon and Pumbaa's Wild Adventure* (1997), *The Lion King II: Simba's Pride* (1998), *Mickey's Magical Christmas: Snowed in at the House of Mouse* (2001), *The Lion King 1½* (2004), and *Behind the Legend: Timon* (2004), as well as in the TV cartoon series

Timon and Pumbaa and *House of Mouse*. He has returned to the stage on occasion, appearing on Broadway in *A Funny Thing Happened on the Way to the Forum* (1996), *Chicago* (1996), *Man of La Mancha* (2002), *Sweet Charity* (2005), and *Curtains* (2007).

St. John, Michelle A Native American actress and singer with credits in Canada, the States, Australia, and New Zealand, she supplied the voice of Pocahontas's best friend Nakoma in *Pocahontas* (1995). The Canadian-born St. John is of the Cree tribe and began her career on the stage in Toronto and in Canadian movies and television. By the 1990s she was working on projects in various countries and recording music for CDs and television programs. St. John's film credits include *Straight Line* (1989), *Where the Spirit Lives* (1989), *Coyote Summer* (1996), *Smoke Signals* (1998), *The Business of Fancydancing* (2002), and *Keeping Quiet* (2010), as well as the TV-movies *Lost in the Barrens II: The Curse of the Viking Grave* (1991), *Conspiracy of Silence* (1991), *Liar, Liar: Between Father and Daughter* (1993), *Spirit Rider* (1993), *Geronimo* (1993), and *White Lies* (1998). She appeared in the television mini-series *By Way of the Stars* (1992) and in the series *Beverly Hills Teens*, *9B*, *Northern Exposure*, *E.N.G.*, *Side Effects*, *Murphy Brown*, and *Tipi Tales*.

Salonga, Lea (b. 1971) A classic beauty with a clear, enthralling singing voice, she has become one of the most famous Asian actresses in the West for her appearances on Broadway and her work in two Disney animated films: the singing voices of Princess Jasmine in *Aladdin* (1992) and the Chinese girl warrior Fa Mulan in *Mulan* (1998). She was born Maria Lea Carmen Imutan Salonga in Manila in the Philippines and by the age of seven was singing in musicals in her native country, recording her first album when she was ten years old, and as a teen had her own Manila television show. She attended Ateneo De Manila University to study dermatology but left college to continue singing and in 1989 made a thrilling London debut as the refugee Kim in the musical *Miss Saigon*, reprising her performance to great acclaim on Broadway in 1991. After doing some musicals in the Philippines, Salonga was back on Broadway in *Les Misérables* (1992) and *Flower Drum Song* (2002). In addition to many recordings, Salonga has sung at Carnegie Hall and other famous venues around the world and has appeared on Philippine and American television. She again did the singing for Jasmine in the videos *Aladdin in Nasira's Revenge* (2001) and *Disney Princesses Enchanted Tales: Follow Your Dreams* (2007), and provided the singing for Mulan in *Mulan II* (2004). Salonga can also be heard in the English language version of the animated Japanese film *Tonari no Totoro* (*My Neighbor Totoro*) (1988). Originally Salonga was cast to do both the speaking and singing voice of the title heroine in *Mulan* but while recording they found that her deep voice used to impersonate a man was not working. So actress Ming-Na was hired to do the speaking Mulan and Salonga's singing was retained.

Sanders, Christopher Michael (b. 1960) An animator and artist who has worked on television series and feature films and now directs, he provided the voice of the rambunctious alien critter Experiment #626, better known as Stitch, in *Lilo & Stitch* (2002) which he co-wrote and co-directed. Born and raised in Colorado and educated at the California Institute of the Arts, he began his career as an artist for Marvel Comics then was hired as an animator for the television cartoon series *Muppet Babies*. Sanders joined Disney in 1987 and worked on the story and/or the animation for such films as *The Rescuers Down Under* (1990), *Beauty and the Beast* (1991), *Aladdin* (1992), *The Lion King* (1994), and *Mulan* (1998). For Dreamworks he directed the animated feature *How to Train Your Dragon* (2010). Sanders first created Stitch in 1985 as a character in a children's book but no publisher would buy it. He returned to the little critter for *Lilo & Stitch* and supplied the voice as well, a tricky job since Stitch speaks no recognized language. The character was also difficult to animate in terms of emotions because there are no pupils in his eyes. The artists had to depend on physical movement of his body and Sanders' squawking sounds to denote what the creature was saying and feeling. Sanders reprised his Stitch in the videos *Stitch! The Movie!* (2003), *Stitch's Great Escape* (2004), *The Lion King 1½* (2004), *The Origin of Stitch* (2005), *Lilo & Stitch 2: Stitch Has a Glitch* (2005), *Leroy & Stitch* (2006), and the TV series *Lilo & Stitch*.

Sanders, George (1906–1972) An urbane character actor with a dry and disapproving air about him, he provided the speaking voice of the soft-spoken, deadly tiger Shere Khan in *The Jungle Book* (1967). George Henry Sanders was born in St. Petersburg, Russia, to English parents, and when the Russian Revolution broke out in 1917 the family returned to London. After attending Brighton College and Manchester Technical College, he pursued various occupations before turning to acting, making his first British movie in 1929. Seven years later he was in Hollywood where he was usually cast as debonair cads and bored aristocrats. Among Sanders' many notable movies are *Lloyd's of London* (1936), *Confessions of a Nazi Spy* (1939), *The Saint Strikes Back* (1939) and three of its sequels, *Rebecca* (1940), *Foreign Correspondent* (1940), *Bitter Sweet* (1940), *The Gay Falcon* (1941) and three of its sequels,

Moon and Sixpence (1942), *The Black Swan* (1942), *The Lodger* (1944), *The Picture of Dorian Gray* (1945), *The Ghost and Mrs. Muir* (1947), *Forever Amber* (1947), *All About Eve* (1950), *Call Me Madam* (1953), *Jupiter's Darling* (1955), *That Certain Feeling* (1956), *Solomon and Sheba* (1959), *Village of the Damned* (1960), *In Search of the Castaways* (1962), *A Shot in the Dark* (1964), *The Quiller Memorandum* (1966), and *The Kremlin Letter* (1970). He appeared is many television series and hosted his own program *The George Sanders Mystery Theatre*. Sanders occasionally acted on the stage, as in the Broadway production of *Conversation Piece* (1934). The tiger Khan in *The Jungle Book* is one of Disney's quietest, most low-key villains and much of this comes from Sanders' understated yet effective performance. The animators copied the actor's nonchalant gestures and facial poses in animating this very gentlemanly but deadly character. Autobiography: *Memoirs of a Professional Cad* (1960); biography: *George Sanders: An Exhausted Life*, Richard VanDerBeets (1993).

Sandler, Ethan (b. 1972) A flexible movie and television actor with a variety of voices, he provided several voices for *Meet the Robinsons* (2007): the beeping bowler-hat–shaped robot DOR-15 known as Doris, the CEO Mr. Smith of InventCo, and the lovably eccentric Robinson family members Uncle Fritz, Aunt Petunia, Cousin Spike, Uncle Dimitri, and Cousin Laszlo. Raised near Seattle, Washington, and educated at Northwestern University, he made his screen debut with *The Chocolate War* (1988), followed by *Adventures in Spying* (1992), *Flushed* (1999), *The Princess Diaries* (2001), *The Bourne Supremacy* (2004), and *The Enigma with a Stigma* (2006). Sandler has appeared on the television series *Sex and the City*, *The $treet*, and *Will & Grace*, but is better remembered as ADA Jeffrey Brandau on *Crossing Jordan*. He also acted in, co-produced, and wrote the series *My Boys*.

Sansom, Ken A familiar character actor and voice artist who has been busy on television since the early 1970s, he provided the voice of the bossy Rabbit in the *Winnie the Pooh* films, videos, and television series since 1988. Sansom has appeared on such TV shows as *The Brady Bunch*, *Mayberry R.F.D.*, *Room 222*, *The Odd Couple*, *All in the Family*, *Columbo*, *Harry O*, *Maude*, *Cannon*, *Charlie's Angels*, *Days of Our Lives*, *Phyllis*, *The Tony Randall Show*, *Baretta*, *Chico and the Man*, *Lou Grant*, *CHiPs*, *Quincy M.E.*, *Remington Steele*, and *Murder, She Wrote*. He was also in several movies, including *The Sting* (1973), *Herbie Rides Again* (1974), *Airport 1975* (1974), and *Funny Lady* (1975). Sansom began his career in television cartoons with the series *The Littles*, followed by such shows as *The Transformers*, *Moon Dreamers*, *The Chipmunks*, and *TaleSpin*, He first voiced Rabbit in the series *The New Adventures of Winnie the Pooh* in 1988, then reprised the role in the series *My Friend Tigger & Pooh* and *The Book of Pooh*, and in several movies and videos, including *Winnie the Pooh Friendship: Tigger-ific Tales* (1988), *Winnie the Pooh and Christmas Too* (1991), *Winnie the Pooh Un-Valentine's Day* (1995), *Pooh's Grand Adventure: The Search for Christopher Robin* (1997), *A Winnie the Pooh Thanksgiving* (1998), *The Tigger Movie* (2000), *Piglet's Big Movie* (2003), *Winnie the Pooh: Springtime with Roo* (2004), *Pooh's Heffalump Movie* (2005), and *Tigger & Pooh and a Musical Too* (2009).

Sarandon, Chris (b. 1942) A handsome leading man whose characters and productions often inspired controversy, he supplied the speaking voice of the "Pumpkin King" Jack Skellington in *The Nightmare Before Christmas* (1993). He was born in Beckley, West Virginia, and as a teenager played professionally in a band before going to West Virginia University and Catholic University of America to study acting. Sarandon performed in regional theatres in the States and Canada and was on Broadway in *The Rothschilds* (1970), *Two Gentlemen of Verona* (1971), and *Censored Scenes from King Kong* (1980). He first gained notice and notoriety as the gay lover in the movie *Dog Day Afternoon* (1975), followed by a variety of roles in such movies as *Lipstick* (1976), *The Sentinel* (1977), *Protocol* (1984), *The Princess Bride* (1987), *Slaves of New York* (1989), *Collision Course* (1989), *Fright Night* (1993), *Terminal Justice* (1996), *Reaper* (2000), *Loggerheads* (2005), and *Multiple Sarcasm*s (2010), as well as many TV-movies, including *The Day Christ Died* (1980), *A Tale of Two Cities* (1980), *Frankenstein* (1987), *The Mayflower Madam* (1987), *Lincoln and the War Within* (1992), and *The Dead Will Tell* (2004). As a child he appeared on the television soap opera *The Guiding Light* and he returned to television as an adult and acted in such series as *Star Trek: Deep Space Nine*, *The Outer Limits*, *The Practice*, *Chicago Hope*, *Felicity*, *ER*, *Judging Amy*, *Law & Order*, and *The Unusuals*. Sarandon returned to Broadway in *Nick & Nora* (1991), *The Light in the Piazza* (2005), and *Cyrano de Bergerac* (2007). Although Sarandon sang in musicals on Broadway, he did not think his singing voice was strong enough for the songs in *The Nightmare Before Christmas* so composer Danny Elfman did the singing for the character of Jack Skellinton.

Sarandon, Susan (b. 1946) The versatile leading lady of films, stage, and television who often plays determined and worldly characters, she voiced Miss Spider in *James and the Giant Peach* (1996) and played the vicious Queen Nerissa in live-action sections of *Enchanted* (2007) and did her vocals for the animated portion. She was born Susan Abigail Tomalin in New York City, and studied theatre at Catholic University of America in Washington, D.C. Although she made her screen debut in *Joe* (1969), Sarandon concentrated on theatre, appearing in the Off Broadway plays *A Coupla White Chicks Sitting Around Talking* (1980) and *Extremities* (1982), and on Broadway in *An Evening with Richard Nixon and ...* (1972). Her early movies include *Lovin' Molly* (1974), *The Front Page* (1974), and *The Great Waldo Pepper* (1975), but it was Sarandon's performance in the cult hit *The Rocky Horror Picture Show* (1975) that brought her the most notoriety. Among her many subsequent movies are *Pretty Baby* (1978), *Atlantic City* (1980), *Loving Couples* (1980), *The Witches of Eastwick* (1987), *Bull Durham* (1988), *Thelma & Louise* (1991), *Lorenzo's Oil* (1992), *The Client* (1994), *Little Woman* (1994), *Dead Man Walking* (1995), *Stepmom* (1998), *Cradle Will Rock* (1999), *Shall We Dance* (2004), *The Lovely Bones* (2009), and *Wall Street: Money Never Sleeps* (2010). Sarandon has appeared on a handful of television series, including *A.D.*, *Malcolm in the Middle*, *Friends*, and *Rescue Me*, and can be heard in the cartoon series *The Simpsons* and in the animated film *Rugrats in Paris: The Movie — Rugrats II* (2000). She returned to the New York Theatre with *The Guys* (2002) and *Exit the King* (2009) and has remained active in many humanitarian causes. She was married for a time to actor Chris Sarandon. The actresses Sissy Spacek, Angelica Huston, and Mary Steenburgen were among the performers considered for the evil Queen Narissa in *Enchanted*, a character in the mold of the great Disney villainesses. At the same time Narissa is a spoof of those wicked characters, something Sarandon was able to do in her live-action scenes and in her vocals in the animated sections. Biographies: *Susan Sarandon: Actress-Activist*, Marc Shapiro (2001); *Susan Sarandon: A True Maverick*, Betty Jo Tucker (2004).

Savage, Keaton A young television actor who has played kids on such series as *Smart Guy*, *Working*, and *Grounded for Life*, he provided the voice for one of the Piggies in *Home on the Range* (2004).

Savage, Randy (b. 1952) A flamboyant wrestling star who has often turned to acting, the "Macho Man" celebrity voiced Dr. Calico's henchman Thug in *Bolt* (2008). He was born Randall Mario Poffo in Columbus, Ohio, the son of professional wrestler Angelo Poffo, and pursued baseball in college and professionally before turning to wrestling. The huge, sun-glassed, bandana-wearing icon was soon a star of both the World Wrestling Foundation (WWF) and World Championship Wrestling (WCW), making many appearances on television in the ring and as a guest star on TV shows. Savage has acted in such television series as *Space Ghost Coast to Coast*, *Walker, Texas Ranger*, and *Nikki*, and in the film *Spider-Man* (2002), He reprised his Thug in the video *Super Rhino* (2009) and his husky voice can be heard in the movie short *Glago's Guest* (2008), and the cartoon series *Family Guy*, *The X's*, *Duck Dodgers*, and *King of the Hill*. Biography: *Randy Savage: The Story of the Wrestler They Call "Macho Man,"* Jacqueline Mudge (1999).

Schaal, Kristen (b. 1978) A pert, quirky comedienne and actress who often writes her own material, she provided the voice of the blue triceratops toy Trixie in *Toy Story 3* (2010). She was born in Longmont, Colorado, and educated at Northwestern University before beginning her career as a stand-up comic in New York City. Schaal's unique brand of comedy soon had her performing in festivals, concerts, and television shows in Europe and the States. She made her screen acting debut in *Kate & Leopold* (2001) and has appeared in other films such as *Adam & Steve* (2005), *Delirious* (2006), *Norbit* (2007), *FCU: Facts Checkers Unit* (2008), *When in Rome* (2010), *Get Him to the Greek* (2010), and *Dinner for Schmucks* (2010). In addition to her appearances on talk shows, comedy specials, and *The Daily Show*, Schaal has acted in many series, including *The Education of Max Bickford*, *Cheap Seats: Without Ron Parker*, *Ugly Betty*, *Six Degrees*, *Law & Order: Criminal Intent*, *Mad Men*, *How I Met Your Mother*, *Horrible People*, and *Modern Family*, although she is probably best known as Mel on *The Flight of the Conchords*. She can be heard in the TV cartoon shows *Freak Show*, *Scott Mateman Presents Scott Bateman Presents*, *Aqua Teen Hunger Force*, and *Xavier: Renegade Angel*, as well as the animated film *Shrek Forever After* (2010). In the original screenplay for *Toy Story 3*, the toy dino Trixie was one of Lotso's gang members; by the final cut she was a friendly dinosaur and one of Bonnie's toys.

Schumacher, Michael (b. 1969) The internationally acclaimed Formula One race car driver, he voiced the Italian race car Michael Schumacker Ferrari in *Cars* (2006). He was born in Hürth-Hermülheim, West Germany, and raced go-carts as a child. He would go on to be the World Champion in Formula One racing seven times. Schumacher's only other voice credit is for the animated French film *Asterix at the Olympic Games* (2008). Biography: *Michael Schumacher: Driven to Extremes*, James Allen (1999).

Scott, Dorothy An actress with a few scattered film and television credits, she provided the voice of the silly Giddy the Elephant in *Dumbo* (1941).

Scott was seen in the movies *The Girl in Room 20* (1946), *The Beginning or the End* (1947), *The Pretender* (1947), and *My Bodyguard* (1980), as well as in an episode of the television series *Barnaby Jones.* Her other voice credit is the TV cartoon series *The Bullwinkle Show.* In various scripts of *Dumbo*, the character is also named "Giggles" and "Fidgety."

Scott, George C. (1927–1999) The respected gravel-voiced actor who played comic and dramatic roles in all media, he provided the voice of the cruel Outback poacher Percival McLeach in *The Rescuers Down Under* (1990). George Campbell Scott was born in Wise, Virginia, and educated at the University of Missouri before serving in the U.S. Marine Corps for four years. He appeared in more than 150 roles in stock stage companies before making a thrilling Manhattan debut in 1957 as *Richard III* for the New York Shakespeare Festival. The following year he was first seen on television in an episode of *Omnibus.* Over the next four decades he acted in dozens of dramatic special and series, including *Kraft Theatre, Playhouse 90, Naked City, The Virginian, East Side/West Side, Hallmark Hall of Fame, Columbo, Mr. President, Traps,* and *New York News*, as well as many made-for-TV movies. Scott's performance in the film *Anatomy of a Murder* (1959) secured his screen career and he would go on to make such successful movies as *The Hustler* (1961), *The List of Adrian Messenger* (1963), *Dr. Strangelove* (1964), *Patton* (1970), *The Hospital* (1971), and *Islands in the Stream* (1977). He often returned to the stage, sometimes directing as well as performing, and he shone in such New York productions as *The Andersonville Trial* (1959), *The Merchant of Venice* (1962), *The Little Foxes* (1967), *Plaza Suite* (1968), *Death of a Salesman* (1975), *Sly Fox* (1976), *Present Laughter* (1982), and *Inherit the Wind* (1996). The character of McLeach in *The Rescuers Down Under* is one of Disney's more straightforward villains without much cunning, brains, or sense of the creative. At the same time he is very deadly in his one-track-mind manner, even willing to kill the boy Cody as easily as he hunts down animals. Scott's performance is deliciously colorful, growling and blustering in a variety of ways to make McLeach almost, but not quite, comic. Memoir: *Love and Madness: My Years with George C. Scott*, Karen Truesdall Riehl (2003); biography: *Rage and Glory: The Volatile Life and Career of George C. Scott*, David Sheward (2008).

Scotti, Vito (1918–1996) A useful television character actor who specialized in foreign types, particularly Italian, he voiced Peppo, the accordian-playing Italian "scat cat" in *The Aristocats* (1970). Vito Giusto Scotti was born in San Francisco, the son of an actress in the Italian theatre, and lived in Naples until the age of seven when he returned to the States. He learned pantomime and commedia dell'arte techniques as a child and began his career doing magic tricks and physical comedy in nightclubs before making his movie debut in 1949 as a Mexican youth in *Illegal Entry.* Scotti first appeared on television in 1950 and would act in over 150 TV comedy and dramatic series over the years, playing everything from Japanese to Russian characters but usually cast as bossy, overbearing Italians. Among his films are *The Black Orchid* (1958), *Two Weeks in Another Town* (1962), *The Courtship of Eddie's Father* (1963), *Captain Newman, M.D.* (1963), *Von Ryan's Express* (1965), *Head* (1968), *Cactus Flower* (1969), *The Boatniks* (1970), *The Godfather* (1972), *Herbie Goes Bananas* (1980), and *Get Shorty* (1995).

Searle, Douglas (1913–1999) A British classical actor who had a long career on both sides of the Atlantic on stage, in films, and on television, he voiced the fatalistic Koala bear Krebbs in *The Rescuers Down Under* (1990) and the bumbling Sultan in *Aladdin* (1992). He was born in London and studied at the Royal Academy of Dramatic Art before making his professional stage debut in 1934. Prior to and after serving in World War II, he played many classical roles at the Birmingham Repertory and the Shakespeare Memorial Theatre at Stratford. Searle also acted and directed at the Stratford Theatre Festival in Canada and made a belated Broadway bow at the age of sixty, later receiving acclaim there for such productions as *The Dresser* (1981) and *Noises Off* (1985). His film and television appearances were limited but memorable, as with the movies *Amadeus* (1984), *Ernest Saves Christmas* (1988), *Ghostbusters II* (1989), and *Almost an Angel* (1990), and the TV series *Amazing Stories, Rags to Riches, Cheers,* and *The Golden Girls.* The character of the Sultan in *Aladdin* was conceived as a kind of an Arabian *Wizard of Oz*, a genial but ineffective ruler. Like many other Disney fathers, he is more enjoyable than admirable. In fact, the Sultan is child-like in his interest in toys and his refusal to deal with important matters of state. He might be irritating if Searle's performance was not so warm and loving.

Sedaris, Amy (b. 1961) A popular television actress and comedienne who sometimes writes her own material, she provided the voice of the tomboy vixen Foxy Loxy in *Chicken Little* (2005). She was born in Endicott, New York, grew up in Raleigh, North Carolina, and started her career in comedy improv troupes. As a member of the Second City and Annoyance Theatre comedy groups in Chicago she was given guest spots on television. Sedaris found national recognition as the quirky Jerri Blank on the Comedy Central series *Strangers with Candy*, then went on to dozens of appearances on talk shows and guest spots on such series as *Just Shoot Me!*, *Sex and the City*, *Monk*, *Sesame Street*, *The Closer*, and *The New Adventures of Old Christine*. Her movie credits include *Maid in Manhattan* (2002), *Elf* (2003), *Strangers with Candy* (2005), *Bewitched* (2005), *Jennifer's Body* (2009), and *Beware the Gonzo* (2010). Sedaris' voice can be heard in the animated movies *Shrek the Third* (2007), *Puberty, the Movie* (2007), and *Space Buddies* (2009). She has written a handful of comedy nonfiction books, some with her brother, the humorist David Sedaris.

Selby, Sarah (1905–1980) A durable character actress who specialized in matronly roles of authority in television shows, she supplied the voice of the snooty Prissy the Elephant in *Dumbo* (1941). She was born in St. Louis, Missouri, and made her film debut in *Dumbo*. Selby acted in thirty movies, including *The Curse of the Cat People* (1944), *The Naughty Nineties* (1945), *A Double Life* (1947), *Perfect Strangers* (1950), *Jim Thorpe—All American* (1951), *Battle Cry* (1955), *Good Morning, Miss Dove* (1955), and *Moon Pilot* (1962), then concentrated on television for the rest of her career. She appeared in such series as *I Love Lucy*, *Dragnet*, *It's a Great Life*, *Father Knows Best*, *Wagon Train*, *The Real McCoys*, *Lassie*, *The Adventures of Ozzie and Harriet*, *Death Valley Days*, *Bonanza*, *Petticoat Junction*, *Green Acres*, *Gunsmoke*, *Family Affair*, and *Rhoda*, but is probably most remembered as Aunt Gertrude in *The Hardy Boys: The Mystery of the Applegate Treasure* and its sequel *The Hardy Boys: The Mystery of the Ghost Farm*.

Selleck, Tom (b. 1945) The tall, macho television and movie star who is also a producer, he provided the voice of the adult inventor Lewis "Cornelius" Robinson in *Meet the Robinsons* (2007). Thomas William Selleck was born in Detroit, Michigan, the son of a real estate executive, and grew up in Los Angeles. He attended the University of Southern California on a basketball scholarship then later trained at the Beverly Hills Playhouse while he started doing some modeling and commercials. Selleck appeared in a number of television series and movies for ten years without getting much attention until he played Magnum in the series *Magnum, P.I.* which ran eight years. His subsequent television credits include *The Closer*, *Friends*, *Boston Legal*, and *Las Vegas*. Among Selleck's film credits are *Midway* (1976), *Coma* (1978), *The Gypsy Warriors* (1978), *Runaway* (1984), *3 Men and a Baby* (1987), *3 Men and a Little Lady* (1990), *Christopher Columbus: The Discovery* (1992), *Open Season* (1995), *In & Out* (1997), *The Love Letter* (1999), and *Killers* (2010), as well as a series of TV-movies based on Robert B. Parker books in which he played the sleuth Jesse Stone. The character of Cornelius in *Meet the Robinsons* is described as "looking like Tom Selleck" by his son Wilbur so that young Lewis will not suspect that the adult inventor Cornelius looks just like Lewis, his real father. When the animated character of Cornelius finally appears in the film, he looks nothing like Selleck but he does have Selleck's voice. Biography: *Tom Selleck: An Unauthorized Biography*, Jason Bonderoff (1983).

Severn, Raymond (1930–1994) A child actor who made films for five years in the 1940s then retired, he supplied the voice, with Leone Le Doux, of the infant prodigy Baby Herbert Weems in the "Baby Weems" segment of *The Reluctant Dragon* (1941). He was born in Johannesburg, South Africa, and when Severn was five years old his family emigrated to California where he and his seven siblings played children's roles in the movies. Severn's film credits are *The Story of Dr. Jenner* (1939), *We Are Not a Alone* (1939), *Foreign Correspondent* (1940), *A Yank at Eton* (1942), *The Man from Down Under* (1943), *A Guy Named Joe* (1943), *The Lodger* (1944), *The Hour Before Dawn* (1944), and *The Suspect* (1944).

Shadix, Glenn (b. 1952) A stout, Southern-flavored character actor and voice artist, he supplied the voice of the (literally) two-faced Mayor of Halloween Town in *The Nightmare Before Christmas* (1993). He was born William Glenn Shadix in Bessemer, Alabama, and studied theatre at Birmingham Southern College before going to New York City where he appeared in several Off Broadway plays, several at the Ensemble Studio Theatre. He made his screen debut in a small role in *The Postman Always Rings Twice* (1981), followed by such films as *Beetlejuice* (1988), *Sunset* (1988), *Heathers* (1989), *Bingo* (1991), *Dark Side of Genius* (1994), *Love Affair* (1994), *Dunston Checks In* (1996), *The Empty Mirror* (1996), *Chairman of the Board* (1998), *Planet of the Apes* (2001), and *The Final Curtain* (2007). Shadix has appeared in such television series as *The Golden Girls*, *Roseanne*, *Seinfeld*, *Empty Nest*, *Night Court*, *Cheers*, *The John Larroquette Show*, *Thanks*, *Carnivale*, and *Sabrina, the Teenage Witch*, and he can be heard on many cartoon series, including *Dinosaurs*, *Life with Louie*, *The Mask*, *Duckman: Private Dick/Family Man*, *Cow and Chicken*, *Hercules: Legendary Journeys*, *Extreme Ghostbusters*, *Time Squad*, *Jackie Chan Adventures*, *Lilo & Stitch*, *The Batman*, *Justice League*, and *Teen Titans*.

Shaffer, Paul (1949) A well-known musician, band leader, comic, and sometime actor, he provided the voice of the hip messenger god Hermes in *Hercules* (1997). Paul Allen Wood Shaffer was born in Thunder Bay, Canada, and educated at the University of Toronto before beginning his career as a keyboard musician in bands on tour and in clubs. Serving as music director for the first Toronto production of *Godspell* in 1972, he went on to work on other musicals and eventually was a member of the band for the television show *Saturday Night Live*. Shaffer's joking in between music sets soon got him attention and he found wide recognition as the musical director, keyboard player, and jokester on the popular talk program *Late Show with David Letterman*. He has made appearances in such films as *This Is Spinal Tap* (1984), *Scrooged* (1988), *Look Who's Talking Too* (1990), *Blues Brothers 2000* (1998), and *Man on the Moon* (1999), and reprised his Hermes on the TV cartoon series *House of Mouse*. The character of Hermes in *Hercule*s is physically based on Schaffer, including the anachronistic glasses the musician wears. At one point in the film, Hermes bangs away on a keyboard, striking a familiar Schaffer pose. Memoir: *We'll Be Here for the Rest of Our Lives: A Swingin' Show-Biz Saga*, with David Ritz (2009).

Shalhoub, Tony (b. 1953) A flexible character actor of stage, screen, and television who usually plays everyman characters who have a bit of a quirk, he voiced Luigi, the Fiat 500 who sells tires in the small town of Radiation Springs, in *Cars* (2006). Anthony Marcus Shalhoub was born in Green Bay, Wisconsin, the son of Lebanese immigrants, and was educated at the University of Southern Main and Yale University for a stage career. He acted in theatre productions in Central Park and Off Broadway and in 1986 made his television and movie debuts. Shalhoub's film credits include *Longtime Companion* (1989), *Barton Fink* (1991), *Addams Family Values* (1993), *I.Q.* (1994), *Big Night* (1996), *Men in Black* (1997), *Primary Colors* (1998), *Spy Kids* (2001), *Men in Black II* (2002), and *Feed the Fish* (2009). He has appeared in many TV-movies and series, including *The X-Files, Frasier, Wings, Ally McBeal,* and *Stark Raving Mad*, but he is most known for his obsessive-compulsive detective Adrian Monk in *Monk* which ran seven years. Shalhoub has often returned to the stage, appearing on Broadway in *The Odd Couple* (1985), *The Heidi Chronicles* (1989), *Conversations with My Father* (1992), and *Lend Me a Tenor* (2010).

Shawn, Wallace (b. 1943) The short, pudgy, nasal character actor who is also a recognized playwright, he voiced Rex the toy dinosaur in *Toy Story* (1994), the irritating boss Gilbert Huph in *The Incredibles* (2004), and three annoying school principals: Mr. Mazur in *A Goofy Movie* (1995), Crosby Stikler in *Teacher's Pet* (2004), and Mr. Fetchit in *Chicken Little* (2005). Wallace Michael Shawn was born in New York City, the son of *The New Yorker* magazine editor William Shawn, and educated at Harvard University and Oxford University before starting a career as a college professor and scholar. He turned to playwriting in the 1970s and a had a handful of original plays and translations of foreign plays produced Off Broadway and in regional theatres across the country. His most notable works include *The Mandrake* (1977), *Marie and Bruce* (1979), *Aunt Dan and Lemon* (1986), *The Fever* (1990), and *The Designated Mourner* (1996). Shawn also took up acting in the 1970s and was cast on the New York stage in character roles, then made a notable screen debut in *Manhattan* (1979). His other movie credits include *My Dinner with Andre* (1981), *The Hotel New Hampshire* (1984), *The Bostonians* (1984), *Radio Days* (1987), *Prick Up Your Ears* (1987), *The Moderns* (1988), *Mrs. Parker and the Vicious Circle* (1994), *Vanya on 42nd Street* (1994), *Clueless* (1995), *My Favorite Martian* (1999), *The Curse of the Jade Scorpion* (2001), *Melinda and Melinda* (2004), and *Fury Vengeance* (2010), but he is most remembered as the obnoxious Vizzini in *The Princess Bride* (1987). Shawn has appeared on many television series, such as *Taxi, The Cosby Show, The Nanny, Clueless, Murphy Brown, Star Trek: Deep Space Nine, Ally McBeal, Sex and the City, Crossing Jordan, The L Word,* and *Gossip Girl*, and can be heard in the cartoon series *King of the Hill, Teamo Supremo, Teacher's Pet, Family Guy,* and *King Fu Panda: Legends of Awesomeness*. Shawn reprised his Rex in *Toy Story 2* (1999), *Toy Story 3* (2010), and in the video *Buzz Lightyear of Star Command: The Adventure Begins* (2000). His voice can also be heard in the animated movies and videos *All Dogs Go to Heaven 2* (1996), *The Jungle Book: Mowgli's Story* (1998), *Tom and Jerry in Shiver Me Whiskers* (2006), *Happily N'Ever After* (2006), and *Scooby-Doo and the Goblin King* (2008).

Shearer, Harry (b. 1943) A comic actor and writer with many television and movie credits but is mostly known for the twenty-one characters he voices on *The Simpsons*, he played the Dog Announcer in *Chicken Little* (2005). Harry Julius Shearer was born in Los Angeles and was a child actor, appearing on early television and in a few films, such as *Abbot and Costello Go to Mars* (1953) and *The Robe* (1953). After attending UCLA and Harvard University for a time, he became a member of a radio comedy group called The Credibility Gap which brought Shearer to the attention of television producers who cast him in *Laverne & Shirley, Saturday Night Live,* and other shows. It was the cult film favorite *This Is Spinal Tap* (1984), which he co-wrote and performed in, that brought Shearer wide recognition. His other numerous movie credits include *The Fish That Saved Pittsburgh* (1979), *My Stepmother Is an Alien* (1988), *The Fisher King* (1991), *Wayne's World 2* (1993), *My Best Friend's Wedding* (1997), *The Truman Show* (1998), *A Mighty Wind* (2003), and *For Your Consideration* (2006). In addition to many appearances on TV talk shows and comedy specials, he has played roles in such series as *The Golden Girls, Murphy Brown, Ellen, Friends, Just Shoot Me!, Jack and Jill, Dawson's Creek*, and *Just for Laughs*. Shearer has voiced *The Simpsons* for over a dozen years, playing such characters as Mr. Burns, Ned Flanders, and Waylon Smithers, and can also be heard in the cartoon series *Animaniacs*, as well as the animated movies and videos *Animalympics* (1980), *Down and Out with Donald Duck* (1987), *Haunted Castle* (2001), and *The Simpsons Movie* (2007),

Sheen, Michael (b. 1969)   A boyish-looking Welsh actor who has found success both on stage and screen, he voiced the nervous Nivens McTwisp, the White Rabbit, in the 2010 version of *Alice in Wonderland*. He was born in Newport, Wales, and studied at the Bristol Old Vic Theatre School before making his London stage debut in 1991. Sheen was praised for his performances in both classic and new plays and he came to Broadway in two of his most acclaimed roles: Mozart in *Amadeus* (1999) and interviewer David Frost in *Frost/Nixon* (2007). He reprised the latter in the 2008 film version which made him well known in the States. Sheen was featured in such movies as *Wilde* (1997), *Bright Young Things* (2003), *The Queen* (2006), and *New Moon* (2009). He has acted in many television specials and series in both Great Britain and in America, ranging from *Gallowglass* in the early 1990s to *30 Rock* in 2010. Sheen's voice can be heard in the videos *Animated Epics: Beowulf* (1998), *Doomwatch: Winter Angel* (1999), and *A Child's Christmas in Wales* (2009).

Shelley, Carole (b. 1939)   A pliable British actress who spent most of her stage and television career in America, she voiced three very different Disney characters: the English spinster goose Amelia Gabble in *The Aristocats* (1970), the motherly Scottish chicken Lady Kluck who is lady-in-waiting to Maid Marian in *Robin Hood* (1973), and the spooky Lachesis, one of the Fates in *Hercules* (1997). Born in London and educated at the Royal Academy of Dramatic Art, she was on the London stage by 1955, appearing in contemporary plays and revues. Shelley first came to the States in 1965 to play the flighty British Pigeon sister Gwendolyn in *The Odd Couple* on Broadway, in the 1968 film, and in the television series. Among her many memorable New York stage appearances are *Absurd Person Singular* (1974), *The Norman Conquests* (1975), *The Elephant Man* (1979), *What the Butler Saw* (1989), *London Suite* (1995), *Cabaret* (1998), *Wicked* (2003), and *Billy Elliot* (2008). Shelley's film credits are limited but she has acted on many dramatic and comedy television series, including *The Avengers, Another World, Spencer: For Hire, The Cosby Show, One Life to Live*, and *Third Watch*. She reprised her creepy Lachesis in the TV cartoon series *Hercules* and in the video *Hercules: Zero to Hero* (1999).

Shen, Freda Foh   An Asian American actress-singer on television since 1975, she provided the voice of Mulan's worried mother La Li in *Mulan* (1998). Shen appeared on the New York stage in such Off Broadway productions as *Plenty* (1982), *Top Girls* (1983), and *Yellow Fever* (1983), as well as on Broadway in *Pacific Overtures* (1976), *The King and I* (1977), *Execution of Justice* (1986), and *Shogun, the Musical* (1990). She made her television debut in an episode of *Khan!*, followed by many other series over the decades, including *The Cosby Show, Silk Stalkings, Party of Five, ER, Chicago Hope, 7th Heaven, Gideon's Crossing, 24, The Practice, JAG, Everwood, Close to Home, Days of Our Lives, House, Grey's Anatomy*, and *Private Practice*. Among her movie credits are *Crossing Delancy* (1988), *Longtime Companion* (1989), *Basic Instinct* (1992), *Daddy's Girl* (1996), *American Virgin* (2000), *Planet of the Apes* (2001), *A Mighty Wind* (2003), *The Ladykillers* (2004), *Red Doors* (2005), *Star Trek* (2009), and *The Mikado Project* (2010). Shen reprised her Fa Li in the video *Mulan II* (2004).

Sheridan, Susan (b. 1947)   A British actress who has voiced many British television, radio, and movie roles, she played the teenage heroine Princess Eilonwy in *The Black Cauldron* (1985) when she was a not-so-young thirty-four years old. Sheridan trained at the Guildhall School of Music and Drama before going on the stage, but it was on the radio that she found fame, voicing the role of Trillian on the popular BBC series *The Hitch Hiker's Guide to the Galaxy* in 1978. That same year she made her television debut, providing children's voices for various programs even though she was thirty years old. Among her British television voice credits are the series *Muzzy, Jimbo and the Jet-Set, Noddy's Toyland Adventures*, and *Animated Tales of the World*, and the specials *Santa's First Christmas* (1992) and *Alex Builds His Farm* (1999). Sheridan continues to act on the stage and is a voice coach in London. Originally actress Hayley Mills was slated to voice Princess Eilonwy in *The Black Cauldron* but she did not sound young enough; instead Sheridan was hired. Eilonwy foreshadows later

Disney princesses in that she is not a helpless victim depending on a hero to save or protect her. Sheridan's engaging but purposeful vocals were essential in creating this new breed of Disney heroine.

Shields, Fred (1904–1974) A nationally-recognized radio announcer who did everything from news coverage to Alka Seltzer commercials, he was the narrator of a handful of Disney shorts and features and provided the voice of the Great Prince of the Forest in *Bambi* (1942). Frederick Hagenstein Shields was born in Kansas City, Missouri, where he ran a theatre group and performed while serving as a radio announcer on the local station. He relocated to Los Angeles and as a radio correspondent covered such events as the arrival of Germany's Graf Zeppelin in 1929. A decade later he was president of the American Federation of Radio Artists and remained one of the top radio announcers in the country until his retirement in 1965. Disney liked Shields' deep, commanding voice and thought it ideal for the character of the Prince in *Bambi*. He wanted the Prince to have a detached, almost cold persona and Shields does this even as he serves as the voice of wisdom for young Bambi. When the Prince tells Bambi that his mother can never be with him again, it is one of the most sobering moments in the history of animation. Shields returned to the Disney studio as narrator in the feature travelogues *Saludos Amigos* (1942) and *The Three Caballeros* (1944), as well as the tongue-in-cheek commentator in the cartoon shorts *How to Play Baseball* (1942), *The New Spirit* (1942), *Pluto and the Armadillo* (1943), *How to Play Golf* (1944).

Shigeta, James (b. 1933) A prolific Asian American actor and singer who has played a variety of roles in films and on television, he supplied the voice of the Chinese General Li who puts his son Li Shang in charge of the new recruits in *Mulan* (1998). He was born in Honolulu, Hawaii, and studied at New York University. After winning first place singing on television's *Ted Mack's Amateur Hour*, he pursued an acting career. Shigeta made his screen debut in 1959 and two years later was the first Asian-American romantic leading man in a Hollywood film: the handsome young hero Wang Ta in *Flower Drum Song* (1961). His subsequent career was a series of ups and downs as the public's taste for Asian characters fluctuated, yet he managed to find work in character parts throughout the next five decades. Among his other movie credits are *Bridge to the Sun* (1961), *Paradise, Hawaii Style* (1966), *Lost Horizon* (1973), *Midway* (1976), *Die Hard* (1988), *Cage* (1989), *China Cry: A True Story* (1990), *Cage II* (1994), *Midnight Man* (1995), *Brother* (2000), *A Ribbon of Dreams* (2002), and *The People I've Slept With* (2009). Shigeta has appeared in dozens of television series, including *Naked City, Dr. Kildare, The Outer Limits, Perry Mason, Ben Casey, It Takes a Thief, Hawaii Five-O, Mission: Impossible, Ironside, Medical Center, Emergency!, Khan!, Kung Fu, Ellery Queen, The Streets of San Francisco, Little House on the Prairie, Police Woman, The Rockford Files, The Love Boat, Simon & Simon, Dragnet, SeaQuest 2032, Babylon 5,* and *Beverly Hills 90210.*

Shirley, Bill (1921–1989) A singer-actor who appeared in mostly B movies in the 1940s and 1950s, he provided the speaking and singing voice of the courageous hero Prince Phillip in *Sleeping Beauty* (1959). He was born in Indianapolis, Indiana, and made his screen debut in *Rookies on Parade* (1941), followed by mostly forgettable roles in such forgotten films as *Ice-Capades* (1941), *Doctors Don't Tell* (1941), *Sailors on Leave* (1941), *Hi, Neighbor* (1942), *Flying Tigers* (1942), *Ice-Capades Revue* (1942), *Three Little Sisters* (1944), *Abbott and Costello Meet Captain Kidd* (1952), and *Sweethearts on Parade* (1953). Aside from voicing the Prince in *Sleeping Beauty*, Shirley's only other memorable credits were singing the title song over the credits of *Dancing in the Dark* (1949) and playing Stephen Foster in *I Dream of Jeanie* (1952). He can be heard on the soundtracks of some movie musicals, doing the singing vocals for Mark Stevens in *I Wonder Who's Kissing Her Now* (1947) and *Oh, You Beautiful Doll* (1949), and singing "On the Street Where You Live" for Jeremy Brett in *My Fair Lady* (1964). Phillip in *Sleeping Beauty* is Disney's first prince with a rounded character, a much more lively and human hero than the royal men in *Snow White and the Seven Dwarfs* and *Cinderella*. Actor-dancer Ed Kemmer was filmed doing the movements of Prince Phillip in *Sleeping Beauty* but it was Shirley's congenial but full-voiced vocals that made the character so appealing.

Shore, Dinah (1916–1994) A favorite singer on the radio, on records, in the movies, and on television for over thirty years, she sang "Two Silhouettes" during an animated sequence in *Make Mine Music* (1946) and was the singing and speaking narrator of the animated "Bongo the Bear" segment in *Fun and Fancy Free* (1947). She was born Frances Rose Shore in Winchester, Tennessee, and studied sociology at Vanderbilt University before taking up singing on the radio. Her recordings with Xavier Cugat's band made her a popular singing star who triumphed on the radio, in such films as *Up in Arms* (1944), *Belle of the Yukon* (1944), *Till the Clouds Roll By* (1946), and *Aaron Slick from Punkin Crick* (1952), and later on in television where she had two of her own variety shows and a TV series *Dinah and Her New Best Friends*. Biography: *Dinah! A Biography of Dinah Shore*, Bruce Cassidy (1979).

Shore, Pauly (b. 1968) A cutting-edge comic and actor who has found success on television and in movies, he voiced Max's teenage friend and computer nerd Bobby Zimmeruski in *A Goofy Movie* (1995). Paul Montgomery Shore was born in Hollywood, California, the son of a comedian and the founder of The Comedy Store in Los Angeles. He began his career on MTV as a host and commentator before getting his own show, *Totally Pauly*. In addition to many talk shows and comedy specials, Shore also appeared on such series as *Married with Children, Fantasy Island, Beverly Hills 90210, Entourage*, and his own sit-com *Pauly*. His movie credits include *Phantom of the Mall: Eric's Revenge* (1989), *Encino Man* (1992), *Class Act* (1992), *In the Army Now* (1994), *Jury Duty* (1995), *Bio-Dome* (1996), *The Curse of the Inferno* (1997), *Red Letters* (2000), *Adopted* (2009), as well as the mockumentary *Pauly Shore Is Dead* (2003) which he also wrote, produced, and directed. He reprised his animated character Bobby in the video sequel *An Extremely Goofy Movie* (2000) and can also be heard in the live-action videos *Casper: A Spirited Beginning* (1997), *Casper Meets Wendy* (1998), and *Dr. Dolittle: Million Dollar Mutts* (2009). Shore often writes his own material and has made some successful comedy records.

Short, Martin (b. 1950) The slightly-built, lively comic actor with dozens of faces and voices, he can be heard as the abandoned and forgetful robot B.E.N. in *Treasure Planet* (2002). Martin Hayter Short was born in Hamilton, Ontario, Canada, the son of an executive and a concert violinist, and educated at McMaster University where he started performing in campus shows. Relocating to Toronto, he appeared in the first professional production there of *Godspell* in 1972. Joining the improv group Second City in 1977, Short worked his way up and was a favorite on the Canadian television series *SCTV*, which was shown in the States. He then appeared frequently on *Saturday Night Live* and eventually his own syndicated program, the mock talk show *Primetime Glick*. In all of these shows, Short also served as one of the writers. He made his film debut in 1979 and over the years shone in comic roles in such movies as *Three Amigos* (1986), *Father of the Bride* (1991), *Father of the Bride Part II* (1995), *Mars Attacks!* (1996), *Jungle to Jungle* (1997), and *The Santa Clause 3: The Escape Clause* (2006). On Broadway he has starred in *The Goodbye Girl* (1993), *Little Me* (1998), and in his mock musical autobiography *Martin Short: Fame Becomes Me* (2006) which he also co-wrote. In addition to *Treasure Planet*, Short also voiced the Disney video *101 Dalmatians: Patch's London Adventure* (2003) and such non–Disney films and videos as *We're Back! A Dinosaur's Story* (1993), *The Pebble and the Penguin* (1995), *Creature Crunch* (1996), *The Prince of Egypt* (1998), *Jimmy Neutron: Boy Genius* (2001), *Barbie as the Princess and the Pauper* (2004), *The Spiderwick Chronicles* (2008), and *Hoodwinked Too! Hood VS. Evil* (2010).

Shulman, Constance (b. 1958) A stage, film, and television actress, she provided the voice for Doug's heartthrob Patti Mayonnaise in *Doug's 1st Movie* (1999). She was born in Johnson City, Tennessee, and educated at the University of Tennessee before working on the stage in New York City, most memorably in the original Off Broadway production of *Steel Magnolias* (1987). Shulman made her screen debut in *Fletch Lives* (1989) and also appeared in *Men Don't Leave* (1990), *McBain* (1991), *Weekend at Bernie's II* (1993), *Sweet and Lowdown* (1999), *A Jersey Christmas* (2008), and *Finding Jean Lewis* (2009). She first voiced Patti in the TV cartoon series *Doug*, then in the revised series *Disney's Doug*.

Silver, Jeffrey (b. 1937) A teenage performer on television who was busy throughout the 1950s then retired from acting, he voiced Nibs, the Lost Boy in the rabbit fur, in *Peter Pan* (1953). He was born in Brooklyn, New York, and as a child was a radio performer, playing the son Alexander Bumstead near the end of the long-running series *Blondie*. Arriving in California in 1948, Silver appeared in such television series as *Space Patrol, Meet Corliss Archer, Dragnet, Waterfront, Climax!, The Loretta Young Show, Cheyenne, Gunsmoke, The Charles Farrell Show, The Bob Cummings Show*, and *Bachelor Father*, as well as the films *The Young Stranger* (1957) and *The Outsider* (1961).

Simanteris, Ross A child actor who has appeared on the television series *CSI: Crime Scene Investigation*, he supplied the voice of one of the three mischievous Piggies in *Home on the Range* (2004). Simanteris can also be heard as one of the young pigs in the cartoon short *A Dairy Tale* (2004), and he did voices for the animated films *Nausicaä of the Valley of the Wind* (1984) and *Ice Age: The Meltdown* (2006), and the video *The Emperor's New Groove 2: Kronk's New Groove* (2005).

Sincere, Jean A stage actress-singer who has also been on television since the early days of the medium, she provided the voice of the little old lady Mrs. Hogenson confounded by insurance company bureaucracy in *The Incredibles* (2004). Sincere was on Broadway in the musicals *Barefoot Boy with Cheek* (1947), *Razzle Dazzle* (1951), *Wonderful Town* (1953), *By the Beautiful Sea* (1954), and *Oh Captain!* (1958). She made her television debut on *The Philco-Goodyear Television Playhouse* in 1949 and over the decades has appeared in such series as *Lux Video Theatre, Cagney & Lacey, St. Elsewhere, The Facts of Life, Newhart, The Wonder Years, Empty Nest, 7th Heaven, The Drew Carey Show, Everybody Loves Raymond, Malcolm in the Middle, Ally McBeal, Frasier, Private Practice,* and *Glee.*

Sinclair, Madge (1938–1995) An actress of Caribbean descent who gave some memorable performances on television, she voiced Simba's mother, the lioness Sarabi, in *The Lion King* (1994). She was born Madge Dorita Walters in Kingston, Jamaica, and worked as a teacher on her native island before going to New York City to pursue an acting career. After appearing in a handful of Off Broadway productions, Sinclair made her screen debut as the Caribbean slave Tituba in the short *The Witches of Salem: The Horror and the Hope* (1972), going on to act in such movies as *Conrack* (1974), *Leadbelly* (1976), *Convoy* (1978), *Star Trek IV: The Voyage Home* (1986), and *Coming to America* (1988). She found more recognition on television, appearing as a regular on the series *Trapper John M.D., Ohara, The Orchid House, Gabriel's Fire, Pros and Cons,* and *Me and the Boys,* as well as in the miniseries *Roots* (1977) and many made-for-TV movies.

Singer, Stuffy (b. 1941) A recognized professional in several sports who spent his childhood and teen years acting on radio, screen, and television, he voiced two of the Lost Boys, Foxy (also called Slightly) and one of the Raccoon Twins, in *Peter Pan* (1953) and was the lead singer for the boys' songs. He was born Simon Singer in Los Angeles and was on radio and television at the age of six. Over the years he appeared on such television series as *Sandy Dreams, Beulah, My Little Margie, The Loretta Young Show, Captain Midnight, Fury, Damon Runyon Theatre, Lassie, Annie Oakley, The Adventures of Jim Bowie, Blondie, Zane Grey Theatre, My Three Sons, Bachelor Father, The Adventures of Ozzie and Harriet, The Patty Duke Show,* and *The Bill Cosby Show*. At the age of nineteen, Singer became more interested in sports, taking up professional table tennis, football, baseball, and eventually handball, becoming a titled champion in the sport. He continued acting until 1970. Like most of the original cast of *Peter Pan*, Singer reprised his two voices in a radio broadcast of the tale on *Lux Radio Theatre* in 1953.

Singerman, Wesley (b. 1990) A child actor who appeared in a few television shows in the 1990s, he later provided the voice of the young time traveler Wilbur Robinson in *Meet the Robinsons* (2007). Wesley Steven Singerman made his television debut at the age of ten in the series *Felicity* and *The Amanda Show*. He voiced the title character in the animated videos *A Charlie Brown Valentine* (2002), *Charlie Brown's Christmas Tales* (2002), and *Lucy Must Be Traded, Charlie Brown* (2003), as well as other characters in *The Little Polar Bear* (2001) and *The Nutcracker and the Mouseking* (2004). As a teenager Singerman acted in the movie *Just for Kicks* (2003) and the television series *7th Heaven*, and as an adult he has played lead guitar for the heavy metal band Fate By Fire.

Siragusa, Peter A large, beefy character actor of television and movies, he supplied the voice of the domineering iguanodon Bruton in *Dinosaur* (2000). The Boston native made his television debut in 1982, going on to play blue-collar types in such series as *Home Improvement, Caroline in the City, Party of Five, The Practice, NYPD Blue, The Closer,* and *Entourage.* Siragusa's movie credits include *Home Alone* (1990), *The Babe* (1992), *While You Were Sleeping* (1995), *The Big Lebowski* (1998), and *Love Don't Cost a Thing* (2003). He can be heard in the animated movies and videos *Home on the Range* (2004), *Mickey's Twice Upon a Christmas* (2004), and *Cloudy with a Chance of Meatballs* (2009).

Smith, Brittany Alyse A television actress who was active during the 1990s, she voiced the Photo Studio Girl in *A Goofy Movie* (1995). Smith appeared in such television series as *Empty Nest, Renegade, NightMan, Chicago Hope,* and *V.I.P.*, as well as in the films *Pinocchio's Revenge* (1996), *Just in Time* (1997), *Treasure of Pirate's Point* (1999), and *One Last Flight* (1999).

Smith, Hal (1916–1994) A prolific voice actor and a favorite face on television for decades, he provided the voice of Goofy for a time after the death of Pinto Colvig in 1967 and one of his last jobs was voicing the horse Phillippe in *Beauty and the Beast* (1991). Harold John Smith was born in Petoskey, Michigan, and grew up in Messena, New York, beginning his career as a disc jockey in Utica. After serving in World War II, Smith went to California and made his screen debut in 1943. By 1952 he was working on television and over the years appeared on hundreds of episodes of such series as *I Married Joan, Bonanza, Have Gun—Will Travel, Dennis the Menace, Perry Mason, Space Angel, the Adventures of Ozzie and Harriet, Death Valley Days, Petticoat Junction, Green Acres, The Dukes of Hazzard,* and *Night Court*, but he is best remembered as Otis the town drunk in *The Andy Griffith Show*. Smith's movie credits include *Walking My Baby Back Home* (1953), *The High Cost of Loving* (1958), *The Apartment* (1960), *The Three Stooges Meet Hercules* (1962), *Son of Flubber* (1963), *The Great Race* (1965), *The Ghost and Mr. Chicken* (1966), *The Million Dollar*

Duck (1971), and *Oklahoma Crude* (1973). He first voiced for Disney when he provided the voice of the Owl in *Winnie the Pooh and the Honey Tree* (1966), a role he reprised in *Winnie the Pooh and the Blustery Day* (1968), *The Many Adventures of Winnie the Pooh* (1973), *Winnie the Pooh Discovers the Seasons* (1981), and *Winnie the Pooh and a Day for Eeyore* (1983), voicing Winnie as well in the last two. Smith voiced the Slob Elephant in *The Jungle Book* (1967), the crass Auctioneer in *The Small One* (1978), Goofy as Jacob Marley in *Mickey's Christmas Carol* (1983), the wacky Gyro Gearloose in *Duck Tales: Treasure of the Golden Suns* (1987) and *Super Duck Tales* (1989), and was heard in such Disney cartoon series as *TaleSpin*, *Adventures of the Gummie Bears*, *The New Adventures of Winnie the Pooh*, *DuckTales*, *Darkwing Duck*, *The Little Mermaid*, and *Bonkers*. Among his many non–Disney animated movies and videos are *The Three Faces of Stanley* (1967), *The Night Before Christmas* (1968), *Santa and the Three Bears* (1970), *Shinbone Alley* (1971), *A Flintstone Christmas* (1977), *Gulliver's Travels* (1979). *Puff and the Incredible Mr. Nobody* (1982), *The Great Bear Scare* (1983), *Frog and Toad Are Friends* (1985), *An American Tail* (1986), *Garfield: His 9 Lives* (1988), and *The Town Santa Forgot* (1993), as well as the cartoon series *The Famous Adventures of Mr. Magoo*, *The Flintstones*, *The Road Runner Show*, *The Pink Panther Show*, *Doctor Dolittle*, *Yogi's Gang*, *Davey and Goliath*, *The New Tom and Jerry Show*, *The Fantastic Four*, *The Smurfs*, *The Littles*, and *Midnight Patrol: Adventures in the Dream Zone*.

Smith, Kai Steel The child actor who voiced the brown-haired Boy in the BnL (Buy-n-Large Corporation) commercial in *WALL-E* (2008), he appeared in the films *Love, Papa* (2008), *Story About a Witch* (2009), and *The Prankster* (2010), as well as in many national television commercials.

Smith, Max (1913–1999) A tenor member of such singing groups as The Sportsmen Quartet and The Mellomen, he was heard on and off screen in a handful of films, such as *Alice in Wonderland* (1951), in which The Mellomen voiced the singing Cards who are painting the roses red, and *Lady and the Tramp* (1955) where they voiced the howling quartet of dogs in the pound. Maxwell Smith was born in Des Moines, Iowa, and as a member of different singing quartets did back up singing for such recording stars as Jo Stafford, Bing Crosby, Doris Day, and Rosemary Clooney. With The Sportsmen Quartet he sang in the movies *Puddin' Head* (1941), *Jingle Belles* (1941), *Lost Canyon* (1942), and *Irish Eyes Are Smiling* (1944), with The Mellomen he was seen and heard in *The Glenn Miller Story* (1954) and *It Happened at the World's Fair* (1963), and he played a singer in such films as *Rebecca of Sunnybrook Farm* (1938), *Ziegfeld Girl* (1941), *Because You're Mine* (1952), and *Love Me or Leave Me* (1955). Smith can also be heard in the Disney animated shorts *The Nifty Nineties* (1941), *Trick or Treat* (1952) and *Toot Whistle Plunk and Boom* (1953), *Pigs Is Pigs* (1954), *Paul Bunyan* (1958), and *Noah's Ark* (1959).

Sohn, Peter An animator and storyboard artist who occasionally does voices for the projects he works on, he provided the voice of the rat Emile, the indiscriminate eater and Remy's brother, in *Ratatouille* (2007). Sohn has served as production artist or animator for the films *The Iron Giant* (1999), *Osmosis Jones* (2001), *Finding Nemo* (2003), *The Incredibles* (2004), *One Man Band* (2005), *Ratatouille*, *WALL-E* (2008), *Up* (2009), and *Leonardo* (2010). He reprised his Emile in the short *Your Friend the Rat* (2007) and can be heard doing voices for minor characters in *The Incredibles*, *Tokyo Mater* (2008), and *George & A. J.* (2009).

Sorensen, Ricky (1946–1994) A young actor on many television shows before retiring at the age of thirty-two, he supplied the few lines spoken by the puppy Spotty in *One Hundred and One Dalmatians* (1961) and, along with Robert and Bruce Reitherman, voiced the young King Arthur, called Wart, in *The Sword in the Stone* (1963). The native of Los Angeles made his television debut at the age of ten on an episode of *My Friend Flicka*, and the next year was on the big screen in *Man Afraid* (1957). Sorensen played preteens, teenagers, and young adults in such films as *Man of a Thousand Faces* (1957), *The Hard Man* (1957), *Tarzan and the Trappers* (1958), *Tarzan's Fight for Life* (1958), *A Lust to Kill* (1959), *Underworld U.S.A.* (1961), *Airport '77* (1977), and *The Cat from Outer Space* (1978). He was more successful in television, acting in several series, including *Perry Mason*, *Death Valley Days*, *The Dona Reed Show*, *Whirlybirds*, *Lawman*, *The Deputy*, *Hazel*, *Walt Disney's Wonderful World of Color*, *Mr. Novak*, *Gidget*, *Please Don't Eat the Daisies*, *The F.B.I.*, *Nanny and the Professor*, and *The Quest*. Sorensen was unhappy with the way his career was going and quit acting in 1978, dying of cancer sixteen years later. The vocal differences between Sorensen and the two Reitherman brothers is evident in *The Sword in the Stone*, Wart's voice going from pre-adolescent soprano to an awkward teenage quality sometimes in the same scene.

Soucie, Kath (b. 1967) A prolific voice actress who can be heard in over 300 episodes of television cartoons, she voiced the mother kangaroo Kanga in the *Winnie the Pooh* shorts, features, videos, and television series. Katherine Soucie was born in Cleveland and studied at the American Academy of Dramatic Arts in New York City before beginning her busy voice career with the TV cartoon series *The Smurfs* in 1981. Soon she was voicing recurring characters in such series as *Jem, Adventures of the Gummie Bears, Timeless Tales from Hallmark, The Real Ghostbusters, Yo Yogi!, Tiny Toon Adventures, Darkwing Duck, The Little Mermaid, Mighty Max. Sonic the Hedgehog, Captain Planet and the Planeteers, Jungle Cubs, 101 Dalmatians: The Series, The Powerpuff Girls, Buzz Lightyear of Star Command, Rugrats, House of Mouse, Kim Possible, The Adventures of Jimmy Neutron: Boy Genius,* and *The Replacements*. Soucie first voiced Kanga in *The Tigger Movie* (2000) and reprised the role in *Mickey's Magical Christmas: Snowed in at the House of Mouse* (2001), *Winnie the Pooh: A Very Merry Pooh Year* (2002), *Piglet's Big Movie* (2003), *Winnie the Pooh: Springtime with Roo* (2004), *Pooh's Heffalump Halloween Movie* (2005), *Pooh's Super Sleuth Christmas Movie* (2007), *Tigger & Pooh and a Musical Too* (2009), and the cartoon series *My Friends Tigger and Pooh*. Also in Disney features she was the voice of one of the Bimbettes in *Beauty and the Beast* (1991), various minor characters in *The Hunchback of Notre Dame* (1996) and *Lilo & Stitch* (2002), and grown-up Wendy in *Return to Never Land* (2002). Souci has been heard in such Disney videos as *Gargoyles: The Heroes Awaken* (1995), *Beauty and the Beast: The Enchanted Christmas* (1997), *Pocahontas II: Journey to a New World* (1998), *An Extremely Goofy Movie* (2000), *Lady and the Tramp II: Scamp's Adventure* (2001), *Kingdom Hearts* (2002), *The Nightmare Before Christmas: Oogie's Revenge* (2004), *The Emperor's New Grove 2: Kronk's New Groove* (2005), *Kingdom Hearts II* (2005), *Bambi II* (2006), and *The Fox and the Hound 2* (2006). Soucie's dozens of other animated movies and videos include *The Little Engine That Could* (1991), *A Flintstone Family Christmas* (1993), *The Tale of Tillie's Dragon* (1995), *Bruno the Kid: The Animated Movie* (1996), *Space Jam* (1996), *A Rugrats Vacation* (1997), *The Brave Little Toaster Goes to Mars* (1998), *The Rugrats Movie* (1998), *Olive, the Other Reindeer* (1999), *The Life and Adventures of Santa Claus* (2000), *Rugrats in Paris: The Movie* (2000), *Recess: School's Out* (2001), *The Trumpet of the Swan* (2001), *Hey Arnold! The Movie* (2002), *Rugrats Go Wild* (2003), *Lionheart* (2003), *The Cat in the Hat* (2003), *The Hobbit* (2003), *Clifford's Really Big Movie* (2004), *Robots* (2005), *Stuart Little 3: Call of the Wild* (2005), *Legend of Frosty the Snowman* (2005), *Curious George* (2006), *Happily N'Ever After* (2006), *Coraline* (2009), and *Green Lantern: First Flight* (2009). Kathryn Beaumont, who had voiced Wendy in *Peter Pan* (1953), recorded all the dialogue for grown-up Wendy in *Return to Never Land*, but the producers were not pleased with it so Soucie was chosen to re-record it for the final print.

Soule, Olan (1909–1994) A character actor with a flexible voice whose sixty-year career included radio, movies, and television, he supplied the voice of the desperate Father who orders his son to sell the donkey in *The Small One* (1978). He was born in La Harpe, Illinois, and began his career at the age of seventeen with a traveling tent show. After doing theatre in Chicago, Soule began working on radio. For ten years he was a regular on the radio soap opera *Bachelor's Children* and for five years he was the commentator on *First Nighter*. He made his screen debut in *It's a Great Feeling* (1949), followed by character parts in such films as *The Lady Takes a Sailor* (1949), *Ma and Pa Kettle Go to Town* (1950), *Destination Big House* (1950), *Peggy* (1950), *Cuban Fireball* (1951), *The Day the Earth Stood Still* (1951), *Bronco Buster* (1952), *The Story of Will Rogers* (1952), *Monkey Business* (1952), *Never Wave at a WAC* (1953), *The Great Diamond Robbery* (1954), *Francis Joins the WACs* (1954), *Dragnet* (1954), *Daddy Long Legs* (1955), *Cult of the Cobra* (1955), *Queen Bee* (1955), *Francis in the Haunted House* (1956), *It Happened at the World's Fair* (1963), *Shock Treatment* (1964), *The Cincinnati Kid* (1965), *The Seven Minutes* (1971), *The Towering Inferno* (1974), *The Apple Dumpling Gang* (1975), and *Homicide* (1991). Soule was even busier on television, appearing in dozens of series, including *My Little Margie, The Millionaire, Captain Midnight, I Love Lucy, The Real McCoys, Bat Masterson, Highway Patrol, The Ann Sothern Show, Dragnet, Schlitz Playhouse, Sugarfoot, Dennis the Menace, The Rebel, Johnny Ringo, Maverick, Wanted: Dead or Alive, The Jack Benny Program, Bachelor Father, Stagecoach West, Alfred Hitchcock Presents, Tales of Wells Fargo, Have Gun—Will Travel, The Untouchables, 77 Sunset Strip, Twilight Zone, Mister Ed, The Andy Griffith Show, Perry Mason, Rawhide, My Favorite Martian, The Farmer's Daughter, Bonanza, The Monkees, The F.B.I., Petticoat Junction, Gunsmoke, The Big Valley, My Three Sons, Dragnet 1967, The Virginian, Arnie, Emergency!, Project U.F.O., Fantasy Island, Battlestar Galactica, The Little House on the Prairie, Dallas,* and *Simon & Simon*. In the 1970s he turned to voice work for TV cartoon series and was heard in such shows as *The New Scooby-Doo Movies, Super Friends, The All-New Super Friends Hour, Challenge of the SuperFriends,* and *SuperFriends: The Legendary Super Powers Show*.

Spacey, Kevin (b. 1959) A smiling, affable actor who has given riveting, intense performances on stage and screen, he voiced the deadly grasshopper leader Hopper in *A Bug's Life* (1998). He was born Kevin Spacey Fowler in South Orange, New Jersey, and was educated at Los Angeles Valley College and Juilliard before staring a career as a stand-up comic in clubs. Spacey made his New York stage debut in 1981 and was noticed the next year for his performance in *Ghosts*. His subsequent performances of note in Manhattan include those in *Long Day's Journey into Night* (1986), *Lost in Yonkers* (1991), *The Iceman Cometh* (1999), and *A Moon for the Misbegotten* (2007). Spacey has also shone in roles on the London stage and in 2003 he was named Artistic Director of the Old Vic Theatre. Although he made his first movie in 1986 and first appeared on television the next year, Spacey did not become a recognized screen star until *American Beauty* (1999). His other memorable films include *Glengarry Glen Ross* (1992), *The Usual Suspects* (1995), *L.A. Confidential* (1997), *The Shipping News* (2001), *Austin Powers in Goldmember* (2002), *Superman Returns* (2006), *21* (2008), and *The Men Who Stare at Goats* (2009). His television credits include the series *The Equalizer, Crime Story, L.A. Law*, and *Wiseguy* and several made-for-TV movies, such as *The Murder of Mary Phagan* (1988), *Fall from Grace* (1990), and *When You Remember Me* (1990). Spacey reprised his Hopper in the animated short *It's Tough to Be a Bug* (1998). Biography: *Looking Closer: Kevin Spacey, the First 50 Years*, Robin Tamblyn (2010).

Spade, David (b. 1964)   The popular stand-up comic with a sharp wit and a sarcastic persona, he provided the voice of the spoiled and smart-aleck Emperor Kuzco who is turned into a llama in *The Emperor's New Groove* (2000). David Wayne Spade was born in Birmingham, Michigan, and grew up in Arizona where he attended Arizona State University to prepare for a business career. Instead he started doing stand-up comedy in clubs and on college campuses, getting the attention of Hollywood and being cast in the movie *Police Academy 4: Citizens on Patrol* (1987). Spade made appearances on such television shows as *The Facts of Life, Baywatch*, and *Alf*, but wide recognition did not come until he became a cast member of *Saturday Night Live* where he impersonated celebrities and also wrote a lot of his material. His other television credits include *Just Shoot Me!, 8 Simple Rules, Carpet Brothers*, and *Rules of Engagement*, and he has appeared in such movies as *The Coneheads* (1993), *Reality Bites* (1994), *Joe Dirt* (2001), *I Now Pronounce You Chuck & Larry* (2007), and *Grown Ups* (2010). Spade reprised his Kuzco in the video *The Emperor's New Groove 2: Kronk's New Groove* (2005) and has voiced characters in the TV cartoon series *Monsters, Beavis and Butt-Head*, and *Father of the Pride*, as well as the animated films *Beavis and Butt-Head Do America* (1996) and *The Rugrats Movie* (1998).

Spall, Timothy (b. 1957)   A short, round character actor who became a favorite in sidekick roles later in his career, he provided the voice of Queen Narissa's henchman Nathaniel in both the animated and live-action sections of *Enchanted* (2007) and the bloodhound Bayard in the 2010 version of *Alice in Wonderland*. Timothy Leonard Spall was born in London, the son of a postal worker and a hairdresser, and trained at the Royal Academy of Dramatic Art before becoming a member of the distinguished Royal Shakespeare Company. After appearing in such famous RSC productions as *The Three Sisters* and *Nicholas Nickleby*, Spall began his television career, eventually getting his own series, and performing in films such as *The Missionary* (1982), *Secrets and Lies* (1996), *Hamlet* (1996), *Topsy-Turvy* (1999), *Love's Labour's Lost* (2000), *Vanilla Sky* (2001), *The Last Samurai* (2003), *Lemony Snicket's A Series of Unfortunate Events* (2004), *Sweeney Todd: The Demon Barber of Fleet Street* (2007), and *The King's Speech* (2010), but he is probably best known as Wormtail/Peter Pettigrew in the *Harry Potter* movies. Spall provided the voices of two rats: Nick in *Chicken Run* (2000) and Scabbers in *Harry Potter and the Prisoner of Azkaban* (2004). Autobiography: *All or Nothing* (2003).

Spann, Aaron (b. 1990)   A child actor who has grown into a voice artist for films and video games, he provided the voices of the two "Lost Boy" Twins in *Return to Never Land* (2002). Spann made his television debut on an episode of *Step by Step* when he was seven, followed by appearances in the series *Meego* and *The Amanda Show*, as well as the TV musical *Geppetto* (2000). He was more frequently heard than seen, voicing characters in the movies *Babe: Pig in the City* (1998), *Baby Geniuses* (1999), *Dinosaur* (2000), and *Chicken Little* (2005), as well as the videos *Jungle Bells* (1999), *The Tangerine Bear: Home in Time for Christmas* (2000), *Recess: All Growed Down* (2003), *The Land Before Time XI: Invasion of the Tinysauruses* (2004), and the cartoon series *The Powerpuff Girls*.

Sparber, Herschel (b. 1943)   A large, deep-voiced character actor on stage, television, and the movies, he voiced the hulking Security Guard in *A Goofy Movie* (1995). He was born in Gary, Indiana, and began his career on the stage, performing in musicals regionally and in New York and appearing on Broadway in *Guys and Dolls* (1992) and *City of Angels* (1992). Sparber made his film debut in 1982 and went on to play thugs and other heavies in a handful of films, such as *King Kong Lives* (1986), *Bloodhounds of Broadway* (1989), *The Birdcage*

(1996), *Scar City* (1998), and *Brother* (2000), but he found more success on television series where he became widely known as the President in *Star Trek: Deep Space Nine* and Uncle Mike Hunter on *Boy Meets World*. Sparber's other television credits include *NYPD Blue, Players, Columbo, That's Life*, and *My Name Is Earl*.

Spence, Bruce (b. 1945) A tall, foreboding character actor who has appeared as sinister types in American, British, and Australian movies, he provided the voice of the Mako shark Chum in *Finding Nemo* (2003). He was born in Auckland, New Zealand, and made his screen debut in 1970, later appearing in many Australian films and television programs. Spence became known internationally for his performances in the movies *Mad Max 2: The Road Warrior* (1981) and *Mad Max Beyond Thunderdome* (1985). His other screen credits include *The Year My Voice Broke* (1987), *Ace Ventura: When Nature Calls* (1995), *The Lord of the Rings: The Return of the King* (2003), *Peter Pan* (2003), *Star Wars: Episode III — Revenge of the Sith* (2005), *Australia* (2008), and *The Chronicles of Narnia: The Voyage of the Dawn Treader* (2010).

Stack, Timothy (b. 1957) A television and film actor and writer usually involved in offbeat projects, he provided the voice of Daddy, the man who rewards Leonard and Spot for finding his daughter's dog, in *Teacher's Pet* (2004). He was born in Doylestown, Pennsylvania, and educated at Boston College before moving to Los Angeles and working with the improv comedy group The Groundlings. Stack made his television debut in an episode of *Lou Grant* in 1981, followed by many other TV series, including *Days of Our Lives, Quincy M.E., Benson, Laverne & Shirley, Reggie, Cagney & Lacey, The Facts of Life, The Paper Chase, Punky Brewster, thirtysomething, Night Court, Doctor Doctor, The Golden Girls, Parker Lewis, Johnny Bago, Seinfeld, Nurses, L.A. Law, Wings, Night Stand, Son of the Beach, Malcolm in the Middle*, and *My Name Is Earl*, as well as the mini-series *The Winds of War* (1983). Among his movie credits are *The Best Little Whorehouse in Texas* (1982), *The Aviator* (1985), *Back to School* (1986), *Martians Go Home* (1989), *Double Trouble* (1992), *Clifford* (1994), *Dear God* (1996), *Idle Hands* (1999), *Cast Away* (2000), *Dumb and Dumber: When Harry Met Lloyd* (2003), *Scary Movie 3* (2003), *Funny Money* (2006), and *Welcome to Paradise* (2007). Stack can be heard in the animated film *The Brave Little Toaster* (1987) and its two sequels. He has written scripts for such television programs as *Saturday Night Live, Doctor Doctor, On Our Own, Family Matters, Son of the Beach*, and *My Name Is Earl*.

Stacy, Michelle (b. 1968) A child performer with only a six-year career, she provided the voice of the orphan heroine Penny who is kidnapped by Madame Medusa in *The Rescuers* (1977). Stacy made her television debut in 1974 and for a short time was in demand for cute, bright-eyed kid roles, as in the films *Logan's Run* (1976), *Gravity* (1976), *Demon Seed* (1977), *Day of the Animals* (1977), and *Airplane!* (1980), as well as a half dozen TV-movies. She also appeared on such television series as *Mannix, Police Woman, Sunshine, The Waltons, The Young Pioneers, Quincy M.E., Eight Is Enough, Wally Brown, The Incredible Hulk, B. J. and the Bear*, and *Richie Brockleman, Private Eye*.

Stalling, Carl W. (1891–1972) A prolific film composer for animated movies who was the composer and/or musical director for over 700 cartoons from the advent of sound to 1966, his only voice credit is doing the sounds of the Walrus in the Mickey Mouse short *Wild Waves* (1930). He was born in Lexington, Missouri, and played piano as a boy. As an adult he got a job playing the theatre organ at a silent film palace in Kansas City where he came to the attention of Walt Disney who was just starting in the animation business. When the young company moved to California, Disney brought Stalling with him and put the composer-arranger in charge of the synchronized music in the early cartoon talkies. Stalling invented the "tick" system in which animators determined the tempo of a cartoon so that the composer could do the music before the film was complete. It was also Stalling who suggested to Disney a series of cartoons built around an existing or original piece of music; these developed into the Silly Symphonies. Among his Disney scores are those for the cartoon shorts *Plane Crazy* (1928), *The Gallopin Gaucho* (1928), *The Barn Dance* (1929), *The Opry House* (1929), *The Barnyard Battle* (1929), *Mickey's Follies* (1929), *The Skeleton Dance* (1929), *Springtime* (1929), and *Haunted House* (1929). After working with Disney for only a few years, Stalling went to Warner Brothers who owned the rights to hundreds of popular songs that could be animated. Stalling usually completed a short score each week, musicalizing hundreds of cartoons for Warners on a regular basis for over twenty years. Biography: *The Life and Music of Carl Stalling*, Anne Marie Guzzo (2002).

Stanger, Kyle (b. 2000) A five-year-old British child with no acting experience, he was chosen from 900 candidates to voice the young purple elephant Lumpy in *Pooh's Heffalump Movie* (2005) and the video sequel *Pooh's Heffalump Halloween Movie* (2005). To date he has no other film or television credits.

Stanley, Florence (1924–2003) A strong-accented, raspy-voiced character actress who worked frequently in television sit-coms, she voiced the cheerful, dog-like Waitress at a wayside diner in *A Goofy Movie* (1995) and radio operator Wilhelmina Bertha Packard in *Atlantis: The Lost Empire* (2001). She was born Florence Schwartz in Chicago and was educated at Northwestern University before making her television debut in 1950 on *Studio One*. For the next fifty years she appeared in hundreds of television episodes ranging from dramas, such as *East Side/West Side*, *NYPD Blue* and *Nurses*, to gothic horror shows like *Dark Shadows*, to such popular sit-coms as *Barney Miller*, *Fish*, *My Two Dads*, and *Cybill*. Stanley made her New York stage debut in 1960 and played supporting roles in ten Broadway productions. She also had small but memorable parts in several films. Stanley reprised her Ms. Packard in the animated series *The House of Mouse* and the video *Atlantis: Milo's Return*, and she can also be heard in the series *Dinosaurs* and *Family Guy*.

Stanton, Andrew (b. 1965) A screenwriter and director of animated films, he has occasionally provided voices as well, such as the helpless Bug who flies into the Bug Zapper in *A Bug's Life* (1998), the Evil Emperor Zurg in *Toy Story 2* (1999), the laid-back loggerhead sea turtle Crush in *Finding Nemo* (2003), and various minor roles in *The Incredibles* (2004), *Cars* (2006), and *WALL-E* (2008). Andrew Christopher Stanton, Jr., was born in Boston, and trained to be an animator but soon turned to writing, contributing to the TV cartoon series *2 Stupid Dogs* and *Mighty Mouse, the New Adventures*, and the screenplays for *Toy Story* (1995), *A Bug's Life*, *Toy Story 2*, *Monsters, Inc.* (2001), *Finding Nemo*, *WALL-E*, and *Toy Story 3* (2010). Stanton was also an executive producer for *Monsters, Inc.*, *Ratatouille* (2007), and *Up* (2009). The character of Crush, who turned out to be one of the most beloved in the multi-character *Finding Nemo*, and his frequent use of "dude" in conversation was the most imitated expression from the movie. The turtle was named after the citrus soft drink, just as his son was named after the beverage Squirt.

Stanton, Harry (1901–1978) A deep-voiced singer with Big Bands who became a character actor in films and on television, he provided the singing voice of the Bass Singer heard in the canoe and the ship in the short *Adventures in Music: Melody* (1953). Stanton sang on screen as himself in the films *Du Barry Was a Lady* (1943) and *Meet the People* (1944), then started playing characters in such movies as *One Too Many* (1950), *When Worlds Collide* (1951), *My Six Convicts* (1952), *The Clown* (1953), *Take the High Ground* (1953), *The Naked Road* (1959), *Riot on Sunset Strip* (1967), *The Secret Life of an American Wife* (1968), and *What's the Matter with Helen?* (1971). He also appeared on several television series, including *I Led 3 Lives*, *Omnibus*, *The Phil Silvers Show*, *The Lloyd Bridges Show*, *The Many Loves of Dobie Gillis*, *Perry Mason*, *The Dick Van Dyke Show*, *Love on a Rooftop*, *Green Acres*, *Petticoat Junction*, and *Bewitched*. Stanton can be heard singing bass in the animated short *Overture to William Tell* (1947).

Stanton, Val (1886–1967) A British character actor and singer in a handful of American films in the 1930s and early 1940s, he voiced the Courier in *The Reluctant Dragon* (1941). He was born Valentine Stanton Burch in London and was on the music hall stage before he emigrated to the States in the 1920s, later appearing on Broadway in the musical *Billie* (1928). Stanton made his screen debut in *Fads and Fancies* (1934), followed by such films as *The Perfect Gentleman* (1935), *Stage Struck* (1936), *Hats Off* (1936), *The Adventures of Robin Hood* (1938), *Mysterious Mr. Moto* (1938), *Prison Train* (1938), *Duke of the Navy* (1942), *This Above All* (1942), and *The Great Impersonation* (1942). He rarely got to sing solo in these but he was featured in the early musical comedy shorts *English as She Is Not Spoken* (1928) and *Cut Yourself a Piece of Cake* (1928) in which he and his brother Ernie Stanton performed musical numbers. Disney legend has it that Val Stanton was the model for Jiminy Cricket.

Stein, Delaney Rose A child actress who supplied the voices of the Young Rapunzel and the Little Girl who places a flower in the well in memory of the missing princess in *Tangled* (2010), she has no other film or television credits.

Steinfeld, Jake (b. 1958) A fitness personality who has acted on occasion, he provided the voice of Git, a member of the colony who was once a lab rat, in *Ratatouille* (2007). The Brooklyn, New York, native was a fitness trainer in Hollywood, helping movie stars build up their bodies for action films, then he had his own television show *Body by Jake* as well as a line of fitness equipment with the same name. Steinfeld played characters on the television series *Simon & Simon*, *Shaping Up*, *Amazing Stories*, *All Is Forgiven*, *The Tracey Ullman Show*, *Dream On*, *Burke's Law*, and his own sit-com *Big Brother Jake*. Among his movie credits are *Cheech & Chong's Next Movie* (1980), *National Lampoon's Movie Madness* (1982), *Into the Night* (1985), *The Money Pit* (1986), *Odd Jobs* (1986), *Tough Guys* (1986), *You Can't Hurry Love* (1988), *Coming to America* (1988), and *Aimee & Jaguar* (1999). He can also be heard in the animated movie *Rock-a-Doodle* (1991) and the TV cartoon series *King of the Hill*.

Steinkellner, Emma A child actress who did the voice of the Little Girl who has lost her dog in *Teacher's Pet* (2004), she has no other film or television credits.

Stepanek, Brian (b. 1971) A television actor who has often turned to voice work, he played the animal shelter guard Martin in *Bolt* (2008). He was born in Cleveland, Ohio, and started his career on the stage in regional theatre. Stepanek made his television debut in 1998 and has been seen on such series as *The West Wing, Six Feet Under, NYPD Blue, CSI: Miami,* and *Brian O'Brian,* but he is mostly known as Arwin on *The Suite Life of Zack and Cody.* He can he heard in several animated television series, including *Transformers, Kim Possible, Phineas and Ferb,* and *Kick Buttowski: Suburban Daredevil,* as well as the films and videos *Charlotte's Web* (2006), *Over the Hedge* (2006), and *Transformers: Beginnings* (2007).

Stevens, Bob (?–1961) A tenor who was a member of the Sportsmen Quartet then sang as one of the Mellomen from 1955 to 1961, he can be heard as part of the canine foursome singing and howling in the pound in *Lady and the Tramp* (1955). Stevens was also part of the Mellomen when they sang in the animated shorts *Paul Bunyan* (1958) and *Noah's Ark* (1959) and he provided some additional voices in *One Hundred and One Dalmatians* (1961). As a member of the Sportsmen Quartet, he sang in the live-action movies *Make Believe Ballroom* (1949) and *Footlight Varieties* (1951) as well as on television on *The Jack Benny Program.* Stevens' other film credits are *Has Anybody Seen My Girl?* (1952), *Love Me or Leave Me* (1955), and *You Can't Run Away from It* (1956).

Stevens, Sally A choral director, contractor, and vocal coach for Hollywood since 1989, she provided the singing voice of the Glowworm in *James and the Giant Peach* (1996). Stevens' many choral music conducting credits include such films as *Edward Scissorhands* (1990), *The Three Musketeers* (1993), *Forrest Gump* (1994), *The Sixth Sense* (1999), *Jurassic Park III* (2001), *Flight of the Phoenix* (2004), *Glory Road* (2005), *Night at the Museum* (2006), *Meet the Robinsons* (2007), and *Where the Wild Things Are* (2009).

Stewart, Bobby A young actor who provided the voice for Baby Bambi in *Bambi* (1942), there is no record of his being in any other film or television program.

Stewart, Nicodemus (1910–2000) An African American character actor of radio, television, and film, he provided the speaking and singing voices of the Straw Hat Crow in *Dumbo* (1941) and the dense Brer Bear in the animated sections of *Song of the South* (1946). He was born Horace Winifred Stewart in New York City, the son of Caribbean immigrants, and worked as a boxer, dancer, and comic before making his screen debut in 1932. His movie credits include *Go West Young Man* (1936), *Dark Manhattan* (1937), *Robin Hood of the Pecos* (1941), *Hit Parade of 1943* (1943), *Cabin in the Sky* (1943), *Stormy Weather* (1943), *Follow the Boys* (1944), *I Love a Bandleader* (1945), *Centennial Summer* (1946), *Carmen Jones* (1954), *St. Louis Blues* (1958), *Silver Streak* (1976), and *Hollywood Shuffle* (1987). Stewart found greater success in radio where he voiced the character of Lightnin' on *The Amos 'n' Andy Show* first on the airwaves then for two years on television. His other TV credits include the series *Ramar of the Jungle, The Jack Benny Program, Ben Casey, Mister Ed,* and *Ironside.* In 1950 he and his wife Edna Stewart founded the Ebony Showcase Theatre in Los Angeles, a venue for African American artists, and ran it for forty-six years. Nick Stewart, as he was sometimes billed, was a versatile voice artist, as witnessed by his sharp-witted, outgoing Crow in *Dumbo* and his slow-witted, lovable lug Brer Bear in *Song of the South.* Stewart can still be heard as Brer Bear on the Disney theme park ride Splash Mountain.

Stewart, Patrick (b. 1940) The popular, balding British actor known to millions of Americans from his *Star Trek* character Captain Jean-Luc Picard on television, he is a respected classical actor whose deep, thrilling voice has been heard in a number of animated films including the boring sheep Mr. Woolensworth who teaches language in *Chicken Little* (2005). Patrick Hewes Stewart was born in Mirfield, England, and left school as a teenager to pursue acting. After working with such prestigious stage companies as the Bristol Old Vic, Lincoln Repertory, and Old Vic, he joined the Royal Shakespeare Company in 1966 and acted with them for twenty-seven years. He made his British television debut in 1964 and his Broadway debut in 1971 when the RSC toured America. Stewart appeared in many classical dramas on both American and British television but it was his portrayal of Picard in *Star Trek: The Next Generation* that made him famous. He reprised the character in films and various television versions of *Star Trek* even as he gave acclaimed performances in other films, television dramas, and on Broadway. Stewart's resonating voice can be heard in the animated movies and videos *Land of Lore: The Throne of Chaos* (1994), *The Pagemaster* (1994), *The Prince of Egypt* (1998), *Animal Farm* (1999), *Jimmy Neutron: Boy Genius* (2001), *Steamboy* (2004), *The Last Dragon* (2004), *The Snow Queen* (2005), and *Bambi II*

(2006), as well as in the series *The Simpsons* and *Family Guy*. Several times Stewart had come close to voicing characters for Disney animated films (he most regrets not playing Jafar in *Aladdin*) but each time his busy film and television schedule kept him from participating. Not until 2005 and *Chicken Little* did he finally voice for Disney. Biography: *Patrick Stewart: The Unauthorized Biography*, James Hatfield (1996).

Stiers, David Ogden (b. 1942)   A favorite television performer and a busy voice actor for Disney, he excels at playing stuffy, high-brow types such as the enchanted clock Cogsworth in *Beauty and the Beast* (1991) but he has provided voices for many other Disney characters as well, including the greedy Governor Ratcliffe and his overeager flunky Wiggins in *Pocahontas* (1995), the kindly Archdeacon in *The Hunchback of Notre Dame* (1996), the Smithsonian scientist Fenton Q. Harcourt in *Atlantis: The Lost Empire* (2001), Stitch's creator Dr. Jumba Jookiba in *Lilo and Stitch* (2002), and the scared cat Mr. Jolly in *Teacher's Pet* (2004). David Atten Ogden Stiers was born in Peoria, Illinois, grew up in Eugene, Oregon, and studied acting at the Actors Workshop in San Francisco before starting his stage career. He was a member of John Houseman's The Acting Company and toured the country in classic plays before appearing in such New York productions as *The Three Sisters* (1973), *The Beggar's Opera* (1973), *Ulysses in Nighttown* (1974), and *The Magic Show* (1974). Stiers made his film debut in 1971 and first appeared on television three years later, playing minor characters in such series as *Charlie's Angels*, *Doc*, *Mary Tyler Moore*, and *The Paper Chase*; then he found fame playing the snooty Major Charles Winchester in *M*A*S*H* for six years. His later television series include *Ally McBeal*, *Love & Money*, *Perry Mason*, *Bull*, *North and South*, *Stephen King's Dead Zone*, and *Two Guys, a Girl and a Pizza Place*. Among Stiers' film credits are *Drive, He Said* (1971), *Oh, God!* (1977), *The Cheap Detective* (1978), *Harry's War* (1981), *The Accidental Tourist* (1988), *Doc Hollywood* (1991), *Shadows and Fog* (1991), *Steal Big Steal Little* (1995), *Everyone Says I Love You* (1996), *Jungle to Jungle* (1997), *The Curse of the Jade Scorpion* (2001), and *Not Dead Yet* (2009). The character of Cogsworth in *Beauty in the Beast* is Stiers' most enduring and endearing character. Originally the enchanted clock was to be voiced by Patrick Stewart but his schedule did not permit him the time. Stiers' vocals for Cogsworth are snooty yet appealing. He reprised his Cogsworth in the videos *Beauty and the Beast: The Enchanted Christmas* (1997), *Belle's Magical World* (1998), *Mickey's Magical Christmas: Snowed in at the House of Mouse* (2001), *Kingdom Hearts II* (2005); his Ratcliffe in *Pocahontas II: Journey to a New World* (1998); and his Dr. Jumba in *Stitch Experiment 626* (2002), *Stitch! The Movie* (2003), *Lilo & Stitch 2: Stitch Has a Glitch* (2005), *Kingdom Hearts: Birth by Sleep* (2010), and the *Lilo & Stitch* TV series. His other animated series include *101 Dalmatians: The Series*, *The Wild Thornberrys*, *House of Mouse*, *American Dragon: Jake Long*, *Justice League*, and *Teacher's Pet*. Stiers has also provided voices for such animated videos and movies as *Toonstruck* (1996), *Spirited Away* (2001), *Uru: Ages Beyond Myst* (2003), *Batman: Mystery of the Batwoman* (2003), *The Cat That Looked at a King* (2004), *Hoodwinked* (2005), *Myst V: End of Ages* (2005), and *Hoodwinked Too! Hood VS. Evil* (2010). His fluent voice has been used as a narrator in several documentaries and in Disney productions such as *Beauty and the Beast* (both the film and the Broadway production), *Winnie the Pooh: Springtime with Roo* (2004), and *Pooh's Heffalump Halloween Movie* (2005).

Stiller, Jerry (b. 1927)   A character actor favorite of stage, screen, and television who can do everything from ethnic comedy to piercing drama, he supplied the voice of the wisecracking parrot Pretty Boy in *Teacher's Pet* (2004). Gerald Isaac Stiller was born in New York City to Austrian Jewish immigrants and was educated at Syracuse University before doing comedy in clubs and with improv groups. He worked as an actor in New York beginning in the 1950s and throughout his career he often returned to the stage, appearing in such Broadway productions as *The Golden Apple* (1954), *Diary of a Scoundrel* (1956), *The Good Woman of Setzuan* (1956), *The Taming of the Shrew* (1957), *The Ritz* (1975), *Passione* (1980), *Hurlyburly* (1984), *Three Men on a Horse* (1993), and *The Three Sisters* (1997). His career took off when he teamed with wife-actress Anne Meara and their comedy act became a favorite in nightclubs and on television, in particular *The Ed Sullivan Show*. Stiller made his television debut in 1956 and over the years acted in such series as *The Courtship of Eddie's Father*, *The Paul Lynde Show*, *Joe and Sons*, *Phyllis*, *Rhoda*, *Hart to Hart*, *Archie Bunker's Place*, *The Love Boat*, *Trapper John M.D.*, *Law & Order*, *Touched by an Angel*, *Sex and the City*, and *Mercy*, although he is probably best remembered as Frank Costanza on *Seinfeld* and Arthur Spooner in *The King of Queens*. He has made many films over the years, including some with his wife Meara and later with their son Ben Stiller. Among them are *Lovers and Other Strangers* (1970), *The Taking of Pelham One Two Three* (1974), *Airport 1975* (1974), *The Ritz* (1976), *Nasty Habits* (1977), *Those Lips, Those Eyes* (1980), *Seize the Day* (1986), *Hairspray* (1988), *Heavy Weights*

(1995), *A Rat's Tale* (1997), *Secret of the Andes* (1999), *My 5 Wives* (2000), *Zoolander* (2001), *Hairspray* (2007), *The Heartbreak Kid* (2007), and *Swinging with the Finkels* (2010), as well as several made-for-TV movies. Stiller can be heard doing voices for the cartoon series *Linus! The Lion-Hearted, Hercules, Crashbox, Teacher's Pet, Odd Job Jack*, and *The Wonder Pets*, and in the animated videos *Hooves on Fire* (1999), *Robbie the Reindeer in Legend of the Lost Tribe* (2002), *The Lion King 1½* (2004), and *Behind the Legend: Timon* (2004). Memoir: *Married to Laughter: A Love Story Featuring Anne Meara* (2000).

Stockwell, Harry (1902–1984)   A singer on Broadway and in a few films, he provided the speaking and singing voice of the Prince in *Snow White and the Seven Dwarfs* (1937). He was born in Kansas City, Missouri, and sang in nightclubs and for stock companies before going to New York City. Stockwell sang in such Broadway musicals as *Broadway Nights* (1929), *Earl Carroll's Vanities* (1931), *As Thousands Cheer* (1933), *George White's Scandals* (1939), and *Marinka* (1945), but his most memorable stage credit was replacing Alfred Drake as Curly in *Oklahoma!* (1943) and playing the role for several years. He made his screen debut in *Here Comes the Band* (1935), followed by such diverse films as *All Over Town* (1937), *Montmartre Madness* (1939), *It Happened to Jane* (1959), and *The Werewolf of Washington* (1973). He is the father of actors Guy Stockwell (1934–2002) and Dean Stockwell (b. 1936). The character of the Prince in *Snow White and the Seven Dwarfs* is the first Disney prince and he is also the least interesting in terms of character and visuals. Like the heroine in the movie, the hero was patterned after live-film footage of a dancer, in this case Louis Hightower, who acted out the character's moves for the camera. Yet the Prince's movements are stiff and not very lifelike, as opposed to Snow White's natural, flowing movement, and facially he is rather blank. The animators were disappointed in the results and some scenes with the Prince were edited out of the movie. (He originally was captured and imprisoned by the Queen then escaped to look for Snow White.) He is not even given a real name, as most later Disney princes. Yet there is something magical, if unreal, about this prince who sings his "One Song" about Snow White. It is indeed his only song but, like much of his character, it suffices.

Stojka, Andre   A voice artist active in television since 1979, he was the voice of the pseudo-intellectual Owl in the *Winnie the Pooh* features and shorts from 1994 to 2006. Stojka began his career as a television producer in the 1960s then began voicing characters in the TV cartoon show *Scooby-Doo and Scrappy-Doo* in 1979, followed by such series as *The Smurfs, Shirt Tales, Challenge of the Go-Bots, Spider-Man, Rainbow Brite, Jonny Quest, Adventures of the Gummi Bears, Darkwing Duck, The Pirates of Dark Water, House of Mouse*, and *The Grim Adventures of Billy & Mandy*. He supplied the voice of Owl in the animated features *The Tigger Movie* (2000) and *Piglet's Big Movie* (2003), as well as in the TV series *The Book of Pooh* and in twenty-one *Winnie the Pooh* videos. Among Stojka's other animated movies and videos are *Rainbow Brite and the Star Stealer* (1985), *Noah's Ark* (1986), *David and Goliath* (1986), *Scooby-Doo and the Ghoul School* (1988), *The Raccoon War* (1994), *The Emperor's New Groove* (2000), *Cinderella II: Dreams Come True* (2002), *The Wacky Adventures of Ronald McDonald: Have Time, Will Travel* (2002), and *Cinderella III: A Twist in Time* (2007).

Strom, Natalie   A child actress who voiced Young Princess Kida in *Atlantis: The Lost Empire* (2001), her only other acting credit is providing the voice for Kid Gloria on the animated television series *The Zeta Project* (2001).

Stuart, Chad (b. 1941)   The British pop singer who, with Jeremy Clyde, made up the popular folk-rock duo Chad and Jeremy, he did the speaking and singing voice for Flaps, one of the Beatles-like vultures, in *The Jungle Book* (1967). He was born David Stuart Chadwick in Windemere, England, and with his partner found moderate success as Chad and Jeremy in Great Britain in the early 1960s. The duo was even more popular in the States with several hit records, appearances on television, and in concert. Stuart appeared on many talk and quiz shows and played variations of himself on the television series *The Dick Van Dyke Show, The Patty Duke Show, Laredo*, and *The Red Skelton Show*. The vultures in *The Jungle Book* were originally to sing a rock-and-roll song but it was thought that the Beatles and the rock sound were a passing fad and the movie would quickly date itself. So the very Beatles-like foursome of vultures break into an old-fashioned style barbershop quartet number called "That's What Friends Are For."

Suarez, Jeremy (b. 1990)   An African American actor on television and in the movies, he voiced the wisecracking bear cub Koda in *Brother Bear* (2003). He was born in Burbank, California, and made his small screen debut on an episode of *Sister, Sister* when he was six years old. That same year he was featured in the film *Jerry Maguire*. Suarez's television credits include the series *Built to Last, Chicago Hope, Beverly Hills 90210*, and *The Bernie Mac Show*, and he has acted in such films as *The Ladykillers* (2004), *Room to Grow* (2005), and *Extreme*

Movie (2008). He reprised his Koda in the video sequel *Brother Bear 2* (2006) and can also be heard in the animated movies and videos *The Land Before Time VIII: The Big Freeze* (2001), *Treasure Planet* (2002), and *The Proud Family Movie* (2005), as well as the animated series *Hey, Arnold!* and *King of the Hill*.

Sullivan, Erik Per (b. 1991)   A child performer on the screen since 1998, he supplied the voice of the sea horse Sheldon in *Finding Nemo* (2003). He was born in Worcester, Massachusetts, and before he was twelve years old he was in the films *Armageddon* (1998), *The Cider House Rules* (1999), *Wendigo* (2001), *Joe Dirt* (2001), and *Unfaithful* (2002). Sullivan was most noticed as Dewey in the TV sit-com *Malcolm in the Middle* for six years. His other movie credits include *Christmas with the Kranks* (2004), *Once Not far from Home* (2006), *Mo* (2007), and *Twelve* (2010).

Sullivan, Nicole (b. 1970)   A comedienne and television actress with extensive voice credits, she provided the voice of adult Franny Robinson, Wilbur's odd but endearing mother, in *Meet the Robinsons* (2007). Nicole Julianne Sullivan was born in New York City, the daughter of a state assemblyman, and educated at Northwest University. She did stand-up comedy in California before beginning her television career on talk shows, comedy specials, and quiz programs, as well as such series as *Herman's Head*, *Diagnosis Murder*, *Party of Five*, *Suddenly Susan*, *Fired Up*, and *According to Jim*, finally finding notoriety as one of the inventive cast members and writers of *MADtv* in 1995. Sullivan stayed with the show for ten years then went on to other series, including *Hot Properties*, *Raines*, *The King of Queens*, *My Boys*, *The Suite Life of Zack and Cody*, *Scrubs*, *Numb3rs*, and *Rita Rocks*. Among her movie credits are *Fairfax Fandango* (1997), *Say You'll Be Mine* (1999), *The Third Wheel* (2002), *Guess Who* (2005), *One Sung Hero* (2006), *Superhero Movie* (2008), and *Black Dynamite* (2009). Sullivan has done voices for the TV cartoon series *Buzz Lightyear of Star Command*, *Stanley*, *Baby Blues*, *Clone High U.S.A.*, *Lilo & Stitch*, *Brandy & Mr. Whiskers*, *Kim Possible*, *Slacker Cats*, *Family Guy*, *The Secret Saturdays*, and *The Penguins of Madagascar*, as well as the animated movies and videos *Buzz Lightyear of Star Command: The Adventure Begins* (2000), *A Baby Blues Christmas Special* (2002), *Kim Possible: A Stitch in Time* (2003), *Kim Possible: So the Drama* (2005), and *The Ant Bully* (2006).

Summer, Cree (b. 1969)   A voice actress who can be heard in over one hundred episodes of television cartoon series since 1983, she provided the voice of Princess Kidagakash "Kida" Nedakh of Atlantis in *Atlantis: The Lost Empire* (2001) as well as in the video sequel *Atlantis: Milo's Return* (2003). She was born Cree Summer Francks in Los Angeles, the son of actor Don Francks, and began her career as a singer before turning to acting and then voice work. Her ability to sound like a slightly-nasal adolescent has allowed her to play teens for nearly thirty years. Summer has voiced recurring characters in dozens of series, including *Inspector Gadget*, *The All New Ewoks*, *The Little Mermaid*, *Tiny Toon Adventures*, *Sonic the Hedgehog*, *Gargoyles*, *Mortal Kombat: Defenders of the Realm*, *Jungle Cubs*, *101 Dalmatians: The Series*, *Pinky, Elmyra & the Brain*, *Sabrina: The Animated Series*, *Batman Beyond*, *Horrible Histories*, *Rugrats*, *Spider-Man*, *Danny Phantom*, *The Buzz on Maggie*, *My Life as a Teenage Robot*, *Transformers: Animated*, and *WordGirl*. Among her many animated videos and movies are *Strawberry Shortcake Meets the Berrykins* (1984), *The Care Bears Movie* (1985), *Tiny Toon Adventures: How I Spent My Vacation* (1992), *Gargoyles: Brothers Betrayed* (1998), *The Rugrats Movie* (1998), *An Extremely Goofy Movie* (2000), *Buzz Lightyear of Star Command* (2000), *Rugrats in Paris* (2000), *Forgotten Realms: Baldur's Gate — Dark Alliance* (2001), *Kermit's Swamp Years* (2002), *Barbie as Rapunzel* (2002), *Lords of Everquest* (2003), *Clifford's Really Big Movie* (2004), *Bambi II* (2006), *Turok: Son of Stone* (2008), and *Curious George II: Follow That Monkey* (2009).

Susskind, Steve (1942–2005)   A character actor who appeared in small roles in many television series, he supplied the voice of the seven-fingered monster Jerry who is the Floor Manager at the factory in *Monsters, Inc.* (2001). He was born in Springfield, Massachusetts, and grew up in Forest Hills, New York. At the age of fifteen he began his career as a singer with the Doo Wop group The Roomates who had some hit records in the early 1960s and appeared on *American Bandstand* and other television shows. Susskind attended New York University and pursued a business career for a time, then went to Los Angeles to become a professional actor. An appearance on an episode of the television sit-com *Archie Bunker's Place* in 1982 was his first of dozens of series, including *The Jeffersons*, *Santa Barbara*, *Jake and the Fatman*, *Knots Landing*, *Tales from the Crypt*, *Married with Children*, *Roseanne*, *NewsRadio*, *Seinfeld*, *Get Real*, *Friends*, *According to Jim*, *Frasier*, and *Jake in Progress*. Among Susskind's film credits are *Friday the 13th Part III* (1982), *Star Trek V: The Final Frontier* (1989), *Round Trip to Heaven* (1992), *Sandman* (1998), and *Dog Gone Love* (2004). He can be heard on the TV cartoon series *Challenge of the GoBots*, *DuckTales*, *Batman*, *The Tick*, and

Godzilla: The Series, as well as the animated films *The Emperor's New Groove* (2000) and *Osmosis Jones* (2001).

Sutherland, John (1910–2001) A Hollywood producer who presented two dozen movies and a few television programs, his only acting credit was providing the voice for the Adult Bambi in *Bambi* (1942). He was born in Williston, North Dakota, and broke into movies as a screenwriter. By 1945 he was producing features, industrials, and educational films, including some animated shorts. In the 1970s he also produced and directed some television programs. Aside from *Bambi*, Sutherland's only other Disney credit was serving as an animator on the Mickey Mouse short *The Beach Party* (1931).

Swardson, Nick (b. 1976) A comic writer and actor in movies and on television, he voiced the over-anxious pigeon Blake who wants to write for television in *Bolt* (2008). Nicholas Swardson was born in Minneapolis, Minnesota, and began his career as a stand-up comic. Comedian-actor Adam Sandler discovered Swardson performing in a club and brought him to Los Angeles where Swardson wrote and appeared in TV comedy specials and some movies as well. His film acting credits include *Almost Famous* (2000), *Pretty When You Cry* (2001), *Malibu's Most Wanted* (2003), *The Benchwarmers* (2006), *I Now Pronounce You Chuck & Larry* (2007), and *Bedtime Stories* (2008). Swardson has appeared on such television series as *Watching Ellie*, *That's My Daughter*, *Cavemen*, and *Reno 911!*

Sweeney, D. B. (b. 1961) A stage, film, and television actor who occasionally voices animated characters, he played the heroic iguanodon Aladar in *Dinosaur* (2000) and the Native American Sitka who is killed by a bear in *Brother Bear* (2003). He was born Daniel Bernard Sweeney in Shoreham, Long Island, New York, and trained at Tulane University and New York University for a stage career. He made his Broadway debut in *The Caine Mutiny Court-Martial* (1983) and his television bow two years later, going on to act in such series as *Lonesome Dove*, *Strange Luck*, *N.Y.P.D. Blue*, *Harsh Realm*, *CSI: Crime Scene Investigation*, *Life as We Know It*, *House*, *Jericho*, *Criminal Minds*, and *24*. Sweeney's movie credits include *Eight Men Out* (1988), *Memphis Belle* (1990), *The Cutting Edge* (1992), *Hear No Evil* (1993), *Spawn* (1997), *Hard Ball* (2001), *The Darwin Awards* (2006), *Two Tickets to Paradise* (2006), *Heatstroke* (2008), and *Fencewalker* (2010). The character of Aladar in *Dinosaur* was originally named Noah, a reference to his saving animals from a natural destruction. Also, the film was conceived as having no dialogue at all, the story told only visually. The studio insisted on dialogue for marketing reasons and much of the fun in the movie comes from the voices such as Sweeney's.

Sweetland, Doug A Pixar animator who was involved in the earliest projects by the company, he provided the non-verbal noises of the magician Presto DiGiotagione and his rabbit assistant Alec Azam in the short *Presto* (2008) which he also wrote and directed. Sweetland worked on the animation for *Toy Story* (1995), *A Bug's Life* (1998), *Toy Story 2* (1999), *Monsters, Inc.* (2001), *Finding Nemo* (2003), *The Incredibles* (2004), and *Cars* (2006), as well as the short *Boundin'* (2003). His only other acting credit is a role in the live-action film *Tracy* (2009).

Swenson, Karl (1908–1978) A beefy, light-haired character actor with many television credits, he provided the voice of the eccentric sorcerer Merlin in *The Sword in the Stone* (1963). He was born in Brooklyn, New York, and began his career on the stage, appearing on Broadway in *A Glass of Water* (1930), *Carrie Nation* (1932), *One Sunday Afternoon* (1933), *House of Remsen* (1934), *It's You I Want* (1935), *Panic* (1935), *A Highland Fling* (1944), and *The Man Who Had All the Luck* (1944). At the same time Swenson was busy on radio, acting in such series as *Cavalcade in America*, *The March of Time*, *Inner Sanctum Mysteries*, *Lorenzo Jones*, *Our Gal Sunday*, *The Adventures of Father Brown*, and *Portia Faces Life*. When this last one went to television, Swenson tried the new medium and over the next two decades appeared in dozens of series, including *Mr. Citizen*, *The United States Steel Hour*, *Robert Montgomery Presents*, *The Walter Winchell File*, *Circus Boy*, *The Adventures of Jim Bowie*, *Leave It to Beaver*, *Cheyenne*, *Bat Masterson*, *Sugarfoot*, *Steve Canyon*, *Bronco*, *Tightrope*, *Rawhide*, *The Rebel*, *Bachelor Father*, *The Rifleman*, *Mr. Lucky*, *Hawaiian Eye*, *Have Gun—Will Travel*, *Ripcord*, *The Untouchables*, *Sam Benedict*, *Laramie*, *77 Sunset Strip*, *Wagon Train*, *Mr. Novak*, *Perry Mason*, *The Big Valley*, *Bonanza*, *Cimarron Strip*, *The Virginian*, *Hawaii Five-O*, *Gunsmoke*, *Lassie*, and *Emergency!*, although he is most remembered as the lumber mill owner Lars Hanson in *Little House on the Prairie*. Among his movie credits are *December 7th* (1943), *Four Boys and a Gun* (1957), *Kings Go Forth* (1958), *The Badlanders* (1958), *The Name on the Bullet* (1959), *Ice Palace* (1960), *The Gallant Hours* (1960), *North to Alaska* (1960), *Judgement at Nuremberg* (1961), *Lonely Are the Brave* (1962), *The Birds* (1963), *The Man from Galveston* (1963), *Major Dundee* (1965), *The Cincinnati Kid* (1965), *Seconds* (1966), *Birth of the Grand Canyon* (1967), *Vanishing Point* (1971), and *Ulzana's Raid* (1972). The character of Merlin in *The Sword in the Stone* is a lively, funny character and, aside from his ability to pull off tricks, there is nothing very mystical about him. Instead Swenson's delivery of the lines is straightforward and matter-of-fact, turning the wizard into an absent-minded but lovable uncle.

Swofford, Ken (b. 1933)   A gruff, red-haired movie and television actor since the early 1960s who specialized in tough, streetwise types, he supplied the voice of diligent Officer White from the Bureau of Animal Safety in *Teacher's Pet* (2004), his last credit before retirement. He was born in DuQuoin, Illinois, and made his television debut on an episode of *Surfside 6* in 1962, going on to appear in dozens of series, including *The Wild Wild West, Daniel Boone, The Virginian, I Spy, Adam-12, The F.B.I., Mission: Impossible, The Streets of San Francisco, Columbo, The Waltons, The Partridge Family, Kung Fu, Paper Moon, Gunsmoke, Switch, Ellery Queen, The Six Million Dollar Man, Hunter, Police Story, The Rockford Files, Fantasy Island, Knots Landing, Knight Rider, Falcon Crest, Simon & Simon, Dynasty, Matlock, Baywatch,* and *Murder, She Wrote,* although he is probably best remembered as Quentin Morloch on *Fame* for two years. Swofford acted in several films, such as *Father Goose* (1964), *The Lawyer* (1970), *The Andromeda Strain* (1971), *Bless the Beasts & Children* (1971), *Skyjacked* (1972), *One Little Indian* (1973), *The Black Bird* (1975), *The Domino Principle* (1977), *S.O.B.* (1981), *Annie* (1982), *Hunter's Blood* (1986), *Black Roses* (1988), *Thelma & Louise* (1991), *The Taking of Beverly Hills* (1991), and *Cops n Robbers* (1995), as well as many made-for-TV movies.

Takei, George (b. 1937)   A popular Asian American actor with fifty years of movie and television credits, he voiced the First Ancestor of the Fa family in *Mulan* (1998). George Hosato Takei was born in Los Angeles and as a child during World War II he and his family were placed in internment camps for Japanese Americans. He later studied architecture at the University of California at Berkeley but a job doing voices for the English version of a Japanese movie got him interested in acting so he transferred to UCLA as a theatre major. While still a student Takei was cast in some television programs and in 1960 he made his screen debut in *Ice Palace*. After appearances in such television series as *Perry Mason, Hawaiian Eye, Death Valley Days, My Three Sons, I Spy,* and *Mission: Impossible,* Takei got the role of his career: Lt. Hikaru Sulu in the original television series *Star Trek*. After the show's three-year run, he returned to the character in the films *Star Trek: The Motion Picture* (1979), *Star Trek II: The Wrath of Khan* (1982), *Star Trek III: The Search for Spock* (1984), *Star Trek IV: The Voyage Home* (1986), *Star Trek V: The Final Frontier* (1989), *Star Trek VI: The Undiscovered Country* (1991), as well as the television series *Star Trek: Voyager* and *Star Trek New Voyages: Phase II*. Takei's other screen credits include *A Majority of One* (1961), *Red Line 7000* (1965), *Walk Don't Run* (1966), *The Green Berets* (1968), *Which Way to the Front?* (1970), *The Magic Pearl* (1997), *The Eavesdropper* (2004), *Ninja Cheerleaders* (2008), and *The Red Canvas* (2009). Among his television series after the run of *Star Trek* are *Hawaii Five-O, Khan!, Chico and the Man, Black Sheep Squadron, General Hospital, Miami Vice, Lightning Force, Kung Fu: The Legend Continues, Space Cases, The Young and the Restless, Scrubs, Malcolm in the Middle, Cory in the House, Jimmy Kimmel Live!, Heroes,* and *The Suite Life on Deck*. Takei reprised his First Ancestor in *Mulan II* (2004) and did voices for several TV cartoon series, including *Jonny Quest, Spider-Man, Hercules, Batman Beyond, The Simpsons, Jackie Chan Adventures, Samurai Jack, Kim Possible, Star Wars: The Clone Wars, Chowder,* and *The Super Hero Squad Show,* as well as the animated videos *Batman Beyond: The Movie* (1999) and *Scooby-Doo and the Samurai Sword* (2009). Autobiography: *To the Stars: The Autobiography of George Takei, Star Trek's Mr. Sulu* (2007).

Tambor, Jeffrey (b. 1944)   A lively, balding, smiling actor on stage, in films, and on television who specializes in offbeat characters, he supplied the voice of the ugly pub thug Big-Nose, who is a romantic at heart and yearns for love, in *Tangled* (2010). Jeffrey Michael Tambor was born in San Francisco and educated at San Francisco State University and Wayne State University. After acting in regional theatres and performing Off Broadway in *Measure for Measure* (1976) and on Broadway in *Sly Fox* (1976), he made his television debut in an episode of *Kojak* in 1977. Two years later he found recognition as Jeffrey P. Brookes II on the series *The Ropers,* followed by such shows as *Barney Miller, Nine to Five, Three's Company, The Love Boat, Mr. Sunshine, The Twilight Zone, Hill Street Blues, Max Headroom, American Dreamer, Everything's Relative, Welcome to the Captain,* and *Twenty Good Years,* but he is best known as the twins George and Oscar Bluth in *Arrested Development* and the sidekick Hank Kingsley in *The Larry Sanders Show*. Tambor made his screen debut in 1979 and has acted in several movies, including *Saturday the 14th* (1981), *The Dream Chasers* (1982), *Mr. Mom* (1983), *Brenda Starr* (1989), *Life Stinks* (1991), *Doctor Dolittle* (1998), *Meet Joe Black* (1998), *There's Something About Mary* (1998), *How the Grinch Stole Christmas* (2000), *Hellboy* (2004), *Superhero Movie* (2008), *Hellboy II: The Golden Army* (2008), and *Operation Endgame* (2010), as well as many TV-movies. He started voicing television cartoon series in the 1990s and can be heard in such shows as *Batman, Dinosaurs, Capitol Critters, Pinky and the Brain, Johnny Bravo, Hercules,* and *Monsters vs. Aliens,* as well as on such animated films and videos as *Jonny's Golden Quest* (1993), *The SpongeBob SquarePants Movie* (2004), and *Pooh's Super Sleuth Christmas Movie* (2007). Tambor returns to the stage on occasion, appearing on Broadway in *Glengarry Glen Ross* (2005) and *La Cage aux Folles* (2011).

Tatasciore, Fred A prolific voice artist who has done many cartoon series and video game characters, he provided the voice of the Troll in the animated section of *Enchanted* (2007). The native New Yorker began voicing for films in 1983 then went on to work on many TV cartoon series, including *Naruto, Star Wars: Clone Wars, What's New, Scooby-Doo?, Avatar: The Last Airbender, Tom Goes to the Mayor, Invader ZIM, Robot Chicken, The Grim Adventures of Billy and Mandy, Ben 10, The Emperor's New School, Wolverine and the X-Men, Chowder, American Dad, Family Guy, Back at the Barnyard,* and *The Secret Saturdays*. Tatasciore can be heard in such animated videos and films as *Curious George* (2006), *The Wild* (2006), *Superman: Brainiac Attacks* (2006), *The Ant Bully* (2006), *Barnyard* (2006), *The Invincible Iron Man* (2007), *Meet the Robinsons* (2007), *Garfield Gets Real* (2007), *Garfield's Fun Fest* (2008), *Madagascar: Escape to Africa* (2008), *Curious George 2: Follow That Monkey* (2009), *Garfield's Pet Force* (2009), *The Princess and the Frog* (2009), and *Tangled* (2010). He can also be heard in over 150 video games.

Taylor, Dub (1907–1994) One of Hollywood and television's most familiar character actors known for playing rural, hayseed types, particularly in westerns, he provided the voice of Digger the Mole in *The Rescuers* (1977). He was born Walter Clarence Taylor II in Richmond, Virginia, and began his career doing comedy in vaudeville. He made a noticeable film debut as one of the eccentric family members in *You Can't Take It with You* (1938) then played the crusty cowhand Cannonball in *The Taming of the West*, a role he returned to in other westerns over the next ten years. Among his other over-one-hundred movies are *Mr. Smith Goes to Washington* (1939), *The Return of Wild Bill* (1940), *The Son of Davy Crockett* (1941), *What's Buzzin', Cousin?* (1943), *Sundown Valley* (1944), *Sagebrush Heroes* (1945), *Lawless Empire* (1945), *Song of the Drifter* (1948), *Across the Rio Grande* (1949), *Riding High* (1950), *Lure of the Wilderness* (1952), *Those Redheads from Seattle* (1953), *Them!* (1954), *Dragnet* (1954), *A Star Is Born* (1954), *Tall Man Riding* (1955), *The Fastest Gun Alive* (1956), *You Can't Run Away from It* (1956), *No Time for Sergeants* (1958), *Street of Darkness* (1958), *Auntie Mame* (1958), *A Hole in the Head* (1959), *Home from the Hill* (1960), *Sweet Bird of Youth* (1962), *Spencer's Mountain* (1963), *Major Dundee* (1965), *The Hallelujah Trail* (1965), *The Cincinnati Kid* (1965), *The Adventures of Bullwip Griffin* (1967), *Bonnie and Clyde* (1967), *The Shakiest Gun in the West* (1968), *The Wild Bunch* (1969), *Death of a Gunfighter* (1969), *The Learning Tree* (1969), *The Flim-Flam Man* (1969), *The Rievers* (1969), *A Man Called Horse* (1970), *Support Your Local Gunfighter* (1971), *Evel Knievel* (1971), *The Getaway* (1972), *Country Blue* (1973), *Tom Sawyer* (1973), *Pat Garrett & Billy the Kid* (1973), *The Fortune* (1975), *Treasure of Matecumbe* (1976), *The Great Smokey Roadblock* (1977), *1941* (1979), *Used Cars* (1980), *Cannonball Run II* (1984), *Back to the Future Part III* (1990), and *Maverick* (1994). Taylor made his television debut in 1951 and over the years was featured in dozens of series such as *The Range Rider, The Roy Rogers Show, I Love Lucy, Cheyenne, Casey Jones, Lawman, Dennis the Menace, Zane Grey Theatre, The Beachcomber, Hazel, My Favorite Martian, Tammy, Please Don't Eat the Daisies, Death Valley Days, The Andy Griffith Show, The Guns of Will Sonnett, Gunsmoke, The Mod Squad, Hawaii Five-O, Bonanza, Emergency!, Walt Disney's Wonderful World of Color, Little House on the Prairie,* and *Designing Women*. Biography: *Dub Taylor*, Frederic P. Miller, Agnes F. Vandome, John McBrewster (2010).

Taylor, Rip (b. 1934) The hyperactive comic dubbed "Master of Mayhem" whose antics are far from subtle, he supplied the voice of Gene, the wacky 3,000-year-old duck genie, in *DuckTales the Movie: The Treasure of the Lost Lamp* (1990). He was born Charles Elmer Taylor in Washington, D.C., and began his career as a stand-up comic in nightclubs where his very physical approach to comedy (silly mustache, outrageous toupees, honking horns, throwing of confetti, and so on) soon made him a favorite in Las Vegas and on television talk shows and variety programs. Taylor was also a popular contestant or judge on quiz shows and over-the-top programs like *The Gong Show* and *The $1.98 Beauty Show*. He sometimes played characters on sit-coms, such as *The Monkees, Life with Bonnie, Sigmund and the Sea Monsters,* and *The Suite Life of Zack and Cody,* and he provided voices for cartoon series, including *The Jetsons, Garfield and Friends, The Addams Family, Bonkers,* and *The Emperor's New School*. Taylor could also be heard in the animated movies and videos *Scooby-Doo Goes Hollywood* (1979), *Tom and Jerry: The Movie* (1992), and *Scooby-Doo and the Monster of Mexico* (2003).

Taylor, Rod (b. 1930) An attractive Australian leading man in American movies and television, he provided the voice of the London canine hero Pongo in *One Hundred and One Dalmatians* (1961). Rodney Sturt Taylor was born in Sydney, Australia, and educated at Sydney Technical and Fine Arts College. While acting on the stage in his native land he found modest success on radio, voicing Tarzan on an Australian children's program, and appeared in the British-made movies *King of the Coral Sea* (1953) and *Long John Silver* (1954). Taylor came to the States in the mid–1950s and made both his American screen and television debut in 1955. His many movies include *The Virgin Queen* (1955), *Hell on Frisco Bay* (1955), *The Catered Affair* (1956), *Giant* (1956), *Raintree County* (1957), *Separate Tables* (1958), *Seven Seas to Calais* (1962), *The V.I.P.s* (1963), *Sunday in New York* (1963), *Hotel* (1967), *Zabriski Point* (1970), *Trader Horn* (1973), *Jamaican Gold* (1979), *A Time to Die* (1982), *Open Season* (1995), and *Inglourious Basterds* (2009), but he is most remembered as the leading man in two classic science fiction movies: *The Time Machine* (1960) and *The Birds* (1963). Taylor was also featured in several television series such as *Studio 57*, *Schlitz Playhouse*, *Playhouse 90*, *Twilight Zone*, *Zane Grey Theatre*, *Hong Kong*, *Bearcats!*, *The Oregon Trail*, *Outlaws*, *Falcon Crest*, and *Walker, Texas Ranger*. The character of Pongo in *One Hundred and One Dalmatians* is very much a low-key, emotionally controlled hero in the British manner. Yet Taylor's vocals are never stuffy or cold. Instead Pogo is very appealing in an almost human, gentlemanly manner. In fact, in many ways he is more human than his "pet" Roger who tends to act more a like dog at times.

Taylor, Russi (b. 1944)   A prolific and versatile voice artist who has played Minnie Mouse in many cartoons, she provided the voices for the duck nephews Huey, Dewey, and Louie and the niece Webbigal "Webby" Vanderquack in *DuckTales the Movie: The Treasure of the Lost Lamp* (1990). She was born in Cambridge, Massachusetts, and made her television debut in 1980 voicing the title character in the animated special *The World of Strawberry Shortcake*, followed by five sequels. Taylor first voiced Minnie Mouse in 1987 in the television special *DTV "Doggone" Valentine* and went on to play the character in sing-along videos, cartoon series such as *Mickey Mouse Works*, *House of Mouse*, and *Mickey Mouse Clubhouse*, and in many animated videos, including *Totally Minnie* (1988), *Runaway Brain* (1995), *The Spirit of Mickey* (1998), *Mickey's New Car* (1999), *Mickey's Once Upon a Christmas* (1999), *Mickey's House of Villains* (2001), *Kingdom Hearts* (2002), *Mickey's Twice Upon a Christmas* (2004), *Mickey's Around the World in 80 Days* (2005), *Kingdom Hearts II* (2005), *Mickey Saves Santa and Other Mousetales* (2006), and *Mickey's Adventures in Wonderland* (2009), as well as a cameo in the film *Who Framed Roger Rabbit* (1988). She first voiced the duck nephews and Webby in the TV cartoon series *DuckTales* and reprised them in such videos as *DuckTales: Treasure of the Golden Suns* (1987), *Sport Goofy in Soccermania* (1987), *Super Duck Tales* (1989), and *DuckTales: The Quest for Gold* (1990). Taylor has provided voices for other characters in many movies and videos, including *Peter and the Magic Egg* (1983), *The Adventures of the American Rabbit* (1986), *My Little Pony: The Movie* (1986), *The Adventures of Ronald McDonald: McTreasure Island* (1989), *The Rescuers Down Under* (1990), *The Jetsons: The Movie* (1990), *Hollyrock-a-Bye Baby* (1993), *A Flintstones Christmas Carol* (1994), *Babe* (1995), *The Tale of Tillie's Dragon* (1995), *The Brave Little Toaster Goes to Mars* (1998), *A Bug's Life* (1998), *Babe: Pig in the City* (1998), *Nine Dog Christmas* (2001), *Cinderella II: Dreams Come True* (2002), *The Fox and the Hound 2* (2006), *Cinderella III: A Twist in Time* (2007), *The Simpsons Movie* (2007), and *Scooby-Doo and the Goblin King* (2008), as well as Daisy Duck in the "Pomp and Circumstance" segment of *Fantasia/2000* (1999), Among her other animated TV series are *Heathcliff*, *The Littles*, *My Little Pony 'n Friends*, *Chip 'n Dale Rescue Rangers*, *TaleSpin*, *Muppet Babies*, *Wild West C.O.W.— Boys of Moo Mesa*, *The Little Mermaid*, *The Critic*, *Timon and Pumbaa*. *Buzz Lightyear of Star Command*, *Kim Possible*, *Clifford's Puppy Days*, *Jakers! The Adventures of Piggley Winks*, and *The Simpsons* in which she voiced Martin Prince for twenty years. Taylor was married to Wayne Allwine, the voice of Mickey Mouse from 1983 to 2001.

Terry, Paul (b. 1987)   The English youth who played the orphan James in the live-action portions of *James and the Giant Peach* (1996) and voiced James in the stop-action section, he retired from acting in 1999 after appearing in the BBC-TV series *Microsoap*. He later majored in German and Engineering at Cardiff University and was bass player for the band Glassapple.

Terry-Thomas (1911–1990)   The distinctive British comic actor known for the gap between his top front teeth that sometimes produced a whistling sound when he spoke, he voiced the loyal if spineless snake Sir Hiss, the crony of Prince John, in *Robin Hood* (1973). He was born Terry Thomas Hoar Stevens in London and was educated at Ardingly College before working as a clerk. He began his performing career in cabarets then found some success entertaining the British troops during World War II with his silly-ass upper-class Englishmen in sketches. After the war he found wider recognition on British television, then became internationally known from the popular films as *Private's Progress* (1956) and *I'm All Right Jack* (1959). Among his other movies are *Lucky Jim* (1957), *Brothers in Law* (1957), *Tom Thumb* (1958), *Too Many Crooks* (1959), *Man in a Cocked Hat* (1959), *Make Mine Mink* (1960), *The Wonderful World of the Brothers Grimm* (1962), *The Mouse on the Moon* (1963), *Those Magnificent Men in Their Flying Machines* (1965), *Munster, Go Home!* (1956), *Kiss the Girls and Make Them Die* (1966), *The Perils of Pauline* (1967), *Where Were You When the Lights Went Out?* (1968), *Don't Raise the Bridge, Lower the River* (1968), *Those Daring Young Men in Their Jaunty Jalopies* (1969), *The Abominable Dr. Phibes* (1971), *Dr. Phibes Rides Again* (1971), *The Cherry Picker* (1974), *Spanish Fly* (1976), and *The Hound of the Baskervilles* (1978). Terry-Thomas appeared on some American television series, such as *Burke's Law*, *The Man from U.N.C.L.E.*, *The Red Skelton Hour*, *The Persuaders*, and *That's Life*, and was featured in the hit British series *The Old Campaigner* in the 1960s. The animators of Disney's *Robin Hood* used the actor's lisp and his look in developing the character of the serpent Sir Hiss. The snake even has a gap between his front teeth, allowing for the lisping sound but also giving his forked tongue a place to slither in and out. Biography: *Bounder! The Biography of Terry-Thomas*, Graham McCann (2009).

Thewlis, David (b. 1963)   A British film actor with a menacing yet magnetic persona, he supplied the voice of the Earthworm in *James and the Giant Peach* (1996). He was born David Wheeler in Blackpool, England, and studied at the Guildhall School of Music and Drama in London before making his British television debut in 1985 and his first film three years later. He found wide recognition for his performance in *Naked* (1993), followed by such movies as *Black Beauty* (1994), *Total Eclipse* (1995), *Restoration* (1995), *DragonHeart* (1996), *The Island of Dr. Moreau* (1996), *Seven Years in Tibet* (1997), *The Big Lebowski* (1998), *Harry Potter and the Prisoner of Azkaban* (2004), *Basic Instinct 2* (2006), *The Boy in the Stripped Pajamas* (2008), *Harry Potter and the Half-Blood Prince* (2009), and *Harry Potter and the Deathly Hallows* (2010).

Thomas, Dave (b. 1949)   The popular comic writer, director, producer, and actor, he first found fame on television then had success in the movies, as with *Brother Bear* (2003) in which he voiced the Canadian moose Tuke. He was born in St. Catherines, Canada, the son of a philosophy professor-author and a musician-composer, was educated at McMaster University. He worked for advertising agencies in Toronto and New York before turning to acting, appearing with the improv comedy troupe Second City in Toronto. Soon the company was known throughout Canada and the States from their television series *SCTV* which Thomas helped write as well. Like the other cast members of *SCTV*, Thomas excelled at impersonating celebrities but he also helped create many original comic characters, none as popular as the oafish Canadian Doug McKenzie who always appeared with his brother Bob (Rick Moranis). The success of *SCTV* led to appearances on *Saturday Night Live* and other television programs, and later he had his own comedy series *The Dave Thomas Comedy Show*. His film credits include *Stripes* (1981), *The Adventures of Bob & Doug McKenzie: Strange Brew* (1983), *Love at Stake* (1987), *Boris and Natasha* (1992), *Coneheads* (1993), *Rat Race* (2001), *Fancy Dancing* (2002), and *Santa's Slay* (2005). Thomas reprised his Tuke in the video sequel *Brother Bear 2* (2006) and provided voices for the TV cartoon series *Raw Toonage*, *Animaniacs*, *The Legend of Tarzan*, *Mission Hill*, *Justice League*, *The Animated Adventures of Bob & Doug McKenzie*, *King of the Hill*, *The Simpsons*, and *Bob & Doug*.

Thomas, Jay (b. 1948)   A familiar television actor and radio talk show host who is also a deft comic, he provided the voice of the obnoxious, controversial Jerry Springer–like TV talk show host Barry Anger in *Teacher's Pet* (2004). He was born Jon Thomas Terrell in Kermit, Texas, and was educated at Gulf Coast Junior College and the University of North Carolina before beginning his career as a radio disc jockey. He made an auspicious television debut in 1979 as Remo DaVinci on seventeen episodes of *Mork & Mindy*, followed by such series as *The Love Boat*, *Family Ties*, *The Golden Girls*, *Open House*, *Married People*, *Ink*, *Katie Joplin*, *The Education of Max Bickford*, *Boston Legal*, and *Cold Case*, but he is more remembered as Jack Stein on *Love & War*, the talk show host Jerry Gold on *Murphy Brown*, and the hockey player Eddie LeBec on *Cheers*. Thomas has appeared in several movies, including *C.H.U.D.* (1984), *The Gig* (1985), *Legal Eagles* (1986), *Little Vegas* (1990), *Straight Talk* (1992), *Mr. Holland's Opus* (1995), *Dirty Laundry* (1996), *A Smile Like Yours* (1997), *Monkey Business* (1998), *Stranger in My House* (1999), *Dragonfly* (2002), *The Santa Clause 2* (2002), *The Santa Clause 3: The Escape Clause* (2006), *Labor Pains* (2009), and *The Pool Boys* (2010), as well as many TV-movies. He can be heard in the television cartoon series *Batman*, *Duckman: Private Dick/Family Man*, *Hercules*, *The Wild Thornberrys*, and *American Dad!*, as well as the animated video *Hercules: Zero to Hero* (1999). Thomas has frequently returned to radio, hosting his own shows in New York and Los Angeles.

Thomas, Jonathan Taylor (b. 1981) A child performer who was very popular on television in the 1990s. he provided the speaking voice of Young Simba in *The Lion King* (1994). He was born Jonathan Taylor Weiss in Bethlehem, Pennsylvania, and when he was four years old his family moved to Sacramento, California, where he started appearing in print ads and television commercials. A role on the short-lived sit-com *The Bradys* led to his getting cast as Randy Taylor on the series *Home Improvement* which ran seven years. At the same time Thomas was featured in such films as *Man of the House* (1995), *Tom and Huck* (1995), *Wild America* (1997), *I'll Be Home for Christmas* (1998), and *Speedway Junky* (1999). His later television credits include *Ally McBeal, Smallville, Veronica Mars,* and *8 Simple Rules,* and the made-for-TV films *Common Ground* (2000) and *An American Town* (2001). Thomas has done voices for the cartoon series *The Oz Kids, The Simpsons,* and *The Wild Thornberrys,* as well as the animated videos *The Raccoon War* (1994), *Christmas in Oz* (1996), *Who Stole Santa?* (1996), *The Adventures of Pinocchio* (1996), *The Nome Prince and the Magic Belt* (1996), *Toto Lost in New York* (1996), *The Tangerine Bear: Home in Time for Christmas* (2000), *Timothy Tweedle the First Christmas Elf* (2000), and *Thru the Moedius Strip* (2005). Biography: *Jonathan Taylor Thomas,* John F. Grabowski (1999).

Thomas, Vanéese Y. A soul and blues singer who has sung on the soundtracks of a few movies, she voiced the Muse Clio in *Hercules* (1997). Thomas appeared and sang in the films *Everyone Says I Love You* (1996) and *Nine* (2009), and can be heard in the animated movie musical *Anastasia* (1997).

Thompson, Bill (1913–1971) A beloved voice actor who started in radio, he played several memorable Disney characters, ranging from the dithering White Rabbit and the dense Dodo in *Alice in Wonderland* (1951) to the wise Professor Owl who taught about music and other subjects in Disney animated shorts. William H. Thompson was born in Terre Haute, Indiana, and became a widely-recognized voice for his different characters on the radio show *Fibber McGee and Molly* in the 1930s and 1940s. He made his screen debut in 1940 and three years later introduced the animated character of Droopy the police dog, a role Thompson would voice in dozens of MGM cartoon shorts. Another recurring character he voiced, the bulldog Spike, was featured in several other MGM shorts. Thompson first worked with the Disney studio in 1951 with *Alice in Wonderland* and for the next thirty years voiced many features and shorts. He provided the voice of the bumbling Mr. Smee and other pirates in *Peter Pan* (1953), the dogs Jock, Bull, and Dashie, as well as the waiter Joe, in *Lady and the Tramp* (1955), the blustering King Hubert in *Sleeping Beauty* (1959), and the British goose Uncle Waldo in *The Aristocats* (1970). Yet Thompson was kept busier in short films, voicing such recurring characters as Ranger J. Audubon Woodlore and Scrooge McDuck, and narrating or playing characters in such memorable Disney cartoons as *How to Catch a Cold* (1950), *Ben and Me* (1953), *Adventures in Music: Melody* (1953), *Toot Whistle Plunk and Boom* (1953), *Spare the Rod* (1954), *No Hunting* (1955), *How to Have an Accident in the Home* (1956), *Duck for Hire* (1957), and *How to Have an Accident at Work* (1959). His Scottish dialect for the Scots terrier Jock in *Lady in the Tramp* is a marvelous piece of comedy without getting too farcical. A few months after voicing the inebriated goose Uncle Waldo in *The Aristocats,* Thompson died of a heart attack at the age of fifty-eight. Thompson's Professor Owl was revived after his death and used as the host for the popular series of *Disney Sing-Along* videos in the 1980s and 1990s.

Thompson, Emma (b. 1959) The highly-acclaimed British actress of stage and screen, she voiced the shrewd Captain Amelia of the spaceship *RLS Legacy* in *Treasure Planet* (2002). She was born in London, the daughter of actors Eric Thompson and Phyllida Law, and was educated at Cambridge University where she was a member of the Footlights Group. After working in radio, Thompson reunited with members of that troupe and began doing comedy skits on television, eventually having a TV special *Cambridge Footlights Revue* (1982). While Robbie Coltrane, Stephen Fry, Hugh Laurie, and others from the group went on to notable careers doing comedy, Thompson made a name for herself in serious roles in television dramas and movies. Among her many notable films (some with her then-husband Kenneth Branagh) are *The Tall Guy* (1989), *Henry V* (1989), *Impromptu* (1991), *Dead Again* (1991), *Howards End* (1992), *Peter's Friends* (1992), *Much Ado About Nothing* (1993), *The Remains of the Day* (1993), *In the Name of the Father* (1993), *Carrington* (1995), *Sense and Sensibility* (1995), *Primary Colors* (1998), *Love Actually* (2003), *Harry Potter and the Prisoner of Azkaban* (2004), *Nanny McPhee* (2005), *Harry Potter and the Order of the Phoenix* (2007), *Brideshead Revisited* (2008), and *Nanny McPhee Returns* (2010), and in many TV-movies, most memorably *Wit* (2001) and *Angels in America* (2003). Thompson occasionally appears on stage as well, as in the London musical *Me and My Girl* (1985), and she has written the scripts or screen adaptations for several of her films and for television. The character of Captain Amelia in *Treasure Planet* was written with Thompson in mind. Her ability to do the classics and contemporary works made her the filmmakers' first choice and, though it is not usually the case, they got their first choice. Biographies: *Emma: The Many Facets of Emma Thompson*, Chris Nickson (1997); *Ken & Em: A Biography of Kenneth Branagh and Emma Thompson*, Ian Shuttleworth (1995).

Tilly, Jennifer (b. 1958) The distinctive movie and television actress with a funny, sexy voice, she provided the voices of the Medusa-like monster Celia Mae in *Monsters, Inc.* (2001) and the clueless but cheerful cow Grace in *Home on the Range* (2004). She was born Jennifer E. Chan in Los Angeles, the daughter of a car salesman and a teacher, and at the age of five moved with her family to British Columbia, Canada. She was educated at Stephens College in Missouri then returned to California and began her television career in 1983, later finding success in the series *Hill Street Blues*. Tilly's other television credits include *It's Garry Shandling's Show, Key West, Moonlighting, Frasier, Out of Practice*, and *CSI: Crime Scene Investigation*, as well as doing voices for such cartoon series as *Pigs Next Door, Family Guy*, and *Hey, Arnold!* She made her film debut in 1984, was noticed for the first time in *The Fabulous Baker Boys* (1989), and received wide acclaim for her performance in *Bullets Over Broadway* (1994). Tilly also appeared in the movies *Let It Ride* (1989), *The Getaway* (1993), *Liar Liar* (1997), *Stuart Little* (1999), *The Cat's Meow* (2001), *The Haunted Mansion* (2003), *Inconceivable* (2008), and *Return to Babylon* (2008). She reprised her Grace in the cartoon short *A Dairy Tale* (2004) and can also be heard in the animated video *Bartok the Magnificent* (1999).

Tisdale, Ashley (b. 1985) A very popular teen actress, singer, and dancer in the new century, she began voicing animated characters when she was ten years old, providing the voice of the ant who is the Lead Blueberry Scout in *A Bug's Life* (1998). Ashley Michelle Tisdale was born in West Deal, New Jersey, and started doing commercials at the age of three. Before she was a teenager she toured in professional productions of *Les Misérables* and *Annie*, then started appearing in television sit-coms, eventually finding wide success in *The Suite Life of Zack and Cody* in 2006. Tisdale found even greater fame as the conniving drama queen Sharpay Evans in the TV-movie *High School Musical* (2005) and reprised the character in the sequels *High School Musical 2* (2007) and *High School Musical 3: Senior Year* (2008). She can be heard in the TV cartoon series *Kim Possible* and *Phineas and Ferb*, Biography: *Ashley Tisdale: Life Is Sweet!*, Grace Norwich (2006).

Tochi, Brian (b. 1959) An Asian American child performer who went on to a long and busy career in films and television, he provided the voice of the Fighting Hyena in *The Lion King* (1994). Brian Keith Tochi was born in Los Angeles and educated at the University of Southern California, UCLA, and the University of California at Irving. He made his television debut at the age of nine and as a boy appeared in such series as *Star Trek, The Brady Bunch, The Partridge Family, Nanny and the Professor, Anna and the King, The Streets of San Francisco, Kung Fu*, and *Marcus Welby, M.D.* Tochi graduated to adult roles in other series, including *Space Academy, Hawaii Five-O, Santa Barbara, Star Trek: The Next Generation*, and *Diagnosis Murder*, and in the 1990s concentrated on TV cartoons, doing voices for such series as *Mortal Kombat: Defenders of the Realm, The Real Adventures of Jonny Quest, Johnny Bravo, The Grim Adventures of Billy & Mandy, Static Shock, Family Guy, Duck Dodgers*, and *Avatar: The Last Airbender*. He was the voice of Leonardo in the three *Teenage Mutant Ninja Turtles* movies and can be heard in the animated films *The Prince of Egypt* (1998), *The Iron Giant* (1999), and *Mulan II* (2004). Tochi has appeared in many live-action films as well, including *The Omega Man* (1971), *The Octagon* (1980), *Revenge of the Nerds* (1984) and two of its video sequels, *Stitches* (1985), *Police Academy 3: Back in Training* (1986), *Police Academy 4: Citizens on Patrol* (1987), *Starship Troopers* (1997), *Fight Club* (1999), *The Boys of Sunset Ridge* (2001), *The Silent Force* (2001), and *Forgetting Sarah Marshall* (2008).

Tom, Lauren (b. 1961) An Asian American actress, singer-dancer, and voice artist with theatre, film, and television credits, she supplied the voice of Younghee, the school girl from Korea, in *Teacher's Pet* (2004). She was born in Chicago and studied dance as a girl, helping her get cast in the touring production of *A Chorus Line* when she was only seventeen years old. She eventually performed in the Broadway production as well, and was featured in such Off Broadway productions as *Family Devotions* (1981), *Non Pasquale* (1983), and *In a Pig's Valise* (1989). and on Broadway in *Doonesbury* (1983) and *Hurlyburly* (1984). Tom made her television debut on two episodes of *The Facts of Life* in 1982, followed by many other series such as *The Equalizer, thirtysomething, Homicide: Life on the Street, Chicago Hope, The Nanny, Grace Under Fire, The Division, My Wife and Kids, Barbershop*, and *Men in Trees*, but she is probably most remembered as Julie on *Friends*. Among her many film credits are *Nothing Lasts Forever* (1984), *Wall Street* (1987), *Cadillac Man* (1990), *The Joy Luck Club* (1993), *When a Man Loves a Woman* (1994), *North* (1994),

With Friends Like These (1998), *Susan's Plan* (1998), *Catfish in Black Bean Sauce* (1999), *Jack the Dog* (2001), *Manhood* (2003), *Bad Santa* (2003), *In Good Company* (2004), *God's Waiting List* (2006), and many TV-movies. In the 1990s, Tom began doing voices for TV cartoons and was heard in such series as *The New Batman Adventures, The Blues Brothers Animated Series, Extreme Ghostbusters, Superman, Teacher's Pet, Pepper Ann, Clerks, Batman Beyond, The Zeta Project, Totally Spies, Samurai Jack, Fillmore!, Kim Possible, Teen Titans, Clifford's Puppy Days, Justice League, Avatar: The Last Airbender, W.I.T.C.H., American Dragon: Jake Long, Codename: Kids Next Door, The Replacements, King of the Hill, Futurama*, and *Kung Fu Panda: Legends of Awesomeness.* Tom also voiced many animated films and videos, including *SubZero* (1998), *The Batman Superman Movie: World's Finest* (1998), *Batman Beyond: The Movie* (1999), *Batman Beyond: Return of the Joker* (2000), *The Wild Thornberrys Movie* (2002), *Kim Possible: The Secret Files* (2003), *Mulan II* (2004), *Kim Possible: So the Drama* (2005), *Codename: Kids Next Door — Operation Z.E.R.O.* (2006), *Bill & Mandy's Big Boogey Adventure* (2007), *The Grim Adventures of KND* (2007), and *Futurama: Bender's Big Score* (2007) and its sequels. She has written fiction, nonfiction, and her own one-woman theatre piece *25 Psychics* which was broadcast on HBO.

Tompkins, Paul F. (b. 1968) A genial comic on television and comedy records who has also acted in various films and series, he supplied the voice of the white-haired pub thug Shorty who dresses as Cupid in *Tangled* (2010). He was born in Philadelphia, the son of a railway worker, and attended Temple University for a time, then did stand-up comedy at The Comedy Works in his home town. Relocating to California, Tompkins found some recognition on the HBO program *Mr. Show with Bob and Dave* and frequently appeared on talk shows, variety programs, and specials on network and cable television. He played characters in such series as *Tenacious D, DAG, The Sarah Silverman Program, Pushing Daisies*, and *Weeds*, and appeared in such films as *Win a Date* (1998), *Anchorman: The Legend of Ron Burgundy* (2004), *There Will Be Blood* (2007), The *Informant!* (2009), and *Drones* (2010), as well as in some TV-movies. Tompkins has done voices for the cartoon series *King of the Hill, Atom TV*, and *Aqua Teen Hunger Force*.

Tondo, Jerry An Asian American stage actor in California who has made a handful of appearances in movies and on television, he voiced the giant but gentle Chinese recruit Chien-Po in *Mulan* (1998). Tondo hails from San Francisco where he participated in the Asian American Theatre before moving to Los Angles where he has been active in the East-West Players, Mark Taper Forum, and other area theatres. He has acted in such television series as *Brothers, Beauty and the Beast*, and *Trapper John, M.D.*, as well as some films, including *Gung Ho* (1986), *Ghost Warrior* (1986), *Scenes from the Class Struggle in Beverly Hills* (1989), *Circuitry Man* (1990), *It's Pat* (1994), *Drop Zone* (1994), and *Nick of Time* (1995). Tondo reprised his Chien-Po in *Mulan II* (2004) and has voiced characters in the TV cartoon series *The Secret Saturdays*.

Tootoosis, Gordon (b. 1941) A Native American actor and activist who has appeared in many films and television shows since the 1970s, he provided the voice of the aged shaman Kekata in *Pocahontas* (1995). He was born on the Poundmaker Reserve in Saskatchewan, Canada, a member of the Cree tribe and the son of John Tootoosis, a co-founder of the National Indian Brotherhood and head of the Federation of Saskatchewan Indian Nations, a position Gordon would later hold. He made his screen debut in *Alien Thunder* (1974), followed by such Hollywood and Canadian films as *Marie Ann* (1978), *Black Robe* (1991), *Leaving Normal* (1992), *Legends of the Fall* (1994), *Pocahontas: The Legend* (1995), *Lone Star* (1996), *Alaska* (1996), *Song of Hiawatha* (1997), *The Edge* (1997), *Bear with Me* (2000), *Reindeer Games* (2000), *Black Point* (2001), *Nobody's Baby* (2001), *The Doe Boy* (2001), *Now and Forever* (2002), *Fugitives Run* (2003), *Seven Times Lucky* (2004), *The Reawakening* (2004), *Hank Williams First Nation* (2005), *Juliana and the Medicine Fish* (2007), *Out in the Cold* (2008), and *The Closer You Get to Canada* (2010), as well as many made-for-TV movies, including *Stone Fox* (1987), *Last Train Home* (1990), *Blood River* (1991), *Lakota Moon* (1992), *Call of the Wild* (1993), *Crazy Horse* (1996), *DreamKeeper* (2003), *Cowboys and Indians: The J. J. Harper Story* (2003), *Bury My Heart at Wounded Knee* (2007), and *Blackstone* (2009). Tootoosis has acted in many television series and mini-series, such as *Red Sarge, Airwolf II, MacGyver, Northern Exposure, Lonesome Dove, Hawkeye, 500 Nations, The X Files, North of 60, MythQuest, Smallville, Into the West, Moccasin Flats, Hank Williams First Nation, Fear Itself, Wapos Bay*, and the British series *Auf Wiedersehen, Pet*.

Torn, Rip (b. 1931) An intense, unpredictable actor of stage, films, and television who is as volatile offscreen as on, he provided the commanding voice of Zeus in *Hercules* (1997). He was born Elmore Rual Torn, Jr., in Temple, Texas, and was educated at Texas A & M University and the University of Texas before working as an oil field roustabout and architectural draftsman. Torn eventually went to

New York City and studied acting with Sanford Meisner and Lee Strasberg and made an auspicious Broadway debut as a replacement for the role of Brick in *Cat on a Hot Tin Roof* in 1956. Over the next forty years he appeared in experimental plays Off Broadway and in American classics on Broadway, most memorably *Sweet Bird of Youth* (1959), *Desire Under the Elms* (1963), *Blues for Mister Charlie* (1964), *Dance of Death* (1971), *The Glass Menagerie* (1975), *Seduced* (1979), and *The Young Man from Atlanta* (1997). Torn made his film debut in 1956 and acted in several movies over the years, including *A Face in the Crowd* (1957), *Pork Chop Hill* (1959), *King of Kings* (1961), *Sweet Bird of Youth* (1962), *The Cincinnati Kid* (1965), *Cotter* (1973), *The Man Who Fell to Earth* (1976), *The Seduction of Joe Tynan* (1979), *Cross Creek* (1983), *Nadine* (1987), *RoboCop 3* (1993), *How to Make an American Quilt* (1995), *Freddy Got Fingered* (2001), *Marie Antoinette* (2006), and *American Cowslip* (2009), but he is best known for playing Chief Agent Zed in *Men in Black* (1997) and its two sequels. Among the dozens of television series he has acted in over the decades are *The Alcoa Hour, Playhouse 90, Alfred Hitchcock Presents, The Untouchables, Ben Casey, The Man from U.N.C.L.E., Dr. Kildare, The John Larroquette Show, The Larry Sanders Show, Will & Grace, The Lyon's Den,* and *30 Rock.* His tough, deep voice can be heard in the animated films *Bee Movie* (2007) and *Cat Tale* (2010). Actors Patrick Stewart, Gregory Peck, John Goodman, and James Belushi were among the stars considered to voice Zeus in *Hercules* but the directors decided on Torn because of his classical sounding (as opposed to contemporary) voice.

Travolta, John (b. 1954)   A popular heartthrob of the 1970s for his clowning on television and his disco dancing on screen, the handsome Italian-Irish actor has matured into a flexible performer who has developed a wide repertoire, including the voice of the canine action-hero Bolt in *Bolt* (2008). Travolta was born in Englewood, New Jersey, and dropped out of school at the age of sixteen to pursue a career in musicals in summer stock. He eventually got on Broadway as a replacement in *Grease* in 1972 and was featured in *Over Here!* (1974) before finding stardom in 1975 as a cute but dense high schooler in the television sit-com *Welcome Back, Kotter.* Travolta secured his fame on screen as the disco-crazy Tony Manero in *Saturday Night Fever* (1977) and as greaser Danny Zuko in *Grease* (1979), then suffered an up-and-down period with a series of flops in the 1980s. In the next decade he established himself as a durable film actor in a variety of roles and genres, in such diverse movies as *Look Who's Talking* (1989) and its two sequels, *Pulp Fiction* (1994), *Phenomenon* (1996), *Primary Colors* (1998), *The Thin Red Line* (1998), *A Love Song for Bobby Long* (2004), *Hairspray* (2007), *The Taking of Pelham 123* (2009), and *From Paris with Love* (2010). The canine Bolt is a curious hero for an animated film. He is a one-dimensional action hero at first but as the movie progresses he loses his artificial bluster and becomes more "human." Biographies: *John Travolta, King of Cool,* Wensley Clarkson (2005); *Fever! The Biography of John Travolta,* Douglas Thompson (1997).

Trousdale, Gary (b. 1960)   The acclaimed animator and director of animated features, he voiced the Old Heretic in *The Hunchback of Notre Dame* (1996). He was born in LaCrescenta, California, and educated at the California Institute of the Arts before beginning to work as an animator in the early 1980s. His first Disney project was *The Black Cauldron* (1985) for which he was an "in-between" artist. Trousdale also contributed to the storyboard for such movies as *Oliver & Company* (1988), *The Little Mermaid* (1989), *The Rescuers Down Under* (1990), and the featurette *The Prince and the Pauper* (1990). His direction of *Beauty and the Beast* (1991) with Kirk Wise put him in the top ranks of animation artists. Trousdale also directed *The Hunchback of Notre Dame, Atlantis: The Lost Empire* (2001), and the shorts *Cranium Command* (1989), *The Madagascar Penguins in a Christmas Caper* (2005), and *Shrek the Halls* (2007).

Trout, Dink (1898–1950)   A radio actor who appeared in a dozen feature films in the 1940s, his last performance was voicing the diminutive, put-upon King of Hearts in *Alice in Wonderland* (1951). He was born Francis Trout in Beardstown, Illinois, and began his career on the stage, making his Broadway debut in 1926. In the 1930s he found success on the radio, playing recurring characters on such shows as *Lum and Abner* and *The Dennis Day Show.* Trout made his first film in 1936 but didn't get noticed until *Scattergood Baines* (1941) in which he played the yokel Pliny Pickett. He reprised the character in *Scattergood Pulls the Strings* (1941) and *Cinderella Swings It* (1943). Trout's other movies include *Gildersleeve's Bad Day* (1943), *It's a Great Life* (1943), *Up in Arms* (1944), *The Doughgirls* (1944), *Irish Eyes Are Smiling* (1944), *The Horn Blows at Midnight* (1945), *Notorious* (1946) and *So Dear to My Heart* (1948). For the Disney short *Bootle Beetle* (1947), Trout did the voice for the clever little insect of the title who always hassles Donald Duck. He reprised the character in three cartoon sequels, *Sea Salts* (1949), *The Greener Yard* (1949), and *Morris the Midget Moose* (1950).

Truitt, Danielle Moné   An African American actress and singer who is also an acting coach, she voiced Tiana's New Orleans friend Georgia in *The Princess and the Frog* (2009). Truitt has appeared in the movies *Fugitive Hunter* (2005), *See Dick Run* (2009), and *Benny Bliss and the Disciples of Greatness* (2009).

Turner, Kathleen (b. 1954) The statuesque, sensual movie actress with a husky voice and a slithering persona, she brought her tongue-in-cheek sultriness to the role of the vampy Jessica Rabbit in *Who Framed Roger Rabbit* (1988). Mary Kathleen Turner was born in Springfield, Missouri, and educated at Southwest Missouri State, the University of Maryland, and the Central School of Speech and Drama in London. She made her New York stage debut in 1977 but soon found work in television and started making movies in 1981. Turner's sizzling performance in *Body Heat* (1981) made her a screen star and she has maintained her popularity through such films as *Romancing the Stone* (1984), *Peggy Sue Got Married* (1986), *The Accidental Tourist* (1988), *War of the Roses* (1989), *V. I. Warshawski* (1991), and *Marley & Me* (2008). She returned to Broadway as a star and was acclaimed for her performances in *Cat on a Hot Tin Roof* (1990), *Indiscretions* (1995), *The Graduate* (2002), and *Who's Afraid of Virginia Woolf?* (2005). Turner has acted in many television series and specials and she reprised her Jessica Rabbit for the film shorts *Tummy Trouble* (1989), *Roller Coaster Rabbit* (1990), and *Trail Mix-Up* (1993), and the video *The Best of Roger Rabbit* (1996). She can also be heard in the animated *Bad Baby* (1997), *National Geographic Kids: Creepy Creatures* (2000), and *Monster House* (2006), as well as on the TV cartoon series *The Simpsons*. The character of the sultry Jessica Rabbit, aside from being vampy and funny in a Mae West kind of way, is a breakthrough for animation: the first truly sensual animated character in a mainstream movie. Also like West, the sex is always mixed with humor so, in a way, Jessica is a satire of sensuality. (Other seductive movie stars that inspired the creators were Lauren Bacall, Rita Hayworth, and Veronica Lake.) Turner's alto speaking voice (Amy Irving did the character's singing) and her perfectly toned phrasing make Jessica a triumph of sound and movement. Memoir: *Send Yourself Roses: Thoughts on My Life, Love, and Leading Roles*, with Gloria Feldt (2008).

Turner, Timothy A child performer whose only film credit is providing the voice of the English lad Christopher Robin in the animated short *Winnie the Pooh and Tigger Too* (1974), his performance was used again in the compilation feature *The Many Adventures of Winnie the Pooh* (1977).

Twillie, Carmen (b. 1950) An African American singer-actress who has sung on and off screen for several movies, she sang solo on the inspiring opening number "Circle of Life" on the soundtrack of *The Lion King* (1994) and voiced the finned creature Undersea Gal in *The Nightmare Before Christmas* (1993). Twillie has sung with various choirs and as a studio singer recorded with Pink Floyd and other artists. She can be heard singing in the animated films and videos *The Swan Princess* (1994), *Beauty and the Beast: The Enchanted Christmas* (1997), *An All Dogs Christmas Carol* (1998), *Rudolph the Red-Nosed Reindeer: The Movie* (1998), *The Tigger Movie* (2000), *The Flintstones: On the Rocks* (2001), and *The Lion King 1½* (2004), as well as the TV cartoon series *All Dogs Go to Heaven: The Series* and *Chowder*. Twillie appeared as well as sang in the films and TV-movies *Solar Crisis* (1990), *Mobsters* (1991), *Vampire in Brooklyn* (1995), *A Walton Easter* (1997), *Dark Blue* (2002), *National Lampoon's Gold Diggers* (2003), *30 Days Till I'm Famous* (2004), *Norbit* (2007), and *License to Wed* (2007), and in the television series *My So-Called Life* and *Nothing Sacred*.

Tyler, Ginny (b. 1932) A voice artist most adept at voicing non-speaking animals, she provided the sounds of the Little Girl Squirrel in *The Sword in the Stone* (1963), the baa-ing of the lambs in the animated sequence of *Mary Poppins* (1964), and the buzzing of the bees in the short *Winnie the Pooh and the Honey Tree* (1966). A native of Seattle, Washington, Tyler made her television debut doing voices for *The Gumby Show* in 1957, followed by such animated series as *The Huckleberry Hound Show*, *Davey and Goliath*, *The New Casper Cartoon Show*, *Space Ghost*, *The Adventures of Gulliver*, *The Fantastic Four*, and *Fred Fintstone and Friends*. She can be heard on the videos *Casper the Friendly Ghost: He Ain't Scary, He's Our Brother* (1979) and *Brer Rabbit's Christmas Carol* (1992), and supplied voices for the movies *Son of Flubber* (1963) and *Doctor Dolittle* (1967).

Unkrich, Lee (b. 1967) A Pixar editor and director who sometimes supplies voices for minor characters in his projects, he was the voice of the red Rock 'Em Sock 'Em Robot in *Toy Story 2* (1999) and the toy Jack in the Box in *Toy Story 3* (2010). Lee Edward Unkrich was born in Cleveland, Ohio, raised in Chagrin Falls, Ohio, and educated at the University of Southern California School of Cinema & Television. After serving as editor for the TV cartoon series *Renegade* he became supervising editor for the films *A Bug's Life* (1998), *Monsters, Inc.* (2001), *Finding Nemo* (2003), and *Cars* (2006). Unkrich was also co-director for *Toy Story 2*, *Monsters, Inc.*, *Finding Nemo*, and solo director for *Toy Story 3* (2010) which he co-wrote. He can be heard doing additional voices in *Monsters, Inc.*, and *Finding*

Nemo. His daughter **Hannah Unkrich** provided the voice for Andy's little sister Molly Davis in *Toy Story 2*.

Ustinov, Peter (1921–2004)   An internationally acclaimed actor, playwright, director, novelist, screenwriter, and raconteur, he voiced both the temperamental lion Prince John and the regal lion King Richard in *Robin Hood* (1973). He was born Peter Alexander Freiherr von Ustinov of Russian, French, Italian, and Ethiopian descent in London, the son of immigrants who fled the Russian Revolution. He grew up speaking several languages, was educated at Westminster School, and trained at the London Theatre Studio before getting work in stock companies. Ustinov made his London stage debut in 1939 and quickly established himself as a very versatile performer with many voices and capable of several different dialects. He began his film career the next year and, while never a leading man, he became an international star as a character actor. Among his notable English-language movies are *Quo Vadis* (1951), *We're No Angels* (1955), *Spartacus* (1960), *Topkapi* (1964), *Viva Max* (1969), *The Treasure of Matecumbe* (1976), *Death on the Nile* (1978), *Evil Under the Sun* (1982), and *Luther* (2003). Ustinov appeared on Broadway in four plays that he wrote and he acted in many television specials and series. He voiced the narration and all the characters in the animated television specials *The Story of Babar, the Little Elephant* (1968) and *Babar Comes to America* (1971) and he can also be heard in *The Mouse and His Child* (1977), *Metamorphoses* (1978), *Tarka the Otter* (1979), *Grendel Grendel Grendel* (1981), *Peep and the Big Wide World* (1988), *The Phoenix and the Magic Carpet* (1995), and *Animal Farm* (1999), as well as the animated series *Doctor Snuggles*. Ustinov's amazing vocal talents can be witnessed in *Robin Hood* where he came up with a thin, sniveling voice for the cowardly Prince John and a deep, commanding one for King Richard. Autobiography: *Dear Me* (1977); biography: *Peter Ustinov: The Gift of Laughter*, John Miller (2003).

Van Rooten, Luis (1906–1973)   A bald-headed character actor whose specialty was playing ethnic types, he did the voices of the quarreling King and the Grand Duke in *Cinderella* (1950). Luis D'Antin Van Rooten was born in Mexico City, Mexico, and grew up in the States where he studied to be an architect at the University of Pennsylvania. After serving in World War II, he turned to the theatre, performing at the Cleveland Playhouse, and then to radio where he voiced many comedies and dramas, including the title character in the series *The Adventures of Nero Wolfe*. In Hollywood, where Van Rooten was usually cast as foreigners, he was featured in such movies as *The Hitler Gang* (1944), *Two Years Before the Mast* (1946), *To the Ends of the Earth* (1948), *Night Has a Thousand Eyes* (1948), *Champion* (1949), *Detective Story* (1951), *My Favorite Spy* (1951), and *The Sea Chase* (1955). Starting in the 1950s he concentrated on television, appearing in dozens of serious and comic series, including *One Man's Family*, *Inner Sanctum*, *The Honeymooners*, *The Loretta Young Show*, *Gunsmoke*, *Perry Mason*, *77 Sunset Strip*, *Peter Gunn*, and *The Defenders*, but his most memorable role was Knobby Walsh in the boxing series *The Joe Palooka Story*. Van Rooten returned to the stage on occasion, appearing on Broadway in *The Number* (1951), *A Touch of the Poet* (1958), and *Luther* (1963), and he wrote three books of comic nonfiction.

Varney, Jim (1949–2000)   A popular character actor who specialized in comic rednecks and goofy country folk, he provided the voice of the easygoing Slinky Dog toy in *Toy Story* (1995) and *Toy Story 2* (1999). Born in Lexington, Kentucky, Varney possessed a high IQ and was able to memorize and mimic television cartoon characters at a young age. By the time he was seventeen he was performing professionally in comedy clubs and acting in various theatres. Going to Nashville, he worked as a comic on local television and in nightclubs where he created the character of Ernest P. Worrell, a raspy-voiced hick whose catch phrase was "KnowhutImean?" As Ernest, Varney eventually became nationally known from network television shows and commercials and he first played his alter-ego on screen in *Ernest Goes to Camp* (1987). Many film sequels followed, as well as television appearances. Ernest became the spokesman for different companies and products and even hosted several *Disneyland* specials. Varney played other roles beside Ernest but most were in a similar vein, such as Evan Earp in both the TV-movie *Rousters* (1983) and the television series, Seaman "Doom and Gloom" Broom in the series *Operation Petticoat*, and Jed Clampett in the film *The Beverly Hillbillies* (1993). He provided the voice of the crusty Jebidiah Allardyce "Cookie" Farnsworth in the Disney animated feature *Atlantis: The Lost Empire* (2001) which came out the year after Varney died of lung cancer. Varney's friend Blake Clark voiced Slinky Dog in *Toy Story 3* (2010).

Venable, Evelyn (1913–1993)   A statuesque beauty who graced two dozen films in the 1930s, she supplied the voice of the Blue Fairy in *Pinocchio* (1940). She was born in Cincinnati, Ohio, and educated at Vassar College and the University of Cincinnati. Venable played leading ladies in Walter Hampden's distinguished theatre company on tour and acted opposite Hampden on Broadway in *Cyrano de Bergerac* in 1932. The next year she made her film debut in *The Cradle Song*, followed by featured roles in such movies as *David Harum* (1934), *Death Takes a Holiday* (1934), *Mrs. Wiggs of the Cabbage Patch* (1934), *The County Chairman* (1935), *The Little Colonel* (1935), *Harmony Lane* (1935), *Vagabond Lady* (1935), *My Old Kentucky Home* (1938), *The Frontiersmen* (1938), and *Lucky Cisco Kid* (1940). After filming *He Hired the Boss* (1943), she retired from show business to raise a family then returned to college, getting a graduate degree at UCLA where she remained as an instructor and director of classic theatre productions. Legend has it that Venable was the model for the Columbia Pictures logo. Disney wanted the role of the Blue Fairy in *Pinocchio* to be beautiful but not glamorous. Dancer Marge Belcher (later film performer Marge Champion), who was the movement model for Snow White, also posed for the Blue Fairy.

von Detten, Erik (b. 1982) An impressive leading man in television with several film credits as well, he supplied the voice of the sadistic neighbor boy Sid Phillips who tortures toys in *Toy Story* (1995). He was born in San Diego, California, and made his film debut at the age of nine. Von Detten played kids and teenagers in *All I Want for Christmas* (1991), *Top Dog* (1995), *Amanda* (1996), and *Leave It to Beaver* (1997), as well as in such TV-movies as *Night Sins* (1993), *A Season of Hope* (1995), *Kidnapped: In the Line of Duty* (1995), *Escape to Witch Mountain* (1995), *A Stranger to Love* (1996), *Things That Go Bump* (1997), *Brink!* (1998), and *Replacing Dad* (1999). He grew up on television, playing recurring roles in *Days of Our Lives*, *Odd Man Out*, *So Weird*, and *Dinotopia*, although he is best remembered as the teenage jock Chris Savage on *Complete Savages*. Von Detten also acted in such series as *ER*, *7th Heaven*, *Meego*, *Raising Dad*, *8 Simple Rules*, *Malcolm in the Middle*, and *Bones*, and he graduated to adult roles in the movies *The Princess Diaries* (2001), *American Girl* (2002), and *Smile* (2005). He started doing voice work when he was twelve and can be heard in the television cartoon series *Life with Louie*, *Recess*, *The Legend of Tarzan*, *Brandy & Mr. Whiskers*, *Avatar: The Last Airbender*, and *Family Guy*, as well as the animated movies and videos *Hercules* (1997), *Tarzan* (1999), and *Recess: School's Out* (2001) and its two sequels. Legend has it that the character of the malicious Sid Phillips in *Toy Story* was based on a Pixar employee also named Phillips who liked to take apart toys and create odd new creatures. He no longer worked at the studio by the time *Toy Story* was made. Sid joins the ranks of one of the most evil of all Disney villains even though he is still a kid. Von Detten reprised his Sid in a cameo role in *Toy Story 3* (2010); Sid is the garbage man picking up the trash outside Andy's house and he still wears the black skull T-shirt from the first movie.

von Oÿ, Jenna (b. 1977) A child actress of television and movies who also is a voice artist and a country music singer, she provided the voice of teenager Stacey, Roxanne's friend and the one who gets her together with Max, in *A Goofy Movie* (1995). She was born Jennifer Jean Von Oÿ in Danbury, Connecticut, and educated at the University of Southern California. She made her television debut at the age of six and as a teenager was a regular on the series *Lenny*, but she is better known as Six LeMeure on *Blossom* for five years and as Stevie Van Lowe on *The Parkers* for five years. Von Oÿ's film credits include *Born on the Fourth of July* (1989), *Turnaround* (2002), and *Dr. Dolittle 3* (2006). She can be heard on the TV cartoon series *Pepper Ann*, *What's with Andy?*, and *Family Guy*.

Vowell, Sarah (b. 1969) A journalist, writer, and radio commentator, she supplied the voice of the super-hero teenager Violet Parr who can disappear and reappear at will in *The Incredibles* (2004). She was born in Muskogee, Oklahoma, was raised in Montana, and was educated at Montana State University and the School of the Art Institute of Chicago. Vowell has reported on various aspects of contemporary life in newspapers, magazines, and radio talk shows and she is most known for her commentary on the PBS radio series *This American Life*. She has been on different television talk shows as well and appeared as a character on the series *Six Degrees* and *Bored to Death*. Vowell is the author of several nonfiction books about a wide range of topics. The idea for the character of Violet in *The Incredibles* came from the comic book superhero Invisible Woman. Director Brad Bird heard Vowell's voice on public radio and thought it perfect for Violet even though the commentator had never acted before. To convince her to take the part, Bird animated a sequence using Vowell's radio voice and sent it to her to watch.

Wahlgren, Kari (b. 1977) A busy voice actress who has provided a variety of voices for over 300 TV cartoon episodes, American versions of *anime* films, and video games, she played the opinionated television network executive Mindy in *Bolt* (2008). She was born in Hoisington, Kansas, and educated at the University of Kansas before appearing on stage in regional theatres. Wahlgren began doing voice work in 1991 when she did the American soundtrack for a Japanese animated film and she went on to provide voices for dozens of others, including many video games based on *anime* characters. She can also be heard in the American cartoon series *Maya & Miguel*, *Curious George*, *American*

Dragon: Jake Long, Super Robot Monkey Team Hyperforce Go!, Kim Possible, The Grim Adventures of Billy and Mandy, Ben 10, Legion of Super-Heroes, Stitch!, Wolverine and the X-Men, Phineas and Ferb, The Life & Times of Tim, and *Kung Fu Pandas: Legends of Awesomeness.* Wahlgren did voices for such movies and videos as *Star Wars: Episode II: Revenge of the Sith* (2005), *The Incredible Hulk: Ultimate Destruction* (2005), *James Bond 007: From Russia with Love* (2005), *Star Wars: Empires at War* (2006), *Spy Hunter: Nowhere to Run* (2006), *Spider-Man 3* (2007), *Shrek the Third* (2007), *The Golden Compass* (2007), *The Little Mermaid: Ariel's Beginnings* (2008), *Prince of Persia* (2008), and *Tangled* (2010).

Wallace, Oliver (1887–1963)   One of Disney's most prolific and accomplished composers and music arrangers, he lent his voice only once to an animated film: as the bar owner Mr. Winky in "The Wind in the Willows" section of *The Adventures of Ichabod and Mr. Toad* (1949). The London-born Wallace received his musical training in England but began his career in California conducting orchestras for silent movies. With the advent of sound he was quickly in demand for composing and arranging music. In 1936 Wallace began working for the Disney studios where he composed and/or supervised the music for hundreds of animated shorts and such features as *Dumbo* (1941) *Cinderella* (1950), *Alice in Wonderland* (1951). and *Peter Pan* (1953). The character of Mr. Winky does not appear in Kenneth Grahame's book *The Wind in the Willows* and in the movie it is a small role but a funny one. The finicky tavern owner sports a Hercule Poirot–like mustache and when he testifies in court he can't help but keep polishing the "bar."

Wallis, Michael (b. 1945)   An historian and a writer about the American Midwest, he provided the voice of the patrol car Sheriff of the small town of Radiator Springs in *Cars* (2006). He was born in St. Louis, Missouri, and educated at the University of Missouri in Columbia before going to work for *Time* magazine. Wallis has written over fifteen books on Americana, covering such historical figures as Davy Crockett, Billy the Kid, and oilman Frank Phillips, as well as many articles for various magazines. His book *Route 66: The Mother Road* (1990) was an important reference source for *Cars* so co-directors John Lasseter and Joe Ranft and some of the production team toured Route 66 with Wallis looking for towns that would serve as the model for Radiator Springs. Wallis' commentary on the trip inspired them to have him do a voice in the film. He reprised his Sheriff in the videos *Mater and the Ghostlight* (2006) and *Tokyo Mater* (2008).

Wallis, Shani (b. 1933)   A bright-eyed British actress-singer of stage, screen, and television, she provided the voice of the alluring Lady Mouse in *The Great Mouse Detective* (1986). She was born in London and was on the stage at the age of four, singing in music halls and acting in plays. After studying at the Royal Academy of Dramatic Art, Wallis was featured in such West End musicals as *Call Me Madam* (1952), *Wonderful Town* (1955), *Finian's Rainbow* (1958), and *Irma La Douce* (1960). She made her Broadway debut in *A Time for Singing* (1966) then two years later shone as Nancy in the film version of *Oliver!* Her other movie credits include *A King in New York* (1957), *Terror in the Wax Museum* (1973), *Round Numbers* (1992), and *Mojave Phone Booth* (2006). Wallis has appeared on American television series since 1965, acting in such shows as *Night Gallery, Gunsmoke, Charlie's Angels, Columbo,* and *The Young and the Restless*.

Walmsley, Jon (b. 1956)   A British child performer who found success on American television, he provided the voice of the English lad Christopher Robin in the short *Winnie the Pooh and the Blustery Day* (1968) and in the compilation feature *The Many Adventures of Winnie the Pooh* (1977). He was born in Blackburn, England, but grew up in the States, making his television debut on an episode of *Combat!* in 1966, and made a notable screen bow as one of the Bower family children in the movie musical *The One and Only, Genuine, Original Family Band* (1968). Appearances in such sit-coms as *My Three Sons* and *The Bill Cosby Show* followed until he found wide recognition as the youth Jason Walton on *The Waltons* in 1971. Walmsley stayed with the series for ten years and acted in all the subsequent *The Waltons* television specials and reunion shows. After the 1980s he concentrated on composing and singing music, appearing in various bands, and occasionally doing voice work, as in the animated videos *Elf Sparkle Meets the Christmas Horse* (2009) and *Elf Sparkle and the Special Red Dress* (2010).

Walton, Mark (b. 1968)   A Disney story artist who has provided voices on occasion, he voiced Barry and Bob, the two over-sexed longhorns who flirt with the dairy cows, in *Home on the Range* (2004), the friendly goose Goosey Loosey in *Chicken Little* (2005), and the hilarious, over-enthusiastic hamster Rhino in *Bolt* (2008). Walton was born in Salt Lake City, Utah, and educated at Utah State University for an art career. By 1999 he was working for Disney on the story boards and characters for such animated films as *Tarzan* (1999), *Home on the Range, Chicken Little,* and *Meet the Robinsons* (2007), as well as the TV cartoon series

Independent Lens. The character of Rhino in *Bolt* was based on producer John Lasseter's pet chinchilla who ran around the house in a plastic ball. The pet and his ball were studied at the studio in order to animate Rhino's movements in the film. The hyperactive hamster turned out to be the comic hit of *Bolt* and one of the funniest sidekicks in recent Disney films. Walton reprised his Rhino in the movie short *Super Rhino* (2009).

Waltrip, Darrell (b. 1947) A championship race car driver, winner of the Winston Cup on three occasions, he provided the voice of the race track commentator Darrell Cartrip in *Cars* (2006). A native of Owensboro, Kentucky, he tied for third in NASCAR's all-time win list. Since retiring, Waltrip has been a broadcaster for NASCAR on the Fox Network.

Warburton, Patrick (b. 1964) A muscular, deep-voiced comic actor of television and film, he has voiced many TV cartoons and played Yzma's thick-headed but lovable henchman Kronk in *The Emperor's New Groove* (2000) and the Alien Cop in *Chicken Little* (2005). He was born in Patterson, New Jersey, the son of an orthopedic surgeon and an actress, and grew up in Huntington Beach, California, where he studied marine biology at Orange Coast College for a time. Warburton then took up modeling, doing commercials, and acting. After appearing in a dozen different television sit-coms he found success as David Puddy on *Seinfeld*. His subsequent television credits include *NewsRadio*, *The Tick*, *8 Simple Rules*, *Less Than Perfect*, and *Rules of Engagement*. Warburton has appeared in a number of movies, such as *The Woman Chaser* (1999), *Scream 3* (2000), *Joe Somebody* (2001), *Men in Black II* (2002), *Get Smart* (2008), and *Made for Each Other* (2009), but he has been more occupied as a voice artist, heard in over 200 TV cartoon episodes, including *Hercules*, *Teacher's Pet*, *Buzz Lightyear of Star Command*, *The X's*, *Kim Possible*, *Robot Chicken*, *Tak & the Power of Juju*, *The Emperor's New School*, *The Venture Bros.*, and *Family Guy*. He reprised his Kronk for the sequel *The Emperor's New Groove 2: Kronk's New Groove* (2005) and he can also be heard in such animated movies and videos as *Buzz Lightyear of Star Command: The Adventure Begins* (2000), *Kim Possible: The Secret Files* (2003), *Home on the Range* (2004), *Hoodwinked!* (2005), *Sky High* (2005), *Open Season* (2006), *Happily N'Ever After* (2006), *Underdog* (2007), *Bee Movie* (2007), *Space Chimps* (2008), and *Hoodwinked Too! Hood vs. Evil* (2010).

Waring, Fred (1900–1984) The long-popular choral director who, with his Pennsylvanians, became known as the Man Who Taught America How to Sing, he and his famous chorale sang the "Trees" section of *Melody Time* (1948). Frederick Malcolm Waring was born in Tyrone, Pennsylvania, and as a teenager started Fred Waring's Banjo Orchestra which continued to perform while he attended Pennsylvania State University where he studied electrical engineering. The band became so popular he left college and led his group to radio jobs and eventually records. Adding a male chorus to the group made Waring even more popular, particularly during World War II when they performed at bond rallies and training camps. After the war, female singers were added and the group became Fred Waring and the Pennsylvanians, appearing on its own radio and television shows. Waring did not invent the electric blender that bears his name, but he financed and promoted it as the Waring Blendor. Memoir: *Fred Waring and the Pennsylvanians*, Virginia Waring (his wife), (2007).

Watanabe, Gedde (b. 1955) An Asian American actor and singer with many television and film credits, he provided the speaking voice of the Chinese recruit Ling in *Mulan* (1998). He was born Gary Watanabe in Ogden, Utah, and grew up in San Francisco where he studied at the American Conservatory Theatre. He first worked on the New York stage, was featured in the Broadway production of *Pacific Overtures* (1976) and Off Broadway in *Dispatches* (1979) and *Poor Little Lambs* (1982), then went to Hollywood where he first gained attention as the Korean Long Duk Dong in the film *Sixteen Candles* (1984). Watanabe's other screen credits include *Gung Ho* (1986), *The Spring* (1989), *Gremlins 2: The New Batch* (1990), *Boys on the Side* (1995), *That Thing You Do!* (1996), *Psycho Sushi* (1997), *Armageddon* (1998), *Guinevere* (1999), *Slackers* (2002), *Alfie* (2004), *Fortune Hunters* (2007), *The Onion Movie* (2008), *Not Forgotten* (2009), and *All Ages Night* (2009). Among the television series he has been on are *Gung Ho!*, *Sesame Street*, *Murphy Brown*, *Newhart*, *Down Home*, *Seinfeld*, *Home Improvement*, and *Sabrina, the Teenage Witch*, but he is most remembered as Nurse Yosh Takata on *ER* for six seasons. He is an accomplished singer but his vocals were considered too trained for the Chinese recruit in *Mulan* so his singing was dubbed by the songs' composer Matthew Wilder. Watanabe reprised his Ling in the video *Mulan II* (2004) and can be heard on the TV cartoon series *Duckman: Private Dick/Family Man*, *Happily Ever After: Fairy Tales for Every Child*, *Rugrats*, *The Simpsons*, *Batman Beyond*, *Family Guy*, *Kim Possible*, and *American Dad*, as well as the videos *The Wacky Adventures of Ronald McDonald: The Visitors from Outer Space* (1999), *Kim Possible: The Secret Files* (2003), and *Scooby-Doo and the Samurai Sword* (2009).

Watson, Allan   A baritone singer who sang on and off screen in a dozen movies in the 1930s and 1940s, he provided the voices of the roly-poly title characters in the Silly Symphony shorts *King Neptune* (1932) and *Santa's Workshop* (1932). Watson can be heard singing on the soundtracks for the live-action movies *Servants' Entrance* (1934) and *Maytime* (1937), and appeared as a singer in *Delicious* (1931), *The Great Ziegfeld* (1936), *Born to Dance* (1936), *Minstrel Days* (1941), *Du Barry Was a Lady* (1943), *Two Girls and a Sailor* (1944), *Bathing Beauty* (1944), and *The Spanish Main* (1945).

Weaver, Blayne (b. 1976)   An actor, writer, and director with a varied set of credits in film and television, he provided the voice of the forever-young Peter Pan in *Return to Never Land* (2002). Blayne Nutron Weaver was born in Bossier City, Louisiana, and while still in high school was cast in the TV-movie *The Flood: Who Will Save Our Children?* (1993). He studied English and Political Science at UCLA and continued acting in television, appearing on the series *JAG*, *Chicago Hope*, *ER*, *The King of Queens*, *MDs*, *NCIS*, and *The Middleman*, as well as the made-for-television movies *The Good Old Boys* (1995) and *Winchell* (1998). Weaver wrote and acted in the films *Maniac* (2001), *Losing Lois Lane* (2004), *Outside Sales* (2006), *Weather Girl* (2009), and *6 Month Rule* (2010), directing the last four as well. He reprised his Peter Pan in the videos *Mickey's Magical Christmas: Snowed in at the House of Mouse* (2001) and *The Lion King 1½* (2004), as well as in the TV cartoon series *House of Mouse*.

Weaver, Dennis (1924–2006)   A popular television actor on the small screen for over fifty years and a veteran of many movies, his last screen credit was providing the voice of the old rancher Abner whose cows are stolen by Alameda Slim in *Home on the Range* (2004). He was born William Dennis Weaver in Joplin, Missouri, educated at the University of Oklahoma, and was an Olympic athlete before becoming a professional actor. He moved to New York City and made his Broadway debut in *Come Back, Little Sheba* (1950) as he was studying at the Actors Studio. Relocating to Hollywood, Weaver appeared in a handful of Westerns between 1952 and 1955 then he found fame as the crusty sidekick Chester Goode on the television series *Gunsmoke*. He remained on the show for nine years then appeared on several other series such as *Dragnet*, *Kentucky Jones*, *Pearl*, *Emerald Point N.A.S.*, *Buck James*, *Lonesome Dove: The Series*, and *Wildfire*, but he was mostly known for his series *McCloud*. Weaver also starred in one of the first made-for-TV movies, the cult favorite *Duel* (1971), followed by many other television films.

Weaver, Doodles (1911–1983)   A wacky radio and television personality with freckles and big ears who also made films and comedy records, he can be heard in three Disney shorts: as various Radio Voices in *Duck Pimples* (1945), the Narrator in the Goofy cartoon *Hockey Homicide* (1945), and the Radio Commentator in *Tennis Racquet* (1949). He was born Winstead Sheffield Weaver in Los Angeles and was educated at Stanford University where he entertained fellow students with his weird animal sounds and practical jokes. He first found recognition in the late 1930s on the radio performing on Rudy Vallee's show and the *Kraft Music Hall*. In 1946 he joined Spike Jones' City Slickers comedy band and as Professor Feitlebaum did comic sports narration and made hilarious noises and comments during songs on radio, television, and on records. Weaver had his own children's television show in Los Angeles then later appeared on national programs in a series of syndicated shorts titled *A Day with Doodles Weaver*. He played character parts in many movies, including *My American Wife* (1936), *A Yank at Oxford* (1938), *Another Thin Man* (1939), *Li'l Abner* (1940), *A Girl, a Guy, and a Gob* (1941), *Reveille with Beverly* (1943), *The Story of Dr. Wassell* (1944), *Carolina Blues* (1944), *Hot Rod Gang* (1958), *Frontier Gun* (1958), *The Rookie* (1959), *The Errand Boy* (1961), *The Nutty Professor* (1963), *Mail Order Bride* (1964), *The Rounders* (1965), *The Road to Nashville* (1967), *The Spirit Is Willing* (1967), *Cancel My Reservation* (1972), *Fugitive Lovers* (1975), *White House Madness* (1975), *The Wild McCullochs* (1975), and *Earthbound* (1981). Weaver also appeared in several television series, including *The Spike Jones Show*, *Maverick*, *Sugarfoot*, *Lawman*, *Have Gun—Will Travel*, *The Donna Reed Show*, *The Andy Griffith Show*, *Laredo*, *Batman*, *My Three Sons*, *Daniel Boone*, *Dragnet 1967*, *Bonanza*, *Starsky and Hutch*, and *Fantasy Island*. Weaver's later years were overshadowed by chronic alcoholism and he committed suicide at the age of seventy-one. His niece is actress Sigourney Weaver.

Weaver, Jackson (1920–1992)   A radio personality and voice artist with only one animated character, but an important one: Smokey the Bear in the Humphrey the Bear animated short *In the Bag* (1956). He was born in New York City and began doing radio in the late 1930s. When the Advertising Council, the media's public service organization, created the character of the gruff but sincere Smokey the Bear in 1947, Weaver provided the voice for the radio and television commercials about fire prevention and continued to do so for three decades, including the 1969 TV cartoon series *Smokey the Bear*. In 1958 he moved to Washington, D.C., where he did a morning radio show with

Frank Harden for thirty-four years, broadcasting up until six days before he died. His only other television credit was an appearance in an episode of *The Big Valley* in 1966.

Weaver, Jason (b. 1979)   An African American actor-singer who has been a professional since his teen years, he provided the singing voice of the young lion cub Simba in *The Lion King* (1994). He was born in Chicago, the son of singer Kitty Haywood, and made his television debut in the made-for-TV movie *The Kid Who Loved Christmas* (1990) and then was featured on the series *Brewster Place, Thea, Smart Guy,* and *Sister, Sister*. Weaver's most acclaimed television performance was playing young Michael Jackson in the TV-movie *The Jacksons: An American Dream* (1992). Among his film credits are *The Long Walk Home* (1990), *The Ladykillers* (2004), *ATL* (2006), and *Love for Sale* (2008). Weaver is also a popular singer who has recorded chart-making albums.

Weaver, Sigourney (b. 1949)   A cool, dark-haired beauty of stage and screen who excels at playing strong, independent women, she provided the voice of the ship's computer in *WALL-E* (2008). She was born Susan Alexander Weaver in New York City, the daughter of a television executive and an actress, and received a superior education at Sarah Lawrence College, Stanford University, and Yale University, performing at the last institution before and after graduation. She made her Manhattan stage debut in 1976 and her screen bow the next year, but it was her performance as Ripley in the sci-fi horror movie *Alien* (1979) that made her famous and she reprised the role in the three sequels. Weaver was featured in such popular films as *The Year of Living Dangerously* (1982), *Ghostbusters* (1984) and its sequel *Ghostbusters II* (1989), *Working Girl* (1988), *Gorillas in the Mist: The Story of Dian Fossey* (1988), *Dave* (1993), *Holes* (2003), *The Village* (2004), and *Avatar* (2009). She returned to the New York stage on occasion and also acted in some television dramas and series. Weaver's voice can be heard in the animated movies and videos *Rabbit Ears: Peachboy* (1993), *The Wild Swans* (1994), *Snow White: A Tale of Terror* (1997), *Happily N'Ever After* (2006), and *The Tale of Despereaux* (2008). Biographies: *Sigourney Weaver*, T. D. Maguffee (1989); *Sigourney Weaver*, Robert Sellers (1992).

Weinger, Scott (b. 1975)   A young, personable, and busy television actor, his most famous role remains the speaking voice of Aladdin in the original 1992 film and its sequels and TV cartoon series. Scott Eric Weinger was born in New York City, the son of an orthopedic surgeon and a teacher, and grew up in Florida and Southern California where he started doing television commercials as a boy. As a teenager he appeared in the television series *Life Goes On, The Family Man,* and *Full House*. At the age of sixteen he first voiced Aladdin, later reprising his performance in the videos *The Return of Jafar* (1994), *Aladdin and the King of Thieves* (1995), *Aladdin's Arabian Adventures* (1998), *Aladdin's Math Quest* (1998), *Aladdin in Nasira's Revenge* (2001), *Mickey's House of Villains* (2001), *Kingdom Hearts I* and *II* (2002 and 2005), and *Jasmine's Enchanted Tales: Journey of a Princess* (2005), as well as the animated TV series *Aladdin* and *House of Mouse*. Scott left acting to receive an education at Harvard University, then returned to show business as a writer and producer, although he still acts in films and on television. He can also be heard in the animated movie *Metoroporisu* (2001) and the video *Farce of the Penguins* (2006). The original Aladdin in folk literature is a young boy in China. The studio wanted to reset the tale in Arabia but kept Aladdin as a thirteen-year-old through much of the movie's development. It was finally decided Aladdin needed to be older, more independent, and rougher; in fact, they saw him as a kind of Indiana Jones character. After auditioning many actors, Weinger was cast and managed to make Aladdin young and appealing even as he was a bit of a playful ruffian.

Weinrib, Lennie (1935–2006)   A prolific voice artist for television cartoons who was also a writer of such shows and a director of teen movies, he provided the voices of the Secretary Bird and the soccer-playing lion King Leonidas in the animated portion of *Bedknobs and Broomsticks* (1971). He was born in the Bronx, New York, and began his career as a stand-up comic. When in California he was cast in the satiric stage musical *Billy Barnes Revue* which transferred to Broadway in 1959. That same year Weinrib started voicing TV cartoons and appearing on live-action series, such as *Peter Gunn, The Spike Jones Show, Alfred Hitchcock Presents, My Favorite Martian, The Dick Van Dyke Show, Laredo,* and *Love, American Style*. Among his many television cartoon credits are *Doctor Dolittle, The Amazing Chan and the Chan Clan, The Flintstones Show, Yogi's Gang, Wait Till Your Father Gets Home, The New Tom and Jerry Show, The New Adventures of Batman, Scooby-Doo and Scrappy-Doo, Voltron: Defender of the Universe, Adventures of the Gummi Bears, The Flintstone Kids, Garfield and Friends,* and *Yo Yogi!*, but he is most known for voicing the title character in the live-action series *H. R. Pufnstuf* which he wrote. In the 1960s Weinrib took up directing movies for a time and helmed the teen flicks *Beach Ball* (1965), *Wild Wild Winter* (1966), and *Out of Sight* (1966).

Weintraub, Carl (b. 1946) A character actor mostly on television since the 1970s, he provided the voice of the Doberman pinscher thug DeSoto in *Oliver & Company* (1988). He made his television debut in 1976 and has appeared on such series as *Police Woman, Barnaby Jones, Hill Street Blues, Remington Steele, Dads, Cagney & Lacey, Baywatch Nights, Days of Our Lives, ER, Judging Amy, 8 Simple Rules,* and *Without a Trace.* Weintrab's film credits include *Beverly Hills Cop* (1984), *Modern Girls* (1986), and *Air Force One* (1997), as well as several TV-movies.

Welker, Frank (b. 1946) One of the most prolific actors in Disney and non–Disney animated films and television, he voiced several non-human characters ranging from the dog-like Footstool in *Beauty and the Beast* (1991) to the gorilla-like Bigfoot in *A Goofy Movie* (1995). Franklin Wendell Welker was born in Denver, Colorado, and educated at Santa Monica College and UCLA. He began his career as a stand-up comic in 1967 and two years later he made his onscreen film debut in *The Trouble with Girls.* After a few more movies he voiced an animated character for the first time, Freddy Jones in the television cartoon series *Scooby Doo, Where Are You?*, a role he would return to hundreds of times over the next forty years. By the end of the 1970s, Welker was voicing dozens of characters for the movies and television and was in great demand; his specialty was coming up with sounds for non-speaking characters. Among his many Disney feature film characters are Dumbo in *Who Framed Roger Rabbit* (1988), Prince Eric's dog Max in *The Little Mermaid* (1989), Joanna the goanna lizard in *The Rescuers Down Under* (1990), the monkey Abu in *Aladdin* (1992), Flit the hummingbird in *Pocahontas* (1995), the cricket Cri-Kee and the horse Khan in *Mulan* (1998), and the monster named Herman Melville in *Doug's First Movie* (1999). He can he heard providing sounds and dialogue in many non–Disney feature movies, including *Gremlins* (1984), *Up the Creek* (1984), *Star Trek III: The Search for Spock* (1984), *My Science Project* (1985), *Troll* (1986), *SpaceCamp* (1986), *The Transformers: The Movie* (1986), *The Golden Child* (1986), *The Trouble with Spies* (1987), *Caddyshack II* (1988), *Hudson Hawk* (1991), *Happily Ever After* (1993), *Super Mario Bros.* (1993), *Stargate* (1994), *The Pagemaster* (1994), *The Santa Clause* (1994), *Mortal Kombat* (1995), *Jumanji* (1995), *Space Jam* (1996), *Cats Don't Dance* (1997), *The Road to El Dorado* (2000), *Jimmy Neutron, Boy Genius* (2001), *The Cat in the Hat* (2003), *Curious George* (2006), and *The Back-up Plan* (2010). Welker has been even busier on television, regularly voicing characters for many TV cartoons, including *The Fantastic Four, Spiderman and His Amazing Friends, G.I. Joe, Inspector Gadget, Dungeons and Dragons, Transformers, DuckTales, Alvin and the Chipmunks, Adventures of the Gummi Bears, TaleSpin, Muppet Babies, Darkwing Duck, Tiny Toon Adventures, Bonkers, Goof Troop, Sonic the Hedgehog, Gargoyles, Animaniacs, The Real Adventures of Jonny Quest, 101 Dalmatians, Buzz Lightyear of Star Command, The Simpsons, Johnny Bravo, Lilo and Stitch, The Adventures of Jimmy Neutron: Boy Genius,* and *Kim Possible.* All in all, Welker can be heard in over 600 movies, videos, and television episodes.

Wen, Ming-Na *see* **Ming-Na**

Wentworth, Martha (1889–1974) A versatile performer dubbed the "Actress of 100 Voices" because of her variety of character voices, she played the Cockney housekeeper Nanny, the cow Queenie, and the goose Lucy in *One Hundred and One Dalmatians* (1961) and the Old Lady Squirrel and the sorcerer hag Madam Mim in *The Sword in the Stone* (1963), as well as the operatic Jenny Wren in the cartoon short *Who Killed Cock Robin?* (1935). She was born Verna Martha Wentworth in New York City and was busy on the radio during the 1930s, acting in everything from thrillers to children's shows. She started making films in the 1930s as well, providing voices for a handful of animated shorts such as *I Haven't Got a Hat* (1935), *I Love to Singa* (1936), *At Your Service Madame* (1936), and *Pigs Is Pigs* (1937). Wentworth started appearing on the screen in the 1940s and acted in many movies, including *Waterloo Bridge* (1940), *Dr. Jekyll and Mr. Hyde* (1941), *Clancy Street Boys* (1943), *A Tree Grows in Brooklyn* (1945), *Santa Fe Uprising* (1946), *Love Nest* (1951), *Young Man with Ideas* (1952), *Jupiter's Darling* (1955), *Blackboard Jungle* (1955), *Good Morning, Miss Dove* (1955), *The Man with the Golden Arm* (1955), *Rock Round the Clock* (1956), *Go, Johnny, Go* (1959), and *The Beatniks* (1960). She made her television debut in 1952 and appeared on such series as *The Dennis Day Show, I Married Joan, Dragnet, Playhouse 90, The Millionaire, Lassie,* and *Perry Mason.* Perhaps Wentworth's finest vocal performance is the funny, vindictive witch Madame Mim in *The Sword in the Stone.* Mim delights in her villainy and her duel of magic with Merlin is a verbal tour de force as well as a visual treat.

West, Adam (b. 1928) A television actor long associated with playing super-heroes, he voiced the fox Leonard in the animated short *Redux Riding Hood* (1997), Ace — Hollywood Chicken Little in *Chicken Little* (2005), and the looney but lovable Uncle Art in *Meet the Robinsons* (2007). He was born William West Anderson in Walla Walla, Washington, grew up in Seattle, and attended

Whitman College and Stanford University before becoming a radio disc jockey. When in the army he worked on military television stations around the world and after his discharge started a local kiddie show in Hawaii. West's first roles in Hollywood were in commercials and mostly television Westerns, and it was not until he had appeared in over forty different series and movies that he was cast as *Batman,* a tongue-in-cheek and very popular live-action series that ran two years in the 1960s. He went on to act in dozens of other television shows but none were as successful as *Batman* so in the 1980s West turned to voice work and was heard in many super-hero cartoon shows such as *The New Adventures of Batman, SuperFriends: The Legendary Super Powers Show, The Super Powers Team: Galactic Guardians, Batman* (2004–2006), and *Batman: The Brave and the Bold*. He can also be heard on many other animated series, including *Rugrats, Histeria!, The Simpsons, Kim Possible,* and *Family Guy.* Autobiography: *Back to the Batcave: The Real Story of the Original Batman Adam West* (2002).

Wheatley, Tom A child performer who provided the voice of the English boy Christopher Robin in *Piglet's Big Movie* (2003), his only other film credit is a small role in *Me and the Big Guy* (1999).

Wheeler, H. A. "Humpy" (b. 1938) A famous promoter of NASCAR auto racing, he voiced Tex, the Cadillac Coupe de Ville who runs the Dinoco oil corporation, in *Cars* (2006). Howard Augustine Wheeler, Jr., was born in Belmont, North Carolina, and played professional football before going into racing. He eventually became president and general manager of Lowe's Motor Speedway, one of the top race tracks in America.

Whitaker, Billy The boy actor who voiced the young, overexcited rabbit Skippy in *Robin Hood* (1973), his only other credit is an episode of the television series *Kipps* in 1960.

Whitaker, Dori A child performer of the 1970s, she voiced the young rabbit Tagalong in *Robin Hood* (1973) and the baby kangaroo Roo in the short *Winnie the Pooh and Tigger Too* (1974) which was reused in the compilation feature *The Many Adventures of Winnie the Pooh* (1977). Her only other credits are the television series *Adam-12* and *Marcus Welby, M.D.,* and the TV movie *Bell, Book and Candle* (1976). She is the sister of actor Billy Whitaker.

White, Lillias (b. 1951) An ample-figured, full-voiced African American singer-actress who has lit up Broadway many times, usually in supporting roles, she provided the voice of the singing Muse Calliope in *Hercules* (1997). The Brooklyn native was educated at City College of New York before working as a backup singer and later a soloist in concerts. White made her New York legit debut in 1975, then went on to replace others in *Barnum* (1981), *Cats* (1985), and *Once on This Island* (1991). Her first wide recognition came as singer Effie in the 1987 revival of *Dreamgirls* (1987) and she also gave memorable performances in *The Life* (1997), *How to Succeed in Business Without Really Trying* (1995), *Dinah Was* (1998), *Chicago* (2006). and *Fela!* (2009). White's other Manhattan musicals include *Rock 'n' Roll: The First 5,000 Years* (1982), *Romance in Hard Times* (1989), *Back to Bacharach and David* (1993), and *Crowns* (2002). She has appeared in a handful of films and some television dramas and series, including three years on *Sesame Street,* but her musical talents have only been enjoyed on the concert and musical stage. White reprised her Calliope in the video *Hercules: Zero to Hero* (1999) and can be heard singing for various characters in the animated film *Anastasia* (1997).

White, Richard (b. 1953) A singer with a full tenor-baritone voice which has been heard in many stage musicals and operas, he provided the singing and speaking voice of the oafish muscleman Gaston in *Beauty and the Beast* (1991). He was born in Oak Ridge, Tennessee, and later moved to Pittsburgh where he began singing professionally. White has sung with the New York City Opera and other theatre and opera companies across the nation and has made several recordings as well. His performance as Ravenal in the Papermill Playhouse production of *Show Boat* was broadcast on Public TV in 1989 and he has appeared on Broadway in revivals of *The New Moon* (1986), *Brigadoon* (1986), *South Pacific* (1987), and *The Desert Song* (1987). The character of Gaston in *Beauty and the Beast* is a unique Disney villain in that he is not ugly and that one doesn't realize he is a villain until halfway through the movie. Gaston does not appear in the original fairy tale but there was a similar character named Avenant in the 1946 French film by Jean Cocteau. British actor Rupert Everett was originally tested for the role but he was not deemed arrogant enough. (Everett later played a similarly arrogant character in *Shrek 2* in 2004). When White was cast and his full-throttle singing voice was utilized, the animators altered Gaston, making him operatic not only in his singing but in all his gestures and moves as well. Among the marvelous aspects of both the animators and White is how Gaston starts to resemble a beast in the last section of the film. White reprised his Gaston on several episodes of the animated TV series *House of Mouse*.

Whitehouse, Paul (b. 1958) A Welsh comic actor and writer who has spent most of his career in British television, he provided the voice of Thackery Earwicket, the volatile March Hare in the 2010 version of *Alice in Wonderland*. He was born in Stanleytown, Wales, and began his career as a comedy performer in revues. Whitehouse made his television debut in 1989 and was a recurring character in such British series and comedy shows as *Harry Enfield's Television Program, The Smell of Reeves and Mortimer, The Fast Show, Happiness, Help, Ruddy Hell! It's Harry and Paul*, and *Bellamy's People*, serving as one of the writers on most of them as well. His handful of movie credits include *Harry Potter and the Prisoner of Azkaban* (2004) and *Finding Neverland* (2004). Whitehouse's versatile voice can be heard in such films and videos as *Hooves of Fire* (1999), *Legend of the Lost Tribe* (2002), *Corpse Bride* (2005), and *Robbie the Reindeer in Close Encounters of the Herd Kind* (2007). The actor improvised many of his lines as the March Hare in *Alice in Wonderland* because director Tim Burton wanted the character to sound spontaneous and in the style of Whitehouse's live comic performances.

Whitman, Mae (b. 1988) A child actress who moved into adult roles and has many credits already in her young career, she supplied the voice of Leslie Dunkling, the student who Leonard loves while she is more interested in his dog, in *Teacher's Pet* (2004). She was born in Los Angeles, the daughter of a movie studio carpenter and an actress, and began performing at the age of three. She made her film debut when she was six years old and has acted in such films as *Bye Bye Love* (1995), *Independence Day* (1996), *One Fine Day* (1996), *The Gingerbread Man* (1998), *Hope Floats* (1998), *An American Rhapsody* (2001), *Going Shopping* (2005), *The Bondage* (2006), *Love's Abiding Joy* (2006), *Boogeyman 2* (2007), *Spring Breakdown* (2009), *Barry Munday* (2010), and *Scott Pilgrim vs. the World* (2010), as well as several made-for-TV movies. Among the television shows she has appeared in are *Friends, Chicago Hope, Judging Amy, Providence, JAG, Cold Case, Arrested Development, Thief, Grey's Anatomy, Desperate Housewives, Ghost Whisperer, ER, In Treatment, The Cleveland Show*, and *Parenthood*, but she is most known as Emma Grace in *State of Grace*. Whitman began doing voices for animation when she was eight. She first voiced Leslie in the TV cartoon series *Teacher's Pet* and can be heard in other series such as *Duckman: Private Dick/Family Man, The Cartoon Cartoon Show, Superman, The Wild Thornberrys, Fillmore!, Johnny Bravo, American Dragon: Jake Long, Avatar: The Last Airbender*, and *Family Guy*. Whitman was the first person to put a voice to Tinker Bell when she made the animated video *Tinker Bell* (2008) and reprised the character in its three sequels. She also voiced the videos and films *Mickey's Once Upon a Christmas* (1999), *The Wild Thornberrys Movie* (2002), *The Jungle Book 2* (2003), and *The Happy Elf* (2005).

Whyte, Joe (b. 1961) A comic improv actor who has appeared in several movies and television shows, he is also a busy voice artist who played the Official in *The Emperor's New Groove* (2000), the gopher baseball player Rodriguez in *Chicken Little* (2005), and the television Reporter in *Meet the Robinsons* (2007). He was born Joseph Walter White in Northridge, California, and was educated at the local campus of the California State University before forming his own improv group. While appearing in many plays and musicals in the Los Angeles area, he started working in animation and voiced various minor characters in such movies as *Tarzan* (1999), *Home on the Range* (2004), *Bolt* (2008), and *The Princess and the Frog* (2009). Whyte can also be heard on several video games.

Wickes, Mary (1916–1995) Although she was rarely cast in a major role, the tall, gawky character actress was one of the most familiar faces in films and on television; her last screen credit was providing the voice of the gargoyle Laverne in *The Hunchback of Notre Dame* (1996). She was born Mary Isabelle Wickenhauser in St. Louis, Missouri, and educated locally at Washington University before working in stock. She made her Broadway debut in 1934 and was cast as busybodies and sidekicks in comedies and musicals such as *Stage Door* (1936), *Stars in Your Eyes* (1939), *The Man Who Came to Dinner* (1939), *Jackpot* (1944), *Hollywood Pinafore* (1945), *Park Avenue* (1946), and *Oklahoma!* (1979). Wickes made her first film in 1935 and over the next sixty years she often stole the show playing wisecracking spinsters, aunts, housekeepers, and secretaries. Among her many movie credits are *The Man Who Came to Dinner* (1942), *Higher and Higher* (1943), *June Bride* (1948), *On Moonlight Bay* (1951), *I'll See You in My Dreams* (1951), *By the Light of the Silvery Moon* (1953), *White Christmas* (1954), *Good Morning, Miss Dove* (1955), *The Music Man* (1962), *The Trouble with Angels* (1966), *Sister Act* (1992), *Sister Act 2: Back in the Habit* (1993), and *Little Women* (1994). Wickes appeared in dozens of television specials and series beginning in 1948, among them *Colgate Theatre, I Love Lucy, Studio One in Hollywood, The Danny Thomas Show, Zorro, Dennis the Menace, Bonanza, The Lucy Show, Julia, The Jimmy Stewart Show, Sigmund and the Sea Monsters, Here's Lucy, Doc, Father Dowling Mysteries*, and *Punky Brewster*. Her only other Disney animated film was *101 Dalmatians* (1961) in which she provided a variety of voices for minor characters. While the gargoyles Victor and Hugo in *The*

Hunchback of Notre Dame were named after the French author of the novel, the female gargoyle Laverne was named after Laverne Andrews, one of the three Andrews Sisters. Wickes died before completing all the vocals for Laverne so actress Jane Withers voiced the remaining lines.

Wilder, Matthew (b. 1953) A movie and television composer, singer, and record producer who has scored both animated and live-action musicals, he provided the singing of the Chinese recruit Ling in *Mulan* (1998) because the voice actor Gedde Watanabe's trained vocals were too polished for the character. He was born Matthew Weiner in New York City and began his career as a singer, finding modest success as part of the Greenwich Village folk duo Matthew and Peter. He found wider success in California where he did back-up singing for Bette Midler and other stars, finally having a hit of his own with a 1983 album that included the chart-climbing song "Break My Stride." After a few more recordings, Wilder turned to composing songs and producing records. In addition to his songs for *Mulan*, his work can be heard in the movies *Tap* (1989), *Pretty Woman* (1990), *The Lizzie McGuire Movie* (2003), *Ella Enchanted* (2004), *It's a Boy Girl Thing* (2006), *He's Just Not That into You* (2009), and *Hannah Montana: The Movie* (2009), as well as the TV series *Dawson's Creek*, *Charmed*, *The Wire*, and *Glee*.

Willard, Fred (b. 1939) The smiling comic actor of television and film who can improvise a variety of types but excels at playing thick-headed, cheerfully obtuse characters, he provided the voice of the alien father Melvin with the "Big Voice" in *Chicken Little* (2005) and Shelby Forthright, the CEO of the Buy-n-Large Corporation, in *WALL-E* (2008) in which his actual image was used at times. He was born in Shaker Heights, Ohio, educated at Virginia Military Institute, and served in the army before becoming a member of the improv group Second City. Willard formed his own comedy group, Ace Trucking Company, then found fame on television as Martin Mull's dense sidekick Jerry on *Fernwood 2-Night* and its spinoff *America 2-Night*. He went on to appear in over 200 episodes of television sit-coms and variety shows, including *Laverne & Shirley*, *Sirota's Court*, *The Love Boat*, *D.C. Follies*, *Roseanne*, *Mad About You*, *Ally McBeal*, *A Minute with Stan Hooper*, *Back to You*, and *Sister, Sister*, though he is most remembered for his Hank MacDougall on *Everybody Loves Raymond*. Willard's movie credits include *Silver Streak* (1976), *Fun with Dick and Jane* (1977), *Americathon* (1979), *Roxanne* (1987), *Austin Powers: The Spy Who Shagged Me* (1999), *The Wedding Planner* (2001), and *Harold & Kumar Go to White Castle* (2004), as well as every "mockumentary" film directed by Christopher Guest, including *This Is Spinal Tap* (1984), *Waiting for Guffman* (1996), *Best in Show* (2000), *A Mighty Wind* (2003) and *For Your Consideration* (2006). He can be heard in such TV cartoon series as *The Simpsons*, *Buzz Lightyear of Star Command*, *The Legend of Tarzan*, *Teamo Supremo*, *Family Guy*, *Dexter's Laboratory*, *Handy Manny*, *Kim Possible*, *The Grim Adventures of Billy and Mandy*, *King of the Hill*, and *Transformers: Animated*.

Williams, Harlan (b. 1962) A stand-up comic and actor who has found notoriety in small but memorable roles in movie comedies, he provided the voice of the Robinson family's hyperactive robot Carl in *Meet the Robinsons* (2007). Harland Michael Williams was born in Toronto, Canada, and attended Sheridan College for a time before dropping out to do stand-up comedy. He eventually moved to Hollywood where he performed at the Laugh Factory, getting enough notice to make appearances on television talk shows and comedy specials. Williams played characters on such television series as *Ellen*, *Simon*, *The Geena Davis Show*, *Las Vegas*, and *My Name Is Earl*, but he got more attention in the movies, including *Dumb & Dumber* (1994), *Down Periscope* (1996), *RocketMan* (1997), *Wag the Dog* (1997), *Half-Baked* (1998), *There's Something About Mary* (1998), *Freddy Got Fingered* (2001), *Sorority Boys* (2002), *Surf School* (2006), and *My Life in Ruins* (2009). He can be heard on such TV cartoon series as *Ned's Newt*, *Gary & Mike*, *Ergo Proxy*, *Slacker Cats*, and *Kick Buttowski: Suburban Daredevil*, as well as in the animated movies and videos *Robots* (2005), *Madagascar: Escape 2 Africa* (2008), and *The Haunted World of El Superbeasto* (2009).

Williams, Joseph (b. 1960) A rock singer-turned-composer of movie and television scores who sometimes performs on the soundtracks of his works, he supplied the singing voice of the adult lion Simba in *The Lion King* (1994). Joseph Stanley Williams was born in Santa Monica, California, the son of acclaimed film composer John Williams and singer-actress Barbara Ruick, and began his career as the lead singer for the popular rock group Toto. After some best-selling albums and an international tour, he departed from Toto and recorded solo with success. Williams' first compositions for the screen were for science fiction films and made-for-TV movies in the 1990s but wider recognition came with his theme music for the television series *Roswell*, followed by such series as *Felicity*, *Surface*, *Windfall*, and *The War at Home*. He composed one section of the music for the movie *Star Wars: Episode VI — Return of the Jedi* (1983) and arranged his father's music for *Star Wars: Episode I — The*

Phantom Menace (1999). Williams appeared as a singer on *Roswell* and reprised his singing for Simba on the video *Mickey's Magical Christmas: Snowed in at the House of Mouse* (2001).

Williams, Laura The singing voice of the lion cub Nala in *The Lion King* (1994), Williams played minor roles in the films *The Boy Who Had Everything* (1984) and *Downtown* (1990) and appeared in two episodes of the television series *Amen*.

Williams, Lucille A screen actress active during the first years of the talkies, she supplied the voice of Perla Mouse in *Cinderella* (1950). Williams played bit or supporting roles in such movies as *Sally's Shoulders* (1928), *Halfway to Heaven* (1929), *Breakfast in Bed* (1930), *Traveling Husbands* (1931), and *Wicked* (1931).

Williams, Rhoda (1930–2006) A child performer on radio, film, and television who matured into a character actress, she voiced the selfish stepsister Drizella in *Cinderella* (1950). Rhoda Elaine Williams was born in Birmingham, Alabama, and by the time she was five years old was in Hollywood playing bit roles in films, such as *Our Gang Follies of 1938* (1937), *National Velvet* (1944), *The Corn Is Green* (1945), and *Our Vines Have Tender Grapes* (1945). She was also performing in radio, voicing the daughter Betty in the radio series *Father Knows Best* from 1949 to 1954. As an adult, Williams played small roles in mostly minor films but was sometimes featured on television, as in the series *Twilight Zone*, *The Dick Van Dyke Show*, *Run for Your Life*, *The Big Valley*, *Dragnet 1967*, and *Marcus Welby, M.D.* Her only other notable voice credit was dubbing Brigitte Bardot's dialogue for the American release of the French film *The Night Heaven Fell* (1958).

Williams, Richard (b. 1933) An animator and designer of movie titles who did voices on occasion, he provided the voice of the elevator attendant Droopy Dog in *Who Framed Roger Rabbit* (1988). He was born in Toronto, Canada, the son of two illustrators, and at the age of sixteen was already a commercial artist. After traveling and painting in Spain he settled in London where he won awards for his animated short *The Little Island* (1959). Williams animated, produced, and directed *A Christmas Carol* (1971), *Raggedy Ann & Andy: A Musical Adventure* (1977), *Ziggy's Gift* (1982), and *The Princess and the Cobbler* (1993), and was animation director for *Who Framed Roger Rabbit*. He also designed the titles for such movies as *What's New Pussycat* (1965), *A Funny Thing Happened on the Way to the Forum* (1966), *Casino Royale* (1966), *Prudence and the Pill* (1968), *The Charge of the Light Brigade* (1968), *Murder on the Orient Express* (1974), and *The Pink Panther Strikes Again* (1976). Williams reprised his Droopy in the short *Tummy Trouble* (1989) and the video *The Best of Roger Rabbit* (1996), and can be heard in *Ziggy's Gift*, *The Princess and the Cobbler*, and *Look Who's Talking Now* (1993). The character of Droopy Dog originated in the 1940s when he was featured as a police dog in twenty MGM shorts voiced by Bill Thompson. Since Thompson had died in 1971, Williams was hired to imitate his voice for *Who Framed Roger Rabbit*. Cory Burton provided the voice for the canine in the Roger Rabbit short *Trail Mix-Up* (1993).

Williams, Robin (b. 1951) The highly eccentric and very popular stand-up-comic-turned-actor who first found fame on television and in concerts, he gave one of his most vibrant and hilarious performances as the voice of the Genie in *Aladdin* (1992). Robin McLauim Williams was born in Chicago and studied at Juilliard before embarking on a successful career as a nightclub comedian, first in small venues then in large concert halls. He became nationally known for his offbeat and quirky performance in the television sit-com *Mork and Mindy* in 1978 and by the 1980s started making films, among his many popular movies being *The World According to Garp* (1982), *Good Morning, Vietnam* (1987), *Dead Poets Society* (1989), *Mrs. Doubtfire* (1993), *The Birdcage* (1996), *Flubber* (1997), *Good Will Hunting* (1997), and *Night at the Museum* (2006). The physical look of the Genie in *Aladdin* was inspired by the line drawings and caricatures by artist Al Hirschfeld but the directors always had Williams in mind for the voice. (The studio wanted Eddie Murphy, John Candy, or Steve Martin.) When Williams was doubtful about the project, the animators took a recording of one of the comic's stand-up routines and animated it with the Genie doing the lines. Williams found the result hilarious and agreed to voice the role. Williams was filmed while in the recording session and was encouraged to ad-lib as much as he liked. The writers incorporated many of these impromptu lines into the script and the animators used many of Williams' physical expressions and gestures in the film, allowing the Genie to change size and shape as dictated by Williams' vocal pyrotechnics. In voicing the Genie, the comic created fifty-two different voices for fifty-two different character impersonations. (These do not include his impersonations of John Wayne, Dr. Ruth Westheimer, George Bush, and others not used in the movie.) The result was perhaps the funniest Disney character ever and a tour de force performance by the acclaimed comic. Because Williams was not a trained singer, parts of the opening song "Arabian Nights" and some other numbers were sung by

Bruce Adler on the soundtrack. Williams reprised his Genie in the videos *Aladdin and the King of Thieves* (1995) and *Aladdin's Math Quest* (1998), as well as the TV series *Great Minds Think for Themselves*. His expressive, versatile voice can be heard in the animated movies and videos *Rabbit Ears: Pecos Bill* (1988), *Rabbit Ears: The Fool and the Flying Ship* (1991), *A Wish for Wings That Work* (1991), *Ferngully: The Last Rainforest* (1992), *From Time to Time* (1992), *Robot* (2005), *Everyone's Hero* (2006), and *Happy Feet* (2006). Biography: *Robin Williams: A Biography*, Andy Dougan (1999).

Williamson, Seth R. and **Shane R.** Two young bothers who shared the voicing of the six-year-old Prince Ralphie at the end of *The Princess and the Frog* (2009), neither have any other film or television credits yet.

Willis, Jack A stage actor with a handful of movie and television credits, he provided the voice of the stuffed toy Frog tied to the front of a truck in *Toy Story 3* (2010). Willis has acted for many prestigious regional theatres across the country, including the American Conservatory Theatre, Arena Stage, American Repertory Theatre, Trinity Repertory Company, and the Dallas Theatre Center. He has appeared on Broadway in *The Old Neighborhood* (1997), *Art* (1998), *The Crucible* (2002), and *Julius Caesar* (2005). Willis' film credits include *Problem Child* (1990), *Love Hurts* (1990), *Free Floaters* (1997), *The Out-of-Towners* (1999), *Cradle Will Rock* (1999), *The Talented Mr. Ripley* (1999), and *Messenger* (2004), as well as the television series *Deadline*, *Law & Order*, *Third Watch*, and *Ed*.

Wilson, Don (1900–1982) The tall, rotund radio and television announcer who usually played himself in his two dozen films, he was the Narrator for the Disney short *Ferdinand the Bull* (1938). He was born in Lincoln, Nebraska, and educated at the University of Colorado where he played football. Wilson began his career singing on local radio in Denver before turning to sportscasting. He was the announcer for a Jack Benny special broadcast in 1934 and the two went on to work together for thirty years on radio then on television, Wilson often the butt of the comic's jokes. He was announcer for other radio shows as well, including programs starring Bing Crosby, Fanny Brice, and Alan Young, and appeared in films in the 1930s and 1940s, including *Broadway Melody of 1936* (1935), *Radio City Revels* (1938), *Two Girls on Broadway* (1940), *The Roundup* (1941), *Thank Your Lucky Stars* (1943), *The Kid from Brooklyn* (1946), *The Chase* (1946), *Larceny* (1948), *Sailor Beware* (1952), and *Niagara* (1953). In addition to his fifteen-year run on *The Jack Benny Program*, Wilson appeared in other television shows, including *The Red Skelton Hour*, *Death Valley Days*, *Harrigan and Son*, and *Batman*, and voiced himself in the animated short *The Mouse That Jack Built* (1959).

Wilson, J. Donald (1904–1984) A scriptwriter and television producer, he was the Narrator for *The Reluctant Dragon* (1941). The Kansas City, Missouri, native wrote stories for magazines, two of which were turned into films: *The Whistler* (1944) and *Key Witness* (1947). Wilson also penned the scripts for the television series *The Whistler* as well as the show *Shotgun Slade* in 1960. He produced the series *Mark Saber* and the television drama *Alarm* (1956). He is not to be confused with the popular radio and television announcer Don Wilson who introduced *The Jack Benny Show*.

Wilson, Owen (b. 1968) The somewhat renegade film writer and actor who brings a unique edge to his characters, he provided the voice of the stock car racer hero Lightning McQueen in *Cars* (2006). Owen Cunningham Wilson was born in Dallas, Texas, the son of a television executive and a photographer, and was educated at the University of Texas at Austin. After writing and acting in the independent film *Bottle Rocket* (1994), he went to Hollywood where he appeared in a variety of movies, including *The Cable Guy* (1996), *Anaconda* (1997), *Armageddon* (1997), *Breakfast of Champions* (1997), *Meet the Parents* (2000), *The Royal Tenenbaums* (2001), *Starsky & Hutch* (2004), *Meet the Fockers* (2004), *The Life Aquatic with Steve Zissou* (2004), *Wedding Crashers* (2005), *Night at the Museum* (2006), *Marley & Me* (2008), *Night at the Museum: Battle of the Smithsonian* (2009), *How Do You Know* (2010), and *Little Fockers* (2010). Wilson reprised his Lightning McQueen in the video *Mater and the Ghostlight* (2006) and can be heard in the animated movies *Fantastic Mr. Fox* (2009) and *Marmaduke* (2010). The character of Lightning McQueen in *Cars* may sound like an homage to actor Steve McQueen who used to race motorcycles but the car is actually named after Pixar animator Glenn McQueen who died in 2002.

Winchell, April (b. 1960) An actress, voice artist, and radio commentator who has been active since 1972, she supplied the voices of the "toon" infant Baby Herman and his mother Mrs. Herman in *Who Framed Roger Rabbit* (1988). April Terri Winchell was born in New York City, the daughter of actor-ventriloquist Paul Winchell, and as a teenager voiced characters for the TV cartoon series *Kid Power*. As an adult she returned to voicing animated characters and worked on hundreds of episodes of such series as *The Legend of Prince Valiant*, *Bonkers*, *Goof Troop*, *Sonic the Hedgehog*, *Swat Kats: The*

Radical Squadron, Mighty Ducks, Timon and Pumbaa, Quack Pack, Jungle Cubs, All Dogs Go to Heaven: The Series, 101 Dalmatians, Hercules, Recess, Pepper Ann, Clerks, The Legend of Tarzan, Teamo Supremo, Lilo & Stitch, Kim Possible, Tak & the Power of Juju, Phineas and Ferb, and *King of the Hill,* but she is probably most known as the voice of Clarabelle the Cow on *Mickey Mouse Works, House of Mouse,* and *Mickey Mouse Clubhouse.* Winchell reprised both Baby Herman and Mrs. Herman in the shorts *Tummy Trouble* (1989), *Roller Coaster Rabbit* (1990), and *Trail Mix-Up* (1993), as well as in the video *The Best of Roger Rabbit* (1996), and can be heard in many other animated films and videos, including *Monster in My Pocket: The Big Scream* (1992), *A Goof Troop Christmas* (1993), *Hollyrock-a-Bye Baby* (1993), *Mighty Ducks the Movie: The First Face-Off* (1997), *Belle's Magical World* (1998), *Pocahontas II: Journey to a New World* (1998), *Antz* (1998), *Mickey's Once Upon a Christmas* (1999), *Alvin and the Chipmunks Meet the Wolfman* (2000), *Recess: School's Out* (2001) and four of its sequels, *Lady and the Tramp II: Scamp's Adventures* (2001), *Mickey's House of Villains* (2001), *Rapsittie Street Kids: Believe in Santa* (2002), *The Hunchback of Notre Dame II* (2002), *Tarzan & Jane* (2002), *Mickey, Donald, Goofy: The Three Musketeers* (2004), *Mulan II* (2004), *Mickey's Twice Upon a Christmas* (2004), *Mickey's Around the World in 80 Days* (2005), *Kim Possible: So the Drama* (2005), *Tarzan II* (2005), *The Emperor's New Groove II: Kronk's New Groove* (2005), *Asterix and the Vikings* (2006), *Queer Duck: The Movie* (2006), *The Fox and the Hound 2* (2006), *Happily N'Ever After* (2007), *Mickey's Treat* (2007), and *The Haunted World of El Superbeasto* (2009). Winchell has also been host and commentator on several radio programs over the years and runs the prestigious advertising company Radio Savant Productions. She has appeared on stage regionally in plays, musicals, and her one-woman show.

Winchell, Paul (1922–2005) A very popular ventriloquist who had a busy career as a character actor and creator of voices for many television shows, he is most remembered today as the voice of Tigger the hyperactive tiger in the *Winnie the Pooh* films and videos. Born Paul Wilchen in New York City, he found fame at the age of twenty-six when he appeared on Edward Bowes' radio program *Original Amateur Hour* with his sidekick dummy Jerry Mahoney. Winchell and Mahoney were featured in early television and later had two shows of their own in which other dummy characters were introduced, most memorably Knucklehead Smiff. Winchell appeared in a few movies without Mahoney and friends but found more success in character parts on television and providing voices for cartoons. Among the TV cartoon series he voiced were *The Jetsons, The Banana Splits Adventure Hour, Wacky Races, Scooby-Doo, Goober and the Ghost Chasers, Yogi's Gang, The Pink Panther Show, Fred Flintstone and Friends, C B Bears, Heathcliff,* and *The Smurfs.* He first voiced the enthusiastic Tigger in the animated short *Winnie the Pooh and the Blustery Day* (1968) and reprised the role in subsequent shorts, features, and the TV cartoon series. Also for Disney, he provided the voice of the hip Chinese Scat Cat Shun Gon in *The Aristocats* (1970) and the zany woodpecker Boomer in *The Fox and the Hound* (1981). Winchell was also a prolific inventor and had many patents, including an early version of an artificial heart. Autobiography: *Winch* (2004).

Wincott, Michael (b. 1958) A stage actor with an unusually raspy voice who has made many films, he provided the voice of the insectoid crew member Scroop in *Treasure Planet* (2002). Michael Anthony Claudio Wincott was born in Toronto, Canada, and trained as an actor at Juilliard in New York City. He acted in several Off Broadway productions, including *Talk Radio* (1987), *Road* (1988), and *States of Shock* (1991), and on Broadway in *Serious Money* (1988) and *The Secret Rapture* (1989). Wincott's first film was *Wild Horse Hank* (1979), followed by such movies as *Circle of Two* (1980), *Nothing Personal* (1980), *Curtains* (1983), *Talk Radio* (1988), *Born in the Fourth of July* (1989), *The Doors* (1991), *Robin Hood: Prince of Thieves* (1991), *1492: Conquest of Paradise* (1992), *Romeo Is Bleeding* (1993), *The Three Musketeers* (1993), *The Crow* (1994), *Alien: Resurrection* (1997), *Gunshy* (1998), *Before Night Falls* (2000), *Along Came a Spider* (2001), *The Count of Monte Cristo* (2002), *The Assassination of Richard Nixon* (2004), *The Diving Bell and the Butterfly* (2007), *What Just Happened* (2008), and *A Lonely Place for Dying* (2009).

Windsor, Barbara (b. 1937) A popular English actress known for her bubble-headed characters in British films and on television, she provided the voice of Mallymkun, the swaggering Dormouse in the 2010 version of *Alice in Wonderland.* She was born Barbara-Ann Deeks in London, the daughter of a costermonger and a dressmaker. She took dance lessons as a young child, and was performing on the stage professionally at the age of twelve. After appearing in some musicals and getting bit parts in films, Windsor found fame as the ditzy Goldie Locks in the movie *Carry on Doctor* (1967) and returned in eight *Carry On* sequels. She later concentrated on television and enjoyed new-found fame as the matriarch Peggy in the series *EastEnders,* remaining with the show for over sixteen years. Autobiography: *All of Me: My Extraordinary Life* (2001).

Winfrey, Oprah (b. 1954) The most powerful African American woman in show business with many producer, actress, and talk show host credits, she served as a consultant on *The Princess and the Frog* (2009) and voiced Tiana's concerned mother Eudora. She was born in Kosciusko, Mississippi, and grew up in Milwaukee where as a teenager she started on local radio. Soon Winfrey was a highly-rated talk show host on Chicago radio then on television, eventually becoming a nationwide favorite as she changed the style and content of the genre. She is a shrewd businesswoman and her production company has presented many television shows, films, and even the Broadway musical *The Color Purple* (2005). It was the 1995 movie version of *The Color Purple* that marked Winfrey's screen acting debut, followed by *Native Son* (1986) and *Beloved* (1998), as well as the TV-movies *The Women of Brewster Place* (1989), *There Are No Children Here* (1993), *Before Women Had Wings* (1997), and *Our Friend, Martin* (1999). She also appeared on the television series *Brewster Place* and *Ellen*, though she is most known for her highly popular talk program *The Oprah Winfrey Show* which has run twenty-five years. Winfrey can be heard in the movie *Charlotte's Web* (2006) and the animated film *Bee Movie* (2007). Biographies: *Oprah*, Kitty Kelley (2010); *Up Close: Oprah Winfrey*, Ilerne Cooper (2008); *Oprah Winfrey: "I Don't Believe in Failure,"* Robin Westen (2005); *The World According to Oprah: An Unauthorized Portrait in Her Own Words*, Ken Lawrence (2005).

Winslowe, Paula (1910–1996) A radio performer in the 1940s and a television actress in the 1950s and 1960s, her first screen credit was voicing Bambi's Mother and one of the Pheasants in *Bambi* (1942). She was born in Grafton, North Dakota, and after marrying radio announcer John Sutherland moved to Los Angeles where she worked as a voice actress at MGM. When Jean Harlow died before completing *Saratoga* (1937), Winslowe supplied some of the late actress' dialogue for the final print. She was heard on such radio shows as *Big Town*, *Lux Radio Theatre*, *The Joe E. Brown Show*, and *Broadway Is My Beat*, but is most remembered for playing Peg Riley in the long-running series *The Life of Riley*. Winslowe also voiced Mrs. Conklin in *Our Miss Brooks* first on radio and then on television. The rest of her career was on the small screen where she appeared in such series as *The Bob Cummings Show*, *I Love Lucy*, *Father Knows Best*, *The George Burns and Gracie Allen Show*, *Rawhide*, *The Jack Benny Program*, *Perry Mason*, *The Adventures of Ozzie and Harriet*, and *Run for Your Life*, as well as providing voices for the animated series *The Flintstones*.

Withers, Jane (b. 1926) A child movie star of the Depression years who was second only to Shirley Temple in popularity, she completed the dialogue for the gargoyle Laverne in *The Hunchback of Notre Dame* (1996) after the death of Mary Wickes. She was born in Atlanta, Georgia, started singing and dance lessons at the age of three, and the next year had her own radio show in Atlanta. Withers' ability to impersonate celebrities of the day brought her to the attention of Hollywood and she was cast as the spoiled brat who plagues Shirley Temple in *Bright Eyes* (1934). Often playing spirited tomboys, she was featured in a series of movie shorts and features, including *Ginger* (1935), *This Is the Life* (1935), *Paddy O'Day* (1935), *Pepper* (1936), *Angel's Holiday* (1937), and *Checkers* (1937). Like Temple, her popularity waned as she grew up and Withers attended the University of Southern California's film school then embarked on an adult career on the screen which consisted mostly of character parts in movies such as *Giant* (1956), *The Heart Is a Rebel* (1958), *The Right Approach* (1961), and *Captain Newman, M.D.* (1963). Withers found much more success on television as Josephine the Plummer in a series of commercials and in such TV series as *Pete and Gladys*, *Bachelor Father*, *The Munsters*, *The Love Boat*, *Hart to Hart*, and *Murder, She Wrote*. She used her talent for impersonation to copy Wickes' voice in *The Hunchback of Notre Dame* and voiced Laverne again in the video sequel *The Hunchback of Notre Dame II* (2002).

Wolfe, Digby (b. 1929) A comedy writer and actor from Great Britain who was active in American television, he supplied the singing and speaking voice of Ziggy, one of the Beatles-like vultures, in *The Jungle Book* (1967). He was born in London and began his career writing musical revues for the stage and comedy sketches for British television shows. Moving to Australia, Wolfe found greater success for his writing and appearances on television, then he relocated to the States where he wrote for *Rowan & Martin's Laugh-In* as well as television specials for Goldie Hawn, John Denver, Shirley MacLaine, and other stars. He appeared in such American sit-coms as *The Munsters*, *The Farmer's Daughter*, *Love on a Rooftop*, *That Girl*, *Occasional Wife*, *I Dream of Jeannie*, and *The Monkees*. Until his retirement in 2004, Wolfe taught comedy writing at the University of New Mexico. The four vultures in *The Jungle Book* do not appear in Kipling's stories. They were added to the movie as a way of having fun with the very popular Liverpool lads who were dominating the music scene. Hence, the Liverpool accents of the four birds.

Wong, B. D. (b. 1962) A multi-talented Asian American actor of stage and screen, he provided the speaking voice of the Chinese Captain Li Shang in *Mulan* (1998). He was born Bradley Darryl Wong in San Francisco and attended San Francisco State College before making his New York Off Broadway debut in 1981. Wong first found fame on Broadway as the sly transvestite Song Liling in *M. Butterfly* (1988), using the name B. D. Wong in the playbill program so that the character's sexual identity remained a secret; he has retained the name in his subsequent appearances on stage, screen and television. Wong's other notable stage credits include *The Tempest* (1989), *You're a Good Man, Charlie Brown* (1999), and *Pacific Overtures* (2004). He became an audience favorite with his performance in the movie *Father of the Bride* (1991) and its sequel, and he has appeared on a variety of television specials and series, including *All American Girl, Oz,* and *Law & Order: Special Victims Unit*. Wong reprised his Shang for the videos *Mulan II* (2004) and *Kingdom Hearts II* (2005) and can be heard in the animated TV series *Happily Ever After: Fairy Tales for Every Child* and *Kim Possible*.

Woodard, Alfre (b. 1952) The acclaimed African American actress of movies and television, she voiced the lemur matriarch Plio in *Dinosaur* (2000). She was born in Tulsa, Oklahoma, and educated at Boston University for a theatre career but after acting in a few productions in New York she was hired for the television drama *The Trial of the Moke* (1978) and was cast in the film *Remember My Name* (1978). Woodard has given memorable performances in such movies as *Cross Creek* (1983), *Extremities* (1986), *Scrooged* (1988), *Miss Firecracker* (1989), *Grand Canyon* (1991), *Passion Fish* (1992), *How to Make an American Quilt* (1995), *Star Trek: First Contact* (1996), *Down in the Delta* (1998), and *Reach for Me* (2009), yet she is just as known for her many TV-movies, including *Go Tell It on the Mountain* (1985), *Mandela* (1987), *A Mother's Courage: The Mary Thomas Story* (1989), *Race to Freedom: The Underground Railroad* (1994), *The Piano Lesson* (1995), *Miss Evers' Boys* (1997), *The Member of the Wedding* (1997), *A Wrinkle in Time* (2003), and *The Water Is Wide* (2006). Woodard's greatest fame has come from her performances in television series, in particular *St. Elsewhere, Desperate Housewives, My Own Worst Enemy,* and *Three Rivers*. She can be heard in the animated TV series *Happily Ever After: Fairy Tales for Every Child* and *Black Panther,* in the video *The Brave Little Toaster to the Rescue* (1997), and the film *The Wild Thornberrys Movie* (2002).

Woods, Ilene (1929–2010) A radio actress and singer in the 1940s, she provided the speaking and singing voice of the title heroine in *Cinderella* (1950). She was born Jacquelyn Ruth Woods in Portsmouth, New Hampshire, and was on stage at the age of two. By the time she was fourteen she had her own radio program in New York City called *The Ilene Woods Show,* then moved to California where she was featured on Jack Carson's radio show *Sealtest Village Store*. Woods' first and only live-action movie was *On Stage Everybody* (1945). Songwriters Mack David and Jerry Livingston had her record their songs for the upcoming *Cinderella* so that Walt Disney could hear them. Over 300 actresses auditioned for the voice of Cinderella but it was that recording of Woods, sent to Disney without her knowing it, that got her the part. Woods appeared as herself on the television series *Of All Things* in 1956 and sang on various TV variety shows before she retired from performing in 1970. After sixty years, Cinderella remains a favorite Disney "princess." She is reticent but not fearful, dreamy but not naive. The statuesque model Helene Stanley posed and was filmed in movement for the Disney animators. Woods' voice seemed to match the regal yet warm persona of the physical character; she looked attractive even covered with cinders and her singing was heavenly even while scrubbing floors.

Woods, James (b. 1947) A tall, lean leading man of stage, films, and television who is often cast in sinister or brooding roles, he supplied the voice of Hades, the conniving god of the underworld, in *Hercules* (1997). James Howard Woods was born in Vernal, Utah, grew up in Warwick, Rhode Island, the son of an U.S. Army Intelligence officer, and attended the Massachusetts Institute of Technology before pursuing an acting career. He appeared in a handful of Off Broadway productions and was seen on Broadway in *The Penny Wars* (1969), *Borstal Boy* (1970), *The Trial of the Catonsville Nine* (1971), and *Finishing Touches* (1973). Woods made his television debut in 1971 and his screen bow the next year, appearing in several movies and series, but he was not widely noticed until his performance in the film *The Onion Field* (1979), followed by such features as *Once Upon a Time in America* (1984), *Against All Odds* (1984), *Salvador* (1986), *Chaplin* (1992), *The Getaway* (1993), *Nixon* (1995), *Ghosts of Mississippi* (1996), *Contact* (1997), *The Virgin Suicides* (1999), *Any Given Sunday* (1999), *Scary Movie 2* (2001), *Riding in Cars with Boys* (2001), and *An American Carol* (2008). His television credits include the mini-series *Holocaust* (1978) and the series *Young Maverick, Fallen Angels, ER,* and *Shark,* as well as voicing characters in the cartoon series *The Simpsons, Family Guy. House of Mouse,* and *Hercules*. Woods reprised his Hades in the last two series, as well as in the videos *Hercules: Zero to Hero* (1999) and *Mickey's House of Villains* (2001), and he can be heard in such animated movies and videos as *Recess: School's Out* (2001), *Final Fantasy: The Spirits Within* (2001), *Rolie Polie Olie: The Great Defender of Fun* (2002), *Robbie the Reindeer in Legend of the Lost Tribe* (2002), *The Easter Egg Adventure* (2004), *Surf's Up* (2007), and *Justice League: Crisis on Two Earths* (2010). Originally the villain Hades in *Hercules* was developed as a character who spoke slowly with sinister pauses. John Lithgow, Jack Nicholson, Willem Dafoe, and David Bowie were among the actors considered for the role. Yet when Woods was cast and voiced the character in a rapid, sarcastic manner, the directors liked it and rethought some of the dialogue. Woods ad-libbed a good deal during the recording sessions and some of it was retained in the movie, especially in the scenes with Megara. The actor based his characterization not on a mythological figure but on a modern-day Hollywood agent and a fast-talking car salesman. Hades ranks as one of Disney's funniest villains and is Woods' favorite role. He returns to play Hades whenever asked, even in the video games based on *Hercules*.

Woodson, William (b. 1917) A deep-voiced character actor whose fifty-year career included radio, films, television, and theatre, he was also a busy voice artist and supplied the voice of the cruel Tanner in the animated short *The Small One* (1978). He was born in San Bernardino, California, and began his career on the stage, eventually appearing on Broadway in the plays *Harriet* (1943), *Othello* (1943), *Cyrano de Bergerac* (1946), and *A Moon for the Misbegotten* (1957). Because of his full, flowing voice he also found work on radio and throughout his long career would often play announcers or serve as narrators for films and television programs. Woodson acted in or narrated such early television shows as *Lights Out, The Philco-Goodyear Television Playhouse, Dick Tracy, Schlitz Playhouse,* and *The Adventures of the Falcon.* He made his screen debut in *The Gallant Blade* (1948) and was seen in such movies as *Vice Squad* (1953), *Not with My Wife You Don't* (1966), *The One and Only, Genuine, Original Family Band* (1968), *More Dead Than Alive* (1969), and *Escape from the Planet of the Apes* (1971), but usually he was heard narrating or announcing in another dozen movies, Woodson also narrated television shows ranging from *The Odd Couple* to the miniseries *The Winds of War* (1983) and its sequel *War and Remembrance* (1988). He was seen in such television series as *This Man Dawson, Route 66, Sea Hunt, The Rifleman, Leave It to Beaver, Have Gun—Will Travel, Dr. Kildare, Bewitched, Perry Mason, F Troop, The Fugitive,* and *The Lucy Show,* and he voiced characters for several TV cartoon series, including *The All-New Super Friends Hour, Battle of the Planets, Challenge of the SuperFriends, Spider-Man, Thundarr the Barbarian, Pandemonium, Garfield and Friends, Tiny Toon Adventures, Capitol Critters,* and *Family Guy.* Woodson retired from acting in 1995 but continued to do radio work and sports broadcasting.

Wooley, Michael-Leon (b. 1966) A large African American actor, singer, and musician with a full, rich voice, he voiced the trumpet-playing alligator Louis in *The Princess and the Frog* (2009). He was born in Fairfax, Virginia, and grew up in Bowie, Maryland, and studied at the American Music and Dramatic Academy in New York City. After touring in the musical *Purlie*, Wooley made his Broadway debut as Big Moe in *Five Guys Named Moe* (1992), followed by *The Music Man* (2000) and *American Buffalo* (2008), as well as providing the singing voice of the man-eating plant Audrey II in *Little Shop of Horrors* (2003). He toured in *Ain't Misbehavin'* and *The Wiz*, and sang in concerts at Carnegie Hall and other venues, as well as in the movie *Dreamgirls* (2006). Wooley's other film credits are *Ghost Town* (2008) and *My Father's Will* (2009), and he has appeared on the television series *Cosby, The Knights of Prosperity, Law & Order: Special Victims Unit,* and voiced the cartoon series *Ugly Americans*. When *The Princess and the Frog* was first being developed, it was hoped that Elton John would voice the character of the musician-alligator and sing his hit song "Crocodile Rock." But in development the concept changed and the gator was patterned after the renowned musician-singer Louis Armstrong; he was named Louis and an original song was written for him in the Armstrong style. Although he is an accomplished musician, Wooley plays the piano so Louis' trumpet playing in *The Princess and the Frog* was done by Terence Blanchard.

Worley, Jo Anne (b. 1937) A loud, expressive comedienne with a multi-octave singing voice, she was a favorite on television and has voiced several cartoons and features, including *Beauty and the Beast* (1991) in which she provided the voice of the enchanted Wardrobe, and *A Goofy Movie* (1995) where she played the overly-respectable principal's secretary Miss Maples. She was born in Lowell, Indiana, and educated at Midwestern State University and Los Angeles City College before performing in revues in California. When the 1961 Los Angeles production *Billy Barnes Revue* transferred to New York, she made her Manhattan debut, staying to make a splash in the revue *The Mad Show* (1966). Her comedy act in New York nightclubs led to her first television appearances, becoming nationally known as one of the zany regulars on *Rowan and Martin's Laugh-In* in 1967. Worley often returns to the regional stage in musicals and comedies even as she continues to appear on such television shows as *Love, American Style; The Love Boat; Murder, She Wrote*; and *Sabrina, the Teenage Witch*. She reprised the Wardrobe in the videos *Belle's Magical World* (1998) and *Kingdom Hearts II* (2005) and provided voices for such animated videos as *Nutcracker Fantasy* (1979), *The Pound Puppies* (1985), *The Elf Who Saved Christmas* (1992), *The Elf and the Magic Key* (1993), and *Kim Possible: The Secret Files* (2003).

Worlock, Frederick (1886–1973) A British character actor active on Broadway in the 1920s and 1930s and a veteran of over eighty Hollywood movies, he supplied the voice of the bumbling Cockney thug Horace in *One Hundred and One Dalmations* (1961). He was born in London and was on the British stage before coming to the States in the early 1920s. Worlock appeared in over two dozen New York stage productions, including *Scaramouche* (1923), *The Moon-Flower* (1924), *She Had to Know* (1925), *Julius Caesar* (1927), *The Furies* (1928), *Hedda Gabler* (1929), *The Truth About Blayds* (1932), *Camille* (1932), *Jezebel* (1933), *Dodsworth* (1934), *Tovarich* (1936), *The Amazing Dr. Clitterhouse* (1937), *King Richard II* (1937), *Suspect* (1940), *Medea* (1949), and *Saint Joan* (1951). He made his American screen debut in 1939 and usually played formidable British or foreign characters in such movies as *Balalaika* (1939), *The Sea Hawk* (1940), *Strange Cargo* (1940), *Moon Over Burma* (1940), *Dr. Jekyll and Mr. Hyde* (1941), *A Yank in the R.A.F.* (1941), *How Green was My Valley* (1941), *The Black Swan* (1942), *Random Harvest* (1942), *Passport to Suez* (1943), *The Lodger* (1944), *National Velvet* (1944), *The Picture of Dorian Gray* (1945), *The Fatal Witness* (1945), *Captain Kidd* (1945), *Forever Amber* (1947), *Love from a Stranger* (1947), *Johnny Belinda* (1948), *Joan of Arc* (1948), *A Connecticut Yankee in King Arthur's Court* (1949), *Jet Over the Atlantic* (1959), *Spartacus* (1960), *The Notorious Landlady* (1962), *Spinout* (1966), and *Airport* (1970). Worlock concentrated on television in the 1950s and 1960s, acting on such series as *Omnibus, The United States Steel Hour, Kraft Theatre, Studio One in Hollywood, Robert Montgomery Presents, The Loretta Young Show, Alfred Hitchcock Presents, Hong Kong,* and *Perry Mason*. The character of the tall and scrawny Horace in *One Hundred and One Dalmations* is a typical bumbling henchman for the Disney villain, in this case Cruella de Vil. Such types usually come in pairs and, in this case, his equally obtuse cohort is the short, pudgy Jasper (J. Pat O'Malley). The fact that these two are supposed to kill and skin the puppies is made less gruesome when one sees how incompetent they are.

Wright, Ben (1915–1989) An American-British actor with a facility for various international accents, he voiced the songwriter Roger Radcliff in *One Hundred and One Dalmations* (1961), the wolf Rama who raises the man-cub Mowgli in *The Jungle Book* (1967), and Prince Eric's advisor Grimsby in *The Little Mermaid* (1989). He was born in London to an English mother and an American father and trained at the Royal Academy of Dramatic Art before serving in the King's Royal Rifle Corps during World War II. Coming to visit the States after the war, he decided to stay and he first worked in radio. Wright then went to Hollywood where his ability to do various dialects allowed him to play a variety of supporting roles in such movies as *Botany Bay* (1953), *The Desert Rats* (1953), *Prince Valiant* (1954), *Prince of Players* (1955), *A Man Called Peter* (1955), *D-Day the Sixth of June* (1956), *Witness for the Prosecution* (1957), *The Wreck of the Mary Deare* (1959), *Journey to the Center of the Earth* (1959), *The Lost World* (1960), *Judgement at Nuremberg* (1961), *Mutiny on the Bounty* (1962), *The Sound of Music* (1965), *Munster, Go Home!* (1966), *The Sand Pebbles* (1966), and *Topaz* (1969). Among his many television credits are the series *Zane Grey Theatre, The Rebel, The Untouchables, Have Gun—Will Travel, Perry Mason, Twilight Zone, Checkmate, Combat!, 77 Sunset Strip, Ben Casey, McHale's Navy, The Outer Limits, Dr. Kildare, The Man from U.N.C.L.E., Get Smart, Bonanza, 12 O'Clock High, The Rat Patrol, It Takes a Thief, The Mod Squad, The Wild Wild West, The Virginian, Hogan's Heroes, Ironside, Barnaby Jones, Emergency!,* and *The Rockford Files*. Wright came out of retirement to audition for the part of the very proper, very stuffy Englishman Grimsby in *The Little Mermaid*. He was cast without the directors even knowing he had voiced Disney characters before. During the recording session someone recognized his voice as that of Roger Radcliff in *One Hundred and One Dalmations*, a movie the animators had grown up on and treasured, and he was treated as a celebrity. Sadly, Wright died before *The Little Mermaid* was released.

Wright, Ralph (1908–1988) A writer who scripted over fifty animated features and shorts for Disney and other companies, he sometimes provided voices as well, such as the gloom-and-doom donkey Eeyore in the shorts *Winnie the Pooh and the Honey Tree* (1966), *Winnie the Pooh and the Blustery Day* (1968), *Winnie the Pooh and a Day for Eyeore* (1983), and in the compilation feature *The Many Adventures of Winnie the Pooh* (1977). He was born in Grants Pass, Oregon, and first worked for

Disney writing the animated short *Goofy's Glider* (1940), followed by dozens of Goofy, Donald Duck, and Pluto cartoons, as well as the minor classic *Lambert the Sheepish Lion* (1952). Wright also contributed to the story and/or screenplays for the Disney features *Bambi* (1942), *Saludos Amigos* (1942), *The Three Caballeros* (1944), *Song of the South* (1946), *Peter Pan* (1953), *Lady and the Tramp* (1955), *Sleeping Beauty* (1959), *The Jungle Book* (1967), *The Aristocats* (1970), and *Bedknobs and Broomsticks* (1971). For other studios he scripted many episodes of the cartoons *Mister Magoo*, *The Dick Tracy Show*, and *Popeye the Sailor*, as well as the animated feature *Gay-Purr-ee* (1962). Wright scripted some live-action nature-adventure movies as well, in particular *Perri* (1957), which he also directed, and *Nikki, Wild Dog of the North* (1961). For many years his co-workers teased Wright about his deep-voiced groan and gloomy way of expressing himself. When it came time to animate the A. A. Milne stories, he was considered a natural for the dour Eeyore and was convinced to voice the character as well as write the scripts. The sad-faced Eeyore often plays a minor role in the original stories but because his voice is so distinctive he is more noticeable in the films. His bleak but accepting view of the world is so consistent that even the fact that his tail keeps falling off is something he has learned to live with.

Wright, Samuel E. (b. 1948)   A deep-voiced African American actor-singer who has given many noteworthy performances in Broadway musicals without ever becoming a star, his voice will be forever remembered from animated television shows and films, particularly the speaking and singing voice of Sebastian the Crab in *The Little Mermaid* (1989) and for introducing the Oscar-winning song "Under the Sea." Wright was born in Camden, South Carolina, and was an acting teacher before making television commercials. He made his Broadway bow as one of the Apostles in the original company of *Jesus Christ Superstar* (1971) and took over leading roles in *Two Gentlemen of Verona* (1972) and *Pippin* (1974). Wright's most accomplished Broadway musical performances were as the uptight, confused father William in *The Tap Dance Kid* (1983) and the majestic King Mufasa in the original cast of *The Lion King* (1997). He has appeared in a handful of live-action television shows and movies, most memorably the musical-bio *Bird* (1988) in which he played Dizzy Gillespie. Wright's other notable Disney voice was that of the strict iguanodon leader Kron in the animated feature *Dinosaur* (2000). The character of the outspoken crab Sebastian was originally to be very British and proper but the songwriters Howard Ashman and Alan Menken suggested a Caribbean-flavored creature to open up musical possibilities. The result was an outstanding performance by Wright and the creation of one of Disney's most beloved characters. He reprised his Sebastian in the videos *Sebastian's Caribbean Jamboree* (1991), *The Little Mermaid II: Return to the Sea* (2000), and *The Little Mermaid: Ariel's Beginning* (2008), as well as in the TV cartoon series *The Little Mermaid*, *Marsupilami*, and *House of Mouse*.

Wright, Will (1891–1962)   A character actor who played craggy-faced, sour old curmudgeons in over one hundred movies and nearly as many television episodes, he voiced the misanthropic Friend Owl in *Bambi* (1942). He was born in San Francisco and, after working as a newspaper reporter, went into vaudeville which led to his screen debut in 1940. Wright played small but noticeable roles in such movies as *Shadow of the Thin Man* (1941), *Sabatour* (1942), *Tales of Manhattan* (1942), *Wildcat* (1942), *The Major and the Minor* (1942), *Wilson* (1944), *Rhapsody in Blue* (1945), *State Fair* (1945), *The Blue Dahlia* (1946), *Blue Skies* (1946), *Mr. Blandings Builds His Dream House* (1948), *Miss Grant Takes Richmond* (1949), *All the King's Men* (1949), *Adam's Rib* (1949), *The Las Vegas Story* (1952), *The Wild One* (1953), *Johnny Guitar* (1954), *The Man with the Golden Arm* (1955), *Johnny Tremain* (1957), *Alias Jesse James* (1959), *Inherit the Wind* (1960), and *Cape Fear* (1962). He first appeared on television in 1953 and went on to act in dozens of series, including *Four Star Playhouse*, *I Love Lucy*, *The Ford Television Theatre*, *Lassie*, *Dragnet*, *December Bride*, *Sugarfoot*, *The Danny Thomas Show*, *Bat Masterson*, *Dennis the Menace*, *Perry Mason*, *Maverick*, and *Bonanza*, but he is most remembered as Doc Bigelow in *Laramie* and the landlord Ben Weaver on *The Andy Griffith Show*. The character of Friend Owl in *Bambi* is that of a lovable curmudgeon, something Wright did so well on screen. Yet the owl is also one of the funniest characters in the movie, mostly because of Wright's comic timing.

Wynn, Ed (1886–1966)   A very distinctive American comic with a lisping voice, fluttering mannerisms, and a silly giggle, who dressed in eccentric costumes, made outrageous puns, and demonstrated ridiculous inventions, he voiced the illogical Mad Hatter in *Alice in Wonderland* (1951). He was born Isaiah Edwin Leopold in Philadelphia, the son of an immigrant who had built up a successful hat company. The son wasn't interested in the family business and as a teenager went into vaudeville, touring the country as part of an act called the Rah Rah Boys. It was in variety that Wynn developed his character of the "perfect fool" and by the 1910s he was playing this character in Broadway revues such as *Ziegfeld Follies* (1914 and 1915), *The Passing Show of 1916*, *Doing Our Bit* (1917), *Over the Top* (1917), and *Shubert Gaieties* (1919), as well as daffy characters in the book musicals *The Deacon and the Lady* (1910), *Sometime* (1918), and *Manhattan Mary* (1927). He became so popular that shows were built around him and even his book musicals, such as *Simple Simon* (1930) and *Hooray for What!* (1937), made concessions to his unique talents. Wynn started producing and directing his musical revues, and sometimes contributed to the sketches and songs, as with *Ed Wynn Carnival* (1920), *The Perfect Fool* (1921), *The Grab Bag* (1924), *The Laugh Parade* (1931), *Boys and Girls Together* (1940), and *Laugh, Town, Laugh* (1942). Wynn was very popular on the radio in the 1930s and on television in the 1950s, and his film career, while limited, stretched from 1927 to 1967. His screen credits include the Disney live-action movies *Babes and Toyland* (1961), *The Absent-Minded Professor* (1961), *Son of Flubber* (1963), *Mary Poppins* (1965), *Those Calloways* (1965), *That Darn Cat!* (1965), and *The Gnome-Mobile* (1967), as well as *Follow the Leader* (1930), *Stage Door Canteen* (1943), *Marjorie Morningstar* (1958), *The Diary of Anne Frank* (1959), and *Cinderfella* (1960). Because of Wynn's many radio performances, his voice was easily recognized by most Americans; so it was something of a breakthrough when Walt Disney let Wynn voice the Mad Hatter, knowing that moviegoers would immediately recognize the star, something that was previously against the studio's policy of using only unknown performers in animated films. Wynn's performance is one of the highlights of *Alice in Wonderland*. His vaudeville comic timing and lisping pronunciation, combined with Lewis Carroll's nonsense lines, create a surreal tea party sequence that is perhaps closer to the original book than any other scene in the movie.

Young, Alan (b. 1919) The beloved leading man of films and television who also voiced animated characters with a Scottish dialect, he provided the voice of Scrooge in *Mickey's Christmas Carol* (1983), the gentle toymaker Hiram Flaversham in *The Great Mouse Detective* (1986), and the miserly Scottish duck millionaire Scrooge McDuck in *DuckTales the Movie: The Treasure of the Lost Lamp* (1990). He was born Angus Young in North Shields, England, and grew up in Edinburgh, Scotland, and later Canada. He began his professional radio career at the age of thirteen and four years later was writing and performing his own show for the Canadian Broadcasting Corporation. Soon he was acting on American radio and in 1944 had his own program, *The Alan Young Radio Show*; in 1950 the program was turned into a television show and ran three years. Young made his film debut in *Margie* (1946) and played genial leading men in movies such as *Chicken Every Sunday* (1949), *Mr. Belvedere Goes to College* (1949), *Aaron Slick from Punkin Crick* (1952), *Androcles and the Lion* (1952), *Gentlemen Marry Brunettes* (1955), *Tom Thumb* (1958), *The Time Machine* (1960), *The Cat from Outer Space* (1978), *Beverly Hills Cop III* (1994), and *The Time Machine* (2002). He has appeared in many television series over the years, including *Death Valley Days*, *Coming of Age*, *Doogie Howser M.D.*, *Coach*, *ER*, and *Sabrina, the Teenage Witch*, but he is most remembered as Wilbur Post who owns a talking horse in *Mr. Ed* which ran five years. Young first started voicing animated characters in the late 1970s and soon was in great demand for cartoon series such as *Spider-Man and His Amazing Friends*, *The Incredible Hulk*, *The Dukes*, *The Smurfs*, *The Chipmunks*, *The Ren & Stimpy Show*, and *Megas XLR*, but it was his Scottish Scrooge McDuck that was most appreciated. Young first voiced McDuck in 1983 in *Mickey's Christmas Carol*, then reprised him in the TV cartoon series *DuckTales*, *Mickey Mouse Works*, and *House of Mouse*, and in the videos *Duck Tales: Treasure of the Golden Suns* (1987), *Super DuckTales* (1989), *Mickey's Once Upon a Christmas* (1999), *Mickey's Twice Upon a Christmas* (2004), and *Mickey's Around the World in 80 Days* (2005). He voiced other characters in such animated videos as *Beauty and the Beast* (1983), *Alice Through the Looking Glass* (1987), *A Flintstone Family Christmas* (1993), and *The Flintstones Christmas in Bedrock* (1996). Autobiography: *Mr. Ed and Me and More!* (2007); Memoir: *There's No Business Like Show Business ... Was* (2006).

Zahn, Steve (b. 1967) A stage, screen, and television leading man who is also an accomplished singer, he voiced the big-hearted pig Runt of the Litter in *Chicken Little* (2005). Steven James Zahn was born in Marshall, Minnesota, the son of a minister, and trained for a theatre career at the Gustavus Adolphus College, the Guthrie Theatre Drama School, and The American Repertory Theatre at Harvard before getting acting jobs Off Broadway and on tour. He made his television debut in 1990 and his first movie two years later but was not noticed until the film *Reality Bites* (1994), followed by such features as *Crimson Tide* (1995), *That Thing You Do!* (1996), *SubUrbia* (1996), *The Object of My Affection* (1998), *You've Got Mail* (1998), *Riding in Cars with Boys* (2001), *National Security* (2003), *Rescue Dawn* (2006), *The Perfect Getaway* (2009), and *Diary of a Wimpy Kid* (2010), as well as providing voices for *Stuart Little* (1999), *Dr. Dolittle 2* (2001), and *Stuart Little 2*

(2002). Zahn has appeared on such television series as *Friends*, *Comanche Moon*, *Monk*, and *Treme*. He returns to the stage on occasion and co-founded the Malaparte Theatre Company.

Zimmer, Norma (1923–2011) A singer who was a regular on television for many years, she voiced the singing-talking White Rose in *Alice in Wonderland* (1951). She was born Norma Beatrice Larsen in Larsen, Idaho, and began her career as a singer with the Norman Luboff Choir, the Peter Ling Chorale, and the Ken Darby Singers, later doing backup vocals for Bing Crosby, Frank Sinatra, and other singers. She then worked as a background singer in Hollywood under her maiden name and then her married name, Norma Zimmer. She sang on the early television variety program *The Meredith Willson Show* in 1949, followed by many musical specials. In 1960 Zimmer was hired by Lawrence Welk to be his "Champagne Lady" and she sang on his television program and on tour for twenty-two years. She can be seen in minor roles (usually as a singer) in such movies as *Mr. Music* (1950), *Singin' in the Rain* (1952), and *Serenade* (1956), and she voiced the title character for the animated holiday short *Suzy Snowflake* (1951). As late as 2009 Zimmer still performed on occasion with veterans of *The Lawrence Welk Show* in Branson, Missouri. Autobiography: *Norma* (1976).

Voice Guide to Disney Animated Films and Characters

The characters from each short and feature film are listed, followed by the actor (if known) who provided the voice for that character. In some musical films the speaking voice and the singing voice are listed separately. Each of the actors listed has a biographical entry in the Voice Actors section.

Feature Films

The Adventures of Ichabod and Mr. Toad (1949)
Mr. Toad: Eric Blore
Cyril Proudbottom: J. Pat O'Malley
Prosecutor: John McLeish
Mole: Colin Campbell
Angus MacBadger: Campbell Grant
Water Rat: Claud Allister
Mr. Winky: Oliver Wallace
Narrator: ("The Wind in the Willows"): Basil Rathbone
Ichabod Crane: (silent)
Katrina Van Tassel: (silent)
Brom Bones: (silent)
Baltus Van Tassel: (silent)
Singing Narrator ("The Legend of Sleepy Hollow"): Bing Crosby

Aladdin (1992)
Aladdin (speaking): Scott Weinger
Aladdin (singing): Brad Kane
Genie: Robin Williams, Bruce Adler
Jasmine (speaking): Linda Larkin
Jasmine (singing): Lea Salonga
Jafar: Jonathan Freeman
Iago: Gilbert Gottfried
Abu: Frank Welker
Sultan: Douglas Searle
Razoul, Captain of the Guards: Jim Cummings
Cave of Wonders: Phil Proctor

Alice in Wonderland (1951)
Alice: Kathryn Beaumont
Mad Hatter: Ed Wynn
Caterpillar/Butterfly: Richard Haydn
Queen of Hearts: Verna Felton
Cheshire Cat: Sterling Holloway
March Hare: Jerry Colonna
Dormouse: James MacDonald
White Rabbit: Bill Thompson
Walrus: J. Pat O'Malley
Carpenter: J. Pat O'Malley
Dodo: Bill Thompson
King of Hearts: Dink Trout
Doorknob: Joseph Kearns
Tweedledum, Tweedledee: J. Pat O'Malley
Bill: Larry Grey
Nesting Mother Bird: Queenie Leonard
The Rose: Doris Lloyd
White Rose: Norma Zimmer
Card: Don Barclay
Card Painters: The Mellomen (Bill Lee, Thurl Ravenscroft, Max Smith, Bill Hamlin)
Alice's Sister: Heather Angel

Alice in Wonderland (2010) animated characters only
Chessur, the Cheshire Cat: Stephen Fry
Absolem, the Blue Caterpillar: Alan Rickman
Nivens McTwisp, the White Rabbit: Michael Sheen
Mallymkin, the Dormouse: Barbara Windsor
Thackery Earwicket, the March Hare: Paul Whitehouse
Bayard the Bloodhound: Timothy Spall
Uilleam, the Dodo Bird: Michael Gough
Jabberwocky: Christopher Lee

The Aristocats (1970)
Duchess (speaking): Eva Gabor
Duchess (singing): Robie Lester
Thomas O'Malley: Phil Harris
Berlioz: Dean Clark
Toulouse: Gary Dubin
Marie: Liz English

Roquefort: Sterling Holloway
Edgar the Butler: Roddy Maude-Roxby
Scat Cat: Scatman Crothers
Shun Gon: Paul Winchell
Billy Bass: Thurl Ravenscroft
Hit Cat: Lord Tim Hudson
Frou-Frou (speaking): Nancy Kulp
Frou-Frou (singing): Ruth Buzzi
Napoleon: Pat Buttram
Lafayette: George Lindsey
Peppo: Vito Scotti
Abigail Gabble: Monica Evans
Amelia Gabble: Carole Shelley
Madame Bonfamille: Hermione Baddeley
Uncle Waldo: Bill Thompson
Le Petit Cafe Cook: Peter Renaday
Lawyer: Charles Lane
Milkman: Peter Renaday
Singer of Title Song: Maurice Chevalier

Atlantis: The Lost Empire (2001)
Milo James Thatch: Michael J. Fox
Commander Lyle Tiberius Rourke: James Garner
Helga Katrina Sinclair: Claudia Christian
Young Princess Kida: Natalie Storm
Adult Princess Kida: Cree Summer
Preston B. Whitmore: John Mahoney
Gaetan "The Mole" Moliere: Corey Burton
Dr. Joshua Strongbear Sweet: Phil Morris
King Kashekim Nedakh: Leonard Nimoy
Vinny Santorini: Don Novello
Audrey Rocio Ramirez: Jacqueline Obradors
Wihelmina Bertha Packard: Florence Stanley
Fenton Q. Harcourt: David Ogden Stiers
Jebidiah Allardyce "Cookie" Farnsworth: Jim Varney

Bambi (1942)
Baby Bambi: Bobby Stewart
Young Bambi: Donnie Dunagan
Adolescent Bambi: Hardie Albright
Adult Bambi: John Sutherland
Bambi's Mother: Paula Winslowe
Young Faline: Cammie King
Adult Faline: Ann Gillis
Young Flower the Skunk: Stan Alexander
Adolescent Flower: Tim Davis
Adult Flower: Sterling Holloway
Young Thumper: Peter Behn
Adult Thumper: Sam Edwards, Tim Davis
Thumber's Mother: Margaret Lee
Great Prince of the Forest: Fred Shields
Aunt Ena: Mary Lansing
Mrs. Quail: Thelma Boardman
Owl Friend: Will Wright
Girl Bunny: Thelma Hubbard
Mr. Mole: Otis Harlan
Chipmunk: Eddie Holden
Mrs. Possum: Mary Lansing
Quail Mother: Thelma Hubbard
Bullfrog: Clarence Nash
Solo Singer on Soundtrack: Donald Novis

Beauty and the Beast (1991)
Belle: Paige O'Hara
Beast: Robby Benson
Gaston: Richard White
Mrs. Potts: Angela Lansbury
Lumiere: Jerry Orbach
Cogsworth: David Ogden Stiers
Chip: Bradley Pierce
Maurice: Rex Everhart
Lefou: Jesse Corti
Wardrobe: Jo Anne Worley
Bimbettes: Mary Kay Bergman, Kath Soucie
Featherduster: Kimmy Robertson
Monsieur D'Arque: Tony Jay
Phillippe: Hal Smith
Bookseller: Alvin Epstein
Stove: Brian Cummings
Footstool: Frank Welker

Bedknobs and Broomsticks (1971) (animated characters only)
Codfish: Bob Holt
Fisherman Bear: Dallas McKennon
Secretary Bird: Lennie Weinrib
King Leonidas the Lion: Lennie Weinrib

The Black Caldron (1985)
Taran: Grant Bardsley
The Horned King: John Hurt
Princess Eilonwy: Susan Sheridan
Dallben: Freddie Jones
Fflewddur Fflam: Nigel Hawthorne
King Eidilleg: Arthur Malet
Gurgi: John Byner
Doli: John Byner
Creeper: Phil Fondacaro
Hen Wen the Pig: (silent)
Orddu: Eda Reiss Merin
Orwen: Adele Malis-Morey
Orgoch: Billie Hayes
Henchmen: Wayne Allwine, James Almanzar
Narrator: John Huston

Bolt (2008)
Bolt: John Travolta
Penny: Miley Cyrus
Mittens: Susie Essman
Rhino: Mark Walton
Dr. Calico: Malcolm McDowell
Director: James Lipton
Agent: Greg Germann
Veteran Cat: Diedrich Bader
Blake: Nick Swardson
Tom: J. P. Manoux
Mindy: Kari Wahlgren
Thug: Randy Savage
Dr. Forrester: Ronn Moss
Young Penny: Chloe Moretz

Penny's Mom: Grey DeLisle
Penny's TV Dad: Sean Donnellan
Vinnie: Lino DiSalvo
Joey: Todd Cummings
Bobby: Tim Mertens
Ester: Kelly Hoover
Martin: Brian Stepanek
Lloyd: Jeff Bennett
Louie: Daran Norris
Billy: Dan Fogelman
Saul: John DiMaggio
Assistant Director: Jenny Lewis

Brother Bear (2003)
Kenai: Joaquin Phoenix
Koda: Jeremy Suarez
Denahi: Jason Raize
Rutt: Rick Moranis
Tuke: Dave Thomas
Sitka: D. B. Sweeney
Tanana: Joan Copeland
Tug: Michael Clarke Duncan
Old Denahi: Harold Gould
Ram #1: Paul Christie
Ram #2: Danny Mastrogiorgio
Old Lady Bear: Estelle Harris
Male Lover Bear: Greg Propps
Female Lover Bear: Pauley Perrette
Foreign Croatian Bear: Darko Cesar
Chipmunks: Bumper Robinson
Inuit Narrator: Angayuqaq Oscar Kawagley

A Bug's Life (1998)
Flik: Dave Foley
Hopper: Kevin Spacey
Queen Atta: Julia Louis-Dreyfus
Princess Dot: Hayden Panettiere
Queen: Phyllis Diller
Molt: Richard Kind
Slim: David Hyde Pierce
Heimlich: Joe Ranft
Francis: Denis Leary
Manny: Jonathan Harris
Gypsy Moth: Madeline Kahn
Rosie: Bonnie Hunt
Tuck and Roll: Michael McShane
P. T. Flea: John Ratzenberger
Dim: Brad Garrett
Mr. Soil: Roddy McDowall
Dr. Flora: Edie McClurg
Thorny: Alex Rocco
Cornelius: David Ossman
Thumper: David L. Lander
Mosquito: Rodger Bumpass
Baby Maggots: Debi Derryberry
Harry the Mosquito: John Lasseter
Lead Blueberry Scout: Ashley Tisdale
Bug Zapper: Andrew Stanton

Cars (2006)
Doc Hudson: Paul Newman
Lightning McQueen: Owen Wilson
Sally Carrera: Bonnie Hunt
Mater: Larry the Cable Guy
Ramone: Cheech Marin
Luigi: Tony Shalhoub
Guido: Guido Quaroni
Flo: Jenifer Lewis
Sarge: Paul Dooley
Sheriff: Michael Wallis
Fillmore: George Carlin
Lizzie: Katherine Helmond
Mack: John Ratzenberger
Red: Joe Ranft
Chick Hicks: Michael Keaton
Van: Richard Kind
Minny: Edie McClurg
The King: Richard Petty
Mrs. The King: Lynda Petty
Harv: Jeremy Piven
Peterbilt: Joe Ranft
No Chuck: Mike Nelson
Jerry Recycled Batteries: Joe Ranft
Darrell Cartrip: Darrell Waltrip
Bob Cutlass: Bob Costas
Tex: Humpy Wheeler
Abominable Snow Plow: John Ratzenberger
Dusty Rust-eze: Ray Magliozzi
Rusty Rust-eze: Tom Maliozzi
Jay Limo: Jay Leno
Michael Schumacher Ferrari: Michael Schumacher
Fred: Andrew Stanton
Junior: Dale Earnhardt, Jr.
Mario Andretti: Mario Andretti
Boost: Jonas Rivera
Snotrod: Lou Romano
Wingo: Adrian Ochoa
DJ: E. J. Holowicki
Kori Turbowitz: Sarah Clark
Tia: Elissa Knight
Mia: Lindsey Collins
Elvis: Sheryl Crow
Woody Car: Tom Hanks
Buzz Lightyear Car: Tim Allen
Hamm Truck: John Ratzenberger
Mike Car: Billy Crystal
Sullivan Truck: John Goodman
Flik Car: Dave Foley
P. T. Flea Car: John Ratzenberger

Chicken Little (2005)
Chicken Little: Zach Braff
Abby Mallard: Joan Cusack
Runt of the Litter: Steve Zahn
Fish Out of Water: Dan Molina
Buck Cluck: Garry Marshall
Foxy Loxy: Amy Sedaris
Mayor Turkey Lurkey: Don Knotts
Mr. Woolensworth: Patrick Stewart

Principal Fetchit: Wallace Shawn
Goosey Loosey: Mark Walton
Dog Announcer: Harry Shearer
Melvin, Alien Dad: Fred Willard
Tina, Alien Mom: Catherine O'Hara
Alien Cop: Patrick Warburton
Ace — Hollywood Chicken Little: Adam West
Morkubine Porcupine: Mark Dindal
Rodriquez: Joe Whyte
Kirby, Alien Kid: Sean Elmore, Evan Dunn, Matthew Josten
Mama Runt: Kelly Hoover
Hollywood Fish: Will Finn
Hollywood Abby: Dara McGarry
Hollywood Runt: Mark Kennedy

Cinderella (1950)
Cinderella: Ilene Woods
Lady Tremaine (Stepmother): Eleanor Audley
Fairy Godmother: Verna Felton
Prince Charming (speaking): William Phipps
Prince Charming (singing): Mike Douglas
Drizella (Stepsister): Rhoda Williams
Anastasia (Stepsister): Lucille Bliss
Gus: James MacDonald
Jaq: James MacDonald
Perla Mouse: Lucille Williams
King: Luis Van Rooten
Lucifer the Cat: June Foray
Bruno the Dog: James MacDonald, Earl Keen
Grand Duke: Luis Van Rooten
Narrator: Betty Lou Gerson

Dinosaur (2000)
Aladar: D. B. Sweeney
Plio: Alfre Woodard
Yar: Ossie Davis
Zini: Max Casella
Suri: Hayden Pantettiere
Kron: Samuel E. Wright
Neera: Julianna Margulies
Bruton: Peter Siragusa
Baylene: Joan Plowright
Eema: Della Reese

Doug's 1st Movie (1999)
Doug Funnie: Thomas McHugh
Skeeter Valentine: Fred Newman
Roger Klotz: Chris Phillips
Patti Mayonnaise: Constance Shulman
Beebe Bluff: Alice Playten
Guy Graham: Guy Hadley
Porkshop: Fred Newman
Mr. Phil Funnie: Doug Preis
Mrs. Theda Funnie: Becca Lish
Judy Funnie: Becca Lish
Principal "Bob" White: Greg Lee
Mr. Bud Dink: Fred Newman
Mr. Chiminy: Chris Phillips
Mr. Swirly: Bruce Bayley Johnson
Herman Melville: Frank Welker

RoboCrusher: Eddie Korbich
Mr. Bill Bluff: Doug Preis
Boomer Bledsoe: Chris Phillips
Al and Moo Sleech: Eddie Korbich
Mayor Tippi Dink: Doris Belack
Ned Cauphee: Fred Newman
Larry: Chris Phillips
Willie White: Doug Preis
Connie Benge: Becca Lish
Elmo: Alice Playten
Chalky Studebaker: Doug Preis
Bluff Assistant: Bob Bottone
Mrs. Perigrew: Fran Brill
Briar Langolier: Melissa Greenspan

Ducktales the Movie: Treasure of the Lost Lamp (1990)
Scrooge McDuck: Alan Young
Huey, Dewey, and Louie: Russi Taylor
Launchpad McQuack: Terence McGovern
Merlock: Christopher Lloyd
Dijon: Richard Libertini
Duckworth: Chuck McCann
Mrs. Featherby: June Foray
Genie: Rip Taylor
Webbigal "Webby" Vanderquack: Russi Taylor
Mrs. Betina Beakley: Joan Gerber

Dumbo (1941)
Dumbo: (silent)
Timothy Mouse: Edward Brophy
Mrs. Jumbo: Verna Felton
Messenger Stork: Sterling Holloway
Ringmaster: Herman Bing
Jim (or Dandy) Crow: Cliff Edwards
Glasses Crow*: Jim Carmichael
Preacher Crow*: James Baskett
Straw Hat Crow*: Nicodemus Stewart
Prissy the Elephant: Sarah Selby
Matriarch Elephant: Verna Felton
Giggles (or Giddy) the Elephant: Dorothy Scott
Catty the Elephant: Noreen Gammill
Skinny: Malcolm Hutton
Clowns: Billy Bletcher, Eddie Holden
Vocalist for "Baby Mine": Betty Noyes
*not confirmed who played which crow

The Emperor's New Groove (2000)
Emperor Kuzco: David Spade
Pacha: John Goodman
Yzma: Eartha Kitt
Kronk: Patrick Warburton
Chicha: Wendie Malick
Chaca: Kellyann Kelso
Tipo: Eli Russell Linetz
Bucky the Squirrel: Bob Bergen
Old Man: John Fiedler
Waitress: Patti Deutsch
Theme Song Guy: Tom Jones
Official: Joe Whyte

Voice Guide to Disney Animated Films and Characters   239

Enchanted (2007) animated characters only
Giselle: Amy Adams
Prince Edward: James Marsden
Queen Narissa: Susan Sarandon
Nathaniel: Timothy Spall
Pip in Andalasia: Jeff Bennett
Pip in New York: Kevin Lima
Bluebird: Emma Rose Lima
Bunny: Teala Dunn
Troll: Fred Tatasciore
Fawn: Emma Rose Lima
Rapunzel: Emma Rose Lima
Narrator: Julie Andrews

Finding Nemo (2003)
Nemo: Alexander Gould
Marlin: Albert Brooks
Dory: Ellen DeGeneres
Crush: Andrew Stanton
Squirt: Nicholas Bird
Gill: Willem Dafoe
Bloat: Brad Garrett
Peach: Allison Janney
Gurgle: Austin Pendleton
Bubbles: Stephen Root
Bruce: Barry Humphries
Anchor: Eric Bana
Deb and Flo: Vicki Lewis
Jacques: Joe Ranft
Nigel: Geoffrey Rush
Chum: Bruce Spence
Mr. Ray: Bob Peterson
Coral: Elizabeth Perkins
Dentist: Bill Hunter
Darla Sherman: Lulu Ebeling
Pearl: Erica Beck
Sheldon: Erik Per Sullivan
Tad: Jordan Ranft
Moonfish School: John Ratzenberger

The Fox and the Hound (1981)
Young Tod: Keith Coogan
Adult Tod: Mickey Rooney
Young Copper: Corey Feldman
Adult Copper: Kurt Russell
Widow Tweed: Jeanette Nolan
Big Mama the Owl: Pearl Bailey
Amos Slade: Jack Albertson
Vixey: Sandy Duncan
Chief: Pat Buttram
Porcupine: John Fiedler
Squeeks the Caterpillar: Jack Angel
Grumpy Badger: John McIntire
Boomer: Paul Winchell
Dinky: Richard Bakalyan

Fun and Fancy Free (1947) animated characters only
Jiminy Cricket: Cliff Edwards
Mickey Mouse: Walt Disney, James MacDonald
Donald Duck: Clarence Nash
Goofy: Pinto Colvig
Willie the Giant: Billy Gilbert
Singing Harp: Anita Gordon
Vocalists ("Fun and Fancy Free"): The Dinning Sisters
Narrator ("Bongo the Bear"): Dinah Shore

A Goofy Movie (1995)
Goofy Goof: Bill Farmer
Max Goof (speaking): Jason Marsden
Max Goof (singing): Aaron Lohr, Laus Høybye
Peter Pete: Jim Cummings
P.J. Pete: Rob Paulsen
Roxanne: Kelly Martin
Bobby Zimmeruski: Pauly Shore
Principal Mazur: Wallace Shawn
Stacey: Jenna von Oy
Powerline: Tevin Campbell
Bigfoot: Frank Welker
Lester: Kevin Lima
Miss Maples: Jo Anne Worley
Waitress: Florence Stanley
Chad: Joey Lawrence
Main Possum Park Emcee: Kevin Lima
Possum Park Emcee: Pat Buttram
Photo Studio Girl: Brittany Alyse Smith
Lester's Grinning Girl: Robyn Richards
Lisa: Julie Brown
Chad: Joey Lawrence
Tourist Kid: Klee Bragger
Security Guard: Herschel Sparber
Wendell: Corey Burton
Mickey Mouse: Wayne Allwine
Donald Duck: Tony Anselmo

The Great Mouse Detective (1986)
Basil of Baker Street: Barrie Ingham
Dr. David Q. Dawson: Val Bettin
Professor Ratigan: Vincent Price
Olivia Flaversham: Susanne Pollatschek
Hiram Flaversham: Alan Young
Fidget: Candy Candido
Mrs. Judson: Diana Chesney
Mouse Queen Moustoria: Eve Brenner
Lady Mouse: Shani Wallis
Miss Kitty Mouse: Melissa Manchester
Toby the Dog: Frank Welker
Felicia the Cat: Frank Welker
Sherlock Holmes: Basil Rathbone (archival sound)
Dr. Watson: Laurie Main
Bar Maid: Ellen Fitzhugh
Bartholomew: Barrie Ingham
Thug Guards: Val Bettin, Wayne Allwine, Walker Edmiston, Tony Anselmo

Hercules (1997)
Young Hercules (speaking): Josh Keaton
Young Hercules (singing): Roger Bart
Adult Hercules: Tate Donovan
Meg: Susan Egan
Philoctetes: Danny DeVito

Hades: James Woods
Pain: Bobcat Goldthwait
Panic: Matt Frewer
Zeus: Rip Torn
Hera: Samantha Eggar
Amphitryon: Hal Holbrook
Alcmene: Barbara Barrie
Hermes: Paul Shaffer
Fates: Amanda Plummer, Carole Shelley, Paddi Edwards
Muses: Cheryl Freeman, La Chanze, Roz Ryan, Lillias White, Vanéese Y. Thomas
Nessus the River Centaur: Jim Cummings
Apollo: Keith David
Cyclops: Patrick Pinney
Titans: Corey Burton
Earthquake Lady: Mary Kay Bergman
Demetrius the Pot Maker: Wayne Knight
Ithicles: Aaron Michael Metchik
Elderly Thebian: Jim Cummings
Tour Bus Guide: Jim Cummings
Wood, Water & Earth Nymphs: Mary Kay Bergman
Narrator: Charlton Heston

Home on the Range (2004)
Maggie: Roseanne Barr
Mrs. Caloway: Judi Dench
Grace: Jennifer Tilly
Alameda Slim: Randy Quaid
Buck: Cuba Gooding, Jr.
Rico: Charles Dennis
Pearl Gesner: Carole Cook
Sheriff Sam Brown: Richard Reihle
Jeb the Goat: Joe Flaherty
Larry the Duck: Marshall Efron
Ollie the Pig: Charlie Dell
Piggies: Bobby Block, Keaton Savage, Ross Simanteris
Wesley: Steve Buscemi
Abner: Dennis Weaver
Willie Brothers (speaking): Sam J. Levine
Willie Brothers (singing): Gregory Jbara, Jason Graae, David Burnham
Lucky Jack: Charles Haid
Audrey the Chicken: Estelle Harris
Rusty the Dog: G. W. Bailey
Junior the Buffalo: Lance DeGault
Annie: Ann Richards
Longhorns Barry and Bob: Mark Walton
Patrick: Patrick Warburton

The Hunchback of Notre Dame (1996)
Quasimodo: Tom Hulce
Frollo: Tony Jay
Esmeralda (speaking): Demi Moore
Esmeralda (singing): Heidi Mollenhauer
Phoebus: Kevin Kline
Victor: Charles Kimbrough
Hugo: Jason Alexander
Laverne: Mary Wickes, Jane Withers
Clopin: Paul Kandel
Archbishop: David Ogden Stiers
Old Heretic: Gary Trousdale
Quasimodo's Mother: May Kay Bergman
Oafish Guard: Bill Fagerbakke
Guards: Jim Cummings, Corey Burton

The Incredibles (2004)
Bob Parr/Mr. Incredible: Craig T. Nelson
Helen Parr/Elastigirl: Holly Hunter
Robert Dashiell "Dash" Parr: Spencer Fox
Violet Parr: Sarah Vowell
Buddy Pine/Syndrome: Jason Lee
Edna "E" Mode: Brad Bird
Lucius Best/Frozone: Samuel L. Jackson
Bomb Voyage: Dominique Louis
Gilbert Huph: Wallace Shawn
Mrs. Hodenson: Jean Sincere
Mirage: Elizabeth Peña
Jack Jack Parr: Eli Fucile, Maeve Andrews
Bernie Kroop: Lou Romano
Principal: Wayne Canney
Tony Rydinger: Michael Bird
Rick Dicker: Bud Luckey
Kari: Bret Parker
Honey: Kimberly Adair Clark
Underminer: John Ratzenberger
Newsreel Narrator: Teddy Newton

James and the Giant Peach (1996) animated characters only
James: Paul Terry
Grasshopper: Simon Callow
Centipede (speaking): Richard Dreyfuss
Centipede (singing): Jeff Bennett
Ladybug: Jane Leeves
Miss Spider: Susan Sarandon
Earthworm: David Thewlis
Glowworm (speaking): Miriam Margolyes
Glowworn (singing): Sally Stevens

The Jungle Book (1967)
Mowgli: Bruce Reitherman
Baloo the Bear: Phil Harris
Bagheera the Panther: Sebastian Cabot
King Louie of the Apes: Louis Prima
Shere Khan the Tiger: George Sanders
Shere Khan (singing): Thurl Ravenscroft
Kaa the Snake: Sterling Holloway
Colonal Hathi: J. Pat O'Malley
Lady Elephant: Verna Felton
Junior: Clint Howard
Buzzie the Vulture: J. Pat O'Malley
Flaps the Vulture: Chad Stuart
Dizzy the Vulture: Lord Tim Hudson
Ziggy the Vulture: Digby Wolfe
Flunkey the Baboon: Leo DeLyon
Akela the Wolf: John Abbott
Rama the Wolf: Ben Wright
Indian Girl: Darleen Carr
Slop Elephant: Hal Smith

Voice Guide to Disney Animated Films and Characters

Lady and the Tramp (1955)
Lady: Barbara Luddy
Tramp: Larry Roberts
Trusty: Bill Baucom
Jock: Bill Thompson
Bull: Bill Thompson
Dachsie: Bill Thompson
Tony: George Givot
Joe: Bill Thompson
Aunt Sarah: Verna Felton
Si and Am: Peggy Lee
Jim Dear: Lee Millar
Darling: Peggy Lee
Beaver: Stan Freberg
Peg: Peggy Lee
Toughy: Dal McKennon
Boris: Alan Reed
Professor: Dal McKennon
Pedro: Dal McKennon
Dog Catcher: Lee Millar
Pound Dogs (singing): The Mellomen (Max Smith, Bill Lee, Thurl Ravenscroft, Bob Stevens)
Solo Carol Singer on the Soundtrack: Donald Novis

Lilo & Stitch (2002)
Lilo: Daveigh Chase
Stitch: Chris Sanders
Nani: Tia Carrere
Jumba: David Ogden Stiers
Pleakley: Kevin McDonald
David Kawena: Jason Scott Lee
Cobra Bubbles: Ving Rhames
Grand Councilwoman: Zoe Caldwell
Captain Gantu: Kevin Michael Richardson
Mrs. Hasagawa: Amy Hill
Rescue Lady: Susan Hegarty

The Lion King (1994)
Young Simba (speaking): Jonathan Taylor Thomas
Young Simba (singing): Jason Weaver
Adult Simba (speaking): Matthew Broderick
Adult Simba (singing): Joseph Williams
Mufasa: James Earl Jones
Scar: Jeremy Irons
Timon: Nathan Lane
Pumbaa: Ernie Sabella
Rafiki: Robert Guillaume
Zazu: Rowan Atkinson
Young Nala (speaking): Niketa Calame
Young Nala (singing): Laura Williams
Adult Nala (speaking): Moira Kelly
Adult Nala (singing): Sally Dworsky
Shenzi: Whoopi Goldberg
Banzai: Cheech Marin
Ed: Jim Cummings
Sarabi: Madge Sinclair
Sarafina: Zoe Leader
Fighting Hyena: Brian Tochi

The Little Mermaid (1989)
Ariel: Jodi Benson
Ursula: Pat Carroll
Prince Eric: Christopher Daniel Barnes
Sebastian: Samuel E. Wright
Scuttle: Buddy Hackett
Flounder: Jason Marin
Louis: Rene Auberjonois
King Triton: Kenneth Mars
Grimsby: Ben Wright
Flotsam and Jetsam: Paddi Edwards
Carlotta: Edie McClurg
Seahorse: Will Ryan
Alana: Kimmy Robertson
Max: Frank Welker

Make Mine Music (1946) animated characters only
Narrator, Willie, Professor Tetti Tatti, Whitey, Isolde, etc. ("Willie the Whale"): Nelson Eddy
Narrator and Casey ("Casey at the Bat"): Jerry Colonna
Singer ("Without You"): Andy Russell
Singer: ("Two Silhouettes"): Dinah Shore
Narrator ("Peter and the Wolf"): Sterling Holloway
Singing Narration ("Johnny Fedora"): The Andrews Sisters
Singing Narration ("The Martins and the Coys"): The Kings Men (Ken Darby, Bud Linn, Rad Robinson, Jon Didson)

The Many Adventures of Winnie the Pooh (1977)
Winnie the Pooh: Sterling Holloway
Tigger: Paul Winchell
Piglet: John Fiedler
Rabbit: Junius Matthews
Eeyore: Ralph Wright
Owl: Hal Smith
Kanga: Barbara Luddy
Roo: Clint Howard, Dori Whitaker
Gopher: Howard Morris
Christopher Robin: Bruce Reitherman, Jon Walmsley, Timothy Turner
Narration: Sebastian Cabot

Mary Poppins (1964) animated characters only
Master of the Hounds: J. Pat O'Malley
Penguins: Dal McKennon, J. Pat O'Malley, Daws Butler
Reporters: Dal McKennon, George Pelling, J. Pat O'Malley, Alan Napier, Sean McClory
Barnyard Horse: Paul Frees
Cow: Marc Breaux
Ram: Bill Lee
Fox: Dal McKennon
Geese: Marni Nixon
Lambs: Ginny Tyler
Hog: Thurl Ravenscroft
Turtle: Daws Butler
Hounds: Alan Napier, George Pelling, Sean McClory
Pearly Drummer: J. Pat O'Malley

Meet the Robinsons (2007)
Lewis: Daniel Hansen, Jordan Fry
Bowler Hat Guy: Stephen J. Anderson

Wilbur Robinson: Wesley Singerman
Michael "Goob" Yagoobian: Matthew Josten
Cornelius: Tom Selleck
Doris: Ethan Sandler
Mildred: Angela Bassett
Lucille Krunklehorn: Laurie Metcalf
Mr. Willerstein: Tom Kenny
Mr. Harrington: John H. H. Ford
Mrs. Harrington: Dara McGarry
Coach: Don Hall
Lizzy: Tracey Miller-Zarneke
Franny: Nicole Sullivan
Young Franny: Jessie Flower
Frankie: Aurian Redson
Receptionist: Dara McGarry
Grandpa Bud: Stephen J. Anderson
Uncle Art: Adam West
Aunt Billie: Kelly Hoover
Carl: Harland Williams
Gaston: Don Hall
Stanley: Paul Butcher
Lefty: Nathan Greno
Spike: Ethan Sandler
Dmitri: Ethan Sandler
Lazlo: Ethan Sandler
Fritz: Ethan Sandler
T-Rex: Joseph Mateo
Tallulah: Stephen J. Anderson
Petunia: Ethan Sandler
Reporter: Joe Whyte

Melody Time (1948) animated characters only
Narrator and Johnny Appleseed: Dennis Day
Old Settler: Dennis Day
Johnny's Angel: Dennis Day
Aracuan Bird: Pinto Colvig
Singer ("Once Upon a Wintertime"): Frances Langford
Singing Narration ("Little Toot"): the Andrews Sisters
Singers ("Blame It on the Samba"): the Dinning Sisters
Singing Narration ("Pecos Bill"): Roy Rogers and the Sons of the Pioneers
Singing Narration ("Trees"): Fred Waring and the Pennsylvanians
Master of Ceremonies ("Melody Time"): Buddy Clark

Monsters, Inc. (2001)
James P. "Sulley" Sullivan: John Goodman
Mike Wazowski: Billy Crystal
Randall Boggs: Steve Buscemi
Boo: Mary Gibbs
Celia Mae: Jennifer Tilly
Roz: Bob Peterson
Abominable Snowman: John Ratzengerger
Fungus: Frank Oz
Needleman: Daniel Gerson
Ms. Flint: Bonnie Hunt
Bile: Jeff Pidgeon
Smitty: Daniel Gerson
George Sanderson: Samuel Lord Black
Jerry Floor Manager: Steve Susskind

Mulan (1998)
Mulan (speaking): Ming-Na
Mulan (singing): Lea Salonga
Shang (speaking): B. D. Wong
Shang (singing): Donny Osmond
Mushu: Eddie Murphy
Yao: Harvey Fierstein
Chi Fu: James Hong
Chien-Po: Jerry Tondo
Ling (speaking): Gedde Watanabe
Ling (singing) Matthew Wilder
Shan-Yu: Miguel Ferrer
Emperor: Pat Morita
Fa Zhou: Soon-Tek Oh
Fa Li: Freda Foh Shen
Grandmother Fa (speaking): June Foray
Grandmother Fa (singing): Marni Nixon
Matchmaker: Miriam Margolyes
General Li: James Shigeta
First Ancestor: George Takei
Khan: Frank Welker
Little Brother: Chris Sanders

The Nightmare Before Christmas (1993)
Jack Skellington (speaking): Chris Sarandon
Jack Skellington (singing): Danny Elfman
Sally: Catherine O'Hara
Dr. Finklestein: William Hickey
Mayor: Glenn Shadix
Oogie Boogie: Ken Page
Lock: Paul Reubens
Shock: Catherine O'Hara
Barrel: Danny Elfman
Santa: Edward Ivory
Zero the Dog: (silent)
Big Witch: Susan McBride
Small Witch: Debi Durst
Corpse Kid: Debi Durst
Corpse Dad: Kerry Katz
Corpse Mom: Debi Durst
Harlequin Demon: Greg Proops
Mr. Hyde: Randy Crenshaw
Man Under the Stairs: Kerry Katz
Behemoth: Randy Crenshaw
Mummy: Sherwood Ball
Undersea Gal: Carmen Twillie
Clown with the Tearaway Face: Danny Elfman
Vampires: Kerry Katz, Sherwood Ball, Randy Crenshaw

Oliver & Company (1988)
Oliver: Joey Lawrence
Jenny Foxworth: Natalie Gregory
Dodger: Billy Joel
Fagin: Dom DeLuise
Sykes: Robert Loggia
Georgette: Bette Midler

Alonzo Ignacio Julio Federico de Tito: Cheech Marin
Einstein: Richard Mulligan
Francis: Roscoe Lee Browne
Rita: Sheryl Lee Ralph
Winston: William Glover
Roscoe: Taurean Blacque
Desoto: Carl Weintraub
Carlo: Frank Welker

One Hundred and One Dalmatians (1961)
Pongo: Rod Taylor
Perdita: Cate Bauer
Roger Radcliff (speaking): Ben Wright
Roger Radcliff (singing): Bill Lee
Anita: Lisa Davis
Cruella de Vil: Betty Lou Gerson
Horace: Frederick Worlock
Jasper: J. Pat O'Malley
Nani or Nanny: Martha Wentworth
Colonel: J. Pat O'Malley
Sergeant Tibbs: David Frankham
Patch: Mickey Maga
Rolly: Barbara Beaird
Lucky: Mimi Gibson
Rover: Barbara Luddy
Spotty: Ricky Sorensen
Towser: Tudor Owen
Danny: George Pelling
Labrador: Ramsay Hill
Princess: Queenie Leonard
Duchess: Marjorie Bennett
Captain: Thurl Ravenscroft
Quiz Master: Tom Conway
Television Announcer: Ramsay Hill
Miss Birdwell: Betty Lou Gerson
Dirty Dawson: Paul Frees
TV Commercial Singer: Lucille Bliss

Peter Pan (1953)
Peter Pan: Bobby Driscoll
Captain Hook: Hans Conried
Wendy: Kathryn Beaumont
John Darling: Paul Collins
Michael Darling: Tommy Luske
Tinker Bell: (silent)
Mr. Smee: Bill Thompson
Mrs. Darling: Heather Angel
Mr. Darling: Hans Conried
Lost Boys:
Cubby/Bear: Robert Ellis
Nibs/Rabbit: Jeffrey Silver
Tootles/Skunk: Tony Butala
Slightly/Foxy: Stuffy Singer
Raccoon Twins: Stuffy Singer, Johnny McGovern
Indian Chief: Candy Candido
Tiger Lily: (silent)
Mermaids: June Foray, Connie Hilton, Margaret Kerry
Narrator: Tom Conway

Pete's Dragon (1977) animated character only
Elliott: Charlie Callas

Piglet's Big Movie (2003)
Piglet: John Fiedler
Tigger: Jim Cummings
Winnie the Pooh: Jim Cummings
Rabbit: Ken Sansom
Eeyore: Peter Cullen
Owl: Andre Stojka
Kanga: Kath Soucie
Roo: Nikita Hopkins
Christopher Robin: Tom Wheatley

Pinocchio (1940)
Pinocchio: Dickie Jones
Geppetto: Christian Rub
Jiminy Cricket: Cliff Edwards
Blue Fairy: Evelyn Venable
J. Worthington Foulfellow: Walter Catlett
Gideon*: Mel Blanc
Stromboli: Charles Judels
Lampwick: Frankie Darro
Cleo the Goldfish: (silent)
Figaro the Kitten: (silent)
Monstro the Whale: (silent)
Coachman: Charles Judels
Carnival Barker: Don Brodie
Rough House Statue: Jack Mercer
*dialogue removed in final print

Pocahontas (1995)
Pocahontas (speaking): Irene Bedard
Pocahontas (singing): Judy Kuhn
John Smith: Mel Gibson
Governor Ratcliffe: David Ogden Stiers
Grandmother Willow: Linda Hunt
Powhatan (speaking): Russell Means
Powhatan (singing): Jim Cummings
Kocoum: James Apaumut Fall
Nakoma: Michelle St. John
Thomas: Christian Bale
Ben: Billy Connolly
Kekata (speaking): Gordon Tootoosis
Kekata (singing): Jim Cummings
Lon: Joe Baker
Meeko: John Kassir
Percy: Danny Mann
Flit: Frank Welker

Pooh's Heffalump Movie (2005)
Winnie the Pooh: Jim Cummings
Lumpy: Kyle Stanger
Tigger: Jim Cummings
Piglet: John Fiedler
Rabbit: Ken Sansom
Eeyore: Peter Cullen
Mama Heffalump: Brenda Blethyn
Kanga: Kath Soucie
Roo: Nikita Hopkins

The Princess and the Frog (2009)
Young Tiana: Elizabeth M. Dampier
Adult Tiana: Anika Noni Rose
Prince Naveen: Bruno Campos
Dr. Facilier: Keith David
Ray the Firefly: Jim Cummings
Louis the Alligator: Michael-Leon Wooley
Lawrence: Peter Bartlett
Mama Odie: Jenifer Lewis
Young Charlotte: Breanna Brooks
Adult Charlotte: Jennifer Cody
"Big Daddy" La Bouff: John Goodman
Eudora: Oprah Winfrey
James: Terrence Howard
Reggie: Ritchie Montgomery
Darnell: Don Hall
Two Fingers: Paul Briggs
Harvey Fenner: Corey Burton
Henry Fenner: Jerry Kernion
Cousin Randy: Randy Newman
Bulford: Michael Colyar
Marlon the Gator: Emeril Lagasse
Ian the Gator: Kevin Michael Richardson
Georgia: Danielle Moné Truitt
Prince Ralphie: Seth R. Williamson, Shane R. Williamson
Stella: Kelly Hoover

Ratatouille (2007)
Remy: Patton Oswalt
Linguini: Lou Romano
Skinner: Ian Holm
Anton Ego: Peter O'Toole
Colette: Janeane Garofalo
Django: Brian Dennehy
Emile: Peter Sohn
Gusteau: Brad Garrett
Horst: Will Arnett
Lalo: Julius Callahan
Larousse: James Remar
Mustafa: John Ratzenberger
Francoise: Julius Callahan
Lawyer Talon Labarthe: Teddy Newton
Pompidou: Tony Fucile
Armbrister Minion: Brad Bird
Health Inspector: Tony Fucile
Television Narrator: Stéphane Roux

The Reluctant Dragon (1941) animated characters only
Dragon: Barnett Parker
Sir Giles: Claud Allister
Boy: Billy Lee
Boy's Father: Barnett Parker
Courier: Val Stanton
Donald Duck: Clarence Nash
Goofy: Pinto Colvig
Baby Weems: Raymond Severn, Leone Le Doux
Baby Weems' Father: Ernie Alexander
Baby Weems' Mother: Linda Marwood
Narrator ("The Reluctant Dragon"): J. Donald Wilson
Narrator ("Baby Weems"): Gerald Mohr
Narrator ("How to Ride a Horse"): John McLeish
FDR: Art Gilmore
Walter Winchell: Eddie Marr

The Rescuers (1977)
Penny: Michelle Stacy
Bernard: Bob Newhart
Miss Bianca (speaking): Eva Gabor
Miss Bianca (singing): Robie Lester
Madame Medusa: Geraldine Page
Mr. Snoops: Joe Flynn
Orville: Jim Jordan
Rufus: John McIntire
Evinrude: James MacDonald
Ellie Mae: Jeanette Nolan
Luke: Pat Buttram
Deadeye the Rabbit: George Lindsey
Gramps: Larry Clemmons
Owl: John Fiedler
Digger the Mole: Dub Taylor
Chairman: Bernard Fox
Brutus and Nero: Candy Candido

The Rescuers Down Under (1990)
Cody: Adam Ryen
Bernard: Bob Newhart
Miss Bianca (speaking): Eva Gabor
Miss Bianca (singing): Robie Lester
McLeach: George C. Scott
Wilbur: John Candy
Jake: Tristan Rogers
Frank: Wayne Robson
Krebbs: Douglas Searle
Red: Peter Firth
Baitmouse: Billy Barty
Francois: Ed Gilbert
Faloo: Carla Meyer
Chairman: Bernard Fox
Joanna: Frank Welker
Nurse Mouse: Russi Taylor
Cody's Mother: Carla Meyer
Doctor: Bernard Fox
Radio Announcer: Peter Greenwood

Return to Neverland (2002)
Jane: Harriet Owen
Peter Pan: Blayne Weaver
Captain Hook: Corey Burton
Smee: Jeff Bennett
Tinker Bell: (silent)
Young Wendy: Harriet Owen
Adult Wendy: Kath Soucie
Edward: Roger Rees
Danny: Andrew McDonough
Cubby: Spencer Breslin
Nibs: Bradley Pierce
Slightly: Quinn Beswick
Twins: Aaron Spann
Toodles: (silent)

Robin Hood (1973)
Robin Hood: Brian Bedford
Little John: Phil Harris
Maid Marian: Monica Evans
Friar Tuck: Andy Devine
Prince John: Peter Ustinov
Sheriff of Nottingham: Pat Buttram
Alan-a-Dale: Roger Miller
Sir Hiss: Terry-Thomas
Lady Cluck: Carole Shelley
King Richard: Peter Ustinov
Trigger the Vulture: George Lindsey
Nutsy the Vulture: Ken Curtis
Captain of the Guards: Candy Candido
Father Sexton: John Fiedler
Mother Church Mouse: Barbara Luddy
Sis the Rabbit: Dana Laurita
Tagalong the Rabbit: Dori Whitaker
Skippy the Rabbit: Willy Whitaker
Otto the Blacksmith: J. Pat O'Malley

Saludos Amigos (1943) animated characters only
Donald Duck: Clarence Nash
Joe Carioca: José Oliveira
Goofy: Pinto Colvig
Narrator: Fred Shields

Sleeping Beauty (1959)
Princess Aurora: Mary Costa
Maleficent: Eleanor Audley
Prince Phillip: Bill Shirley
Flora: Verna Felton
Fauna: Barbara Jo Allen
Merryweather: Barbara Luddy
King Stefan: Taylor Holmes
King Hubert: Bill Thompson
Maleficent's Goons: Pinto Colvig, Candy Candido
Owl: Dal McKennon
Narrator: Marvin Miller

Snow White and the Seven Dwarfs (1937)
Snow White: Adriana Caselotti
Queen/Old Witch: Lucille LaVerne
Doc: Roy Atwell
Grumpy: Pinto Colvig
Happy: Otis Harlan
Sleepy: Pinto Colvig
Sneezy: Billy Gilbert
Bashful: Scotty Mattraw
Dopey: Eddie Collins
Prince: Harry Stockwell
Magic Mirror: Moroni Olsen
Huntsman: Stuart Buchanan
Birds: Purv Pullen, Marion Darlington

So Dear to My Heart (1949) animated character only
Wise Old Owl: Ken Carson
Adult Jeremiah/Narrator: John Beal

Song of the South (1946) animated characters only
Brer Rabbit: Johnny Lee
Brer Fox: James Baskett
Brer Bear: Nicodemus Stewart
Birds: Babette, Cherie, and Peggy De Castro

The Sword in the Stone (1963)
Wart: Ricky Sorenson, Richard Reitherman, Robert Reitherman
Merlin: Karl Swenson
Sir Ector: Sebastian Cabot
Sir Kay: Norman Alden
Madame Mim: Martha Wentworth
Archimedes: Junius Matthews
Sir Pelinore: Alan Napier
Scullery Maid: Barbara Jo Allen
Wolf: James MacDonald
Black Bart: Thurl Ravenscroft
Girl Squirrel: Ginny Tyler
Old Lady Squirrel: Martha Wentworth

Tangled (2010)
Rapunzel: Mandy Moore
Young Rapunzel: Delaney Rose Stein
Flynn Rider: Zachary Levi
Madame Gothel: Donna Murphy
Stabbington Brothers: Ron Perlman
Pug Thugs:
Hook-Hand Thug: Brad Garrett
Big-Nose Thug: Jeffrey Tambor
Shorty Thug: Paul F. Tompkins
Vlad: Richard Kiel
Maximus the Horse: (silent)
Pascal the Chameleon: (silent)
Captain of the Guard: M. C. Gainey
King: (silent)
Queen: (silent)
Little Girl: Delaney Rose Stein

Tarzan (1999)
Young Tarzan: Alex D. Linz
Adult Tarzan: Tony Goldwyn
Jane Porter: Minnie Driver
Kala: Glenn Close
Professor Archimedes Q. Porter: Nigel Hawthorne
Mr. Clayton: Brian Blessed
Kerchak, the Gorilla King: Lance Henriksen
Terk: Rosie O'Donnell
Young Tantor: Taylor Dempsey
Adult Tantor: Wayne Knight
Tantor's Mother: Patti Deutsch
Mungo: Michael Perl

Teacher's Pet (2004)
Spot Helperman/Scott Leadready II/Scott Manly-Manning: Nathan Lane
Dr. Ivan Krank: Kelsey Grammer
Leonard Amadeus Helperman: Shaun Fleming
Mrs. Mary Lou Moira Angela Darling Helperman: Debra Jo Rupp
Mr. Jolly: David Ogden Stiers
Pretty Boy: Jerry Stiller
Dennis: Paul Reubens

Adele: Megan Mullally
Ian Wazselewski: Rob Paulsen
Principal Crosby Strickler: Wallace Shawn
Barry Anger: Jay Thomas
Mrs. Boogin: Estelle Harris
Marsha/Marcia: Genie Francis
John/Juan: Anthony Geary
Blue Fairy: Rosalyn Landor
Daddy: Timothy Stack
Little Girl: Emma Steinkellner
Beefeater: David Maples
Officer White: Ken Swofford
Leslie Dunkling: Mae Whitman
Conductor: Kevin Michael Richardson
Boy: Patrick Dorn

The Three Caballeros (1945) animated characters only
Donald Duck: Clarence Nash
Joe Carioca: José Oliveira
Panchito: Joaquin Garay
Aracuan Bird: Pinto Colvig
Narrator ("The Cold Blooded Penguin"): Sterling Holloway
Narrators: Fred Shields, Frank Graham

The Tigger Movie (2000)
Tigger: Jim Cummings
Winnie the Pooh: Jim Cummings
Piglet: John Fiedler
Rabbit: Ken Sansom
Eeyore: Peter Cullen
Owl: Andre Stojka
Kanga: Kath Soucie
Roo: Nikita Hopkins
Christopher Robin: Tom Attenborough
Narrator: John Hurt

Toy Story (1995)
Woody: Tom Hanks
Buzz Lightyear: Tim Allen
Andy: John Morris
Mr. Potato Head: Don Rickles
Rex: Wallace Shawn
Slinky Dog: Jim Varney
Hamm: John Ratzenberger
Bo Peep: Annie Potts
Sid Phillips: Erik von Detten
Molly: Hannah Unkrich
Sergeant: R. Lee Emery
Lenny the Binoculars: Joe Ranft
Mr. Spell: Jeff Pidgeon
Shark: Jack Angel
Andy's Mom: Laurie Metcalf
Hannah Phillips: Sarah Freeman
Mr. Spell: Jeff Pidgeon
TV Announcer: Penn Jillette
Sid's Mom: Mickie McGowan
Pizza Planet Guard: Phil Proctor

Toy Story 2 (1999)
Woody: Tom Hanks
Buzz Lightyear: Tim Allen
Jessie: Joan Cusack
Stinky Pete the Prospector: Kelsey Grammer
Andy: John Morris
Mr. Potato Head: Don Rickles
Mrs. Potato Head: Estelle Harris
Rex: Wallace Shawn
Slinky Dog: Jim Varney
Hamm: John Ratzenberger
Bo Peep: Annie Potts
Al the Toy Collector: Wayne Knight
Andy: John Morris
Andy's Mom: Laurie Metcalf
Sergeant: R. Lee Emery
Evil Emperor Zurg: Andrew Stanton
Barbie: Jodi Benson
Geri the Cleaner: Jonathan Harris
Mr. Spell: Jonathan Pidgeon
Wheezy the Penguin (speaking): Joe Ranft
Wheezy the Penguin (singing): Robert Goulet
Molly: Hannah Unkrich
Blue Rock 'Em Sock 'Em Robot: John Lasseter
Red Rock 'Em Sock 'Em Robot: Lee Unkrich
Flik the Ant: Dave Foley
"Woody's Roundup" Announcer: Corey Burton

Toy Story 3 (2010)
Woody: Tom Hanks
Buzz Lightyear: Tim Allen
Jessie: Joan Cusack
Lots-O-Huggin' Bear: Ned Beatty
Andy: John Morris
Mr. Potato Head: Don Rickles
Mrs. Potato Head: Estelle Harris
Rex: Wallace Shawn
Slinky Dog: Blake Clark
Hamm: John Ratzenberger
Ken: Michael Keaton
Barbie: Jodi Benson
Bookworm: Richard Kind
Trixie: Kristen Schaal
Dolly: Bonnie Hunt
Mr. Pricklepants: Timothy Dalton
Stretch the Octopus: Whoopi Goldberg
Andy's Mom: Laurie Metcalf
Sergeant: R. Lee Emery
Molly: Beatrice Miller
Buttercup: Jeff Garlin
Bonnie: Emily Hahn
Chunk: Jack Angel
Twitch: John Cygan
Frog: Jack Willis
Chatter Telephone: Teddy Newton
Jack-in-the-Box: Lee Unkrich
Bonnie's Mother: Lori Alan
Sparks: Jan Rabson
Chuckles the Clown: Bud Luckey
Peatrice: Amber Kroner
Peanelope: Brianna Maiwand
Spanish Mode Buzz Lightyear: Javier Fernandez Peña

Young Andy: Charlie Bright
Baby Molly: Hannah Unkrich
Aliens: Jeff Pidgeon
Janitor: Bob Peterson
Sid Phillips the Garbage Man: Erik von Detten

Treasure Planet (2002)
Jim Hawkins: Joseph Gordon-Levitt
Young Jim: Austin Majors
John Silver: Brian Murray
B.E.N.: Martin Short
Mr. Arrow: Roscoe Lee Browne
Onus: Corey Burton
Billy Bones: Patrick McGoohan
Morph: Dane A. Davis
Sarah Hawkins: Lauri Metcalf
Dr. Doppler: David Hyde Pierce
Captain Amelia: Emma Thompson
Hands: Michael McShane
Scroop: Michael Wincott
Narrator: Tony Jay

Up (2009)
Carl Fredrickson: Edward Asner
Russell: Jordan Nagai
Charles Muntz: Christopher Plummer
Dug: Bob Peterson
Alpha: Bob Peterson
Beta: Delroy Lindo
Gamma: Jerome Ranft
Omega: Josh Cooley
Young Ellie: Elie Docter
Young Carl: Jeremy Leary
Foreman Tom: John Ratzengerger
Construction Worker Steve: Danny Mann
Police Officer Edith: Mickie McGowan
Nurse George: Donald Fullilove
Nurse AJ: Jess Harnell
Campmaster Strauch: Pete Docter
Kevin: Pete Docter
Newsreel Announcer: David Kaye

WALL-E (2008)
WALL-E: Ben Burtt
EVE: Elissa Knight
Captain McCrea: Jeff Garlin
Shelby Forthright: Fred Willard
AUTO: (computer generated)
John: John Ratzenberger
Mary: Kathy Najimy
Ship's Computer: Sigourney Weaver
M-O: Ben Burtt

Who Framed Roger Rabbit (1988) animated characters only
Roger Rabbit: Charles Fleischer
Jessica Rabbit (speaking) Kathleen Turner
Jessica Rabbit: (singing): Amy Irving
Baby Herman (off screen): Lou Hirsch
Baby Herman (on screen): April Winchell
Psycho: Charles Fleischer
Stupid: Fred Newman
Droopy Dog: Richard Williams
Smart Ass: David Lander
Greasy: Charles Fleischer
Mrs. Herman: April Winchell
Benny the Cab: Charles Fleischer
Betty Boop: Mae Questel
Bugs Bunny: Mel Blanc
Donald Duck: Tony Anselmo
Mickey Mouse: Wayne Allwine
Minnie Mouse: Russi Taylor
Goofy: Tony Pope
Daffy Duck: Mel Blanc
Yosemite Sam: Joe Alaskey
Porky Pig: Mel Blanc
Sylvester: Mel Blanc
Tweety Bird: Mel Blanc
Foghorn Leghorn: Joe Alaskey
Pinocchio: Peter Westy
Woody Woodpecker: Cherry Davis
Dumbo: Frank Welker
Hippo: Mary T. Radford
Wolf: Tony Pope
Lena Hyena: June Foray
Singing Sword: Frank Sinatra (archival sound)
Judge Doom as a Toon: Christopher Lloyd

Film Shorts

All of the Disney sound shorts featuring favorites Mickey Mouse, Donald Duck, Pluto, Chip and Dale, Goofy, and so on are listed, as well as shorts that offered other characters. The Silly Symphony shorts are also included and indicated as such. These were usually musical cartoons with little or no dialogue and the characters often were silent as the music was primary so voice actors were rarely needed. Shorts that were part of a feature-length anthology film, such as "Peter in the Wolf" in *Make Mine Music* and "Pecos Bill" from *Melody Time*, are included in the features section.

Adventures in Music: Melody (1953)
Professor Owl: Bill Thompson
Bass Singer: Harry Stanton

African Diary (1945)
Goofy/Narrator: Pinto Colvig

All in a Nutshell (1949)
Donald Duck: Clarence Nash
Chip: James MacDonald
Dale: Dessie Flynn

Alpine Climbers (1936)
Mickey Mouse: Walt Disney
Donald Duck: Clarence Nash

Goofy: Pinto Colvig
Saint Bernard: unknown

Aquamania (1961)
Goofy: Pinto Colvig
Goofy Jr.: Kevin Corcoran
Narrator: John Dehner

Arctic Antics (1930) Silly Symphony
Seals, walruses, polar bears, penguins: silent

The Army Mascot (1942)
Pluto: Pinto Colvig
Gunther Goat: unknown

The Art of Self-Defense (1941)
Goofy: George Johnson
Narrator: John McLeish

The Art of Skiing (1941)
Goofy: George Johnson
Narrator: John McLeish

The Autograph Hound (1939)
Donald Duck: Clarence Nash
Security Guard: Billy Bletcher
Mickey Rooney: unknown
Sonja Henie: unknown
Shirley Temple: unknown
The Ritz Brothers: unknown

Autumn (1930) Silly Symphony
Crow, skunk, porcupine, beavers, ducks, etc.: silent

Babes in the Woods (1932) Silly Symphony
Two Dutch children, witch, gnomes, etc.: silent

Baggage Buster (1941)
Goofy: George Johnson

The Band Concert (1935)
Donald Duck: Clarence Nash
Mickey Mouse: silent

The Barn Dance (1929)
Mickey Mouse: Walt Disney
Minnie Mouse: Marcellite Garner
Pete: Billy Bletcher

The Barnyard Battle (1929)
Mickey Mouse: silent
Cats: silent

The Barnyard Broadcast (1931)
Mickey Mouse: Walt Disney
Minnie Mouse: Marcellite Garner
Pluto; unknown
Cat: unknown

The Barnyard Concert (1930)
Mickey Mouse: Walt Disney
Three Birds: unknown
Piglets: unknown

Barnyard Olympics (1932)
Mickey Mouse: Walt Disney
Minnie Mouse: Marcellite Garner
Pete: Billy Bletcher

Bath Day (1946)
Minnie Mouse: Ruth Clifford
Figaro: Clarence Nash
Lucifer: unknown
Alley Cats: unknown

The Beach Party (1931)
Mickey Mouse: Walt Disney
Minnie Mouse: Marcellite Garner
Horace Horsecollar: unknown
Clarabelle Cow: unknown
Pluto: unknown

Beach Picnic (1939)
Donald Duck: Clarence Nash
Pluto: Lee Millar

Bearly Asleep (1955)
Donald Duck: Clarence Nash
Humphrey the Bear: James MacDonald

The Bears and the Bees (1932) Silly Symphony
Big Bear, Bear Cubs: silent

Bee at the Beach (1950)
Donald Duck: Clarence Nash
Bee: unknown

Bee on Guard (1951)
Donald Duck: Clarence Nash
Bee Guard: unknown

Beezy Bear (1955)
Donald Duck: Clarence Nash
Humphrey the Bear: James MacDonald
Ranger J. Audubon Woodlore: Bill Thompson

Ben and Me (1953)
Amos Mouse: Sterling Holloway
Benjamin Franklin: Charles Ruggles
Thomas Jefferson: Hans Conried
Governor Keith: Bill Thompson

The Big Bad Wolf (1934) Silly Symphony
Big Bad Wolf: Billy Bletcher
Little Red Riding Hood: unknown
Practical Pig: Pinto Colvig
Fifer Pig: Dorothy Compton
Fiddler Pig: Mary Moder
Granny: unknown

The Big Wash (1948)
Goofy: Pinto Colvig
Dolores the Elephant: unknown

Billposters (1940)
Donald Duck: Clarence Nash
Goofy: Pinto Colvig
Goat: silent

The Bird Store (1932) Silly Symphony
Canary, cat, Marx Brothers birds, etc.: silent

Birds in the Spring (1933) Silly Symphony
Otto the bird, rattlesnake, father bird, etc.: silent

Birds of a Feather (1931) Silly Symphony
Chick, hawk, crows, etc.: silent

The Birthday Party (1931)
Mickey Mouse: Walt Disney
Minnie Mouse: Marcellite Garner
Chef: unknown

Blue Rhythm (1931)
Mickey Mouse: Walt Disney
Minnie Mouse: Marcellite Garner
Pluto: unknown
Horace Horsecollar: unknown
Clarabelle Cow: unknown

Boat Builders (1938)
Mickey Mouse: Walt Disney
Goofy: Pinto Colvig
Donald Duck: Clarence Nash
Minnie Mouse: Marcellite Garner

Bone Bandit (1948)
Pluto: Pinto Colvig
Gopher: unknown

Bone Trouble (1940)
Pluto: Lee Millar
Butch the Bulldog: unknown

Bootle Beetle (1947)
Bootle Beetle: Dink Trout
Donald Duck: Clarence Nash
Young Beetle: unknown

Boundin' (2003)
Jackalope: (silent)
Lamb: (silent)
Narrator: Bud Luckey

The Brave Engineer (1950)
Narration and Casey Jones: Jerry Colonna
Singing Narration: The King's Men (Ken Darby, Bud Linn, Rad Robinson, Jon Didson)

Brave Little Tailor (1938)
Mickey Mouse: Walt Disney
Minnie Mouse: Marcellite Garner
King: unknown
Giant: unknown

Broken Toys (1935) Silly Symphony
Sailor Doll: Tommy Bupp
Girl Doll: unknown.
Fields Doll: unknown
Police Doll: unknown
Zazu Pitts Doll: unknown
Shirley Temple Doll: unknown

Bugs in Love (1932) Silly Symphony
Boy Bug, Girl Bug, crow, etc.: silent

Building a Building (1933)
Mickey Mouse: Walt Disney
Minnie Mouse: Marcellite Garner
Pegleg Pete: Billy Bletcher

Bumble Bee (1949)
Pluto: Pinto Colvig
Bumble Bee: unknown

The Busy Beavers (1931) Silly Symphony
Clever Beaver, beavers, etc.: silent

The Cactus Kid (1930)
Mickey Mouse: Walt Disney
Minnie Mouse: Marcellite Garner
Pedro (Pete): Billy Bletcher

Californy 'er Bust (1945)
Goofy: Pinto Colvig
Narrator: John McLeish

Camp Dog (1950)
Pluto: Pinto Colvig
Bent-Tail the Coyote: unknown
Bent-Tail, Junior: unknown

Camping Out (1934)
Mickey Mouse: Walt Disney
Minnie Mouse: Marcellite Garner
Horace Horsecollar: unknown
Clarabelle Cow: unknown

Canine Caddy (1941)
Pluto: Pinto Colvig
Mickey Mouse: Walt Disney
Gopher: unknown

Canine Casanova (1945)
Pluto: Pinto Colvig
Dinah the Dachshund: unknown
Dogcatcher (Pete): Billy Bletcher

Canine Patrol (1945)
Pluto: Pinto Colvig
Baby Turtle: unknown

Cannibal Capers (1930) Silly Symphony
Cannibals, lion, etc.: unknown

Canvas Back Duck (1953)
Donald Duck: Clarence Nash
Boxer Peewee Pete: Billy Bletcher
Huey, Dewey, Louie: Clarence Nash
Little Boy: unknown

Casey Bats Again (1954)
Casey, his nine daughters: unknown

The Castaway (1931)
Mickey Mouse: Walt Disney
Gorilla, lion, alligator, turtle: unknown

Cat Nap Pluto (1948)
Pluto: Pinto Colvig
Figaro: Clarence Nash
Pluto Sandman: unknown
Figaro Sandman: unknown

The Cat's Out (131) Silly Symphony
Cat, bird, giant animals: silent

The Chain Gang (1930)
Mickey Mouse: Walt Disney
Hound Dogs: Pinto Colvig
Guards: unknown

Chef Donald (1941)
Donald Duck: Clarence Nash
Radio announcer: unknown

Chicken Little (1943)
Chicken Little: Frank Graham
Cocky Locky: Frank Graham
Foxy Loxy: Frank Graham
Turkey Lurkey: Frank Graham
Ducks: Clarence Nash
Chickens: Florence Gill
Narrator: Frank Graham

The China Plate (1931) Silly Symphony
Emperor, Mandarin boy and girl, musicians, dancers, etc.: silent

The China Shop (1934) Silly Symphony
Shop owner, china figurines, etc.: silent

Chip an' Dale (1947)
Chip: James MacDonald
Dale: Dessie Flynn
Donald Duck: Clarence Nash

Chips Ahoy (1956)
Donald Duck: Clarence Nash
Chip: James MacDonald
Dale: Dessie Flynn

Clock Cleaners (1937)
Mickey Mouse: Walt Disney
Donald Duck: Clarence Nash
Goofy: Pinto Colvig
Stork: unknown

The Clock Store (1931) Silly Symphony
Clocks, clock figures, etc.: silent

The Clock Watcher (1945)
Donald Duck: Clarence Nash

Clown of the Jungle (1947)
Donald Duck: Clarence Nash
Aracuan Bird: Pinto Colvig
Narrator: unknown

Cock o' the Walk (1935) Silly Symphony
Country Rooster, Prize Fighter Rooster, Hen: unknown

Cold Storage (1951)
Pluto: Pinto Colvig
Stork: unknown

Cold Turkey (1951)
Pluto: Pinto Colvig
Milton the Cat: unknown

Cold War (1951)
Goofy: Pinto Colvig
Mrs. Goofy: unknown

Commando Duck (1944)
Donald Duck: Clarence Nash

Contrary Condor (1944)
Donald Duck: Clarence Nash
Mother Condor: Florence Gill
Baby Condor: Florence Gill

The Cookie Carnival (1935) Silly Symphony
Gingerbread Boy: Pinto Colvig
Girl Cookie: unknown

Corn Chips (1951)
Donald Duck: Clarence Nash
Chip: James MacDonald
Dale: Dessie Flynn

The Country Cousin (1936) Silly Symphony
Morty Citymouse: unknown
Abner Countrymouse: unknown

A Cowboy Needs a Horse (1956)
Young Boy: silent
Singing narration: Disney chorus

Crazy Over Daisy (1950)
Donald Duck: Clarence Nash
Daisy Duck: Gloria Blondell
Chip: James MacDonald
Dale: Dessie Flynn

Crazy with the Heat (1947)
Donald Duck: Clarence Nash
Goofy: Pinto Colvig
Oasis Soda Fountain Proprietor: Paul Frees

Cured Duck (1945)
Donald Duck: Clarence Nash
Daisy Duck: Gloria Blondell

Daddy Duck (1948)
Donald Duck: Clarence Nash
Joey, the Baby Kangaroo: unknown
Nagging Social Worker: unknown

The Delivery Boy (1931)
Mickey Mouse: Walt Disney
Minnie Mouse: Marcellite Garner
Pluto: unknown

Der Fuehrer's Face (1942)
Donald Duck: Clarence Nash
Nazi Officer: unknown

Destino (2003)
Singer: Dora Luz

Dog Watch (1945)
Pluto: Pinto Colvig
Rat: unknown

The Dognapper (1934)
Dognapper (Pegleg Pete): Billy Bletcher
Mickey Mouse: Walt Disney
Donald Duck: Clarence Nash
Minnie Mouse: unknown
Minnie's Pekinese: unknown

Don Donald (1937)
Donald Duck: Clarence Nash
Donna (Daisy) Duck: Clarence Nash

Donald and Pluto (1936)
Donald Duck: Clarence Nash
Pluto: Pinto Colvg

Donald and the Wheel (1961)
Donald Duck: Clarence Nash
Spirit of Progress, Senior: Thurl Ravenscroft
Spirit of Progress, Junior: unknown

Donald Applecore (1952)
Donald Duck: Clarence Nash
Chip: James MacDonald
Dale: Dessie Flynn

Donald Duck and the Gorilla (1944)
Donald Duck: Clarence Nash
Ajax the Gorilla: unknown
Huey, Dewey, Louie: Clarence Nash
Radio Voice: Unknown

Donald Gets Drafted (1942)
Donald Fauntleroy Duck: Clarence Nash
Sgt. Pete: Billy Bletcher
Officer: John McLeish

Donald in Mathmagic Land (1959)
Donald Duck: Clarence Nash
Narrator and the Spirit of Adventure: Paul Frees

Donald's Better Self (1938)
Donald Duck: Clarence Nash
Donald's Angel: Thelma Boardman
Donald's Devil: Don Brodie

Donald's Camera (1941)
Donald Duck: Clarence Nash
Chipmunk: unknown
Woodpecker: unknown

Donald's Cousin Gus (1939)
Donald Duck: Clarence Nash
Gus the Goose: unknown
Barking Hot Dog: Pinto Colvig

Donald's Crime (1945)
Donald Duck: Clarence Nash
Daisy Duck: Gloria Blondell

Donald's Decision (1942)
Donald Duck: Clarence Nash
Donald's Angel: Thelma Boardman
Donald's Devil: Don Brodie

Donald's Diary (1954)
Donald Duck: Clarence Nash
Daisy Duck: Gloria Blondell
Narrator and Donald's Internal Monologue: Leslie Denison

Donald's Dilemma (1947)
Donald Duck: Clarence Nash
Daisy Duck: Gloria Blondell
Psychiatrist: unknown

Donald's Dog Laundry (1940)
Donald Duck: Clarence Nash
Pluto: Lee Millar

Donald's Double Trouble (1946)
Donald Duck: Clarence Nash
Daisy Duck: Gloria Blondell
Donald's Look-a-Like: Leslie Denison

Donald's Dream Voice (1948)
Donald Duck: Clarence Nash
Daisy Duck: Ruth Clifford
Suave Donald: Leslie Denison

Donald's Garden (1942)
Donald Duck: Clarence Nash
Gopher: unknown

Donald's Gold Mine (1942)
Donald Duck: Clarence Nash
Burro: unknown

Donald's Golf Game (1938)
Donald Duck: Clarence Nash
Huey, Dewey, Louie: Clarence Nash
Grasshopper: unknown

Donald's Happy Birthday (1949)
Donald Duck: Clarence Nash
Huey, Dewey, Louie: Clarence Nash

Donald's Lucky Day (1939)
Donald Duck: Clarence Nash
Black cat: unknown

Donald's Nephews (1938)
Donald Duck: Clarence Nash
Huey, Dewey, Louie: Clarence Nash

Donald's Off Day (1944)
Donald Duck: Clarence Nash
Huey, Dewey, Louie: Clarence Nash

Donald's Ostrich (1937)
Donald Duck: Clarence Nash
Hortense the Ostrich: Pinto Colvig
Lady Chef on Radio: Elvia Allman
Villain on Radio: Billy Bletcher

Donald's Penguin (1939)
Donald Duck: Clarence Nash
Baby Penguin: unknown

Donald's Snow Fight (1942)
Donald Duck: Clarence Nash
Huey, Dewey, Louie: Clarence Nash

Donald's Tire Trouble (1943)
Donald Duck: Clarence Nash

Donald's Vacation (1940)
Donald Duck: Clarence Nash
Chipmunks, Bear: unknown

Don's Fountain of Youth (1953)
Donald Duck: Clarence Nash

Huey, Dewey, Louie: Clarence Nash
Alligator: unknown

Double Dribble (1946)
Goofy: Pinto Colvig

Dragon Around (1954)
Donald Duck: Clarence Nash
Chip: James MacDonald
Dale: Dessie Flynn

Drip Dippy Donald (1948)
Donald Duck: Clarence Nash

The Duck Hunt (1932)
Mickey Mouse: Walt Disney
Pluto: Pinto Colvig

Duck Pimples (1945)
Donald Duck: Clarence Nash
Harold King/Mystery Writer: Doodles Weaver
Detective Hennessey: Billy Bletcher
Radio characters: Doodles Weaver

Dude Duck (1951)
Donald Duck: Clarence Nash
Rover Boy the Horse: unknown

Dumb Bell of the Yukon (1946)
Donald Duck: Clarence Nash
Daisy Duck: unknown
Mother Bear: unknown
Baby Bear: unknown

Early to Bed (1941)
Donald Duck: Clarence Nash

Education for Death (1943)
Hans the German Boy: unknown
Adolf Hitler: Adolf Hitler (archival sound)
Narrator: Art Smith

Egyptian Melodies (1931) Silly Symphony
Spider, mummies, soldiers: unknown

Elmer Elephant (1936) Silly Symphony
Elmer Elephant: unknown
Tillie Tiger: Bernice Hansen

The Eyes Have It (1945)
Private Donald Duck: Clarence Nash
Pluto: Pinto Colvig

Fall Out — Fall In (1943)
Donald Duck: Clarence Nash

Farmyard Symphony (1938) Silly Symphony
Rooster, Chicken, Farmer, Farmer's Wife: unknown
Bull: Billy Bletcher

Father Noah's Ark (1933) Silly Symphony
Noah, Noah's Sons and their Wives, Mother Noah: unknown

Father's Are People (1951)
Father (Goofy): Pinto Colvig
Junior: Bobby Driscoll

Father's Day Off (1953)
Goofy: Pinto Colvig
Mrs. Goofy: unknown

Father's Lion (1952)
George Geef (Goofy): Pinto Colvig
Junior: Bobby Driscoll
Lion: unknown

Father's Week End (1953)
Goofy: Pinto Colvig
Junior: Bobby Driscoll

Ferdinand the Bull (1938)
Ferdinand: Milt Kahl
Narrator: Don Wilson

Fiddling Around (1930) aka *Just Mickey*
Mickey Mouse: Walt Disney

Figaro and Cleo (1943)
Figaro the Kitten: Clarence Nash
Cleo the Goldfish: silent
Maid: unknown

Figaro and Frankie (1947)
Minnie Mouse: Ruth Clifford
Figaro the Kitten: Clarence Nash
Frankie the Canary: unknown
Butch the Bulldog: unknown

Fire Chief (1940)
Fire Chief Donald Duck: Clarence Nash
Huey, Dewey, Louie: Clarence Nash

The Fire Fighters (1930)
Mickey Mouse: Walt Disney
Minnie Mouse: Marcellite Garner
Horace Horsecollar: unknown
Cat: unknown

First Aiders (1944)
Minnie Mouse: Ruth Clifford
Pluto: Pinto Colvig
Figaro the Kitten: Clarence Nash

Fishin' Around (1931)
Mickey Mouse: Walt Disney
Pluto: Pinto Colvig
Game Warden: unknown

Flowers and Trees (1932) Silly Symphony
Two trees in love, jealous tree stump, etc.: silent

Flying Jalopy (1943)
Donald Duck: Clarence Nash
Ben Buzzard: unknown

The Flying Mouse (1934) Silly Symphony
Bat: Clarence Nash
Mouse, Butterfly Fairy, Spider: unknown

The Flying Squirrel (1954)
Donald Duck: Clarence Nash
Flying Squirrel: unknown

Food for Feudin' (1950)
Pluto: Pinto Colvig
Chip: James MacDonald
Dale: Dessie Flynn

For the Birds (2000)
Large Bird: Ralph Eggleston

For Whom the Bulls Toil (1953)
Goofy: Pinto Colvig
Narrator and Mexican fans: Joaquin Garay

Foul Hunting (1947)
Goofy: Pinto Colvig
Duck: unknown

The Fox Hunt (1931) Silly Symphony
Fox, hunters: unknown

The Fox Hunt (1938)
Mickey Mouse: Walt Disney
Goofy: Pinto Colvig
Donald Duck: Clarence Nash
Clara Cluck: Florence Gill
Horace Horsecollar: unknown

Frank Duck Brings 'em Back Alive (1946)
Goofy: Pinto Colvig
Frank Duck (Donald Duck): Clarence Nash
Lion: unknown

Freewayphobia No. 1 (1965)
Goofy: Pinto Colvig
Narrator: Paul Frees

Frolicking Fish (1930) Silly Symphony
Octopus, other sea creatures: silent

Fun with Mr. Future (1982)
Mr. Future: unknown

Funny Little Bunnies (1934) Silly Symphony
Bunnies: unknown

The Gallopin' Gaucho (1928)
Mickey Mouse: Walt Disney
Minnie Mouse: Walt Disney
Pete: Billy Bletcher
Ostrich: unknown

A Gentleman's Gentleman (1941)
Mickey Mouse: Walt Disney
Pluto: Lee Millar

Geri's Game (1997)
Geri: Bob Peterson

Get Rich Quick (1951)
George Geef (Goofy): Pinto Colvig
Mrs. Geef: unknown

Giantland (1933)
Mickey Mouse/Jack and the Beanstalk: Walt Disney
Giant: unknown
Minnie Mouse: Marcellite Garner
Mickey's Nephews: unknown

The Goddess of Spring (1934) Silly Symphony
Persephone, Devil: unknown

Golden Eggs (1941)
Donald Duck: Clarence Nash
Rooster: unknown
Hens: Florence Gill

The Golden Touch (1935) Silly Symphony
King Midas: Billy Bletcher
Elf: unknown

Goliath II (1960)
Goliath II: Kevin Corcoran
Goliath I: J. Pat O'Malley
Goliath's Mother: Barbara Jo Allen
Raja the Tiger: Mel Blanc
Eloise: Verna Felton
Mouse: Paul Frees
Narrator: Sterling Holloway

Good Scouts (1938)
Donald Duck: Clarence Nash
Huey, Dewey, Louie: Clarence Nash

A Good Time for a Dime (1941)
Donald Duck: Clarence Nash
Daisy Duck: unknown

Goofy and Wilbur (1939)
Goofy: George Johnson
Wilbur the Grasshopper: unknown

Goofy Gymnastics (1949)
Goofy: Pinto Colvig
Narrator: John McLeish

Goofy's Freeway Troubles (1965)
Goofy: Pinto Colvig
Narrator: Paul Frees

Goofy's Glider (1940)
Goofy: George Johnson
Narrator: John McLeish

The Gorilla Mystery (1930)
Mickey Mouse: Walt Disney
Minnie Mouse: Marcellite Garner
Gorilla: unknown

Grand Canyonscope (1954)
Donald Duck: Clarence Nash
Ranger J. Audubon Woodlore: Bill Thompson
Mountain lion: unknown

The Grasshopper and the Ants (1934) Silly Symphony
Grasshopper: Pinto Colvig
Queen Ant: unknown

The Greener Yard (1949)
Donald Duck: Clarence Nash
Bootle Beetle: Dink Trout
Beetle's Son: unknown

Grin and Bear It (1954)
Donald Duck: Clarence Nash
Humphrey the Bear: James MacDonald
Ranger J. Audubon Woodlore: Bill Thompson

The Grocery Boy (1932)
Mickey Mouse: Walt Disney
Minnie Mouse: Marcellite Garner
Pluto: Pinto Colvig

Gulliver Mickey (1934)
Mickey Mouse: Walt Disney
Mickey's Nephews: unknown
Giant Spider: unknown

The Haunted House (1929)
Mickey Mouse: Walt Disney
Grim Reaper Skeleton, ghosts, etc.: unknown

Hawaiian Holiday (1937)
Mickey Mouse: Walt Disney
Minnie Mouse: Marcellite Garner
Goofy: Pinto Colvig
Donald Duck: Clarence Nash
Pluto: Pinto Colvig

Hello Aloha (1952)
Mr. Geef (Goofy): Pinto Colvig

Hell's Bells (1929) Silly Symphony
Satan, Cerebus, demons: unknown

The Hockey Champ (1939)
Donald Duck: Clarence Nash
Huey, Dewey, Louie: Clarence Nash

Hockey Homicide (1945)
Goofy: Pinto Colvig
Referee "Clean Game" Kinney: unknown
Bertino and Ferguson: unknown
Narrator: Doodles Weaver

Hold That Pose (1950)
Goofy: Pinto Colvig
Bear: unknown

Home Defense (1943)
Donald Duck: Clarence Nash
Huey, Dewey, Louie: Clarence Nash

Home Made Home (1951)
Goofy: Pinto Colvig
Narrator: John McLeish

Honey Harvester (1949)
Donald Duck: Clarence Nash
Bee: unknown

Hook, Lion and Sinker (1950)
Donald Duck: Clarence Nash
Mountain lion: unknown
Lion cub: unknown

Hooked Bear (1956)
Humphrey the Bear: James MacDonald
Ranger J. Audubon Woodlore: Bill Thompson

How to Be a Detective (1952)
Johnny Eyeball, Private Eye (Goofy): Pinto Colvig
Sheriff Al Muldoon (Pete): Billy Bletcher
The Dame: June Foray

How to Be a Sailor (1944)
Goofy: Pinto Colvig
Narrator: John McLeish

How to Dance (1953)
Goofy: Pinto Colvig
Musicians: Firehouse Five Plus Two

How to Fish (1942)
Goofy: George Johnson
Narrator: John McLeish

How to Have an Accident at Work (1959)
Donald Duck: Clarence Nash
J. Fate: Bill Thompson

How to Have an Accident in the Home (1956)
Donald Duck: Clarence Nash
J. Fate: Bill Thompson

How to Play Baseball (1942)
Goofy: George Johnson
Narrator: Fred Shields

How to Play Football (1944)
Goofy: Pinto Colvig
Coach: unknown

How to Play Golf (1944)
Goofy: Pinto Colvig
Narrator: Fred Shields

How to Ride a Horse (1950)
Goofy: Pinto Colvig
Narrator: John McLeish

How to Sleep (1953)
Goofy: Pinto Colvig
Scientist: unknown

How to Swim (1942)
Goofy: George Johnson
Narrator: John McLeish

I'm No Fool as a Pedestrian (1956)
Jiminy Cricket: Cliff Edwards

I'm No Fool Having Fun (1957)
Jiminy Cricket: Cliff Edwards

I'm No Fool in Water (1957)
Jiminy Cricket: Cliff Edwards

I'm No Fool with a Bicycle (1956)
Jiminy Cricket: Cliff Edwards

I'm No Fool with Fire (1956)
Jiminy Cricket: Cliff Edwards

In Dutch (1946)
Pluto: Pinto Colvig
Dinah the Dachshund: unknown
Major: Pinto Colvig

In the Bag (1956)
Humphrey the Bear: James MacDonald
Ranger J. Audubon Woodlore: Bill Thompson
Smokey the Bear: Jackson Weaver

Inferior Decorator (1948)
Donald Duck: Clarence Nash
Bee: unknown

It's Tough to Be a Bird (1969) animated characters only
M. C. Bird/Narrator: Richard Bakalyan
Soprano: Ruth Buzzi

Jack and Old Mac (1956)
Old MacDonald: unknown
Mrs. MacDonald: unknown
Animal musicians: unknown

Jack-Jack Attack (2005)
Jack-Jack Parr: Eli Fucile
Buddy Pine/Syndrome: Jason Lee
Agent Rick Dicker: Bud Luckey
Kari McKeen: Bret Parker

The Jazz Fool (1929)
Mickey Mouse: Walt Disney
Horace Horsecollar: unknown

Jungle Rhythm (1929)
Mickey Mouse: Walt Disney
Parrot: Walt Disney
Other animals: unknown

Just Dogs (1932) Silly Symphony
Pluto: Pinto Colvig
Puppy: unknown

Just Mickey see ***Fiddling Around***

The Karnival Kid (1929)
Mickey Mouse: Walt Disney
Minnie Mouse: Marcellite Garner
Barker: unknown
Two singing cats: unknown

King Neptune (1932) Silly Symphony
King Neptune: Allan Watson
Mermaids: Marcellite Garner

The Klondike Kid (1932)
Pierre (Pegleg Pete): Billy Bletcher
Mickey Mouse: Walt Disney
Pluto: Pinto Colvig
Minnie Mouse: Marcellite Garner
Goofy: Pinto Colvig

A Knight for a Day (1946)
Squire Cedric (Goofy): Pinto Colvig
Sir Lionsteak: Pinto Colvig
Sir Cumference: Pinto Colvig
Princess Esmerelda: unknown

Lambert, the Sheepish Lion (1952)
Lambert: unknown
Stork: Sterling Holloway
Lambert's Mother: unknown
Narrator: Sterling Holloway

The Legend of Coyote Rock (1945)
Pluto: Pinto Colvig
Coyote: unknown

Lend a Paw (1941)
Mickey Mouse: Walt Disney
Pluto: Pinto Colvig
Pluto's Angel: Pinto Colvig
Kitten: unknown
Bianca the Goldfish: silent

Let's Stick Together (1952)
Donald Duck: Clarence Nash
Spike the Bee: Bill Thompson
Spike's Wife: June Foray

Lighthouse Keeping (1946)
Donald Duck: Clarence Nash
Marblehead the Pelican: unknown

Lion Around (1950)
Donald Duck: Clarence Nash
Huey, Dewey, Louie: Clarence Nash
Mountain lion: unknown

Lion Down (1951)
Goofy: Pinto Colvig
Mountain lion: unknown

The Litterbug (1961)
Donald Duck: Clarence Nash
Narrator: John Dehner

Little Hiawatha (1937) Silly Symphony
Little Hiawatha: unknown

The Little House (1952)
Narrator: Sterling Holloway

The Little Whirlwind (1941)
Mickey Mouse: Walt Disney
Minnie Mouse: Thelma Boardman

Lonesome Ghosts (1937)
Mickey Mouse: Walt Disney
Goofy: Pinto Colvig
Donald Duck: Clarence Nash
Short Ghost: Billy Bletcher
Other ghosts: unknown

Lucky Number (1951)
Donald Duck: Clarence Nash
Huey, Dewey, Louie: Clarence Nash

Lullaby Land (1933) Silly Symphony
Baby, Toy Dog, Sandman, etc.: unknown

The Mad Doctor (1933)
Mickey Mouse: Walt Disney
Pluto: Pinto Colvig
Mad Scientist: unknown

The Mad Dog (1932)
Mickey Mouse: Walt Disney
Pluto: Pinto Colvig

Magician Mickey (1937)
Mickey Mouse: Walt Disney
Donald Duck: Clarence Nash
Goofy: Pinto Colvig

Mail Dog (1947)
Pluto: Pinto Colvig
Rabbit: unknown

The Mail Pilot (1933)
Mickey Mouse: Walt Disney
Pete: Billy Bletcher
Minnie Mouse: Marcellite Garner

Man's Best Friend (1952)
Goofy: Pinto Colvig
Bowser the Puppy: unknown

Melody see ***Adventures in Music: Melody***

Merbabies (1938) Silly Symphony
Merbabies, Whale, etc.: unknown

The Merry Dwarfs (1929) Silly Symphony
Dwarfs: unknown

Mickey and the Seal (1948)
Mickey Mouse: James MacDonald
Pluto: Pinto Colvig
Baby Seal: unknown

Mickey Cuts Up (1931)
Mickey Mouse: Walt Disney
Minnie Mouse: Marcellite Garner
Pluto: Pinto Colvig

Mickey Down Under (1948)
Mickey Mouse: James MacDonald
Pluto: Pinto Colvig
Emu: unknown

Mickey in Arabia (1932)
Mickey Mouse: Walt Disney
Minnie Mouse: Marcellite Garner
Pete: Billy Bletcher

Mickey Plays Papa (1934)
Mickey Mouse: Walt Disney
Pluto: Pinto Colvig
Baby: unknown

Mickey Steps Out (1931)
Mickey Mouse: Walt Disney
Minnie Mouse: Marcellite Garner
Pluto: Pinto Colvig

Mickey's Amateurs (1937)
Mickey Mouse: Walt Disney
Donald Duck: Clarence Nash
Goofy: Pinto Colvig
Clara Cluck: Florence Gill

Mickey's Birthday Party (1942)
Mickey Mouse: Walt Disney
Minnie Mouse: Thelma Boardman
Pluto: Pinto Colvig
Donald Duck: Clarence Nash
Clara Cluck: Florence Gill
Clarabelle Cow: unknown
Horace Horsecollar: unknown

Mickey's Choo-Choo (1929)
Mickey Mouse: Walt Disney
Minnie Mouse: Marcellite Garner

Mickey's Christmas Carol (1983)
Ebeneezer Scrooge (Scrooge McDuck): Alan Young
Bob Cratchit (Mickey Mouse): Wayne Allwine
Nephew Fred (Donald Duck): Clarence Nash
Jacob Marley's Ghost (Goofy): Hal Smith
Christmas Past (Jiminy Cricket): Eddie Carroll
Christmas Present (Willie the Giant): Will Ryan
Christmas Future (Pete): Will Ryan
Belle (Daisy Duck): Patricia Parris
Tiny Tim: Dick Billingsley
Collectors for the Poor: Hal Smith, Will Ryan
Gravedigger: Wayne Allwine

Mickey's Circus (1936)
Mickey Mouse: Walt Disney
Minnie Mouse: Marcellite Garner
Donald: Clarence Nash
Seal: unknown

Mickey's Delayed Date (1947)
Mickey Mouse: Walt Disney
Minnie Mouse: Ruth Clifford
Pluto: Pinto Colvig

Mickey's Elephant (1936)
Mickey Mouse: Walt Disney
Bobo the Elephant: unknown
Pluto: Pinto Colvig

Mickey's Fire Brigade (1935)
Mickey Mouse: Walt Disney
Donald Duck: Clarence Nash
Goofy: Pinto Colvig
Clarabelle Cow: Elvia Allman

Mickey's Follies (1929)
Mickey Mouse: Walt Disney
Minnie Mouse: Marcellite Garner
Patricia Pig: unknown

Mickey's Gala Premiere (1933)
Mickey Mouse: Walt Disney
Minnie Mouse: Marcellite Garner
Pluto: Pinto Colvig
Pegleg Pete: Billy Bletcher
Laurel and Hardy, Marx Bothers, Mae West, Jimmy Durante, and other stars: unknown

Mickey's Garden (1935)
Mickey Mouse: Walt Disney
Pluto: Pinto Colvig

Mickey's Good Deed (1932)
Mickey Mouse: Walt Disney
Spoiled Brat: unknown
Pluto: Pinto Colvig

Mickey's Grand Opera (1936)
Mickey Mouse: Walt Disney
Pluto: Pinto Colvig
Donald Duck: Clarence Nash
Clara Cluck: Florence Gill
Clarabelle Cow: unknown

Mickey's Kangaroo (1935)
Mickey Mouse: Walt Disney
Kangaroo: unknown
Pluto: Pinto Colvig

Mickey's Man Friday (1935)
Mickey Mouse: Walt Disney
Friday: Billy Bletcher

Mickey's Mechanical Man (1933)
Mickey Mouse: Walt Disney
Minnie Mouse: Marcellite Garner
Robot: Unknown
Kongo Killer the Gorilla: unknown

Mickey's Mellerdrammer (1933)
Uncle Tom (Mickey Mouse): Walt Disney
Minnie Mouse: Marcellite Garner
Simon Legree (Horace Horsecollar): Billy Bletcher
Eliza (Clarabelle Cow): Elvia Allman
Goofy: Pinto Colvig

Mickey's Nightmare (1932)
Mickey Mouse: Walt Disney
Minnie Mouse: Marcellite Ganer
Goofy: Pinto Colvig

Mickey's Orphans (1931)
Mickey Mouse: Walt Disney
Minnie Mouse: Marcellite Garner
Pluto: Pinto Colvig
Orphan Kittens: unknown

Mickey's Pal Pluto (1933)
Mickey Mouse: Walt Disney
Minnie Mouse: Marcellite Garner
Pluto: Pinto Colvig
Pluto's Good Conscience: unknown
Pluto's Bad Conscience: unknown
Kittens: unknown

Mickey's Parrot (1938)
Mickey Mouse: Walt Disney
Radio Announcer: unknown
Pluto: Pinto Colvig
Parrot: unknown

Mickey's Polo Team (1936)
Mickey Mouse: Walt Disney
Donald Duck: Clarence Nash
Goofy: Pinto Colvig
Big Bad Wolf: Billy Bletcher
Clarabelle Cow: unknown
Laurel and Hardy, Clark Gable, W. C. Fields, Shirley Temple and other stars: unknown

Mickey's Revue (1932)
Mickey Mouse: Walt Disney
Minnie Mouse: Marcellite Garner
Pluto: Pinto Colvig
Horace Horsecollar: unknown
Goofy: Pinto Colvig

Mickey's Rival (1936)
Mickey Mouse: Walt Disney
Minnie Mouse: Marcellite Garner
Mortimer Mouse: unknown

Mickey's Service Station (1935)
Mickey Mouse: Walt Disney
Pete: Billy Bletcher
Donald Duck: Clarence Nash
Goofy: Pinto Colvig

Mickey's Steam Roller (1934)
Mickey Mouse: Walt Disney
Minnie Mouse: Marcellite Garner
Mickey's Nephews: unknown

Mickey's Trailer (1938)
Mickey Mouse: Walt Disney
Donald Duck: Clarence Nash
Goofy: Pinto Colvig

Midnight in a Toy Shop (1930) Silly Symphony
Spider, toys: unknown

Mike's New Car (2002)
Mike: Billy Crystal
Sulley: John Goodman

Mr. Duck Steps Out (1940)
Donald Duck: Clarence Nash
Daisy Duck: Clarence Nash
Huey, Dewey, Louie: Clarence Nash

Mr. Mouse Takes a Trip (1940)
Mickey Mouse: Walt Disney
Train Conductor (Pete): Billy Bletcher
Pluto: Lee Millar

Modern Inventions (1937)
Donald Duck: Clarence Nash
Robot Butler: Billy Bletcher
Robot Barber Chair: Cliff Edwards
Robot Nurse Maid: unknown

Monkey Melodies (1930) Silly Symphony
Monkeys, hippo, alligator, and other animals: unknown

The Moose Hunt (1931)
Mickey Mouse: Walt Disney
Pluto: Pinto Colvig
Moose: unknown

Moose Hunters (1937)
Mickey Mouse: Walt Disney
Donald Duck: Clarence Nash
Goofy: Pinto Colvig

More Kittens (1936) Silly Symphony
Orphan kittens, St. Bernard, other animals: unknown

Morris, the Midget Moose (1950)
Old Bootle Beetle/Narrator: Dink Trout
Morris the Moose: unknown
Thunderclap the Moose: unknown
Balsam the Moose: unknown

Moth and the Flame (1938) Silly Symphony
Boy moth, girl moth, other moths: unknown

Mother Goose Goes Hollywood (1938) Silly Symphony
Laurel and Hardy, Marx Brothers, W. C. Fields, Charlie McCarthy and other stars: unknown

Mother Goose Melodies (1931) Silly Symphony
Old King Cole, Humpty Dumpty, Little Miss Muffett and other nursery rhyme characters: unknown

Mother Pluto (1936) Silly Symphony
Pluto: Pinto Colvig
Hen: Florence Gill
Grasshopper, rooster and other animals: unknown

Motor Mania (1950)
Mr. Walker/Mr. Wheeler (Goofy): Pinto Colvig
Narrator: John McLeish

Moving Day (1936)
Mickey Miuse: Walt Disney
Pete: Billy Bletcher
Goofy: Pinto Colvig
Donald Duck: Clarence Nash

Music Land (1935) Silly Symphony
Various musical instruments: unknown

Musical Farmer (1932)
Mickey Mouse: Walt Disney
Minnie Mouse: Marcellite Garner
Pluto: Pinto Colvig

The New Neighbor (1953)
Donald Dick: Clarence Nash
Pete: Billy Bletcher
Pete's Dog: unknown

The New Spirit (1942)
Donald Duck: Clarence Nash
Radio Announcer: Fred Shields
Singers: Cliff Edwards, The Sportsmen Quartet

The Nifty Nineties (1941)
Mickey Mouse: Walt Disney
Minnie Mouse: Thelma Boardman
Fred: Fred Moore
Ward: Ward Kimball
Chickens: Florence Gill
Singers: Thurl Ravenscroft, Max Smith, John Rarig, Bill Days

Night (1930) Silly Symphony
Owls, fireflies, frogs, moths, frogs and other animals: unknown

The Night Before Christmas (1933) Silly Symphony
Singing Narrator: Donald Novis
Santa Claus, toys and children: unknown

No Hunting (1955)
Donald Duck: Clarence Nash
Grandpa Duck: Bill Thompson
Ranger: Bill Thompson

No Sail (1945)
Donald Duck: Clarence Nash
Goofy: Pinto Colvig

No Smoking (1951)
George Geef (Goofy): Pinto Colvig

Off His Rockers (1992)
Boy: silent
Rocking Horse: silent

Officer Duck (1939)
Officer Donald Duck: Clarence Nash
Tiny Tom (Pete): unknown

Oilspot and Lipstick (1987)
Junk monster, junk objects: silent

The Old Army Game (1943)
Private Donald Duck: Clarence Nash
Sgt. Pete: Billy Bletcher

Old King Cole (1933) Silly Symphony
Old King Cole and other nursery rhyme characters: unknown

Old MacDonald Duck (1941)
Donald Duck: Clarence Nash

The Old Mill (1937) Silly Symphony
Owl, mice, birds and other animals: unknown

Old Sequoia (1945)
Forest Ranger Donald Duck: Clarence Nash
Beavers: unknown

The Olympic Champ (1942)
Goofy: Pinto Colvig
Narrator: John McLeish

On Ice (1935)
Mickey Mouse: Walt Disney
Goofy: Pinto Colvig
Minnie Mouse: Marcellite Garner
Donald Duck: Clarence Nash
Pluto: Pinto Colvig

The Opry House (1929)
Mickey Mouse: silent

Orphans' Benefit (1934)
Mickey Mouse: Walt Disney
Donald Duck: Clarence Nash
Clara Cluck: Florence Gill
Goofy: Pinto Colvig
Horace Horsecollar: unknown

Orphans' Benefit (1941)
Mickey Mouse: Walt Disney

Donald Duck: Clarence Nash
Clara Cluck: Florence Gill
Orphans: unknown

Orphans' Picnic (1936)
Mickey Mouse: Walt Disney
Donald Duck: Clarence Nash
Orphans: unknown

Out of Scale (1951)
Donald Duck: Clarence Nash
Chip: unknown
Dale: unknown

Out of the Frying Pan into the Firing Line (1942)
Minnie Mouse: Thelma Boardman
Mickey Mouse: Walt Disney
Pluto: Pinto Colvig

Out on a Limb (1950)
Donald Duck: Clarence Nash
Chip: unknown
Dale: unknown

Pantry Pirate (1940)
Pluto: Lee Millar
Mammy Twoshoes the Cook: Lillian Randolph

Partly Cloudy (2009)
Peck the Stork: Tony Fucile
Gus the Cloud: Tony Fucile
Female Cloud: Lori Richardson
Human Mom: Lori Richardson

Paul Bunyan (1958)
Paul Bunyan: Thurl Ravenscroft
Babe the Ox: silent
Cal McNab: unknown
Chris Crosshaul: unknown
Shot Gunderson: unknown
Joe Muffaw: unknown

Peculiar Penguins (1934) Silly Symphony
Peter Penguin, Polly Penguin: unknown

The Pelican and the Snipe (1944)
Monte the Pelican: unknown
Vidi the Snipe: unknown
Narrator: Sterling Holloway

Pests of the West (1950)
Pluto: Pinto Colvig
Bent-Tail the Coyote: unknown
Junior Coyote: unknown

The Pet Store (1933)
Mickey Mouse: Walt Disney
Minnie Mouse: Marcellite Garner
Beppo the Gorilla: unknown
Tony: unknown

The Picnic (1930)
Mickey Mouse: Walt Disney
Minnie Mouse: Marcellite Garner
Rover (Pluto): unknown

The Pied Piper (1933) Silly Symphony
Pied Piper, children and citizens, singing narrators: unknown

Pioneer Days (1930)
Mickey Mouse: Walt Disney
Minnie Mouse: Marcellite Garner
Indians: unknown

Plane Crazy (1928)
Mickey Mouse: Walt Disney
Minnie Mouse: Walt Disney

The Plastics Inventor (1944)
Donald Duck: Clarence Nash
Radio Announcer: unknown

Playful Pan (1930) Silly Symphony
Pan the Satyr, flowers and animals: unknown

Playful Pluto (1934)
Mickey Mouse: Walt Disney
Pluto: Pinto Colvig

The Plowboy (1929)
Mickey Mouse: Walt Disney
Minnie Mouse: Marcellite Garner
Horace Horsecollar: unknown
Clarabelle Cow: unknown

Pluto and the Armadillo (1943)
Pluto: Pinto Colvig
Mickey Mouse: Walt Disney
Armadillo: unknown
Narrator: Fred Shields

Pluto and the Gopher (1950)
Pluto: Pinto Colvig
Gopher: Pinto Colvig
Minnie Mouse: Ruth Clifford

Pluto at the Zoo (1942)
Pluto: Pinto Colvig
Lion, gorilla, kangaroo and other zoo animals: unknown

Pluto, Junior (1942)
Pluto: Pinto Colvig
Pluto, Junior: unknown

Plutopia (1951)
Pluto: Pinto Colvig
Mickey Mouse: James MacDonald
Milton the Cat: Jim Backus
Cat: unknown

Pluto's Blue Note (1947)
Pluto: Pinto Colvig
Music Store Proprietor: Billy Bletcher

Pluto's Christmas Tree (1952)
Pluto: Pinto Colvig
Mickey Mouse: James MacDonald, Edward Brophy
Minnie Mouse: Ruth Clifford
Donald Duck: Clarence Nash

Chip: James MacDonald
Dale: Dessie Flynn
Goofy: Pinto Colvig

Pluto's Dream House (1940)
Pluto: Lee Millar
Mickey Mouse: Walt Disney
Magic Lamp: Billy Bletcher
Radio Cooking Show voice: Elvia Allman

Pluto's Fledgling (1948)
Pluto: Pinto Colvig
Orville the Baby Bird: unknown

Pluto's Heart Throb (1950)
Pluto: Pinto Colvig
Dinah the Dachshund: unknown
Butch the Bulldog: unknown

Pluto's Housewarming (1947)
Pluto: Pinto Colvig
Turtle: unknown
Butch the Bulldog: unknown

Pluto's Judgement Day (1935)
Pluto: Pinto Colvig
Mickey Mouse: Walt Disney
Kitten: Clarence Nash
Cat Prosecutor: Billy Bletcher
Cat Judge: Clarence Nash

Pluto's Kid Brother (1946)
Pluto: Pinto Colvig
K. B.: unknown
Butch the Bulldog: unknown
Dogcatcher: unknown

Pluto's Party (1952)
Pluto: Pinto Colvig
Mickey Mouse: James MacDonald
Minnie Mouse: Ruth Clifford
Mickey's Nephews: unknown

Pluto's Playmate (1941)
Pluto: Lee Millar
Baby Seal: unknown

Pluto's Purchase (1948)
Pluto: Pinto Colvig
Mickey Mouse: James MacDonald
Butch the Bulldog: unknown

Pluto's Quin-Puplets (1937)
Pluto: Pinto Colvig
Fifi: unknown
Puppies: unknown

Pluto's Surprise Package (1949)
Pluto: Pinto Colvig
Turtle: unknown

Pluto's Sweater (1949)
Minnie Mouse: Ruth Clifford
Pluto: Pinto Colvig
Figaro the Kitten: unknown

The Pointer (1939)
Mickey Mouse: Walt Disney
Pluto: Lee Millar
Bear: unknown

Polar Trappers (1938)
Pluto: Pinto Colvig
Donald Duck: Clarence Nash
Penguin: unknown

The Practical Pig (1939) Silly Symphony
Big Bad Wolf: Billy Bletcher
Practical Pig: Pinto Colvig
Fifer Pig: Dorothy Compton
Fiddler Pig: Mary Moder

Presto (2008)
Presto DiGiotagione the Magician: Doug Sweetland
Alec Azam the Rabbit: Doug Sweetland

Primitive Pluto (1950)
Pluto: Pinto Colvig
Primo, Pluto's Primitive Instinct: unknown
Bunny, bear: unknown

The Prince and the Pauper (1990)
Mickey Mouse/Prince Mickey: Wayne Allwine
Goofy: Bill Farmer
Donald Duck: Tony Anselmo
Pluto: Bill Farmer
Captain of the Guard (Pete): Arthur Burghardt
Horace Horsecollar: Bill Farmer
Clarabelle Cow: Elvia Allman
Archbishop: Frank Welker
Weasels: Bill Farmer, Charles Adler
Two Kids: Rocky Krakoff, Tim Eyster
Dying King: Frank Welker
Narrator: Roy Dotrice

Private Pluto (1943)
Private Pluto: Pinto Colvig
Drill Sgt. Pete: unknown
Chip: James MacDonald
Dale: Dessie Flynn

Pueblo Pluto (1949)
Pluto: Pinto Colvig
Mickey Mouse: James MacDonald
Ronnie the Pup: unknown

Puppy Love (1933)
Mickey Mouse: Walt Disney
Minnie Mouse: Marcellite Garner
Pluto: Pinto Colvig
Fifi: unknown

The Purloined Pup (1946)
Police Officer Pluto: Pinto Colvig
Ronnie the Pup: unknown
Butch the Bulldog: unknown

Puss-Cafe (1950)
Pluto: Pinto Colvig
Milton the Cat: unknown
Richard the Cat: unknown

Put-Put Troubles (1940)
Pluto: Lee Millar
Donald Duck: Clarence Nash
Frog: unknown

R'coon Dawg (1951)
Pluto: Pinto Colvig
Mickey Mouse: James MacDonald
Raccoon: unknown

Redux Riding Hood (1997)
Wolf: Michael Richards
Red Riding Hood: Lacey Chabert
Doris, Mrs. Wolf: Mia Farrow
Thompkins: Jim Cummings
Woodsman: Fabio
Lil Wolf: Phil Fondacaro
Grandma: June Foray
Otis, the Boss: Don Rickles
Leonard Fox: Adam West
Narrator: Garrison Keillor

Rescue Dog (1947)
Pluto: Pinto Colvig
Seal Pup: unknown

The Riveter (1940)
Donald Duck: Clarence Nash
Foreman (Pete): Billy Bletcher

The Robber Kitten (1935) Silly Symphony
Ambrose the Kitten/Butch: unknown
Dirty Bill: Billy Bletcher

Roller Coaster Rabbit (1990)
Roger Rabbit: Charles Fleischer
Baby Herman (on screen): April Winchell
Baby Herman (off screen): Lou Hirsch
Jessica Rabbit: Kathleen Turner
Droopy Dog: Corey Burton
Mrs. Herman: April Winchell
Bull: Frank Welker

Rugged Bear (1953)
Humphrey the Bear: James MacDonald
Donald Duck: Clarence Nash

Runaway Brain (1995)
Mickey Mouse: Wayne Allwine
Dr. Frankenollie: Kelsey Grammer
Minnie Mouse: Russi Taylor
Pluto: Bill Farmer
Julius: Jim Cummings

The Saga of Windwagon Smith (1961)
Windwagon Smith: Rex Allen
Mayor Crum: J. Pat O'Malley
Molly Crum: unknown
Singers: Sons of the Pioneers
Jasper and Horace: unknown

Santa's Workshop (1932) Silly Symphony
Santa Claus: Allan Watson
Santa's Secretary: Pinto Colvig
Elves: unknown

Scrooge McDuck and Money (1967)
Scrooge McDuck: Bill Thompson
Heuy, Dewey, Louie: unknown
Singers: The Mellomen (Thurl Ravenscroft, Bill Lee, Bill Cole, Gene Merlino)

Sea Salts (1949)
Donald Duck: Clarence Nash
Mac Bootle Beetle: Dink Trout

Sea Scouts (1939)
Donald Duck: Clarence Nash
Heuy, Dewey, Louie: Clarence Nash

Self-Control (1938)
Donald Duck: Clarence Nash
Hen: Florence Gill
Woodpecker, caterpillar and other animals: unknown
Radio Voice of Uncle Smiley: unknown

Shanghaied (1934)
Mickey Mouse: Walt Disney
Minnie Mouse: Marcellite Garner
Pirate Pete: Billy Bletcher

Sheep Dog (1949)
Pluto: Pinto Colvig
Bent-Tail the Coyote: unknown
Bent-Tail Junior: unknown

The Shindig (1930)
Mickey Mouse: Walt Disney
Minnie Mouse: Marcellite Garner
Horace Horsecollar: Walt Disney
Clarabelle Cow: Marcellite Garner
Patricia Pig: unknown
Hippo, dachshund and other animals: unknown

The Simple Things (1953)
Mickey Mouse: James MacDonald
Pluto: Pinto Colvig
Seagull: unknown

The Skeleton Dance (1929) Silly Symphony
Four dancing skeletons, bats, cats and other animals: unknown

Sky Trooper (1942)
Donald Duck: Clarence Nash
Pete: unknown

The Sleepwalker (1942)
Pluto: Pinto Colvig
Dinah the Dachshund: unknown

Sleepy Time Donald (1947)
Donald Duck: Clarence Nash
Daisy Duck: Ruth Clifford

Slide, Donald, Slide (1949)
Donald Duck: Clarence Nash
Bee: unknown

The Small One (1978)
Boy: Sean Marshall
Father: Olan Soule
Tanner: William Woodson

Auctioneer: Hal Smith
Guard: Joe Higgins
Potter: Thurl Ravenscroft
Joseph: Gordon Jump

Social Lion (1954)
Lion: unknown
Various Citizens: Paul Frees

Society Dog Show (1939)
Pluto: Pinto Colvig
Mickey Mouse: Walt Disney
Fifi: unknown
Judge: unknown

Soup's On (1948)
Donald Duck: Clarence Nash
Huey, Dewey, Louie: Clarence Nash

Spare the Rod (1954)
Donald Duck: Clarence Nash
Huey, Dewey, Louie: Clarence Nash
Pygmy cannibals: Pinto Colvig
Narrator and Voice of Child Psychology: Bill Thompson

The Spider and the Fly (1931) Silly Symphony
Spider, houseflies, dragonflies and other insects: unknown

The Spirit of '43 (1943)
Donald Duck: Clarence Nash

Springtime (1929) Silly Symphony
Grasshoppers, frogs, insects, flowers, etc.: unknown

Springtime for Pluto (1944)
Pluto: Pinto Colvig
Spirit of Spring: unknown

Squatter's Rights (1946)
Mickey Mouse: Walt Disney
Pluto: Pinto Colvig
Chip: unknown
Dale: unknown

Steamboat Willie (1928)
Mickey Mouse/Willie: Walt Disney
Minnie Mouse: Walt Disney
Captain Pete: unknown
Parrot: Walt Disney
Goat and other animals: unknown

The Steeplechase (1933)
Mickey Mouse: Walt Disney
Minnie Mouse: Marcellite Garner
Colonel: unknown
Staple Hands: unknown

Straight Shooters (1947)
Donald Duck: Clarence Nash
Huey, Dewey, Louie: Clarence Nash

Summer (1930) Silly Symphony
Dragonflies, butterflies, beetles and other insects: unknown

Susie, the Little Blue Coupe (1952)
Susie: unknown
Various owners, police, etc.: unknown
Narrator: Sterling Holloway

Symphony Hour (1942)
Mickey Mouse: Walt Disney
Sylvester Macaroni (Pete): Billy Bletcher
Clara Cluck: Florence Gill
Donald Duck: Clarence Nash
Goofy: Pinto Colvig
Radio Announcer: John McLeish

A Symposium on Popular Songs (1962)
Professor Ludwig Von Drake: Paul Frees

T-Bone for Two (1942)
Pluto: Pinto Colvig
Butch the Bulldog: unknown

Tea for Two Hundred (1948)
Donald Duck: Clarence Nash
Ants: Pinto Colvig

Teachers Are People (1952)
Goofy: Pinto Colvig
George: unknown
Children: unknown
Narrator: Alan Reed

Tennis Racquet (1949)
Goofy: Pinto Colvig
Radio Commentator: Doodles Weaver

El Terrible Toreador (1929) Silly Symphony
Mexican bar maid, Officer, Toreador: unknown

Test Pilot Donald (1951)
Donald Duck: Clarence Nash
Chip: unknown
Dale: unknown

They're Off (1948)
Snapshot: unknown
Old Moe: unknown
Various Goofy characters: Pinto Colvig

Three Blind Mouseketeers (1936) Silly Symphony
Tall Mouseketeer: Pinto Colvig
Other Two Mouseketeers: unknown
Captain Katt: Billy Bletcher

Three for Breakfast (1948)
Donald Duck: Clarence Nash
Chip: unknown
Dale: unknown

The Three Little Pigs (1933) Silly Symphony
Big Bad Wolf: Billy Bletcher
Practical Pig: Pinto Colvig, Walt Disney
Fifer Pig: Dorothy Compton
Fiddler Pig: Mary Moder

Three Little Wolves (1936) Silly Symphony
Big Bad Wolf: Billy Bletcher
Practical Pig: Pinto Colvig

Fifer Pig: Dorothy Compton
Fiddler Pig: Mary Moder

Three Orphan Kittens (1935) Silly Symphony
Three Orphan Kittens: unknown
Maid, daughter of the house: unknown

Thru the Mirror (1936)
Mickey Mouse: Walt Disney
Queen of Cards: unknown
King of Cards: unknown

Tiger Trouble (1945)
Goofy: Pinto Colvig
Elephant: unknown
Tiger: unknown

Timber (1941)
Donald Duck: Clarence Nash
Pierre (Pete): Billy Bletcher

Toby Tortoise Returns (1936) Silly Symphony
Toby Tortoise, Max Hare, Mae West: unknown

Tomorrow We Diet (1951)
George Geef (Goofy): Pinto Colvig
Mirror Goofy: unknown

Toot Whistle Plunk and Boom (1953)
Professor Owl: Bill Thompson
Bird Students: unknown
Singers: The Mellomen (Bill Lee, Thurl Ravenscroft, Max Smith, Bill Hamlin)

The Tortoise and the Hare (1935) Silly Symphony
Toby Tortoise: unknown
Max Hare: unknown

Touchdown Mickey (1932)
Mickey Mouse: Walt Disney
Goofy: Pinto Colvig
Pluto: Pinto Colvig
Alley Cats: unknown

Toy Tinkers (1949)
Donald Duck: Clarence Nash
Chip: James MacDonald
Dale: Dessie Flynn

Trader Mickey (1932)
Mickey Mouse: Walt Disney
Pluto: Pinto Colvig
Cannibal Chief: Pinto Colvig

Traffic Troubles (1931)
Mickey Mouse: Walt Disney
Minnie Mouse: Marcellite Garner
Pegleg Pete: Billy Bletcher
Officer: unknown

Trail Mix-Up (1993)
Roger Rabbit: Charles Fleischer
Baby Herman (on screen): April Winchell
Baby Herman (off screen): Lou Hirsch
Jessica Rabbit: Kathleen Turner
Droopy Dog: Corey Buton
Mrs. Herman: April Winchell

Bear: Frank Welker
Beaver: Frank Welker

Trailer Horn (1950)
Donald Duck: Clarence Nash
Chip: unknown
Dale: unknown

The Trial of Donald Duck (1948)
Donald Duck: Clarence Nash
Pierre: unknown

Trick or Treat (1952)
Donald Duck: Clarence Nash
Witch Hazel: June Foray
Huey, Dewey, Louie: Clarence Nash

Trombone Trouble (1944)
Donald Duck: Clarence Nash
Trombonist (Pegleg Pete): Billy Bletcher
Jupiter: John McLeish
Vulcan: John McLeish

Truant Officer Donald (1941)
Donald Duck: Clarence Nash
Huey, Dewey, Louie: Clarence Nash

The Truth About Mother Goose (1957)
Little Jack Horner: unknown
Mary Quite Contrary: unknown
Queen Elizabeth: unknown
Narrator: John Dehner

Tugboat Mickey (1940)
Captain Mickey Mouse: Walt Disney
Goofy: Pinto Colvig
Donald Duck: Clarence Nash

Tummy Trouble (1989)
Roger Rabbit: Charles Fleischer
Baby Herman (on screen): April Winchell
Baby Herman (off screen): Lou Hirsch
Droopy Dog: Richard Williams
Jessica Rabbit: Kathleen Turner
Orderly: Corey Burton

Two Chips and a Miss (1952)
Chip: unknown
Dale: unknown
Clarice: unknown

Two Gun Goofy (1952)
Goofy: Pinto Colvig
Pistol Pete: Billy Bletcher

Two-Gun Mickey (1934)
Mickey Mouse: Walt Disney
Minnie Mouse: Marcellite Garner
Pegleg Pete: Billy Bletcher

Two Weeks Vacation (1952)
Goofy: Pinto Colvig
Mechanic: unknown

The Ugly Duckling (1931) Silly Symphony
Ugly Duckling, Mother Hen, Chicks: unknown

The Ugly Duckling (1939) Silly Symphony remake
Ugly Duckling, Mother Hen. Chicks, Swan: unknown

Uncle Donald's Ants (1952)
Donald Duck: Clarence Nash
Ants: Pinto Colvig

Up a Tree (1955)
Donald Duck: Clarence Nash
Chip: unknown
Dale: unknown

The Vanishing Private (1942)
Private Donald Duck: Clarence Nash
Sgt. Pete: Billy Bletcher
General: unknown

Victory Vehicles (1943)
Goofy: George Johnson
Narrator: Fred Shields

The Village Smithy (1942)
Donald Duck: Clarence Nash
Jenny the Donkey: unknown

Vincent (1982)
Vincent Malloy: unknown
Vincent's Mother: unknown
Narrator: Vincent Price

Water Babies (1935) Silly Symphony
Water nymphs, animals: silent

The Wayward Canary (1932)
Mickey Mouse: Walt Disney
Minnie Mouse: Marcellite Garner
Canary: unknown
Pluto: Pinto Colvig

Wet Paint (1946)
Donald Duck: Clarence Nash
Susie the Bird: unknown

The Whalers (1938)
Mickey Mouse: Walt Disney
Donald Duck: Clarence Nash
Pluto: Pinto Colvig
Whale: unknown

When the Cat's Away (1929)
Mickey Mouse: Walt Disney
Minnie Mouse: Marcellite Garner
Tom Cat: unknown
Parrot: unknown

Who Killed Cock Robin? (1935) Silly Symphony
Jenny Wren: Martha Wentworth
Judge Owl: Billy Bletcher
Dan Cupid: unknown
Cock Robin: unknown

The Whoopee Party (1932)
Mickey Mouse: Walt Disney
Minnie Mouse: Marcellite Garner
Goofy: Pinto Colvig
Horace Horsecollar: unknown
Patricia Pig: unknown

Wide Open Spaces (1947)
Donald Duck: Clarence Nash
Motel Proprietor: Billy Bletcher

Wild Waves (1930)
Mickey Mouse: Walt Disney
Minnie Mouse: Marcellite Garner
Walrus: Carl W. Stalling
Seal, pelicans and other animals: unknown

Window Cleaners (1940)
Donald Duck: Clarence Nash
Pluto: Lee Millar
Bee: unknown

Winnie the Pooh and the Blustery Day (1968)
Winnie the Pooh: Sterling Holloway
Tigger: Paul Winchell
Piglet: John Fiedler
Rabbit: Junius Matthews
Eeyore: Ralph Wright
Owl: Hal Smith
Kanga: Barbara Luddy
Roo: Clint Howard
Gopher: Howard Morris
Christopher Robin: Jon Walmsley
Narrator: Sebastian Cabot

Winnie the Pooh and the Honey Tree (1966)
Winnie the Pooh: Sterling Holloway
Piglet: John Fiedler
Rabbit: Junius Matthews
Eeyore: Ralph Wright
Owl: Hal Smith
Kanga: Barbara Luddy
Roo: Clint Howard
Gopher: Howard Morris
Christopher Robin: Bruce Reitherman
Narrator: Sebastian Cabot

Winter (1930) Silly Symphony
Bears, raccoons, moose, groundhogs and other animals: unknown

Winter Storage (1949)
Donald Duck: Clarence Nash
Chip: unknown
Dale: unknown

The Wise Little Hen (1934) Silly Symphony
Wise Little Hen: Florence Gill
Peter Pig: Pinto Colvig
Donald Duck: Clarence Nash

Wonder Dog (1950)
Pluto: Pinto Colvig
Dinah the Dachshund: unknown
Butch the Bulldog: unknown

Woodland Cafe (1937) Silly Symphony

Fireflies, centipedes, beetles and other insects: unknown

Working for Peanuts (1953)
Donald Duck: Clarence Nash
Chip: James MacDonald
Dale: Dessie Flynn
Dolores the Elephant: unknown

The Worm Turns (1937)
Mickey Mouse: Walt Disney
Dog Catcher (Pete): Billy Bletcher
Pluto: Pinto Colvig

Wynken, Blynken and Nod (1938) Silly Symphony
Three sleepy children: unknown

Ye Olden Days (1933)
Minstrel Mickey Mouse: Walt Disney
Ye Princess Minnie Mouse: Marcellite Garner
Ye Prince: unknown
Goofy: Pinto Colvig
Clarabell Cow: unknown
King: unknown

Voice Guide to Favorite Disney Characters

Stars of Theatrical Cartoon Shorts

(also includes voices for the TV cartoon series based on the shorts)

Characters	Voices
Mickey Mouse	Walt Disney, James MacDonald, Wayne Allwine
Minnie Mouse	Walt Disney, Marcelitte Garner, Thelma Boardman, Ruth Clifford, Russi Taylor
Donald Duck	Clarence Nash, Tony Anselmo
Daisy Duck	Clarence Nash, Gloria Blondell, June Foray, Kath Soucie, Diane Michelle, Russi Taylor, Tress MacNeille
Huey, Dewey, Louie	Clarence Nash, Russi Taylor, Tony Anselmo, Jeannie Elias
Scrooge McDuck	Bill Thompson, Alan Young
Goofy	Pinto Colvig, George Johnson, Bill Farmer, Will Ryan, Tony Pope
Pluto	Pinto Colvig, Lee Millar, Bill Farmer
Chip	James MacDonald, Tress MacNeille
Dale	Dessie Flynn, Corey Burton, Tress MacNeille
Pete	Billy Bletcher, Will Ryan, Jim Cummings
Clarabelle Cow	Marcellite Garner, Elvia Allman, April Winchell
Horace Horsecollar	Walt Disney, Billy Bletcher, Bill Farmer
Big Bad Wolf	Billy Bletcher, Tony Pope, Michael Richards, Jim Cummings
Winnie the Pooh	Sterling Holloway, Hal Smith, Jim Cummings
Tigger	Paul Winchell, Will Ryan, Jim Cummings
Piglet	John Fiedler, Travis Oates
Eeyore	Ralph Wright, Peter Cullen, Jim Cummings
Owl	Hal Smith, Andre Stojka
Rabbit	Junius Matthews, Will Ryan, Ken Sansom
Kanga	Barbara Luddy, Patricia Parris, Kath Soucie, Tress MacNeille
Roo	Clint Howard, Jerome Beidler, Nikita Hopkins, Max Burkholder
Christopher Robin	Bruce Reitherman, Jon Walmsley, Timothy Turner, Tim Hoskins, Brady Bluhm, Frankie J. Galasso, Tom Attenborough, Tom Wheatley, William Green, Paul Tiesler

Princesses and Heroines

Alice	*Alice in Wonderland*—1951 (Kathryn Beaumont)
Ariel	*The Little Mermaid* (Jodi Benson)
Aurora	*Sleeping Beauty* (Mary Costa)
Belle	*Beauty and the Beast* (Paige O'Hara)
Cinderella	*Cinderella* (Ilene Woods)
Dot	*A Bug's Life* (Hayden Panttiere)
Eilonwy	*The Black Cauldron* (Susan Sheridan)
Esmeralda	*The Hunchback of Notre Dame* (Demi Moore, Heidi Mollenhauer)
Faline	*Bambi* (Cammie King, Ann Gillis)

Voice Guide to Favorite Disney Characters

Characters	Voices
Giselle	*Enchanted* (Amy Adams)
Helen Parr	*The Incredibles* (Holly Hunter)
Jane	*Return to Neverland* (Harriet Owen)
Jane Porter	*Tarzan* (Minnie Driver)
Jasmine	*Aladdin* (Linda Larkin, Lea Salonga)
Jenny Foxworth	*Oliver & Company* (Natalie Gregory)
Jessie	*Toy Story 2* and *Toy Story 3* (Joan Cusack)
Kida	*Atlantis: The Lost Empire* (Cree Summer, Natalie Storm)
Lady	*Lady and the Tramp* (Barbara Luddy)
Lilo	*Lilo & Stitch* (Daveigh Chase)
Maid Marian	*Robin Hood* (Monica Evans)
Miss Bianca	*The Rescuers* and *The Rescuers Down Under* (Eva Gabor, Robie Lester)
Mulan	*Mulan* (Ming-Na, Lea Salonga)
Nala	*The Lion King* (Moira Kelly, Niketa Calame, Laura Williams, Sally Dworsky)
Penny	*Bolt* (Miley Cyrus)
Penny	*The Rescuers* (Michelle Stacy)
Pocahontas	*Pocahontas* (Irene Bedard, Judy Kuhn)
Rapunzel	*Tangled* (Mandy Moore)
Sally Carrera	*Cars* (Bonnie Hunt)
Sally	*The Nightmare Before Christmas* (Catherine O'Hara)
Snow White	*Snow White and the Seven Dwarfs* (Adriana Caselotti)
Tiana	*The Princess and the Frog* (Anika Noni Rose, Elizabeth M. Dampier)
Wendy Darling	*Peter Pan* (Kathryn Beaumont)

Princes and Other Traditional Heroes

Aladdin	*Aladdin* (Scott Weinger, Brad Kane)
Bambi	*Bambi* (Hardie Albright, John Sutherland, Donnie Dunagan)
Bernard	*The Rescuers* and *The Rescuers Down Under* (Bob Newhart)
Bob Parr	*The Incredibles* (Craig T. Nelson)
Bolt	*Bolt* (John Travolta)
Buzz Lightyear	*Toy Story*, *Toy Story 2* and *Toy Story 3* (Tim Allen)
Cody	*The Rescuers Down Under* (Adam Ryen)
Copper	*The Fox and the Hound* (Corey Feldman, Kurt Russell)
Doug Funnie	*Doug's 1st Movie* (Thomas McHugh)
Dumbo	*Dumbo* (silent)
Flik	*A Bug's Life* (Dave Foley)
Flynn Ryder	*Tangled* (Zachary Levi)
Hercules	*Hercules* (Tate Donovan, Josh Keaton, Roger Bart)
James	*James and the Giant Peach* (Paul Terry)
Jim Hawkins	*Treasure Planet* (Joseph Gordon-Levitt)
John Smith	*Pocahontas* (Mel Gibson)
Kenai	*Brother Bear* (Joaquin Phoenix)
Leonard Helperman	*Teacher's Pet* (Shaun Fleming)
Lewis	*Meet the Robinsons* (Daniel Hansen, Jordan Fry)
Max Goof	*A Goofy Movie* (Jason Marsden, Aaron Lohr, Laus Høybye)
Milo James Hatch	*Atlantis: The Lost Empire* (Michael J. Fox)
Mowgli	*The Jungle Book* (Bruce Reitherman)
Nemo	*Finding Nemo* (Alexander Gould)
Oliver	*Oliver & Company* (Joey Lawrence)
Pacha	*The Emperor's New Groove* (John Goodman)
Peter Pan	*Peter Pan* (Bobby Driscoll)
Peter Pan	*Return to Neverland* (Blayne Weaver)
Pinocchio	*Pinocchio* (Dickie Jones)
Prince	*Snow White and the Seven Dwarfs* (Harry Stockwell)
Prince Charming	*Cinderella* (William Phipps, Mike Douglas)
Prince Edward	*Enchanted* (James Marsden)

268 Voice Guide to Favorite Disney Characters

Characters	*Voices*
Prince Eric	*The Little Mermaid* (Christopher Daniel Barnes)
Prince Naveen	*The Princess and the Frog* (Bruno Campos)
Prince Phillip	*Sleeping Beauty* (Bill Shirley)
Robin Hood	*Robin Hood* (Brian Bedford)
Shang	*Mulan* (B.D. Wong, Donny Osmond)
Simba	*The Lion King* (Jonathan Taylor Thomas, Matthew Broderick, Jason Weaver, Joseph Williams)
Taran	*The Black Cauldron* (Grant Bardsley)
Tarzan	*Tarzan* (Tony Goldwyn, Alex D. Linz)
Tod	*The Fox and the Hound* (Keith Coogan, Mickey Rooney)
Wart	*The Sword in the Stone* (Ricky Sorenson, Richard Reitherman, Robert Reitherman)
Wilbur Robinson	*Meet the Robinsons* (Wesley Singerman)
Woody	*Toy Story, Toy Story 2* and *Toy Story 3* (Tom Hanks)

Non-Traditional Heroes and Heroines

Aladar	*Dinosaur* (D. B. Sweeney)
Basil of Baker Street	*The Great Mouse Detective* (Barrie Ingham)
Beast	*Beauty and the Beast* (Robby Benson)
Carl Fredrickson	*Up* (Edward Asner)
Chicken Little	*Chicken Little* (Zach Braff)
Dragon	*The Reluctant Dragon* (Barnett Parker)
Ichabod Crane	*The Adventures of Ichabod and Mr. Toad* (silent)
Jack Skellington	*The Nightmare Before Christmas* (Chris Sarandon, Danny Elfman)
James P. Sullivan	*Monsters, Inc.* (John Goodman)
Johnny Appleseed	*Melody Time* (Dennis Day)
Kuzco	*The Emperor's New Groove* (David Spade)
Linguini	*Ratatouille* (Lou Romano)
Lightning McQueen	*Cars* (Owen Wilson)
Maggie	*Home on the Range* (Roseanne)
Mike Wazowski	*Monsters, Inc.* (Billy Crystal)
Mr. Toad	*The Adventures of Ichabod and Mr. Toad* (Eric Blore)
Mrs. Caloway	*Home on the Range* (Judi Dench)
Quasimodo	*The Hunchback of Notre Dame* (Tom Hulce)
Remy	*Ratatouille* (Patton Oswalt)
Roger Rabbit	*Who Framed Roger Rabbit* (Charles Fleischer)
Scrooge McDuck	*Ducktales the Movie: Treasure of the Lost Lamp* (Alan Young)
Sir Giles	*The Reluctant Dragon* (Claud Allister)
Spot	*Teacher's Pet* (Nathan Lane)
WALL-E	*WALL-E* (Ben Burtt)

Human Villains and Villainesses

Alameda Slim	*Home on the Range* (Randy Quaid)
Bowler Hat Guy	*Meet the Robinsons* (Stephen J. Anderson)
Brom Bones	*The Adventures of Ichabod and Mr. Toad* (silent)
Buddy Pine	*The Incredibles* (Jason Lee)
Captain Hook	*Peter Pan* (Hans Conried)
Captain Hook	*Return to Neverland* (Corey Burton)
Charles Muntz	*Up* (Christopher Plummer)
Clayton	*Tarzan* (Brian Blessed)
Cruella de Vil	*One Hundred and One Dalmatians* (Betty Lou Gerson)
Dr. Facilier	*The Princess and the Frog* (Keith David)
Dr. Ivan Krank	*Teacher's Pet* (Kelsey Grammer)
Edgar	*The Aristocats* (Roddy Maude-Roxby)
Frollo	*The Hunchback of Notre Dame* (Tony Jay)
Gaston	*Beauty and the Beast* (Richard White)
Jafar	*Aladdin* (Jonathan Freeman)
John Silver	*Treasure Planet* (Brian Murray)

Characters	Voices
Lady Tremaine	*Cinderella* (Eleanor Audley)
Lyle Tiberius Roarke	*Atlantis: The Lost Empire* (James Garner)
Madame Gothel	*Tangled* (Dona Murphy)
Madame Medusa	*The Rescuers* (Geraldine Page)
Madame Mim	*The Sword in the Stone* (Martha Wentworth)
McLeach	*The Rescuers Down Under* (George C. Scott)
Queen	*Snow White and the Seven Dwarfs* (Lucille LaVerne)
Queen Narissa	*Enchanted* (Susan Sarandon)
Ratcliffe	*Pocahontas* (David Ogden Stiers)
Shan-Yu	*Mulan* (Miguel Ferrer)
Sid Phillips	*Toy Story* (Erik von Detten)
Skinner	*Ratatouille* (Ian Holm)
Stromboli	*Pinocchio* (Charles Judels)
Sykes	*Oliver & Company* (Robert Loggia)
Yzma	*The Emperor's New Groove* (Eartha Kitt)

Non-Human Villains and Villainesses

Chick Hicks	*Cars* (Michael Keaton)
Dr. Finklestein	*The Nightmare Before Christmas* (William Hickey)
Hades	*Hercules* (James Woods)
Hopper	*A Bug's Life* (Kevin Spacey)
Horned King	*The Black Cauldron* (John Hurt)
Jabberwocky	*Alice in Wonderland*—2010 (Christopher Lee)
Judge Doom	*Who Framed Roger Rabbit* (Christopher Lloyd)
Kaa	*The Jungle Book* (Sterling Holloway)
Kron	*Dinosaur* (Samuel E. Wright)
Lots-O-Huggin' Bear	*Toy Story 3* (Ned Beatty)
Maleficent	*Sleeping Beauty* (Eleanor Audley)
Merlock	*Ducktales the Movie: Treasure of the Lost Lamp* (Christopher Lloyd)
Monstro	*Pinocchio* (silent)
Oogie Boogie	*The Nightmare Before Christmas* (Ken Page)
Prince John	*Robin Hood* (Peter Ustinov)
Queen of Hearts	*Alice in Wonderland*—1951 (Verna Felton)
Randall Boggs	*Monsters, Inc.* (Steve Buscemi)
Ratigan	*The Great Mouse Detective* (Vincent Price)
Scar	*The Lion King* (Jeremy Irons)
Shere Kahn	*The Jungle Book* (George Sanders, Thurl Ravenscroft)
Sheriff	*Robin Hood* (Pat Buttram)
Stinky Pete	*Toy Story 2* (Kelsey Grammer)
Ursula	*The Little Mermaid* (Pat Carroll)

Heroes' and Heroines' Sidekicks and Friends

Abby Mallard	*Chicken Little* (Joan Cusack)
Angus MacBadger	*The Adventures of Ichabod and Mr. Toad* (Campbell Grant)
Baloo	*The Jungle Book* (Phil Harris)
Bashful	*Snow White and the Seven Dwarfs* (Scotty Mattraw)
B.E.N.	*Treasure Planet* (Martin Short)
Colonel	*One Hundred and One Dalmatians* (J. Pat O'Malley)
Crush	*Finding Nemo* (Andrew Stanton)
Cyril Proudbottom	*The Adventures of Ichabod and Mr. Toad* (J. Pat O'Malley)
Dawson	*The Great Mouse Detective* (Val Bettin)
Doc	*Snow White and the Seven Dwarfs* (Roy Atwell)
Dodger	*Oliver & Company* (Billy Joel)
Dopey	*Snow White and the Seven Dwarfs* (Eddie Collins)
Dory	*Finding Nemo* (Ellen DeGeneres)
Emile	*Ratatouille* (Peter Sohn)
Evinrude	*The Rescuers* (James MacDonald)

Characters	Voices
Fish Out of Water	*Chicken Little* (Dan Molina)
Flounder	*The Little Mermaid* (Jason Marin)
Flower	*Bambi* (Stan Alexander, Tim Davis, Sterling Holloway)
Friar Tuck	*Robin Hood* (Andy Devine)
Genie	*Aladdin* (Robin Williams, Bruce Adler)
Genie	*Ducktales the Movie: Treasure of the Lost Lamp* (Rip Taylor)
Geppetto	*Pinocchio* (Christian Rub)
Grace	*Home on the Range* (Jennifer Tilly)
Grumpy	*Snow White and the Seven Dwarfs* (Pinto Colvig)
Gurgi	*The Black Cauldron* (John Byner)
Gus	*Cinderella* (James MacDonald)
Happy	*Snow White and the Seven Dwarfs* (Otis Harlan)
Hugo	*The Hunchback of Notre Dame* (Jason Alexander)
Jake	*The Rescuers Down Under* (Tristan Rogers)
Jaq	*Cinderella* (James MacDonald)
Jiminy Cricket	*Pinocchio* (Cliff Edwards)
Koda	*Brother Bear* (Jeremy Suarez)
Launchpad McQuack	*Ducktales the Movie: Treasure of the Lost Lamp* (Terence McGovern)
Laverne	*The Hunchback of Notre Dame* (Mary Wickes, Jane Withers)
Little John	*Robin Hood* (Phil Harris)
Louis	*The Princess and the Frog* (Michael-Leon Wooley)
Lucius Best	*The Incredibles* (Samuel L. Jackson)
Mater	*Cars* (Larry the Cable Guy)
Maximus	*Tangled* (silent)
Mittens	*Bolt* (Susie Essman)
Mole	*The Adventures of Ichabod and Mr. Toad* (Colin Campbell)
Mushu	*Mulan* (Eddie Murphy)
Orville	*The Rescuers* (Jim Jordan)
P. J. Pete	*A Goofy Movie* (Rob Paulsen)
Pip	*Enchanted* (Jeff Bennett, Kevin Lima)
Pumbaa	*The Lion King* (Ernie Sabella)
Ray	*The Princess and the Frog* (Jim Cummings)
Rhino	*Bolt* (Mark Walton)
Runt of the Litter	*Chicken Little* (Steve Zahn)
Russell	*Up* (Jordan Nagai)
Scuttle	*The Little Mermaid* (Buddy Hackett)
Sergeant Tibbs	*One Hundred and One Dalmatians* (David Frankham)
Skeeter Valentine	*Doug's 1st Movie* (Fred Newman)
Sleepy	*Snow White and the Seven Dwarfs* (Pinto Colvig)
Slinky Dog	*Toy Story, Toy Story 2* and *Toy Story 3* (Jim Varney, Blake Clark)
Sneezy	*Snow White and the Seven Dwarfs* (Billy Gilbert)
Terk	*Tarzan* (Rosie O'Donnell)
Thomas O'Malley	*The Aristocats* (Phil Harris)
Thumper	*Bambi* (Sam Edwards, Tim Davis, Peter Behn)
Timon	*The Lion King* (Nathan Lane)
Timothy Mouse	*Dumbo* (Edward Brophy)
Tinker Bell	*Peter Pan* (silent)
Tito	*Oliver & Company* (Cheech Marin)
Tramp	*Lady and the Tramp* (Larry Roberts)
Victor	*The Hunchback of Notre Dame* (Charles Kimbrough)
Water Rat	*The Adventures of Ichabod and Mr. Toad* (Claud Allister)
Wilbur	*The Rescuers Down Under* (John Candy)
Zini	*Dinosaur* (Max Casella)

Villains' and Villainess' Sidekicks and Accomplices

Alpha	*Up* (Bob Peterson)
Barrel	*The Nightmare Before Christmas* (Danny Elfman)
Banzai	*The Lion King* (Cheech Marin)

Characters   *Voices*
Creeper   *The Black Cauldron* (Phil Fondacaro)
Dijon   *Ducktales the Movie: Treasure of the Lost Lamp* (Richard Libertini)
Ed   *The Lion King* (Jim Cummings)
Fidget   *The Great Mouse Detective* (Candy Candido)
Gaetan Moliere   *Atlantis: The Lost Empire* (Corey Burton)
Horace   *One Hundred and One Dalmatians* (Frederick Worlock)
Iago   *Aladdin* (Gilbert Gottfried)
Jasper   *One Hundred and One Dalmatians* (J. Pat O'Malley)
Joanna   *The Rescuers Down Under* (Frank Welker)
Kronk   *The Emperor's New Groove* (Patrick Warburton)
Lawrence   *The Princess and the Frog* (Peter Bartlett)
Lefou   *Beauty and the Beast* (Jesse Corti)
Lock   *The Nightmare Before Christmas* (Paul Reubens)
Lucifer   *Cinderella* (June Foray)
Meg   *Hercules* (Susan Egan)
Molt   *A Bug's Life* (Richard Kind)
Nathaniel   *Enchanted* (Timothy Spall)
Pain   *Hercules* (Bobcat Goldthwait)
Panic   *Hercules* (Matt Frewer)
Shenzi   *The Lion King* (Whoopi Goldberg)
Shock   *The Nightmare Before Christmas* (Catherine O'Hara)
Sir Hiss   *Robin Hood* (Terry-Thomas)
Smee   *Peter Pan* (Bill Thompson)
Smee   *Return to Neverland* (Jeff Bennett)
Snoops   *The Rescuers* (Joe Flynn)
White Rabbit   *Alice in Wonderland*—1951 (Bill Thompson)

Fathers, Mothers, Teachers and Protectors

Andy's Mom   *Toy Story, Toy Story 2* and *Toy Story 3* (Laurie Metcalf)
Bagheera   *The Jungle Book* (Sebastian Cabot)
Bambi's Mother   *Bambi* (Paula Winslowe)
Big Daddy La Bouff   *The Princess and the Frog* (John Goodman)
Big Mama Owl   *The Fox and the Hound* (Pearl Bailey)
Blue Fairy   *Pinocchio* (Evelyn Venable)
Buck Cluck   *Chicken Little* (Garry Marshall)
Dallben   *The Black Cauldron* (Freddie Jones)
Django   *Ratatouille* (Brian Dennehy)
Doc Hudson   *Cars* (Paul Newman)
Duchess   *The Aristocats* (Eva Gabor, Robie Lester)
Emperor   *Mulan* (Pat Morita)
Eudora   *The Princess and the Frog* (Oprah Winfrey)
Fa Zhou   *Mulan* (Soon-Tek Oh)
Fairy Godmother   *Cinderella* (Verna Felton)
Fauna   *Sleeping Beauty* (Barbara Jo Allen)
Fflewddur Fflam   *The Black Cauldron* (Nigel Hawthorne)
Flora   *Sleeping Beauty* (Verna Felton)
Goofy Goof   *A Goofy Movie* (Bill Farmer)
Grandmother Fa   *Mulan* (June Foray, Marni Nixon)
Grandmother Willow   *Pocahontas* (Linda Hunt)
Gusteau   *Ratatouille* (Brad Garrett)
Hiram Flaversham   *The Great Mouse Detective* (Alan Young)
Kala   *Tarzan* (Glenn Close)
Kerchak   *Tarzan* (Lance Henrikson)
Mama Odie   *The Princess and the Frog* (Jenifer Lewis)
Marlin   *Finding Nemo* (Albert Brooks)
Maurice   *Beauty and the Beast* (Rex Everhart)
Mrs. Jumbo   *Dumbo* (Verna Felton)
King Nedakh   *Atlantis: The Lost Empire* (Leonard Nimoy)

Characters	Voices
King Stefan	*Sleeping Beauty* (Taylor Holmes)
Merlin	*The Sword in the Stone* (Karl Swenson)
Merryweather	*Sleeping Beauty* (Barbara Luddy)
Mufasa	*The Lion King* (James Earl Jones)
Mrs. Helperman	*Teacher's Pet* (Debra Jo Rupp)
Mrs. Potts	*Beauty and the Beast* (Angela Lansbury)
Nani	*Lilo & Stitch* (Tia Varrere)
Perdita	*One Hundred and One Dalmatians* (Cate Bauer)
Philoctetes	*Hercules* (Danny DeVito)
Pongo	*One Hundred and One Dalmatians* (Rod Taylor)
Powhatan	*Pocahontas* (Russell Means, Jim Cummings)
Professor Porter	*Tarzan* (Nigel Hawthorne)
Rafiki	*The Lion King* (Robert Guillaume)
Rufus	*The Rescuers* (John McIntire)
Sir Ector	*The Sword in the Stone* (Sebastian Cabot)
Sultan	*Aladdin* (Douglas Searle)
Triton	*The Little Mermaid* (Kenneth Mars)
Wendy	*Return to Neverland* (Kath Soucie)
Widow Tweed	*The Fox and the Hound* (Jeanette Nolan)
Yar	*Dinosaur* (Ossie Davis)
Zeus	*Hercules* (Rip Torn)

Pets and Other Animal Companions

Abu	*Aladdin* (Frank Welker)
Archimedes	*The Sword in the Stone* (Junius Matthews)
Bruno	*Cinderella* (James MacDonald, Earl Keen)
Cleo	*Pinocchio* (silent)
Dashsie	*Lady and the Tramp* (Bill Thompson)
Dug	*Up* (Bob Peterson)
Elliott	*Pete's Dragon* (Charlie Callas)
Figaro	*Pinocchio* (silent)
Flit	*Pocahontas* (Frank Welker)
Georgette	*Oliver & Company* (Bette Midler)
Jock	*Lady and the Tramp* (Bill Thompson)
Kevin	*Up* (Pete Docter)
Max	*The Little Mermaid* (Frank Welker)
Meeko	*Pocahontas* (John Kasir)
Morph	*Treasure Planet* (Dane A. Davis)
Mr. Jolly	*Teacher's Pet* (David Ogden Stiers)
Pascal	*Tangled* (silent)
Percy	*Pocahontas* (Danny Mann)
Pretty Boy	*Teacher's Pet* (Jerry Stiller)
Trusty	*Lady and the Tramp* (Bill Baucon)
Roquefort	*The Aristocats* (Sterling Holloway)
Si & Am	*Lady and the Tramp* (Peggy Lee)
Stitch	*Lilo & Stitch* (Chris Sanders)
Zazu	*The Lion King* (Rowan Atkinson)
Zero	*The Nightmare Before Christmas* (silent)

Miscellaneous Favorites

Absolem	*Alice in Wonderland*— 2010 (Alan Rickman)
Al	*Toy Story 2* (Wayne Knight)
Alan-a-Dale	*Robin Hood* (Roger Miller)
Anastasia	*Cinderella* (Lucille Bliss)
Andy	*Toy Story, Toy Story 2* and *Toy Story 3* (John Morris)
Anton Ego	*Ratatouille* (Peter O'Toole)
Atta	*A Bug's Life* (Julia Louis-Dreyfus)
Baby Herman	*Who Framed Roger Rabbit* (Lou Hirsch, April Winchell)

Voice Guide to Favorite Disney Characters 273

Characters	*Voices*
Boo	*Monsters, Inc.* (Mary Gibbs)
Brer Bear	*Song of the South* (Nicodemus Stewart)
Brer Fox	*Song of the South* (James Baskett)
Brer Rabbit	*Song of the South* (Johnny Lee)
Bruce	*Finding Nemo* (Barry Humphries)
Buck	*Home on the Range* (Cuba Gooding, Jr.)
Captain McCrea	*WALL-E* (Jeff Garlin)
Caterpillar	*Alice in Wonderland*—1951 (Richard Haydn)
Centipede	*James and the Giant Peach* (Richard Dreyfus)
Charlotte	*The Princess and the Frog* (Jennifer Cody, Breanna Brooks)
Cheshire Cat	*Alice in Wonderland*—1951 (Sterling Holloway)
Chessur	*Alice in Wonderland*—2010 (Stephen Fry)
Cogsworth	*Beauty and the Beast* (David Ogden Stiers)
Colette	*Ratatouille* (Janeane Garofalo)
Colonel Hathi	*The Jungle Book* (J. Pat O'Malley)
Crows	*Dumbo* (James Baskett, Cliff Edwards, Nicodemus Stewart)
Drizella	*Cinderella* (Rhoda Williams)
Edna E. Mode	*The Incredibles* (Brad Bird)
EVE	*WALL-E* (Elissa Knight)
Fagin	*Oliver & Company* (Dom DeLuise)
Foulfellow	*Pinocchio* (Walter Catlett)
Francis	*A Bug's Life* (Denis Leary)
Frank	*The Rescuers Down Under* (Wayne Robson)
Goob Yagoobian	*Meet the Robinsons* (Matthew Josten)
Grasshopper	*James and the Giant Peach* (Simon Callow)
Guido	*Cars* (Guido Quaroni)
Gypsy	*A Bug's Life* (Madeline Kahn)
Hamm	*Toy Story, Toy Story 2* and *Toy Story 3* (John Ratzenberger)
Heimlich	*A Bug's Life* (Joe Ranft)
Jessica Rabbit	*Who Framed Roger Rabbit* (Kathleen Turner, Amy Irving)
Joe Carioca	*Saludos Amigos* and *The Three Caballeros* (Jose Oliveira)
King Louie	*The Jungle Book* (Louis Prima)
Lampwick	*Pinocchio* (Frankie Darro)
Lost Boys	*Peter Pan* (Tony Butala, Robert Ellis, Johnny McGovern, Jeffrey Singer, Stuffy Silver)
Louis	*The Little Mermaid* (Rene Auberjonois)
Luigi	*Cars* (Tony Shalhoub)
Lumiere	*Beauty and the Beast* (Jerry Orbach)
Mad Hatter	*Alice in Wonderland*—1951 (Ed Wynn)
March Hare	*Alice in Wonderland*—1951 (Jerry Colonna)
Mayor	*The Nightmare Before Christmas* (Glenn Shadix)
Miss Spider	*James and the Giant Peach* (Susan Sarandon)
Mr. Potato Head	*Toy Story, Toy Story 2* and *Toy Story 3* (Don Rickles)
Panchito	*The Three Caballeros* (Joaquin Garay)
Peg	*Lady and the Tramp* (Peggy Lee)
Penguins	*Mary Poppins* (Dal McKennon, J. Pat O'Malley, Daws Butler)
Phoebus	*The Hunchback of Notre Dame* (Kevin Kline)
Powerline	*A Goofy Movie* (Tevin Campbell)
Pub Thugs	*Tangled* (Brad Garrett, Jeffrey Tambor, Paul F. Tompkins, Richard Kiel)
Ramone	*Cars* (Cheech Marin)
Rex	*Toy Story, Toy Story 2* and *Toy Story 3* (Wallace Shawn)
Rico	*Home on the Range* (Charles Dennis)
Roger Radcliff	*One Hundred and One Dalmatians* (Ben Wright, Bill Lee)
Scat Cat	*The Aristocats* (Scatman Crothers)
Sebastian	*The Little Mermaid* (Samuel E. Wright)
Sheriff	*Cars* (Michael Wallis)
Stabbington brothers	*Tangled* (Ron Perlman)
Vultures	*The Jungle Book* (Chad Stuart, J. Pat O'Malley, Lord Tim Hudson, Digby Wolfe)
Willie the Giant	*Fun and Fancy Free* (Billy Gilbert)
Willie the Whale	*Make Mine Music* (Nelson Eddy)

BIBLIOGRAPHY

Biographical works on individual performers are listed at the end of the person's entry.

Bailey, Adrian. *Walt Disney's World of Fantasy.* New York: Everest House, 1982.

Bain, David, and Bruce Harris. *Mickey Mouse: Fifty Happy Years.* New York: Harmony, 1977.

Barrier, Michael. *Hollywood Cartoons: American Animation in Its Golden Age.* New York: Oxford University Press, 2003.

Blitz, Marcia. *Donald Duck.* New York: Harmony, 1979.

Contemporary Theatre, Film and Television: Who's Who in the Theatre. Vols. 1–41. Detroit: Gale Research, 1978–2002.

Cotter, Bill. The *Wonderful World of Disney Television.* New York: Hyperion, 1997.

Dunning, John. *Tune in Yesterday: The Ultimate Encyclopedia of Old-Time Radio.* Englewood Cliffs, NJ: Prentice-Hall, 1976.

Erickson, Hal. *Television Cartoon Shows: An Illustrated Encyclopedia*, 1949–1993. Jefferson, NC: McFarland, 1995.

Eyles, Allen. *Walt Disney's "The Three Little Pigs."* New York: Simon and Schuster, 1986.

Finch, Christopher. *The Art of Walt Disney.* New York: Harry N. Abrams, 1973.

Grant, John. *Encyclopedia of Walt Disney Animated Characters.* New York: Hyperion, 1998.

Hischak, Thomas S., and Mark A. Robinson. *The Disney Song Encyclopedia.* Lanham, MD: Scarecrow, 2009.

_____. *The Oxford Companion to the American Musical: Theatre, Film and Television.* New York: Oxford University Press, 2008.

Holliss, Richard, and Brian Sibley. *The Disney Studio Story.* New York: Crown, 1988.

_____. *Walt Disney's Mickey Mouse: His Life and Times.* New York: Harper and Row, 1986.

_____. *Walt Disney's "Snow White and the Seven Dwarfs" and the Making of a Classic Film.* New York: Simon and Schuster, 1987.

Johnston, Ollie, and Frank Thomas. *The Disney Villain.* New York: Hyperion, 1993.

Katz, Ephraim. *The Film Encyclopedia,* 3d ed. New York: HarperPerennial, 1998.

Lawson, Tim, and Alisa Pearsons. *The Magic Behind the Voices: A Who's Who of Cartoon Voice Actors.* Jackson: University Press of Mississippi, 2004.

Lenburg, Jeff. *The Encyclopedia of Animated Cartoons.* New York: Facts on File, 1991.

_____. *Who's Who in Animated Cartoons.* New York: Applause, 2006.

Maltin, Leonard. *The Disney Films,* 4th ed. New York: Disney, 2000.

_____. *Of Mice and Magic: A History of American Animated Cartoons.* New York: McGraw-Hill, 1980.

March, Julia, and Victoria Taylor, eds. *Pixarpedia.* New York: DK, 2009.

O'Brien, Flora. *Walt Disney's Donald Duck: 50 Years of Happy Frustration.* Tucson, AZ: HP, 1984.

Parker, John, ed. *Who's Who in the Theatre.* 16 eds. London: Pitman, 1912–1977.

Schickel, Richard. *The Disney Version,* rev. ed. New York: Touchstone, 1986.

Smith, Dave. *Disney A to Z: The Official Encyclopedia,* 3d ed. New York: Disney, 2006.

Thomas, Bob. *Disney's Art of Animation: From Mickey Mouse to "Hercules."* New York: Hyperion, 1997.

Thomas, Frank, and Ollie Johnson. *Disney Animation: The Illusion of Life.* New York: Abbeville, 1981.

Walker, John, ed. *Halliwell's Who's Who in the Movies.* New York: HarperCollins, 2006.

Webb, Graham. *The Animated Film Encyclopedia.* Jefferson, NC: McFarland, 2000.

Weber, Francis. *Mickey's Golden Jubilee.* Los Angeles: Junipero Sierra, 1979.

Wright, Jean Ann. *Voice-Over for Animation.* Burlington, MA: Focal, 2009.

INDEX

Numbers in ***bold italics*** indicate the voice actor main entry.

Abbott, John *3*
Adams, Amy *3*
Adler, Bruce *3–4*, 226
Adler, Charles *4*
Adlon, Pamela *4*
Adventures in Music: Melody 116, 200, 210
The Adventures of Ichabod and Mr. Toad 8, 28, 36, 50, 92, 143, 148, 159–60, 173, 174
Aladdin 3, 4, 10, 11, 52, 57, 59, 61, 74, 79, 81, 90, 112, 115, 122, 129, 142, 167, 170, 186, 189, 202, 217, 220, 221, 225
Alan, Lori *4–5*
Alaskey, Joe *5*
Albertson, Jack *5*
Albright, Hardie *5*
Alden, Norman *5–6*
Alexander, Ernie *6*
Alexander, Jason *6*
Alexander, Stan *6*
Alice in Wonderland (1951) 10, 16, 20, 45, 72, 93, 94, 97, 100–101, 111, 113, 124, 130, 132, 148, 159, 196, 210, 213, 217, 232–33, 234
Alice in Wonderland (2010) 80–81, 90, 124, 127, 145, 179, 192, 198, 223, 227
All in a Nutshell 75
Allen, Barbara Jo *6–7*
Allen, Rex *7*
Allen, Tim *7–8*
Allister, Claud *8*
Allman, Elvia *8*
Allwine, Wayne *8*, 62, 208
Almanzar, James *8–9*
Anderson, Stephen J. *9*
Andretti, Mario *9*
Andrews, Julie *9*, 122
Andrews, Maeve *9*
Andrews Sisters *9–10*, 224
Angel, Heather *10*
Angel, Jack *10*
Anselmo, Tony *10–11*, 153
Aquamania 48, 57
The Aristocats 14, 34, 42, 43, 50, 64, 69, 70, 81, 96, 100, 103, 111, 119, 120, 127, 129, 139, 174, 176, 189, 192, 210, 227, 232

Arnett, Will *11*
The Art of Self-Defense 143
The Art of Skiing 109, 143
Asner, Ed *11–12*
Atkinson, Rowan *12*
Atlantis: The Lost Empire 32, 42, 52, 77, 82–83, 97, 133, 150, 155, 157, 167, 200, 202, 203, 204, 213, 215
Attenborough, Tom *12*
Atwell, Roy *12*
Auberjonois, Rene *12–13*
Audley, Eleanor *13*
The Autograph Hound 43

Backus, Jim *13–14*
Baddeley, Hermione *14*
Bader, Diedrich *14*
Bailey, G.W. *15*
Bailey, Pearl *15*
Bakalyan, Richard *15*
Baker, Joe *15–16*
Bale, Christian *16*
Ball, Sherwood *16*
Bambi 5, 6, 15, 21, 28, 54, 55, 65, 67, 87, 95, 100, 103, 111, 116, 122, 126, 153, 157, 193, 201, 205, 228, 232
Bana, Eric *16*
Barclay, Don *16*
Bardsley, Grant *16–17*
The Barn Dance 83, 199
Barnes, Christopher Daniel 17
The Barnyard Battle 199
The Barnyard Broadcast 83
Barrie, Barbara *17*
Bart, Roger *17*
Bartlett, Peter *17–18*
Barty, Billy *18*
Baskett, James *18*
Bassett, Angela *18–19*
Bath Day 44
Baucom, Bill *19*
Bauer, Cate *19*
The Beach Party 205
Beach Picnic 145
Beaird, Barbara *19*
Beal, John *19*
Beatty, Ned *19–20*
Beaumont, Kathryn *20*, 197

Beauty and the Beast 3, 10, 11, 23, 24, 48–49, 51, 70, 71, 74, 77, 107, 115, 121–22, 129, 142, 158–59, 160, 167, 170, 173, 180, 186, 195, 197, 202, 213, 221, 222, 230
Beck, Erica *20*
Bedard, Irene *20–21*
Bedford, Brian *21*
Bedknobs and Broomsticks 101, 121, 143, 220, 232
Behn, Peter *21*
Belack, Doris *21–22*
Bellboy Donald 143
Ben and Me 100, 183, 210
Bennett, Jeff *22*
Bennett, Marjorie *22*
Benson, Jodi *22–23*, 158
Benson, Robby *23*
Bergen, Bob *23–24*
Bergman, Mary Kay *24*
Beswick, Quinn *24*
Bettin, Val *24*
The Big Bad Wolf 46, 147
Billingsley, Dick *24–25*
Bing, Herman *25*
Bird, Brad 9, *25*, 125, 216
Bird, Michael *25*
Bird, Nicholas *25*
Black, Sam *25*
The Black Cauldron 8, 17, 35, 61, 76, 97, 105, 109, 112, 134, 144, 176, 192, 213
Blacque, Taurean *25*
Blanc, Mel *25–26*
Blessed, Brian *26*
Bletcher, Billy *26–27*
Blethyn, Brenda *27*
Bliss, Lucille *27*
Block, Bobby *27*
Blondell, Gloria *27–28*
Blore, Eric *28*, 160
Boardman, Thelma *28*
Bolt 9, 14, 22, 29, 52, 53, 57, 61, 62, 70, 76, 84, 93, 102, 115, 123, 128, 130, 135, 141, 144, 149, 150, 156, 175, 188, 201, 205, 213, 216, 217–18, 223
Bone Trouble 145
Bottone, Bob *28*
Braff, Zach *28*

275

Bragger, Klee **28**
The Brave Engineer 45, 112, 117
Brave Little Tailor 83, 148
Breaux, Marc **28–29**
Brenner, Eve **29**
Breslin, Spencer **29**
Briggs, Paul **29**
Bright, Charles **29**
Brill, Fran **29**
Broderick, Matthew 28, **29–30**
Brodie, Don **30**
Broken Toys 32
Brooks, Albert **30**
Brooks, Breanna **30**
Brophy, Edward **30–31**
Brother Bear 4, 9, 23, 29, 31, 41, 42, 48, 49, 59, 65, 71, 91, 93, 94, 96, 102, 113, 138, 142, 144, 149, 165, 166, 167, 170, 171, 172, 180, 203, 205, 209
Brown, Julie **31**
Browne, Roscoe Lee **31**
Buchanan, Stuart **31**
A Bug's Life 10, 23, 25, 31, 59, 61, 71, 76, 83, 96, 104, 112, 116, 120, 122, 124, 131, 132, 140, 142, 143, 157, 160, 163, 165, 166, 170, 172, 173, 174, 179, 181, 198, 200, 205, 208, 211, 214
Bumpass, Rodger **31–32**
Bupp, Tommy **32**
Burghardt, Arthur **32**
Burnham, David **32**
Burton, Corey **32–33**, 75, 225
Burtt, Ben **33**
Buscemi, Steve **33**
Butala, Tony **33**
Butcher, Paul **33–34**
Butler, Daws **34**
Buttram, Pat **34**
Buzzi, Ruth **34–35**
Byner, John **35**

Cabot, Sebastian **35**
Calame, Niketa **35**
Caldwell, Zoe **35**
Callaghan, Julius **35–36**
Callas, Charlie **36**
Callow, Simon **36**
Campbell, Colin **36**
Campbell, Tevin **36–37**
Camping Out 83
Campos, Bruno **37**
Candido, Candy **37**
Candy, John **37–38**, 225
Canney, Wayne **38**
Carlin, George **38**
Carmichael, Jim **38**
Carr, Darleen **38**
Carrere, Tia **38–39**
Carroll, Eddie **39**
Carroll, Pat **39**
Cars 8, 9, 10, 23, 31, 38, 43, 45, 48, 49, 50, 63, 66, 71, 76, 85, 96, 98, 101, 104, 114, 116, 118, 122, 127, 128, 132, 133, 135, 136, 140, 142, 154, 155, 157, 165, 166, 167, 171, 172, 173, 174, 179, 181, 188, 191, 200, 205, 214, 217, 218, 222, 226
Carson, Ken **39–40**

Casella, Max **40**
Caselotti, Adriana 3, 24, **40–41**
Catlett, Walter **41**
Cesar, Darko **41**
Chabert, Lacey **41**
Chase, Daveigh **41–42**
Chesney, Diana **42**
Chevalier, Maurice **42**, 160
Chicken Little 4, 28, 52–53, 61, 65, 69, 74, 76, 85, 87, 91, 93, 102, 110, 112, 115, 118, 138, 141, 146, 147, 158, 166, 189, 191, 198, 201–202, 217, 218, 221, 223, 224, 233
Chip an' Dale 75
Chips Ahoy 75
Christian, Claudia **42**
Christie, Paul **42**
Cinderella 13, 16, 27, 54, 63–64, 72, 76–77, 84, 111, 114, 132, 148, 174, 193, 215, 217, 225, 229
Clark, Blake **42–43**, 215
Clark, Buddy **43**
Clark, Dean **43**
Clark, Kimberly Adair **43**
Clark, Sarah **43**
Clemmons, Larry **43**
Clifford, Ruth **43–44**
Close, Glenn **44**
Clown of the Jungle 46
Coburn, James **44**
Cody, Jennifer **44**
Collins, Eddie **44–45**
Collins, Lindsey **45**
Collins, Paul **45**
Colonna, Jerry **45**
Colvig, Pinto **45–46**, 109, 195
Colyar, Michael **46**
Compton, Dorothy **46**
Connolly, Billy **46–47**
Conried, Hans 32, **47**
Contrary Condor 87
Conway, Tom **47**
Coogan, Keith **47–48**
Cook, Carole **48**
Cooley, Josh **48**
Copeland, Joan **48**
Corcoran, Kevin **48**
Corn Chips 75
Corti, Jesse **48–49**
Costa, Mary **49**
Costas, Bob **49**
Crazy Over Daisy 28
Crenshaw, Randy **49**
Crosby, Bing **49–50**
Crothers, Scatman **50**
Crow, Sheryl **50**
Crystal, Billy 7, **50–51**, 89, 178
Cullen, Peter 51
Cummings, Brian **51**
Cummings, Jim **51–52**, 106
Cummings, Todd **52**
Cured Duck 28
Curtis, Ken **52**
Cusack, Joan **52–53**
Cygan, John **53**
Cyrus, Miley **53**, 149

Dafoe, Willem **53**, 230
Dalton, Timothy **53–54**
Dampier, Elizabeth **54**

Darby, Ken **117**
Darlington, Marion **54**
Darro, Frankie **54**
David, Keith, **54–55**
Davis, Cherry **55**
Davis, Dane A. **55**
Davis, Lisa **55**
Davis, Ossie **55**
Davis, Tim **55–56**
Day, Dennis **56**
Days, Bill **56**
De Castro Sisters **56**
DeGault, Lance **56**
DeGeneres, Ellen **56–57**
Dehner, John **57**
DeLisle, Grey **57**
Dell, Charlie **58**
DeLuise, Dom **58**
DeLyon, Leo **58**
Dempsey, Taylor **58**
Dench, Judi **58–59**
Denison, Leslie **59**
Dennehy, Brian **59**
Dennis, Charles **59**
Derryberry, Debi **59–60**
Destino 132
Deutsch, Patti **60**
Devine, Andy **60**
DeVito, Danny **60–61**
Diller, Phyllis **61**
Di Maggio, John **61**
Dindal, Mark **61**
Dinning Sisters **61**
Dinosaur 40, 55, 136, 156, 163, 168, 175, 195, 198, 205, 229, 232
DiSalvo, Lino **61**
Disney, Walt 8, 19, 28, 33, 40, 42, **61–62**, 100, 109, 123, 132, 139, 153, 169, 182, 199, 229, 232
Docter, Elie **62**
Docter, Pete **62**
Dodson, Jon **117**
Donald and the Wheel 174
Donald Gets Drafted 143
Donald in Mathmagic Land 80
Donald's Better Self 28, 30
Donald's Crime 28
Donald's Decision 30
Donald's Diary 59
Donald's Dilemma 28
Donald's Double Trouble 28, 59
Donald's Dream Voice 44, 59
Donald's Ostrich 8, 46
Donnellan, Sean **62**
Donovan, Tate **62–63**
Dooley, Paul **63**
Dotrice, Roy **63**
Douglas, Mike **63–64**
Doug's First Movie 21, 28, 29, 92, 94, 109, 118, 125, 130, 142, 154, 166, 168, 169, 194, 221
Dreyfuss, Richard **64**
Driscoll, Bobby **64**
Driver, Minnie **64**
Dubin, Gary **64–65**
Duck for Hire 210
Duck Pimples 219
DuckTales: The Movie—Treasure of the Lost Lamp 10, 77, 84, 128, 130, 139, 142, 167, 207, 208, 233

Dumbo 25, 27, 30, 31, 38, 67, 72, 82, 100–101, 106, 143, 157, 174, 188–89, 190, 201, 217
Dunagan, Donnie **65**
Duncan, Michael Clarke **65**
Duncan, Sandy **65**
Dunn, Evan **65**
Dunn, Teala **65–66**
Durst, Debi **66**
Dworsky, Sally **66**

Earhardt, Dale, Jr. **66**
Ebeling, Lulu **66**
Eddy, Nelson **66**
Edmiston, Walker **66–67**
Edwards, Cliff **39**, **67**
Edwards, Patti **67**
Edwards, Sam **67–68**
Efron, Marshall **68**
Egan, Susan **68**
Eggar, Samantha **68**
Eggleston, Ralph **68**
Elfman, Danny **68–69**
Ellis, Robert **69**
Elmer Elephant 95, 112
Elmore, Sean **69**
The Emperor's New Groove 9, 11, 23, 31, 60, 61, 73, 89, 94, 96, 97, 110, 115, 117, 129, 134, 135, 142, 146, 198, 203, 205, 218, 223
Enchanted 3, 9, 22, 65, 129, 137, 138, 159, 188, 198, 207
English, Liz **69**
Epstein, Alvin **69**
Ermey, R. Lee **69–70**
Essman, Susie **70**
Evans, Monica **70**
Everhart, Rex **70**
Eyster, Tim **70–71**

Fabio **71**
Fagerbakke, Bill **71**
Fall, James Apaumut **71**
Fantasia 92, 143, 148
Fantasia/2000 8, 11, 41, 121
Farmer, Bill **71**
Farrow, Mia **72**
Fathers Are People 64
Father's Lion 64
Father's Week End 64
Feldman, Corey **72**
Felton, Verna **72**
Ferdinand the Bull 111, 112, 226
Ferrer, Miguel **72–73**
Fiedler, John **73**
Fierstein, Harvey **73–74**
Finding Nemo 16, 20, 25, 27, 30, 45, 53, 56–57, 66, 68, 75, 81, 83, 90, 96, 101, 104, 105, 107, 123, 128, 131, 135, 140, 157, 163, 164, 165, 167, 171, 173, 174, 182, 184, 196, 199, 200, 204, 205, 214
Finn, Will **74**
The Fire Fighters 83
First Aiders 44
Firth, Peter **74**
Fitzhugh, Ellen **74**
Flaherty, Joe **74**
Fleischer, Charles **74–75**
Fleming, Shaun **75**

Flint, Shelby **75**
Flower, Jessie **75**
Flynn, Dessie **75**
Flynn, Joe **75–76**
Fogelman, Dan **76**
Foley, Dave **76**
Fondacaro, Phil **76**
For the Birds 68
For Whom the Bulls Toil 82
Foray, June **76–77**
Ford, John H.H. **77**
Fox, Bernard **77**
Fox, Michael J. **77–78**
Fox, Spencer **78**
The Fox and the Hound 5, 10, 15, 25, 34, 43, 48, 65, 72, 73, 142, 156, 182, 184, 227
Francis, Genie **78**
Frankham, David **78**
Freberg, Stan **78–79**
Freeman, Cheryl **79**
Freeman, Jonathan **79**
Freeman, Sarah **79**
Frees, Paul **79–80**
Frewer, Matt **80**
Fry, Jordan **80**, 95
Fry, Stephen **80–81**
Fucile, Eli **81**
Fucile, Tony **81**
Fullilove, Donald **81**
Fun and Fancy Free 39, 41, 46, 61, 62, 67, 86, 89, 132, 153, 193

Gabor, Eva **81**
Gainey, M.C. **81–82**
Gallant, Jim **82**
The Gallopin' Gaucho 199
Gammill, Noreen **82**
Garay, Joaquin **82**
Garlin, Jeff **82**
Garner, James **82–83**
Garner, Marcellite **83**
Garofalo, Janeane **83**
Garrett, Brad **83–84**
Geary, Anthony 78, **84**
Gerber, Joan **84**
Geri's Game 165, 173
Germann, Greg **84**
Gerson, Betty Lou **84–85**
Gerson, Daniel **85**
Gibbs, Mary **85**
Gibson, Mel **85**
Gibson, Mimi **85–86**
Gilbert, Billy **86**
Gilbert, Ed **86**
Gill, Florence **86–87**
Gillis, Ann **87**
Gilmore, Art **87**
Givot, George **87**
Glover, William **87**
Goldberg, Whoopi **87–88**
Golden Eggs 87
The Golden Touch 26, 148
Goldthwait, Bobcat **88**
Goldwyn, Tony **88–89**
Goliath II 7, 25, 48, 72, 80, 100, 159
Gooding, Cuba, Jr. **89**
Goodman, John 33, **89**
Goofy and Wilbur 109

Goofy Gymnastics 143
A Goofy Movie 8, 11, 28, 31, 32, 34, 36–37, 52, 71, 74, 103, 123, 129, 131, 137, 138, 163, 178, 191, 194, 195, 198, 200, 216, 221, 230
Goofy's Freeway Troubles 80
Goofy's Glider 143, 232
Gordon, Anita **89**
Gordon-Levitt, Joseph **89–90**
Gottfried, Gilbert **90**
Gough, Michael **90**
Gould, Alexander **90–91**
Gould, Harold **91**
Goulet, Robert **91**
Graae, Jason **91**
Graham, Frank **91**
Grammer, Kelsey **91–92**
Grant, Campbell 92
The Grasshopper and the Ants 46
The Great Mouse Detective 8, 11, 24, 29, 37, 42, 61, 66, 74, 106, 133, 134, 169, 170, 174, 217, 233
The Greener Yard 213
Greenspan, Melissa **92**
Greenwood, Peter **92**
Gregory, Natalie **92**
Greno, Nathan **93**
Grey, Larry **93**
Guillaume, Robert **93**

Hackett, Buddy **93**
Hadley, Guy **93–94**
Hahn, Emily **94**
Haid, Charles, **94**
Hall Don **94**
Hamlin, Bob **94**
Hanks, Tom **94–95**
Hansen, Bernice **95**
Hansen, Daniel **95**
Harlan, Otis **95**
Harnell, Jess **95–96**
Harris, Estelle **96**
Harris, Jonathan **96**
Harris, Phil 86, **96–97**
The Haunted House 199
Hawthorne, Nigel **97**
Haydn, Richard **97**
Hayes, Billie **97**
Hegarty, Susan **97–98**
Helmond, Katherine **98**
Henricksen, Lance **98**
Hercules 6, 10, 11, 17, 24, 29, 31, 32, 45, 52, 54, 59, 60–61, 62–63, 67, 68, 71, 79, 80, 88, 100, 113, 115, 118, 119, 128, 142, 145, 167, 168, 170, 172, 185, 191, 192, 210, 212–13, 216, 222, 229–30
Heston, Charlton **98**
Hickey, William **98–99**
Higgins, Joe **99**
Hill, Amy **99**
Hill, Ramsay **99**
Hilton, Connie **99**
Hirsch, Lou **99–100**
Hockey Homicide 112, 219
Holbrook, Hal **100**
Holden, Eddie **100**
Holloway, Sterling 46, **100–101**
Holm, Ian **101**
Holmes, Taylor **101**

Holowicki, E.J. *101*
Holt, Bob *101*
Home on the Range 11, 15, 27, 32, 33, 48, 56, 58, 59, 68, 71, 74, 89, 91, 94, 96, 108, 115, 126, 128, 142, 170, 171, 177, 179, 183, 188, 194, 195, 211, 217, 218, 219, 223
Hong, James *102*
Hoover, Kelly *102*
Hopkins, Nikita *102*
How to Be a Sailor 143
How to Catch a Cold 210
How to Dance 116
How to Have an Accident at Work 210
How to Have an Accident in the Home 210
How to Play Baseball 109, 193
How to Play Golf 193
How to Swim 109, 143
Howard, Clint *103*
Howard, Terrence *103*
Høybye, Laus *103*
Hubbard, Thelma *103*
Hudson, Lord Tim *103–104*
Hulce, Tom *104*
Humphries, Barry *104*
The Hunchback of Notre Dame 6, 10, 11, 23, 24, 29, 31, 32, 45, 52, 59, 71, 74, 81, 104, 107–108, 112, 116, 117, 119, 142, 147, 148, 167, 170, 172, 197, 202, 213, 223–24, 228
Hunt, Bonnie *104*
Hunt, Linda *104–105*
Hunter, Bill *105*
Hunter, Holly *105*
Hurt, John *105*
Huston, John *105–106*
Hutton, Malcolm *106*

In the Bag 219
The Incredibles 9, 25, 38, 43, 62, 68, 78, 81, 101, 105, 107, 123, 125, 131, 154, 155, 157, 163, 165, 167, 171, 173, 174, 178, 181, 191, 194, 196, 200, 205, 216
Ingham, Barrie *106*
Irons, Jeremy *106*
Irving, Amy *106–107*, 214
It's Tough to Be a Bird 15, 35, 116
It's Tough to Be a Bug 76, 198
Ivory, Edward *107*

Jack-Jack Attack 81, 125, 132, 181
Jackson, Samuel L. *107*
James and the Giant Peach 22, 36, 64, 126, 135, 155, 187, 201, 208, 209
Janney, Allison *107*
Jay, Tony *107–108*
Jbara, Gregory *108*
Jillette, Penn *108*
Joel, Billy *108–109*
Johnson, Bruce Bayley *109*
Johnson, George *109*
Jones, Dickie *109*
Jones, Freddie *109–10*
Jones, James Earl *110*
Jones, Tom *110*

Jordan, Jim 37, *110*
Josten, Matthew, *110–11*
Judels, Charles *111*
Jump, Gordon *111*
The Jungle Book 3, 35, 38, 43, 58, 72, 86, 96–97, 100–101, 103–104, 111, 160, 170, 174, 176, 186–87, 196, 203, 228, 231, 232

Kahl, Milt *111–12*
Kahn, Madeline *112*
Kandel, Paul *112*
Kane, Brad *112*
Kassir, John *112–13*
Katz, Kerry *113*
Kawagley, Angavuqaq Oscar *113*
Kaye, David *113*
Kearns, Joseph *113*
Keaton, Josh *113–14*
Keaton, Michael *114*
Keen, Earl *114*
Keever, Douglas *114*
Keillor, Garrison *114*
Kelly, Moira *114–15*
Kelso, Kellyann *115*
Kennedy, Mark *115*
Kenny, Tom *115*
Kernion, Jerry *115*
Kerry, Margaret *115*
Kiel, Richard *115–16*
Kimball, Ward *116*, 148
Kimbrough, Charles *116*
Kind, Richard *116*
King, Cammie *116–17*
King Neptune 83, 219
The King's Men *117*
Kitt, Eartha *117*
Kline, Kevin *117*
Knight, Elissa *118*
Knight, Wayne *118*
Knotts, Don *118*
Kopf, Kim *118*
Korbich, Eddie *118–19*
Krakoff, Rocky *119*
Kroner, Amber *119*
Kuhn, Judy *119*
Kulp, Nancy *119*

LaChanze *119*
Lady and the Tramp 19, 72, 78–79, 87, 109, 111, 124, 126, 132, 143, 145, 157, 173, 174, 175, 180, 196, 201, 210, 232
Lagasse, Emeril *119–20*
Lambert the Sheepish Lion 100–101, 232
Lander, David L. *120*
Landor, Rosalyn *120*
Lane, Charles *120*
Lane, Nathan *121*
Langford, Frances *121*
Lansbury, Angela *121–22*
Lansing, Mary *122*
Larkin, Linda *122*
Larry the Cable Guy *122*
Lasseter, John 7, 114, *122–23*, 218
Laurita, Dana *123*
LaVerne, Lucille *123*
Lawrence, Joseph *123*
Leader, Zoe *124*

Leary, Denis *124*
Leary, Jeremy *124*
Le Doux, Leone *124*, 190
Lee, Bill *124*
Lee, Billy *124*
Lee, Christopher *124–25*
Lee, Greg *125*
Lee, Jason *125*
Lee, Jason Scott *125*
Lee, Johnny 18, *125–26*
Lee, Margaret *126*
Lee, Peggy *126*, 145
Leeves, Jane *126*
LeGault, Lance *126–27*
Leno, Jay *127*
Leonard, Queenie *127*
Lester, Robie *127*
Levi, Zachary *127*
Levine, Sam J. *127–28*
Lewis, Jenifer *128*
Lewis, Jenny *128*
Lewis, Vicki *128*
Libertini, Richard *128–29*
Lilo and Stitch 10, 20, 23, 29, 35, 38–39, 41, 96, 97, 99, 102, 125, 140, 142, 167, 177, 178, 186, 197, 202
Lima, Emma Rose *129*
Lima, Kevin *129*
Lindo, Delroy *129*
Lindsey, George *129*
Linn, Bud *117*
Linnetz, Eli Russell *129*
Linz, Alex D. *129–30*
The Lion King 11, 12, 29–30, 35, 52, 66, 81, 87, 93, 97, 106, 110, 114, 121, 124, 135, 170, 173, 185, 186, 195, 210, 211, 214, 220, 224, 225
Lipton, James *130*
Lish, Becca *130*
The Litterbug 57
The Little Mermaid 4, 10, 12–13, 17, 22–23, 39, 61, 67, 74, 81, 86, 93, 129, 136, 137, 140, 158, 167, 180, 185, 213, 221, 231, 232
The Little Whirlwind 28
Lloyd, Christopher *130*
Lloyd, Doris *130*
Loggia, Robert *130–31*
Lohr, Aaron *131*
Louis, Dominique *131*
Louis-Dreyfus, Julia *131*
Luckey, Bud *131–32*
Luddy, Barbara *132*
Luske, Tommy 115, *132*
Luz, Dora *132*

MacDonald, James 8, 62, *132–33*
Maga, Mickey *133*
Maglionni, Tom and Ray *133*
Mahoney, John *133*
Main, Laurie *133*
Maiwand, Brianna *133*
Majors, Austin *133–34*
Make Mine Music 9–10, 45, 66, 100, 111, 117, 148, 174, 184, 193
Malet, Arthur *134*
Malick, Wendie *134*
Malis-Morey, Adele *134*

Manchester, Melissa *134*
Mann, Danny *134–35*
Manoux, J.P. *135*
The Many Adventures of Winnie the Pooh 43, 100, 103, 138, 149, 174, 196, 214, 217, 231
Margolyes, Miriam *135–36*
Margulies, Julianna *136*
Marin, Cheech *136*
Marin, Jason *136*
Marples, David *135*
Marr, Eddie *136*
Mars, Kenneth *136–37*
Marsden, James *137*
Marsden, Jason, *137*
Marshall, Garry *137–38*
Marshall, Sean *138*
Martin, Kellie *138*
Marwood, Linda *138*
Mary Poppins 9, 16, 28–29, 34, 62, 79, 85, 111, 124, 134, 139, 143, 153, 159, 163, 174, 214
Mastrogiorgio, Danny *138*
Mateo, Joseph *138*
Matthews, Junius C. *138–39*
Mattraw, Scotty *139*
Maude-Roxby, Roddy *139*
McBride, Susan *139*
McCann, Chuck *139*
McClory, Sean *139–40*
McClurg, Edie *140*
McDonald, Kevin *140*
McDonough, Andrew *140*
McDowall, Roddy *140–41*
McDowell, Malcolm *141*
McElroy, Niki *141*
McGarry, Dara *141*
McGoohan, Patrick *141–42*
McGovern, Johnny *142*
McGovern, Terence *142*
McGowan, Mickie *142*
McHugh, Thomas *142*
McIntire, John *142–43*, 156
McKennon, Dal *143*
McLeish, John *143*
McShane, Michael *143*
Means, Russell *143–44*
Meet the Robinsons 9, 18, 33, 61, 71, 75, 76, 77, 80, 93, 94, 95, 102, 111, 115, 123, 138, 141, 144, 146, 147, 175, 181, 187, 190, 195, 201, 204, 207, 217, 221, 223, 224
Melody Time 10, 43, 46, 56, 61, 64, 111, 121, 153, 159, 181, 218
Mercer, Jack *144*
Merin, Eda Reiss *144*
Mertens, Tim *144*
Metcalf, Laurie *144–45*
Metchik, Aaron Michael *145*
Meyer, Carla *145*
Mickey's Amateurs 86
Mickey's Birthday Party 28, 86
Mickey's Christmas Carol 8, 24, 39, 61, 153, 185, 196, 233
Mickey's Fire Brigade 8, 112
Mickey's Follies 83, 199
Mickey's Grand Opera 86
Mickey's Mellerdrammer 8
Mickey's Nightmare 83
Mickey's Orphans 83

Mickey's Revue 46
Mickey's Rival 83
Mickey's Steamroller 83
Mickey's Surprise Party 83
Midler, Bette *145*
Millar, Lee *145*
Millar, Lee, Jr. *145–46*
Miller, Beatrice *146*
Miller, Marvin *146*
Miller, Roger *146*
Miller-Zarneke, Tracey *146*
Ming-Na *146–47*, 186
Mr. Duck Steps Out 43
Moder, Mary *147*
Mohr, Gerald *147*
Molina, Dan *147*
Mollenbauer, Heidi *147*
Monsters, Inc. 7, 10, 23, 25, 31, 33, 44, 50–51, 62, 68, 71, 85, 89, 91, 104, 123, 131, 135, 142, 155, 162, 165, 166, 170, 171, 172, 173, 174, 179, 181, 200, 204, 205, 211, 214
Montgomery, Ritchie *147–48*
Moore, Demi *148*
Moore, Fred *148*
Moore, Mandy *148–49*
The Moose Hunt 46
Moranis, Rick *149*, 209
More Kittens 173
Moretz, Chloe *149*
Morita, Pat *149*
Morris, Howard *149–50*
Morris, John *150*
Morris, Phil *150*
Morris the Midget Moose 213
Moss, Ronn *150*
Mulan 11, 24, 29, 41, 66, 72, 73, 77, 89, 93, 97, 102, 135, 139, 146–47, 149, 151–52, 156, 158, 160, 167, 176, 186, 192, 193, 206, 212, 218, 221, 224, 229
Mullally, Megan *150–51*
Mulligan, Richard *151*
Murphy, Donna *151*
Murphy, Eddie *151–52*, 225
Murray, Brian *152*

Nagai, Jordan *152*
Najimy, Kathy *152–53*
Napier, Alan *153*
Nash, Clarence 11, *153*
Nelson, Craig T. *153–54*
Nelson, Mike *154*
The New Spirit 193
Newhart, Bob *154*, 181
Newman, Fred *154*
Newman, Paul 8, *154–55*
Newman, Randy *155*
Newton, Teddy *155*
The Nifty Nineties 28, 56, 87, 95, 116, 148, 173, 174, 196
The Night Before Christmas 157
The Nightmare Before Christmas 16, 49, 66, 68, 98, 107, 113, 139, 150, 158, 162, 170, 171, 173, 177, 187, 190, 214
Nimoy, Leonard *155–56*
Nixon, Marnie *156*
No Hunting 210
Noah's Ark 80, 124, 174, 196, 201

Nolan, Jeanette 143, *156*
Norris, Daran *156*
Novello, Don *156–57*
Novis, Donald *157*
Noyes, Betty *157*

Obradors, Jacqueline *157*
Ochoa, Adrian *157*
O'Donnell, Rosie *157–58*
Oh, Soon-Tek *158*
O'Hara, Catherine *158*
O'Hara, Paige *158–59*
Oliveira, José *159*
Oliver & Company 25, 31, 58, 61, 74, 81, 87, 92–93, 108–109, 119, 123, 129, 130–31, 135, 145, 151, 172, 173, 213, 221
Olsen, Moroni *159*
The Olympic Champ 109, 143
O'Malley, J. Pat *159–60*, 231
One Hundred and One Dalmatians 16, 19, 22, 27, 47, 55, 78, 79, 84, 85, 99, 111, 124, 127, 132, 133, 143, 159, 161, 162, 163, 174, 196, 201, 208, 221, 231
The Opry House 199
Orbach, Jerry *160*
Orphan's Benefit 86
Osmond, Donny *160*
Ossman, David *160*
Oswalt, Patton *160–61*
O'Toole, Peter *161*
Out of the Frying Pan Into the Fire 28
Owen, Harriet *161*
Owen, Tudor *161*
Oz, Frank *161–62*

Page, Geraldine *162*
Page, Ken *162*
Palmer, Garrett *162–63*
Panettiere, Hayden *163*
Pantry Pirate 38, 172–73
Parker, Barnett *163*
Parker, Bret Brook *163*
Parris, Patricia *163*
Partly Cloudy 81, 178
Paul Bunyan 124, 174, 196, 201
Paulsen, Rob *163–64*
Pelling, George *164*
Peña, Elizabeth *164*
Peña, Javier Fernández *164*
Pendleton, Austin *164*
The Penguin and the Snipe 100
Perkins, Elizabeth *164–65*
Perl, Michael *165*
Perlman, Ron *165*
Perrette, Pauley *165*
Peter Pan 10, 20, 33, 37, 45, 47, 64, 69, 76, 99, 111, 115, 132, 142, 148, 174, 194, 195, 197, 210, 217, 232
Pete's Dragon 36, 138
Peterson, Bob *165*
Petty, Richard *165–66*
Phillips, Chris *166*
Phipps, William *166*
Phoenix, Joaquin *166*
Pidgeon, Jeff *166–67*
Pierce, Bradley *167*
Pierce, David Hyde *167*

Piglet's Big Movie 51, 73, 102, 187, 197, 203, 222
Pinney, Patrick *167*
Pinocchio 25–26, 30, 31, 41, 54, 67, 92, 109, 111, 144, 148, 183, 215–16
Piven, Jeremy *167*
Plane Crazy 199
Playten, Alice *168*
Plowright, Joan *168*
Plummer, Amanda *168*
Plummer, Christopher *168–69*
Pluto and the Armadillo 193
Plutopia 13
Pluto's Christmas Tree 44, 75
Pluto's Dream House 8, 145
Pluto's Playmate 145
Pluto's Sweater 44
Pocahontas 15, 16, 20–21, 38, 45, 46, 52, 71, 74, 85, 97, 104–105, 112, 119, 135, 144, 186, 202, 212, 221
The Pointer 145
Pollatschek, Susanne *169*
Pooh's Heffalump Movie 27, 49, 51, 73, 102, 187, 199
Pope, Tony *169*
Potts, Annie *169*
The Practical Pig 43, 46, 147
Preis, Doug *169*
Presto!, 205
Price, Vincent 107, *169–70*
Prima, Louis *170*
The Prince and the Pauper 4, 8, 11, 32, 63, 70–71, 119, 213
The Princess and the Frog 17, 29, 30, 32, 37, 44, 46, 52, 54, 55, 89, 94, 102, 103, 113, 115, 119–20, 128, 147, 148, 155, 170, 176, 178, 182–83, 207, 214, 223, 226, 228, 230
Private Pluto 75, 132
Proctor, Phil *170*
Professor Tall and Mr. Small 143
Proops, Greg *170–71*
Pullen, Purv *171*
Puppy Love 83
Put-Put Trouble 43

Quaid, Randy *171*
Quaroni, Guido *171*
Questrel, Mae *171–72*

Rabson, Jan *172*
Radford, Mary T. *172*
Raize, Jason *172*
Ralph, Sheryl Lee *172*
Randolph, Lillian *172–73*
Ranft, Jerome *173*
Ranft, Joe *173*
Ranft, Jordan *173*
Rarig, John *173*
Ratatouille 11, 25, 35, 45, 48, 59, 76, 81, 83–84, 97, 101, 123, 131, 132, 155, 160–61, 165, 171, 173, 174, 176, 178, 181, 183, 196, 200
Rathbone, Basil 36, 106, 113, *173–74*
Ratzenberger, John *174*
Ravenscroft, Thurl *174–75*
Redson, Aurian *175*

Redux Riding Hood 41, 71, 72, 76, 77, 114, 177, 179, 221
Reed, Alan *175*
Rees, Roger *175*
Reese, Della *175–76*
Reitherman, Bruce *176*, 196
Reitherman, Richard *176*
Reitherman, Robert *176*, 196
The Reluctant Dragon 6, 8, 43, 57, 87, 124, 136, 138, 143, 147, 148, 163, 190, 200, 226
Remar, James *176*
Renaday, Pete *176–77*
The Rescuers 34, 37, 43, 73, 75, 76, 77, 81, 93, 110, 111, 127, 129, 132–33, 142–43, 154, 156, 162, 199, 207
The Rescuers Down Under 18, 37, 61, 74, 77, 81, 86, 92, 115, 127, 129, 145, 154, 173, 180, 181, 185, 186, 189, 208, 213, 221
Return to Never Land 20, 22, 24, 29, 32, 140, 161, 163, 167, 175, 197, 198, 219
Reubens, Paul *177*
Rhames, Ving *177*
Richards, Ann *177*
Richards, Michael *177–78*
Richards, Robyn *178*
Richardson, Kevin Michael *178*
Richardson, Lori *178*
Rickles, Don *178–79*
Rickman, Alan *179*
Riehle, Richard *179*
Rivera, Jonas *179*
The Robber Kitten 26–27
Roberts, Larry *180*
Robertson, Kimmy *180*
Robin Hood 21, 34, 37, 43, 52, 60, 70, 73, 97, 111, 123, 129, 132, 146, 160, 192, 208–209, 215, 222
Robinson, Bumper *180*
Robinson, Rad *117*
Robson, Wayne *180*
Rocco, Alex *180–81*
Rogers, Roy *181*
Rogers, Tristan *181*
Roller Coaster Rabbit 75, 100, 214, 227
Romano, Lou *181*
Rooney, Mickey *181–82*
Root, Stephen *182*
Rose, Anika Noni *182–83*
Roseanne 183
Roux, Stéphane *183*
Rub, Christian *183*
Ruggles, Charles *183–84*
Runaway Brain 92, 208
Rupp, Debra Jo *184*
Rush, Geoffrey *184*
Russell, Andy *184*
Russell, Kurt *184*
Ryan, Roz *184–85*
Ryan, Will *185*
Ryen, Adam *185*

Sabella, Ernie *185–86*
The Saga of Windwagon Smith 7, 159
St. John, Michelle *186*

Salonga, Lea *186*
Saludos Amigos 31, 111, 153, 159, 193, 232
Sanders, Christopher Michael *186*
Sanders, George *186–87*
Sandler, Ethan *187*
Sansom, Ken *187*
Santa's Workshop 148, 219
Sarandon, Chris *187*
Sarandon, Susan *187–88*
Savage, Keaton *188*
Savage, Randy *188*
Schaal, Kristen *188*
Schumacher, Michael *188*
Scott, Dorothy *188–89*
Scott, George C. *189*
Scotti, Vito *189*
Sea Salts 213
Sea Scouts 38, 43
Searle, Douglas *189*
Sedaris, Amy *189–90*
Selby, Sarah *190*
Self-Control 87
Selleck, Tom *190*
Severn, Raymond 124, *190*
Shadix, Glenn *190*
Shaffer, Paul *190–91*
Shalhoub, Tony *191*
Shawn, Wallace *191*
Shearer, Harry *191–92*
Sheen, Michael *192*
Shelley, Carole *192*
Shen, Freda Foh *192*
Sheridan, Susan *192–93*
Shields, Fred *193*
Shigeta, James *193*
The Shindig 83
Shirley, Bill *193*
Shore, Dinah *193*
Shore, Pauly *194*
Short, Martin *194*
Shuflman, Constance *194*
Silver, Jeffrey *194*
Simanteris, Ross *194*
Sincere, Jean *194–95*
Sinclair, Madge *195*
Singer, Stuffy *195*
Singerman, Wesley *195*
Siragusa, Peter *195*
The Skeleton Dance 199
Sleeping Beauty 7, 13, 37, 45, 49, 55, 72, 79, 101, 111, 132, 143, 146, 173, 174, 193, 210, 232
Sleepy Time Donald 44
The Small One 99, 111, 138, 174, 196, 197, 230
Smith, Brittany Alyse *195*
Smith, Hal *195–96*
Smith, Kai Steel *196*
Smith, Max *196*
Snow White and the Seven Dwarfs 12, 24, 30, 31, 40–41, 44–46, 54, 62, 64, 86, 92, 95, 111, 123, 132, 139, 148, 151, 159, 166, 171, 193, 203
So Dear to My Heart 19, 39–40, 54, 64
Sohn, Peter *196*
Song of the South 18, 56, 62, 64, 111, 125, 201, 232

Sorenson, Ricky 176, **196**
Soucie, Kath 20, **196–97**
Soule, Olan **197**
Spacey, Kevin **197–98**
Spade, David 28, **198**
Spall, Timothy **198**
Spann, Aaron **198**
Sparber, Herschel **198–99**
Spare the Rod 210
Spence, Bruce **199**
Sport Goofy in Soccermania 10, 81, 129, 169, 185, 208
Springtime 199
Springtime for Pluto 174
Stack, Timothy **199**
Stacy, Michelle **199**
Stalling, Carl W. **199**
Stanger, Kyle **199**
Stanley, Florence **200**
Stanton, Andrew 30, **200**
Stanton, Harry **200**
Stanton, Val **200**
Steamboat Willie 27, 62, 132
Stein, Delaney Rose **200**
Steinfeld, Jake **200**
Steinkellner, Emma **201**
Stepanek, Brian **201**
Stevens, Bob **201**
Stevens, Sally **201**
Stewart, Bobby **201**
Stewart, Nicodemus **201**
Stewart, Patrick 12, 26, 137, **201–202**
Stiers, David Ogden **202**
Stiller, Jerry **202–203**
Stockwell, Harry **203**
Stojka, Andre **203**
Strom, Natalie **203**
Stuart, Chad **203**
Suarez, Jeremy **203–204**
Sullivan, Erik Per **204**
Sullivan, Nicole **204**
Summer, Cree **204**
Susskind, Steve **204–205**
Sutherland, John **205**
Swardson, Nick **205**
Sweeney, D.B. **205**
Sweetland, Doug **205**
Swenson, Karl **205–206**
Swofford, Ken **206**
The Sword in the Stone 6, 7, 15, 35, 111, 132, 138–39, 153, 174, 176, 196, 205, 214, 221
Symphony Hour 86

Takei, George **206**
Tambor, Jeffrey **206–207**
Tangled 61, 81, 83, 93, 115, 127, 144, 148–49, 151, 165, 200, 206, 207, 212
Tarzan 9, 10, 11, 23, 26, 44, 52, 58, 59, 60, 64, 88, 94, 97, 115, 118, 128, 129, 157–58, 165, 170, 216, 217, 223
Tatasciore, Fred **207**
Taylor, Dub **207**
Taylor, Rip **207**
Taylor, Rod **207–208**
Taylor, Russi 8, 11, **208**
Teachers Are People 175

Teacher's Pet 4, 63, 75, 78, 84, 92, 96, 120, 121, 135, 151, 163, 177, 178, 184, 191, 199, 201, 202, 206, 209, 211, 223
Tennis Racquet 219
Terry, Paul **208**
Terry-Thomas **208–209**
Thewlis, David **209**
Thomas, Dave 149, **209**
Thomas, Jay **209**
Thomas, Jonathan Taylor **210**
Thomas, Vanéese Y. **210**
Thompson, Bill **210**
Thompson, Emma **210–11**
The Three Caballeros 46, 82, 91, 100, 111, 132, 148, 153, 159, 193, 232
The Three Little Pigs 26, 46, 111, 147, 148
Three Little Wolves 46, 147, 148
The Three Mouseketeers 46
Three Orphan Kittens 173
The Thrifty Pig 147
The Tigger Movie 12, 49, 51, 73, 102, 105, 187, 197, 203, 214
Tilly, Jennifer **211**
Tisdale, Ashley **211**
Tochi, Brian **211**
Tom, Lauren **211–12**
Tompkins, Paul F. **212**
Tondo, Jerry **212**
Toot, Whistle, Plunk and Boom 94, 116, 124, 174, 196, 210
Tootoosis, Gordon **212**
Torn, Rip **212–13**
The Tortoise and the Hare 40, 43
Toy Story 7, 10, 20, 59, 62, 66, 68, 69–70, 71, 79, 94, 108, 123, 132, 142, 144, 150, 155, 165, 166, 167, 169, 170, 172, 173, 174, 178–79, 191, 200, 205, 215, 216
Toy Story 2 7, 10, 20, 22, 23, 24, 25, 31, 32, 52, 59, 62, 71, 76, 91, 92, 94, 96, 118, 122, 123, 132, 142, 144, 150, 155, 157, 165, 166, 169, 170, 171, 173, 174, 179, 191, 200, 205, 214, 215
Toy Story 3 4, 7, 10, 19–20, 22, 29, 43, 52, 53, 82, 87, 94, 96, 101, 104, 111, 114, 116, 119, 123, 131, 133, 142, 144, 146, 150, 163, 165, 172, 174, 188, 191, 200, 214, 216, 226
Trail Mix-Up 75, 100, 155, 214, 215, 225, 227
Travolta, John **213**
Treasure Planet 10, 11, 23, 31, 32, 55, 89–90, 107, 115, 128, 133, 141, 142, 143, 144, 152, 167, 170, 194, 204, 210–11, 227
Trick or Treat 94, 124, 174, 196
Trombone Trouble 143
Trousdale, Gary **213**
Trout, Dink **213**
Truitt, Danielle Moné **213–14**
Tummy Trouble 75, 100, 214, 225, 227
Turner, Kathleen 107, **214**
Turner, Timothy **214**
Twillie, Carmen **214**
Tyler, Ginny **214**

The Ugly Duckling 112
Unkrich, Hannah **215**
Unkrich, Lee **214–15**
Up 11–12, 23, 48, 62, 68, 81, 95, 101, 113, 131, 124, 129, 135, 152, 155, 165, 166, 168, 172, 173, 174, 179, 181, 196, 200
Ustinov, Peter **215**

Van Rooten, Luis **215**
Varney, Jim 43, **215**
Venable, Evelyn **215–16**
von Detten, Erik **216**
von Oy, Jenna **216**
Vowell, Sarah **216**

Wahlgren, Kari **216–17**
Wallace, Oliver **217**
WALL-E 5, 23, 33, 45, 62, 68, 82, 96, 101, 118, 123, 141, 142, 152, 162, 166, 172, 174, 178, 196, 200, 220, 224
Wallis, Michael **217**
Wallis, Shani **217**
Walmsley, Jon **217**
Walton, Mark **217–18**
Waltrip, Darrell, **218**
Warburton, Patrick **218**
Waring, Fred **218**
Watanabe, Gedde **218**, 224
Watson, Allan **219**
Watson, Blayne **219**
Weaver, Dennis **219**
Weaver, Doodles **219**
Weaver, Jackson **219–20**
Weaver, Jason **220**
Weaver, Sigourney **220**
Weinger, Scott 122, **220**
Weinrib, Lennie **220**
Weintraub, Carl **221**
Welker, Frank **221**
Wentworth, Martha **221**
West, Adam **221–22**
Wheatley, Tom **222**
Wheeler, H.A. **222**
Whitaker, Billy **222**
Whitaker, Dori **222**
White, Lilias **222**
White, Richard **222**
Whitehouse, Paul **222–23**
Whitman, Mae **223**
Whitmire, Steve **223**
Who Framed Roger Rabbit 5, 8, 10, 11, 25–26, 34, 52, 55, 74, 77, 82, 99, 106, 120, 130, 154, 163, 169, 171, 172, 208, 214, 221, 225, 226
Who Killed Cock Robin?, 27, 221
The Whoopee Party 46
Whyte, Joe **223**
Wickes, Mary **223–24**, 228
Wild Waves 199
Wilder, Matthew **224**
Willard, Fred **224**
Williams, Harlan **224**
Williams, Joseph **224–25**
Williams, Laura **225**
Williams, Lucille **225**
Williams, Rhoda **225**
Williams, Richard **225**
Williams, Robin 3–4, **225–26**

Williamson, Seth R. *226*
Williamson, Shane R. *226*
Willis, Jack *226*
Wilson, Don *226*
Wilson, J. Donald *226*
Wilson, Owen *226*
Winchell, April *226–27*
Winchell, Paul *227*
Wincott, Michael *227*
Window Cleaners 145
Windsor, Barbara *227–28*
Winfrey, Oprah *228*
Winnie the Pooh and the Blustery Day 43, 73, 100, 103, 112, 132, 138, 149, 196, 217, 227, 231
Winnie the Pooh and the Honey Tree 43, 100, 103, 132, 138, 143, 149, 176, 196, 214, 231
Winnie the Pooh and Tigger Too!, 43, 100, 103, 132, 214, 222
Winslowe, Paula *228*
The Wise Little Hen 86, 153
Withers, Jane 224, *228*
Wolfe, Digby *228*
Wong, B.D. *229*
Woodard, Alfre *229*
Woods, Ilene *229*
Woods, James *229–30*
Woodson, William *230*
Wooley, Michael-Leon *230*
Worley, Jo Anne *230–31*
Worlock, Frederick *231*
Wright, Ben *231*
Wright, Ralph *231–32*
Wright, Samuel E. *232*
Wright, Will *232*
Wynn, Ed *232–33*

Young, Alan *233*

Zahn, Steve *233–34*
Zimmer, Norma *234*

www.ingramcontent.com/pod-product-compliance
Lightning Source LLC
Chambersburg PA
CBHW081543300426
44116CB00015B/2738